CALIFORNIA HERITAGE

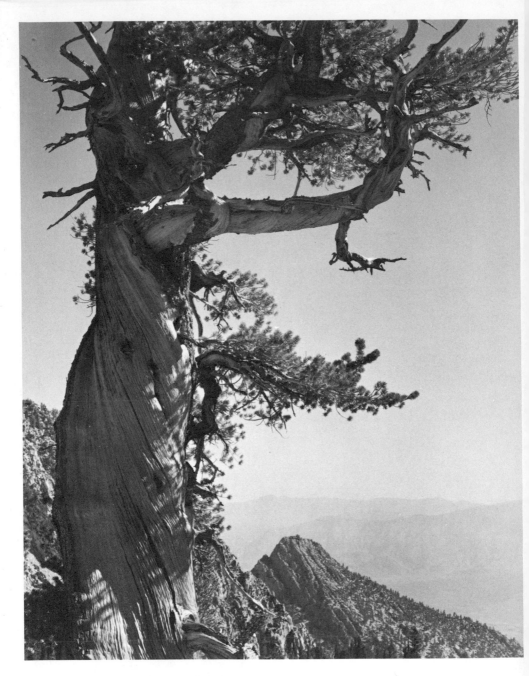

PINE TREE *by Cedric Wright*

CALIFORNIA
HERITAGE

AN ANTHOLOGY OF
HISTORY AND LITERATURE
BY JOHN AND LAREE CAUGHEY

F. E. PEACOCK PUBLISHERS

Itasca, Illinois

For permission to reprint selections as indicated we thank these copyright holders:
Robinson Jeffers: "The Inquisitors," *The Double Axe and Other Poems,* © 1948.
Arthur H. Clark Co.: "How the Earth Was Made" and "Mouse Steals Fire," Gifford and Block, *Californian Indian Nights Entertainments,* ©1930.
Indiana University Press: "Dance Mad," Theodora Kroeber, *The Inland White,* ©1959.
Houghton Mifflin Co.: "The Grass on the Mountains," Mary Austin, *The American Rhythm,* ©1923 by Harcourt Brace & Co.; "The Bindle Stiff," Wallace Stegner, *The Preacher and the Slave,* ©1950.
University of California Press: "Acorn Cookery" and "Mono Basketry," C. Hart Merriman, *Studies of the California Indians,* ©1955; "First Travelers through the Land," F. J. Teggart, *The Portolá Expedition,* ©1911; "Los Angeles River and Plain," H. E. Bolton, *Juan Crespi, Missionary Frontiersman,* ©1927; "The Captain and the Friar," Bolton, *Anza's California Expeditions,* ©1930; "The Death of Junípero Serra," Bolton, *Historical Memoirs of New California,* ©1926; "News and Gossip from Santa Barbara," G. P. Hammond, *The Larkin Papers,* ©1951; "Tragedy at Donner Lake," F. J. Teggart, *Diary of Patrick Breen,* ©1916; "Bulletin from Yerba Buena," L. C. Powell, *Philosopher Pickett,* ©1942; "Los Angeles and Santa Barbara in 1860-61," W. H. Brewer, *Up and Down California,* ©1930 by Yale University Press; "Crime and Punishment in Los Angeles," W. B. Rice, *The Los Angeles Star,* ©1947; "The California Clipper," R. A. Rydell, *Cape Horn to the Pacific,* ©1952; "Reform Governor," G. E. Mowry, *The California Progressives,* ©1951; "The Sierra Nevada," F. E. Matthes, *The Incomparable Valley,* ©1950; "Expulsion of the Japanese," tenBroeck, Barnhart and Matson, *Prejudice, War, and the Constitution,* © 1954; "A Way of Life," Theodora Kroeber, *Ishi in Two Worlds,* © 1961.
Hampton Institute: "Ishi, the Last Yahi," *Southern Workman,* ©1917.
California Historical Society: "Glimpses of the Coast" and "Along the Coast in 1602," H. R. Wagner, *Spanish Voyages to the Northwest Coast of America,* ©1929; "Life and Customs," C. L. Camp, *James Clyman, American Frontiersman,* ©1928; "Battle of San Pasqual," G. W. Ames, Jr., *A Doctor Comes to California,* ©1943.
Aimee F. Chapman Luginbuehl: "The Governor's Lady," C. E. Chapman, *History of California, the Spanish Period,* ©1921.
Brandt & Brandt: "The Church Robbers," A. de Fierro Blanco [W. Nordhoff], *The Journey of the Flame,* ©1933 Houghton Mifflin Co., ©1961 Mary Williams.
University of Colorado Press: "The Significance of the Borderlands," *The Trans-Mississippi West,* ©1930.
Fine Arts Press: "Trapping in the Sacramento Valley," M. S. Sullivan, *The Travels of Jedediah Smith,* ©1934; "A Visit to Fort Ross," M. E. Wilbur, *Duflot de Mofras' Travels on the Pacific Coast,* ©1937.
Saunders Press: "Rancho Patrocinio del Alisal," R. F. Axe, *Nach dem Sacramento,* ©1938.
Huntington Library: "Life on the Ranchos," R. G. Cleland, *The Cattle on a Thousand Hills,* ©1941; "The Utopia of Madame Modjeska," R. V. Hine, *California's Utopian Colonies,* ©1953.
Columbia University Press: "On the Trail," Read and Gaines, *Gold Rush,* ©1944.
The Ward Ritchie Press: "The Panama Lottery," J. W. Caughey, *Seeing the Elephant,* ©1951.
Pacific Historical Review: "California at Last," J. W. Caughey, "The Jacob Y. Stover Narrative," ©1937; "Mining Methods in Catgut Cañon," E. H. Carpenter, Jr., "Mark Twain to the Editors," ©1949; "Perspective on the Pacific," J. C. Parish, "Introductory Editorial," ©1932; "The Clampers," C. I. Wheat, "The Clampers," ©1949.
Edwin S. Morby and Arturo Torres-Rioseco: "San Francisco Vignettes," V. Pérez Rosales, *California Adventure,* ©1947.
The Colt Press: "Take Your Bible in One Hand," G. R. Stewart, Jr., *Take Your Bible in One Hand,* ©1939.
Alfred A. Knopf, Inc.: "The Lucky Louse, or Blood Will Tell," G. E. Dane, *Ghost Town,* ©1941; "The Passing of a Literary Frontier," Franklin Walker, *San Francisco's Literary Frontier,* ©1939; "The Way of a Historian," Oscar Lewis, *I Remember Christine,* ©1942; "On Beetle Rock," Sally Carrighar, *One Day on Beetle Rock,* ©1944.
Harvard University Press: "The Mines in Retrospect," R. W. Paul, *California Gold,* ©1947 the President and Fellows of Harvard College.
Kern County Historical Society: "The Expansive Power of Beans," Boyd and Rogers, *San Joaquin Vignettes,* ©1955.
Stanford University Press: "The Slim Princess," Jerry MacMullen, *Paddle-Wheel Days in California,* © 1944; "The Mooney Case," Richard H. Frost, *The Mooney Case,* © 1968.
Academy Library Guild: "The Watch," A. R. Rojas, *The Lore of the California Vaquero,* ©1958.
Wallace Smith: "The Stockton Gang Plow," *Garden of the Sun,* ©1939.
Viking Press, Inc.: "The City That Was," Will Irwin, *The City That Was,* ©1906 B. W. Huebsch & Co.; "And It Came to Pass," John Steinbeck, *The Grapes of Wrath,* ©1939 John Steinbeck; "The Slide Area," Gavin Lambert, *The Slide Area,* ©1959 Gavin Lambert.
Isabel W. Chase: "The Color of the Desert," J. S. Chase, *California Desert Trails,* ©1919 J. Smeaton Chase.
Rolf K. McPherson: "Dedication of the Temple," A. S. McPherson, *This Is That,* ©[1923] Echo Park Evangelistic Association.
James Rorty: "California Dissonance," Sterling, Taggard, and Rorty, *Continent's End,* ©1925.
Rogers Company: "The People's Jester," Will Rogers' column, ©1932.
Liveright Publishing Corp.: "The Ghost of Billy the Kid," Edwin Corle, *Mojave,* ©1934.
Jake Zeitlin: "China Boy," Idwal Jones, *China Boy,* ©1936 Primavera Press.
William Saroyan: "Fresno," William Saroyan, *The Saroyan Special,* ©1934.
Carey McWilliams: "South of the Tehachapi," Carey McWilliams, *Southern California Country,* ©1946.
Little, Brown & Co.: "Whispering Glades," Evelyn Waugh, *The Loved One,* ©1948.
New Directions: "They Were Putting Up the Statue," Lawrence Ferlinghetti, *A Coney Island of the Mind,* ©1955, 1958 Lawrence Ferlinghetti.
City Lights Books: "A Supermarket in California," Allen Ginsberg, *Howl and Other Poems,* ©1956, 1958 Allen Ginsberg.
Marzani & Munsell, Inc.: "The Sign-up," Abraham Polonsky, *A Season of Fear,* ©1956 Abraham Polonsky.
Remi Nadeau: "The Spiralling Growth of Los Angeles," Remi Nadeau, *Los Angeles from Mission to Modern City,* ©1961.
Jim Murray: "H₂O 'Malley, or, Let 'em Drink Beer," Los Angeles *Times,* ©1962.
Robinson Jeffers: "The Inquisitors," *The Double Axe and Other Poems,* © 1948. *Prejudice, War, and the Constitution,* © 1954; "A Way of Life," Theodora Kroeber, *Ishi in Two Worlds,* © 1961. fornia, © 1944; "The Mooney Case," Richard H. Frost, *The Mooney Case,* © 1968.
Harper & Row: "Hyperion to a Satyr," Aldous Huxley, *Tomorrow and Tomorrow,* © 1956.
Grossman Publishers: "The Soil Beneath the Blacktop," *California Revolution,* © 1968.
Prentice-Hall: "Home Is a Freeway," Neil Morgan, *California Syndrome,* © 1969.
World Publishing Company: "Capricious Million," Gladwin Hill, *Dancing Bear,* © 1968.
Jack Jones: "Watts Was Called 'Mudtown,' " © 1965.
Ed Cray: "The Curious Incident of the Raided Mosque," © 1965.
Ramparts: "The Organizer's Tale," © 1966.
Sierra Club: "Winning a Reprieve," *Not Man Apart,* © 1965.

TO JOHN, SUSIE, DONNA, MARC, AND JOHN
CALIFORNIANS OR SOMETIMES CALIFORNIANS

Preface

AMONG the states California possessed the greatest diversity of scene and resources. It offers a multitude of environments, climates in the plural, and has proved itself capable of supporting many radically different ways of living.

California also has a complex and varied history. When discovered, exactly half a century after Columbus, it had an Indian population much more numerous than the continental average north of Mexico and a way of life distinguishably Californian. The Spaniards waited until 1769 to return and with missionaries, soldiers, and a few settlers to establish an outpost of empire. The Spanish colony became a Mexican province, still pastoral. Americans filtered in, annexed the trade, and witnessed the change of flag. Gold carried California headlong into a new era which, as it turned out, was merely the first in a succession of skyrocketing changes.

The redshirted miner gave place to the railroad builder, he in turn to the real estate boomer, the health seeker, and the orange grower. The surge was carried forward by oil, the movies, and the automobile, the tourist industry, shipbuilding and airplane construction, industrialized agriculture, gargantuan aqueducts and freeways, and science and technology focussed on missiles and space probes. En route there were abrasions in race relations, with the aged and the young, with the poor, between labor, management, and the consumer, and upon the environment.

Alongside this eventful past California came to have a voluminous commentary, some of it sober history, much of it lyrical and analytical description, some of it indubitably creative writing. Dana, Frémont, Harte, Stevenson, Muir, Austin, London, Jeffers, Steinbeck—these are merely a start on a roll call of the gifted and inspired who contributed an outpouring to match the richness of the state's geography and history.

Here we bring together some of the best of this writing. Our selections are ranged in ten clusters, beginning with the Indians and continuing to the contemporary. Each section progresses from particularized writings to more reflective views. As the supply of historical or creative writing varies from period to period, so does the ratio of our selections. Each selection was picked because it would be rewarding in and of itself, but also for its contribution to the unit and the whole.

We see at least three uses for this book. Because each selection has its own integrity, some readers may want to dip in at random. Others, we hope, will read a section at a sitting for an insight into that sector of the California experience. Those who consume from cover to cover will have a quick tour through the state's history and its literature. Our ulterior motive is to spark broader reading. The first leads are to the books from which the components of this collection are drawn, and following the last selection is a tabulation of Other Books To Read, in clusters pertinent to each section. The recent texts in California history offer many more suggestions, surpassed, however, by what is in stock in the great and good libraries of Californiana.

Throughout our engagement in this enterprise we had generous help from friends almost innumerable. Booklovers volunteered suggestions, and librarians assisted in the search. We particularly thank the participating photographers and, in an adjacent art field, Ward Ritchie, who designed the book. To the writers, 143 in number, whose names are ranged alphabetically on the closing pages, we are most indebted. They and the broader ranks of contributors on California themes made possible such a gathering as this.

J. & L. C.

Contents

Illustrations

xiv

CALIFORNIA HERITAGE

1

THE INDIANS

Up to 1769, roughly two hundred years ago, the only Californians were Indians. Through the Spanish period, the Mexican period, and the American conquest, Indians continued to outnumber everyone else. Only with the avalanche of migration in the gold rush were they reduced to a minority. For another generation they were a factor of some importance in politics, economy, land ownership, and public safety. The state has Indians today, though they are but a fraction of one per cent of the population, and many are so integrated into the general culture as to be unrecognizable. Nevertheless, in the state's history the Indians have a substantial place and one that increases in importance as one reads back into the earlier chapters. Beyond the threshold of the written record, in what we call the prehistoric, Indian occupancy stretches back, not forever, but fifty or seventy-five or perhaps a hundred times as far as the combined Spanish, Mexican, and American epochs.

As found by the Spaniards, these Indians were living in a state of such abysmal ignorance and simplicity that they made a very poor impression. Of the Diegueños at Coyote Canyon, for instance, Pablo Font remarked in 1776, "they are so savage, wild and dirty, disheveled, ugly, small, and timid, that only because they have the human form is it possible to believe that they belong to mankind."

This picture somewhat maligns these first Californians. It is true they contented themselves with houses that were flimsy and small. They wore little clothing. Their personal possessions were

2

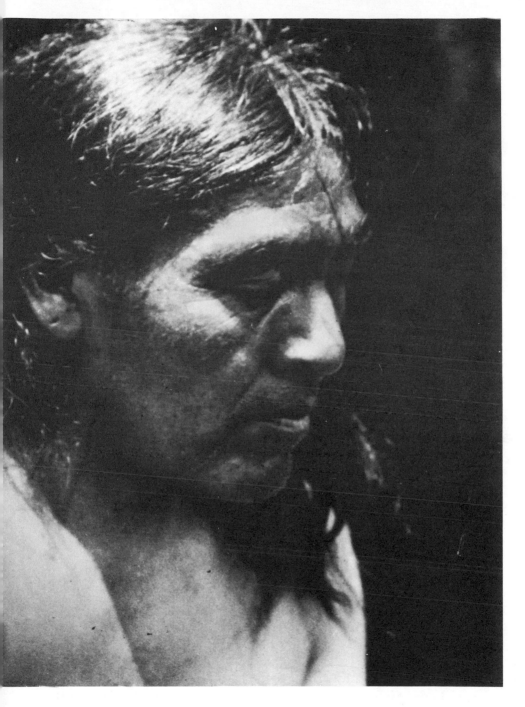

I S H I

meager. They did more trapping and snaring than hunting. They put little emphasis on war and less on government. Except along the Colorado they did not till the soil. They had no metals and most of them made no pottery. They appeared to be going through life emptyhanded. And the Spanish missionaries sometimes despaired over how much would have to be taught them before they could be Christians and useful subjects of the Spanish monarch.

The American pioneers, most of whom were conditioned against Indians by the national tradition and the experience of wresting other parts of the continent from fiercer and more warlike natives, heartily agreed. In allusion to the local habit of grubbing for roots and larvae, and unaware that in the main the roots were wanted as fibers for basket making, the early Americans contemptuously called them Digger Indians and moved callously toward exterminating them. Inevitably the early comment stresses the primitiveness and the deficiencies in the Indian way of life.

When anthropologists came on the scene, they saw the Californians in a better light. They praised the dietary made possible by the ingenious process of sweetening the acorn, the highly developed art of basketry, the intricate fraternal organizations, the thorough knowledge of the environment, particularly the plant life, and even the sensible adjustment of conventions in dress to the realities of the climate.

Through archeological search and collection of specimens for museum display a partial inventory of the material culture of these Indians has been assembled. So measured, the attainments are less prepossessing than for the Eskimo, the Northwest Coast tribes, the Iroquois, the Five Civilized Tribes, the Plains Indians after the adoption of the horse, or the Pueblo, not to mention the Aztecs and the Maya. In part the poor showing is because the acorn process was more idea than mechanism. The important thing was the formula which called for a hot rinse to remove the tannic acid.

Most fortunately for their reputation, the California Indians had a rich literature. Solely oral, it consisted of stories usually peopled by Coyote, Mouse, Eagle, and their brethren, all possessed with human qualities and characteristics. Although some

4

of the tales are short and simple, others are complex and would tax the memory of most modern readers. Yet they were preserved by being told, remembered, retold, and thus perpetuated. Literally hundreds of such stories have been collected.

Some of the stories probe the most difficult problems—how the world began, where man came from, the question of good and evil. Some have a quiet moral, such as the one in which Coyote challenges the Los Angeles River to a race. Others tackle history —how man got fire, how the languages originated, why buckeye wood makes a good fire drill, how the Indians learned about salmon. Many of these tales have humor as a pervasive element as in the Yokuts' explanation of the origin of the mountains and with the fun-loving people described in "Dance Mad." They give much information on how the Indians lived, and they also provide excellent insights into the Indian patterns of thought and behavior.

The Mary Austin poem here presented is a sort of transition from the Indians' own literature to what others have written about them. She labels it "translated from the Paiute." Since the medium is verse, we assume a touch of poetic license, but present also is the appreciation that one creative artist felt toward another. By temperament she understood "the brown shy quiet people" and caught their emotions and yearnings.

The writing on the Indians from outside their society is divisible into two parts. First there was writing by men who were informed, even expert, but could not claim to be versed in the science of studying and fathoming a primitive society. Examples are not lacking of criticism and execration. George Nidever, for instance, relates very calmly how when he came to California in 1833, he let two Indians pass him on the trail, waited until they were "lined up," and killed them both with one shot. This was in the Sierra, but he was avenging the killing of his brother a year earlier, east of the Rockies, and by quite different Indians. In the 1850's the editor of the Los Angeles *Star* advocated a concerted campaign on the Indians from east and west with the laudable purpose of driving them all into Great Salt Lake. Such sentiments were not uncommon, but ordinarily are more illuminating on the commentator than the subject.

The Boscana, Wilson, and Bancroft passages here reproduced have more constructive purpose. Gerónimo Boscana, one of the later Franciscan missionaries, did a free translation of an Indian myth and garnished it with a kindly but exasperated description of his neophytes. Writing some eighteen years after the closing of the missions, Benjamin D. Wilson saw much more capacity in the Indians than did the majority of his contemporaries. Another thirty-five years later, the Indians had been all but overwhelmed by the force and violence of the whites. Hubert Howe Bancroft spelled out the record and expressed his value judgment on this tragedy of which we must be custodians, absorbing it into our tradition and morality.

More recently, the science of anthropology having come into its own, the California Indians and their culture have had scientific description and analysis. The essay on their food habits deals with a typifying fundamental in their way of life. The shorter reminiscent account of the actual preparation and serving of the acorn mush has an attention to detail that bespeaks the careful scientist. The description of basketry is lyrical in praise of the weaver's skill and the good design and engineering of the water basket. This praise is all the more impressive since it goes to the Mono on the east flank of the Sierra, good journeywomen weavers, but less renowned than the Pomo on the coast above Russian River. The tribute to Ishi, also the work of a man habituated to the scientific method, is unusual in its personal flavor, its attention to Ishi the human being, not just the native informant. Additionally it is a commentary on one price of advancing civilization.

This group of selections reaches toward a balanced view of the earliest Californians. Later selections have much more on the subject, notably those from Ascensión, Costansó, Crespi, Fages, Lapérouse, Vancouver, Smith, Bidwell, and Bunnell.

A Way of Life

BY THEODORA KROEBER

The California Indian was a true provincial. He was also an introvert, reserved, contemplative, and philosophical. He lived at ease with the supernatural and the mystical which were pervasive in all aspects of life. He felt no need to differentiate mystical truth from directly evidential or "material" truth, or the supernatural from the natural: one was as manifest as the other within his system of values and perceptions and beliefs. The promoter, the boaster, the aggressor, the egoist, the innovator, would have been looked at askance. The ideal was the man of restraint, dignity, rectitude, he of the Middle Way. Life proceeded within the limits of known and proper pattern from birth through death and beyond. Its repetitive rhythm was punctuated with ritual, courtship, dance, song, and feast, each established according to custom going back to the beginning of the world, an event which, along with subsequent events having to do with setting the way of life, was well known and fully recounted in the peoples' oral but elaborate and specific histories.

It was not an easy life, but it was a good one. There were lean times, but the lean like the fat times were shared with family, friends, and tribe. Life was as it had always been.

Theodora Kroeber, *Ishi in Two Worlds*
(Berkeley, University of California Press, 1961), 23.

How the Earth Was Made

AS TOLD BY THE YUKI

The Yuki lived among the redwoods in the northern part of Mendocino County.

In the beginning everything was water. On the water, in a fleck of foam, a down feather circled. From this came a voice and sing-

7

ing. This was the creator Taikomol who was to make the world. His name means He-who-goes-alone. With him was the god Coyote. After a time the god who was in the feather came to look like a man. All the time that he was taking on the appearance of a man he was singing. Then he made a basket from parts of his own body. From this basket he made the earth which he fastened and strengthened with pine pitch. Then he traveled over it four times from north to south with Coyote hanging to his body. Next he fastened the four corners of the earth and made the sky from the skins of four whales. Then he made people by laying sticks of wood in a house overnight. In the morning these sticks had turned into people.

Taikomol wanted people to live forever, but Coyote's son died and was buried. The god offered to bring him to life, but Coyote said that the dead should remain dead and for that reason people do not come to life again after they die.

Edward W. Gifford and Gwendoline Harris Block, eds.,
Californian Indian Nights Entertainments
(Glendale, Arthur H. Clark Company, 1930), 82.

Origin of the Mountains

AS TOLD BY THE YOKUTS

The Yokuts were spread over most of the San Joaquin Valley, a location central to this story. The recorder, Stephen Powers, came early to California and traveled widely among the Indians.

Once there was a time when there was nothing in the world but water. About the place where Tulare Lake is now, there was a pole standing far up out of the water, and on this pole perched a hawk and a crow. First one of them would sit on the pole a while, then the other would knock him off and sit on it himself. Thus they sat on top of the pole above the waters for many ages. At length they wearied of the lonesomeness, and they created the birds which prey on fish such as the kingfisher, eagle, pelican, and others. Among them was a very small duck, which dived down

8

to the bottom of the water, picked its beak full of mud, came up, died, and lay floating on the water. The hawk and the crow then fell to work and gathered from the duck's beak the earth which it had brought up, and commenced making the mountains. They began at the place now known as Ta-hí-cha-pa Pass, and the hawk made the east range, while the crow made the west one. Little by little, as they dropped in the earth, these great mountains grew athwart the face of the waters, pushing north. It was a work of many years, but finally they met together at Mount Shasta, and their labors were ended. But, behold, when they compared their mountains, it was found that the crow's was a great deal the larger. Then the hawk said to the crow, "How did this happen, you rascal? I warrant you have been stealing some of the earth from my bill, and that is why your mountains are the biggest." It was a fact, and the crow laughed in his claws. Then the hawk went and got some Indian tobacco and chewed it, and it made him exceedingly wise. So he took hold of the mountains and turned them round in a circle, putting his range in place of the crow's; and that is why the Sierra Nevada is larger than the Coast Range.

Stephen Powers, *Tribes of California*
(Washington, 1877), 383-384.

Coyote and the Water

AS TOLD BY THE GABRIELINO

The Gabrielino occupied most of Los Angeles and Orange counties. They are so called because in mission days they came under the influence and control of Mission San Gabriel. Hugo Reid, a Scotch pioneer in southern California and husband of a Gabrielino woman, included this story in a series on the Indians contributed to the Los Angeles Star in 1851.

A Coyote, which, like all the rest of his kin, considered himself as the most austere animal on the face of the earth, not even excepting man himself, came one day to the margin of a small river. Looking over the bank, on seeing the water run so slow, he addressed it in

9

a cunning manner, "What say you to a race?" "Agreed to," answered the water very calmly. The Coyote ran at full speed along the bank until he could hardly stand from fatigue and on looking over the bank saw the water running smoothly on.

He walked off with his tail between his legs and had something to reflect upon for many a day afterwards.

Hugo Reid, *The Indians of Los Angeles County*
(Los Angeles, 1926), 33,
reprinting from the Los Angeles *Star*, 1851.

Mouse Steals Fire

AS TOLD BY THE MIWOK

The Miwok had their home in Marin County.

A long time ago, in the very beginning of things, the people in the hills were freezing, for they had no fire with which to keep warm. They gathered in their assembly house to talk over what they could do. There were Black Goose, White Goose, Lizard, Coyote, Mouse, and many others. It was Lizard, sitting on the rock outside of the assembly house, who discovered fire emerging from an assembly house in the valley below.

Later, Mouse, the Flute-player, slipped away unnoticed to go and steal some of the fire from the valley people. He took with him four of his flutes. When he arrived at the assembly house in the valley he found Bear, Rattlesnake, Mountain Lion, and Eagle guarding all the entrances. But Mouse managed, nevertheless, to get into the house. He climbed on top of the house, and while Eagle slept he cut two of his wing feathers which were covering the smoke hole, and slipped in.

Once in, he began to play his flute for the people. The music soon lulled them to sleep, and, when they were all snoring, Mouse safely filled his four flutes with fire and escaped.

When the people awoke they search all over the hills for the one who had stolen fire from them.

Eagle sent Wind, Rain, and Hail in pursuit, for they were considered the swiftest travelers among the valley people. Finally Hail came up to Mouse, but Mouse had concealed his flutes under a buckeye tree just before Hail overtook him, and so denied having the fire. Hail believed him and departed.

Because Mouse placed his flutes of fire under the buckeye tree, there remains to this day fire in the buckeye tree, and people today obtain their fire with a drill of buckeye wood.

After Hail's departure, Mouse resumed his journey with his four flutes of fire. He met Coyote, who had become impatient fearing some dreadful fate had befallen Flute-player, and had gone out to find him.

Arrived home, Mouse sat on top of the assembly house, playing his flutes and dropping coals through the smokehole.

Coyote interrupted him, however, before he was finished, and so it is that the people who sat in the middle of the house received fire. Those people now cook their food and talk correctly. The people who sat around the edge of the room did not get any fire and today when they talk their teeth chatter with the cold. That is the way the languages began. If Coyote had not interrupted and Mouse had been able to finish playing all his flutes of fire, everyone would have received a share of fire and all would have spoken one language.

Indians today talk many different languages for the reason that all did not receive an equal share of fire.

Edward W. Gifford and Gwendoline Harris Block, eds.,
Californian Indian Nights Entertainments
(Glendale, Arthur H. Clark Company, 1930), 135-136.

Dance Mad

AS TOLD BY THE WINTU

The Wintu inhabited the Sacramento Valley and the mountains surrounding the Trinity Alps. Theodora Kroeber accompanied her husband, anthropologist A. L. Kroeber, on many of his field trips. She is an accomplished psychologist.

It sometimes happens when many people are gathered together for dancing and singing and feasting that one or another of those who are dancing does not stop when the others stop, does not eat or sleep or rest, but goes on dancing and dancing. He goes dance mad.

Once long ago a whole people went dance mad, dancing while the moons and seasons came and went, dancing all around the world.

It began one day of spring after the heavy winds had quieted and the bare ground was green with young clover, in a village on Swift Creek, midway between the top edge of the world where the three principal rivers are small streams and the lower edge of the world where these rivers, wide and deep, flow together to make the Nom-ti-pom—that is, the Sacramento River—and empty into the sea. This village, like the sea and the rivers, was old, its people unchanged in their ways since the world was made.

The occasion was a feast celebrating the initiation into full womanhood of Nomtaimet, the daughter of one of the village families. Nomtaimet's father and mother had neglected nothing of the customary observances and training belonging to this period in a girl's life. They knew that it is an important and indeed a dangerous time for her, and for others, too, if she does not learn to keep its prohibitions, to follow its complex ritual, and to behave with decorum.

Nomtaimet's mother built for her daughter a little house. Here, separated from the family but close by, she lived alone during the moons of her initiation. She fasted and kept to herself, seeing only her mother and her mother's mother, who brought her food, bathed her, combed her hair, and cared for her, for she was not allowed, by old custom, to touch herself. She left the little house only after dark, and then briefly, keeping her head covered and her face screened from sight all the time she was outside. She spent the long days and nights inside and alone, doing only those tasks appropriate to her state, learning from her mother and her grandmother the role and behavior of a good woman and wife.

She learned that on the day and the night before her husband should go to hunt or fight or gamble, she must help him to avoid her and by no means tempt him to sleep with her, for this would spoil his luck. She learned that she must again help him to avoid her during all of her moon periods until she was an old woman unable to bear him children, that she must live in her own separate house during these time, apart from her husband. There were further rules of continence and food prohibitions which she must faithfully follow each time she should be with child. Each rule and prohibition came embedded in ritual, song, and story, and these, too, she learned.

When the long moons of learning and fasting and praying came to an end, her mother and her grandmother were more than satisfied with her behavior and her knowledge. They and her father, and her mother's and her father's brothers and sisters, made a feast in her honor, sending runners to invite the people from villages all up and down Swift Creek to come to feast and dance and sing with them.

Her young friends, boys and girls, had sung to her often in the evening outside her little house to let her know she was not forgotten, but she never broke the rule—she neither looked out nor showed herself nor answered them. They were as happy to have her back as she was to be there, and now the young married women came up and talked to her as if she was already a grown woman and one of their group.

Nomtaimet emerged from her long seclusion pale, much changed, and very beautiful. The old as well as the young exclaimed at her beauty, while the old recalled that a girl is never so beautiful as at this time when she is newly returned to the world from her long initiation. She was carefully dressed for her great day. Her new buckskin shirt was elaborately ornamented with shells and beads. In her ears were enormous polished shell earrings and about her neck many strings of beads which half covered her breasts. Her hair, washed and shining, hung in two thick braids tied with mink. She carried rattles made from deer's hooves and a slender willow staff given her by the young married women to symbolize her coming of age.

The women who were not taken up with cooking or caring for children gathered around Nomtaimet, admiring her. First one man and then another joined them until someone said, "We should dance—we are enough to make a circle dance." Holding hands

13

and singing, they formed a moving circle around Nomtaimet, dancing the old circle dance which had been the coming of age dance for girls since the beginning of time.

Hearing the singing and the familiar rhythm of the shuffling side step of the dance, the old men and women came from their fires and their houses, and the children who were big enough to dance came with them, all of them joining the moving circle which grew bigger and bigger. The only ones not dancing were the women who were pounding acorns or stirring the food which was being cooked in large baskets in preparation for the feast. One by one even they put down their pestles and their stirring paddles and became part of the circle. They circled and sang until above the stamp of their dancing feet came the echo of distant voices and the silken sound of arrows flying swiftly overhead. The dancing stopped while the people from the neighboring villages appeared from behind the hills, running, shouting, and singing, the young men among them releasing arrows to whir, level, over the heads of the dancers.

In this way the guests came to the village, and there were greetings and talking and laughing until Nomtaimet's father invited them all to eat.

It was a great feast. For ten days and ten nights they ate and sang and danced. At last the feasting was over. The tenth night of singing and dancing came and went. But the pale dawn of the eleventh day found all those people still dancing. They kept right on dancing, all of them. They went dance mad.

In a long line, singing as they went, they danced up the trail leading out of the village to the east. Soon the last house was left behind and they were dancing among the hills they knew, the hills of home, up and over them until they could no longer see their houses. Through briars and chaparral, over rocks and rough ground, up and down hill, they danced on and on.

It is possible to retrace much of their dancing journey around the world, for it is known that they came to the Trinity River, the first of the great rivers, and that they forded this river as they forded all streams—by dancing straight across them. On the far side of the Trinity there is a flat, open and bare today as it was then, where the dancers again formed in a circle and danced the round dance. In a line once more, they danced on east through a gap in the hills to the Hayfork and across it and up the steep ridge beyond. At the top of the ridge they found a spring, Paukaukunmen. Here they stopped to rest and drink from the spring. You can still see the large basins in the rocks where they sat. This was their first resting place.

From Paukaukunmen, they danced down the other side of the ridge. They might have become faint from hunger, except that they learned to gather berries and to catch small animals without breaking the rhythm of their dance, crossing ridge after ridge, fording small streams, and so finding themselves at last on the banks of Middle River, the McCloud. Here they made their second resting place.

By this time their moccasins were cut to pieces and nothing much but belts and a few maple bark and buckskin shreds of aprons remained of their clothes. They did not try to replace their worn-out clothing; instead they filled their pouches with clays and dyes for face and body paint, and for the rest of their dancing trip they wore no clothes at all, keeping their faces and bodies freshly painted.

The dancers were far, far from home now, farther than any of them had ever been, in country they knew only from the tales told them by the old ones. The old ones themselves knew only so much as was learned from an occasional meeting with strangers who had, rarely and at some earlier time, wandered west as far as Swift Creek—strangers who spoke in the same tongue and observed the same way of life, but who nonetheless lived far from the center of the world and close to the borderland of peoples of other ways and tongues. The dancers found the Middle River Country much as they had been told it was, that is to say, a rich country of many people and many deer, of bushes loaded with hazelnuts and berries of many sorts. There was an abundance for all, and they hunted and gathered and ate there by the river, growing fat and sleek while they made friends with the people of the Middle River. One of the things they learned from their new friends was to catch and cook salmon—something which, strange as it seems now, they had not known about.

With this fresh salmon diet they felt new strength and new

power, and they set off dancing again. They were no longer interested in hunting and gathering; they wished only to dance and dance, and then to fish and cook and eat more salmon. So now they danced close beside one stream or another, wherever the salmon were best, learning the names of the many different kinds of salmon, their size and appearance and their favorite rivers. Dancing and fishing, they went farther and farther downstream as the season drew on and the salmon swam shorter distances upstream to spawn.

Having left home in the time of winds and new clover, they had by now passed the warm moons dancing and spearing salmon. As the leaves began to dry and fall from the trees, the dancers were on the banks of the third great river, the Pitt; and dancing far, far to the south, they came where the rivers join for their trip to the sea. They were in country different from any they knew even by report from the old ones, a country whose people spoke in a tongue they did not understand. The land on both sides of the lower Sacramento River stretches as far as eye can see, marshy, swampy, full of water birds. They danced through the marshes and swamps and among the water birds until there came to them the smell of salt on the air. Leaving the marshes behind, they danced down the Sacramento where it broadens at its mouth. And they stood and watched it empty into the sea.

Wearied at last of watching, they danced again, this time on the lower rim of the earth where the river meets the sea. Keeping to the rim, they turned their backs to the river, dancing away from the Nom-ti-pom toward the north. The time of the dead leaves was past. The fog moon came and went, and it was already the time of the mud moon and of frosts. They saw all about them storms and rain and floods, but there on the lower rim of the earth there were no storms, and they continued to dance along its sometimes rocky, sometimes sandy shore.

The season of storms and cold, like the other seasons, came and went, blown away by the big winds of the awakening earth. And now the dancers turned inland, away from the sea, dancing and half blown towards home. They reached Swift Creek as the new clover was making a green mat over the earth, just as it had done

when Nomtaimet first came out of her seclusion at the beginning
of the dance journey.

The dancers were home, and the dance madness was no longer
on them. It had lasted through all the moons and seasons and had
carried them all around the world. As long as she lived, Nomtaimet told her children, as her children's children tell even today,
of the feast her father made for her, and of the dance madness
that came after it.

Theodora Kroeber, *The Inland Whale*
(Bloomington, Indiana University Press, 1959), 77-84.

The Grass on the Mountain

FROM THE PAIUTE

*The Paiute were to be found in the mountains and desert country
along the eastern border of California and across Nevada and
Utah, which is named after them. When she lived at Independence
in Owens Valley, Mary Austin had contact with them.*

> Oh, long, long
> The snow has possessed the mountains.
>
> The deer have come down and the big-horn,
> They have followed the Sun to the south
> To feed on the mesquite pods and the bunch grass.
> Loud are the thunder drums
> In the tents of the mountains.
> Oh, long, long
> Have we eaten chia seeds
> And dried deer's flesh of the summer killing.
> We are wearied of our huts
> And the smoky smell of our garments.
>
> We are sick with desire of the sun
> And the grass on the mountain.

Mary Austin, *The American Rhythm*
(New York, Harcourt Brace and Company, 1923), 70.

A Missionary Reflects on His Charges

BY GERONIMO BOSCANA

Gerónimo Boscana came to California in 1806 and served as missionary until his death in 1831. His Chinigchinich *is accounted by far the most informative document on the California Indians written by any of the Franciscans.*

No doubt these Indians passed a miserable life, ever idle, and more like the brutes, than rational beings. They neither cultivated the ground, nor planted any kind of grain; but lived upon the wild seeds of the field, the fruits of the forest, and upon the abundance of game. It is really surprising, that during a lapse of many ages, with their reason and experience, they had not advanced one iota in improving the things that would have been useful and convenient for them; for instance, in agriculture; in planting and cultivating those seeds which were most appreciated—also trees around their dwellings, bearing such fruit as they were obliged to bring from a great distance. But no! nothing of the kind! and in no part of the province was to be found aught but the common, spontaneous, productions of the earth.

It cannot be denied, that these Indians, like all the human race, are the descendents of Adam; endowed with reason, or in other words, with a soul. When we read of the ancients—of their having transplanted trees which were wild, thus increasing their abundance, and quality, and of their planting seeds, which improved by cultivation, we cannot but wonder that a knowledge so important was unknown here until the missionary fathers came amongst them, and introduced the planting of wheat, corn, beans, and other grains, that are now so abundant every where. I consider these Indians, in their endowments, like the soul of an infant, which is merely a will, accompanied with passions—an understanding not exercised, or without use; and for this reason, they did not comprehend the virtue of prudence, which is the result of time and reason—of the former, by experience, and the latter, by dissertation. Although ripe in years, they had no more experience than when in childhood—no reasoning powers, and therefore followed blindly in the footsteps of their predecessors.

Their occupation consisted in the construction of the bow and arrow, in hunting for deer, rabbits, squirrels, rats, etc., which not only provided them with food, but *clothing*, if so it can be called. Their usual style of dress, was a small skin thrown over the shoulders, leaving the remaining portion of their person unprotected; but the females formed a kind of cloak out of the skins of rabbits, which were put together after this manner. They twisted them into a kind of rope, that was sewed together, so as to conform to the size of the person, for whom it was intended, and the front was adorned with a kind of fringe, composed of grass, which reached down to the knees; around the collar it was adorned with beads, and other ornaments, prized by the Indians.

They passed their time in plays, and roaming about from house to house, dancing and sleeping; and this was their only occupation, and the mode of life most common amongst them from day to day. The old men, and the poorer class, devoted a portion of the day to constructing house utensils, their bows and arrows, and the several instruments used in making their baskets; also nets of various dimensions, which were used for sundry purposes, such as for catching fish and wild fowl, and for carrying heavy burdens on their backs, fastened by a strap passed across the forehead. In like manner, the females used them for carrying their infants.

The women were obliged to gather seeds in the fields, prepare them for cooking, and to perform all the meanest offices, as well as the most laborous. It was painful in the extreme, to behold them, with their infants hanging upon their shoulders, groping about in search of herbs or seed, and exposed as they frequently were to the inclemency of the weather. Often it was the case that they returned home severely fatigued, and hungry, to cook the fruits of their toil, but, perhaps, there would be no wood, the fire extinguished, and their lazy husband either at play or sleeping, so that again they would be obliged to go out into the cold for fuel. When the brutal husband came home, or awoke from his sluggishness, he expected his meal, and if not prepared at the moment, invectives and ill treatment were the universal consequence. Poor creatures! more unfortunate than slaves! They were in such subjection, that for the most trifling offence, punishment was the result, and oftentimes death; but, thank Heaven! since the intro-

19

duction of the Christian religion among this unhappy race, the females have received more liberty and better treatment. The most wonderful of God's blessings enjoyed among them, was the great facility with which they underwent their accouchement, when it would seem as if they endured no suffering.

From the translation of Gerónimo Boscana's "Chinigchinich" in Alfred Robinson, *Life in California* (New York, 1846), 285-288.

The Indian as Workman

BY BENJAMIN D. WILSON

Benjamin D. Wilson, a pioneer of the class of 1841, became an important rancher, vineyardist, and subdivider in Los Angeles and vicinity. He also held several public offices. The selection that follows is drawn from a report which he filed in 1852 as United States Indian agent for southern California.

The Indian laborers and servants are "domesticated;" mix with us daily and hourly; and, with all their faults, appear to be a necessary part of the domestic economy. They are almost the only house or farm servants we have. The San Luiseño is the most sprightly, skillful, and handy; the Cahuilla plodding, but strong, and very useful with instruction and watching.

When at work, they will do without ardent spirits, but *must* have it on Saturday night and Sunday. Very little of the money earned during the week goes for meat and bread—their chief want with it is for drink and cards. They are universal gamblers, and inveterately addicted to the vice; consequently their clothing continually changes hands. Yet, I have met with some who do not drink, and have an aspiration to decency. Some, again, are idle and vagabonds; but I have rarely found them unwilling to work, when well paid.

If it be true that they cannot do half the work a white man can, 'tis equally true that custom at best never allows them more than half the wages of the latter, and, generally, much less than half. The common pay of Indian farm hands is from eight to ten dollars per month; and one dollar per day the highest in the towns—but few pay so much. No white man here, whether American, Sonoranian, or Californian, will work for such wages, nor anything like it.

That better wages merely would make the Indian here a better man, is doubtful. With more money, he would only pursue his evil tastes to greater excess. When their weekly *juegos* (plays) were restrained by the magistrates, and only allowed at distant intervals they were much better off; and then, too, liquor shops were not so common. In some streets of this little city, almost every other house is a grog-shop for Indians. They have, indeed, become sadly deteriorated, within the last two years; and it may be long, very long, before a sound public opinion will speak like the potent voice of the Mission Fathers.

But, let us remember, these same Indians built all the houses in the country, and planted all the fields and vineyards. There is hardly any sort of ordinary work for which they do not show a good-will.

Under the Missions, they were masons, carpenters, plasterers, soapmakers, tanners, shoemakers, blacksmiths, millers, bakers, cooks, shepherds, agriculturists, horticulturists, viñeros, vaqueros —in a word, filled all the laborious occupations known to civilized society. Their work must have been rudely executed sometimes, it may well be supposed; and they have forgotten much they once knew. But they acquired the rudiments of a practical knowledge which has outlived their good teachers, and contributed much to the little improvement this section of country has reached in eighteen years.

They are inferior only to the American in bodily strength, and might soon rank with the best Californian and Sonoranian in all the arts necessary to their physical comfort. They teach the American, even, how to make an adobe (sun-dried brick), mix the *lodo* (mud mortar), put on the *brea* (pitch) for roof—all these, recondite arts to the new beginner, yet very important to be

known, when there are no other building materials. They understand the mysteries of irrigation, the planting season, and the
harvest. Poor unfortunates! they seldom have farms of their own
to till, or a dwelling to shelter them from the rain!

John W. Caughey, ed.,
The Indians of Southern California in 1852
(San Marino, Huntington Library, 1952), 21-23.

Extermination of the Indians

BY HUBERT HOWE BANCROFT

*Hubert Howe Bancroft reached California in the gold rush and
found his personal bonanza as a book dealer and publisher. As a
sideline he became a collector of Californiana. Out of this activity
arose the Bancroft Library, now at Berkeley, the chief arsenal for
research on the history of the Far West. Bancroft also plunged into
writing the history of this half continent, employing such help as
he could find. The result was a seven-and-a-half-foot shelf of books
styled his* WORKS *with a third of the thirty-nine volumes trained
on California. Though published more than seventy years ago,
the Bancroft History is still the most cited work in its field.*

That part of the early intercourse between aboriginal Americans
and Europeans which properly belongs to history may be briefly
given. For short work was made of it in California. The savages
were in the way; the miners and settlers were arrogant and impatient; there were no missionaries or others present with even
the poor pretense of soul-saving or civilizing. It was one of the
last human hunts of civilization, and the basest and most brutal
of them all.

We do not know why the Digger Indians of California were so
shabbily treated by nature; why with such fair surroundings they
were made so much lower in the scale of intelligence than their
neighbors; but being low, and unsophisticated, in a measure

harmless until trodden upon, surely it was not a mark of high merit on the part of the new comers to exterminate them so quickly. They were without houses or dress, with hardly any knowledge of agriculture, and almost devoid of religious ideas, roaming through forest and plain in search of roots and berries, small game and fish, improvident and dependent wholly on the products of the seasons. Split into petty bands, they were kept apart by a confusing multiplicity of tongues.

The professed aim of the early missionaries, to spread civilization, would appear to have discovered a prolific field; but indolent in mind as well as body, the natives offered no encouragement, and the fathers soon adopted the plan of extending the pupillage system of Mexico into actual serfdom on this remote frontier. Gathered partly by force from their hunting-fields and haunts, with their nomadic allurements, the Indians were set to toil on plantations; not severely, for friar rule was tempered by religion; but without any incentives or hopes beyond those of a slave, and maintained in a politic condition of ignorance and abjection. The sale and decay of the missions brought further hardships to the fold. A few had acquired sufficient knowledge of settled customs to remain either as hangers-on of the colonists or to manage a field or cattle range of their own. The rest drifted back among their roaming kindred to revel in savage freedom, with many a fresh vice to poison the good nature of an abasing indifference. Imbued with a certain taste for the comforts of their former life, notably for meat, they found additional incentive for horse and cattle stealing, partly in retaliation for the overbearing manners and harsh treatment so often experienced from their Mexican masters. This feeling had in many directions grown bitter, and during the conquest by the United States it led to a more menacing attitude, marked by atrocities.

In the southern half of the state the wild Indians were practically restricted to the Coast range and valleys eastward. On the lower San Joaquin and beyond, the influence of the missions faded into a still fainter impress left by occasional contact with settled outposts, and with kidnappers from missions and pueblos. The gold discovery brought them a share of affluence, but the increased intercourse with white adventurers led to degrading habits, particularly drunkenness and prostitution, which acquired further virulence from the fostered taste for finery, and the disposition to linger round mining camps to pick up cast-off clothing and refuse. The attendant train of disease produced sadder havoc in their ranks than sword or famine.

The most prominent feature of their contact with the gold-seekers was abuse on the part of white men, and consequent retaliation. A hatred for Indians was acquired on the plains, from which the milder tribes of California had to suffer. Then followed the rush of miners into regions hitherto claimed as tribal ranges, with consequent encounters, and the slaughter or repulse of less strong intruders, many of whom found to their cost that the confidence inspired by the milder natives of the lower Sacramento was misplaced when applied to the fiercer clans of the north and of the hills. The old practice of kidnapping continued in force, partly owing to the high price of labor, partly for immoral purposes.

Race antagonism, for much of which the Mexicans were responsible, brought on many evil complications; later came maltreatment by agents, with embezzlement of presents and property pertaining to the wards, and disregarded treaties and criminal neglect by the government. The indifference and errors of the latter were a main cause for the many wanton outrages.

Thus it is that the California valley cannot grace her annals with a single Indian war bordering on respectability. It can boast, however, a hundred or two of as brutal butcherings, on the part of our honest miners and brave pioneers, as any area of equal extent in our republic. The poor natives of California had neither the strength nor the intelligence to unite in any formidable numbers; hence, when now and then one of them plucked up courage to defend his wife and little ones, or to retaliate on one of the many outrages that were constantly being perpetrated upon them by white persons, sufficient excuse was offered for the miners and settlers to band and shoot down any Indians they met, old or young, innocent or guilty, friendly or hostile, until their appetite for blood was appeased.

Hubert Howe Bancroft, *History of California*
(San Francisco, 1884-1890), VII, 474-477.

The Food Problem
of the California Indians

BY A. L. KROEBER

Although his interests encompassed the whole field of anthropology and more, A. L. Kroeber has special eminence in the study of the Indians of California. For many years he headed the University of California's distinguished department of anthropology, his students were in the forefront of research on the Californians, his own investigations were often in this field, and he systematized the knowledge available in the cyclopedic Handbook from which the following selection is drawn.

The California Indians are perhaps the most omnivorous group of tribes on the continent. The corn, salmon, buffalo, reindeer, or seal which formed the predominant staple in other regions, did indeed have a parallel in the acorn of California; but the parallel is striking rather than intrinsic.

To begin with, the oak is absent from many tracts. It does not grow in the higher mountains, in the desert, on most of the immediate coast; and it is at best rare in districts like the baked plains inhabited by the southern Yokuts valley tribes, a fact that may help to explain the permanent association and commingling of the majority of these tribes with their foothill neighbors. It is true that at worst it is rarely a far journey to an abundant growth of acorn-bearing trees anywhere in California; but the availability of such supplies was greatly diminished by the habits of intense adherence to their limited soil followed by the great majority of divisions.

Then, where the acorn abounded, the practices both of collecting and of treating it led directly to the utilization also of other sources of nourishment. The farmer may and does hunt, or fish, or gather wild growths; but these activities, being of a different order, are a distraction from his regular pursuits, and an adjustment is necessary. Either the pursuit of wild foods becomes a subsidiary activity, indulged in intermittently as leisure affords, and from the motive of variety rather than need, or a sexual or seasonal division becomes established, which makes the same people in part, or for part of the year, farmers and in part hunters. An inclination of this sort is not wanting in many districts of California. The dry and hot summer makes an outdoor life in the hills, near the heads of the vanishing streams, a convenience and a pleasure which coincide almost exactly with the opportunity to hunt and to gather the various natural crops as they become available from month to month. The wet winter renders house life in the permanent settlement in a valley or on a river correspondingly attractive, and combines residence there with the easiest chance to fish the now enlarged streams on an extensive scale, or to pursue the swarms of arrived water fowl.

But this division was not momentous. The distances ranged over were minute. Fishing was not excluded among the hills. Deer, rabbits and gophers could be hunted in the mild winter as well as in summer. And while acorns and other plant foods might be garnered each only over a brief season, it was an essential part of their use that much of their preparation as well as consumption should be spread through the cycle of the calendar.

Further, the food resources of California were bountiful in their variety rather than in their overwhelming abundance along special lines. If one supply failed, there were a hundred others to fall back upon. If a drought withered the corn shoots, if the buffalo unaccountably shifted, or the salmon failed to run, the very existence of peoples in other regions was shaken to its foundations. But the manifold distribution of available foods in California and the working out of corresponding means of reclaiming them prevented a failure of the acorn crop from producing similar effects. It might produce short rations and racking hunger, but scarcely starvation. It may be that it is chiefly our astounding ignorance of all the more intimate and basal phases of their lives that makes it seem as if downright mortal famine had been less often the portion of the Californian tribes than of those in most other regions of the continent. Yet, with all allowance for this potential factor of ignorance in our understanding, it does appear that such catastrophes were less deep and less regularly recurring. Both formulated and experiential tradition are nearly silent on actual famines, or refer to them with rationalizing abstraction.

26

The only definite cases that have come to cognizance, other than for a few truly desert hordes whose slender subsistence permanently hung by a thread, are among the Mohave, an agricultural community in an oasis, and among the Indians of the lower Klamath, whose habits, in their primal dependence on the salmon, approximated those of the tribes of the coasts north of California.

The gathering of the acorn is like that of the pine nut; its leaching has led to the recognition of the serviceability of the buckeye once its poison is dissolved out; the grinding has stimulated the use of small hard seeds, which become edible only in pulverized form. The securing of plant foods in general is not separated by any gap of distinctive process from that of obtaining grasshoppers, caterpillars, maggots, snails, mollusks, crawfish, or turtles, which can be got in masses or are practically immobile: a woman's digging stick will procure worms as readily as bulbs. Again, it is only a step to the taking of minnows in brooks, of gophers, or lizards, or small birds: the simplest of snares, a long stick, a thrown stone even, suffice with patience, and a boy can help out his grandmother. The fish pot is not very different from the acorn receptacle, and weirs, traps, stiff nets, and other devices for capturing fish are made in the same technique of basketry as the beaters, carriers, and winnowers for seeds. Even hunting was but occasionally the open, outright affair we are likely to think. Ducks were snared and netted, rabbits driven into nets, even deer caught in nooses and with similar devices. There is nothing in all this like the difference between riding down buffalo and gathering wild rice, like the break from whale hunting to berry picking, from farming to stalking deer.

The California Indian, then, secured his variety of foods by techniques that were closely interrelated, or, where diverse, connected by innumerable transitions. Few of the processes involved high skill or long experience for their successful application; none entailed serious danger, material exposure, or even strenuous effort. A little modification, and each process was capable of successful employment on some other class of food objects. Thus the activities called upon were distinguished by patience, simplicity, and crude adaptability rather than by intense endeavor and accurate specialization; and their outcome tended to manifold distribution

27

and approximate balance in place of high yields or concentration along particular but detached lines.

The human food production of aboriginal California will accordingly not be well understood until a really thorough study has been made of all of the activities of this kind among at least one people. The substances and the means are both so numerous that a recapitulation of such data as are available is always only a random, scattering selection.

Observers have mentioned what appealed to their sense of novelty or ingenuity, what they happened to see at a given moment, or what their native informants were interested in. But we rarely know whether such and such a device is peculiar to a locality or widespread, and if the former, why; whether it was a sporadic means or one that was seriously depended on; and what analogous ones it replaced. Statements that this tribe used a salmon harpoon, another a scoop net, a third a seine, a fourth poison, and that another built weirs, give us in their totality some approximation to a picture of the set of activities that underlie fishing in California as a whole: but for each individual group the statement is of little significance, for it is likely that those who used the nets used the spear and poison also, but under distinctive conditions; and when they did not, the question is whether the lack of one device is due to a more productive specialization of another, or to natural circumstances which made the employment of this or that method from the common stock of knowledge impracticable for certain localities.

There is, however, one point where neither experience nor environment is a factor, and in which pure custom reigns supreme: the animals chosen for the list of those not eaten. Myth, magic, totemism, or other beliefs may be at the bottom; but every tribe has such an index, which is totally unconnected with its abilities, cultural or physical, to take food.

Among the Yokuts, one animal stands out as edible that everywhere in northern California is absolute taboo and deadly poison: the dog. The Yurok give as their formal reason for not drinking river water that a large stream might contain human foetuses or a dead dog. The Yokuts did not shrink from eating dogs.

Coyote flesh was generally avoided, whether from religious

28

reverence or magical fear is not clear. Grizzly-bear meat was also viewed askance. The bear might have devoured human flesh, which would be near to making its eater a cannibal. Besides, in all probability, there was a lurking suspicion that a grizzly bear might not be a real one, but a transformed bear doctor. The disposition of the animal showed itself in the muscular fibers bristling erect when the flesh was cut, the Yokuts say. Brown bears had fewer plays of the imagination directed upon them, but even their meat was sometimes avoided. Birds of prey and carrion from the eagle down to the crow were not eaten. Their flesh, of course, is far from palatable; but it is these very birds that are central in Yokuts totemism, and the rigid abstinence may have this religious motivation. All reptiles were unclean to the southern Yokuts, as to the Tübatulabal; but the northern tribes exercised a peculiar discrimination. The gopher snake, water snakes, and frogs were rejected, but lizards, turtles, and, what is strangest of all, the rattlesnake, were fit food to the Chukchansi. There is a likely alien influence in this, for the neighboring Miwok probably, and the Salinans to the west certainly, ate snakes, lizards, and even frogs. On the other hand, the southern Yokuts relished the skunk, which when smoked to death in its hole was without offensive odor; while to the Miwok and Salinans it was abomination.

A. L. Kroeber, *Handbook of the California Indians*
(Washington, 1925), 523-526.

Acorn Cookery

BY C. HART MERRIAM

C. Hart Merriam was originally a biologist. He published significantly in that field, for instance in his Review of the Grizzly and Big Brown Bears of North America *(1918). A few years earlier his interest turned to the Indians of California, and he budgeted about six months a year to visiting and questioning them. The information he assembled is precisioned and therefore graphic. In the acorn cooking here described one modern element*

*has intruded—the cloth used to line the rinsing basin. In all else
the method was purely primitive.*

Near the northwest corner of Mono Lake I once watched two
squaws cook acorn mush for a band of about twenty Indians. The
acorns had been first reduced to meal by hammering with stone
pestles in deeply worn mortar pits dug out of the solid rock and
had been sifted in the winnowing baskets by an adroit motion
which separates the fine from the coarse—a motion the novice can
never get. It was then "leached" to take away the bitter taste.
This was done by allowing the water to filter through it in a
primitive but ingenious way. The place selected was a dry sandy
knoll. Here a shallow hole a foot deep and four or five feet in
diameter was dug and lined with two pieces of cloth, laid over one
another at right angles. The meal was placed on the cloth and
large basketfuls of water were laboriously brought from a neigbor-
ing stream, carried up the hill, and poured over the meal, which
was patted by the hands until thoroughly wet. The water sank
through into the porous sand and was replaced by fresh basketfuls
until, after repeated tastings, the women found the bitterness
sufficiently washed out. The meal was then scraped together by
the hands and heaped up in irregular masses; part was at once
put into a large basket to cook; the remainder was afterwards
made into cakes for future use and laid in the sun to dry.

The cooking basket was filled a little more than half full of
water and placed near the fire. Then four hot stones, six or eight
inches in diameter, were taken out of the fire by means of two
sticks and dropped into the basket. Almost immediately the water
began to boil and the mush to thicken. During the twenty minutes or half-hour required for the cooking one of the squaws stirred
it slowly with a stick, apparently to prevent the stones from resting on one spot long enough to burn the basket. The stuff boiled
exactly like porridge, throwing up multitudes of miniature volcanoes and spluttering as if over hot coals. When it was done, the
second squaw filled two small bowl-shaped baskets with water to
receive and rinse the hot stones, which the first squaw fished out
with a flat stick. Quickly and dexterously the old squaw washed
off the adhering mush before the water got too hot for her hands

and tossed the stones back into the fire. The contents of the small baskets, which had now become thin porridge, were then poured into the thicker mush in the big basket and stirred, giving the whole the desired consistency. This completed the operation.

On cooling, the acorn mush jellies; and if put in a moderately cool place, it keeps for some days. Its color is drab or drab pink, and it has no particular taste when fresh. It always seemed to me that a little salt and a good deal of cream and sugar would improve it mightily. Still, it is eaten without seasoning or sweetening and with evident relish. In summer, if kept too long, it ferments and gives off a sour liquid of a disagreeable odor. Among the Mono Paiute it is not an everyday food but a luxury, for the reason that they have to go so far to obtain the acorns; but it is today the staple food of numerous tribes in northwestern California, of Indians of the west flank of the Sierra, and of many of the Luiseño and other "Mission" tribes in the southern part of the state.

C. Hart Merriam, *Studies of the California Indians*
(Berkeley, University of California Press, 1955), 117-118.

Mono Basketry

BY C. HART MERRIAM

Some of the Mono still survive, and so does their name applied to Mono Lake and the surrounding basin. They are a branch of the Paiute.

Most of the utensils of the Mono Paiute, including dishes, water bottles and vessels for cooking, are baskets made by their own hands, as of old. These baskets may be classed by forms or uses into a dozen categories: cradles or papoose baskets, large cornucopia-shaped burden baskets, snowshoe-shaped winnowing baskets, scoop-shaped winnowing baskets, spoon-shaped baskets with handles for collecting pine nuts, deep bowl-shaped baskets for cooking; individual mush bowls; ribbed trinket baskets; jugs and bottles for holding and carrying water, deep cylindrical baskets for collecting worms; small flat, oval seed paddles, with a handle,

31

for knocking seeds off standing plants; and small conical baskets worn by the squaws as hats, and also used for gathering berries and fruit.

Some of the baskets are plain; others ornamented with intricate, striking, and beautiful designs, woven in black and red. The black is the split root of the brake-fern (Pteris), the red the inner bark of the redbud (Cercis). Besides these, some of the coarser baskets, particularly the large conical ones for carrying burdens, are ornamented by simply leaving the bark on some of the willow strands of which they are composed.

The best and finest of the Mono Paiute baskets are those made for cooking. They may be large or small, with straight-flaring or rounded sides, but all have flat bottoms and all are of what Professor Mason calls the "three-rod foundation" type. This class includes the ceremonial baskets—the most sacred and precious possessions of the tribe. The designs on these are symbolic, but their meaning is exceedingly difficult to ascertain. At one time I thought the ceremonial baskets should be put in a class by themselves, but the difficulty of discriminating between some of them and some of the ordinary cooking baskets is so great that no hard and fast line can be drawn. The ceremonial baskets are used for cooking acorn meal at certain ceremonial feasts, and are now sometimes used also for cooking the ordinary pine-nut soup—a sign of the waning respect for aboriginal rites.

These water bottles (o-sa, o-sa-ha) are of various shapes and sizes; they hold from half a gallon to twelve or fifteen gallons each. The larger ones are for camp use only, being much too heavy, when full of water, to be carried on horseback. They are always broad and spindle-shaped, a form beautifully adapted for use when lying on the ground. The lower or bottom part is much longer than the upper, which is given off at such an angle that, when one side rests flat on the ground, the mouth is thrown upward so far that the bottle can be filled nearly full without spilling. If the point of the bottom is sunk just a little in the sand, it will lie on its side quite full without letting any water escape. But this is by no means the only advantage of the spindle shape, for when the basket is full, the weight is so delicately adjusted (the broad middle part acting as a fulcrum) that the slightest pressure on the mouth is sufficient to tilt it down enough to let the water flow out—a most convenient arrangement for filling other receptacles and also for drinking when one is reclining on the ground. On the desert at the east end of Mono Lake I have seen a baby crawl to one of these bottles, take the mouth in its mouth, tilt it down and drink its fill, without touching a hand to the bottle. When let go, the bottle immediately tipped back to its former position without the loss of a drop. A more simple, efficient, and ingenious device would be hard to find. . . .

The big camp bottles, when full, are exceedingly heavy. In carrying them the body is inclined forward so as to distribute the weight over the back, and they are kept from slipping down by a broad band which passes over the forehead. I have seen a squaw, who had taken one to a small stream to fill, find herself unable to lift it in position alone; but when assisted, and once the heavy burden was in place, she walked slowly off with it and climbed the hill to her camp, perhaps an eighth of a mile distant. In summer they are usually tucked into the brush at one corner of the wickiup, sheltered from the direct rays of the sun. . . .

Winnowing baskets (te'-ma) are large, flat, broadly subtriangular or snowshoe-shaped baskets, more or less concave or scooped and nearly always ornamented by one or more bands, sometimes with rather elaborate designs. They are of two principal types: slightly concave, deepest in the middle or deeply concave, deeply scooped at or near the big end. They have many uses, such as winnowing grain and seeds, sifting meal made from acorns and nuts of the nut pine, separating the fine meal from the coarse, winnowing fly larvae so that the skins are blown away leaving the meat or kernels, and so on. The women become exceedingly skillful in their use and it is interesting to watch them work. The large te'-mas, deeply scooped near the broad end, are used for winnowing grain and other heavy seeds, which are tossed up to allow the wind to carry off the chaff.

The shallow winnowing baskets are of two kinds, compactly woven and openly woven. The openly woven ones are used for roasting pine nuts. Coals from the fire and a quantity of the nuts are thrown into the basket, and it is adroitly agitated, something after the manner of a popcorn shaker, until the nuts are sufficiently

33

roasted. This blackens the interior but does not seem to burn it injuriously. The compactly woven ones are used for separating the fine meal from the coarse after the acorns or pine nuts have been pounded in stone mortars. The movement is graceful and very skillful.

Scoop-shaped baskets, used as pinon scoops, resemble the winnowing baskets but are coarser, deeper, and usually much narrower.

The cooking baskets (opa, opa-che-da) are bowl-shaped coiled baskets of the 3-rod foundation type, with relatively small flat bottoms. Most of them are beautifully made, and many are handsomely decorated. The ceremonial baskets are usually of this order and their designs are sacred and symbolic. They are the finest baskets made by the Paiute. In the older ones the designs are usually simple, but strong and highly effective. In some of the modern ones they are more diffuse and much less artistic. Some of the small ones, now made to sell, are overloaded with design and the design is brought down over the bottom—a thing I have never seen in an old Paiute basket. They are examples of modern degenerate work, which is common among tribes which make baskets for the trade instead of for their own use. Nevertheless, such baskets find a ready market and bring good prices, so that there is very little incentive for continuing the old styles.

C. Hart Merriam, *Studies of the California Indians*
(Berkeley, University of California Press, 1955), 118-122.

Ishi, the Last Yahi

BY T. T. WATERMAN

T. T. Waterman, University of California anthropologist and museum curator, wrote also on such topics as the religious practices of the Diegueños and the ethnogeography of the Yurok. His essay on Ishi has the added quality of being a personal tribute to a respected friend.

I often feel that it is hard to tell the story of Ishi in such a way as to convince people of its reality. He has been described as the last survivor of a tribe that remained in the Stone Age until the twentieth century. I should like to tell enough of the history of his little group to explain how it was possible for them to remain "primitive." In spite of the fact that in 1910 he was still living in the age of stone, he was himself a rare character, with a mind of unusual caliber.

First of all I should like to tell you something about his tribe. It is the old story of an Indian people being crowded by the whites. In this case, however, the Indians most concerned were already a small group surrounded by enemies when the whites came into the country. They called themselves simply Yahi (people) as Indian tribes mostly do, and this has come to be used as their tribal name. The Yahi were not numerically as strong as the surrounding peoples, and had for some generations been driven to follow a prowling life. They frequented a very wild area along Mill and Deer creeks, east of the Sacramento River in northern California. Their fastnesses lay in the hills just to the east of the great level stretches of the Sacramento Valley. The country here is an old lava formation and is accordingly a region of cliffs and wild gorges, with numerous dusky glens and duskier caves, the canyon floors and slopes of the hills overgrown with a perfect tangle of scrub.

In this wild region the Yahi roved about safe from intrusion, and lived securely in their own empire except for the fact that at infrequent intervals snow and heavy weather brought them to the verge of starvation. Under such circumstances they were forced to pay flying visits to the sunny lands of their richer neighbors in the valley. The memory of old scores still unsettled on each side always made these trips an occasion for violence. Long before the coming of the whites the Yahi had learned one principle very thoroughly. It was, in plain language, this: "When outnumbered, scoot for Deer Creek." Consequently, when the white invasion began, the Yahi escaped the fate of the other Indian tribes. The valley Indians became hangers-on of civilization and lost in some cases even the memory of their old life. The Yahi followed their time-honored rule and took refuge in their foothill fastnesses. As the Indian tribes of the valley were replaced by white settlers, the Yahi transferred to the white "valley people" the bitter hostility they had already learned to feel. So they remained a "wild" tribe.

The history of this wild tribe has in it a good deal of the pathetic. The whites were not satisfied to let them alone. It grew to be the custom to blame every miscarriage of plans to the presence of these "wild" Indians. If sheep strayed or were eaten by pumas, the settlers preferred in most cases to believe that the Indians had made way with them. If provisions were taken from outlying camps, Indians could always be conjured up to take the blame. Even if freshets drowned the onion patches, or if potato bugs got away with the "spuds," it was felt in some dim way that Indians were probably at the bottom of it. In more tragic cases, where murders were committed in out-of-the-way places, nothing could convince the settlers of the Indians' innocence. By 1860 there came to be a sort of war between the whites and the Indians, in which most of the aggression was on the part of the whites. The rest is a story I almost hate to tell.

The men into whose hands fell the adjusting of relations between the whites and the Yahi Indians showed at times a ferocity that is almost incredible. It was of course unavoidable that there should be friction. In a general way, and sentiment aside, the old Indian way of life had in every case to be done away with. When Columbus landed on San Salvador, there was only one Indian to each twenty-four square miles of North America (speaking in general averages). The outlook for humanity as a whole demanded that this Indian population be displaced and crowded together. It was inevitable that intensive farming should replace the haphazard husbandry and roving habits of the Indians. The pity was that this "displacing" was never done systematically, nor was it ever done by the recognized agents of government. Recognized government took a hand in every case only after the displacing had already been made an accomplished fact by traders and trappers along the frontier. The "frontiersman" is not quite so romantic and Homeric a figure as the novelists would make us believe. The truth is that he is always irresponsible, usually indifferent, frequently ignorant, and in some cases thoroughly brutalized. I might cite three or four instances in connection with the Yahi.

A party of whites, in April 1871, pursued a band of Indians with dogs. They located them in a cave across a narrow gulch, and shot a number of them, finally entering the cave itself. Here they found a lot of dried meat, and some small children. The hero of the occasion, being a humane man, a person of fine sensibilities and delicacy of feeling, could not bear to kill these babies—at any rate, not with the heavy 56-calibre Spencer rifle he was carrying. "It tore them up too bad." *So he shot them with his 38-calibre Smith and Wesson revolver.* The names of several men who were in this party are in my notes. The bodies later disappeared. Another informant, referring to an occasion some years later, told me of finding a cave with marks of occupation, ashes, and human teeth. From his description of the locality I gathered that he was describing the same cave. Apparently the survivors had returned and cremated the dead, according to their tribal custom.

In the fall of 1865 a party of whites looking for scalps (the whites did the scalping then in California, not the Indians) spied a party of Yahi encamped. There were men, women, children, babies, and dogs—a whole tribe, or what was left of one. Just before daybreak the whites separated into two parties and closed in on the Indians from two sides. The stage was set for one act in the drama of the Yahi tribe. When the firing began the startled Indians, avoiding one party, ran into the other. An informant of mine who visited the scene of the "skirmish" some time later counted forty-three skeletons. Only a few Indians escaped.

On good authority I can report the case of an old prospector-pioneer-miner-trapper of this region who had on his bed even in recent years a blanket lined with Indian scalps. These he had taken years before. He had never been a Government scout, soldier, or officer of the law. The Indians he had killed he had killed purely on his own account. No reckoning was at any time demanded of him.

It is important to note these facts, for they explain what would otherwise be almost incredible. By 1870 or soon after, the Yahi tribe had been reduced to a few individuals. They disappeared from sight, and for forty years we have practically no account of them. I say practically, for as a matter of fact they were seen on at least half a dozen occasions during this time. I might cite one or two. A good man and true, who is now well known to me, was deer hunting as a lad, about twenty-five years ago, on Big Antelope Creek. The following curious incident happened. In working about a buckeye thicket, he heard noises. He sent his dog in to rout out whatever was in there. The dog came out frightened, so he went in himself. The plain fact was that he had run on to a party of the wild Indians, though all he could see at first were objects moving through the brush trying to get away from him. They finally began to shoot at him with bows. Three arrows were fired at him. One went through his hatbrim, grazing his face, and broke off on a boulder in front of him. He has the arrow yet, and showed it to me. In trying to get away, they dropped among other things a complete arrow-making outfit. This outfit is now in our Museum. On other occasions they were more clearly seen, so that it is not true that they totally disappeared. It is a very curious fact that when individuals at rare intervals reported such incidents as the one I have mentioned it created no interest, for they were simply put down as liars. So the presence of "wild" Indians persisted through a long period as a sort of local tradition or myth. The incidents when they were seen were not even reported in the papers.

It seems almost impossible that in a thickly settled region like California, this group could go on living their own primitive life. Yet they did so. It is perfectly certain that they had nothing to do with the whites directly. They carried on an independent existence. They profited, however, by picking up certain property around abandoned camps, as they naturally would. Thus they got bits of metal which they used for tools, and some cloth. They also preferred to make arrow points out of bottle glass, rather than out of the native obsidian rock. They hunted with the bow and arrow, for two reasons. In the first place they did not understand firearms, and seemingly never had had any in their possession. In the second place the bow was silent. In the river they speared fish in the primitive way, smoking it over a fire and storing it away for winter. I have seen the framework of the brush hut they used for this purpose. In the summer they slipped out of their retreat, and went to the eastward as far as Mount Lassen and on its upper slopes they hunted in peace until the snow drove them down. We know this peak now as California's only active volcano but in those days it was silent and still. Most of their time they spent in Deer Creek canyon, within a few miles of the valley, in the midst of its thickest jungles of scrub oak and brush. Here they fished and hunted, gathered acorns and seeds, and managed an independent existence. That they were not discovered is due to their experience with the whites, and to the fact that there were only a few of them. This, in connection with the character of their country, enabled them to keep out of sight for more than a generation.

Fifteen miles in an air line from their foothill stronghold, trains on the Southern Pacific Railroad passed daily back and forth. Yet in their rugged canyon, where the scrub oak and poison oak are so thick that the explorer can make only two miles a day through it (I speak from experience) they passed long years safe from detection. The story of how the small remnants of a tribe were finally discovered and became scattered, I have told in another place. I merely want to insist here that the last survivor, who fell into my hands in 1910, was still a stone-age Indian, as unaccustomed to the ways of civilization as could well be imagined.

I should like to tell something of my acquaintance with Ishi, especially those incidents which illustrate the character of the man and shed light on his peculiar viewpoint. I may begin by speaking of railroad trains. Our friendship started at Oroville, California, where loneliness and hunger had driven Ishi to come into a slaughterhouse near town. In bringing him down to the University, where his home was to be for the rest of his life, it was necessary to take the train. Behold Ishi and myself, an attendant Indian, and some hundreds of interested palefaces, waiting on the platform for the train to come in. As Number Five appeared in the distance and came whistling and smoking down the humming rails in a cloud of dust, Ishi wanted to get behind something. We were standing some distance from the track as it was, for I felt that he might be afraid of the engine. My charge however wanted to hide *behind* something. He had often seen trains. Later he told us in his own language that he had in his wanderings seen trains go by in the distance. But he did not know they ran on tracks. When he saw them he always lay down in the grass or behind a

39

bush until they were out of sight. He visualized a train as some devil-driven, inhuman prodigy. Security lay not in keeping off of the right-of-way, but in keeping out of its sight.

Here is another fact that illustrates his personal attitude. To a primitive man, what ought to prove most astonishing in a modern city? I would have said at once, the height of the build-ings. For Ishi, the overwhelming thing about San Francisco was the number of people. That he never got over. Until he came into civilization, the largest number of people he had ever seen together at any one time was five! At first a crowd gathered around him alarmed him and made him uneasy. He never entirely got over his feeling of awe, even when he learned that everybody meant well. The big buildings he was interested in. He found them edifying, but he distinctly was not greatly impressed. The reason, as far as I could understand it, was this. He mentally compared a towering twelve-story building not with his hut in Deer Creek, which was only four feet high, but with the cliffs and crags of his native mountains. He had something in some way analogous stored up in his experience. And to see five thousand people at once was something undreamed of, and it upset him.

Which is to be considered more interesting and surprising, *per se*, an ordinary trolley car or an automobile? For Ishi, the trolley car, every time. I stupidly expected him to grow excited over his first automobile, as I did over mine, in the year 1898. For Ishi, of course, both were plain miracles. Both the auto and the streetcar were agitated and driven about by some supernatural power—one as much as the other. The street car, however, was the bigger of the two, it had a gong which rang loudly at times, and moreover was provided with an attachment which went "shoo!" and blew the dust away when the airbrakes were released. Ishi would watch trolley cars by the hour.

Aeroplanes, by the way, he took quite philosophically. We took him down to Golden Gate Park to see Harry Fowler start to fly across the continent. When the plane was trundled out and the engines started, the Indian was surprised and amused at the uproar they created. The machine was finally launched, and after a long circuit, soared back above our heads. As it came overhead we particularly called his notice to it. He was mildly interested.

"*Saltu?*" he said interrogatively, nodding toward the plane a thousand feet skyward, "White man up there?" When we said yes he laughed a bit, apparently at the white man's funny ways, and let it pass. Either he was ready to expect anything by that time, or else his amazement was too deep for any outward expression. Like most "nature-people," he was inclined to preserve his dignity in the face of the unfamiliar or the overwhelming, giving very little sign. Under equivalent stimulation of course the paleface dances about and squeals.

Ishi was however jarred completely out of his equanimity, amazed past speech or movement, by a window shade. On the morning of his second day at the Museum, I found him trying to raise the shade to let the sunlight in. It gave me a queer feeling to realize that never in his experience, either in his canyon home or in the Oroville jail (the first thirty hours of civilization he spent as an honored guest at Butte County's penal establishment) had he encountered the common roller shade. He tried to push it to one side and it would not go. He tried pushing it up and it would not stay. I showed him how to give it a little jerk and let it run up. The subsequent five minutes he utilized for reflection. When I came back at the end of that time, he was still trying to figure out where the shade had gone.

Concerning foods he had certain prejudices which he was never able to overcome. For example he politely asked to be excused from gravies and sauces. He did not take at all kindly to the notion of boiling food. Fried, baked, roasted, broiled, or raw he could understand. He did not like those processes which lead to semiliquids. No milk if you please for Ishi, and no eggs unless they were hard boiled. All such things, he said, lead to colds in the head! The real basis of his dislike seemed to be their aesthetic effect. I have often wondered since just how far our eating habits may be considered messy. He wanted his food dry and clean appearing. For drink he liked only transparent beverages, that could not have anything concealed about them. Tea was his idea of the proper drink.

I should like to say that in all his personal habits he was extraordinarily neat. At his first dinner he behaved as many another man has done under similar circumstances. He waited patiently until someone let him know, by setting the example, whether a given dish was to be consumed with the aid of a spoon, a knife, some kind of a fork, or with the plain fingers. Then he calmly did likewise. His actions were always in perfectly good taste. Even during his first days in civilization, he could be taken comfortably into any company. He had a certain fastidiousness which extended to all his belongings. His effects were kept carefully in order. Not only his apparel, but his arrow-making appliances, his bow, and his other impediments, were always in perfect array. During the time he lived at my home a certain member of my family constantly urged me to model my own behavior in such respects after the Indian's shining example.

Ishi, moreover, was remarkably clever with his hands. In his own way he was a fine workman. He made bows of perfect finish. He could chip arrow-points to perfection out of any of the materials which give a conchoidal fracture—obsidian, flint, agate, or bottle glass. Some of his handsomest specimens were made out of bromo-seltzer bottles. No more beautiful arrow-points exist than the ones he made. His finished arrow—point, shaft, and feathering—is a model of exquisite workmanship.

On the whole he took very kindly to civilization. He seemed apprehensive at times that we would send him back ultimately to his wilderness. Once when we were planning with much enthusiasm to take him on a camping trip, to revisit with him his foothill home, he filed a number of objections. One was that in the hills there were no chairs. A second was, that there were no houses or beds. A third was, that there was very little to eat. He had been cold and gone empty so often, in the hills, that he had few illusions left. In camp, however, he proved to be a fine companion. He could swim and wash dishes and skylark with anybody, and out-walk everybody.

He convinced me that there is such a thing as a gentlemanliness which lies outside of all training, and is an expression purely of an inward spirit. It has nothing to do with artificially acquired tricks of behavior. Ishi was slow to acquire the tricks of social contact. He never learned to shake hands but he had an innate regard for the other fellow's existence, and an inborn considerateness, that surpassed in fineness most of the civilized breeding with which I am familiar. His life came to a close as the result of an over susceptibility to tuberculosis, to which he was at some time or other exposed, and to which he never developed the slightest immunity. He contributed to science the best account he could give of the life of his people, as it was before the whites came in. To know him was a rare personal privilege, not merely an ethnological privilege. I feel myself that in many ways he was perhaps the most remarkable personality of his century.

T. T. Waterman, in *Southern Workman,*
XLVI (1917), 528-537.

2

THE COMING
OF THE SPANIARDS

CALIFORNIA's recorded history began in the 1530's when some of Cortés' men, and then the great conquistador himself, ventured as far as the peninsula. They found it hard going, so much that they gave up their project of occupying it. But exploration continued and in 1542 Juan Rodríguez Cabrillo made discovery of San Diego Bay, ran with some thoroughness the coast as far as the turn at Point Concepcion, and sailed on perhaps as far as the Oregon line. North of the point he was out of sight of land much of the time and he made no landings. He did, however, gain a fair idea of the trend of the coast and the general nature of the country.

Nothing contained in the report of this expedition stimulated an immediate follow-up. Nor did Francis Drake's visit, thirty-seven years later, when he tarried for a few weeks with his ship-load of Spanish treasure, waiting the proper season for crossing the Pacific. Using Manila galleons late in the century the Spaniards made two disastrous attempts to reconnoiter at Morro Bay and near Point Reyes. In 1602 Sebastián Vizcaíno carried out a much more thorough inspection. Retracing Cabrillo's course, he blithely renamed bays and islands with names that would persist —San Diego, Santa Catalina, San Pedro, Santa Monica, Santa Barbara, Monterey, and many more. His one landing north of Point Concepcion became the climax of his voyage. His mission was to find a port of call for the Manila galleons on their long voyage back to Mexico. With its timber, water, and fertile soil,

44

HEADLANDS, BIG SUR *by Cedric Wright*

the southern end of Monterey Bay impressed him as ideal for the purpose. His report emphasized this finding. Spain waited 167 years before proceeding to occupy the land, but all through this century and two-thirds it was a fixed idea among Spanish official-dom that the Port of Monterey was California's crowning asset.

Meanwhile, pearl fishers occasionally went to Baja California and in 1697 the Jesuits, under a special contract with the king, opened a mission frontier there. The land was forbidding and the natives were exceedingly backward. A wave of revolt in the 1730's set back the work, and the picture in general was not bright enough to prompt expansion northward.

Finally in 1769 reasons of imperial policy brought a decision to advance to Vizcaíno's Port of Monterey. Expeditions set out by sea and by land and for the first time a Spanish force marched through the land north from San Diego. Gaspar de Portolá and his men experienced earthquakes at Rio Santa Ana de los Temblores. They discovered the Los Angeles River and Plain and the San Fernando Valley. They met a simple people, sometimes a bit lightfingered, but always hospitable, and occasionally a nuisance in their zeal to entertain. They found bears in abundance near San Luis Obispo and farther north they came upon great sequoias. Crossing the Santa Lucia Mountains, they followed the Salinas to the ocean. The latitude was right, but from horseback the southern curve of Monterey Bay looked so open that they assumed Vizcaíno's port must be farther on. Thus they came to their great discovery, San Francisco Bay.

With a long and difficult supply route from Mexico and with the Indians in possession of no recognizable surplus, the Spanish colonizers had a most discouraging beginning. Early in 1770 Portolá was on the verge of pulling them all back to Mexico. They stuck it out. In mid-decade the viceroy improved the supply serv-ice by sea, and Juan Bautista de Anza opened a land route from Sonora. Over it he brought a reinforcement of some 240 men, women, and children and a herd of cattle which in time would guarantee an adequate food supply for all.

By the late eighteenth century Spain was seldom prodigal in its outlay for extending its empire. Initial subsidy for missions, pre-sidios, pueblos, and possibly for ranchos was one thing, but as soon as possible all but the military posts were expected to become self-supporting. Furthermore, the purpose in California was to set up a token occupation of the coastal strip to stall off possible British or Russian encroachments and to give protection in depth to the profitable colonies to the south. Accordingly, after the first ten or a dozen years imperial support was minimized and the colony was left to the momentum of its earlier impulse.

The explorers, from Cabrillo and Drake to Portolá and Anza, came on a great adventure. For one noteworthy figure it is securely established that he was romantic and fiction-minded. He is the man who gave California her name. We do not know who he was or exactly when or where he did the christening, though it occurred on the peninsula and before any penetration farther north. For a long time there was wild surmise about the derivation of the name. Now it is established that it came from a well-known book, Ordóñez de Montalvo's *Las sergas de Esplandián*, and California's anonymous benefactor had the genius and sentiment to see its appropriateness.

On the early voyages the record is very sketchy. Most of the men were not literate. That also was true later—none of Los Angeles' first citizens could so much as sign their names. Yet even in these early snatches, the quality of the writing often shows through. The journal of the Cabrillo expedition is spare and dignified yet eloquent. Drake's chaplain is much more voluble, and Vizcaíno's Franciscan is informal and chatty. No detail is so small or so human that it escapes him.

Portolá's own journal suggests a most taciturn man. But by his day imperial Spain had developed a strong tradition of paper work. Her frontier agents were required not merely to perform but to file detailed reports. This applied to civil and military officers and doubly to the missionaries, who customarily reported both in their capacity as employees of the government and as churchmen responsible to their superiors in the Franciscan order. This writing bulks large and, because its purpose was to inform the authorities in Spain and New Spain, it consists primarily of matter-of-fact narratives of steps taken and problems encountered, and descriptions of natives, climate, terrain, vegetation, and water supply, almost always in terms of the potential for empire building in the Spanish style, through missions, presidios, pueblos, and ranchos.

For Portolá's march, thus, we have not only his terse account but a detailed diary by engineer Miguel Costansó, a trail diary by Fray Juan Crespi, and a number of letters. On the Anza expeditions there was writing enough to permit a five-volume documentary, one volume of which is given over in its entirety to the trail diary of Fray Pablo Font.

The foremost writer of this epoch was the California Boswell, Fray Francisco Paloú. He came with the reinforcements in 1772, was made vice-president of the missions, and succeded to the presidency in 1784. He prepared a multi-volume memoir, a sourcebook on Spanish California in its critical decade. His most famous work is a biography of his life-long friend, Fray Junípero Serra, first president of the missions and California's most revered hero. In Serra, Paloú had a compelling character, a vivid personality, a man of infinite devotion and determination, a great force in the establishment of this Spanish outpost. It is appropriate that the first real example of California letters should be this biography published in Mexico in 1787.

Commencing with Jean François Gallup de Lapérouse, foreign visitors began inspection of California and performed the traditional service of their class by recording data that natives and nationals often thought too commonplace to mention. George Vancouver, first English mariner to describe San Francisco, found material deficiencies but much that was admirable about Indians and Spaniards. Many of the writers quoted in the Pastoral section fall in this same category of foreign visitor.

In the twentieth century occurred something approaching a revolution in the writing about Spanish California. Researchers discovered Spain's colonial archives as an added resource for the study of this epoch. Some of them also inspected the terrain covered and attempted wherever possible to follow the trail of their particular pioneer. Still another innovation was to study what happened in isolated California not just as a bit of local history but in relationship to larger forces and what was going on in the rest of the world. The anecdote from Charles E. Chapman's *History of California*, slight though the episode was, is the richer for details and insights that he got through archival research. Walter Nordhoff's contribution is fiction but based on familiarity with the region and people of Baja California and on use of scholarly publications. Author or editor of more than a score of volumes pertaining to the northern Spanish borderlands, Herbert E. Bolton was himself a pioneer in assessing the significance of the Spanish achievement in the belt from Florida and Georgia across the continent to California.

The California of Queen Calafia

BY GARCI RODRIGUEZ ORDONEZ DE MONTALVO

At the time of the conquest of Mexico one of the more popular books in Spain was a melodramatic thriller, Las sergas de Esplandián, *by Garci Rodríguez Ordóñez de Montalvo. In it Ordóñez introduced a placename which one of his many readers saw fit to apply to a supposed island. This island turned out to be a peninsula and, with its mainland extension, has ever since been known as California.*

Know ye that on the right hand of the Indies there is an island called California, very near the Terrestrial Paradise and inhabited by black women without a single man among them and living in the manner of Amazons. They are robust of body, strong and passionate in heart, and of great valor. Their island is one of the most rugged in the world with bold rocks and crags. Their arms are all of gold, as is the harness of the wild beasts which, after taming, they ride. In all the island there is no other metal.

They live in well-excavated caves. They have ships in which they go to raid other places, and the men they capture they carry off with them, later to be killed as will be told. At other times, being at peace with their opponents, they consort with them freely and have carnal relations from which it results that many of them become pregnant. If they give birth to a female they keep her, but if to a male they kill him. The reason for this, as is known, is that they are firmly resolved to keep the males at so small a number that without trouble they can control them with all their lands, saving those thought necessary to perpetuate the race.

In this island called California, with the great roughness of the land and the multitude of wild animals, are many griffins the like of which are not found in any other part of the world. In the season when the griffins give birth to their young, these women cover themselves with thick hides and go out to snare the little griffins, taking them to their caves where they raise them. And being quite a match for these griffins, they feed them the men taken as prisoners and the males to which they have given birth. All this is done with such skill that the griffins become thoroughly accustomed to them and do them no harm. Any male who comes to the island is killed and eaten by the griffins. Even if the latter are gorged they do not fail to seize them, fly high in the air with them, and, when tired of carrying them, let them fall to their death.

Over this island of California rules a queen, Calafía, statuesque in proportions, more beautiful than all the rest, in the flower of her womanhood, eager to perform great deeds, valiant and spirited, and ambitious to excel all those who have ruled before her.

Translated from Garci Rodríguez Ordóñez de Montalvo,
Las sergas de Esplandián (c. 1510).

Glimpses of California

FROM THE RELATION OF THE VOYAGE
OF JUAN RODRIGUEZ CABRILLO

Juan Rodríguez Cabrillo was the first mariner to reach the coast of American California. The journal is cast in the third person, but is usually credited to him and, after his death, to Bartolomé Ferrelo, the chief pilot.

On the following Thursday [September 28, 1542] . . . they discovered a closed and very good port which they named San Miguel [San Diego Bay]. It is in 34⅓ degrees. After anchoring they went ashore where there were some people, all of whom fled except three, to whom presents were given. By signs they said that farther inland people like the Spaniards [a reference doubtless to the Melchior Díaz and Alarcón expeditions] had passed, and they indicated great fear. That night they went ashore to fish with a net, and some Indians began to shoot arrows at them and wounded three.

The next morning they moved farther into the port, which is large, and brought back two boys who understood nothing by signs. They gave them shirts and sent them away.

The following morning three big Indians came to the ships and said by signs that people like us were going about in the interior, bearded, clothed, and armed like those on the ships. They made signs that they had crossbows and swords. They made gestures with the right arm as if lancing, ran about as if on horseback, and made signs that they were killing many Indians. For this reason they feared them. These people are well-built and big. They wear skins of animals. . . .

At daybreak on Saturday, October 7, they anchored . . . at an island [Catalina] and went ashore with the ship's boat to see if there were people. As the boat neared land many Indians came out of the grass and bushes, shouting, dancing, and making signs to come ashore. Seeing the women fleeing, they made signs not to be afraid. Shortly these Indians were reassured, put down their bows and arrows, launched a fine canoe carrying eight or ten Indians, and came out to the ships. They gave them beads and other presents with which they were well pleased. . . .

On Sunday, October 8, they crossed to the mainland and a large bay [San Pedro] which they named Bay of Smokes because of the many smokes they saw there. . . . This bay is in 35 degrees and is a good port, and the country is good, with many valleys, plains, and groves of trees. . . .

On Tuesday [near Point Mugu] they saw a town with large houses like those of New Spain. Many fine canoes each with twelve or thirteen Indians came to the ships. They told of Christians going about in the interior . . . and indicated that they could be reached in seven days. Juan Rodríguez determined to send two Spaniards into the interior [but instead] sent a letter. . . . They named this town "Pueblo de las Canoas." These Indians wear

51

skins of animals, are fishermen, and eat raw fish and also maguey.
. . . Here they took possession and remained until Friday, the
thirteenth. . . .

They continued their voyage . . . and always there were many
canoes because that coast is heavily populated. Many Indians
boarded the ships, pointed out the towns, and told their names:
Xuco, Bis, Sopono, Alloc, Xabaagua, Xocotoc, Potoltuc, Nacbuc,
Quelqueme, Misinagua, Misesopano, Elquis, Coloc, Mugu,
Xagua, Anacbuc, Partocac, Susuquei, Quanmu, Gua, Asimu,
Aguin, Casalic, Tucumu, and Yncpupu. . . . All this coast is thickly
settled. All these Indians brought them many sardines, fresh and
very good. . . .

On November 16 at a turn in the coast they came to a great bay
which appeared to have a port and river. All that day and night
and the next day they beat about until they saw that there was no
river or shelter. In order to take possession they dropped anchor in
forty-five fathoms but did not dare go ashore because of the heavy
surf. This bay [Monterey] is at 39 degrees and its entire shore is
covered with pines down to the water. They named it "La Baya de
los Pinos." . . .

The following Saturday they ran [south] along the coast and
by night found themselves off Cape San Martin. All this coast is
very bold and there is a great swell and the land is very high.
The mountains reach the sky and the sea beats upon them. When
sailing along close to shore it seems as if they would fall on the
ships. . . .

While wintering at the island La Posesión [San Miguel], on
January 3, 1543, Juan Rodríguez, captain of these ships, departed
this life from a fall which he had at this island when they were
there before in which he broke an arm near the shoulder. He left
as captain the chief pilot, Bartolomé Ferrelo, a native of the
Levant. At the time of his death he charged them not to abandon
the exploration of as much as possible of all that coast. They named
the island Juan Rodríguez.

Translated from the facsimile in Henry R. Wagner,
Spanish Voyages to the Northwest Coast of America
(San Francisco, California Historical Society, 1929),
450-463.

Drake and His Plate of Brasse

BY FRANCIS FLETCHER

On Drake's famous voyage round the world, Francis Fletcher was accredited as chaplain, an odd rank on what was almost a pirate ship. The paragraphs quoted are his account of the California stopover. The text of the inscription is from the Plate of Brasse now on display in the Bancroft Library.

This country our gencrall named *Albion*, and that for two causes; the one in respect of the white bancks and cliffes, which lie toward the sea; the other, that it might haue some affinity, euen in name also, with our owne country, which was sometime so called.

Before we went from thence, our generall caused to be set vp, a monument of our being there; as also of her maiesties, and successors right and title to that kingdome, namely, a plate of brasse, fast nailed to a great and firme post; whereon is engrauen her graces name, and the day and yeare of our arriuall there, and of the free giuing vp, of the prouince and kingdome, both by the king and people, into her maiesties hands; together with her highnesse picture, and armes in a piece of sixpence currant English monie, shewing it selfe by a hole made of purpose through the plate: vnderneath was likewise engrauen the name of our generall &c.

The Spaniards neuer had any dealing, or so much as set a foote in this country; the vtmost of their discoueries, reaching onely to many degrees Southward of this place.

And now, as the time of our departure was perceiued by them to draw nigh, so did the sorrowes and miseries of this people, sceme to themselues to increase vpon them; and the more certaine they were of our going away, the more doubtfull they shewed themselues, what they might doe; so that we might easily iudge that that ioy (being exceeding great) wherewith they receiued vs at our first arriual, was cleane drowned in their excessiue sorrow for our departing: For they did not onely loose on a sudden all mirth, ioy, glad countenance, pleasant speeches, agility of body, familiar reioycing one with another, and all pleasure what euer flesh and bloud might bee delighted in, but with sighes and sorrowings, with heauy hearts and grieued minds, they powred out wofull complaints and moanes, with bitter teares and wringing of their hands, tormenting themselues. And as men refusing all comfort, they onely accounted themselues as cast-awayes, and those whom the gods were about to forsake: So that nothing we could say or do, was able to ease them of their so heauy a burthen, or to deliuer them from so desperate a straite, as our leauing of them did seeme to them that it would cast them into.

Howbeit seeing they could not still enjoy our presence, they (supposing vs to be gods indeed) thought it their duties to intreate vs that being absent, we would yet be mindfull of them, and making signes of their desires, that in time to come wee would see them againe, they stole vpon vs a sacrifice, and set it on fire erre we were aware; burning therein a chaine and a bunch of feathers. We laboured by all meanes possible to withhold or withdraw them but could not preuaile, till at last we fell to prayers and singing of Psalmes, whereby they were allured immediately to forget their folly, and leaue their sacrifice vnconsumed, suffering the fire to go out, and imitating vs in all our actions; they fell a lifting vp their eyes and hands to heauen as they saw vs do.

The 23. of Iuly they tooke a sorrowfull farewell of vs, but being loath to leaue vs, they presently ranne to the tops of the hils to keepe vs in their sight as long as they could, making fires before and behind, and on each side of them, burning therein (as is to be supposed) sacrifices at our departure.

Francis Fletcher, in *The World Encompassed by Sir Francis Drake* (London, 1628), 79-81.

The Plate of Brasse

BEE IT KNOWNE VNTO ALL MEN BY THESE PRESENTS

IVNE 17 1579

BY THE GRACE OF GOD AND IN THE NAME OF HERR

MAIESTY QVEEN ELIZABETH OF ENGLAND AND HERR

SVCCESSORS FOREVER I TAKE POSSESSION OF THIS

KINGDOME WHOSE KING AND PEOPLE FREELY RESIGNE

THEIR RIGHT AND TITLE IN THE WHOLE LAND VNTO HERR

MAIESTIES KEEPEING NOW NAMED BY ME AN TO BEE

KNOWNE VNTO ALL MEN AS NOVA ALBION

FRANCIS DRAKE

Along the Coast in 1602

BY ANTONIO DE LA ASCENSIÓN

Fray Antonio de la Ascension was the official chronicler for the expedition led by Sebastián Vizcaíno in 1602 for the examination of the California coast.

A few leagues farther, they saw a large island, almost twelve leagues away from the mainland, and went to inspect it. This was the day of the martyr Santa Catalina, and for this reason it was named "Santa Catalina." They anchored near it November 28 [November 25], but before reaching it another very much larger island southwest of it was seen, but as this was somewhat distant, they left it to be explored on the return. As the ships were approaching the Isla de Santa Catalina to cast anchor, the Indian inhabitants began to raise smokes on the beach, and when they saw they had anchored, the women, children, and old men began to shout and make demonstrations of joy in proof of their happiness. They came running to the beach to receive the guests who were arriving.

As soon as the ships anchored and the sails were furled, the *General* ordered the *Almirante* to go ashore and take with him Father Antonio, Captain Peguero with some soldiers from the *Capitana*, and Captain Alarcon with twenty-four soldiers, all armed with harquebuses and with their matches lit, to see what the Indians wanted, what there was in the island, and to bring back the information at once. When those who were with the *Almirante* landed, many old men, women, and children came up with much familiarity, friendship and affability, just as if they had seen Spaniards before. Our people asked them by signs for water. They at once brought a rush barrel full of water, which was good, and said that the spring from which they took it was somewhat distant. With this news they returned to the ships to pass the night. The following day the *General* ordered a tent to be set up on land in which Fathers Andrés and Antonio should say mass, Father Tomás being now sick. Then all went to hear mass. On this occasion a great number of young Indians had assembled, well built and robust, all naked. The day before these had been fishing in some small well-built canoes of boards fastened together, with their poops and bows like barks. Some of these canoes were so large that they would hold more than twenty people. In the small ones there are ordinarily three when they go fishing, two men with their paddles and two-bladed oars, seated or on their knees, one in the stern and the other in the bow, and a boy between to throw out such water as the canoe might make. They paddle on one side and the other in such unison and concert that they go flying. . . .

The boys and girls are white and blond, and all are affable and smiling. These Indians and those of the islands make use for their living quarters of some houses made like cabins. They cover these with a mat of rushes very closely woven, something like Moorish mats, which they set up on some great upright forked poles. They are so spacious that each will hold fifty people. I think that a family lives in each one. As the houses are portable, they remove them to other places whenever it seems advisable. Neither rain nor the sun penetrates them. The vessels and pitchers in which they keep water are made of reeds. In the island there is a great quantity of something like potatoes, and small *xicamas*, which the Indians carry to the mainland to sell. They live by buying, selling and bartering. They showed us some pieces of the blue metal with which they paint themselves like the one I spoke of before. In this island and in those near by there are many Indians and many settlements and houses like those described.

The soldiers ran all over the island and in one part of it fell in with a place of worship or temple where the natives perform their sacrifices and adoration. This was a large flat patio and in one part of it, where they had what we would call an altar, there was a great circle all surrounded with feathers of various colors and shapes, which must come from the birds they sacrifice. Inside the circle there was a figure like a devil painted in various colors, in the way the Indians of New Spain are accustomed to paint them. At the sides of this were the sun and the moon. When the soldiers reached this place, inside the circle there were two large crows larger than ordinary ones, which flew away when they saw strangers, and alighted on some near-by rocks. One of the soldiers, seeing their size, aimed at them with his harquebus, and discharging it, killed them both. When the Indians saw this they began to weep and display great emotion. In my opinion, the Devil talked to them through these crows, because all the men and women hold them in great respect and fear. I saw with my own eyes some Indian women cleaning some fish on the beach for food for themselves and their husbands and children. Some crows came up to them and took this out of their hands with their bills, while they remained quiet without speaking a word or frightening them away, and were astonished to see the Spaniards throw stones at them. . . .

These Indians are very light-fingered and clever, and in stealing anything and in putting it in safety are ingenious. If it were not for being prolix in this chapter, I would relate here some of their transactions with us; I believe that they beat the gypsies in cunning and dexterity. Many of them wished to go with us, but this did not seem advisable, and so they were made to leave the ships and remain in their country. . . .

When the fleet was in sight of the mainland, and near one of the islands, which was named "Santa Barbara," the first of the channel, a canoe came flying out from the mainland with four men propelling it. Aboard was an Indian with his son and other Indians who accompanied him, who gave us to understand that he was the king or lord of that country. This canoe came up to the *Capitana*, and with great assiduity and swiftness made three turns around it, all those on board singing in their language in the manner and the tone in which the Indians of New Spain sing in their *mitotes*, or dances. They then came up to the ship and the principal Indian or petty king, grasping the end of the rope which was passed to them, came aboard without any suspicion or fear whatever, and the first thing he did on entering the ship was to make another three turns around the waist, singing in the same tone. This ceremony being concluded, standing before the *General* and the rest, he commenced a long harangue in his language, of which we could understand not a word. Having finished this, he explained by intelligible signs that the people of the Isla de Santa Catalina had notified him by four posts in canoes that the ships had arrived there and that the people on board wore clothes and beards and were kind-hearted and of good demeanor, having entertained them and given them many things, and that he should come to see us. By reason of this news he had come there to offer his country and what entertainment he could supply if we wished to receive it. He begged and prayed us to come to the shore with the ship, saying that he would provide us with everything necessary. As he did not see any women on the ship, he asked by signs if we had any, pointing to his private parts and giving us clearly to understand what he wished to say. The *General* told him he did not have any, nor were they necessary. The Indian then importuned the *General* with more energy for all to go ashore, promising to give each one ten women to serve them and entertain them. At this all of us laughed very much and the chief, thinking that we were deriding him, and that we thought he would not do what he promised, renewed his offers, and asked the *General* to send ashore a soldier in the canoe in which he had come to see with his own eyes if it was true that he could comply with what he had promised, saying that he would remain as a hostage with his son while the soldier went and returned to inform himself about the truth of it. The *General* held a council about this, and it was decided that as it was already night nothing should be done until the following day, but that when it was dawn, some should go ashore to see if there was a safe and commodious port where the ships could remain at anchor, and if there was one, they would go there, and that the Indian should go back to his country that night to make the necessary arrangements. With this they dismissed him, the *General* having given him some things. He went away well paid and contented with the good behaviour and kindness which he saw in those whom he expected to have as guests on the following day, and to get something ready with which to entertain them.

Within an hour after the chief had gone back to his country a southeast wind came up, one they had not enjoyed before in all the time they had been sailing. As it was a stern wind it seemed to the *General* and the others that they should take advantage of the opportunity which Our Lord had provided, and that on the return voyage they could come back to see what the Indian chief wanted and had promised.

Translated in Henry R. Wagner,
Spanish Voyages to the Northwest Coast of America (San Francisco, California Historical Society, 1929), 234-242.

First Travelers through the Land

BY MIGUEL COSTANSO

*Engineer Miguel Costansó was official navigator and cosmog-
rapher for Portolá's march toward Monterey. He succeeds quite
well in probing the thoughts and emotions of the Indians as well
as in recording the experiences of the Spaniards. His diary may be
appropriately read with that of Fray Juan Crespi (see pg. 66).*

The departure [from San Diego] having been fixed for the 14th
of July [1769] the governor ordered out six soldiers and a corporal
to explore the country for the distance of the first two days'
marches. These soldiers left on the morning of the 12th, and returned on the afternoon of the following day with the information
that they had found a watering-place sufficient for the men and
horses at a distance of six or seven leagues. . . .

Friday, July 28.—We pitched our camp on the left bank of the
[Santa Ana] river. To the right there is a populous Indian village;
the inhabitants received us with great kindness. Fifty-two of them
came to our quarters, and their captain or cacique asked us by
signs which we understood easily, accompanied by many entreaties, to remain there and live with them. [He said] that they
would provide antelopes, hares, or seeds for our subsistence, that
the lands which we saw were theirs, and that they would share
them with us.

At this place we experienced a terrible earthquake, which was
repeated four times during the day. . . . To this place we gave the
name of Río de los Temblores. . . .

Thursday, August 3.—We forded the Río de la Porciúncula, which
descends with great rapidity from the canyon through which it
leaves the mountains and enters the plain. . . .

Friday, August 4—From the Ojo de Agua de los Alisos [Sycamore
Spring], skirting the mountains, over a good level road covered
with grass, we reached the Ojos de Agua del Berrendo [Deer
Spring], a name we gave the place because we caught there one

of these animals alive—its leg had been broken on the preceding afternoon by a musket-shot from a volunteer soldier who had not been able to overtake it. The watering-place was situated in a hollow surrounded by low hills near the seacoast. Here we found an Indian village [and the inhabitants were] very good-natured. They came at once to our quarters with trays of seeds, nuts, and acorns; to these presents we responded with our strings of glass beads, which they hold in high esteem. . . .

Monday, August 14.—We reached the coast, and came in sight of a real town [Ventura]—the most populous and best arranged of all we had seen up to that time—situated on a tongue or point of land, right on the shore which it was dominating, and it seemed to command the waters. We counted as many as thirty large and capacious houses, spherical in form, well built, and thatched with grass. We judged from the large number of people that came out to meet us, and afterwards flocked to the camp, that there could not be less than four hundred souls in the town.

These natives are well built and of a good disposition, very agile and alert, diligent and skillful. Their handiness and ability were at their best in the construction of their canoes made of good pine boards, well joined and calked, and of a pleasing form. They handle these with equal skill, and three or four men go out to sea in them to fish, as they will hold eight or ten men. They use long double-bladed paddles and row with indescribable agility and swiftness. All their work is neat and well finished, but what is most worthy of surprise is that to work the wood and stone they have no other tools than those made of flint; they are ignorant of the use of iron and steel, or know very little of the great utility of these materials, for we saw among them some pieces of knives and sword-blades which they used for no other purpose than to cut meat or open the fish caught in the sea. We saw, and obtained in exchange for strings of glass beads and other trinkets, some baskets or trays made of reeds, with different designs; wooden plates and bowls of different forms and sizes, made of one piece so that not even those turned out in a lathe could be more successful. . . .

60

Sunday, August 20.—All the land that we examined, along the road as well as from our camp, is exceedingly pleasing, with an abundance of pasture, and covered with live-oaks, willows, and other trees, giving indications of fertility and of [a capacity] to produce whatever one might desire to sow.

The natives, not content with making us presents of their eatables, wished, furthermore, to give us a feast, thus manifesting the mutual rivalry and contention between the towns to excel each other in gifts and festivities, in order to merit our approval and praise. In the afternoon the leaders and caciques of each town came, one after the other, adorned according to their custom —painted and decked with feathers, having in their hands some split canes with the motion and noise of which they marked time for their songs, and the rhythm for the dance, so regularly and so uniformly that there was no discord.

The dancing continued all the afternoon, and we had hard work to rid ourselves of [our visitors]. Finally we sent them away, earnestly recommending them, by means of signs, not to come back during the night to disturb us; but in vain. At nightfall they returned with a large retinue of clowns or jugglers, playing whistles, the noise of which grated upon the ears. It was to be feared that they would stampede our horses, and, for this reason, the commander, with his officers and some soldiers, went out to receive them. These gave the natives some glass beads, and intimated to them that if they came back to disturb our sleep, they would no longer be our friends and we would give them a bad reception. This was a sufficient measure to cause them to retire and to leave us in peace for the remainder of the night. . . .

Thursday, August 31.—The natives here were poor—they had no houses and we doubted if this place was their permanent abode. They honored us with a dance, and it was the first place where we saw the women dance. Two of these excelled the others; they had a bunch of flowers in their hands, and accompanied the dance with various graceful gestures and movements without getting out of time in their songs. . . .

Thursday, September 7.—In this canyon we saw troops of bears; they had the land plowed up and full of the holes which they make

61

in searching for the roots they live on, which the land produces. The natives also use these roots for food, and there are some of a good relish and taste. Some of the soldiers, attracted by the chase because they had been successful on two other occasions, mounted their horses, and this time succeeded in shooting one. They, however, experienced the fierceness and anger of these animals—when they feel themselves to be wounded, headlong they charge the hunter, who can only escape by the swiftness of his horse, for the first burst of speed is more rapid than one might expect from the bulk and awkwardness of such brutes. Their endurance and strength are not easily overcome, and only the sure aim of the hunter, or the good fortune of hitting them in the head or heart, can lay them low at the first shot. The one they succeeded in killing received nine bullet wounds before it fell, and this did not happen until they hit him in the head. Other soldiers mounted on mules had the boldness to fight one of these animals. They fired at him seven or eight times and, doubtless, he died from the wounds, but he maimed two of the mules, and, by good fortune, the men who were mounted upon them extricated themselves.

The canyon was given the name of Los Osos [The Bears].

Saturday, September 16.—We entered through the canyon which allowed us passage into the mountains, following it now on one side and now on the other as the lay of the land permitted. This canyon was very narrow; in some places the hills surrounding it were cut away at the foot, and were all inaccessible, not only to the men but even to goats and deer. . . .

Wednesday, September 20.—From the top of the hill we commanded the mountain range, which extended in all directions, without seeing its end on any side—a sad outlook for these poor travelers, tired and worn out by the fatigue of the journey, by the task of clearing rough passages and breaking roads through hills, woods, dunes, and swamps. The cold began to be felt; we had already many soldiers afflicted with scurvy and rendered incapable of service, the toil of which increased for those who remained on their feet. . . .

Saturday, September 30.—From our camp we could hear the sound of the ocean, but we could not see the shore. Therefore, desirous of knowing on what part of the coast we were, and convinced that we could not be very far from the desired port of Monterey, . . . our commander resolved that the scouts should set out promptly to explore the coast and the mouth of the river. . . .

Tuesday, October 3.—The scouts returned in the afternoon and said that they had not seen a port, either to the north or south of the Punta de Pinos; they did see, however, a small bay lying between the said Punta de Pinos and another point farther to the south. . . .

Wednesday, October 4.—Our commander, somewhat confused by these reports, determined to call a meeting of his officers to consider what action was most suitable in the present exigency. He drew attention to the scarcity of provisions that confronted us; to the large number of sick we had among us (there were seventeen men half-crippled and unfit for work) ; to the season, already far advanced; and to the great suffering of the men who remained well, on account of the unlimited work required in looking after the horses, and watching them at night, in guarding the camp, and in the continual excursions for exploration and reconnoissance. The meeting was held after we had heard the mass of the Holy Ghost, and all the officers voted unanimously that the journey be continued, as this was the only course that remained, for we hoped to find—through the grace of God—the much desired port of Monterey, and in it the packet *San Joseph* which would relieve our needs; and, if God willed that in the search for Monterey we should all perish, we would have performed our duty towards God and man, laboring together until death for the success of the undertaking upon which we had been sent. . . .

Sunday, October 15.—We directed our course to the north-north-west, without withdrawing far from the coast, from which we were separated by some high hills very thickly covered with trees which some said were savins. They were the largest, highest, and straightest trees that we had seen up to that time; some of them were four or five yards in diameter. The wood is of a dull, dark, reddish color, very soft, brittle, and full of knots.

Tuesday, October 31.—The hills which prevented our passage along the shore, although easy of access for the ascent, had, on the other side, a very difficult and rough descent. The pioneers went out in the morning with the sergeant to make a road over it, and afterwards, at eleven o'clock, we followed him with the pack-animals.

From the summit we saw to the northwest a large bay formed by a point of land which extended a long distance into the sea, and about which many had disputed on the preceding day, as to whether or not it was an island; it was not possible at that time to see it as clearly as now on account of the mist that covered it. Farther out, about west-northwest from us, seven rocky, white islands could be seen; and, casting the eye back upon the bay, one could see farther to the north some perpendicular white cliffs. Looking to the northeast, one could see the mouth of an estuary which appeared to extend inland. In consideration of these indications we consulted the sailing-directions of the pilot Cabrera Bueno, and it seemed to us beyond all question that what we were looking upon was the port of San Francisco; and thus we were convinced that the port of Monterey had been left behind. . . .

Sunday, December 10.—Before leaving this bay we erected a cross upon the beach with an inscription cut on the wood which said: "Dig! At the foot thou wilt find a writing." This writing is hereinafter transcribed word for word.

"The land-expedition which set our from San Diego on July 14, 1769, under the command of the governor of California, Don Gaspar de Portolá, entered the Canal de Santa Bárbara on August 9; it passed the Punta de la Concepción on the 27th of the same month; and reached the foot of the Sierra de Santa Lucía on September 13; it entered this mountain range on the 17th of the same month; it completed the passage of the mountain range, going completely round it, on October 1; and on the same day came in sight of the Punta de Pinos. On the 7th of the same month, having already examined the Punta de Pinos, and the bays to the north and south of it, without finding any indications of the port of Monterey, it decided to go forward in search of the port. On October 30 the expedition came in sight of the Punta de los Reyes, and the seven Farallones of the port of San Francisco. The expedition endeavored to reach the Punta de los Reyes, but some immense estuaries, which extend inland an extraordinary distance, and which forced it to make a very wide circuit, and other difficulties (the greatest being the lack of provisions) made it necessary for the expedition to turn back, believing that the port of Monterey might possibly be found within the Sierra de Santa Lucía, and fearing that the port might have been passed without having been seen. The expedition turned back from the farthest point of the Estero de San Francisco on November 11; it passed the Punta de Año Nuevo on the 19th of the same month; and arrived again at this Punta and Ensenada de Pinos on the 27th of the same month. From that day to the present—December 9—the expedition was engaged in searching within the mountains for the port of Monterey, skirting the side towards the sea, in spite of its ruggedness—but in vain. Finally, now disappointed and despairing of finding the port, after so many endeavors, labors, and hardships, and without other provisions than fourteen sacks of flour, the expedition sets out to-day from this bay for San Diego. Pray thou Almighty God to guide it, and, sailor, may his Divine Providence take thee to a port of safety.

"At this Ensenada de Pinos, on the 9th day of December, 1769. . . .

"The commanders of the packets—whether the *San Joseph* or *El Principe*—are requested, that if within a few days after the date of the writing they should land on this shore, and inform themselves of its contents, and of the unhappy circumstances of the expedition, they should sail close to the shore, and follow it to San Diego, so that if the expedition should have good fortune to catch sight of one of the two vessels, and should be able, by means of signals made by flags or gunshots, to indicate the place where the expedition may be, it might aid them with provisions, if that were possible.

"May God be glorified."
We set out on the march, the weather being clear and cold.

From the diary of Miguel Costansó,
in Frederick J. Teggart, ed., *The Portolá
Expedition of 1769-1770* (Berkeley, University of California Press, 1911), passim.

Los Angeles River and Plain

BY JUAN CRESPI

*Fray Juan Crespi came up from Baja California with the first de-
tachment by land, joined the Portolá march toward Monterey,
and as the only Franciscan to make this entire journey was commissioned to write the composite diary for the trip. He accompanied Fages to the San Joaquin Valley in 1772 and sailed with
Pérez to the Northwest Coast in 1774, compiling detailed journals
for these trips. His assigned mission was Carmel.*

Wednesday, August 2 [1769].—We set out from the valley in the
morning and followed the same plain in a westerly direction.
After traveling about a league and a half through a pass between
low hills, we entered a very spacious valley, well grown with
cottonwoods and alders, among which ran a beautiful river from
the north-northwest, and then, doubling the point of a steep hill,
it went on afterwards to the south. Toward the north-northeast
there is another river bed which forms a spacious water-course,
but we found it dry. This bed unites with that of the river, giving
a clear indication of great floods in the rainy season, for we saw
that it had many trunks of trees on the banks. We halted not very
far from the river, which we named Porciúncula. Here we felt
three consecutive earthquakes in the afternoon and night. We
must have traveled about three leagues to-day. This plain where
the river runs is very extensive. It has good land for planting all
kinds of grain and seeds, and is the most suitable site of all that
we have seen for a mission, for it has all the requisites for a large
settlement.

As soon as we arrived about eight heathen from a good village came to visit us; they live in this delightful place among the trees on the river. They presented us with some baskets of pinole made from seeds of sage and other grasses. Their chief brought some strings of beads made of shells, and they threw us three handfuls of them. Some of the old men were smoking pipes well made of baked clay and they puffed at us three mouthfuls of smoke. We gave them a little tobacco and glass beads, and they went away well pleased.

Thursday, August 3.—At half-past six we left the camp and forded the Porciúncula River, which runs down from the valley, flowing through it from the mountains into the plain. After crossing the river we entered a large vineyard of wild grapes and an infinity of rosebushes in full bloom. All the soil is black and loamy, and is capable of producing every kind of grain and fruit which may be planted. We went west, continually over good land well covered with grass. After traveling about half a league we came to the village of this region, the people of which, on seeing us, came out into the road. As they drew near us they begin to howl like wolves; they greeted us and wished to give us seeds, but as we had nothing at hand in which to carry them we did not accept them. Seeing this, they threw some handfuls of them on the ground and the rest in the air.

We traveled over another plain for three hours, during which we must have gone as many leagues. In the same plain we came across a grove of very large alders, high and thick, from which flows a stream of water about a buey in depth. The banks were grassy and covered with fragrant herbs and watercress. The water flowed afterwards in a deep channel towards the southwest. All the land that we saw this morning seemed admirable to us. We pitched camp near the water. This afternoon we felt new earthquakes, the continuation of which astonishes us. We judge that in the mountains that run to the west in front of us there are some volcanos, for there are many signs on the road which stretches between the Porciúncula River and the Spring of the Alders, for the explorers saw some large marshes of a certain substance like pitch; they were boiling and bubbling, and the pitch came out mixed with an abundance of water. They noticed that the water runs to one side and the pitch to the other, and that there is such an abundance of it that it would serve to caulk many ships. This place where we stopped is called the Spring of the Alders of San Estevan.

From the diary of Juan Crespi,
in Herbert E. Bolton, ed., *Fray Juan Crespi,*
Missionary Explorer (Berkeley, University of California Press, 1927), 146-149.

The Captain and the Friar

BY PEDRO FONT

The following passage from Fray Pedro Font's diary of the second Anza expedition effectively introduces both Anza and Font. It suggests the potential friction between state and church even in a unitary system such as the Spanish empire, or perhaps it is an example of how, in the rigors of a long period in the field, nerves can get frayed.

Tuesday, February 6, [1776]—I awoke again suffering from my mouth, but I was somewhat relieved afterward by touching the sores with a little powder of verdigris. The animals were rounded up for our journey, but we suspended the march and remained here because the day was very cloudy and unpleasant. The wind blew fiercely and threatened rain, and after noon rain began to fall. At night, after supper, I saw a light in the room in which Señor Anza and I slept, and went to see who had lighted it, because in the presidio there was such a scarcity of candles, as of everything else, that we were careful not to light candles unless it was necessary. I found that the cook had lighted it because he was awaiting Señor Ansa, to ask him if he should prepare the olla to march next day, as had been ordered, though he did not prepare it because it was raining. I returned to the room where we all were, in which the three fathers and Señor Ribera slept, and where we ate and passed most of the day because in the presidio there was no other habitation. I asked who had lit the candle and why, and right here and in front of everybody I made my complaint to Señor Ansa, telling him that it was hard on me that he should never tell me what he had decided, when he told it to the servants, with whom he talked about these and others things, sometimes very intimately, whereas with me he always maintained great haughtiness and reserve. He replied to me:

"Well, why do you wish, your Reverence, that I should tell you what I decide? I am under no obligation to do so."

"Yes, I know that you are not obliged to do so," I replied, "nor I to demand it; but it appears to me natural that you should tell me, as a companion, what you decide, in order that I may not be caught unprepared, for I also have to travel. It is for this reason that I would be glad to know about it, and not to interfere in your decisions. Indeed, you know very well that up to now I have not interfered in delays or marches, because it is your business to decide them, as I said to you the day when we arrived at Santa Ana, the 6th of October, when you asked me my opinion as to whether we should remain at the pueblo or at the river, after you had given orders to halt at the river. I understand you, and I know you do not like to take counsel with anybody; and I also know that you are under no obligation to do what I may ask of you, as I experienced on the 1st of December, when I requested you to move the camp to Palma's ranchería and you did not wish to do it. And yet, although you do not communicate your plans to me in order that I may give my opinion, since it is not my business and I know that you do not have to accept it, at least it would be pleasant if, as a friend, you should tell me what you decide by way of conversation and for my guidance."

To this he replied that I was complaining without reason, for he was now telling me what he had decided. I answered:

"It is true that you are telling me of it, but only at the last minute when everybody already knows it, and when I see it, as happened with the messenger whom you dispatched from the Puerto de San Carlos on the 25th of December; and with the decision to come to San Diego of which you told me on the night of January 6th, after everybody else already knew about it."

"Well, Father," he said, "your Reverence must know that my having been delayed here is because I saw that your Reverence was ill, for so far as I was concerned I would have started."

I replied that I was grateful for this favor, although up to the present he had not intimated any such thing to me; and that he must understand that I did not wish him to be delayed on my account, for since before leaving San Miguel I had said that I did not wish him to retard his marches on my account for a single day. And so I concluded:

"If we are waiting only for that let us start now at once, or to-morrow morning, even if it rains."

I said this because at San Miguel he several times decided to begin the journey and failed to do so on various pretexts that arose, under cover of which the march was delayed, because his wife wished it and he had the opportunity to give her this pleasure. In fact, I became ill during those days, and Señor Ansa, having decided to begin the journey on September 28, asked me if I were ready to travel, saying if not he would suspend the march until I should recover. I replied that he must not wait on my account, for I trusted in God that I should get better on the way.

Now, the Señora wished a little further delay, and thought she would obtain it through my being ill. For this reason she charged Doña Cathalina Ortiz, wife of Don Manuel Monteagudo, in whose house I was lodging, to persuade me to object to traveling until I was better. To this suggestion I replied that if Señor Ansa had decided to begin the march it must not be delayed on my account. Doña Cathalina said to me:

"Father, Doña Ana Regina Serrano would be very glad if they would wait at least one day more, and this could easily be brought about if you would say so, for you are ill." To this I replied:

"I also would be glad, not so much because I am ill as for another reason; but assuming that the decision has been made I did not wish to say anything." Doña Cathalina agreed with me and said:

"Well, Father, tell me plainly what your opinion is."

Thinking that this was a private conversation which we were having, I said to her:

"Señora, my opinion is that since we are now at the presidio of San Miguel, and that we have already delayed so many days, for other reasons we might as well delay one day more. Then we would set out from the presidio and begin the march on the day of that Holy Prince, after the people have heard Mass, which perhaps we might sing; and I perhaps might be able to say a few words to the people. To me this would seem better, as I already have suggested to Señor Ansa. But if he has already decided on something different and paid no attention to my suggestion, I have nothing more to say except that I do not wish it said that we have delayed on my account."

This conversation ended, Doña Cathalina went straightway to Ansa's house to relate to him what I had said; and in a short time Señor Ansa came to me, saying:

"So your Reverence has decided that we should start on the feast of San Miguel?"

"Señor," I replied, "why should I decide that? Doña Cathalina, in a casual conversation, asked my opinion, and I told her what I thought, but without opposing myself to your decision."

"Well, Father," he said, "we will do as your Reverence says."

"You will do what you wish," I replied, "and let us understand that this is not my decision; nor do I wish that you should delay the march a single day on my account."

"No, Father," he said, "but I also think that what your Reverence says is best."

Señor Ansa then left, and in a short time Doña Cathalina returned and said to me:

"Doña Ana and I thank you, because they are waiting one day more."

"Well, what have I got to do with that?" I replied.

"Much," she answered, "because Don Juan did not wish to wait, but now he is waiting because your Reverence desires it so."

"Señora," I said, "I wish neither this nor that, but only what Don Juan may wish."

"Well, Father," she replied, "as soon as Don Juan arrived at his house he said, 'Oh, dear, now I am going to wait one day more, because I must please the father; and he has decided it thus, because he wishes to have his say before setting out'," alluding to the sung Mass and the exhortation which I had suggested and he had opposed.

I have related all this at length in order to show how these lords are accustomed to resort to pretexts with the friars, making friends of them when it suits their convenience, but paying no attention to them at other times, when they do not need them.

Pedro Font, Diary, in Herbert E. Bolton,
Anza's California Expeditions
(Berkeley, University of California Press, 1930), IV, 218-224.

The Death of Junipero Serra

BY FRANCISCO PALOU

Fray Francisco Palou, closest associate of the founding president of the California missions, here reports to his superior the circumstances of Junipero Serra's death. Several insights are offered. One is Palou's distress over Serra's extreme asceticism. Another is the insistence of the Indians on a distribution of relics from the missionary who had meant so much to them.

Mission San Carlos, September 7, 1784

Hail Jesus, Mary and Joseph!
Very Reverend Father Guardian, Fray Juan Sancho
Reverend Father Guardian:

On the 28th of August just passed, God was pleased to take to eternity the soul of my ever-loved and honored father, the father president and founder of these new missions, Fray Junípero Serra.

His death was much regretted by all of us, and to me especially, as his pupil, although an unworthy one, it was a matter of extreme grief and sorrow because of the loss of so great a master, both learned and holy. God wished to give me the consolation of being present at his death by a mere chance. This was that when I was at the mission of Our Father San Francisco more than forty leagues north of here, the deceased father wrote me, intimating to me that he wished to talk over with me the news that your Reverence had communicated to him regarding the intention of the illustrious bishop of Sonora to have the reverend Dominican fathers come to occupy these new missions. I started at once, leaving at that mission my father companion Fray Pedro Cambón, and also leaving the boat anchored in the harbor. I arrived at this

72

mission of San Carlos de Monterey on the afternoon of the 18th
of the month of August. I found my beloved father happy, and
with no other ill health than his old lung trouble and the swelling of the feet from which, as your Reverence knows, he has
suffered for more than twenty years without doing the least thing
to help it. I found him as zealous as ever, preaching the gospel to
the neophytes and catechumens, and singing with them as always, chiefly the verses for the Assumption of the Blessed Mary,
whose octave it then was and on whose day, the 15th, his Reverence had chanted Mass and preached in most solemn fashion.

We discussed the question, and decided that it would be best
for me to go to the College to see if I could get information on the
matter of these missions. I regretted very deeply going so far from
his Reverence, as I told him, and especially under the present circumstances, since in a short time some decision as to the illustrious
bishop's intention might come. But he encouraged me, and told
me that he had already written to your Reverence that I would
embrace the opportunity of the ship to come, adding, "In remaining as I do, I offer you to God for His holy love and in accordance with His holy will." With this decided, we discussed the
details, making notes of whatever we judged desirable until the
sailing.

On the 22d, when the ship arrived at this port, his lungs felt
more congested, although he paid no attention to it, in spite of the
fact that there was some internal change, for on the 20th he had
prepared to make again or to renew his general confession, as he
had done many times with me. I attributed this to the fact that
he was doing it because of my departure, but I immediately
changed my opinion, because at night he had a fever, and had it
still on the morning of the 27th. However he got up and recited
the Divine Office up to and including the terce, rising as if nothing
had happened. He asked me to administer the holy viaticum to
him before any misfortune could happen that would deprive
him of this spiritual consolation, adding that it was to be in the
church. I told him that it was not necessary for it to be carried
out with all the ceremony possible. He gave me such reasons,
sprung from his profound humility and religious fervor, that I had
to yield to his desires, and on his own feet he went to church, about

73

a hundred yards distant, accompanied by the whole town of neophytes, the commander of the presidio, and part of the troops. Kneeling near the chancel, he prepared to receive the consecration of the viaticum. As I began the hymn to summon the Host the sick father began the *Tantum Ergo* with the sonorous voice he always used, as if nothing were the matter, affecting us all so deeply that we could not follow him in the singing. I administered the holy viaticum with the ceremonies of the manual of the Order, and when the service was finished he remained in the same posture on his knees, thanking the Lord. When this was concluded he returned to the cell or little room in his quarters, leaving us all amazed and edified.

At night he had a higher fever and asked me to administer extreme unction to him, which I did without his having taken to his bed. He repeated with us the penitential psalms and the litany. He spent the night partly seated on the floor, the greater part on his knees, saying that he rested better thus. On the 28th the fever continued, though he did not take to his bed, but remained seated in an Indian chair with great calmness. The captain of the packet, Don Joseph Cañizares, and the chaplain, Don Cristóbal Díaz, came to see him. When his Reverence recognized them he was very much pleased, thanked them for their visit, and gave them a close embrace, telling the father chaplain that he would give him the closest one since he was a priest of Jesus Christ. He said some words to edify them, at which they were greatly moved, showing it by the tears in their eyes. At one o'clock, when those gentlemen and the rest were with the father, he told me to sprinkle him with holy water because great fear had begun to come over him, and for his consolation to pray for the acceptance of his soul. I did so, his Reverence replying with all the litanies. When I had finished he exclaimed, all filled with joy, "Thanks be to God, now the fear has completely left me. Now I am not afraid. I am already well. We will go and have a little broth." Then he walked to the table and took a bowl of broth. Afterward he began to pray the evening prayers, and when they were ended he said he wished to rest a little. He took off only his mantle and reclined on the planks covered with only a blanket, which were his usual bed. I then went out to pray, and on entering again because of my great anxiety,

I found him already sleeping in the Lord, without having made the slightest sign.

As soon as the news was made public it spread through all the town, everybody mourning the death of their dead father. Everybody crowded to see him, and it was necessary to close the gate, in order to place him in the coffin that he himself had ordered made, for the day before he sent for the carpenter of the presidio without our knowing it and asked him to make a box large enough to bury him in. He complied and I did not see it until they brought it to me. As soon as he died his body was placed in it, taking it from the bed or platform on which he died, without removing his habit, by the order of the chaplain of the boat and the captain, who were present at all this. Then the Indians whom the dead father had baptized and confirmed brought roses and other flowers with which to adorn his dead body, and weeping at his death they did not want to go away. At night we took his body to the church, with a procession formed by all the town and the six soldiers of the guard, one of whom stayed on watch all night with many Indian neophytes and some sailors.

When the father died all were eager for some little thing that he had used. I promised that I would comfort them all so that they might not do anything unseemly, but in spite of this and of the sentinels at night, they cut off bits of the habit that served as a shroud and much of the hair from his tonsure. The following day Father Fray Buenaventura Sitjar, to whom I had written the day before, arrived from the mission of San Antonio, twenty-five leagues distant, to administer the sacraments. From San Antonio he informed the mission of San Luís, twice as far away, but on account of the distance Father Fray Antonio Paterna did not arrive in time for the burial, but did come for the formal honors. I did not write to the other missions because of the great distance, nor to the two in the North, because Father Naboa was ill, and my companion, Fray Pedro Cambón, was alone. For the reasons stated Father Mathías Noriega and I alone of the missionaries were present at his death.

The following day, which was Sunday, with the aid of Father Fray Buenaventura Sitjar and the father chaplain, we chanted the vigil, and immediately afterwards I said Mass for the body

75

present, the chaplain and Father Fray Mathías acting as assistants and Fray Buenaventura singing in the choir with the Indian choristers. Many people were present, not only from the mission but also from the ship, including the captain and officers, only the prisoners being left on board. The commander of the presidio did the same with his troops, and the adjutant inspector, who was present on a tour of inspection, came like all the others to pay honor to the deceased father. Only the governor was not there, he being in San Francisco forty leagues away.

In the afternoon the burial took place with all solemnity. The procession went by way of the plaza, making four stops and singing at each a response. The soldiers carried the body, the rest going with tapers in their hands. When we arrived at the church we sang lauds with all the ceremony of the ritual of the Order. All were eager to honor the deceased, the royal presidio as well as the packet which was anchored in the bay, whose captain, because of the great love and esteem that he felt for the deceased, had him paid the honors of a general, ordering a salute fired every half hour. The presidio replied with a similar salute, and although the mission is a league away, the salutes were heard, which, together with the tolling of the bells, moved us all. They did the same on the day of the honors, which was the 4th of September, the same people, officers and soldiers being present. Father Fray Antonio Paterna, who arrived at this mission on the 31st, also took part in them. We chanted the vigil and celebrated Solemn High Mass, and when it was ended I said a few words to commend the dead father to God, thanking Him for the honors that He had bestowed upon him.

Although I was forgetful of the fact that I had been asked for some mementoes of the deceased father, which they said they wanted for relics, they did not forget. On the contrary, they importuned me to such an extent that I was forced to give up his tunic, which I told them they must make into scapulars and bring them to me to bless, together with their cords. They did this, and when I distributed them I explained that they were the scapular and girdle of Our Father San Francisco, in return for which they should pray for a season for the soul of the dead father. In this way I satisfied the eager worshippers and interceded for the soul of the dead father if, indeed, he needs our prayers and petitions. For this purpose I communicated the news to all the missions, and I am doing so to your Reverence, so that in the sacred and apostolic College they may make their prayers, and may communicate it to the other colleges and to our sacred province of Mayorca, to whose provincial I hope to write if God gives me life to send some diaries that my dear dead father lector told me a short time before his death it would be well to send, although he did not order me to do so. I am not sending them at present because the ship is leaving as soon as possible, and I must send a report by it although there is time for only a short one. I hope also that you will communicate the news to the illustrious Señor Verger, bishop of Linares, and to all the father's other acquaintances, that they may commend him to God. We are doing the same here because, in spite of the fact that in accordance with his exemplary life he departed from it by death piously, we believe these prayers will be worthy in the eyes of God.

I here pray that He may spare your life for the many years that are due you. Mission of San Carlos de Monte Rey, September 7, 1784.

Your Reverence's most humble servant and the humblest of your brothers.

FRAY FRANCISCO PALOU (Rubric).

Francisco Paloú to Fray Juan Sancho.
Translated in Herbert E. Bolton, ed., *Historical Memoirs*
of New California (Berkeley, 1926), IV, 354-361.

Life in California in 1786

BY JEAN FRANCOIS GALLUP DE LAPEROUSE

At the head of a French scientific mission encircling the globe Jean François Gallup de Lapérouse tarried for a fortnight at Monterey. In the South Pacific his ship went down with all aboard. Fortunately for posterity he had sent home a copy of his journal including his California account and the statement of his views— uncomplimentary—on the mission system.

We cast anchor on the evening of September 14, two leagues out, in view of the presidio [of Monterey] and of two ships that were in port. They had fired guns every quarter hour in order to let us find the anchorage, which the fog was hiding from us. . . .

M. Fages, commandant of the fort and of the two Californias, had already received orders to welcome us as though ours were ships of his nation. He executed these orders with grace and interest which deserve warmest acknowledgement. He would take nothing from us but words of thanks. Beef, vegetables, and milk were sent aboard in abundance. The commander of the two corvettes and the commandant of the fort competed to serve us. Each wished to have the exclusive privilege of filling our needs, and when the time came to settle the account we had to insist that payment be received. The vegetables, milk, and chickens, and the work of the soldiers helping us take on wood and water were given gratis, and the beeves, sheep, and grain were set at a price so low that it was evident that they gave us a bill only because we insisted. In addition, M. Fages opened everything to us. His house was ours and his servants were entirely at our disposal.

The fathers from Mission San Carlos, two leagues from Monterey, came to the presidio. They were as obliging to us as were the officers of the fort and the two frigates. They invited us to go and dine with them and promised to help us know in detail the regime of their missions, the mode of life of the Indians, their arts, their new customs, and in general all that could interest the curiosity of travelers. We accepted with pleasure these offers which we would have hesitated to solicit. It was arranged that we should set off the next morning. M. Fages wished to accompany us, and he took the responsibility of providing us horses. After crossing a small plain covered with bands of cattle and in which were only a few trees to protect these animals from the rain or too great heat, we climbed some hills and heard the sound of several bells which announced our arrival. The priest had been notified by a rider sent ahead by the governor.

We were received as the lords of the parish making their first entrance into their lands. The president of the missions, wearing his cope and sprinkler in hand, awaited us at the door of the church, which was illuminated as for the greatest feast day. He conducted us to the foot of the high altar, where he intoned the *Te Deum* in thanks for the success of our voyage.

Before entering the church we had crossed a plaza where Indians of both sexes were ranged in line. Their expressions revealed no astonishment and left us to doubt that we were the subject of their conversation during the rest of the day. The church is a regular fort, although covered with thatch. It is dedicated to St. Charles and ornamented with reasonably good pictures, copies of Italian originals. There is a picture of hell, in which the painter seems to have shared the imagination of Calot. As it is absolutely necessary to make a strong impression on the minds of the new converts I am persuaded that such a picture has never been more useful in any country and that it would be impossible for a Protestant cult which proscribes images and almost all the other ceremonies of our church to make any progress among this people. I doubt that the picture of paradise, which is opposite to that of hell, produces on them an equally good effect. . . .

On leaving the church we passed the same file of Indians; they had not left their post during the *Te Deum*. The children were a little apart and formed in groups before the house of the missionaries, which faces the church, together with the storerooms. On the right is the Indian village, consisting of about fifty huts which lodge the 740 persons of both sexes, children included, who make up Mission San Carlos, or of Monterey.

These huts are the most miserable that one could find anywhere. They are round, six feet in diameter by four in height. Sticks of the size of an arm, fixed in the ground and coming together in an arch at the top, are the framework. Eight or ten mats of straw badly arranged on these sticks more or less protect the occupants from the wind or rain. When the weather is fair, these huts are left half uncovered. The only precaution is to have two or three mats of straw in reserve.

The exhortations of the missionaries have never been able to change the general architecture of the two Californias. The Indians say that they like the open air, that it is better to set fire to your house whenever you are eaten up by too many fleas, and to be able to build another in less than two hours. . . .

The Indians, as also the missionaries, rise with the sun. They go to prayers and mass, which lasts an hour. During that time there is being prepared in the middle of the plaza, in three great kettles, out of barley which has been roasted before being ground, that kind of gruel which the Indians call *atole*, of which they are most fond, although it is not seasoned with butter or salt and would be for us a most insipid meal.

Each hut sends to get the ration for all its people in a bark vase [an urn-shaped basket]. There is no confusion or disorder, and when the caldrons are empty, they distribute the scrapings to the children who have best learned the catechism lessons. The meal lasts three quarters of an hour, after which they all go to their work. Some go to till the land with oxen, others work in the garden, each according to the needs of the community and always under the supervision of one or two of the religious.

The women are only charged with the care of their households and of their children and to roast and grind the grains. This operation is more laborious and tedious, because they have no other means but to crush the grain on a stone with a pestle. M. de Langle, observing this operation, presented his mill to the missionaries. It would be difficult to render them a greater service. With it four women can do the work of a hundred. It will release time for spinning wool and for weaving rough cloth. But thus far the padres, more occupied with heavenly than worldly interests, have neglected to introduce even the most useful arts. They are so ascetic themselves, that they have not a single chamber with heat, although the winter here is sometimes rigorous. The greatest anchorites never practiced a more edifying life. (Note: Father Fermín de Lasuén, president of the missions of New California, is one of the most estimable and respected men I have ever met. His gentleness, charity, and love for the Indians are beyond expression.)

At noon the bells announce dinner. The Indians leave their work and send for their ration in the same basket as for breakfast. This second stew is thicker than the first, having wheat, corn, peas, and beans added to it. The Indians call it *pozole*. They go back to work from two o'clock to four or five. Then they go to evening prayers, which last about an hour, and then follows another ration of *atole* like that at breakfast. These three distributions subsist a large number of Indians. Perhaps we should adopt this most economical soup in our years of famine. Some seasoning could be added to it. The whole science of this cuisine is in roasting the grain before grinding it. As the Indian women have no pottery or metal vessels for this operation, they do it with basketry trays and glowing coals. They turn the trays with such dexterity and quickness that they manage to puff and crack the grains without singeing the tray, though it is most combustible. The best roasted coffee does not approach the perfection of toasting that the Indians know how to give their grain. It is distributed [for roasting] every morning, and the least irregularity with the issue is punished with the lash, but it is rare that anyone exposes herself to such punishment.

These punishments are administered by Indian magistrates called *caciques*. In each mission there are three, chosen by the people from those whom the missionaries have not excluded. To give a fair idea of the office we should say that these caciques, like the heads of the quarters, are passive instruments carrying out the wishes of their superiors, and their principal functions are to serve as beadles in the church and to maintain order and rectitude there. The women are never whipped in public but in a closed room far enough removed so that their cries will not by any chance rouse a compassion which might lead the men to revolt. The latter, on the contrary, are exposed to the view of all their fellows so that their punishment may serve as an example. The usually beg for mercy; the executor then reduces the force of the blows, but the number is always irrevocably fixed. . . .

The missionaries, well persuaded through prejudice and perhaps through experience that the minds of these people are almost never developed, for this reason treat them as children and admit only a few to the communion. These are the geniuses of this people, who, like Descartes and Newton, have enlightened their time and compatriots by informing them that four and four make eight, a calculation beyond the capacity of their brethren. The mission program is not designed to lift this veil of ignorance. Everything there is directed toward obtaining the rewards of the other life, and the most ordinary arts, such as the medicine of our villages, are not practiced here. . . .

New California, of which the settlement farthest north is San Francisco, in latitude 37^d 58′, has no limits, according to the governor, except those of America itself. In going almost to Mount St. Elias our ships did not reach it limits. To the pious motives which first induced Spain to expend large sums for the construction of these presidios and missions are now added powerful reasons of state, which could turn the attention of the government to this rich part of America where otter skins are as common as in the Aleutians and the other parts frequented by the Russians. . . .

New California, in spite of its fertility, does not yet have a single agricultural settler. A few soldiers married to Indian women living in the forts or scattered out as squads of guards at the different missions are the only representatives of Spain in this part of America. California is no less attractive than Virginia on the other side of the continent except that it is farther from Europe. Proximity to Asia should make up for that, and I believe that good laws and unrestricted commerce would soon procure her some colonists. The possessions of Spain are so extensive that it is impossible to believe that none of them will grow. The many celibates of both sexes, vowed to that estate by the principle of perfection, and the government's constant policy of admitting only one religion and of using the most violent methods to maintain it will continue to be an obstacle to all development.

Translated from Jean François Gallup de Lapérouse,
Voyage autour du monde (Paris, 1797), I, 249-283.

First Report on San Francisco

BY GEORGE VANCOUVER

George Vancouver of the British navy was sent to the Pacific because of a Spanish-British clash at Nootka, near the forty-ninth parallel. He improved the opportunity to explore, chart much of the Pacific coast, apply a multitude of names, and visit Hawaii and California. In this Spanish province, like Lapérouse, he expected more improvements than he found. He entered San Francisco Bay in November, 1792.

82

The Spanish commandant . . . had been some time on the beach in the rain before we anchored, for the purpose of instantly affording us any assistance in his power to supply. A message to this effect was brought by three of the native Indians who spoke Spanish, and who came on board in a canoe of the country; which with another, (though perhaps the same) seen crossing the harbour the evening we entered it, were the only Indian vessels we had met with, and were without exception the most rude and sorry contrivances for embarkation I had ever beheld. . . . The wind now blew strong with heavy squalls from the s.w. and in the middle of this spacious inlet the sea broke with much force; notwithstanding which, as soon as these people had delivered their message, they crossed the inlet for the purpose of catching fish, without seeming to entertain the least apprehension for their safety. They conducted their canoe or vessel by long double-bladed paddles, like those used by the Esquimaux.

The s.w. wind attended by much rain, blew very hard until the morning of the 17th, when the weather becoming more moderate I visited the shore. . . .

Whilst engaged in allotting to the people their different employments, some saddled horses arrived from the commandant with a very cordial invitation to his habitation; which was accepted by myself and some of the officers. We rode up to the Presidio, an appellation given to their military establishments in this country, and signifying a *safe guard*. The residence of the friars is called a Mission. We soon arrived at the Presidio, which was not more than a mile from our landing place. Its wall, which fronted the harbour, was visible from the ships; but instead of the city or town, whose lights we had so anxiously looked for on the night of our arrival, we were conducted into a spacious verdant plain, surrounded by hills on every side, excepting that which fronted the port. The only object of human industry which presented itself, was a square area, whose sides were about two hundred yards in length, enclosed by a mud wall, and resembling a pound for cattle. Above this wall the thatched roofs of their low small houses just made their appearance. On entering the Presidio, we found one of its sides still uninclosed by the wall, and very indifferently fenced in by a few bushes here and there, fastened to stakes in the ground. The unfinished state of this part, afforded us an opportunity of seeing the strength of the wall, and the manner in which it was constructed. It is about fourteen feet high, and five feet in breadth, and was first formed by uprights and horizontal rafters of large timber, between which dried sods and moistened earth were pressed as close and as hard as possible; after which the whole was cased with the earth made into a sort of mud plaster, which gave it the appearance of durability, and of being sufficiently strong to protect them, with the assistance of their fire-arms, against all the force which the natives of the country might be able to collect.

The Spanish soldiers composing the garrison amounted, I understood, to thirty-five; who, with their wives, families, and a few Indian servants, composed the whole of the inhabitants. Their houses were along the wall, within the square, and their fronts uniformly extended the same distance into the area, which is a clear open space, without buildings or other interruptions. The only entrance into it, is by a large gateway; facing which, and against the centre of the opposite wall or side, is the church; which, though small, was neat in comparison to the rest of the buildings. This projects further into the square than the houses and is distinguishable from the other edifices, by being white-washed with lime made from sea-shells; as there has not yet been any lime-stone or calcareous earth discovered in the neighborhood. On the left of the church, is the commandant's house, consisting,I believe, of two rooms and a closet only, which are divided by massy walls, similar to that which encloses the square, and communicating with each other by very small doors. Between these apartments and the outward wall was an excellent poultry house and yard, which seemed pretty well stocked; and between the roof and ceilings of the rooms was a kind of lumber garret: these were all the conveniences the habitation seemed calculated to afford. The rest of the houses, though smaller, were fashioned exactly after the same manner; and in the winter, or rainy seasons, must at the best be very uncomfortable dwellings. For though the walls are a sufficient security against the inclemency of the weather, yet the windows, which are cut in the front wall, and look into the square, are destitute of glass, or any other defence that does not at the same time exclude the light.

84

The apartment in the commandant's house, into which we were ushered, was about thirty feet long, fourteen feet broad, and twelve feet high; and the other room, or chamber, I judged to be of the same dimensions, excepting in its length, which appeared to be somewhat less. The floor was of the native soil raised about three feet from its original level, without being boarded, paved, or even reduced to an even surface: the roof was covered in with flags and rushes, the walls on the inside had once been white-washed; the furniture consisted of a very sparing assortment of the most indispensable articles, of the rudest fashion, and of the meanest kind; and ill accorded with the ideas we had conceived of the sumptuous manner in which the Spaniards live on this side of the globe.

It would, however, be the highest injustice, notwithstanding that elegancies were wanting, not to acknowledge the very cordial reception and hearty welcome we experienced from our worthy host; who had provided a refreshing repast, and such an one as he thought likely to be most acceptable at that time of the day; nor was his lady less assiduous, nor did she seem less happy than himself, in entertaining her new guests.

On approaching the house we found this good lady, who, like her spouse, had passed the middle age of life, decently dressed, seated cross-legged on a mat, placed on a small square wooden platform raised three or four inches from the ground, nearly in front of the door, with two daughters and a son, clean and decently dressed, sitting by her; this being the mode observed by these ladies when they receive visitors. The decorous and pleasing behaviour of the children was really admirable, and exceeded any thing that could have been expected from them under the circumstances of their situation, without any other advantages than the education and example of their parents; which however seemed to have been studiously attended to, and did them great credit. This pleasing sight added to the friendly reception of our host and hostess, rendered their lowly residence no longer an object of our attention; and having partaken of the refreshments they had provided, we remounted our horses in order to take a view of the surrounding country before we returned on board to dinner, where Señor Sal and his family had promised to favor me with their good company, and who had requested my permission to increase their party by the addition of some other ladies in the garrison.

Our excursion did not extend far from the Presidio, which is situated as before described in a plain surrounded by hills. This plain is by no means a dead flat, but of unequal surface; the soil is of a sandy nature, and was wholly under pasture, on which were grazing several flocks of sheep and herds of cattle; the sides of the surrounding hills, though but moderately elevated, seemed barren, or nearly so; and their summits were composed of naked uneven rocks. Two small spaces in the plain, very insecurely inclosed, were appropriated to kitchen gardens; much labour did not appear to have been bestowed either in the improvement of the soil, in selecting the quality of the vegetables, or in augmenting their produce; the several seeds once placed in the ground, nature was left to do the rest without receiving any assistance from manual labour.

Senr. Sal having been made acquainted with the difficulties we had to encounter in removing our wood to the sea side, politely offered us the carts he had for the use of the Presidio; but on their being produced I was greatly disappointed, as they were by no means so well calculated as the miserable straw canoes for the service they were intended to perform.

Thus, at the expence of very little examination, though not without much disappointment, was our curiosity satisfied concerning the Spanish town and settlement of St. Francisco. Instead of finding a country tolerably well inhabited and far advanced in cultivation, if we except its natural pastures, the flocks of sheep, and herds of cattle, there is not an object to indicate the most remote connection with any European, or other civilized nation.

This sketch will be sufficient, without further comment, to convey some idea of the inactive spirit of the people, and the unprotected state of the establishment at this port, which I should conceive ought to be a principal object of the Spanish crown, as a key and barrier to their more southern and valuable settlements on the borders of the north pacific. Should my idea of its importance be over-rated, certain it is, that considered solely as an establishment, which must have been formed at considerable expence, it possesses no other means for its protection than such as

86

have been already described; with a brass three-pounder mounted on a rotten carriage before the presidio, and a similar piece of ordnance which (I was told) was at the s.e. point of entrance lashed to a log instead of a carriage; and was the gun whose report we heard the evening of our arrival. Before the presidio there had formerly been two pieces of ordnance, but one of them had lately burst to pieces.

George Vancouver, *A Voyage of Discovery to the North Pacific Ocean* (London, 1798), II, 4-9.

The Governor's Lady

BY CHARLES E. CHAPMAN

Charles E. Chapman headed a procession of doctoral candidates in history at the University of California who had the benefit of Native Sons of the Golden West fellowships. He was in Spain for two years gathering materials for his dissertation on the founding of Spanish California and calendaring a large body of manuscripts pertaining to the history of the Pacific slope of North America. Later as professor at Berkeley his major interest turned to Latin American history.

By 1782 the last group of settlers who had come by the Anza route had established themselves in their new homes. In that year, too, the fiery but lovable Catalan, Pedro Fages, arrived, to begin his second term of office as governor of the new province. . . .

Governor Fages, some years before, had married Eulalia de Callis, a Catalan lady of quality who was even more of a firebrand than was the good Don Pedro himself. When Fages went to Alta California for the second time, Doña Eulalia and her son Pedro remained behind. Fages very much wanted them to be with him, and wrote a number of letters which have a peculiarly modern sound in their demonstration of the meagre reach of his marital authority. For example, he wrote to Captain José Antonio de Roméu in Sonora to "use his influence" to induce Doña Eulalia to come; evidently he despaired of his own powers of persuasion.

Doña Eulalia at first refused, but both Neve and Roméu joined forces to assure her that Alta California was not wholly barbarous, wherefore she consented to join her husband there. As far as Loreto she was escorted by Captain Joaquín Cañete. There, in May 1782, she was met by Fages. Between July 1782 and January 1783, Doña Eulalia made the long journey to Monterey. The whole trip was something in the nature of a royal progress, for there was a succession of receptions in her honor given by the missionaries, soldiers, settlers, and even the Indians. Indeed, her coming was a great event. Not only was she the wife of the governor, but she was also the first lady of rank and social standing who had ever visited the province.

However Doña Eulalia may have enjoyed the attentions showered upon her, she was shocked by conditions as she found them. In particular she was distressed by the number of naked Indians that she saw. Thereupon she began impulsively to give away both her own clothes and those of Don Pedro, until the latter pointed out to her that she could not replenish their wardrobe; there were no shops in Alta California. That checked Doña Eulalia's reckless generosity, though it is true that she continued to deserve a reputation for charity. She managed to "endure" Alta California until after the birth of her daughter (August 3, 1784). Then she announced that she had had enough. And straightway there was trouble.

Unable to persuade Don Pedro to allow her to pack herself and her children off to New Spain, Doña Eulalia resorted to coercive measures against her legal lord and master. She exiled him from her apartments, and during three months made him keep his distance, hardly so much as communicating with him. Finding that Fages did not respond to absent treatment, Doña Eulalia became suspicious, and at length, convinced, though without justifiable grounds, that Fages was paying altogether too much attention to a servant girl whom he had picked up among the Indians of the Colorado. Thereupon she broke silence with Fages, and accused him of infidelity in a torrent of words. Moreover, she rushed into the street and "told everybody," vowing that she would get a divorce. The friars tried to reconcile her, and said that they found no grounds for a divorce. She responded that she would go to the *infierno* (Hell) before she would go again to Fages. The friars ordered her to stay at home in seclusion for a while and to do no more talking.

The above incident took place in February 1785. It came at a time when Fages was obliged by gubernatorial duty to make a trip to the south. He therefore asked Father Noriega to take care of Doña Eulalia at Mission San Carlos during his absence. Father Noriega consented, and sent for Doña Eulalia, but she refused to go, locking herself and her babies in her room. Then the much-tried Don Pedro showed *his* temper. He broke down the door, and when his gentle helpmeet still refused to go to the mission threatened to tie her up and take her. So Doña Eulalia *went*. She made the friars pay for her humiliation. During her stay at the mission they could not manage her at all. She put on display some of her outbreaks in the church itself, to the great scandal of all who witnessed them. Indeed, the friars became so much out of patience with her that at one time they threatened to flog her and put her in chains. They did not yield to the impulse, however.

At length, after a quarrel of about a year, Fages and his wife were reconciled, in September 1785. The governor had desired it, all along, for he was in fact devoted to Doña Eulalia. The latter became satisfied that her charges against Fages were unfounded, and consented to return to him. From this time forth, there is no further evidence of untoward incidents between them,—but it is likely under the circumstances that they occurred, for Doña Eulalia did not give up her attempts to get away from Alta California. In the very next month after their reconciliation she wrote a petition to the *Audiencia* of Guadalajara asking for Fages' removal on the alleged ground of his ill-health. Fages did not know of the petition until after it had been sent. He then made every effort to head it off, and was successful. The documents do not say what happened in the meantime at the gubernatorial residence.

Doña Eulalia seems finally to have won the fight. Early in 1790 Fages himself asked to be relieved. His petition was granted, and José Antonio de Roméu was appointed in his place. In the fall of 1790, as soon as the news reached Monterey, Eulalia and her children took the San Blas boat, and left the province. Fages had been told that he need not await the coming of his successor, but he stayed on for another year, until October or November 1791. He probably joined his family in Mexico City, and is supposed to have died in 1796.

Charles E. Chapman, *A History of California, the Spanish Period* (New York, The Macmillan Company, 1921), 397-400.

The Church Robbers

BY ANTONIO DE FIERRO BLANCO
[WALTER NORDHOFF]

When The Journey of the Flame *appeared in 1933 there was much speculation on who was behind the penname Fierro Blanco. Posthumously Walter Nordhoff confessed to the honor, and a second printing in 1955 so records it. The book was written out of a substantial knowledge gained from reading and long association with the* viejos *of Baja California.*

Soon after I gentled my first wild gelding came the great robbery of our Mission Church of San Borromeo, the Friend of Christ. This Cathedral was of adobe and shabby, with much of the outer plastering fallen off; for Father Blood-of-Christ had taught from the beginning: "The exterior matters little. It is what lies within which God values."

Some said that this father spoke of the soul, but such were not in favor with our monks, and if too loud-mouthed risked what was not pleasant to think of.

Within our church was the richest shrine for a thousand miles. On our Gulf Coast the *mareas* [spring tides] cast up great heaps of pearl oysters, which belonged, of course, to him who found them; but of all found, San Borromeo received his part. Therefore, in front of our Virgin were bowls full of the finest pearls. Before the Saints, also, were figures in silver and even in gold, with much jewelry from mothers who had sick children, and from those who asked intercession for whatever cause. From all the coast north and south came gold and silver figures, or jewelry from those who were fortunate or unfortunate, needing protection for what they had, or help if in misery. San Borromeo refused no request, or, if he refused, then only because of fault in him who asked.

All these vast treasures lay in sight and unprotected, since the Cathedral's Founder had said: "God will protect that He values." Therefore the doors of this church were never closed, and only God Himself, or perhaps those of His Saints deputed for such labor, watched all this wealth.

Three times had come robbers. First a Spaniard, whom like all of the meaner class from Spain, we called *"Gachupin"* [pig], for they value money above honor, and life more than valor.

Entering at night, he filled a bag with pearls from the Virgin's altar. We found him next morning, fallen on the Cathedral steps with an apoplexy. When he was taken up, he said the Virgin had placed the Infant Christ from her arms into those of San Borromeo, and stepping from her Shrine had followed him to the door. Laid by our priests before the High Altar, he died in a torment of shudders, and we, who had been called to watch, wondered at the power of God. Of all the pearls he had taken not one was lost. One great brilliant, the Madonna Charm, fallen from the bag this Spanish thief carried, had rolled behind a stone step. This step being displaced by one who trod upon it, the pearl was by the providence of God revealed to an honest man who returned it to our padres.

The second robbery was by a man who had dug a cellar in which to store yams. Since the Topa Chisera [the Wizard Gopher] had been given by Father Blood-of-Christ the earth for its dwelling, all excavation for houses was forbidden lest it emerge and injure men. But this man dug his cellar secretly, and being found out, became sullen and resisted our church.

As he explained afterwards, he entered by the open front door since it could not but please our Saints to see a worshiper come at night, when the lazy sleep. Having asked intercession of Mary, Mother of God, for the success of his robbery—for being drowsy at this time she might promise aid for his purpose without investigation—he took no pearls from her altar.

"Regarding adornments a woman is merciless," this thief said. "Therefore perhaps it was that She abandoned Her Infant and followed to punish that Spanish robber. But San Borromeo was a man, a jolly old soul, who had also his weaknesses if the stories one hears be true. Little I thought he would grudge me a trifle of his wealth. Then, having taken what I needed of gold and silver, I went out the back door thinking: "These Saints are great people. What do they know of back doors, even though perhaps the flatteries in my prayers have not dulled their watchfulness regarding the front door?"

As this thief passed by the priests' path behind the church, a rabid skunk bit his ankle. He went to our padres for aid, and while they worked over him a golden figure of Saint Peter dropped from a hole in his pocket. The priest laid the thief before the High Altar, as was our custom for sacrilege, and he died in torment, refusing the Sacrament and spitting upon the Body of Christ offered him —since, as he said, "if these Saints have betrayed me in spite of my flatteries, why consider them more?"

The third robber was a sailor from our Mission galleon. He took all our silver and gold figures aboard this ship, and as it was sailing time he thought himself safe from pursuit. But his ship refused to move. It had grounded upon a sandbar, and a great storm arising, all were nearly drowned. Therefore another sailor, who had known of the theft, and had been refused a part, told the galleon's captain, and all church treasures were recovered.

As for the sacrilegious thief, they hoisted him by his left leg to the masthead, and there he hung until he died. The Saints could thus see that his pockets, being upside down, were empty; and by their permission the ship sailed off contentedly like a great bird. It was noted at that time that a land breeze carried the galleon out, as if our Saints were glad to be rid of its crew; for wind from the land by day is most unusual with us.

Within my memory is the last great robbery of our shrine. He who stole had first prayed before the altars, since we found there mud from his feet. Then with pieces torn from the priests' vestments he had bound the eyes of all our Saints, even of the Infant Jesus in his Mother's arms. Thus having deceived the Virgin and Saints by praise, and blinded them with bandages, he took everything of value from them—pearls, jewelry, and figures, both silver and gold. We were like a swarm of bees deprived of their honey when, next morning, we heard of this sacrilege, but the padres soothed us, saying: "This robber will die as have all others. We must, therefore, intercede with the Virgin that she deliver his soiled soul from the Topa Chisera." This they said, but we knew they prayed God for vengeance both on his body and on his soul, since they held continuous Mass day and night.

On this morning I saddled a half-wild stallion, and after I had mounted my bit broke. This was the more curious because it was recently made by me of new iron; but we later found it had been so filed as to break easily. Nor could I, being still only half-grown, hold my great brute with his hackamore. He began more in play than in viciousness, but having run a mile from our village, he put his nostrils to the ground for a moment and seemed to go crazy. At furious speed he charged up a narrow horse trail which rose rapidly along the slopes of San Pablo Mountain, and following the scent which excited him, plowed a way through thorn scrub to the ridge-top. Thence by goatlike leaps he bore me down into the chasm made by the great earthquake which had split San Pablo's dome, at the time Father Blood-of-Christ allotted to the Topa Chisera its earth dwelling.

Quickly, when my stallion came to a mare grazing on the small flat, I slipped off; leaving the enamored pair to their mating, and glad to escape unhurt from flying heels and savage teeth.

Then, wondering how a neighbor's mare could be so far from home, I glanced around; and never have I been more affrighted. In front of a small fire sat a man melting up silver figures from our shrine. Before melting, he had cut off their heads, which lay in a heap near him. Doubtless he had thought: "Who knows about these Saints? They may spy upon me even though their heads be melted. Better let their heads lie here."

"Help yourself, Princeling," he called to me, pointing to the piles of heads. Was it the Virgin called your stallion here?"

I went to him dragging my feet, and covered with a cold sweat which ran down my body in streams. That he had lured me here through his brood mare I knew. That he would kill me was certain, and with these silver heads in my pockets our priests would condemn my soul to Hell forever. Was it not I who had led in all deviltry since I could walk? Was not the color of my hair an indication of my final resting-place? Many a woman had so told me, for red hair is not a sign of grace. There is no Saint known having hair of that color.

I should have killed him where he sat, but was so paralyzed through fear that I forgot the dagger at my side, and its uses. When a boy is under twelve years old, he lacks vigor to attack a grown man. Moreover, at that time I had never killed anyone, and though carefully taught I lacked practice. Learning alone has little value. A man may know by heart the two hundred Spanish name-colors of horses, and yet be easily tumbled off by any old brood mare.

Since that day I have always believed that, if a boy ever called me father, it would go hard with me if I could find no man upon whom that boy could practice his dagger thrusts. Many a boy of spirit and usefullness has died for lack of such practice. My master's mother was right. These are days of too much thought and too little action. It still angers me to think that I might have spent an eternity in Hell while this sacrilegious thief lived his life out in a house of three rooms, all with doors, because those who taught me my dagger stopped at theory.

"Hold the ladle, *cuñado*" [brother-in-law], he said to me; for so all church robbers call each other, being by marriage related to Satanna, the wife of Satan. The man smiled at me with that cold politeness with which the well-bred welcome one they are about to destroy. That smile, I learned as a boy deceives only those who hope against hope, and die a dozen deaths while waiting for their end. Thus he dallied with me, and had not Saints' heads lain heaped between us with their threat of Hell fires, I would have been but as an entrapped fly, to which the spider approaches ever stroking and petting its victim, but still a bloodsucker.

I poured the molten silver into dry clay moulds, with every drop damning my soul. Small bricks they were, such as fit easily into pack-bags. Even I pocketed, laughing, a great pearl flipped to me across our fire; "the Madonna's Charm," which had been set in the Virgin's hair.

"Did the Virgin weep much," the church robber asked, "when Father Talk-Much uncovered Her eyes?" And we chuckled finely together as I told him of the Virgin's frock wetted by tears She had shed over the loss of Her pearls. I was but a boy, yet I could then joke with death, as afterwards when grown up. A boy must die bravely, for he is a man, though only half-grown.

"Let the Virgin seek other pearls," he exclaimed, "and when you are older you may take them all yourself. As for me, I am not a Spaniard and know when I have enough. By tomorrow I shall be at La Paz, mourning deeply for the sacrilege at San José del Arroyo, and promising the Virgin a double portion of all pearls I may find in shell-heaps this winter.

" 'By the Eyes of the Saints,' I shall swear hereafter," this vile thief continued. "No oath of that sort need be kept since I blinded them."

Thus we laughed and talked, I doing my share gaily while my hair was damp with fear-sweat, and my buckskin underclothing drenched as well.

When our melting was done, and dozens of small, easily carried bricks of gold and silver lay around us, the robber yawned, stretching his arms; and to taunt my helplessness with a dagger, said: "Were it not that I must reach La Paz tomorrow, I would sleep for an hour before eating."

And I, not to be ashamed, answered: "A boy is always hungry; and I must be returning, or they may come for me, since I left without orders. Let us eat at once."

Over the cooking he wasted much time to torment me, concealing what he fried from my sight, and keeping the boiling olla hidden by his body so I might imagine all things unsafe. Then, without shame, when all was ready, he poured into my earthen cup from his palm a handful of poison powder; and, breaking a twig, said:

"Stir it well. This sugar dissolves slowly but is none the less sweet."

I tasted it, and bitter as death though the tea was, I answered gaily: "You found then also the priests' sugar loaf. Little chance they give us poor devils to taste white sugar!"

Though my throat was parched almost beyond swallowing, I ate heartily to hold back the poison, and entertained this thief with stories of my adventures, so that, as I had hoped, he lost caution in laughter. Therefore I got a chance to pour half of my cup contents down my chest armor, where it trickled from chest to legs and ran down even into my foot protectors. In those days we wore *guaraches*, not shoes, and in driving wild cattle put on overshoes which covered our legs to the knees.

"How your gang of young *cabrones* [hellions] will miss you!" he exclaimed, holding his fat paunch with one hand in order to laugh more easily, and with his left rolling a long cigarette of corn husk and tobacco coyote. Thus he kept his right hand always free and near a knife handle, in case I attempted resistance. Both to take his eyes off me at moments and to ensure his death should he repeat these stories to others, I had told him of the adventures of Padre Anselmo and the Virgin's frock, which I had watched, but never dared even to hint at before, since this padre was of high repute and not given to forgiveness. Also concerning an adventure of the tenth son of our Governor Verdugo. There was little I did not know of our great people, and much aid have I derived from such knowledge; though chiefly from a reputation thus gained for holding my tongue.

With the first poison pang—since, not knowing what he had given me, I dared not simulate its pains earlier—I rose, staggering and holding my belly.

"I am ill!" I cried, weeping like a baby. "Take me to my mother!"

"So soon?" he asked, puzzled; but as I began to bellow loudly, he led up both horses, saying: "These foreigners lack endurance for poisons, it seems."

Princeling and foreigner they called me because my father was an Irish King. This poisoner knew he must get me away from his melting-place before the venom he had given me rendered me unconscious. Otherwise, searching the hills for me, men might trail me to his den, and by our tracks understand his part in my death and thus locate the real church robber.

With one foot in my saddle stirrup and left hand on my stallion's hackamore, I pretended to swoon, calling loudly, "I cannot mount!" so that he might boost me up. Then, while both his hands were occupied in lifting me, I struck him full in his throat, back of the windpipe; turning my knife so as to open the wound, that his life-blood might find no impediment.

Never in my whole life have I seen such surprise in any man's face. In spite of my poison pains I laughed.

"Princeling yourself!" I called to him, for he knew this nick-name was one I hated. Had not his poison been griping me, I would have stayed to watch his death. A full-blooded man dies slowly, and to have taunted him would have eased my own passing; but it best suited me to reach our village alive, and thus save my soul, which otherwise the Madonna's Charm I carried in my pocket would cost me.

While I mounted my stallion, the church robber's mare was loose and restless, being fed full of corn in readiness for the long ride to La Paz. Terrified by the blood and her master's sudden fall to the ground, she started for San José del Arroyo on full gallop. My stallion, seeing his whole *manada* vanishing, gave chase with equal spirit, and conscious or unconscious I still clung to my saddle. Passing my grandfather's house, I fell off by choice; and, spurned by my horse's heels, shot in through the open doorway and landed at my mother's feet, calling as I lost my senses:

"The church treasure! The robber poisoned me and I killed him!"

Then, content to die, I dropped my hold on life and knew no more except pain, until I was past danger.

They drenched me with more milk than any twin calves ever sucked, and our padres prayed over me. One, indeed, who was learned in such things, and possibly practiced them, gave me a cure which helped. Though as always it was chiefly that I was tough and too young for dissipations to have weakened me.

Over my buckskin underwear, drenched with fear-sweat and the tea I had poured down my chest armor, my mother worked all that night long, to prevent stiffening of the deer hide; doubling the *gamuza* [tanned buckskin] and pulling it this way and that to keep it from hardening. So women must do when their men hunt wild cattle or are hunted.

The church treasure they recovered without loss of a pearl.

Truly God protects that He values. But the church robber's body had been privately removed. His family was influential, and none dared to disgrace it or risk his nine brothers' daggers.

Antonio de Fierro Blanco [Walter Nordhoff],
The Journey of the Flame
(Boston, Houghton Mifflin Co., 1933), 26-36.

The Significance of the Borderlands

BY HERBERT E. BOLTON

Herbert E. Bolton, for forty years the stroke of the California crew of historians, had three passions: the oneness of Western Hemisphere history, the significance of the Spanish borderlands, and the publication of important original documents. The excerpts from Crespi, Font, and Palóu are plucked from the long shelf of his translations. The paragraphs that follow relate California to her sister provinces in the Spanish borderlands.

Spain had long talked of advancing her settlements to Alta California. Lower California and Pimería Alta (southern Arizona) had been occupied at the end of the seventeenth century. Vizcaíno had chased elk in Carmel Valley and boosted the "fine harbor of Monterey." Zealous friars painted in glowing colors the missionary field awaiting them in the populous towns along the Santa Barbara Channel. If only the king would help, what a harvest they would reap! But there was a vast desert gap to cross, and the king always had more pressing tasks in other corners of the hemisphere. So California waited until an emergency should arise.

That emergency came when Russia threatened to extend her settlements from Alaska down the Pacific Coast. Carlos III was not a man who temporized, and he proceeded to occupy Alta California. Square-jawed Gálvez organized the expedition. Its immediate purpose was to hold the harbor of Monterey, for the Golden Gate and San Francisco Bay had not yet been discovered. In command of the enterprise went Portolá. At the head of the immortal missionary band was Junípero Serra, a man remarkable among all pioneers in American history.

98

With vigor the plan was put into execution. San Diego was occupied as a half-way base in the summer of 1769; a year later the flag of Spain floated over Monterey Bay. Between these two strategic points a celebrated chain of missions was begun. Meanwhile Portolá discovered the Golden Gate and San Francisco Bay. Anza now opened a land route from Sonora, and a year later, in a superb feat of frontiering, he led over the same trail a colony of two hundred and forty persons to found San Francisco, on what Father Font, the diarist, called "that prodigy of nature . . . the harbor of harbors."

The Russian threat had forced the Spanish frontier one long notch higher; the ubiquitous English now gave it another hoist. British traders began to swarm the waters of the North Pacific. Thereupon Spain extended California even to Nootka Sound (now in British Columbia), establishing there a slender presidio and a little mission. But England shook her fist, the cards were stacked against Spain, and she withdrew to San Francisco.

Outposts so scattered called for lines of communication. Men who dared were not lacking, and Spain's frontiersmen, under the direction of the great viceroy Bucareli, proceeded to tie the border provinces together. The pathfinding energy displayed in the last quarter of the eighteenth century was scarcely less vigorous than that of the golden days of the sixteenth. Level-headed Anza had opened a route from Sonora to California. Santa Fé now became the hub of long exploratory spokes thrust forth to connect the new outposts with the old. Fearless Garcés, prince of lonely wanderers, showed a way from Santa Fé to Los Angeles. Escalante, on a similar mission, made his prodigious odyssey of two thousand miles from Santa Fé through Colorado, Utah, and Arizona and back to Santa Fé. De Mézières, Vial, and their associates, blazed communication lines connecting Santa Fé with San Antonio, Natchitoches, and St. Louis. Finally, in an effort to connect Louisiana with Spain's Nootka settlement, men sent out from St. Louis ascended the Missouri River as far as the Yellowstone. . . .

All these salients—La Florida, Texas, Louisiana, and California —in origin were defensive outposts, and so they were regarded by Spain. To hold them she utilized especially her two typical frontier institutions, the presidio and the mission.

99

The presidio was a soldier garrison. It might be composed of ten men or two hundred, according to the need. Its function was to give military protection to its district, sending out detachments here, there, and yonder, scouting, chasing Indians, ejecting intruders. Temporary garrisons might occupy the merest shacks. Important and permanent presidios were provided with fortifications. The most substantial of all the northern line was the one at St. Augustine. Presidios, temporary or permanent, were scattered all along the frontier of New Spain. Port Royal, San Agustín, Apalache, Pensacola, New Orleans, the Arkansas Post, St. Louis, Natchitoches, Los Adaes, San Antonio, La Bahía, San Sabá, San Juan Bautista, Ojinaga, El Paso, Santa Fé, Janos, Tubac, Tucson, Altar, and the four in Alta California—San Diego, Santa Barbara, Monterey, and San Francisco—were the more notable of the presidios of the northern borderlands. But numerous other points, all the way from Georgia to San Francisco were occupied for longer or shorter periods, as occasion demanded.

Beside the presidial soldier went the missionary. The mission was par excellence a frontier institution. The missionary was an agent not only of the Church, but of the State as well. His primary business was to save souls and spread Spanish civilization among the heathen. The heathen were to be found on the frontier, beyond the established settlements. Here was the missionary's proper field of endeavor. As soon as his pioneer work among the Indians on one frontier was done, he was expected to turn his flock over to the parish clergy and move on to a new tribe, farther in the wilderness.

Theoretically at least, the State was just as anxious as the Church to Christianize and civilize the heathen. But it cost money to run Indian schools (for such the missions were) and the king's money had to be spent where it was most needed. The missionary field was unlimited, and the friars were always pulling at the rein. Not all the demands made on the royal treasury could be satisfied, and those most urgent first got attention. On the frontiers endangered by foreign foes there was a double need. Soldiers sent there could keep out Europeans and protect the missions. Many times the sovereigns had to turn deaf ears to missionary appeals for funds and permission to go to work among outlying tribes. But when political danger coincided with missionary opportunity, the friars had their way. Then they went beside the soldier to help hold the endangered frontier for Spain, at the same time that they saved souls and spread Spanish civilization.

In fact, the friars often cleverly turned foreign danger to their own account. They saw on some international border a tribe outside the Christian fold. They begged for funds and permission to go. Neither was forthcoming. Then a rumor was heard of impending foreign aggression. Stationed on the frontier, and first to hear the rumors, the friars reported them to the viceroy. They wielded good pens and their words carried weight. The outcome, often, was a new defensive advance of soldier and missionary, to hold the border against a threatening European neighbor. . . .

The soldier and the missionary were the primary agencies by which defensive expansion was effected. It was all the better if civil settlers could be had, to supplement the work of the leather-jacket and the friar. So small civil colonies generally were added. Such a colony went to San Agustín, one to Santa Fé, another to San Antonio, and still others to California. The presidio and mission became nuclei around which ranchers settled on generous land grants. Retired presidial soldiers generally became settlers in the vicinity of their posts. Roman history was repeated here.

Thus these slender defensive and missionary outposts took root in the soil. As a result, nearly every stable presidio, and many missions, slowly grew into permanent settlements. Most of the old Spanish towns along the frontier, like St. Augustine, San Antonio, Tucson, San Diego, Los Angeles, Santa Barbara, Monterey, and San Francisco have grown from small beginnings as presidios or missions or both.

Such in brief were these northern borderlands, as viewed from the standpoint of the Spanish Empire. In Madrid, in Lima, in Buenos Aires, in Mexico, they were regarded as defensive and missionary fringes. The real Spanish America lay to the south of them.

Herbert E. Bolton, "Defensive Spanish Expansion and the Significance of the Borderlands," *The Trans-Mississippi West* (Boulder, University of Colorado, 1930), 19-25.

3

PASTORAL

IN THE LATTER PART of the Spanish period California re-
lapsed into a much more placid existence. The colony was about as
large as imperial policy required, the assignment to those on the
station was essentially a holding operation, and growth and
change were no more than nominal. After the turn of the century
Spain became increasingly neglectful of the province; government ships ceased to come with any regularity and the Californians were left more to their own devices. In the quarter century
of Mexico's sovereignty the neglect continued, though it was
Mexico that secularized the missions, made the bulk of the rancho
land grants, and opened the door for a lawful import-export trade.

Government officials and missionaries through most of this
period continued to file reports. These materials have not attracted any such attention as Bolton, Wagner, Chapman, and
Priestley gave to the earlier Spanish source materials. Americans
and other foreigners infiltrated the province and many of them set
down some account of their experiences. The format is usually
straight narration and description, usually quite unpretentious
though sometimes moving and noteworthy for the information
contained.

First came the sea-otter poachers after pelts to take to the excellent market in China. Because the best hunting was at un-
frequented parts of the coast and because trade would be in violation of the law, these people had minimal contact with the Spanish
settlements. Yet William Shaler comments on the nature of the
Spanish regime and George W. Eayrs eloquently denounces the

A RANCH IN THE COAST RANGES *by Edward Weston*

Spanish restrictions as well as the seizure of his property. Count Rezanov also came to trade and loaded his ship with supplies for the Russians in Alaska. For the record his ill-fated romance with Doña Concepción was far more noteworthy.

Beaver trappers such as Jedediah Smith could be quoted on their contacts with the officials of Mexican California. They also carried out some of the earliest inspections of the interior, here represented in Smith's comments on Indians and bears in the Sacramento Valley. Richard Henry Dana and Prudencia Higuera offer complementary descriptions of the hide trade, and John Coffin Jones, though with an eye to much else, affords a glimpse into the life of a resident trader. The French visitor Eugene Duflot de Mofras and John Bidwell, one of the first of the pioneer settlers by the overland route, describe Fort Ross and Sutter's New Helvetia on the northern fringes of the Mexican province. John C. Frémont waxes lyrical over the flower-decked Central Valley as seen by his party emerging from the snows of the Sierra. The perils of the overland journey are starkly related in Patrick Breen's diary. He was a member of the Donner party, which was delayed en route and then snowed in just short of the Sierra summit.

James Clyman, overland pioneer, William H. Emory, army officer, and Carl Meyer, Argonaut from Switzerland, with some inner balancing of praise and criticism suggest the nature of life in the pastoral era.

In this body of writing at least two works have literary distinction, Dana's *Two Years Before the Mast* and Frémont's *Report*. Dana's reason for writing was to describe the lot of the working-man at sea and if possible to bring about an improvement. To our good fortune he included an intimate picture of California and the Californians. Content had much to do with this book's success, but Dana also wrote so well that his book has had frequent use as a model of style and reaches some modern readers on that basis.

Frémont first entered California in the winter of 1843-1844, and before coming again in 1845 he filed a book-length report. An official account and published as a government document, it was much more: a story of adventure, a description of scenes new to American readers and a commentary on unfamiliar types such as fur trade veterans, western Indians of several cultures, and the

Californians as sampled at Sutter's Fort and southward. In addition, Frémont knew how to write with precision and with dash.

A later generation of fictionists discovered this pastoral era as ineffably idyllic. Gertrude Atherton in her *Splendid Idle Forties* saw it in this perfection, and Stewart Edward White was even more successful in evoking this image and bringing it to popular acceptance. There may be question whether this performance was a service to history, yet it was in tune with Bancroft's *California Pastoral* and Nellie van de Grift Sánchez' *Spanish Arcadia*, and it was substantially confirmed in Robert Glass Cleland's *Cattle on a Thousand Hills*.

First American Report

BY WILLIAM SHALER

William Shaler came to the California coast in 1803 and again the next year to collect sea-otter pelts for the market in China. He was not the first American on the scene, but was the first to write a report. He is in error on some points, as in thinking himself the first navigator to visit Catalina, and other of his remarks are open to question, but he was writing on the basis of direct observation.

On the 24th of February [1805], I arrived without any remarkable occurrence on the coast of California, where we got plentiful supplies of provisions as usual, and were not unsuccessful in our collections of furs. The 14th of March, I paid a visit to the island of Santa Catalina, where I had been informed, by the Indians, that there was a good harbour. We remained there a few days only to ascertain that point. We found the harbour [Avalon] every thing that could be desired, and I determined that, after collecting all the skins on the coast, I would return to it and careen the ship, which she was by this time greatly in want of. After completing our business on the coast, we returned to Santa Catalina, and anchored in the harbour on the 1st of May. As I was the first navigator who had ever visited and surveyed this place, I took the liberty of naming it after my much respected friend, M. De Roussillon. We warped the ship into a small cove, and landed the cargo and every thing moveable, under tents that we had previously prepared for their reception. The Indian inhabitants of this island, to the amount of about 150 men, women, and children, came and encamped with us, and readily afforded us every aid in their power. . . .

By the 9th of June, the ship was again rigged with a jury mizenmast, our cargo on board, and we were again ready for sea. On the 12th, we bid adieu to our Indian friends, and left Port Roussillon with the intention of running down the coast, and, if we found the ship not to leak so much as to be unsafe, to run for the Sandwich Islands, where I determined to leave her, and to take passage in some north-west fur trader for Canton. . . .

The Spanish population of the Californias is very inconsiderable; by the best information I could obtain, it hardly exceeds 3000 souls, including the garrisons, among which, even the latter, the officers excepted, there are very few white people: it principally consists of a mixed breed. They are of an indolent, harmless disposition, and fond of spiritous liquors. That they should not be industrious, is not surprising; their government does not encourage industry. For several years past, the American trading ships have frequented this coast in search of furs, for which they have left in the country about 25,000 dollars annually, in specie and merchandize. The government have all used their endeavors to prevent this intercourse, but without effect, and the consequence has been a great increase of wealth and industry among the inhabitants. The missionaries are the principal monopolizers of the fur trade, but this intercourse has enabled the inhabitants to take part in it. At present, a person acquainted with the coast may always procure abundant supplies of provisions. All these circumstances prove, that, under a good government, the Californias would soon rise to ease and affluence. . . .

The plan of civilization in the missions is to instruct the Indians in the Catholic religion, the Spanish language, the necessary arts, agriculture, etc.; but the notion of private property is not admitted among them; so that each mission forms an indivisible society, of which the fathers are the kings and pontiffs. The missionaries of the Franciscan order, in Upper California, have salaries of 400 dollars per annum; the Dominicans that are established below have but 350 dollars. The missions of California may be considered as so many valuable estates or plantations belonging to the king of Spain, and capable, in case of a conquest of this country, of furnishing abundant supplies of all kinds of provisions, horses, etc. . . .

The Spaniards have complete possession of the peninsula of California; but that is not the case above: there their domination is bounded by the Sierra Madre, which in no part is far removed from the coast; so that in reality they are masters of the maritime part of the country only. Beyond that range of mountains the country is remarkably fine, well watered, and covered with forests. These they have not as yet been able to penetrate, on account of their being thickly inhabited by warlike tribes of Indians. . . .

The mutual jealousies and selfish policy of the great European powers have been the causes that some of the most beautiful regions of the universe have long languished under the degrading shackles of ignorance and superstition; and the Spanish monarchy has been so long left to the quiet enjoyment of the finest part of the new world, that they have been at full liberty to extend their conquests there in every direction, without any other obstacles than the feeble opposition of the native savages. Any of the great maritime powers that should determine to give independence to New Spain, or wrest it from the Spanish dominion, would naturally seek to establish themselves in California, from whence, as a place of arms, they might carry on their operations against that defenceless kingdom with a certainty of success. This the Spaniards have doubtless forseen, and been beforehand in occupying it, with a view of forming a barrier to those valuable possessions. The foregoing shows that what they have yet done has had a directly contrary effect. They have, at a great expense and considerable industry, removed every obstacle out of the way of an invading enemy; they have stocked the country with such multitudes of cattle horses, and other useful animals, that they have no longer the power to remove or destroy them; they taught the Indians many of the useful arts, and accustomed them to agriculture and civilization; and they have spread a number of defenceless inhabitants over the country, whom they never could induce to act as enemies to those who should treat them well, by securing to them the enjoyments of liberty, property, and a free trade which would almost instantaneously quadruple the value of their actual possessions: in a word they have done every thing that could be done to render California an object worthy the attention of the great maritime powers; they have placed it in a situation to want nothing but a good government to rise rapidly to wealth and importance.

The conquest of this country would be absolutely nothing; it would fall without an effort to the most inconsiderable force; and as the greatest efforts that the Spanish government would be capable of making towards its recovery would be from the shores of New Spain, opposite the peninsula, a military post, established at the bay of Angels, and that of San Diego fortified and defended by a competent body of troops would render such an attempt ineffectual. The Spaniards have few ships or seamen in this part of the world; the arsenal of San Blass would be their only resource on such an occasion, and that might be very easily destroyed. But, admitting that the inactivity of the invaders should permit them to transport troops over to the peninsula, those that come from New Spain could not be very formidable, either in point of numbers or courage, and they would have to penetrate through Lower California where they would not find even water in their march: all the other resources of that desolate country could be easily removed out of their way. They could not march round the head of the gulf: the natural obstacles to such an expedition would be very numerous; and they must besides force their way through many warlike nations of savages.

An expedition by sea to Upper California would be equally difficult for them; the bad weather they must encounter in winter, and the great length of the passage in summer, on account of the prevailing northwest winds, would render it a very precarious undertaking. In a word, it would be as easy to keep California in spite of the Spaniards, as it would be to wrest it from them in the first instance.

William Shaler, "Journal of a Voyage from China
to the Northwestern Coast of America
Made in 1804," *American Register*, III (1808), 136-175.
Reprinted with introduction by Lindley Bynum (Claremont, 1935).

An International Romance

BY NIKOLAI PETROVICH REZANOV,
GEORG HEINRICH VON LANGSDORFF,
GEORGE SIMPSON,
AND FRANCIS BRET HARTE

Nikolai Petrovich Rezanov, chamberlain of the Czar, headed the Russian expedition that visited San Francisco in 1806 for the purpose of opening a trade that would supply the Russian outpost in Alaska. Georg Heinrich von Langsdorff, engineer, served also as interpreter. Sir George Simpson, governor of the Hudson's Bay Company, visited California in the interest of his trading company, some thirty-five years later, and, as he records, unintentionally brought tidings to Doña Concepción. Francis Bret Harte, better known for his stories of the gold camps, was one of many to bring together the several pieces of the story.

REZANOV: Embracing at once the opportunity offered by a favoring wind and tide to enter the puerto on the following morning [March 28, 1806, o.s.: April 8, 1806, n.s.], and the suspicious nature of the Spanish government being known to me, I thought it best to go straight through the gate and by the fort, in view of our desperate situation. I deemed it useless to send in and ask for permission to enter, since, in the event of refusal, we should necessarily perish at sea, and decided that two or three cannon-balls would make less difference to us than refusal.

With all sails full, we ran for the puerto. As we neared the fort a great commotion was observed among the soldiers, and when abreast of it one of them asked, through a speaking trumpet, "What ship is that?" "Russian," we replied. They shouted to us several times to anchor, but we merely replied, "Si, señor; si, señor," and simulated an active effort to comply with their demand, but in the mean time we had passed the fort and were running up the puerto, and at a cannon-shot's distance complied.

LANGSDORFF: At the Presidio . . . we were received in the most hospitable manner by Señora Argüello, esposa of the commandante permanente, and her family. . . .

Their simple, natural cordiality captivated us to such a degree that we forthwith desired to become acquainted with each individual member of the family, and to learn the name of each one, having at once formed a strong attachment for them, and becoming interested in their personal welfare.

The Señora Argüello was the mother of fifteen children, and of these thirteen were living at this time. Some of the sons were absent upon military duty, and the others were at home. Of the grown-up unmarried daughters, the Doña Concepción most particularly interested us. She was distinguished for her vivacity and cheerfulness, her love-inspiring and brilliant eyes and exceedingly beautiful teeth, her expressive and pleasing features, shapeliness of figure, and for a thousand other charms, besides an artless natural demeanor. Beauties of her kind one may find, though but seldom, only in Italy, Portugal, and Spain. . . .

Our intimate association daily with the Argüello family, the music and dancing, the sports, aroused in the mind of Rezanov some new and important speculations. These led to the formation of a plan of a very different nature from the original scheme for the establishment of commercial relations.

The bright sparkling eyes of Doña Concepción had made upon him a deep impression, and pierced his inmost soul. He conceived the idea that through a marriage with the daughter of the commandante of the Presidio de San Francisco a close bond would be formed for future business intercourse between the Russian American Company and the provincia of Nueva California. He had therefore decided to sacrifice himself, by wedding Doña Concepción, to the welfare of his country, and to bind in friendly alliance both Spain and Russia.

REZANOV: Seeing that our situation was not getting better, expecting every day that some serious unpleasantness would arise, and having but little confidence in my own men, I decided that I should assume a serious bearing where I had before been but formally polite and gracious.

Associating daily with and paying my addresses to the beautiful Spanish señorita, I could not fail to perceive her active, venturesome disposition and character, her unlimited and overweening desire for rank and honors, which, with her age of fifteen years, made her, alone among her family, dissatisfied with the land of her birth. She always referred to it jokingly; thus, as "a beautiful country, a warm climate, an abundance of grain and cattle,—and nothing else."

I described Russia to her as a colder country, but still abounding in everything, and she was willing to live there, and at length I imperceptibly created in her an impatient desire to hear something more explicit from me, and when I proffered my hand, she accepted.

My proposal was a shock to her parents, whose religious upbringing was fanatical. The difference in religion, besides the prospective separation from their daughter, was, in contemplation, a dreadful blow to them.

They sought the counsel of the misioneros, who did not know what to do. The parents forced their daughter to church and had her confessed. They urged her to refuse me, but her brave front finally quieted them all. The holy padres decided to leave the final decision to the throne of Rome.

Not being able to bring about the marriage, I had a written conditional agreement made, and forced a betrothal. Consent was given on condition that the agreement be kept secret pending the decision of the pope. Thereafter my deportment in the house of Comandante Argüello was that of a near relative, and I managed this puerto of his Catholic majesty as my interests called for.

SIMPSON: Among the persons whom we met this afternoon was a lady of some historical celebrity. Von Resanoff, having failed, as elsewhere stated, in his attempt to enter the Columbia River in 1806, continued his voyage as far as San Francisco, where besides purchasing immediate supplies for Sitka, he endeavoured, in negotiation with the comandante of the district and the governor of the province, to lay the foundation of a regular intercourse between Russian America and the California settlements. In order to cement the national union, he proposed uniting himself with the Donna Conception Arguello, one of the commandant's daughters, his patriotism clearly being its own reward, if half of Langsdorff's description was correct: "She was lively and animated, had spark-

ling, love-inspiring eyes, beautiful teeth, pleasing and expressive features, a fine form, and a thousand other charms; yet her manners were perfectly simple and artless."

The chancellor, who was himself of the Greek Church, regarded the difference of religion with the eyes of a lover and a politician, but as his imperial master might take a less liberal view of the matter, he posted away to St. Petersburgh with the intention, if he should there be successful, of subsequently visiting Madrid for the requisite authority to carry his schemes into full effect. But the Fates, with a voice more powerful than that of emperors and kings, forbade the bans, and Von Resanoff died, on his way to Europe, at Krasnoyarsk in Siberia of a fall from his horse.

Thus at once bereaved of her lover, and disappointed in her hope of becoming a pledge of friendship between Russia and Spain, Donna Conception assumed the habit, but not, I believe, the formal vows, of a nun, dedicating her life to the instruction of the young and the consolation of the sick. This little romance could not fail to interest us; and, notwithstanding the ungracefulness of her conventional costume and the ravages of an interval of time, which had tripled her years, we could still discover in her face and figure, in her manners and conversation, the remains of those charms which had won for the youthful beauty Von Resanoff's enthusiastic love and Langsdorff's equally enthusiastic admiration.

Though Donna Conception apparently loved to dwell on the story of her blighted affections, yet, strange to say, she knew not, till we mentioned it to her, the immediate cause of the chancellor's sudden death. This circumstance might, in some measure, be explained by the fact, that Langsdorff's work was not published before 1814; but even then, in any other country than California, a lady who was still young would surely have seen a book which, besides detailing the grand incident of her life, presented at the same time so gratifying a portrait of her charms.

BRET HARTE:
Forty years on wall and bastion swept the hollow idle breeze,
Since the Russian eagle fluttered from the California seas;
Forty years on wall and bastion wrought its slow but sure decay,

And St. George's Cross was lifted in the port of Monterey;
And the citadel was lighted, and the hall was gayly drest,
All to honor Sir George Simpson, famous traveler and guest.
Far and near the people gathered to the costly banquet set,
And exchanged congratulations with the English baronet;
Till the formal speeches ended, and amidst the laugh and wine
Someone spoke of Concha's lover—heedless of the warning sign.
Quickly then cried Sir George Simpson: "Speak no ill of him,
    I pray.
He is dead. He died, poor fellow, forty years ago this day—
Died while speeding home to Russia, falling from a fractious horse.
Left a sweetheart, too, they tell me. Married, I suppose, of course!
Lives she yet?" A death-like silence fell on banquet, guests, and
    hall,
And a trembling figure rising fixed the awe-struck gaze of all.
Two black eyes in darkened orbits gleamed beneath the nun's
    white hood;
Black serge hid the wasted figure, bowed and stricken where it
    stood.
"Lives she yet?" Sir George repeated. All were hushed as Concha
    drew
Closer yet her nun's attire. "Señor, pardon, she died too!"

LANGSDORFF: On November 27th I arrived at Krasnoyarsk, a toler-ably regular built town, on the river Yenisei. It stands in a beauti-ful and fertile valley, and there are five hundred houses and four churches. It was rendered remarkable to me as having been the place where Count Resanov lost his life in the preceding March. I stopped for the night at Krasnoyarsk, and in the morning visited the tomb of Resanov. It is a large stone, in the fashion of an altar, but without any inscription.

RUSSELL: When the first convent and seminary for females in California was founded at Monterey in 1851 by the Dominican Sisters, the Doña Concepción, though sixty years of age, was the first novice to enter. On April 11, 1851, she received the white habit of Saint Dominic at the hands of Bishop José Sadoc Alemany, and with it the name of María Dominga. This convent, opened under the protection of Saint Catherine of Siena, was in 1854 moved to Benicia, and there Sor María Dominga lived until her death on December 23, 1857. Two days later the body was laid to rest in the convent cemetery.

Rezanov's narrative is in T. C. Russell, ed., *The Rezanov Voyage to Nueva California in 1806* (San Francisco, 1926), 11, 36-37, 97-99; Langsdorff's in T. C. Russell, *Langsdorff's Narrative of the Rezanov Voyage* (San Francisco, 1927), 40-42, 85-86, 144; George Simpson, *Narrative of a Journey round the World* (London, 1847); Francis Bret Harte, "Concepción de Argüello," *Collected Works* (Boston, 1902).

A Smuggler's Complaint

BY GEORGE W. EAYRS

In the second decade of the nineteenth century, with sailings from Mexico interrupted, California stood in need of the trade which the sea-otter men could supply. Such trade was, however, contrary to Spanish law, and upon occasion the law was enforced. In spelling as well as in business, Eayrs was a contrabander, though the phonetic approach will usually give the answer, as for instance that "Captn Arwayus Sun" means "Captain Argüello's son." His lament is eloquent testimony on the state of the trade, the life of the traders, and to some extent on life in the province.

Sn Deago October 8—1813

Moste Noble & Excellent Sir, Vice Roy of Mexico—

Being a Prisoner in this place and moste disagreeably situated, I have to deplore of Your Excellency as spedy relief as the nature of my captivity and dificulty of the times will admit of—My ship was taken possession of, by an armed party in a long Boat from the Ship Flora Dⁿ Nicolas Noe belonging to Lima—I used no means of defence whatever, my sole visit here being for supplis—

Since being a Prisoner, I have been treated inhumanely, even so if the two Countrys had been at War—It is but about leaven Years since (by being left at Monterrey I passed this whole Continent, Via Mexico & the Havana, and I must confess I was treated with humanity—I have commanded the Ship Mercury, since January 1808, nearly six Yeaˢ my Trade has been chiefly with the

114

Russian Governor & the Savages on the N West Coast of America, In the Winter seasons, when the Weather has been blustering, I have run as far South as California for the purpose of Supplys, & one Year was imployed hunting Furs from Columbies River to this Coast—It is true, I have made a little Traffic with the Californians, & have not the least wish to conceal my whole Trade in this six Years, whatever damage it may lay me liable to—

From the highest to the lowest Officers on this—Coast, has been the means of my makeing any Trade here, & have Intreated me to bring them things for the Cultivation, & other articles that they was nearly in distress for—I have supplyed the Clergy for the articles of Religion, from their great intreaties, not being able on account of the Revolution on the Continent to obtain them—I have taken in pay Provisions & a few Furs, have cover'd many a naked one, and receiv'd the produce of his land in pay—I have no doubt but there is some in high Office here, should Your Excellency request the truth of them, relate to You just the same facts—

It is several months since my Ship was taken, & in this time I have had to content my self with being plundered, I say plnᵣ for I can call it by no other name—It is but a few Days since, I arrived at this Place—where I was informed I was at liberty & could write to the Vice Roy—

Suffice it to say, & I humbly beg Your Excellency—will generously take my affair into consideration—should the case happen in Spain at a time of want, and be indulged by the highest Officers of the Kingdom, justice would be done—

Haveing ben nearly seven months at the Russian settlement in Latᵈ 57° North for the purpose of Repairing my ship, had nearly expended all my Provisions from which Plase I sailed for this Coast on the 28 April—I directed my Course for the Russian settlement on New Albian in Latᵈ 39 or 40° North, for the purpose of landing six Hogheads of molasses, & some Cloathing that the Governor had pute on board my ship for that purpose, he likewise pute on board, . . . a Box containing six Gold & Silver Watches, one of which was made a Present to him by the Emperor, all these to be left at Canton—for Repairs—The Cloaths I landed, but the Molasses, the Russian Commandᵣ could not take, haveing no Boat fit for the purpose   After landing these Goods set sail for Monterrey, at which place I lay off two Days, but being a thik fog could not enter, when I set Sail for Point Conception, I stoped at the Mission of S^{nt} Luis, where by the friendly Pardra, I obtained two Bullocks—twelve Hogs & salt to Salt the same—I made no tarry, but set stail for P^t Conception, where I arrived on the first of April June [sic], and I set my People to filling up Water, and cutting Oak fer the purpose of completing the Repairs of my Ship—The only thing that I obtained here was one Sheep, when the Ship Flo^a made hir appearance at Noon—The next morning at Day light, my ship was taken possession of as before Related—my first Officer and two men was taken from my Ship, & I ordered to S^{nt} Barbara—my Ship arrived long before the Flo^a & I had it completly in my power to retain my Ship again, but my determination was, to use no hostile means, not withstanding it was done to me—

I have a Young Female with me which I have had several Years, with whom I esteem equal the same as if I was lawfully married to hir, and a Daughter, only twenty five Days old when the Ship was taken—The second Day after I arr^d at this Place, I was Ordered on Shore with my little Family, & after overhawling my Trunks &c, was permitted to take them with me, with some Articles of Cookery—I had likewise a small Indian Boy that I Bo^t at Columbies River, five Years since, him I also took with me—On the 19 June I was sent for early in the morning by Arwayus [Argüello's] Son—said for the purpose of giveing in my Deposition—I soon after Repaired to Cap^{tn} Arwayus House, little thinking what Base business was going on—A Kind of a Deposition was Written, but I no not what—while this was doing, I once wished to return to the House I lived at, but that was denied me—After completing this, I was sent to my House in company with Cap^{tn} Arwayus Sun, The First Officer, the Boatswain and Clark, of D^n Nicolas Noe's Ship, said by the Governors of Monterreys orders, to rehistory all my Bagage for Gold &c my whole Cloathing with my Girls, was hove on the Ground—the same things that was given me when I landed, was now taken from me—even part of my Girl's shoes, with Handf^s & other things was taken—What was the basest of all, I found on my arrival at the House, my Girl packing up hir things & looking as if she had been beeten, she informed me, while I was absent, a Padre, several Girls, Dr Nicolas, Clark & others, had been there and ordered hir to pack up and leave the House amedeatly, that I was in confinment and would never see hir more—hir Indian Boy was taken from hir, notwithstanding sick in Bed, & I have never since seen him, and in all probability had I not return'd to my House as I did, both my Girl and Daughter would been secreted away, where I should never more hird of them again—while at S^{nt} Barbara, I found the Sailors of both Ships, selling the Plunder they had made of my Cargo, & likewise my Cloaths, I presume a flemish Acct—will be given of my Cargo—

I send Yours Excellency here inclosed, an Invoice of the Mercury's Cargo, Provisions &c—The Furs I cannot estimate their Value, nor the Ship. The six Hogsheads of Molasses is going to ruin at S^{nt} Barbara, & the six Watches I presume, will be of as little Value, as they cannot be repaired on this Continent—Those things belonging to the Russian Govenor, what ever may be concluded on my Ship & Property, according to the Laws of Nations, I think they aught to be restored to the owner again—There is likewise a small Box & a packet of Papers, directed to the R^n Governo^r contents unkown to me—About the 15 of Septr I was ordered to depart amediately for S^{nt} Deago, where I now remain, it is reported to me that Spain is at War with the United States—The last accounts I had from America, they was at peace with all Europe excepting England.

I expect that N. America will not go to War with Spain, unless forced by Britain, should she not; my earnest wish is, that I may be permitted to proceed on to Mexico & lay my case before Your Excellency, leaving my Girl and little Child under the protection of some Mission—The turbelent state the whole Globe is in at present, makes it dificult to determing what to do, but I beg that I may have as spedy a conclution on Your Excellency's part as Posable, that I may lay my affair before the American Government—

Should the United States be oblige to go to War with Spain, I can expect nothing, In which case, I earnestly request the humanity of Your Excellency, to permit me to depart for the Russian Settlement, this will save—great expence to Your Excellency, and relave both me and my little Family from distress and Prison—

God grant Your Excellency will take my case spedily into consideration—

> I remain honoured Sir, Your
> Moste Obedient, moste humble
> GEORGE W. EAYRS
> [RUBRICA]

George W. Eayrs, MS Letter, Los Angeles Public Library;
published in Charles F. Lummis, *Flowers of Our Lost Romance*
(Boston, 1929), 147-152.

Trapping in the Sacramento Valley

BY JEDEDIAH SMITH

Jedediah Smith is the foremost of American pathfinders. From a trappers' rendezvous near Great Salt Lake he ventured southwestward in 1826 and made the first transcontinental entry to California. His exit was by the Central Valley and across the Sierra, the first crossing on record. The next year he was back again and this time left on the northern route, pioneering land travel to Oregon. Only fragments of his journals have survived. From these come the following selections describing his experiences along the Sacramento.

21st March [1828] NW 7 Miles crossing the several channels of Red Bank Creek and encamp within 3 Miles of the Yaloo. After encamping I went with the trappers down to the river where they set their traps. The indians were numerous and in one place I came uppon them before they had an opportunity to run off and gave them some Beads according to my common custom. The squaws had their baskets filled with young Pea vine and from what I could observe I think their principal supports consi[s]ts of Acorns, Grass, Pea vines, Roots and what few fish and water fowl they are able to take.

If Missionaries could be useful in Civilizing and Christianizing any indians in the World their efforts should be turned toward this valley. The indians are numerous honest and peaceable

118

in their dispositions. They live in a country where the soil is good and the climate pleasant with the exception of 2 or 3 months in the winter when there is too much rain. There is seldom any frost and I have seen snow but once in the valley of the Buenaventura.

A great many of these indians appear to be the lowest intermediate link between man and the Brute creation. In the construction of houses they are either from indolence or from a deficiency of genius inferior to the Beaver and many of them live without any thing in the shape of a house and rise from their bed of earth in the morning like the animals around them and rove about in search of food. If they find it it is well if not they go hungry. But hunger does not teach them providence. Each day is left to take care of itself . . . degraded ignorant as these indians must be and miserable as the life appears which they lead it is made more apparent by a contrast with the country in which they are placed a country one would think rather calculated to expand than restrain the energies of man a country where the creator has scattered a more than ordinary Share of his bounties. . . .

29th March N 6 Miles and encamp on the river. I was obliged to cross many Slous of the River that were verry miry and passed great numbers of indians who were engaged in digging Roots. I succeeded in giving to them some presents. they were small in size and apparently verry poor and miserable. The most of them had little Rabit Skin Robes. 11 Beaver taken.

30th March The Party remained in camp and I went up the river with one man to examine the country. About 1 Mile above camp a creek came in 20 yards called Pen-min wide deep and Muddy. Along its banks were many dirt Lodges having the entrance at the top. As we passed along the little children reminded me of young wolves or Prairae dogs. They would sit and gaze at us until we approached near to them when they would drop down into their holes. Some of the indians appeared much frightened as we came in sight while others scarcely quit their Work (digging roots) to look at us. . . .

April 1st The trappers all came in one trap lost by Beaver. In the evening several of us went out hunting for there was considerable sign of Bear Deer Elk and Antelope in the neighborhood. Mr. [Martin] McCoy and J[oseph] Palmer killed a large Grizly

Bear in tolerable order and on opening him found nearly in the center of the lights a stone Arrow head together with about 3 inches of the Shaft attached to it. The men brought that part of the lights containing the arrow into camp. The wound appeared perfectly healed and closed around the arrow. 3 indians who came with us to camp were busily employed on the share of Meat alloted to them and on the entrails of the Bear. They filled themselves so completely that they were puffed up like Bladders. One of those indians had a spear with a stone head like that of an Arrow but 5 or 6 times as large. The handle was about 6 feet Long. . . .

5th April W N W 7 Miles Turned out from the river and 5 miles from camp crossed a Creek 20 yards wide running West. Rapid but fordable. I called it Black Sand Creek. My encampment was on the River bank. Many indians came as near the camp as I would permit and sat down. I gave them some presents. They were naked but had not the miserable appearance of those below. They were under the impression that the horses could understand them and when they were passing they talked to them and made signs as to the men. . . .

7th April . . . In the vicinity was considerable appearance of game and particularly bear. In the evening we shot several Bear and they ran into thickets that were convenient. Several of us followed one that was Badly wounded into a thicket. We went on foot because the thicket was too close to admit a Man on horse back.

As we advanced I saw one and shot him in the head when he immediately [tumbled] fell—Apparently dead. I went in to bring him out without loading my gun and when I arrived within 4 yards of the place where the Bear lay the man that was following me close behind spoke and said "He is alive." I told him in answer that he was certainly dead and was observing the one I had shot so intently that I did not see one that lay close by his side which was the one the man behind me had reference to. At that moment the Bear sprang towards us with open mouth and making no pleasant noise.

Fortunately the thicket was close on the bank of the creek and the second spring I plunged head foremost into the water. The Bear ran over the man next to me and made a furious rush on the third man Joseph Lapoint. But Lapoint had by good fortune a Bayonet fixed on his gun and as the Bear came in he gave him a severe wound in the neck which induced him to change his course and run into another thicket close at hand. We followed him there and found another in company with him. One of them we killed and the other went off Badly wounded.

I then went on horse Back with two men to look for another that was wounded. I rode up close to the thicket in which I supposed him to be and rode round it several times halloeing but without making any discovery. I rode up for a last look when the Bear sprang for the horse. He was so close that the horse could not be got underway before he caught him by the tail. The Horse being strong and much frightened exetered himself so powerfully that he gave the Bear no opportunity to close uppon him and actually drew him 40 or 50 yards before he relinquished his hold.

The Bear did not continue the pursuit but went off and [I] was quite glad to get rid of his company on any terms and returned to camp to feast on the spoils and talk of the incidents of our eventful hunt. 16 Beaver taken. . . .

Jedediah Smith, Journal, in Maurice S. Sullivan, ed.,
The Travels of Jedediah Smith (Santa Ana, California, 1934), 72-78.

Trading with the Californians

BY RICHARD HENRY DANA

Because of eye trouble Richard Henry Dana was advised to interrupt his studies at Harvard. He signed on as a sailor on a ship putting out for California and the hide trade. Out of this experience rounding the Horn and droghing hides along the California coast came Two Years Before the Mast, *a plea for better treatment of the sailor and a vivid description of life at sea and in this particular trade. From the perspective of his later efforts in law, politics, and foreign service, Dana was inclined to dismiss* Two Years Before the Mast *as a boy's work. It, nevertheless, is his claim to fame.*

We returned by sundown, and found the *Loriotte* at anchor within a cable's length of the *Pilgrim*. The next day we were "turned-to" early, and began taking off the hatches, overhauling the cargo, and getting everything ready for inspection. At eight, the officers of the customs, five in number, came on board, and began over-hauling the cargo, manifest, etc. The Mexican revenue laws are very strict, and require the whole cargo to be landed, examined, and taken on board again; but our agent, Mr. R——, had suc-ceeded in compounding with them for the last two vessels, and saving the trouble of taking the cargo ashore. The officers were dressed in the costume which we found prevailed through the country—a broad-brimmed hat, usually of a black or dark brown color, with a gilt or figured band round the crown, and lined in-side with silk; a short jacket of silk or figured calico, (the Euro-pean skirted body-coat is never worn;) the shirt open in the neck; rich waistcoat, if any; pantaloons wide, straight, and long, usually of velvet, velveteen or broadcloth; or else short breeches and white stockings. They wear the deer-skin shoe, which is of a dark brown color, and (being made by Indians) usually a good deal orna-mented. They have no suspenders, but always wear a sash round the waist, which is generally red, and varying in quality with the means of the wearer. Add to this the never-failing cloak, and you have the dress of the Californian. This last garment, the cloak, is always a mark of the rank and wealth of the owner. The "gente de razon," or aristocracy, wear cloaks of black or dark blue broad-cloth, with as much velvet and trimmings as may be; and from this they go down to the blanket of the Indian, the middle classes wearing something like a large table-cloth, with a hole in the middle for the head to go through. This is often as coarse as a blanket, but being beautifully woven with various colors, is quite showy at a distance. Among the Spaniards there is no working class; the Indians being slaves and doing all the hard work;) and every rich man looks like a grandee, and every poor scamp like a broken-down gentleman. I have often seen a man with a fine fig-ure and courteous manners, dressed in broadcloth and velvet, with a noble horse completely covered with trappings; without a *real* in his pockets, and absolutely suffering for something to eat.

The next day, the cargo having been entered in due form, we

began trading. The trade-room was fitted up in the steerage, and furnished out with the lighter goods, and with specimens of the rest of the cargo; and M——, a young man who came out from Boston with us, before the mast, was taken out of the forecastle, and made supercargo's clerk. He was well qualified for the business, having been clerk in a counting-house in Boston. He had been troubled for some time with the rheumatism, which unfitted him for the wet and exposed duty of a sailor on the coast. For a week or ten days all was life on board. The people came off to look and to buy —men, women, and children; and we were continually going in the boats, carrying goods and passengers—for they have no boats of their own. Everything must dress itself and come aboard and see the new vessel, if it were only to buy a paper of pins. The agent and his clerk managed the sales, while we were busy in the hold or in the boats. Our cargo was an assorted one; that is, it consisted of everything under the sun. We had spirits of all kinds, (sold by the cask,) teas, coffee, sugar, spices, raisins, molasses, hardware, crockery-ware, tin-ware, cutlery clothing of all kinds, boots and shoes from Lynn, calicoes and cottons from Lowell, crapes, silks; also, shawls, scarfs, necklaces, jewelry, and combs for the ladies; furniture; and in fact, everything that can be imagined, from Chinese fire-works to English cart-wheels—of which we had a dozen pairs with their iron rims on.

The Californians are an idle, thriftless people, and can make nothing for themselves. The country abounds in grapes, yet they buy bad wine made in Boston and brought round by us, at an immense price, and retail it among themselves at a *real* (12½ cents) by the small wineglass. Their hides too, which they value at two dollars in money, they give for something which costs seventy-five cents in Boston; and buy shoes (as like as not, made of their own hides, which have been carried twice round Cape Horn) at three and four dollars, and "chicken-skin boots'' at fifteen dollars apiece. Things sell, on an average at an advance of nearly three hundred per cent upon the Boston prices. This is partly owing to the heavy duties which the government, in their wisdom, with the intent, no doubt, of keeping the silver in the country, has laid upon imports. These duties, and the enormous expenses of so long a voyage, keep all merchants, but those of heavy capital, from engaging in the trade. Nearly two thirds of all the articles imported into the country from round Cape Horn, for the last six years, have been by the single house of Bryant, Sturgis & Co., to whom our vessel belonged and who have a permanent agent on the coast.

This kind of business was new to us, and we liked it very well for a few days, though we were hard at work every minute from daylight to dark, and sometimes even later.

By being thus continually engaged in transporting passengers with their goods, to and fro, we gained considerable knowledge of the character, dress, and language of the people. The dress of the men was as I have before described it. The women wore gowns of various texture—silks, crape, calicoes, etc.—made after the European style, except that the sleeves were short, leaving the arm bare, and that they were loose about the waist, having no corsets. They wore shoes of kid, or satin, sashes or belts of bright colors, and almost always a necklace and ear-rings. Bonnets they had none. I only saw one on the coast, and that belonged to the wife of an American sea-captain who had settled in San Diego and had imported the chaotic mass of straw and ribbon as a choice present to his new wife. They wear their hair (which is almost invariably black, or a very dark brown) long in their necks, sometimes loose, and sometimes in long braids; though the married women often do it up on a high comb. Their only protection against the sun and weather is a large mantle, which they put over their heads, drawing it close round their faces, when they go out of doors, which is generally only in pleasant weather. When in the house or sitting out in front of it, which they often do in fine weather, they usually wear a small scarf or neckerchief of a rich pattern. A band, also, about the top of the head, with a cross, star, or other ornament in front, is common. Their complexions are various, depending—as well as their dress and manner—upon their rank; or, in other words, upon the amount of Spanish blood they can lay claim to. Those who are of pure Spanish blood, having never intermarried with the aborigines, have clear brunette complexions, and sometimes even as fair as those of English women. There are but few of these families in California, being mostly those in official stations, or who, on the expiration of their offices, have settled here upon property which they have acquired; and others who have been banished for state offences. These form the aristocracy; intermarrying, and keeping up an exclusive system in every respect. They can be told by their complexions, dress, manner, and also by their speech; for, calling themselves Castilians, they are very ambitious of speaking the pure Castilian language, which is spoken in a somewhat corrupted dialect by the lower classes. From this upper class they go down by regular shades, growing more and more dark and muddy, until you come to the pure Indian, who runs about with nothing upon him but a small piece of cloth, kept up by a wide leather strap drawn round his waist. Generally speaking, each person's caste is decided by the quality of the blood, which shows itself, too plainly to be concealed, at first sight. Yet the least drop of Spanish blood, if it be only of quatroon or octoon, is sufficient to raise them from the rank of slaves, and entitle them to wear a suit of clothes—boots, hat, cloak, spurs, long knife, and all complete, though coarse and dirty as may be,—and to call themselves Españolos, and to hold property, if they can get any.

The fondness for dress among the women is excessive, and is often the ruin of many of them. A present of a fine mantle, or of a necklace or pair of ear-rings gains the favor of the greater part of them. Nothing is more common than to see a woman living in a house of only two rooms, and the ground for a floor, dressed in spangled satin shoes, silk gown, high comb, and gilt, if not gold, ear-rings and necklace. If their husbands do not dress them well enough, they will soon receive presents from others. They used to spend whole days on board our vessel, examining the fine clothes and ornaments, and frequently made purchases at a rate which would have made a seamstress or waiting-maid in Boston open her eyes.

Next to the love of dress, I was most struck with the fineness of the voices and beauty of the intonations of both sexes. Every common ruffian-looking fellow, with a slouched hat, blanket cloak, dirty underdress, and soiled leather leggings, appeared to me to be speaking elegant Spanish. It was a pleasure simply to listen to the sound of the language, before I could attach any meaning to it. They have a good deal of the Creole drawl, but it is varied with an occasional extreme rapidity of utterance in which they seem to skip from consonant to consonant, until, lighting upon a broad, open vowel, they rest upon that to restore the balance of sound. The women carry this peculiarity of speaking to a much greater extreme than the men, who have more evenness and stateliness of utterance. A common bullock-driver, on horseback, delivering a message, seemed to speak like an ambassador at an audience. In fact, they sometimes appeared to me to be people on whom a curse had fallen, and stripped them of everything but their pride, their manners, and their voices.

Another thing that surprised me was the quantity of silver that was in circulation. I certainly never saw so much silver at one time in my life, as during the week that we were at Monterey. The truth is, they have no credit system, no banks, and no way of investing money but in cattle. They have no circulating medium but silver and hides—which the sailors call "California bank notes." Everything that they buy they must pay for in one or the other of these things. The hides they bring down dried and doubled, in clumsy ox-carts, or upon mules' backs, and the money they carry tied up in a handkerchief,—fifty, eighty, or an hundred dollars and half dollars.

Richard Henry Dana, *Two Years before the Mast* (New York, 1840), 92-98.

Trading with the Americans

BY PRUDENCIA HIGUERA

The twelve-year-old girl responsible for this vivid account of trading with the Americans was about fifty years older when she wrote it. Its feel, however, is authentic.

In the autumn of 1840 my father lived near what is now called Pinole Point, in Contra Costa County, California. I was then about twelve years old, and I remember the time because it was then that we saw the first American vessel that traded along the shores of San Pablo Bay. One afternoon a horseman from the Peraltas, where Oakland now stands, came to our ranch, and told my father that a great ship, a ship "with two sticks in the center," was about to sail from Yerba Buena into San Pablo and Suisun, to buy hides and tallow.

The next morning my father gave orders, and my brothers, with the peons, went on horseback into the mountains and smaller valleys to round up all the best cattle. They drove them to the beach, killed them there, and salted the hides. They tried out the tallow in some iron kettles that my father had bought from one of the Vallejos, but as we did not have any barrels, we followed the common plan in those days. We cast the tallow in round pits about the size of a cheese, dug in the black adobe and plastered smooth with clay. Before the melted tallow was poured into the pit an oaken staff was thrust down in the center, so that by the two ends of it the heavy cake could be carried more easily. By working very hard we had a large number of hides and many pounds of tallow ready on the beach when the ship appeared far out in the bay and cast anchor near another point two or three miles away. The captain soon came to our landing with a small boat and two sailors, one of whom was a Frenchman who knew Spanish very well, and who acted as interpreter. The captain looked over the hides, and then asked my father to get into the boat and go to the vessel. Mother was much afraid to let him go, as we all thought the Americans were not to be trusted unless we knew them well. We feared they would carry my father off and keep him a prisoner. Father said, however, that it was all right: he went and put on his best clothes, gay with silver braid, and we all cried, and kissed him good-by, while mother clung about his neck and said we might never see him again. Then the captain told her: "If you are afraid, I will have the sailors take him to the vessel, while I stay here until he comes back. He ought to see all the goods I have, or he will not know what to buy." After a little my mother let him go with the captain, and we stood on the beach to see them off. Mother then came back, and had us all kneel down and pray for father's safe return. Then we felt safe.

He came back the next day, bringing four boat-loads of cloth, axes, shoes, fish-lines, and many new things. There were two grindstones, and some cheap jewelry. My brother had traded some deerskins for a gun and four tooth-brushes, the first ones I had ever seen. I remember that we children rubbed them on our teeth till the blood came, and then concluded that after all we liked best the bits of pounded willow root that we had used for brushes before. After the captain had carried all the hides and tallow to his ship he came back, very much pleased with his bargain, and gave my father, as a present, a little keg of what he called Boston rum. We put it away for sick people.

After the ship sailed my mother and sisters began to cut out new dresses, which the Indian women sewed. On one of mine mother put some big brass buttons about an inch across, with eagles on them. How proud I was! I used to rub them hard every day to make them shine, using the tooth-brush and some of the pounded egg-shell that my sisters and all the Spanish ladies kept in a box to put on their faces on great occasions. Then our neighbors, who were ten or fifteen miles away, came to see all the things we had bought. One of the Moragas heard that we had the grindstones, and sent and bought them with two fine horses.

Soon after this I went to school, in an adobe, near where the town of San Pablo now stands. A Spanish gentleman was the teacher, and he told us many new things, for which we remember him with great respect. But when he said the earth was round we all laughed out loud, and were much ashamed. That was the first day, and when he wrote down my name he told me that I was certainly "La Cantinera, the daughter of the regiment." Afterward I found out it was because of my brass buttons. One girl offered me a beautiful black colt she owned for six of the buttons, but I continued for a long time to think more of those buttons than of anything else I possessed.

MARTINEZ

Prudencia Higuera.
Century, XLI (1890), 192-193.

News and Gossip from Santa Barbara

BY JOHN COFFIN JONES

Like many merchants in the Pacific trade, John Coffin Jones was a Bostonian. He served as United States consul at Honolulu in the 1830's, meanwhile basing his trade there. Having married a daughter of Carlos Carrillo, he spent five years in Santa Barbara before returning to Boston.

After leaving you at Monterey I landed at this place in thirty six hours and was made happy by finding my wife and friends all well. Sta Barbara, like Monterey, is looking miserable indeed; if I had not a wife to make me cumfortable in this desolate quarter of the globe, and ware compeled, here to anchor on shore, I should be strongly tempted to hasten my departure from this land of sorrows by the force, either, of pistol or brandy. . . .

I wrote you a fiew days since by a Courier dispatched by Alcalda of this place and tho' I have nothing new to communicate at the present time, I cannot suffer the Alert to depart, without one line, meer[l]y to report, that I am yet in the land of the living and move and have a being. I have had hard work however, for the last month, to keep soul and body together, for the want of sufficient of the eatible things of this world to sustain nature. It is now impossible to obtain any thing of the food kind in the way of meat or bread; beans and jirkey, of last years produce, are now the only articles of sustinence that support the people at the present time. As both of those articles are my aversion, and to attempt to eat either of them I should conceive an act of deliberate suecide, I therefore generally fare hard; indeed I may say I only live at present by gun, which affords one pleasure and the wherewithall to satisfy the palate. There is plenty of Corn to be obtained, on which I could feast should it make its appearance in the shape of a good old Yankee pudding or even a hoe cake baked before a negroes shins, but when it comes before me in the form of such horrible cakes as constitutes the bread of this country, ye Gods, at the very sight of them, my throat becoms as dry as the clnk of a lime kiln, and to attempt to pass one of them into my inner man would be as impossible, as to find a fit man in California for Governor of the Department. I hope you are doing better at the North, and if you can finde any butter, for the love of Jesus, do purchase me some without regard to price and send it by first opportunity. . . .

Should a cargo of lumber be wanted can you furnish it immediately, and would it be safe to take it off at this season from

Santa Cruz. . . . If you want the Draft, send me the form you wish it made out in. I draw on my agent Ebenzr Chadwick Esq, Boston at thirty days. . . .

I return you the No of the Poleynesian [a Honolulu newspaper] which contains the Presidents Message and am much obliged to you for the loan of it. . . .

There is no news whatever at this part of the Coast. The new General [Micheltorena] has not yet reached this place, tho we have been expecting him here the last fortnight; report says he left the Angelos on the 17th and that he will be here on the 24th with all his ragamuffin troops; I hope to God they will be swallowed up by a flood of an earth quacke before they shall have been permited to enter the Pueblo of Santa Barbara. From all accounts the General is a mild, affable and apparntly, well disposed man, but devoid of all energy, stability, force, or resolution, the very last man that should have been sent to guide the destinies of California; he appears to be very fickle, arid very undecided in his movments, and if reports speaks true, not over stocked with the one indispensable requisite to make a good Soldier. The troops, you have already receved a sample of by the California, they consist of body of leperos and laddrones, and I am told, with a fiew exceptions, wretched and miserable as are the soldiers, their officers, if there can be any beings more loathsome and dispicable, they are so. What a prospect for California, after the introduction of such a body of felons; it is intended, no doubt, to be made the Botany Bay of Mexico. If there was a speck of courage or of moral honesty in the Californians, they would rise en massé and drive these wretches from their shores; but no, these pusilanimous souls quail at the very thought, and without a murmur they will no doubt, suffer themselves to be ridden over and ridden down by this and fresh importation from the great resavoir in Mexico till they will scarcely dare to peep about themselves, to ascertain wether they really have an actual existence.

The people are proposing here to give the General a ball soon after his arrival. It will be at Mr Thompsons, but not intended to be very splendid. There is not the means to get up anything very nice or extra. There is also a great want of females for a dance. It will probably cost about 350 Dollars, all in Cash. . . .

130

I can only say that the taking of Monterey by Comd. [Thomas ap Catesby] Jones, without any orders, on the mere supposition, that a war existed between the U States and Mexico, is a proceeding, so st[r]ange & so unaccountable, that the more I think of it, the more I am puzzled to reconsile it with the act of any one but that of a mad man. What will be the effect, God only knows. For my own part, I apprehend the worst consequences; the American interest in this Coast and in Mexico, will have received a shock from which it will take years to recover, and her Character, which God knows, has always been quite low enough, in the estimation of the Mexicans will, if possible, sink lower, even into perfect insignificance. Since the surrender of Monterey, . . . I have drawn my head within my shell, and sneak about like a condemned criminal. The people here cannot be convinced that all is settled; they think the surrender of Monterey only a sham, for some purpose yet unknown but that the stripes will soon be posited again when the people may least suspect it.

The only hope I have, is, that all is not amicably settled, but that after the reception of the insulting letter to Mr Webster, the U States will consider it, as it actually is, a decliration of war on the part of Mexico, and that eir this, hostilities have actually commenced.

Excerpts from letters to Thomas Oliver Larkin,
July 16, Nov. 17, 1841, Oct. 22, Nov. 5, 1842,
in George P. Hammond, ed., *The Larkin Papers*
(Berkeley, University of California Press,
1951), I, 96, 133-135, 300-301, 310-311.

A Visit to Fort Ross

BY EUGENE DUFLOT DE MOFRAS

Eugène Duflot de Mofras was sent by the French government to make an inspection of Mexico and Alta California in 1840. The publication of his Travels *made him an authority overnight in Paris. He retained an interest in the lands he had visited and published occasional articles on them until his death in 1884.*

The Russians, with the consent of the Spanish authorities, founded their colony at Bodega in 1812, and since Mexico became independent this has never been contested. The Russian flag has never been lowered, ships of other nations have landed there without restraint and—from personal observation aboard a three-master—it is evident that every time a Russian vessel sails from Bodega to Monterey or San Francisco she pays a tonnage tax, as if coming from a foreign port.

Russian farms produce about 2,500 fanegas of wheat (1407 hectoliters), which may be purchased at a lower price from the Spaniards or at the missions, especially those of San José and Santa Clara. Recently it has seemed advantageous to purchase all supplies of wheat and fresh jerked meat from them, and so in September, 1841, 3,500 head of cattle and part of the outlying farms were sold to M. Sutter. De Rotchev, governor at Fort Ross, departed from California on January 1, 1842, aboard the brig *Constantin*, after sending to Sitka what colonists were no longer needed after farming had been abandoned. His affairs were left in charge of M. Nicolai, who resides near Bodega at Khliebnikov's farm, two leagues away.

During my sojourn in California the Russian establishments were in their prime. The nucleus of the population consisted of 800 Russians, or rather Asiatic Russians, around whom had gathered tribes of Indians who worked indifferently for a small stipend. The Russians, however, treated the Indians with the utmost kindliness, paid them fair wages, and never abused them. To keep unfriendly tribes under control, the Russians formed a military organization that also protects all Spaniards residing north of San Francisco who are in danger of raids by natives who devastate the southern country, steal animals, and sometimes kill the settlers. . . .

Near the sea European fruit trees thrive, as do tobacco plants, vines, vegetables, and grains. Wheat planted on slopes with western exposure suffers, however, from fog. Along the coast crops grow more rapidly and more abundantly than on the plains where the two farms of Khliebnikov and Jorge are situated and where the land is heavily wooded. Kostromitinov's farm has superior pasturage, while that of Don Jorge produces remarkable vineyards.

Fort Ross with its gardens has a superb location. Nothing can surpass the picturesque and spectacular setting which the forests of mammoth pines that form its background supply. Ross is built in the form of a quadrilateral, 80 meters broad. In the center of this enclosure the governor's house, the officers' quarters, the arsenal, barracks, stores, and a Greek chapel surmounted by a cross and pleasant little bells, are situated. The palisade is formed by heavy timbers, is 4 meters high, and is pierced by an opening surmounted by carronades. At opposite corners rise two hexagonal bastions two stories high, equipped with six cannon. At the other leading settlements such as those of Kostromitinov, Vasili [or] Khliebnikov, and Don Jorge Chernik, the workshops, farms, barracks, and officers' quarters are surrounded by gardens, and are built of wood attractively ornamented. The houses, which the Russians call *isbas*, resemble those found in Muscovite villages. Port Bodega consists of only two or three small houses owned by the pilots and the port captain, but it has extensive warehouses that hold such supplies as grain, kegs of wine, hides, and what rigging and equipment are required by ships. Each farm has its bathhouses, commodious quarters for the Indians, windmills, handmills, sawmills, granaries, and rooms for drying tobacco. Extensive shops for joiners' work, forging, coopers' work, and ships' carpenters have been established at the foot of Fort Ross near the small creek where ships anchor. . . .

From a personal standpoint, appreciation of the amicable welcome that was invariably accorded our party by the Russian officials during our visits in 1841 cannot be too warmly expressed. The governor of Ross, Alexander de Rotchev, his wife, née Princess Gazarin, M. Kostromitinov, head of the counting-house at Sitka, Captain Sagoskin, commander of the sloop *Hélène*, and M. Wosnesenki, scientist of the Academy at St. Petersburg, exerted themselves at all times to make our visit at their settlements agreeable.

In addition to our reception, which was almost European, they materially assisted in the exploration of various parts of the country by placing at our disposal skiffs, canoes, and soldiers, and by assembling for our use numerous relays of excellent horses. Such attentions and courtesies are specially appreciated by travelers who have passed long months of privation, relying for companion ship solely on miserable Indians. Anyone who has led the dreary life of a trapper—the life of "the long carabine"—or has been pursued by the yells of savages, can fully appreciate the joy of a choice library, French wines, a piano, and a score of Mozart. It is indeed a privilege to take this opportunity to express publicly gratitude to the Russian officers for their regal hospitality.

Eugène Deflot de Mofras, *Exploration du territoire de l'Orégon,*
des Californies et de la mer Vermeille
(Paris, 1844); translated in Marguerite Eyer Wilbur, ed.,
Duflot de Mofras' Travels on the Pacific Coast
(Santa Ana, 1937), II, 4-7, 10.

Sutter's Fort

BY JOHN BIDWELL

As a young man in 1841 John Bidwell was a leader of the first party to come overland to California with purpose of settling. He worked for John Sutter, developed a ranch of his own in the Sacramento Valley, was prominent in the early gold mining, in urging the building of a railroad, and in politics. The description here quoted is of California as he remembered it many years later.

Nearly everybody who came to California made it a point to reach Sutter's Fort. Sutter was one of the most liberal and hospitable of men. Everybody was welcome—one man or a hundred, it was all the same. He had peculiar traits: his necessities compelled him to take all he could buy, and he paid all he could pay; but he failed to keep up with his payments. And so he soon found himself immensely—almost hopelessly—involved in debt. His debt to the Russians amounted at first to something near one hundred thousand dollars. Interest increased apace. He had agreed to pay in wheat, but his crops failed. He struggled in every way, sowing large areas to wheat, increasing his cattle and horses, and trying to build a flouring mill. He kept his launch running to and from the bay, carrying down hides, tallow, furs, wheat, etc., returning with lumber sawed by hand in the redwood groves nearest the bay and other supplies. On an average it took a month to make a trip. The fare for each person was five dollars, including board. Sutter started many other new enterprises in order to find relief from his embarrassments; but, in spite of all he could do, these increased. Every year found him worse and worse off; but it was partly his own fault. He employed men—not because he always needed and could profitably employ them, but because in the kindness of his heart it simply became a habit to employ everybody who wanted employment. As long as he had anything he trusted any one with everything he wanted—responsible or otherwise, acquaintances and strangers alike. Most of the labor was done by Indians, chiefly wild ones, except a few from the Missions who spoke Spanish. The wild ones learned Spanish so far as they learned anything, that being the language of the country, and everybody had to learn something of it. The number of men employed by Sutter may be stated at from 100 to 500—the latter number at harvest time. Among them were blacksmiths, carpenters, tanners, gunsmiths, vaqueros, farmers, gardeners, weavers (to weave coarse woolen blankets), hunters, sawyers (to saw lumber by hand, a custom known in England), sheep-herders, trappers, and, later, mill-wrights and a distiller. In a word, Sutter started every business and enterprise possible. He tried to maintain a sort of a military discipline. Cannon were mounted, and pointed in every direction through embrasures in the walls and bastions. The soldiers were Indians, and every evening after coming from work they were drilled under a white officer, generally a German, marching to the music of fife and drum. A sentry was always at the gate, and regular bells called men to and from work.

Harvesting, with the rude implements, was a scene. Imagine three or four hundred wild Indians in a grain field, armed, some with sickles, some with butcher-knives, some with pieces of hoop iron roughly fashioned into shapes like sickles, but many having only their hands with which to gather by small handfuls the dry and brittle grain; and as their hands would soon become sore, they resorted to dry willow sticks, which were split to afford a sharper edge with which to sever the straw. But the wildest part was the threshing. The harvest of weeks, sometimes of a month, was piled up in the straw in the form of a huge mound in the middle of a high, strong, round corral; then three or four hundred wild horses were turned in to thresh it, the Indians whooping to make them run faster. Suddenly they would dash in before the band at full speed, when the motion became reversed, with the effect of plowing up the trampled straw to the very bottom. In an hour the grain would be thoroughly threshed and the dry straw broken almost into chaff. In this manner I have seen two thousand bushels of wheat threshed in a single hour. Next came the winnowing, which would often take another month. It could only be done when the wind was blowing, by throwing high into the air shovelfuls of grain, straw, and chaff, the lighter materials being wafted to one side, while the grain, comparatively clean, would descend and form a heap by itself. In this manner all the grain in California was cleaned. At that day no such thing as a fanning mill had ever been brought to this coast.

The kindness and hospitality of the native Californians have not been overstated. Up to the time the Mexican régime ceased in California they had a custom of never charging for anything; that is to say, for entertainment—food, use of horses, etc. You were supposed, even if invited to visit a friend, to bring your blankets with you, and one would be very thoughtless if he traveled and did not take a knife with him to cut his meat. When you had eaten, the invariable custom was to rise, deliver to the woman or hostess the plate on which you had eaten the meat and beans —for that was about all they had—and say, *"Muchas gracias, Señora"* ("Many thanks, madame"); and the hostess as invariably replied, *"Buen Provecho"* ("My it do you much good"). The Missions in California invariably had gardens with grapes, olives, figs, pomegranates, pears, and apples, but the ranches scarcely ever had any fruit. When you wanted a horse to ride, you would take it to the next ranch—it might be twenty, thirty, or fifty miles—and turn it out there, and sometime or other in reclaiming his stock the owner would get it back. In this way you might travel from one end of California to the other.

The ranch life was not confined to the country, it prevailed in the towns too. There was not a hotel in San Francisco, or Monterey, or anywhere in California, till 1846, when the Americans took the country. The priests at the Missions were glad to entertain strangers without charge. They would give you a room in which to sleep, and perhaps a bedstead with a hide stretched across it, and over that you would spread your blankets.

At this time there was not in California any vehicle except a rude California cart; the wheels were without tires, and were made by felling an oak tree and hewing it down till it made a solid wheel nearly a foot thick on the rim and a little larger where the axle went through. The hole for the axle would be eight or nine inches in diameter, but a few years' use would increase it to a foot. To make the hole, an auger, gouge, or chisel was sometimes used, but the principal tool was an ax. A small tree required but little hewing and shaping to answer for an axle. These carts were always drawn by oxen, the yoke being lashed with rawhide to the horns. To lubricate the axles they used soap (that is one thing the Mexicans could make), carrying along for the purpose a big pail of thick soapsuds which was constantly put in the box or hole; but you could generally tell when a California cart was coming half a mile away by the squeaking. I have seen the families of the wealthiest people go long distances at the rate of thirty miles or more a day, visiting in one of these clumsy two-wheeled vehicles. They had a little framework around it made of round sticks, and a bullock hide was put in for a floor or bottom. Sometimes the better class would have a little calico for curtains and cover. There was no such thing as a spoked wheel in use then. Somebody sent from Boston a wagon as a present to the priest in charge of the Mission of San José, but as soon as summer came the woodwork shrunk, the tires came off, and it all fell to pieces. There was no one in California to set tires. When Governor Micheltorena was sent from Mexico to California he brought with him an ambulance, not much better than a common spring wagon, such as a marketman would now use with one horse. It had shafts, but in California at that time there was no horse broken to work in them, nor was there such a thing known as a harness; so the governor had two mounted vaqueros to pull it, their reatas being fastened to the shafts and to the pommels of their saddles. The first wagons brought into California came across the plains in 1844 with the Townsend or Stevens party. They were left in the mountains and lay buried under the snow till the following spring, when Moses Schallenberger, Elisha Stevens (who was the captain of the party), and others went up and brought some of the wagons down into the Sacramento Valley. No other wagons had ever before reached California across the plains.

John Bidwell, "In California before the Gold Rush,"
Century, XLI (1890), 169-173.

Life and Customs, 1845

BY JAMES CLYMAN

A Rocky Mountain fur man in the 1820's, a soldier in the Black Hawk War in 1832, and a California pioneer by way of Oregon in 1845, James Clyman was an all-around westerner. He also was an inveterate diarist, with very frank comment on the scene and people around him.

The —— Callifornians are a proud Lazy indolent people doing nothing but ride after herds or from place to place without any appearant object   The Indians or aboriginees do all the drudgery and labour and are kept in state of Slavery haveing no or Receeving no compensation for their labour except a scanty allowance of subsistance during the time they [are] actually imployed and perhaps a cotton Shirt and wool sufficient to make a coarse Blanket which they spin and weave in their own way   Their method of manufacturing is simple and curious   They beat the wool with two sticks in place of cards and when it is beaten enough they spin it with a stick and lay the warp by driveing a number of small sticks in the ground it [is] raised by letting a stick run through sufficiently to pass a smal ball through and brought up with the same stick   of course their fabrick is coarse but they make it very durable   The californian Plough is a curiosity in agriculture being made of a forked branch of a tree one prong of which answers for a handle the other for a Land side mould Board Coulter & all haveing a small piece of Iron on the forward part about the size of a mans hand and half an inch thick   Harrow no such thing known

A small Quantity of wheat a patch of corn and Beans—with

some garden vegetables constitute all the agracultural products of the main bulk of the californians not half sufficient for a supply and a greate portion of the inhabitants live exclusively on Beef and mutton both of which are remarkably fine and fat but want the fine flour and vegetables to make a good meal for an American Several kinds of red peppers are grown in greate abundance and enter largely into the californian cookery so much so as to nearly strangle a Forigner and you find it necesary to have a good apatite to swallow a meal   no such thing as a good flouring mill is to be found but every family have a small hand mill on which they mash their grain when they have any to mash and a coarse sive for a Bolt   Their bread is made in thin wafer like cakes and baked slowly untill they are as hard as a sea buisket   Thier sheep are small and produce a small Quantity of coarse wool along the back the belly being entirely bare   Their cattle are of a good size and handsomely built   some farms or Ranches have from Five to Twenty thousand head of neat stock on them with large stocks of horses and sheep   no such thing as a woolen Factory is known nor in fact a manufactory of any kind or discription and even a coarse woolen hat sells from five to eight dollars   The trade of the country is carried on by some Eight or ten vessels fitted out from Boston with dry goods which they sell at from three to five hundred percent advance on prime cost and take Hides and Tallow in return   The tallow is generally sold in the south american mining districts and the hides salted and carried home   it usually takes about Three year to make a trading trip of this kind

The govornment of this province has like all the spanish american govornments gone through several Revolutions and changes But I believe every change has been for the worse and all though it took a recent change about one year since no change is preciev-able except that the revenue has fallen into the hands of other persons   The revenue is small and wholey used up by the col-lectors not a cent going to the central government   no such thing as a court of Justice is known higher than an Alcaldas court which is equivalent to a Justice of the peace in the United States and [the] alcalda is bound by no Law but his own oppinions which decides all differences

In Fact the civil the Military and all parts of the Government are weak imbecile and poorly organized and still less respected and in fact but little needed as the inhabitants live so Isolated as to have but little intercourse with each other and therefore few difficulities to settle

The forigners which have found their way to this country are mostly a poor discontented set of inhabitants and but little education hunting for a place as they [want] to live easy   only a few of them have obtained land and commenced farming and I do not hear of but one man that has gone to the trouble and Expence to get his tittle confirmed and fixed beyond altiration and dispute

In speaking of the govorment of california I must say that it is the most free and easy govorment Perhaps on the civilized globe   no Taxes are imposed on any individual what ever   I saw nor heard of no requrement for Roade labour no Military tax no civil department to support no Judiciary requiring pay and in every respect the people live free   you may support Priest or not at your pleasure and if your life and property are not Quite so safe as in some other countries you have the pleasure of using all your earnings   And strange as it may seem I never saw a spanish Californian that was mechanic of any kind or discription and how they formerly made   made   out to cultivate any land is a mistery to me not yet solved   nor do I recolect of seeing during my stay in this povince one single instance of a californian having a rail or stone fence all their fencing being made of Brush or willows woven in the form of a Basket and in some few Instances they had taken root and made a living fence and ware they cut and set in the proper season most of them would live——

Entry for December 1, 1845, in James Clyman's Diary, in Charles L. Camp, ed., *James Clyman, American Frontiersman* (San Francisco, California Historical Society, 1928), 186-188; available also in an enriched edition (Portland, 1960), 185-186.

Down from the Sierra

BY JOHN CHARLES FREMONT

Though seldom breaking a trail that was really new, John Charles Frémont moved so spectacularly and wrote about his travels with

such élan that he became famous as the great pathfinder. An instance in point is his winter crossing of the Sierra Nevada in 1844. The simpler course and much the safer would have been to wait three or four months. Having made the rash decision, Frémont carried it out resourcefully and indomitably. The passage here quoted greets the warm, flowered, and populated lower Sacramento Valley with understandable enthusiasm.

We continued down the right bank of the river, traveling for a while over a wooded upland, where we had the delight to discover tracks of cattle. To the southwest was visible a black column of smoke, which we had frequently noticed in descending, arising from the fires we had seen from the top of the Sierra. From the upland we descended into broad groves on the river, consisting of the evergreen, and a new species of white oak, with a large tufted top, and three to six feet in diameter. Among these was no brushwood; and the grassy surface gave to it the appearance of parks in an old, settled country. Following the tracks of the horses and cattle in search of people, we discovered a small village of Indians. Some of these had on shirts of civilized manufacture, but were otherwise naked, and we could understand nothing from them; they appeared entirely astonished at seeing us.

We made an acorn meal at noon, and hurried on, the valley being gay with flowers, and some of the banks being absolutely golden with the California poppy (Eschscholtzia crocea). Here the grass was smooth and green, and the groves very open, the large oaks throwing a broad shade among sunny spots.

Shortly afterward we gave a shout at the appearance on a little bluff of a neatly built adobe house with glass windows. We rode up, but, to our disappointment, found only Indians. There was no appearance of cultivation, and we could see no cattle, and we supposed the place had been abandoned. We now pressed on more eagerly than ever; the river swept round in a large bend to the right, the hills lowered down entirely; and, gradually entering a broad valley, we came unexpectedly into a large Indian village, where the people looked clean, and wore cotton shirts and various other articles of dress. They immediately crowded around us, and we had the inexpressible delight to find one who spoke a little in different Spanish, but who at first confounded us by saying there were no whites in the country; but just then a well-dressed Indian came up, and made his salutations in very well spoken Spanish. In answer to our inquiries he informed us that we were upon the Rio de los Americanos (the River of the Americans), and that it joined the Sacramento River about ten miles below. Never did a name sound more sweetly! We felt ourselves among our country-men; for the name of "American," in these distant parts, is applied to the citizens of the United States.

To our eager inquiries he answered, "I am a vaquero (cowherd) in the service of Captain Sutter, and the people of this *rancheria* work for him." Our evident satisfaction made him communicative, and he went on to say that Captain Sutter was a very rich man, and always glad to see his country people. We asked for his house. He answered that it was just over the hill before us and offered, if we would wait a moment, to take his horse and conduct us to it. We readily accepted his civil offer. In a short distance we came in sight of the fort, and, passing on the way the house of a settler on the opposite side (a Mr. Sinclair), we forded the river; and in a few miles were met a short distance from the fort by Captain Sutter himself. He gave us a most frank and cordial reception—conducted us immediately to his residence—and under his hos-pitable roof we had a night of rest, enjoyment, and refreshment, which none but ourselves could appreciate. But the party left in the mountains with Mr. Fitzpatrick were to be attended to; and the next morning, supplied with fresh horses and provisions, I hurried off to meet them. On the second day we met, a few miles below the forks of the Rio de los Americanos; and a more forlorn and pitiable sight than they presented cannot well be imagined. They were all on foot—each man, weak and emaciated, leading a horse or mule as weak and emaciated as themselves. They had experienced great difficulty in descending the mountains, made slippery by rains and melting snows, and many horses fell over precipices and were killed; and with some were lost the packs they carried. Among these was a mule with the plants which we had collected since leaving Fort Hall, along a line of two thousand miles' travel. Out of sixty-seven horses and mules with which we commenced crossing the Sierra only thirty-three reached the Valley of the

Sacramento, and they only in a condition to be led along. Mr. Fitzpatrick and his party, traveling more slowly, had been able to make some little exertion at hunting, and had killed a few deer. The scanty supply was a great relief to them; for several had been made sick by the strange and unwholesome food which the preservation of life compelled them to use. We stopped and encamped as soon as we met; and a repast of good beef, excellent bread, and delicious salmon, which I had brought along, were their first relief from the sufferings of the Sierra and their first introduction to the luxuries of the Sacramento. It required all our philosophy and forbearance to prevent plenty from becoming as hurtful to us now as scarcity had been before.

> John Charles Frémont, *Report of the Exploring Expedition to the Rocky Mountains* (Washington, 1845), 376-378.

Tragedy at Donner Lake

FROM THE DIARY OF PATRICK BREEN

The marooning of the Donner party in the Sierra in the winter of 1846 stands as the most harrowing episode in the history of the West. Other fragmentary testimonies have survived, but Patrick Breen's diary, brief though its entries are, is the only one approaching a day-to-day account of the experience.

Friday Nov. 20th 1846   Came to this place on the 31st of last month that it snowed   we went on to the pass   the snow so deep we were unable to find the road, when within 3 miles of the summit   then turned back to this shanty on the Lake, Stanton came one day after we arriveed here   we again took our teams & waggons & made another unsuccessful attempt to cross in company with Stanton   we returned to the shanty it continuing to snow all the time we were here   we now have killed most part of our cattle having to stay here untill next spring & live on poor beef without bread or salt   it snowed during the space of eight days with little intermission, after our arrival here, the remainder of time up to this day was clear & pleasant frezeing at night the snow nearly gone from the valleys.

Sat. 21st   Fine morning   wind N:W   22 of our company are about starting across the mountain this mor[n]ing including Stanton & his indians,   some clouds flying   thawed to day wnd E.

Sunday 22nd   Froze hard last night   this a fine clear morning, wind E.S.E   no account from those on the mountains.

Monday 23rd   Same weather   wind W   the Expedition across the mountains returned after an unsuccsful attempt. . . .

Sunday 29th   Still snowing now about 3 feet deep,   wind W killed my last oxen to day   will skin them tomorrow   gave another yoke to Fosters   hard to get wood.

Monday 30th   Snowing fast   wind W   about 4 or 5 feet deep, no drifts   looks as likely to continue as when it commenced   no liveing thing without wings can get about.

December 1st Tuesday   Still snowing   wind W   snow about 5½ feet or 6 deep   difficult to get wood   no going from the house completely housed up   looks as likely for snow as when it commenced, our cattle all killed But three or four them, the horses & Stantons mules gone & cattle suppose lost in the snow   no hopes of finding them alive.

Wedns. 2nd.   Continues to snow   wind W   sun shineing hazily thro the clouds   dont snow quite as fast as it has done snow must be over six feet deep   bad fire this morning.

Thursd. 3rd   Snowed a little last night   bright and cloudy at intervals all night, to day cloudy   snows none   wind S.W. warm but not enough so to thaw snow lying deep allround   expecing it to thaw a little to day   the forgoing written in the morning   it immediately turned in to snow & continued to snow all day & likely to do so all night.

Friday 4th   Cloudy that is flying clouds   neither snow or rain this day   it is a relief to have one fine day,   wind E by N no sign of thaw   freezeing pretty hard   snow deep. . . .

Sund. 6th   The morning fine & clear   now some cloudy wind S-E   not much in the sunshine,   Stanton & Graves manufactureing snow shoes for another mountain scrabble   no account of mules. . . .

Wedns. 9th   Commenced snowing about 11 o'clock   wind

N:W snows fast took in Spitzer yesterday so weak that he cannot rise without help caused by starveation all in good health some having scant supply of beef Stanton trying to make a raise of some for his Indians & self not likely to get much. . . .

Wed'd 16th Fair & pleasant Froeze hard last night & the company started on snow shoes to cross the mountains wind S.E looks pleasant.

Thursd. 17th Pleasant sunshine to day wind about S.E Bill Murp[hy] returned from the mountain party last evening Bealis died night before last Milt. & Noah went to Donnos 8 day since not returned yet, thinks they got lost in the snow, J. Denton here to day. . . .

Sund. 20 Night clear froze a little now clear & pleasant wind N by W thawing a little Mrs Reid here, no account of Milt. yet Dutch Charley started for Donoghs turned back not able to proceed tough times, but not discouraged our hopes are in God. Amen.

Mond. 21 Milt. got back last night from Donos camp sad news. Jake Donno Sam Shoemaker Rinehart, & Smith are dead the rest of them in a low situation Snowed all night with a strong S-W wind to day cloudy wind continues but not snowing, thawing sun shineing dimly in hope it will clear off. . . .

Friday 25th began to snow yesterday about 12 o'clock snowed all night & snows yet rapidly wind about E by N Great difficulty in getting wood John & Edwd. has to get [it] I am not able offered our prayers to God this Cherimass morening the prospect is apalling but hope in God *Amen*

Jany. 1st 1847 We pray the God of mercy to deliver us from our present calamity if it be his Holy will Amen. Commencd. snowing last night does not snow fast wind S:E sun peeps out at times provisions geting scant dug up a hide from under the snow yesterday for Milt. did not take it yet. . . .

Sund. 3rd Continues fair in day time freezeing at night wind about E Mrs. Reid talks of crossing the mountains with her children provisions scarce.

Mond. 4th Fine morning looks like spring thawing now about 12 o clock wind S:E Mrs. Reid Milt. Virginia & Eliza

started about ½ hour ago with prospect of crossing the mountain
may God of Mercy help them   left ther children here   Tom
with us Pat with Keysburg & Jas with Gravese's folks, it was difficult for Mrs. Reid to get away from the children. . . .

Friday 8th   Fine morning   wind E   froze hard last night
very cold this morning   Mrs. Reid & company came back this
mor[n]ing   could not find their way on the other side of the
Mountain   they have nothing but hides to live on   Martha is to
stay here   Milt. & Eliza going to Donos   Mrs. Reid & the 2 boys
going to their own shanty & Virginia   prospects dull   may God
relieve us all from this difficulty if it is his Holy will Amen. . . .

Sund. 17th   Fine morning   sun shineing clear   wind S.S.E.
Eliza came here this morning, sent her back again to Graves
Lanthrom crazy last night so Bill says, Keyburg sent Bill to get
hides off his shanty & carry thim home this morning,   provisions
scarce   hides are the only article we depend on, we have a little
meat yet,   may God send us help.

Mond. 18th   Fine day clear & pleasant   wind W, thawing
in the sun   Mrs. Murphy here to day   very hard to get wood.

Tuesd. 19th   Clear & pleasant   thawing a little in the sun
wind S.W.   Peggy & Edward sick last night by eating some meat
that Dolan threw his tobacco on, pretty well to day (praise God
for his Blessings,)   Lanthrom very low   in danger if relief dont
soon come   hides are all the go, not much of any other in camp. . . .

Thursd. 21   Fine morning   wind W   did not freze quite so
hard last night as it has done,   John Battice & Denton came this
morning with Eliza   she wont eat hides   Mrs. Reid sent her back
to live or die on them.   Milt. got his toes froze   the Donoghs are
all well. . . .

Satd. 30th   Fine pleasant morning   wind W   beginning to
thaw in the sun   John & Edwd. went to Graves this morning   the
Graves seized on Mrs Reids goods untill they would be paid   also
took the hides that she & family had to live on,   she got two pieces
of hides from there & the ballance they have taken   you may
know from these proceedings what our fare is in camp   there is
nothing to be got by hunting yet perhaps there soon will.   God
send it   Amen. . . .

146

Frid. February 5th   Snowd. hard all untill 12 o clock at night wind still continud to blow hard from the S. W: to day pretty clear a few clouds only   Peggy very uneasy for fear we shall all perrish with hunger   we have but a little meat left & only part of 3 hides has to support Mrs. Reid   she has nothing left but one hide & it is on Graves shanty   Milt is livig there & likely will keep that hide   Eddys child died last night.

Satd. 6th   It snowd. faster last night & to day than it has done this winter & still continues without an intermission   wind   S.W.

Murphys folks or Keysburgs say they cant eat hides   I wish we had enough of them   Mrs Eddy very weak.

Sund. 7th   Ceasd. to snow last after one of the most severe storms we experienced this winter the snow fell about 4 feet deep. I had to shovel the snow off our shanty this morning it thawd so fast & thawd. during the whole storm.   to day it is quite pleasant   wind S. W.   Milt here to day says Mrs Reid has to get a hide from Mrs. Murphy & McCutchins child died 2nd of this month. . . .

Frid. 12th   A warm thawey morning   wind S.E.   we hope with the assistance of Almighty God to be able to live to see the bare surface of the earth once more. O God of Mercy grant it if it be thy holy will Amen. . . .

Sund 14th   Fine morning but cold before the sun got up, now thawing in the sun   wind S E   Ellen Graves here this morning John Denton not well   froze hard last night   John & Edwd. E burried Milt. this morning in the snow.

Mond. 15   Moring cloudy untill 9 o clock   then cleared off warm & sunshine   wind W.   Mrs Graves refusd. to give Mrs Reid any hides   put Suitors pack hides on her shanty would not let her have them   says if I say it will thaw it then will not, she is a case. . . .

Frid. 19th   Froze hard last night   7 men arrived from Colifornia yesterday evening with som provisions but left the greater part on the way   to day clear & warm for this region some of the men are gone to day to Donnos Camp   will start back on Monday. . . .

Tuesd. 23   Froze hard last night   to day fine & thawey has the appearance of spring all but the deep snow   wind S:S.E.

shot Towser do day & dressed his flesh   Mrs Graves came here this morning to borrow meat dog or ox   they think I have meat to spare but I know to the contrary   they have plenty hides   I live principally on the same. . . .

Thursd. 25th   Froze hard last night   fine & sunshiney to day   wind W.   Mrs Murphy says the wolves are about to dig up the dead bodies at her shanty, the nights are too cold to watch them, we hear them howl.

Frid. 26th   Froze hard last night   today clear & warm   Wind S:E.   blowing briskly   Marthas jaw swelled with the tooth-ache;   hungry times in camp, plenty hides but the folks will not eat them   we eat them with a tolerable good apetite. Thanks be to Almighty God.   Amen   Mrs Murphy said here yesterday that thought she would commence on Milt. & eat him. I dont that she has done so yet, it is distressing   The Donnos told the California folks that they commence to eat the dead people 4 days ago, if they did not succeed that day or next in finding their cattle then under ten or twelve feet of snow & did not know the spot or near it, I suppose they have done so ere this time.

Satd. 27th   Beautiful morning sun shineing brilliantly, wind about S. W.   the snow has fell in debth about 5 feet but no thaw but [in] the sun in day time it freezing hard every night,   heard some geese fly over last night   saw none.

Sund.   28th   Froze hard last night   to day fair & sunshine wind S.E.   1 solitary Indian passed by yesterday   come from the lake   had a heavy pack on his back   gave me 5 or 6 roots re-sembleing onions in shape   taste some like a sweet potatoe, all full of little tough fibres.

Mond. March the 1st   So fine & pleasant   froze hard last night   there has 10 men arrived this morning from Bear Valley with provisions   we are to start in two or three days & cash our goods here   there is amongst them some old [hands]   they say the snow will be here untill June.

Diary of Patrick Breen, edited by Frederick J. Teggart (Berkeley, University of California Press, 1910), 273-284; a slightly different rendition is in George R. Stewart, *Ordeal by Hunger* (second edition, Boston, 1960), 323-335.

Vaquero

BY WILLIAM H. EMORY

William H. Emory was one of the officers under Kearny in his march into New Mexico and on to California. One of his achievements was a beautifully executed mapping of the route followed, together with a report on the march, from which the following paragraphs are drawn. Emory later had important assignments in boundary surveying and in the Civil War.

The captured horses were all wild and but little adapted for immediate service, but there was rare sport in catching them, and we saw for the first time the lazo thrown with inimitable skill. It is a saying in Chihuahua that "a Californian can throw the lazo as well with his foot as a Mexican can with his hand," and the scene before us gave us an idea of its truth. There was a wild stallion of great beauty which defied the fleetest horse and the most expert rider. At length a boy of fourteen, a Californian, whose graceful riding was the constant subject of admiration, piqued by repeated failures, mounted a fresh horse, and, followed by an Indian, launched fiercely at the stallion.

His lareat darted from his hand with the force and precision of a rifle ball, and rested on the neck of the fugitive; the Indian, at the same moment, made a successful throw, but the stallion was too stout for both, and dashed off at full speed, with both ropes flying in the air like wings. The perfect representation of Pegasus, he took a sweep, and followed by his pursuers, came thundering down the dry bed of the river. The lazos were now trailing on the ground, and the gallant young Spaniard, taking advantage of the circumstance, stooped from his flying horse and caught one in his hand. It was the work of a moment to make it fast to the pommel of his saddle, and by a short turn of his own horse, he threw the stallion a complete somerset, and the game was secure.

William H. Emory, *Notes of a Military Reconnoissance*,
30th Cong., 1 sess., *Senate Exec. Doc. No. 7* (Washington, 1848), 97.

Rancho Patrocinio del Alisal

BY CARL MEYER

*Carl Meyer was one of those forty-niners who came more to ob-
serve than to mine. A clue is that he tarried as long as he did at
William E. P. Hartnell's country place. With all the cultivation
that was carried on, it would appear to have been more hacienda
than rancho, but California usage is inexorable and rancho it was.
In another passage Meyer gives as rich a description of a Mexican
pack train as he achieves here of life at Patrocinio del Alisal.*

Rancho Patrocinio del Alisal is over thirty *leguas* in circumference; it is a whole duchy. Eight thousand head of cattle and several
thousand horses and sheep graze here. . . .

   Agriculture is not carried on extensively at Patrocinio del Alisal
nor at other California ranchos. Cultivated fields, or *milpas*, are
seen only here and there. Lack of trained workmen and the very
profitable business of cattle raising have stifled any further agricultural pursuits. Mr. Hartnell would be delighted to have European settlers on his rancho; the advantages which he is prepared to
offer to them would surpass anything which has ever been anticipated in such contracts.

   At the time of the missions California produced 100,000 barrels of wine yearly and the same amount of brandy; today barely
enough is produced for the market. Mr. Hartnell owns a large
piece of vineyard which, however, is in such a neglected state that
the vines are rapidly becoming destroyed or growing wild. On the
other hand the vegetable garden of the rancho, which can be easily
watered, leaves nothing to be desired. Under the care of a French
gardener it produces during the whole year the most varied and
delicious native and foreign vegetables. It gave me particular
pleasure to walk between the green garden beds, reaching now
and again for a radish, gooseberry, current or strawberry, and with
everything else of which I had been deprived for so long growing
right at hand.

   The sight of the native garden plants is also pleasing. The eye
lingers with pleasure on the casaba melon (*cresentia cujete*), on
the vine-covered earth-wall, on the dark green *ruqueta bed*, or on

the pepper plant which chokes my praise in my mouth by its tongue-burning pod and without which life for the California ranch dweller is as impossible as for the Mexican. If he be offered both a pepper pod and a strawberry-like *granadita*, he will disdain the latter. *Chile verde* must never be absent from his table; it is like the white bread of the Frenchman. Without chili all food is tasteless, and without chili his customs would be less fiery. Fiery customs are to be found wherever pepper grows. At Patrocinio del Alisal I had opportunity enough to observe this again, not, however, without variations.

Mr. Hartnell is a born Englishman. He has been in this country for thirty years and is happily married to a Californian who presented him with twenty-two children, fourteen of whom are still living, the oldest son being twenty-seven years old and the youngest being baptized at the time of my stay at the rancho. Mr. Hartnell was educated in Germany and speaks all modern languages very fluently. He left nothing undone to have his children educated according to his standards and always kept a European tutor for this purpose. I was not surprised therefore to find thoroughly educated people and everything which makes society pleasant in the middle of a broad prairie in this far corner of the world. Every child had a musical training and brass and stringed instruments were played, from the French horn to the piano. Every evening suitable instruments were heard together and signalled the beginning of the *tertulia*.

The whole household takes part in a California *tertulia*, even the servants have the pleasure of looking on. It is a most liberal, but at the same time very aristocratic entertainment. The richly dressed members of the family, together with the friends of the house favored as *compadres* and *comadres*, and the other guests, sit along the walls of a spacious room. Respects are paid whereby a thousand compliments, a thousand wishes and a thousand pretty words are wasted. *"Beso las manos!"* and *"Beso las pies!"* [I kiss your hands! I kiss your feet!] passes from mouth to mouth and the most animated conversation is developed. But the young *dons* and *donzellas* become too restless during this, they want music, song, games and dancing. Everyone takes his turn at the piano and as he who can play should also be able to sing the stranger is quickly told, "No excuse, *Señor*, the *Señorita* will accompany you." To earn applause it is only necessary to sing any strange song, which has a cheerful sound, because they like entertainment in music and song.

A *cigarillo*, rolled by the *Señorita's* deft fingers, is the stranger's reward for his cheerful song. He is indeed unfortunate if he does not like to smoke and does not accept the *cigarillo "con mil gracias"* and *"con mucho gusto,"* and smoke it to the health of its beautiful donor; for then she will never bestow her favor upon him, even if he be an Apollo! Only the men take part in the national card game and while they are amusing themselves at this the young people play *juegas de prendas*, a popular forfeit game. Soon everyone joins in, for one would certainly be a foolish fellow to wish to miss this entertainment in which the redeeming of the forfeit frequently affords unforgetable memories. The *fandango*, without which the *tertulia* cannot be concluded, brings everyone together again to increase the pleasure of the group to its highest point.

The traveler soon learns that the dance in Spanish-America is unavoidable, even more than that, it has become the law of society here, the most universal pleasure embodied in a natural law, for the Spanish dance is a circling of its charming object. Just like the planets around the sun it is a picture of life, of attraction and repulsion. The Spanish-American dances as long as he lives and "I have enough of dancing" would mean for him "Oh, I am tired of living!" He allows no opportunity for dancing to pass; how could a *tertulia* be ended without dancing? These graceful movements, this casting of glances by the "lightly tanned sunburnt ones" and this light, skillful handclasping and interweaving of the odd figures of the Spanish dances would never end if it were not that the *matrone* of the house has the prerogative of announcing the midnight hour to the group and no one wishes to be the last to leave the parlor.

Night on a California or Mexican Rancho brings something unpleasant with it about which not a word would be said if its cause were not generally known in the country and if it were not an endemic evil: it is what one might call "flea-fever." Hardly has one gone to bed when a whole band of these small devilish fleas pursue their bloody maneuvers on one's sensitive skin driving away sleep and torturing a man to madness. One breaks out in a martyr's sweat and because of this and the continual throwing off of the covers one runs the risk of contracting a fever. It is almost impossible to rid the body entirely of these vermin during the day so these blood-related parasites also join in the pleasant entertainment of the *Tertulia*.

> Many women, many fleas,
> Many fleas, much itching
> Thought they cause you secret pain
> You dare not complain!

No hesitancy is shown on the rancho in speaking of this country-wide misfortune, even in the presence of ladies, and the stranger whose skin is not yet leathery enough to withstand it is unreservedly pitied. During a conversation not the least hesitation is shown in making certain gestures [scratchings] as it would be impossible to refrain from doing so. These body beasts are more effective than the quintessence of Spanish pepper, the most imperative means for creating and stimulating southern customs!

Carl Meyer, Nach dem Sacramento (Aarau, 1856),
translated by Ruth Frey Axe (Claremont, 1938) 60-64.

Life on the Ranchos

BY ROBERT GLASS CLELAND

For many years Robert Glass Cleland headed the Huntington Library research staff in southwestern history. The following selection is from the most cited of his books, The Cattle on a Thousand Hills, *a social and economic history of southern California's transition to American ways.*

The carefree life of the California rancheros a hundred years ago has been the theme of so many colorful descriptions that one hesitates to dwell upon the subject further; but the chapter would not be complete without some reference to it. From an economic and social point of view the great ranchos of the period had much in common with the medieval English manor. Except for a few luxuries obtained from trading vessels on the coast, each ranch was virtually a self-sustaining economic unit. Large numbers of Indians, recruited chiefly from the fast-decaying mission communities, served as *vaqueros*, artisans, farm laborers, and domestic servants in return for simple but abundant food, primitive shelter, and a scant supply of clothing. Some of the native families lived in the *indiada*, a cluster of primitive huts built near the main adobe *casa*, while others dwelt in small villages, called rancherias, widely scattered over the state.

The homage paid a California don, both by members of his family and by his retainers, was not unlike that once accorded a feudal lord. The members of his household were often numbered by the score. He provided a home for a host of poor relations, entertained strangers, as well as friends, with unwearying hospitality, and begat as many sons and daughters as the Hebrew patriarchs of old.

On large estates an army of Indian women were required for domestic service. "Each child (of whom there were sixteen) has a personal attendant," said Señora Vallejo of her household staff, "while I have two for my own needs; four or five are occupied in grinding corn for tortillas, for so many visitors come here that three grinders do not suffice; six or seven serve in the kitchen, and five or six are always washing clothes for the children and other servants; and, finally, nearly a dozen are employed at sewing and spinning."

The chronic dearth of money, characteristic of the entire Spanish-Mexican period, forced the Californians to resort to barter in virtually all their business dealings. Trade between the ranchers and foreign vessels, as portrayed so vividly by Richard Henry Dana in his *Two Years Before the Mast*, depended almost exclusively on this method of exchange. But the system applied with equal universality to domestic transactions as well. Contracts and promissory notes were often made payable in terms of cattle, hides or tallow; judges levied fines and judgments in the same commodities; and even the smallest amount of merchandise—a few yards of cloth, a pound of sugar, a box of raisins, a handful of cigars—was purchased with the standard of currency of the province, the ubiquitous cattle hide, known, from Alaska to Peru, as the "California bank note."

Free from the pressure of economic competition, ignorant of the wretchedness and poverty indigenous to other lands, amply supplied with the means of satisfying their simple wants, devoted to "the grand and primary business of the enjoyment of life," the Californians enjoyed a pastoral, patriarchal, almost Arcadian existence until a more complicated and efficient civilization invaded their "demiparadise." One who knew by experience the simplicity and contentment of California ranch life a hundred years ago [W. A. Hawley] drew, for less fortunate generations, the following picture of its quiet charm:

"The *rancho* lay beyond the mountain range and extended over rolling hills and little valleys. A creek flowed through it, and on the banks were many sycamores. Shaded by oaks was the long, low adobe house, with its red tiled roof and wide veranda. Behind the fence of chaparral was the orchard and the melon patch, and beyond the orchard was the meadow, golden with buttercups in the early spring. In the open fields, dotted with oaks, the rich alfilerilla grew, and on the hillsides were the wild grasses which waved like billows as the breezes from the distant ocean blew across them. The sameness of recurring events of each succeeding year never seemed monotonous, but brought repose, contentment and peace. When the dew was still on the grass, we would mount our horses and herd the cattle if any had strayed beyond the pasture. In the wooded cañons where the cool brooks flowed, and where the wild blackberries grew, we ate our noon day meal and rested. And as the hills began to glow with the light of the setting sun we journeyed homeward. When the long days of summer came, we ate our evening meal beneath the oaks, and in the twilight we listened to the guitar and the songs of our people. In the autumn we harvested the corn and gathered the olives and the grapes.

"Those were the days of long ago. Now all is changed by modern progress; but in the simple ranch life of the older time there was a contented happiness which an alien race with different temperament can never understand."

Robert Glass Cleland, *The Cattle on a Thousand Hills*
(San Marino, Huntington Library, 1941), 42-45.

4

THE CONQUEST

As early as 1808 William Shaler published a report on California that might have been read as a proposal for American annexation. Within a score of years the beaver trappers were entering the province by the overland routes and the hide traders had carried out a commercial annexation. Soon there was more open talk about acquisition by the United States, and Andrew Jackson, Daniel Webster, and other notables gave the matter thought and some effort. Mexico, however, though neglectful of her northwestern province, was not ready to cede it away. In 1842 the standing instructions to the commander of the Pacific squadron of the United States Navy were disclosed when Commodore Thomas ap Catesby Jones, in the belief that the United States and Mexico were at war, landed at Monterey and raised the Stars and Stripes. Persuaded the next day that there was no war, he apologized as best he could. His capture did not count.

Four years later the peace was broken again. At Sonoma in northern California a group of disaffected Americans defied Mexican authority and raised the Flag of the Bear. Something of the motivation and a bit of the haphazard nature of this movement are revealed in the proclamation by William B. Ide. Meanwhile, on the other side of the continent, in the belt between the Nueces and the Rio Grande, patrols of Mexican and American troops had clashed, and on the basis of this incident President Polk called on Congress to declare that a state of war existed. California was not an immediate cause of the war, but to acquire the province was an American war aim and the campaigning was conducted accordingly. Commodore Sloat sailed to Monterey and on July 7 took

GOLDEN GATE *by Ansel Adams*

possession and raised the American flag. The Navy continued the conquest by proclamations and flag raisings at Yerba Buena, Sonoma, Sutter's Fort, and San Jose. The Californians did not resist, and the Bear Flag men dissolved their republic and volunteered as auxiliary troops. On August 17, after the Stars and Stripes were raised at Los Angeles, Commodore Stockton could proclaim American possession of the entire province.

In September, however, what began as trivial friction with the occupation forces at Los Angeles expanded into a general uprising. Stockton landed sailors at San Pedro to march on Los Angeles, only to be ignominiously repulsed in the Battle of the Old Woman's Gun. In December General Stephen W. Kearny and his dragoons, after their long march from Missouri, ran into the resistance fighters at San Pasqual. The regulars held the field but suffered most of the casualties. Army, navy, and auxiliaries such as Frémont's battalion then tried to pull together to suppress the southern California revolt. Joining forces, Kearny and Stockton moved north from San Diego to strike again at the insurgents. Edwin Bryant's commentary on the march with Frémont and Charles E. Pickett's on military alarums in the north may seem marginal to the real campaigning, yet it was a show of force rather than heavy fighting that re-established American control. A token is that the Californians chose to capitulate to Frémont, slowly approaching from the northwest, rather than to Kearny and Stockton with their heavier armament. After four months the province once again was under control.

An inter-service imbroglio involving Kearny, Stockton, and Frémont as principals held the stage in 1847. On February 2, 1848, the Treaty of Guadalupe Hidalgo made formal transfer of California to the United States. Ten days earlier James Marshall struck gold at Coloma on the South Fork of the American River, with consequences that are a chapter to themselves. One important result was to hasten the shift from military government to civilian control and eventually to statehood. In fact, by August, 1849, the Californians were electing delegates to a constitutional convention, and a few weeks later this convention completed its work. Its members marked the occasion with solemnity and more exuberant celebration.

158

Sloat had proclaimed that the United States was taking permanent possession. The treaty in 1848 gave official confirmation. Late in 1849 by drafting a constitution and promptly translating it into an operating government, the Californians served notice that they were ready for statehood. The national authorities were too much involved in sectional controversy to give heed immediately, but on September 9, 1850, the state was legitimatized and its Senators and Congressmen were welcomed to their seats.

All histories of California relate how the province was seized, then had to be reconquered, and how in rapid order it moved on to become the thirty-first state. The change of flag may well have been as important as any event in the entire history of the state. Some historians so record it, though there is strong temptation to give top billing to the gold discovery and rush as considerably more distinctive. Less frequently a historian says flatly that the American seizure was an act of aggression, though Josiah Royce, native son, philosopher, and historian, makes this point emphatically.

The Bear Flag Proclamation

BY WILLIAM B. IDE

At sixty William B. Ide was one of the oldest of the Bear Flaggers. After electing him commandant, they deeply offended him by turning to Frémont as leader. Through Ide's high-flown language one may discern, though not with absolute clarity, the purpose of the Bears.

To all persons, Citizens of Sonoma, requesting them to remain at peace, and to follow their rightful occupations without fear of Mollestation.

The Commander in Chief of the Troops assembled at the Fortress of Sonoma give his inviolable pledge to all persons in California not found under arms that they shall not be disturbed in their persons, their property or social relations one to another by men under his command.

He also solemnly declares his object to be First, to defend himself and companions in arms who were invited to this country by

159

a promise of Lands on which to settle themselves and families who were also promised a "Republican Government," who, when having arrived in California were denied even the privilege of buying or renting Lands of their friends, who instead of being allowed to participate in or being protected by a "Republican Government" were oppressed by a "Military Despotism," who were even threatened, by "proclamation" from the Chief officer of the aforesaid Despotism, with extermination if they would not depart out of the Country; leaving all their property, their arms and beasts of burden, and thus deprived of the means of flight or defence. We were to be driven through deserts, inhabited by hostile Indians to certain destruction. To overthrow a "Government" which had seized upon the property of the Missions for its individual aggrandizement; which has ruined and shamefully oppressed the labouring people of California, by their enormous exactions on goods imported into this country; is the determined purpose of the brave men who are associated under his command.

He also solemnly declares his object in the Second place to be to invite all peaceable and good Citizens of California who are friendly to the maintenance of good order and equal rights (and I do hereby invite them to repair to my camp at Sonoma without delay) to assist us in establishing and perpetuating a "Republican Government" which shall secure to all; civil and religious liberty; which shall detect and punish crime; which shall encourage industry virtue and literature; which shall leave unshackled by Fetters, Commerce, Agriculture, and Mechanism.

He further declares that he relies upon the rectitude of our intentions; the favor of Heaven and the bravery of those who are bound to, and associated with him, by the principle of self preservation; by the love of truth; and by the hatred of tyranny—for his hopes of success.

He further declares that he believes that a Government to be prosperous and happifying in its tendency must originate with its people who are friendly to its existence. That its Citizens, are its Guardians, its officers are its Servants, and its Glory their reward.

Signed *William B. Ide*

Head Quarters Sonoma June 15th 1846.

Manuscript HM 4116, Huntington Library.

To the Inhabitants of Callifornia

BY JOHN D. SLOAT

In July, 1846, John D. Sloat was the rather reluctant instrument of destiny. Consul Larkin thought he should have taken possession for the United States a couple of days earlier, but raise the flag he did on July 7 to the accompaniment of this reassuring proclamation.

To the inhabitants of Callifornia

The central Government of Mexico having commenced hostilities against the United States of America, by invading the territory, and attacking the troops of the United States stationed at the north side of the Rio Grande, with a force of seven thousand men under General Ariste, which army was totally destroyed, and all their Artillery, Baggage & & captured on the 8th and 9th May last, by a force of two thousand three hundred men under the command of General Taylor; and the city of Matamoras taken and occupied by the forces of the United States.

The two nations being actually at war, by this transaction, I shall hoist the standard of the United States at Monterey immediately, and carry it throughout California.

I declare to the inhabitants of California that altho' I come in arms with a powerful force, I do not come among them as enemy to California; but on the contrary I come as their best friend; as henceforward California will be a portion of the United States; and its peacable inhabitants will enjoy the same rights and privileges as the citizens of any other portion of that nation, with all the rights and privileges they now enjoy, together with the privileges of choosing their own magistrates and other officers for the administration of Justice among themselves; and the same protection will be extended to them, as to any other state of the union.

They will also enjoy a permanent Government, under which life, property, and the constitutional right and lawful security to worship the creator in a way most congenial to each ones sense of duty, will be secure which unfortunately the central Government of Mexico cannot afford them, destroyed as her internal resources are by the internal factions and corrupt officers who create constant revolutions to promote their own interests, and oppress the people.

Under the flag of the United States, California will be free from all such troubles and expense, consequently the country will rapidly advance and improve both in agriculture and commerce as of course the revenue laws will be the same in California as in all other parts of the United States; affording them all manufactures and produce of the United States free of any duty; and all foreign goods at one quarter the duty they now pay, a great increase in the value of real estate and the products of California.

With the great interest and kind feelings I know the Govt. and people of the United States possess towards the citizens of California, the country cannot but improve more rapidly than any other on the continent of America.

Such of the inhabitants of California whether natives or foreigners as may not be disposed to accept the high privileges of Citizenship and to live peacably under the free Government of the United States will be allowed time to dispose of their property and to remove out of the country if they choose, without any restriction, or remain in it, observing strict neutrality.

With full confidence in the honor and integrity of the inhabitants of the country, I invite the judges, Alcaldes, and other Civil officers to retain their office, and to Execute their functions as heretofore, that the public tranquility may not be disturbed; at least until the Government of the Territory can be more definitely arranged.

All persons holding titles of real estate or in quiet possession of lands under colour of right, shall have their titles and rights guaranteed them.

All churches and the property they contain, in possession of the clergy of California shall continue in the same rights and possession they now enjoy.

All provisions and supplies of every kind furnished by the inhabitants for the use of the United States Ships and soldiers, will be paid for their rates and no private property will be taken for public use without just compensation at the moment.

United States Ship Savannah
Harbour of Monterey, July 6th 1846

> *Signed* JOHN D. SLOAT
> Commander in Chief of the
> United States Naval forces
> in the Pacific Ocean
>
> From a contemporary manuscript copy
> in the Pony Express Museum.

Fremont and His Volunteers

BY FRED WALPOLE

Low in funds and in health, Fred Walpole left England in 1844 on a voyage aimed to restore his health if not his fortune. The journey of four years and 83,000 miles took him to California just when the United States was taking over. The coincidence resulted in this candid observation on Frémont and his men.

During our stay Captain Fremont and his party arrived, preceded by another troop of American horse. It was a party of sea-men mounted, who were used to scour the country to keep off marauders. Their efficiency as sailors, they being nearly all English, we will not question. As cavalry they would probably, have been singularly destructive to each other. Their leader, however, was a fine fellow, and one of the best rifle-shots in the States. Fremont's party naturally excited curiosity. Here were true trappers, the class that produced the heroes of Fenimore Cooper's best works. These men had passed years in the wilds, living on their own resources: they were a curious set. A vast cloud of dust appeared first, and thence in long file emerged this wildest wild party. Fremont rode a-head, a spare active-looking man, with such an eye! He was dressed in a blouse and leggings, and wore a felt hat. After him came five Delaware Indians, who

were his body-guard, and have been with him through all his wanderings: they had charge of two baggage-horses. The rest, many
of them blacker than the Indians, rode two and two, the rifle held
by one hand across the pommel of the saddle. Thirty-nine of them
are his regular men, the rest are loafers picked up lately; his original men are principally backwoodsmen from the State of Ten-
nessee, and the banks of the upper waters of the Missouri. He has
one or two with him who enjoy high reputations in the Prairies.
Kit Carsons is as well known there as the Duke is in Europe. The
dress of these men was principally a long loose coat of deer-skin,
tied with thongs in front; trousers of the same, of their own manufacture, which, when wet through, they take off, scrape well inside with a knife, and put on as soon as dry; the saddles were of
various fashions, though these and a large drove of horses, and a
brass field-gun, were things they had picked up about California.
The rest of the gang were a rough set; and perhaps their private,
public, and moral characters had better not be too closely examined. They are allowed no liquor, tea and sugar only; this, no
doubt, has much to do with their good conduct, and the discipline
too is very strict. They were marched up to an open space on the
hills near the town, under some large firs, and there took up their
quarters in messes of six or seven in the open air. The Indians lay
beside their leader. One man, a doctor, six foot six high, was an
odd looking fellow. May I never come under his hands!

The party, after settling themselves, strolled into the town. and
in less than two days passed in drunkenness and debauchery, three
or four were missing. . . . They were accordingly marched away
into those wilds of which they seemed much better citizens. In
justice, however, to the Americans, I must say they seemed to
treat the natives well, and their authorities extended every protection to them. One of the gang was very uncivil to us, and threw
on us the withering imputation of being Britishers, with an intensity of scorn that must have been painful to himself; on inquiry he was found to be a deserter from the Marines. In fact, the
most violently Yankee were discovered to be English fellows, of
high principles, of course. One day returning from a ride a party of
us were galloping hard in pursuit of a jackal, when a man rode up
to us, an ill-looking little old fellow, and asked us who we were,

adding, "I came up thinking you were Mexicans, to stop you; as you are not, you may proceed." Fancy the fellow, six to one!

The butts of the trappers' rifles resemble a Turkish musket, therefore fit light to the shoulder; they are very long and very heavy; carry ball about thirty-eight to the pound. A stick a little longer than the barrel is carried in the bore, in which it fits tightly; this keeps the bullet from moving, and in firing, which they do in a crouching position, they use it as a rest.

Fred *Walpole, Four Years in the Pacific
in Her Majesty's Ship Collingwood*
(London, 1849), II, 215-218.

From the Diary of an Alcalde

BY WALTER COLTON

Coming to California as chaplain of the U.S.S. Congress, *Walter Colton on July 28, 1846, was named alcalde of Monterey. That meant, in short, that he was the government of the town and district. He made regulations and enforced them. He put drunks and gamblers to toiling on public works. He pyramided fines into a hall useful as a courthouse, school, and the seat for the constitutional convention of 1849. He edited the first newspaper. And he found time to keep a diary.*

Saturday, Aug. 15, 1846.   To-day the first newspaper ever published in California made its appearance. The honor, if such it be, of writing its Prospectus, fell to me. It is to be issued on every Saturday, and is published by Semple and Colton. Little did I think when relinquishing the editorship of the North American in Philadelphia, that my next feat in this line would be off here in California. My partner is an emigrant from Kentucky, who stands six feet eight in his stockings. He is in a buckskin dress, a foxskin cap; is true with his rifle, ready with his pen, and quick at the type-case.

He created the materials of our office out of the chaos of a small concern, which had been used by a Roman Catholic monk in printing a few sectarian tracts. The press was old enough to be preserved as a curiosity; the mice had burrowed in the balls; there were no rules, no leads, and the types were rusty and all in pi. It was only by scouring that the letters could be made to show their faces. A sheet or two of tin were procured, and these, with a jack-knife, were cut into rules and leads. Luckily we found, with the press, the greater part of a keg of ink; and now came the main scratch for paper. None could be found, except what is used to envelop the tobacco of the cigar smoked here by the natives. A coaster had a small supply of this on board, which we procured. It is in sheets a little larger than the common-sized foolscap. And this is the size of our first paper, which we have christened the Californian.

Though small in dimensions, our first number is as full of news as a black-walnut is of meat. We have received by couriers, during the week, intelligence from all the important military posts through the territory. Very little of this has transpired; it reaches the public for the first time through our sheet. We have, also, the declaration of war between the United States and Mexico, with an abstract of the debate in the senate. A crowd was waiting when the first sheet was thrown from the press. It produced quite a little sensation. Never was a bank run upon harder; not, however, by people with paper to get specie, but exactly the reverse. One-half of the paper is in English, the other in Spanish. The subscription for a year is five dollars; the price of a single sheet is twelve and a half cents; and is considered cheap at that.

Friday, Sept. 4, 1846. I empannelled to-day the first jury ever summoned in California. The plaintiff and defendant are among the principal citizens of the country. The case was one involving property on the one side, and integrity of character on the other. Its merits had been pretty widely discussed, and had called forth an unusual interest. One-third of the jury were Mexicans, one-third Californians, and the other third Americans. This mixture may have the better answered the ends of justice, but I was apprehensive at one time it would embarrass the proceedings; for the plaintiff spoke in English, the defendant in French, the jury, save the Americans, Spanish, and the witnesses all the languages known to California. But through the silent attention which prevailed, the tact of Mr. Hartnell, who acted as interpreter, and the absence of young lawyers, we got along very well.

The examination of the witnesses lasted five or six hours; I then gave the case to the jury, stating the questions of fact upon which they were to render their verdict. They retired for an hour, and then returned, when the foreman handed in their verdict, which was clear and explicit, though the case itself was rather complicated. To this verdict, both parties bowed without a word of dissent. The inhabitants who witnessed the trial, said it was what they liked—that there could be no bribery in it—that the opinion of twelve honest men should set the case forever at rest. And so it did, though neither party completely triumphed in the issue. One recovered his property, which had been taken from him by mistake, the other his character, which had been slandered by design. If there is any thing on earth besides religion for which I would die, it is the right of trial by jury.

Tuesday, Sept. 15, 1846. The citizens of Monterey elected me to-day alcalde, or chief magistrate of this jurisdiction—a situation which I have been filling for two months past, under a military commission. It has now been restored to its civil character and functions. Their election is undoubtedly the highest compliment which they can confer; but this token of confidence brings with it a great deal of labor and responsibility. It devolves upon me duties similar to those of mayor of one of our cities, without any of those judicial aids which he enjoys. It involves every breach of the peace, every case of crime, every business obligation, and every disputed land-title within a space of three hundred miles. From every other alcalde's court in this jurisdiction there is an appeal to this, and none from this to any higher tribunal. Such an absolute disposal of questions affecting property and personal liberty, never ought to be confined to one man. There is not a judge on any bench in England or the United States, whose power is so absolute as that of the alcalde of Monterey.

Walter Colton, Three Years in California
(New York, 1850), 32-33, 47-48, 55.

Battle of San Pasqual

FROM THE DIARY OF JOHN S. GRIFFIN

A surgeon with Stephen W. Kearny's dragoons on their long trek to California, John S. Griffin was present at the battle of San Pasqual and at the best vantage point to tally the damages inflicted on the Americans. After the war he pursued his career in Los Angeles.

5th-6th, 7th, 8th, 9th, 10th, 11th [December, 1846].

6th—We were all afoot about 2 A.M. and expected to surprise the party of Mexicans, though we had been in the rain all night our arms were not reloaded, but boots and saddles was the word, and off we put in search of adventure, in two miles from our camp we met Gallespie with his company, which fell in—in our rear— Major Swords was left back with the baggage, and thirty men. Another party some 10 or 15 men were left back with Gallespies four pounder. This reduced our fighting men to about 85 all told —with these and two howitzers we marched forward. The morning was excessively cold, and we felt it more as the most of us were wet to the skin. After passing over a mountain and traveling as near as I can judge some ten or eleven miles we came in sight of the enemys fires. We marched down the mountain   so soon as we arrived on the plain the shout and charge was commenced from the advance. After runing our jaded and broken down mules and horses some ¾ or a mile, the Enemy fired on us. The balls whistled about most infernally for a while but the light was not sufficient, for me to distinguish any thing like a line of the Enemy,   on my left however from the flashing of the guns I could see that there was a considerable row, and in a few moments the Enemy broke and, we found they had made a stand in front of a Ranchereo. This was called St Pasqual. At this time a fellow came dashing by, and I saw he was a Mexican   several shots were fired at him when he fell   I think as well as I·could judge by the light, day was just breaking—it was Lt Beal of the Navy who fired the shot. At this time another fellow came dashing by presenting with his hat &c a most Mexican look—when bang went a dragoon pistol—but missed   another dragoon who happened to be near—drew his sabre and was about cutting the man down when I yelled out to him to stop as the man was one of Gallespies party—by this time we were very much disordered—our men some being mounted on fresh horses, and others on poor and broken down mules could not come. Capt Moor however ordered the charge to be continued and it was in the most hurly burly manner—not more than ten or fifteen men being in line and not over forty all together on they went however—the Enemy continued to retreat for about ½ mile further when they rallied and came at us like devils with their lances—being mounted on swift horses—and most of our fire arms having been discharged or missed fire from the rain of the night previous, our advance was perfectly at their mercy. The men wheeled, and by this time a howitzer being near rallied on the gun, and drove the enemy off—Hammond was the first wounded man I saw, he had been in the advance with Moore—and got a lance wound on the left side between the 8th and 9th ribs—I told him to go a little farther to the rear and I would attend to him. At this time I was sepperated from him—when the Genl saw me and told me he was wounded and wished my services, shortly after the devils got around me, and like to have fixed my flint— but I got off by dropping my gun which I snapped at a fellow and drawing an empty pistol—this answered the purposes of a loaded one—I then met Capt Galespie who told me he was wounded he bleeding most profusely, the wound being in front directly over the heart. Capt Gibson next called on me and in a few moments I found I had my hands full. Capt Johnston who led the first charge was killed by a gun shot wound in the head. I was told this was the only man of ours who—received any injury from gun shot— Moor was killed far in the advance leading the second charge and Hammond I was told received his wound in attempting to rescue Moor—a man by name of [Frank] Menard, of Capt Emorys party was killed, one of Gallespies men, 2 Sergts—1 Copl and 11 privates of Dragoons and one missing—supposed to be killed—we lost one of our Howitzers in this action, the mules in it ran wild and ran off with the piece. There [were] but three men with it and one was killed and the other two desperately wounded—upon the whole we suffered most terribly in this action 4 officers wounded one Sergt. one Copl and 10 privates, and Mr Robedeaux our interpreter—in all 35 men killed and wounded and I should think there was not to exceed fifty men who saw the enemy—We took two prisoners. The Enemy I think must have suffered as much as we did.

This was an action where decidedly more courage than conduct was showed   The first charge was a mistake on the part of Capt Johnston, the 2nd on the part of Capt Moor. After the Genl was wounded and the men were rallied he was anxious for another charge but was persuaded not to risk it. We drove the enemy from the field and encamped. All that day was engaged in dressing the wounded.

On the 7th we left again on our march. Small parties of the Enemy hanging about in sight all day. in the evening we passed the Ranch of St Bernard, and killed some chickens for our wounded and drove some cattle off with us. When we had marched some miles from the Ranch the enemy again appeared and made another rush, to occupy a hill, where they could annoy us. They got to the top of the hill about the time we got half way up when the fight commenced and after two or three minutes the rascals ran, leaving three of their spears on the field. We occupied these heights as a camp for that night   on the 8th we saw some commotion on the plain—in a short time a flag of truce was sent to us by Picot the commander of the Mexicans,   with some sugar & tea—a change of clothing for Capt Gallespie—which had been sent to Gallespie from St Diago, and he had taken them with the prisoners The capture of these three men we now found out caused the commotion on the plain in the morning   We exchanged our prisoner for one of the men taken, and learned from him that Commodore Stockton refused to send us a reinforcement. The Genl then determined to march out at all hazzards but in a council of officers, the Navy officers pledged themselves so strongly that Stockton would send relief, and on account of the wounded, the Genl consented to remain—in the evening Lt Beal of the Navy with Carson started again as an express to Stockton. We burnt all of our baggage so as to have as little encumbrance as possible, dismounted the men and determined to perform the rest of the march on foot. We left our camp on the battle field of the 6th with 6 ambulances with wounded. The enemy are constantly hanging around us but are very careful not to come within gun shot—9th We remained in camp, nothing going on the Enemy perading about on the mountains and the other side of the vally—We are reduced to mule meat—it does not go so coarse—after all some of my poor fellows have as many as 8 wounds on a side 3 are run through the arm—generally—they seem to aim with their lances so as to strike a man near the kidneys.

10th Sergt [John] Cox died this morning his wound on the left side, just above the crista of the Illeum [ilium]—he had singultus [hiccups] for several hours before death and vomited bloody water. We remain in camp to day waiting in case reinforcements be sent, if they are not sent we march in the morning at all hazzards. On the evening of the 10th we were grazing our animals at the foot of the hill near our camp—when we saw the Mexicans driving a band of wild horses toward us. Capt Gilispie who has been in this country during the war, immediately told us what they were up to. Their plan was to run them full speed among our animals, and in that way to take off all we had—in half an hour we saw them coming full speed—the wild devils with sheep skins & other things of that sort tied to their tails, it certainly presented one of the most beautiful sights we had ever beheld—but as we were warned of their intentions, we were prepared. We waited a few moments so as to entice some of the rascals in gun shot if possible, and then quietly drove our animals out of the way throwing out a strong body of men to meet the rascals if they should come within reach of our guns.—by a shout the drove of wild horses was turned One mule however with a sheep skin tied to his tail was so imprudent as to come within gun shot, forty balls I was told struck him, yet he did not fall, and was finally driven on the hill where we were encamped and butchered. This was a god send to us as the mule was fat, and that which we had been eating was not equal by any means to stall fed beef. The Genl ordered all things to be in readiness for marching in the morning. We all went to bed firmly convinced that we should be obliged to fight our way to St. Diago.

George Walcott Ames, Jr., ed.,
A Doctor Comes to California
(San Francisco, California Historical Society, 1943), 45-49.

A Christmas in the
Santa Ynez Mountains

BY EDWIN BRYANT

*Edwin Bryant crossed the continent in 1846, the year of the Don-
ner tragedy, but with a packing company that got in well before
the passes closed and in time to take part in the conquest. As a
volunteer under Frémont, he did more marching than fighting.
Yet with the unusual weather that California can conjure up, this
kind of campaigning could be arduous. Bryant's* What I Saw in
California *came out just in time to titilate the gold seekers and
provide them some help on the overland route.*

December 24.—Cloudy and cool, with an occasional sprinkling
rain. Our route to-day lay directly over the St. Ynes mountain, by
an elevated and most difficult pass. The height of this mountain
is several thousand feet. We reached the summit about twelve
o'clock, and our company composing the advance-guard, we encamped about a mile and a half in advance of the main body of the
battalion, at a point which overlooks the beautiful plain of Santa
Barbara, of which, and the ocean beyond, we had a most extended
and interesting view. With the spyglass, we could see in the plain
far below us, herds of cattle quietly grazing upon the green herbage that carpets its gentle undulations. The plain is dotted with
groves, surrounding the springs and belting the small water-
courses, of which there are many flowing from this range of mountains. Ranchos are scattered far up and down the plain, but not
one human being could be seen stirring. About ten or twelve miles
to the south, the white towers of the mission of Santa Barbara raise
themselves. Beyond, is the illimitable waste of waters. A more
lovely and picturesque landscape I never beheld. On the summit of
the mountain, and surrounding us, there is a growth of hawthorn,
manzanita, (in bloom,) and other small shrubbery. The rock is
soft sandstone and conglomerate, immense masses of which, piled
one upon another, form a wall along the western brow of the
mountain, through which there is a single pass or gateway about

eight or ten feet in width. The descent on the western side is pre-
cipitous, and appears almost impassable. Distance 4 miles.

December 25.—Christmas-day, and a memorable one to me.
Owing to the difficulty in hauling the cannon up the steep acclivi-
ties of the mountain, the main body of the battalion did not come
up with us until twelve o'clock, and before we commenced the
descent of the mountain a furious storm commenced, raging with
a violence rarely surpassed. The rain fell in torrents and the wind
blew almost with the force of a tornado. This fierce strife of the
elements continued without abatement the entire afternoon, and
until two o'clock at night. Driving our horses before us we were
compelled to slide down the steep and slippery rocks, or wade
through deep gullies and ravines filled with mud and foaming torrents of water, that rushed downwards with such force as to carry
along the loose rocks and tear up the trees and shrubbery by the
roots. Many of the horses falling into the ravines refused to make
an effort to extricate themselves, and were swept downwards and
drowned. Others, bewildered by the fierceness and terrors of the
storm, rushed or fell headlong over the steep precipices and were
killed. Others obstinately refused to proceed, but stood quaking
with fear or shivering with cold, and many of these perished in
the night from the severity of the storm. The advance party did
not reach the foot of the mountain and find a place to encamp
until night—and a night of more impenetrable and terrific darkness I never witnessed. The ground upon which our camp was
made, although sloping from the hills to a small stream, was so
saturated with water that men as well as horses sunk deep at
every step. The rain fell in such quantities that fires with great
difficulty could be lighted, and most of them were immediately
extinguished.

The officers and men belonging to the company having the cannon in charge, labored until nine or ten o'clock to bring them down
the mountain, but they were finally compelled to leave them.
Much of the baggage also remained on the side of the mountain,
with the pack mules and horses conveying them; all efforts to
force the animals down being fruitless. The men continued to
straggle into the camp until a late hour of the night;—some crept
under the shelving rocks and did not come in until the next morn-

ing. We were so fortunate as to find our tent, and after much difficulty pitched it under an oak-tree. All efforts to light a fire and
keep it blazing proving abortive, we spread our blankets upon the
ground and endeavored to sleep, although we could feel the cold
streams of water running through the tent and between and
around our bodies.

In this condition we remained until about two oclock in the
morning, when the storm having abated I rose, and shaking from
my garments the dripping water, after many unsuccessful efforts
succeeded in kindling a fire. Near our tent I found three soldiers
who had reached camp at a late hour. They were fast asleep on
the ground, the water around them being two or three inches deep;
but they had taken care to keep their heads above water by using
a log of wood for a pillow. The fire beginning to blaze freely, I
dug a ditch with my hands and a sharp stick of wood, which
drained off the pool surrounding the tent. One of the men, when
he felt the sensation consequent upon being "high and dry,"
roused himself, and sitting upright, looked around for some time
with an expression of bewildered amazement. At length he
seemed to realize the true state of the case, and exclaimed in a tone
of energetic soliloquy:

"Well, who *wouldn't* be a soldier and fight for California?"

"You are mistaken," I replied.

Rubbing his eyes he gazed at me with astonishment, as if having
been entirely unconscious of my presence; but reassuring himself he said:

"How mistaken?"

"Why," I answered, "you are not fighting for California."

"What the d——l then am I fighting for?" he inquired.

"For TEXAS."

"Texas be d——d; but hurrah for General Jackson!" and with
this exclamation he threw himself back again upon his wooden
pillow, and was soon snoring in a profound slumber.

Making a platform composed of sticks of wood upon the soft
mud, I stripped myself to the skin, wringing the water from each
garment as I proceeded. I then commenced drying them by the
fire in the order that they were replaced upon my body, an employment that occupied me until daylight, which sign, above

the high mountain to the east, down which we had rolled rather than marched yesterday, I was truly rejoiced to see. Distance 3 miles.

Edwin Bryant, *What I Saw in California*
(New York, 1848), 379-382.

Bulletin from Yerba Buena

BY CHARLES E. PICKETT

Charles E. Pickett was so loquacious that he got the nickname "Philosopher." He was also feisty and continually embroiled in battles of words which sometimes lapsed into physical contact. In the letter here quoted his uninhibited comment is about what others had been doing and failing to do.

You may have gathered from my last letter that things were getting in a muss with us, and now I regret to add that the thing is too true. Yerba Buena is a perfect hell, all in a fever, the animosity and bad feeling of three or four different parties raging at once, and heaven only knows where the end will be. All law, justice and common sense has been thrown aside with us, and as a consequence, anarchy and misrule is reigning supreme. Wherefore is this you will ask. I answer, because Capts. Mervine and Hull *both* and *neither* of whom are in command here, are men of very weak intellect and no judgment. The whole of their operations are conducted either through the blind random suggestions of their own minds, or directed by a set of ignorant and knavish advisers, whom they have allowed to worm and fawn themselves into their good graces and opinions. Some objected to Capt. Montgomery's administration, because he allowed certain improper things to be done. But few of us here now of any correct thinking, but sadly regret his leaving and wish much for his return. . . .

The war has begun and ended here since you left. Some rumours were prevalent in town about six weeks since of a party of Californians in this vicinity, and great preparations made to prevent an attack on the town, which was kept in a constant ferment and state of alarm, the soldiers and citizens being round up for battle nearly every night by Grannies Mervine and Hull, who have not slept 6 nights for that time. And although such fears were felt for the safety of the place yet small parties were constantly going out to the Mission and beyond. Bartlett with six men went to the Mission, where he danced all night and next day proceeded to Sanchez with his Bacqueros for cattle, and whilst in the act of surrounding a band of beeves in the prairie, was pounced on by the Californians and made prisoner together with all his men. Our efficient commanders here did not stir a soldier to go in pursuit, and not till nearly three weeks after, and until the arrival of Capt. Weber here with a party of 35 men, was a force organized under Capt. Marston to go out. Capt. Bailar Smith, with volunteers from Yerba Buena, together with Weber and Marston's company, composed a force of about 100 men.

These proceeded—having one cannon, which was a great bore and trouble—on the track of the enemy, whom they found in the woods just this side of Santa Clara. At the time the fight commenced Weber and Smith were absent scouting with a few men each but managed on hearing the firing to get back safely. But such a battle! O shades of Alexander and Bounaparte! hide your faces whilst it is told. The Californians were 120 in all, mounted on good horses, which they took good care should keep them out of the range of the shot, which caused our forces to waste a vast deal of ammunition to no purpose. Finding nothing could be done there, our army marched on towards the Mission, the Californians, surrounding them in the mustard on every side, and presenting only a single man in a spot to be fired at, each exchanging shot at from a quarter to half mile distant. A halt was ordered every few hundred yards, when a broadside was blazed away; doing considerable damage to the mustard stalks. When the cannon was to be fired, a man would mount on it, sight with his hand the direction of the enemy, when jumping down, off she was banged. The result of the day's fight was two men on our side got a slight scratch one not drawing blood, and one killed and two badly wounded on the other side.

Preparations were about being made by the volunteers to go and attack their camp that night, but a flag of truce came in and demanded an armistice, proposing terms of treaty, provided their grievances were redressed. . . .

I am just informed that the wounded men on our side were not touched by the enemy, as they at first supposed and so reported, but hurt themselves in the oak bushes. And it is even doubted whether the Californians recd. any injury. The fight lasted several hours. And the treaty which was made half way between the Mission and the oaks, in sight of the two armies, lasted nearly one whole day.

A Devil of a rumpus is kicked up about the first issue from the Star office. Hull is much incensed in reference to the two articles signed Yerba Buena—called on Jones for the author, who told him it was me, and required the editor to apologize in his next paper for inserting such articles. Jones has talked pretty plainly to the Capt., rather daring him to interfere with the liberty of the press, and has written him a note in reference to the course [upon which] he (Hull) expects his paper shall be conducted, intimating that no apology is to be given, and that $5000 per month is to be charged to the U. States in case it is ordered to be stopped. Hull also objected to other matter, or rather his advisers do for him. The poor man is in a perfect fever and wants to leave; he says he does not know what his authority is here, as he is styled Commander of Northern District of California, Gov., etc., but finds that Mervine takes all command when he pleases. In fact nobody here, neither officers soldiers nor citizens, know who is in command. Nor do we know what rules, laws, regulations, etc., we are governed by, the Alcalde doing as he pleases, and Hull sanctioning all.

They are full of lawsuits both at Sonoma and the Pueblo as well as here; and great opposition and bad feeling in respect to the way law is administered. The fact is, I begin to think that José Le Cruz Sanchez' prophecy will be true about our fighting amongst ourselves, which you recollect he made at the time he asked you about going to the Islands on the brig. All the volunteers up this way are more than ever opposed to the Navy officers having anything to do with them.

Those about the Pueblo, whose time will be out soon, say that unless a better state of command is not placed here, that none will enlist again, and if any necessity exist for an armed force, they will act on their own hook in the business. In this place we are all so worried and disgusted at the state of affairs for some weeks past, that if the vote were put tomorrow for every officer and soldier of the Navy to go aboard and stay there, and let us get 25 volunteers in the barracks, it would carry by a large majority. . . .

From a letter from Charles E. Pickett
to William Heath Davis, Jan. 11, 1847,
in Lawrence Clark Powell, *Philosopher Pickett*
(Berkeley, University of California Press, 1942), 139-146.

The Closing Scenes of the Convention

BY BAYARD TAYLOR

Bayard Taylor was sent to cover the gold rush for the New York Tribune. *His dispatches, somewhat revised, made up* Eldorado, *one of the most felicitous firsthand descriptions of California in '49. Well demonstrating the speed at which the community was moving, a convention to frame a state government assembled at Monterey in the fall of 1849. It did its job remarkably well and earned the celebration which Taylor describes.*

The day and night immediately preceding the dissolution of the Convention far exceeded in interest all the former period of its existence. I know not how I can better describe the closing scenes than by the account which I penned on the spot, at the time:

The Convention yesterday (October 12) gave token of bringing its labors to a close; the morning session was short and devoted only to the passing of various miscellaneous provisions, after which an adjournment was made until this morning, on account of the Ball given by the Convention to the citizens of Monterey. The members, by a contribution of $25 each, raised the sum of $1,100 to provide for the entertainment, which was got up in return for that given by the citizens about four weeks since.

The Hall was cleared of the forum and tables and decorated with young pines from the forest. At each end were the American colors, tastefully disposed across the boughs. Three chandeliers,

178

neither of bronze nor cut-glass, but neat and brilliant withal, poured their light on the festivities. At eight o'clock—the fashionable ball-hour in Monterey—the guests began to assemble, and in an hour afterward the Hall was crowded with nearly all the Californian and American residents. There were sixty or seventy ladies present, and an equal number of gentlemen, in addition to the members of the Convention. The dark-eyed daughters of Monterey, Los Angeles and Santa Barbara mingled in pleasing contrast with the fairer bloom of the trans-Nevadian belles. The variety of feature and complexion was fully equalled by the variety of dress. In the whirl of the waltz, a plain, dark, nun-like robe would be followed by one of pink satin and gauze; next, perhaps, a bodice of scarlet velvet with gold buttons, and then a rich figured brocade, such as one sees on the stately dames of Titian.

The dresses of the gentlemen showed considerable variety, but were much less picturesque. A complete ball-dress was a happiness attained only by the fortunate few. White kids could not be had in Monterey for love or money, and as much as $50 was paid by one gentleman for a pair of patent-leather boots. Scarcely a single dress that was seen belonged entirely to its wearer, and I thought, if the clothes had power to leap severally back to their respective owners, some persons would have been in a state of utter destitution. For my part, I was indebted for pantaloons and vest to obliging friends. The only specimen of the former article which I could get belonged to an officer whose weight was considerably more than two hundred, but I managed to accommodate them to my proportions by a liberal use of pins, notwithstanding the difference of size. Thus equipped, with a buff military vest, and worsted gaiters with very square toes, I took my way to the Hall in company with Major Smith and his brother.

The appearance of the company, nevertheless, was genteel and respectable, and perhaps the genial, unrestrained social spirit that possesed all present would have been less had there been more uniformity of costume. Gen. Riley was there in full uniform, with the yellow sash he won at Contreras; Majors Canby, Hill and Smith, Captains Burton and Kane, and the other officers stationed in Monterey, accompanying him. In one group might be seen Capt. Sutter's soldierly moustache and clear blue eye; in another, the erect figure and quiet, dignified bearing of Gen. Vallejo. Don Pablo de la Guerra, with his handsome, aristocratic features, was the floor manager, and gallantly discharged his office. Conspicuous among the native members were Don Miguel de Pedrorena and Jacinto Rodriguez, both polished gentlemen and deservedly popular. Dominguez, the Indian member, took no part in the dance, but evidently enjoyed the scene as much as any one present. The most interesting figure to me was that of Padre Ramirez, who, in his clerical cassock, looked on until a late hour. If the strongest advocate of priestly gravity and decorum had been present, he could not have found in his heart to grudge the good old padre the pleasure that beamed upon his honest countenence.

The band consisted of two violins and two guitars, whose music made up in spirit what it lacked in skill. They played, as it seemed to me, but three pieces alternately, for waltz, contra-dance and quadrille. The latter dance was evidently an unfamiliar one, for once or twice the music ceased in the middle of a figure. Each tune ended with a funny little squeak, something like the whistle of the octave flute in *Robert le Diable*. The players, however, worked incessantly, and deserved good wages for their performance. The etiquette of the dance was marked by that grave, stately courtesy, which has been handed down from the old Spanish times. The gentlemen invariably gave the ladies their hands to lead them to their places on the floor; in the pauses of the dance both parties stood motionless side by side, and at its conclusion the lady was bravely led back to her seat.

At twelve o'clock supper was announced. The Court Room in the lower story had been fitted up for this purpose, and, as it was not large enough to admit all the guests, the ladies were first conducted thither and waited upon by a select committee. The refreshments consisted of turkey, roast pig, beef, tongue, and *pâtés*, with wines and liquors of various sorts, and coffee. A large supply had been provided, but after everybody was served, there was not much remaining. The ladies began to leave about two o'clock, but when I came away, an hour later, the dance was still going on with spirit.

The members met this morning at the usual hour, to perform the last duty that remained to them—that of signing the Constitution. They were all in the happiest humor, and the morning was so bright and balmy that no one seemed disposed to call an organization. Mr. Semple was sick, and Mr. Steuart, of San Francisco, therefore called the meeting to order by moving Capt. Sutter's appointment in his place. The Chair was taken by the old pioneer, and the members took their seats around the sides of the hall, which still retained the pine trees and banners left from last night's decorations. The windows and doors were open, and a delightful breeze came in from the Bay, whose blue waters sparkled in the distance. The view from the balcony in front was bright and inspiring. The town below—the shipping in the harbor—the pine-covered hills behind—were mellowed by the blue October haze, but there was no cloud in the sky, and I could plainly see, on the northern horizon, the mountains of Santa Cruz and the Sierra de Gavilan.

After the minutes had been read, the Committee appointed to draw up an Address to the People of California was called upon to report, and Mr. Steuart, Chairman, read the Address. Its tone and sentiment met with universal approval, and it was adopted without a dissenting voice. A resolution was then offered to pay Lieut. Hamilton, who is now engaged in engrossing the Constitution upon parchment, the sum of $500 for his labor. This magnificent price, probably the highest ever paid for a similar service, is on a par with all things else in California. As this was their last session, the members were not disposed to find fault with it, especially when it was stated by one of them that Lieut. Hamilton had written day and night to have it ready, and was still working upon it, though with a lame and swollen hand. The sheet for the signers' names was ready, and the Convention decided to adjourn for half and hour and then meet for the purpose of signing.

I amused myself during the interval by walking about the town. Everybody knew that the Convention was about closing, and it was generally understood that Capt. Burton had loaded the guns at the fort and would fire a salute of thirty-one guns at the proper moment. The citizens, therefore, as well as the members, were in an excited mood. Monterey never before looked so bright, so happy, so full of pleasant expectation.

About one o'clock the Convention met again; few of the members, indeed, had left the hall. Mr. Semple, although in feeble health, called them to order, and after having voted Gen Riley a salary of $10,000, and Mr. Halleck, Secretary of State, $6,000 a year, from the commencement of their respective offices, they proceeded to affix their names to the completed Constitution. At this moment a signal was given; the American colors ran up the flagstaff in front of the Government buildings, and streamed out on the air. A second afterward the first gun boomed from the fort, and its stirring echoes came back from one hill after another, till they were lost in the distance.

All the native enthusiasm of Capt. Sutter's Swiss blood was aroused; he was the old soldier again. He sprang from his seat, and, waving his hand around his head, as if swinging a sword, exclaimed: "Gentlemen, this is the happiest day of my life. It makes me glad to hear those cannon: they remind me of the time when I was a soldier. Yes, I am glad to hear them—this is a great day for California!" Then, recollecting himself, he sat down, the tears streaming from his eyes. The members with one accord gave three tumultuous cheers, which were heard from one end of the town to the other. As the signing went on, gun followed gun from the fort, the echoes reverberating grandly around the bay, till finally, as the loud ring of the *thirty-first* was heard, there was a shout: "That's for California!" and everyone joined in giving three times three for the new star added to our Confederation. . . .

All were in happy and satisfied mood, and none [more] so than the native members. Pedrorena declared that this was the most fortunate day in the history of California. Even Carillo, in the beginning one of our most zealous opponents, displayed a genuine zeal for the Constitution, which he helped to frame under the laws of our Republic.

Thus closes the Convention; and I cannot help saying, with Capt. Sutter, that the day which sees laid the broad and liberal foundation of a free and independent State on the shores of the Pacific is a great day for California. As an American, I feel proud and happy—proud that the Empire of the West, the commerce of the great Pacific, the new highway to the Indies, forming the last link in that belt of civilized enterprise which now clasps the world, has been established under my country's flag; and happy that in all the extent of California, from the glittering snows of the Shaste to the burning deserts of the Colorado, no slave shall ever lift his arm to make the freedom of that flag a mockery.

The members of the Convention may have made some blunders in the course of their deliberations; there may be some objectionable clauses in the Constitution they have framed. But where was there ever a body convened under such peculiar circumstances?— where was ever such harmony evolved out of so wonderful, so dangerous, so magnificent a chaos? The elements of which the Convention was composed were no less various, and in some respects antagonistic, than those combined in the mining population. The questions they had to settle were often perplexing, from the remarkable position of the country and the absence of all precedent. Besides, many of them were men unused to legislation. Some had for years past known no other life than that of the camp; others had nearly forgotten all law in the wild life of the mountains; others again were familiar only with that practiced under the rule of a different race. Yet the courtesies of debate have never been wantonly violated, and the result of every conflict of opinion has been a quiet acquiescence on the part of the minority. Now, at the conclusion, the only feeling is that of general joy and congratulation.

Thus we have another splendid example of the ease and security with which people can be educated to govern themselves. From that chaos whence, under the rule of a despotism like the Austrian, would spring the most frightful excesses of anarchy and crime, a population of freemen peacefully and quietly develops the highest form of civil order—the broadest extent of liberty and security. Governments, bad and corrupt as many of them are, and imperfect as they all must necessarily be, nevertheless at times exhibit scenes of true moral sublimity. What I have to-day witnessed has so impressed me; and were I a believer in omens, I would augur from the tranquil beauty of this evening—from the clear sky and the lovely sunset hues on the waters of the bay—more than all, from the joyous expression of every face I see—a glorious and prosperous career for the STATE OF CALIFORNIA!

Bayard Taylor, *Eldorado, or, Adventures in the Course of Empire* (London, 1850), I, 159-164, 166-168.

The Conquerors and
Their Consciences

BY JOSIAH ROYCE

*Born at Grass Valley in the Mother Lode country in 1855 and edu-
cated at the state university, Josiah Royce went on to Harvard and
became a philosopher. In the 1880's he was commissioned to do a
history of California for the American Commonwealth series. Instead of going back to the beginnings and carrying up to date of
publication, he chose to concentrate on the ten bustling years
from the Bear Flag Revolt to the Second Vigilance Committee. The
choice permitted more thoroughness and deeper reflection, as is
indicated by the following excerpt.*

The American as conqueror is unwilling to appear in public as
a pure aggressor; he dare not seize a California as Russia has seized
so much land in Asia, or as Napoleon, with full French approval,
seized whatever he wanted. The American wants to persuade not
only the world, but himself, that he is doing God service in a peaceable spirit, even when he violently takes what he has determined
to get. His conscience is sensitive, and hostile aggression, practiced
against any but Indians, shocks this conscience, unused as it is to
such scenes. Therefore Semple and Ide, and the cautious secretary
of state, and the gallant captain, and the venerable senator, all
alike, not only as individuals, but also as men appealing for approval to their fellow-countrymen at large, must present this sinful undertaking in private and in public as a sad, but strictly
moral, humane, patriotic, enlightened, and glorious undertaking.
Other peoples, more used to shedding civilized blood, would have
swallowed the interests of the people of twenty such Californias
as that of 1846, without a gasp. The agents of such nations would
have played at filibustering without scruple, if they had been instructed to adopt that plan as the most simple for getting the land
desired; or they would have intrigued readily, fearlessly, and
again without scruple, if that plan had seemed to their superiors
best for the purpose. But our national plans had to be formed so
as to offend our squeamish natures as little as possible. Our national

conscience, however, was not only squeamish, but also, in those days, not a little hypocritical. It disliked, moreover, to have the left hand know what the right hand was doing, when both were doing mischief. And so, because of its very virtues, it involved itself in disastrously complex plots.

All the actors concerned worked, namely, in the fear of this strictly virtuous, of this almost sanctimonious public opinion,—a public opinion that was at the same time, both in the North and in the South, very sensitive to flattery, very ambitious to see our territory grow bigger, and very anxious to contemplate a glorious national destiny. Moreover, all these our agents not only feared the public, but participated themselves in the common sentiments. Hence we find the Polk cabinet elaborately considering, not merely how to prosecute successfully their intended aggressive war, just as the leaders of any other rapacious nation would have considered such a matter, but also how to put their war into harmony with the enlightened American spirit. And, in the autumn of 1845, their pious plans were apparently well formed. To Mexico the Slidell mission should be sent, with its offer to purchase California. This would be a liberal offer, and, if it ever became public, would set us right as a powerful and generous nation in the eyes of the world, while it would give us in the mean time a chance to get California for nothing, by the completion of our intrigue in that territory and by the act of its own people. The beautiful and business-like compromise thus planned would set at one our national conscience and our national shrewdness; it would be not only magnanimous, but inexpensive. Yet even this compromise must be carefully expressed by the honorable secretary of state in such language as would not offend the sensitive American spirit, in case, by some accident, the whole scheme should some day come plainly to light. Larkin must be instructed that we had "no ambitious aspirations to gratify," and that we only desired to arouse in the California breast "that love of liberty and independence so natural to the American continent."

But this combination of the Slidell mission with the Larkin dispatch, a combination whose genuine character has not hitherto been properly understood by the historians of the Mexican War, was not more characteristic of our nation than was the combination by which the pious plan was defeated. One active and not overcautious young agent, who had good reason to know the importance of the crisis, and who was not altogether unwilling to turn it to account for various private ends, was in California just then, and received certain advices in a confidential "family cipher;" and these advices somehow, whether wholly by his own fault or also by the fault of his father-in-law, led him to thwart the carefully prepared plans of the government. In acting as he did, he not only became for the moment a filibuster, pure and simple, but he endangered our whole scheme by, perhaps unwittingly, doing his best to drive California directly into the arms of England. Either because England really was not anxious for California just then, or because her agents in the Pacific were not sufficiently on the alert, this result was averted, yet not in consequence of the gallant captain's undertaking, but only through Sloat's arrival with the news of those hostilities on the Rio Grande which superseded all previous plots and pretenses, and which, "by the act of Mexico," as our veracious president declared, forced us, unwilling, conscientious, and humane as we were, into an unequal contest with a physically puny foe.

Meanwhile, the gallant captain's undertaking, although a plain violation of his orders, was itself not un-American in its forms and methods, at least in so far as they were reported to the public. He felt himself, after all, to be a peaceful and scientific gentleman, who shunned war, and loved the study of nature. He was a type of our energy and of our mild civilization, in the presence of crafty and wily Spaniards, who, as he somehow persuaded either himself or his followers, had incited the Indians of the unknown Klamath wilderness against him, had threatened the ripening wheat-fields of his countrymen, and at last had begun marching against his own party with an armed force. This armed force, marching against him, was indeed not at the moment to be seen in the whole territory by any human eye; but its asserted existence nevertheless thenceforth justified him in the clearer eyes of heaven and his absent fellow countrymen. So at least he himself and the venerable senator would seem in all sincerity to have felt; and the public, by the nomination of the young hero to the presidency in 1856, and by the large vote then polled in his favor, set their seal of approval also upon the verdict of his conscience.

But when hostilities had once begun, the men who were not in the state secrets were as American and as moral as those who were initiated. To them the whole thing appeared partly as a glorious revolution, a destined joy for the eyes of history-reading posterity, a high and holy business; and partly as a missionary enterprise, destined to teach our beloved and erring Spanish-American brethren the blessings of true liberty. The Bear Flag heroes interpreted the affair, in their way also, to a large and representative American public; and these heroes, like their betters, show us what it is to have a national conscience sensitive enough to call loudly for elaborate and eloquent comfort in moments of doubt, and just stupid enough to be readily deluded by mock-eloquent cant. The result of the whole thing is that although, in later years, the nation at large has indeed come to regard the Mexican War with something of the shame and contempt that the "Biglow Papers" and the other expressions of enlightened contemporary opinion heaped upon the unworthy business, still, in writing California history, few have even yet chosen to treat the acts of the conquest with the deserved plainness of speech, while, in those days, the public both in the South and in the whole of the West, together with a considerable portion of the public elsewhere, was hoodwinked by such methods as were used, and so actually supposed our acquisition of the new territory to be a God-fearing act, the result of the aggression and of the sinful impotence of our Spanish neighbors, together with our own justifiable energy, and our devotion to the cause of freedom. It is to be hoped that this lesson, showing us as it does how much of conscience and even of personal sincerity can coexist with a minimum of effective morality in international undertakings, will some day be once more remembered; so that when our nation is another time about to serve the devil, it will do so with more frankness, and will deceive itself less by half-unconscious cant. For the rest, our mission in the cause of liberty is to be accomplished through a steadfast devotion to the cultivation of our own inner life, and not by going abroad as missionaries, as conquerors, or as marauders, among weaker peoples.

Josiah Royce, *California* (Boston, 1886), 151-156.

5

GLINTS OF GOLD

WITH NO PAUSE FOR ADJUSTMENT to the great new fact of being part of the United States, California plunged into the more compelling excitement of the gold rush. Suddenly the province swarmed with adventurers from all the states and most of the nations. With this flood of new manpower, new initiative, and suddenly abundant purchasing power, the community rushed headlong into a social revolution that was at once a binge and a constructive advance.

An accidental find of gold at Coloma on January 24, 1848, triggered all this. At the time the episode seemed so trivial that discoveror James Marshall and his companions, thinking back on it, had trouble fixing the exact date. At first the follow-up was insignificant, but by late spring gold fever was sweeping San Francisco and Monterey. A few months later it was pulling men to the diggings from the rest of California and from much of the Pacific area. With plenty of elbowroom and an abundance of surface deposits these forty-eighters led a carefree, crime-free life. At year's end, however, the problems of society were beginning to assert themselves, including robbery and assault and how to maintain order and to improvise law.

As of the close of 1848 the urge to join the rush was taking powerful hold in the Midwest, the East, and on the far side of the Atlantic. Covered wagons more numerous than in all earlier years put together took the overland routes. Ships exceeding all prior traffic rounded Cape Horn. A new service featuring steamers and an alleged connection at Panama was the choice of those who wanted to make the best time.

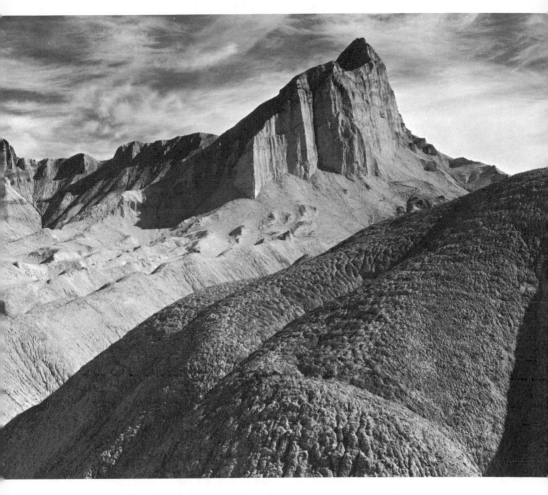

MANLY BEACON, DEATH VALLEY *by Ansel Adams*

Alonso Delano, later to be a favorite California writer, and J. Goldsborough Bruff, the most ambitious of all the trail diarists, describe scenes and experiences on the most favored route. R. R. Taylor writes feelingly about the way chance ruled at Panama. Jacob Y. Stover, after a narrow escape from disaster en route, expresses the pure bliss of at last reaching California. And William Lewis Manly, unassuming hero of the rescue of the Bennett-Arcane party from Death Valley, recreates the ordeal of being lost in the desert.

Many of the forty-niners who crossed the Plains or Mexico or the Isthmus or rounded Cape Horn had high consciousness that they were making history and partly on that account many of them traveled with notebook in hand. Among the overlanders their journals range from the bare bones of Sheldon Young's log to Bruff's wonderfully prolix testament. For many of them the entries reveal that the daily routine was a monotonous "hitched up, drove, made camp." The passengers at sea had a longer and greater monotony. Their journals start off gravely descriptive and then, all too often, descend to shipboard gossip and trivia. The passengers by Panama with two or three stops en route were at their best as letter writers. All told, the traveling forty-niners did a prodigious amount of recording. On the subsequent experiences of life in the mines and in the towns and cities that served the mines they were much less voluble. Most of these accounts are at best the raw materials of history and have been mined as such. Other bits and pieces are rather to be assayed as literature, as attempts to communicate the emotional impact of gold rush experience.

The gold rush gave Californians their first real opportunity to write for publication. Eastern publishers welcomed and even commissioned California manuscripts, and local newspapers, magazines, and book publishers vied for copy. The response was a flowering of writing, some of it exotic, but most of it focused on gold rush California. Such history as was written was introverted upon current events. Alongside this matter-of-fact chronicling there now appeared for the first time a companion venturing into fiction and poetry, most of which was directed to the selfsame scenes and themes.

In the fullness of California writing the miner's life is an ever-recurrent theme. Sometimes the treatment is reportorial as in Charles Howard Shinn's narrative of the Scotch Bar case. Often it picks up the joshing and the broad humor the miners favored. So it is in the Thomes-Stewart account of the Bible-bearing Yankee Argonauts and in G. Ezra Dane's recreation of a tale from Columbia. Occasionally the method is analytical, here represented by Rodman W. Paul's comparison of the Bret Harte-Mark Twain-Joaquin Miller picture with the hard facts of mining as a business.

The books from which the last two excerpts are drawn neatly illustrate the commingling of history and literature. Paul's *California Gold* perspicaciously inspects the forty-niner as miner. Dane's *Ghost Town* looks almost exclusively at the miner when he was not at work. The one applies the method of the graduate seminar, the other of E Clampus Vitus. The one rests on data unexceptionably historical, the other derives from sources literary and folklore. Each accomplishes what its author set out to do. It is when the two are brought into conjunction that the Mother Lode prospector stands forth as the whole man.

The Discovery

BY JAMES W. MARSHALL,
HENRY W. BIGLER, AND
AZARIAH SMITH

James W. Marshall has undying fame as the gold discoverer. He was boss of the crew building the sawmill at Coloma, and Henry Bigler and Azariah Smith were two of the young Mormons working with him. Their several notes, variously dated, illustrate how fitful human memory is and how difficult the reconstruction of an event, even an extraordinary one.

MARSHALL: While we were in the habit at night of turning the water through the tail race we had dug for the purpose of widening and deepening the race, I used to go down in the morning to see what had been done by the water through the night; and about half past seven o'clock on or about the 19th of January—I am not quite certain to a day, but it was between the 18th and 20th of that month—1848, I went down as usual, and after shutting off the water from the race, I stepped into it, near the lower end, and there, upon the rock, about six inches beneath the surface of the water, I discovered the gold. I was entirely alone at the time. I picked up one or two pieces and examined them attentively; and having some general knowledge of minerals, I could not call to mind more than two which in any way resembled this—*sulphuret of iron*, very bright and brittle; and *gold*, bright, yet malleable; I then tried it between two rocks, and found that it could be beaten into a different shape, but not broken. I then collected four or five pieces and went up to Mr. Scott (who was working at the carpenter's bench making the mill wheel) with the pieces and said, "I have found it."

"What is it?" inquired Scott.

"Gold," I answered.

"Oh! no," returned Scott, "that can't be."

I replied positively—"I know it to be nothing else."

Mr. Scott was the second person who saw the gold. W. J. Johnston, A. Stephens, H. Bigler, and J. Brown, who were also working in the mill yard, were then called up to see it. Peter L. Wimmer, Mrs. Jane Wimmer, C. Bennet, and I. Smith, were at the house; the latter two of whom were sick; E. Persons and John Wimmer, (a son of P. L. Wimmer), were out hunting oxen at the same time. About 10 o'clock the same morning, P. L. Wimmer came down from the house, and was very much surprised at the discovery, when the metal was shown him; and which he took home to show his wife, who, the next day, made some experiments upon it by boiling it in strong lye, and saleratus; and Mr. Bennet by my directions beat it very thin.

Four days afterwards, I went to the Fort for provisions, and carried with me about three ounces of the gold, which Capt. Sutter and I tested with *nitric acid*. I then tried it in Sutter's presence by taking three silver dollars and balancing them by the dust in the air, then immersed both in water, and the superior weight of the gold satisfied us both of its nature and value.

BIGLER: Monday 24th this day some kind of mettle was found in the tail race that looks like goald first discovered by James Martial, the Boss of the Mill.

Sunday 30th Clear and has been all the last week our metal has been tride and prooves to be goald it is thought to be rich we have pict up more than a hundred dollars woth last week.

SMITH: This week mr. Marshall found some pieces of (as we all suppose) Gold, and he has gone to the Fort, for the purpose of finding out. it is found in the raceway in small pieces; some have been found that would weigh five dollars.

Sunday February the 6th Mr. Marshall has returned with the fact that it is Gold; and captain Sutter came here wednesday with Johnston, for the purpose of looking at the mine, where the gold is found; and got enough for a ring. . . .

Monday Feb. the 14th The past week I did not work but three days and a half. Mr. Marshall grants us the privilege of picking up Gold odd spells and Sundays, and I have gathered up considerable. When we shut down the gates the gold is found in the bottom of the tale race. Sunday Feb. 20th The fore part of the past week it rained and I did not work but four days, and I have been drilling a rock which is in the race, and blasting, which pleases the Indians very much to see the rock which is very hard, split open so easy. Today I picked up a little more of the root of all evil. Sunday March the 12th The two past weeks, as usial, I have been to work on the mill; and last sunday I picked up two dollars and a half, below this place about two miles. Today we started the mill, and sawed up one log and are pining it on the forebay. The mill runs very well; but the back water hinders some, and the tale race will have to be dug some deeper.

Sunday March the 19th Last week we ran the mill some and it cuts well, makeing beautifull plank. Today I crossed the river and went down it to hunt for Gold, and found some. . . .

. . . Tuesday March the 28th Last Sunday I with three others went down the river on the other side and picked up considerable Gold. . . .

Monday Appr. 3d Yesterday I with some others, again went down the river and picked up some more Gold. Friday April the 7th I have worked four days this week; but today I am laying by. Brothers Brown, Stephens, and Bigler started today for the Fort but I thought that I would stay and work. Mr. Marshall has gave

193

us the privilege of hunting Gold and haveing half we find, and we are a going to improve the opportunity. I have something like thirty dollars of it now.

James W. Marshall, in Hutchings' *California Magazine*,
II (1857), 199-201; Henry W. Bigler, Diary,
and Azariah Smith, Diary, reproduced in
Elisabeth L. Egenhoff, *The Elephant
as They Saw It* (San Francisco, 1949), 31-33.

A Violent Attack of the Gold Fever

BY JAMES H. CARSON

For a special edition of the San Joaquin Republican *(Stockton) in 1852 old-timer James H. Carson contributed a lushly reminiscent account. On any other subject his writing would be classed as hyperbole and bombast, but on the initial symptoms of the gold fever it passes for sober truth.*

I was at that time (1848) a resident of the then flourishing City of Monterey. The months of April and May had carried off many of our inhabitants—not to their long homes, but to the gold mines. Many of the old fellows who had put the whole golden report down as "dod drat" humbug, had one after another gone to the mines. Some had left privately to prevent the remainder from laughing at them, while others, bordering on insanity, raved around crying for pick-axe, shovel and pan had started off at railway speed. The month of May, with all her flowers and balmy air had approached, and I an unbeliever still. One day I saw a form, bent and filthy, approaching me, and soon a cry of recognition was given between us. He was an old acquaintance and had been one of the first to visit the mines. Now he stood before me: his hair hung out of his hat—his chin with beard was black, and his buckskins reached to his knees; an old flannel shirt he wore, which may a bush had tore.

Yes, Billy, I can see you yet, just as you stood before me on that sunny tenth day of May looking so much like the devil with that great bag of the Tempter on your back. Then he told me that it was gold, and that he had made it in five weeks at Kelsy's and the dry diggins (where Placerville now is). I could not believe it but told him the proof would be in his bag, which was soon opened, and out the metal tumbled; not in dust or scales, but in pieces ranging in size from that of a pea to hen's eggs; and, says he, "this is only what I picked out with a knife." There was before me proof positive that I had held too long to the wrong side of the question. I looked on for a moment; a frenzy seized my soul; unbidden my legs performed some entirely new movements of Polka steps—I took several—houses were too small for me to stay in; I was soon in the street in search of necessary outfits; piles of gold rose up before me at every step; castles of marble, dazzling the eye with their rich appliances; thousands of slaves, bowing to my beck and call; myriads of fair virgins contending with each other for my love, were among the fancies of my fevered imagination. The Rothschilds, Girards and Astors appeared to me but poor people; in short, I had a very violent attack of the Gold Fever.

One hour after I became thus affected, I was mounted on an old mule, armed with wash hand basin, fire shovel, a piece of square iron pointed at one end, a blanket, rifle, a few yards of jerked beef, and a bag of *penola*, and going at high-pressure mule speed for the "diggin's."

No roads marked the way to the traveller in California then: but, guided by the sun and well-known mountain peaks, we proceeded on our journey. No ferries were in operation for our passage across the deep and rapid streams. The site of the now beautiful and flourishing city of Stockton, was then alone in its native greatness; no steamboat's whistle was heard to startle the affrighted elk, nor had the newsboys' call been heard, or solemn bell called forth the sons of prayer. But still there was a little mud. Heedless of all difficulties, on, on I sped, until Mormon Island, on the South Fork, brought me up. Some forty or fifty men were at work with the cradle machines, and were averaging about 8 oz. per day to the man. But a few moments passed before I was knee deep in water, with my wash-basin full of dirt, plunging it about endeavoring to separate the dirt from the gold. After washing some fifty pans of dirt, I found I had realised about four bits' worth of gold. Reader, do you know how an hombre feels when the gold fever heat has suddenly fallen to about zero? I do. Kelsey's and the old dry diggings had just been opened, and to them I next set out; a few hours' ride brought me to the Indian-trading camp of Captain Weber's famed company, where I saw sights of gold that revived the fever again. I saw Indians giving handsful of gold for a cotton handkerchief or a shirt—and so great was the income of the Captain's trading houses that he was daily sending out mules packed with gold, to the settlements.

James H. Carson, *Recollections of the California Mines* (Stockton, 1852), 4-5.

Excitement at Monterey

BY WALTER COLTON

Shortly after the happenings here reported, Walter Colton was off to the mines himself, more to look than to dig, it is true.

Tuesday, June 20, 1848. My messenger sent to the mines, has returned with specimens of the gold; he dismounted in a sea of upturned faces. As he drew forth the yellow lumps from his pockets, and passed them around the eager crowd, the doubts, which had lingered till now, fled. All admitted they were gold, except one old man, who still persisted they were some Yankee invention, got up to reconcile the people to the change of flag. The excitement produced was intense; and many were soon busy in their hasty preparations for a departure to the mines. The family who had kept house for me caught the moving infection. Husband and wife were both packing up; the blacksmith dropped his hammer, the carpenter his plane, the mason his trowel, the farmer his sickle, the baker his loaf, and the tapster his bottle. All were off for the mines, some on horses, some on carts, and some on crutches, and one went in a litter. An American woman, who had recently established a boarding-house here, pulled up stakes, and was off before her lodgers had even time to pay their bills. Debtors ran, of course. I have only a community of women left and a gang of prisoners, with here and there a soldier, who will give his captain the slip at the first chance. I don't blame the fellow a whit; seven dollars a month, while others are making two or three hundred a day! that is too much for human nature to stand.

Saturday, July 15, 1848. The gold fever has reached every servant in Monterey; none are to be trusted in their engagement beyond a week, and as for compulsion, it is like attempting to drive fish into a net with the ocean before them. Gen. Mason, Lieut. Lanman, and myself, form a mess; we have a house, and all the table furniture and culinary apparatus requisite; but our servants have run, one after another, till we are almost in despair: even Sambo, who we thought would stick by from laziness, if no other cause, ran last night; and this morning, for the fortieth time, we had to take to the kitchen, and cook our own breakfast. A general of the United States Army, the commander of a man-of-war, and the Alcalde of Monterey, in a smoking kitchen, grinding coffee, toasting a herring, and peeling onions! These gold mines are going to upset all the domestic arrangements of society, turning the head to the tail, and the tail to the head. Well, it is an ill wind that blows nobody any good: the nabobs have had their time, and now comes that of the "niggers." We shall all live just as long, and be quite as fit to die.

Walter Colton, *Three Years in California*
(New York, 1850), 246-248.

How Dry Diggings Became Hangtown

BY E. GOULD BUFFUM

A Mexican War veteran who had done garrison duty in Baja California and Los Angeles, E. Gould Buffum rushed off to the mines as soon as his enlistment expired. He is sharp on the mining life, the restlessness of the prospectors ever alert to rumors of richer diggings, the hardships and discomforts of camp life, the disaster of illness, the exorbitant prices. He was one of the first and the few to expostulate against the lynch law of the impromptu tribunals.

A scene occurred about this time that exhibits in a striking light, the summary manner in which "justice" is dispensed in a com-

197

munity where there are no legal tribunals. We received a report on the afternoon of January 20th, [1849], that five men had been arrested at the dry diggings, and were under trial for a robbery. The circumstances were these:—A Mexican gambler, named Lopez, having in his possession a large amount of money, retired to his room at night, and was surprised about midnight by five men rushing into his apartment one of whom applied a pistol to his head, while the others barred the door and proceeded to rifle his trunk. An alarm being given, some of the citizens rushed in, and arrested the whole party. Next day they were tried by a jury chosen from among the citizens, and sentenced to receive thirty-nine lashes each, on the following morning. Never having witnessed a punishment inflicted by Lynch-law, I went over to the dry diggings on a clear Sunday morning, and on my arrival, found a large crowd collected around an oak tree, to which was lashed a man with a bared back, while another was applying a raw cowhide to his already gored flesh. A guard of a dozen men, with loaded rifles pointed at the prisoners, stood ready to fire in case of an attempt being made to escape. After the whole had been flogged, some fresh charges were preferred against three of the men— two Frenchmen, named Garcia and Bissi, and a Chileno, named Manuel.

These were charged with a robbery and attempt to murder, on the Stanislaus River, during the previous fall. The unhappy men were removed to a neighboring house, and being so weak from their punishment as to be unable to stand, were laid stretched upon the floor. As it was not possible for them to attend, they were tried in the open air, in their absence, by a crowd of some two hundred men, who had organized themselves into a jury, and appointed a *pro tempore* judge. The charges against them were well substantiated, but amounted to nothing more than an attempt at robbery and murder; no overt act being even alleged. They were known to be bad men, however, and a general sentiment seemed to prevail in the crowd that they ought to be got rid of. At the close of the trial, which lasted some thirty minutes, the Judge put to vote the question whether they had been proved guilty. A universal affirmative was the response; and then the question, "What punishment shall be inflicted?" was asked. A brutal-looking fellow in the crowd, cried out, "Hang them." The proposition was seconded, and met with almost universal approbation. I mounted a stump, and in the name of God, humanity, and law, protested against such a course of proceeding; but the crowd, by this time excited by frequent and deep potations of liquor from a neighboring groggery, would listen to nothing contrary to their brutal desires, and even threatened to hang me if I did not immediately desist from any further remarks. Somewhat fearful that such might be my fate, and seeing the utter uselessness of further argument with them, I ceased, and prepared to witness the horrible tragedy. Thirty minutes only were allowed the unhappy victims to prepare themselves to enter on the scenes of eternity. Three ropes were procured, and attached to the limb of a tree. The prisoners were marched out, placed upon a wagon, and the ropes put round their necks. No time was given them for explanation. They vainly tried to speak, but none of them understanding English, they were obliged to employ their native tongues, which but few of those assembled understood. Vainly they called for an interpreter, for their cries were drowned by the yells of a now infuriated mob. A black handkerchief was bound around the eyes of each; their arms were pinioned, and at a given signal, without priest or prayer-book, the wagon was drawn from under them, and they were launched into eternity. Their graves were dug ready to receive them, and when life was entirely extinct, they were cut down and buried in their blankets. This was the first execution I ever witnessed.—God grant that it may be the last!

E. Gould Buffum, *Six Months in the Gold Mines*
(Philadelphia, 1850), 83-85.

The Argonauts on the March

BY ALONSO DELANO

In the fifties Alonso Delano became one of California's most respected businessmen and a much enjoyed writer and artist, inclined toward the humorous. In more serious vein he wrote one of the most lucid descriptions of the overland rush, from which a few early excerpts are here produced.

199

May 22   A little before noon we saw the grass-covered sand hills which bounded the valley of the Platte, and we were some hours in *ascending* the gentle slope to them. It appeared to me that from the time we left the Little Blue, we were gradually ascending, so that the Platte seemed really to flow through higher ground than the tributaries of the Kanzas; and that should a canal be cut from the Platte, it would descend to the Blue, through a series of locks. As we rose to the apex of the last hill, the broad valley of the Platte lay before us, as level as a floor, and the great artery of the Missouri, with its turbid, muddy waters, a mile in width, divided by Grand Island, came in sight. Here, too, was a scene of active life. Here the road from Old Fort Kearny united with the St. Joseph road, and for the whole distance in view, up and down the river, before and behind us, long trains were in motion or encamped on the grassy bottom, and we could scarcely realize that we were in an Indian country, from the scene of civilized life before us, and this was all caused by the magic talisman of gold. . . .

May 25   . . . The day opened cold, raw and windy, and the drive was extremely disagreeable. I was shut up in my wagon, suffering intensely from pain, thirst, and feverish excitement, and at night I had recourse to my usual comforters, blue-pill and oil. At evening the wind went down, and the sun showed his glorious face once more, like an old but long absent friend, above the blanket-clouds, and promised a fair day on the morrow. Distance, fourteen miles.

May 26   The morrow came, and although there was a heavy frost, the sun came out according to promise. The day, for a wonder, was calm, and the genial atmosphere, together with the effect of the apothecary shop in my bowels, made me feel that disease was subdued.

During the day we passed a poor fellow who had fallen from his wagon, which passed over him, breaking his leg in two places. Doctor Gillespie, of Captain Tutt's company, kindly set it, and the unfortunate man once more turned his face homeward—a long and dubious journey for one in his condition. Distance, sixteen miles. . . .

May 30 Morning dawned gloomily enough. It seemed as if a water spout was discharging its floods upon us. Our rain storms at home were only gentle showers compared with this. The wind blew a hurricane, and our cattle, when grazing, kept moving off, apparently in hopes of getting away from the storm, and it was absolutely necessary to keep driving them back almost constantly to prevent them from straying off. Finding it impossible to keep them together, and as they could not eat, from the fury of the storm, we drove them in, where they stood all day under the lee of the wagons, tied to the wheels. . . . It took us till nearly noon to cook our breakfasts. Our stoves were put into our tents, and the covers of boxes, or stray pieces of wood in the wagons, were used to start a fire, and then buffalo chips were heaped upon the stoves until they got dry enough to burn, and in this way we contrived to do our cooking. The comforts of home crowded on our memories, and many a sigh was given for those we had left behind. . . . It continued to rain without cessation through the day, and we turned into our damp beds with a feeling of cheerlessness, though not dispirited. Distance, nothing.

May 31 . . . We left our encampment about eight o'clock, and drove slowly all day. We constantly met groups of men, inquiring for lost cattle, and our own train was carefully scanned, to see if some missing ox had been replaced by theirs. Among the unfortunate ones, one company, having an hundred head, lost seventy; another, out of eighteen, lost nine; and we passed two wagons with families, who had only three oxen tied to the wheels. It was a kind of *terra firma* shipwreck, with the lamentable fact, that the numerous craft sailing by were unable to afford the sufferers any relief. . . .

We saw buffalos for the first time in considerable numbers, on the opposite side of the fork, and were much amused in seeing the emigrants, who had crossed, dashing in upon them in gallant style. One was shot in our sight. Not only was the chase exciting, but witnessing it was extremely so; and as the herd dashed off, we could scarcely repress a desire to be after them; but this was impossible, for a broad and dangerous stream was between us. . . .

June 3 . . . Loading our wagons too heavily with cumbrous and weighty articles, and with unnecessary supplies of provisions, had been a general fault, and the cattle began to exhibit signs of fatigue. We resolved, therefore, to part with everything which was not absolutely necessary, and to shorten the dimension of our wagons so that they would run easier. . . . We were compelled to throw away a quantity of iron, steel, trunks, valises, old clothes, and boots . . . ; and I may observe here that we subsequently found the road lined with cast-off articles, piles of bacon, flour, wagons, groceries, clothing, and various other articles, which had been left, and the waste and destruction of property was enormous. . . . On leaving home, we were under the impression that corn meal would not keep on the plains without first being kiln-dried; that butter-crackers and flour would not keep well, and that our bread-stuffs must necessarily be in the shape of hard bread. This we found was a false impression, and that a little care in airing occasionally would preserve meal, flour, hams, and indeed anything, as well as in a store room at home. . . . Instead of suffering on the plains, the trip can be made by taking the proper precautions, with comparative comfort and safety.

Alonso Delano, *Across the Plains and Among the Diggings*
(Auburn, New York, 1854), 47, 55-60, 62-64.

On the Trail

BY J. GOLDSBOROUGH BRUFF

J. Goldsborough Bruff joined the gold rush with the intention of producing a thorough description of the overland route, complete with maps and realistic sketches, by which all future emigrants could have safe conduct to the mines. He endured extraordinary sufferings en route, amassed voluminous notes and sketches, but could find no publisher who would rise to the challenge. His most detailed of all gold rush narratives, now the foundation document for the overlanders of 1849, consequently languished in manuscript for ninety-five years.

[*July*] 8. . . . we moved on, and the train had only gone its length, when I was called, and informed that a member, who had, last night complained of indisposition was now dangerously ill: This was strange, as no report had been made to me of his illness, and the mules were called in, hitched up, and the train put in motion before I was told of the disaster. I immediately wheeled the train to the right, moved down a few hundred yards, and corralled, on the banks of the river. On walking back to the tent of the unfortunate man, I found the wagon of his messmates standing there, and the Surgeon attending him. The D^r told me he had all the symptoms of Asiatic cholera. His messmates said that for several days he had complained of indisposition, and had also drank of *Slew* water, which I had cautioned the men against using. At 11 A.M. he was deranged, saying he was not afraid to die, and requesting his friends to shoot him. . . .

At 1 P.M. poor Bishop died, of Cholera.—The first casualty in the Company, sudden and astounding, was this very mysterious and fatal visitation. Yesterday, in presence of the deceased, I remarked how very fortunate we had been, in all respect[s], and trusted we might continue so. The messmates of the deceased laid him out, sewed him up in his blue blanket, and prepared a bier, formed of his tent-poles. I had a grave dug in a neighboring ridge, on left of the trail, about 400 yards from it. Dry clay and gravel, and coarse white sand-stone on the next hill, afforded slabs to line it with, making a perfect vault. I sat 3 hours in the hot sun, and sculptured a head and foot stone; and filled the letters with blacking from the hub of a wheel.

I then organized a funeral procession, men all in clean clothes and uniforms, with music, (a key-bugle, flute, violin and accordian) and two and two, with the Stars & stripes over the body, we marched to the measured time of the dirge, deposited the body of our comrade in the grave, an elderly gentleman read the burial service, and we filled up the grave, erected the stones, and returned to camp. Capt. McNulty, his Lieutenant, and a firing party of 8 men in uniform (N.Y. Comp) came back some distance & participated in the last rites over the adventurer's grave. The sun shed his declining rays over the closing scene. (*Lowered the body into the grave with bridle-reins.*) . . .

[*July*] 17.—(*Commences clear & very warm Calm.*) Very early this morning I sent the mules 7 miles up Deer Creek, under guard of 20 men—to graze, and a party to cut grass & bring down. Hauled the seine, in Platte, a[nd] caught a number of fine fish. A Company with ox-wagons, crossed the ferry this morning. Our wheels much shrunk—repairing & strengthening them.

The abandonment and destruction of property here—at Deer Creek, is extraordinary: true, a great deal is heavy cumbrous, useless articles: A Diving bell and all the apparatus, heavy anvils, iron and steel, forges, bellows, lead, &c. &c. and provissions;—bacon in great piles, many chords of it—good meat. Bags of beans, salt, &c. &c. Trunks, chests, tools of every description, clothing, tents, tent-poles, harness, &c. &c.

I took advantage of the piles of bacon here, and had all mine trimmed of fat and the rusty exterior and the requisite amount of pounds replaced by choice cuts from the abandoned piles. Was told of a man here, who a few days ago offered a barrel of sugar for sale, for about threble its cost, price—and unable to obtain that, he poured Spirits of turpentine in it, and burnt it up. The spirit of selfishness has been here beautifully developed—Discarded effects generally rendered useless:—Camp utensils & vessels broken, kegs & buckets stove, trunks chopped with hatchets, & saws & other tools all broken. A considerable accumulation of ox-chains & yokes. . . .

[*July*] 21. . . . Drove from 7 A.M. till 11 A.M. and nooned. 2 P.M. moved on again, over a high and steep sand-hill, very heavy drag, ascended higher, and gained the level mountain top, and fairly in line, on the summit, when, at 3 P.M. two dark clouds one from the S.W. and the other from the N.W. met over head, and (*Hail Storm*) discharged their contents on our devoted heads. Rain fell in a perfect sheet, blinding and appalling lightning, and crashing thunder. In a few seconds from the commencement of this tempest, the hail suddenly descended, like large gravel in immense quantities, thrown down upon us.—then Hail-stones of extraordinary size, not only cut and bruised the men, whose faces and hands were bleeding, but it also cut the mules. I thought that in my younger days, in the tropics, and at sea, I had seen some tall storms, but this one beat all my experience. . . .

Aug. 11. . . . Moved down, at 6 A.M. 4 miles, to the banks of "Bear river," a beautiful stream: Level and broad bottoms, with plenty of grass. Caught a number of fine large fish. Banks of stream lined with willows. Found here, many ox-camps, and many others, driving on. . . .

This would be a magnificent spot for a Settlement, apparently; but timber is distant, and the traders say that snow falls here to the depth of 4 feet. . . .

As my camp was close to the edge of the stream, I spread my blanket under the concavity formed in a group of willows, and at midnight laid down, and slept soundly, till a little before day, when some animal about the size of a pointer dog, ran hastily over me, treading on my breast & awakening me.—I presumed it was only a small wolf, and drew my blanket over my face, and finished my repose—till 6 A.M. when called to breakfast. Cold night. . . .

[*Aug.*] 31st. . . . Passed 8 dead oxen, 6 do mules, 1 dying horse, and 1 do lame & abandon'd Quite unwell.—Overtook Mr. Hunt,— of Peoria, Ill. who kindly invited me to get in his wagon, where I slept soundly till he halted, late in the afternoon, at a beautiful stream gushing out from under a rocky cliff, where the road descends a considerable & stony hill, & turns suddenly to the left. —After which, in a few hundred yards, it turns to the right, Several Ox companies here—Men, women, children, and animals enjoying the clear cool water. This is the valley of the "Hot Springs"—(several hot springs farther along). (13 *ms.*) I supped with my kind Illinoisian friends,—and the pleasure of ladies company, to-boot. After supper and a short chat, I lit my pipe, bade my friends adieu, and rode on, after night, to overtake my old comrades—ahead. . . .

[*Oct.*] 11 . . . Road winding to avoid large rocks and immense fir trees. A cart following, with a yoke of small and very lean oxen; these steep ascents are almost too much for them.—Road W.S.W.

over a level mountain-top, ¾ ms. A mule fell, but raised, and proceeded. A tedious road for the poor mules. Passed a *house*-wagon,
drawn by 3 yoke of oxen & 2 small cows.—3 ladies with them.—
This wagon was termed by the emigrants,—the '*Steam-boat*,'—
The body had side projections, above the wheels, and in front was
a stove, the pipe sticking out of the top.—A family of the name of
Allford, were the proprietors. . . .

Some of my team so weak, that they could not keep up, and did
not reach us for some time after I halted. A lady in the "*Steamboat*" wagon, has an infant born a month since, in these mountains. Here I was compelled, on account of the mules, to camp.
Condemned a defective wagon, & distributed the cargo and mules.
Sun Set cloudy, light Wind N. Temp. 56° While grazing, at night,
a mule fell over a rock, and was jamed, keel-up, between a couple
of parallel rocks. With great difficulty extricated the *critter*,—
buised & skinned.—A horse also bruised by the rocks, 1 mule
died. . . .

Oct. 20. . . . A very rocky dusty place; I took a hearty draught of
cold mountain water, eat a handful of crackers, smoked my pipe,
and made a fire. At the foot of an immense fur tree, where the
rocks in the road were so irregular that I might lay in dust in a
hollow, with some ease, in shape of letter S, and there spread my
blanket & placed my saddle-pillow; some fragments of a wagon—
and a wheel,—hub on flame, soon afforded me warmth and light,
by which I wrote up my brief notes, buttond up my over coat, and
quickly slept sound. Report of rifles, in the adjacent hills, answered
by people here,—hunters lost. . . .

[*Oct.*] 25. . . . It is a queer sight now, to observe the straggling
emigrants coming up and going in. Wagons of every kind, oxen,
horses, mules, bulls, cows, and people,—men, women, & children,
all packed. A few weeks travel has wrought a great change in their
circumstances.—Many of them I recognize as old acquaintances
as far back as Pittsburgh, and all along our western waters, and
over the long travel. Large companies, fine animals, a great
amount of provisions & stores, and smiling faces; were now a scat-

tered, broken, selfish stragglers, dusty in faces and dress, and many of them, thin with hunger, as well as anxiety.

J. Goldsborough Bruff, Diary, in Georgia Willis Read
and Ruth Gaines, eds. *Gold Rush: The Journals,
Drawings, and Other Papers of J. Goldsborough Bruff*
(New York, 1944), I, 33-34, 46-47, 49, 87-88,
159, 214-215, 232, 240-241.

The Panama Lottery

BY R. R. TAYLOR

R. R. Taylor well illustrates that not all the forty-niners were rollicking and carefree. He made the steamer trip on borrowed money, and constantly weighing on him was the responsibility to earn for the wife and family waiting for his return. Thus the delay at Panama was something which he literally could not afford.

July 24, 1849

My Dear Wife:

Today has been the most exciting day I think I ever spent. I have had more pending upon a *game of chance* than I ever had before, or probably ever shall again. To explain. When I last wrote you I had almost concluded to leave here in the "Wilhelmine." Mr. Burnham wished to do so & urged me hard to go. But I felt I could not afford the time to go in a sailing craft. I felt the necessity of getting into some situation where I could be earning something for you, & if I did not go in a steamer it would very likely be three months before I got to California. Finally therefore, I positively refused to go in any other way until I was certain no passage could be got in the steamer, & Mr. Burnham reluctantly staid.

From the moment of the arrival of the "Panama" I kept my eye on the movements of the agents, in order that no tickets should be sold without my knowledge. I made it a rule to be about the office of the company at least every two hours in the day, & nothing escaped my attention. At last it was given out yesterday afternoon just before the closing of the office that the tickets remaining would be disposed of to-day. At daylight I was "on hand," confident of being able to get near enough to the front of the crowd to get a ticket. But a new notice came out. Persons wishing tickets were to register their names & then they were to draw lots for the 50 tickets to be disposed of. Fifty pieces of paper were to be numbered & put into a hat, & as there were over a hundred applications there were of course to be as many blanks as there was a surplus of names. I should have said that the Oregon having arrived on Saturday greatly damaged, Mr. Burnham & Foster had both been lucky enough to get a job repairing her for which they were to get well paid & get a free passage up in her when she goes which will be sometime in August. They had therefore gone to "Toboga" an island some 12 miles down the bay, & I was left to run my chance alone. The stake you will see was a great one;—if I drew a blank, I must take a sailing vessel & run my risk of getting to California, "sometime" in a crowded hold, with the worst fare possible, or remain 3 or 4 weeks longer in this miserable place, for the Oregon & perhaps after all not get a passage in her—if I won I should probably get to California in 3 weeks.

The drawing was to take place at one o'clock & the intermediate time was an exciting period for me. A great crowd was collected to witness the drawing & a good deal of trouble was experienced in correcting the list & making sure that none were there who already had tickets, or who were known to be speculators etc. Lt. [Edward F.] Beale, whose name you will see in the papers often, presided at the hat, & when my name was called & he put in his hand, I believe my heart fairly stood still. He drew *a ticket* & the way I jumped about and shook hands with friends & acquaintances who crowded around with their congratulations was "a caution." Had he drawn a blank, I am afraid I should have sunk under it—my spirits & my courage which I have managed thus far to preserve good, would have deserted me under so great a disappointment. But thank Heaven this was not reserved for me.

A letter from Panama by R. R. Taylor,
in John W. Caughey, ed., *Seeing the Elephant*
(Los Angeles, The Ward Ritchie Press, 1951), 45-47.

California at Last

BY JACOB Y. STOVER

Jacob Y. Stover was one of several hundred forty-niners who attempted a southwestern short-cut from Salt Lake. They started with a guide, split into a dozen or more groups, and fanned out into the mountain-obstructed desert of the Great Basin. Some of these wanderers entered Death Valley. Stover's group turned south a little sooner, struck the trail of their guide, Jefferson Hunt, and straggled across the Mojave Desert to the happy ending here described.

We went in the evening on the desert and travelled all night. Next day it rained on us, it gave us water to drink but made it slippery to walk. The second night I shall never forget. We were sleepy, tired and hungry. We went five to ten miles and stopped to rest; we burned grease wood and then lay or stood around to get warm. This was in December.

We at last got to the Mojave River. The third night, which was dry, we found a deep hole that had water in it; we drank and what horses we had left drank. We lay down on the sand and gravel and slept good. Next morning we got up and ate a bite and started up the river. It had been a little cloudy and misty down where we were; we hadn't gone more than a mile or so when all at once we saw the water coming three or four feet high abreast, carrying with it sticks, brush and logs, and on top six inches of foam. We ran to the nearest bank and just made it. Part of our men were way down below. We hallooed to them so they got out on the same side that we did.

We travelled up the stream all day but did not make very good headway, there being so much brush on the mountain side. Hunt's trail we could see now and then on the other side. Night came on we were on the wrong side of the river. The river was getting down. We went to the water edge, stripped off our clothes, waded over, got some wood, made a fire, warmed ourselves, and slept there for the night. We came to the conclusion that a cloud had bursted. We could see the mountain covered white with snow.

Next morning we started on Hunt's trail, got two or three miles when Jim and I (ahead as usual) came on two fine fat steers, drove them a few rods, were thinking of having some fine beef when we met a man hunting them. He said he was sent out with provision for us. He took us up to his wagon. We saw some tallow where he had been frying his fat beef. I think it was half an inch thick and as big as the bottom of the frying pan. We got hold of it about the same time, broke it about the middle I guess—we didn't measure it, but ate it down and looked for more. That tasted as good as pie did at home.

But we did not stop at that; we took our butcher knives, cut off chunks and put them on the coals and broiled them, wet up corn meal, put on flat rocks, and were in the business by the time the rest got there. They followed suit as quick as they saw what was going on. The man sat and looked on. We filled ourselves, then we commenced to ask him how far it was to California. He said, "Oh, you can get there tomorrow."

You better believe we felt good to think that only one more day and we would see that long-looked for place. He told us to take what meal we wanted and meat, so we did. The man went on out to meet more hungry people.

We started down the creek, crossing the creek every few rods, then wading in water, till we began to get hungry again. We stopped and baked on stones and cooked the meat on sticks and ate everything he had given us, then started on.

About sun down we got out of the canon to the loveliest place I ever saw; everything looked so nice and warm; the frogs were singing and the birds too; it seemed like we had passed into a new world. We went about one hundred and sixty rods and came to an oak grove; the wind had blown the leaves up against a log and made us a bed; we thought we would not reject the offer. We spread our blankets and turned in for the night. We were up at daylight on the road, the birds were singing; I can't describe the joy and happiness we all felt. Everything seemed so lovely.

In the afternoon we got to the first ranch, it was called Poka-mongo Ranch in Spanish; in English, Negro Ranch. The owner was a negro. We came to the house, stacked our blankets in a pile, and went up where he was making wine of grapes and in rather a novel way to us. He had a beef hide with a hole in the center of the hide, four forks planted in the ground and four poles run through holes cut in the edge of the hide, which bagged down so it would hold two or three bushels of grapes. He had two forks, one on each side of the skin, and a pole tied from one fork to the other. Two buck Indians, stripped off naked, took hold of this pole with their hands and tramped the grapes. The wine would run. We ate grapes then went at the wine, caught it in our tin cups, as we all had one apiece. The old negro stood and looked on. We drank it as fast as the Indians could tramp it for awhile. The old negro after awhile said, "Gentlemen, you have had a hard time of it, I know, but de first ting you know you will know noting. You are welcome to it."

The old negro was right. They began to tumble over and the wine came up as fast as it went down. He got a spade and gave it to me, told me to dig holes at their mouths. So I did. Finally Dr. Downer and I were the only ones left on our feet. The sun was about one hour high was the last thing I recollect. Sometime in the night I waked up and found myself lying on my back, the stars shining in my face. I felt cold. How came I to be lying on the grass? I felt around for my blankets. I began to realize my situation seeing the rest of the company lying as I had left them. I looked around, found my blankets, went to bed.

Now this spree was on Christmas day. In the morning when we all got up we felt pretty good but awfully hungry. The old negro sent two of his buckaries out to fetch in a beef for us. They brought in one. We soon had beef and corn meal, ate what we could, thanked him and started for Los Angeles.

John W. Caughey, ed., "The Jacob Y. Stover Narrative,"
Pacific Historical Review, VI (1937), 175-177.

Rescue from Death Valley

BY WILLIAM LEWIS MANLY

As a hired teamster for the Bennett and Arcane families, young Lewis Manly was in the caravan of forty-niners moving south-westward from Salt Lake. Having reached an oasis in Death Valley, Bennett thought it best to send Manly and John Rogers ahead

to learn the correct route to the settlements. With great difficulty
they made it in, bought a mule and two horses and a small amount
of supplies, and headed back into the desert. The account picks up
in the course of their return to the camp at Bennett Wells.

Starting early we made the summit about noon, and from here we
could see the place where we found a water hole and camped the
first night after we left the wagons. Down the steep cañon we
turned, the same one in which we had turned back with the
wagons, and over the sharp broken pieces of volcanic rock that
formed our only footing we hobbled along with sore and tender
feet. We had to watch for the smoothest place for every step, and
then moved only with the greatest difficulty. The Indians could
have caught us easily if they had been around, for we must keep
our eyes on the ground constantly and stop if we looked up and
around. But we at last got down and camped on some spot where
we had set out twenty-five days before to seek the settlements.
Here was the same little water hole in the sand plain, and the same
strong sulphur water which we had to drink the day we left. The
mule was turned loose dragging the same piece of rawhide she
had attached to her when we purchased her, and she ranged and
searched faithfully for food finding little except the very scattering bunches of sage brush. She was industrious and walked around
rapidly picking here and there, but at dark came into camp and
lay down close to us to sleep.

There was no sign that any one had been here during our absence, and if the people had gone to hunt a way out, they must
either have followed the Jayhawker's trail or some other one. We
were much afraid that they might have fallen victims to the Indians. Remaining in camp so long it was quite likely they had
been discovered by them and it was quite likely they had been
murdered for the sake of the oxen and camp equipage. It might
be that we should find the hostiles waiting for us when we reached
the appointed camping place, and it was small show for two
against a party. Our mule and her load would be a great capture
for them. We talked a great deal and said a great many things at
that camp fire, for we knew we were in great danger, and we had

many doubts about the safety of our people, that would soon be decided, and whether for joy or sorrow we could not tell.

From this place, as we walked along, we had a wagon road to follow, in soft sand, but not a sign of a human footstep could we see, as we marched toward this, the camp of the last hope. We had the greatest fears the people had given up our return and started out for themselves and that we should follow on, only to find them dead or dying. My pen fails me as I try to tell the feelings and thoughts of this trying hour. I can never hope to do so, but if the reader can place himself in my place, his imagination cannot form a picture that shall go beyond reality.

We were some seven or eight miles along the road when I stopped to fix my moccasin while Rogers went slowly along. The little mule went on ahead of both of us, searching all around for little bunches of dry grass, but always came back to the trail again, and gave us no trouble. When I had started up again I saw Rogers ahead leaning on his gun and waiting for me, apparently looking at something on the ground. As I came near enough to speak I asked what he had found and he said—"Here is Captain Culverwell, dead." He did not look much like a dead man. He lay upon his back with arms extended wide, and his little canteen, made of two powder flasks, lying by his side. This looked indeed as if some of our saddest forebodings were coming true. How many more bodies should we find? Or should we find the camp deserted, and never a trace of the former occupants.

We marched toward camp like two Indians, silent and alert, looking out for dead bodies and live Indians, for really we more expected to find the camp devastated by those rascals than to find that it still contained our friends. To the east we could plainly see what seemed to be a large salt lake with a bed that looked as if of the finest whitest sand, but really a wonder of salt crystal. We put the dreary steps steadily one forward of another, the little mule the only unconcerned one of the party, ever looking for an odd blade of grass, dried in the hot dry wind, but yet retaining nourishment, which she preferred.

About noon we came in sight of the wagons, still a long way off, but in the clear air we could make them out and tell what they were, without being able to see anything more. Half a mile was the distance between us and the camp before we could see very plainly, as they were in a little depression. We could see the covers had been taken off, and this was an ominous sort of circumstance to us, for we feared the depredations of the Indians in retaliation for the capture of their squashes. They had shot our oxen before we left and they have slain them this time and the people too.

We surely left seven wagons. Now we could see only four and nowhere the sign of an ox. They must have gone ahead with a small train and left these four standing after dismantling them.

No signs of life were anywhere about, and the thought of our hard struggles between life and death to go out and return, with the fruitless results that now seemed apparent, was almost more than human heart could bear. When should we know their fate? When should we find their remains, and how learn of their sad history if we ourselves should live to get back again to settlements and life? If ever two men were troubled, Rogers and I surely passed through the furnace.

We kept as low and as much out of sight as possible, trusting very much to the little mule that was ahead, for we felt sure she would detect danger in the air sooner than we, and we watched her closely to see how she acted. She slowly walked along looking out for food, and we followed a little way behind, but still no decisive sign to settle the awful suspense in which we lived and suffered. We became more and more convinced that they had taken the trail of the Jayhawkers, and we had missed them on the road, or they had perished before reaching the place where we turned from their trail.

One hundred yards now to the wagons and still no sign of life, no positive sign of death, though we looked carefully for both. We fear that perhaps there were Indians in ambush, and with nervous, irregular breathing we counsel what to do. Finally Rogers suggested that he had two charges in his shotgun and I seven in the Coll's [Colt] rifle, and that I fire one of mine and await results before we ventured any nearer, and if there are any of the red devils there we can kill some of them before they get to us. And now both closely watching the wagons I fired the shot. Still as death and not a move for a moment, and then as if by magic a man came out from under a wagon and stood up looking all around, for he did not see us. Then he threw up his arms high over his head and shouted—"The boys have come! The boys have come!" Then other bare heads appeared, and Mr. Bennett and wife and Mr. Arcane came toward us as fast as ever they could. The great suspense was over and our hearts were first in our mouths, and then the blood all went away and left us almost fainting as we stood and tried to step. Some were safe perhaps all of those nearest us, and the dark shadow of death that had hovered over us, and cast what seemed a pall upon every thought and action, was lifted and fell away a heavy oppression gone. Bennett and Arcane caught us in their arms and embraced us with all their strength, and Mrs. Bennett when she came fell down on her knees and clung to me like a maniac in the great emotion that came to her, and not a word was spoken. If they had been strong enough they would have carried us to camp upon their shoulders. As it was they stopped two or three times, and turned as if to speak, but there was too much feeling for words; convulsive weeping would choke the voice.

All were a little calmer soon, and Bennett soon found voice to say;—"I know you have found some place, for you have a mule," and Mrs. Bennett through her tears, looked staringly at us as she could hardly believe our coming back was a reality, and then exclaimed:—"Good boys! O, you have saved us all! God bless you forever! Such boys should never die!" It was some time before they could talk without weeping. Hope almost died within them, and now when the first bright ray came it almost turned reason from its throne. A brighter, happier look came to them than we had seen, and then they plied us with questions, the first of which was: —"Where were you?"

We told them it must be 250 miles yet to any part of California where we could live. Then came the question;—"Can we take our wagons?" "You will have to walk," was our answer, for no wagons could go over that unbroken road that we had traveled. As rapidly and carefully as we could we told them of our journey and the long distance between the water holes; that we had lost no time and yet had been twenty-six days on the road; that for a long distance the country was about as dry and desolate as the region we had crossed east of this camp. We told them of the scarcity of grass, and all the reasons that had kept us so long away from them.

215

We inquired after the others whom we had left in camp when we went away, and we were told all they knew about them. Hardly were we gone before they began to talk about the state of affairs which existed. They said that as they had nothing to live on but their oxen it would be certain death to wait here and eat them up, and that it would be much better to move on a little every day and get nearer and nearer the goal before the food failed. Bennett told them they would know surely about the way when the boys returned, and knowing the road would know how to manage and what to expect and work for, and could get out successfully. But the general opinion of all but Mr. Bennett and Mr. Arcane and their families was, as expressed by one of them:—"If those boys ever get out of this cussed hole, they are d--d fools if they ever come back to help anybody."

Some did not stay more than a week after we were gone, but took their oxen and blankets and started on. They could not be content to stay idly in camp with nothing to occupy their minds or bodies. They could see that an ox when killed would feed them only a few days, and that they could not live long on them, and it stood them in hand to get nearer the western shore as the less distance the more hope while the meat lasted. Bennett implored them to stay as he was sure we would come back, and if the most of them deserted him he would be exposed to the danger of the Indians, with no hope of a successful resistance against them.

But the most seemed to think that to stay was to die, and it would be better to die trying to escape than to set idly down to perish. These men seemed to think their first duty was to save themselves, and if fortunate, help others afterwards, so they packed their oxen and left in separate parties, the last some two weeks before. They said that Capt. Culverwell went with the last party. I afterward learned that he could not keep up with them and turned to go back to the wagons again, and perished, stretched out upon the sand as we saw him, dying all alone, with no one to transmit his last words to family or friends. Not a morsel to eat, and the little canteen by his side empty. A sad and lonely death indeed!

There was no end to the questions about the road we had to answer, for this was uppermost on their minds, and we tried to

216

tell them and show them how we must get along on our return. We told them of the great snow mountains we had seen all to the north of our road, and how deep the snow appeared to be, and how far west it extended. We told them of the black and desolate ranges and buttes to the south, and of the great dry plains in the same direction. We told them of the Jayhawkers trail; of Fish's dead body; of the salt lake and slippery alkali water to which we walked, only to turn away in disappointment; of the little sheets of ice which saved our lives; of Doty's camp and what we knew of those gone before; of the discouraged ones who gave us their names to send back to friends; of the hawk and crow diet; of my lameness; of the final coming out into a beautiful valley, in the midst of fat cattle and green meadows, and the trouble to get the help arranged on account of not knowing the language to tell the people what we needed. They were deeply impressed that my lameness had been a blessing in disguise, or we would have gone on to the coast and consumed more time than we did in walking slowly to favor the cripple knee. Our sad adventures and loss of the horses in returning were sorrowfully told and we spoke of the provisions we had been able to bring on the little mule which had clambered over the rocks like a cat; that we had a little flour and beans, and some good dried meat with fat on it which we hoped would help to eke out the poorer fare and get them through at last. They were so full of compliments that we really began to think we had been brought into the world on purpose to assist some one, and the one who could forecast all things had directed us, and all our ways, so that we should save those people and bring them to a better part of God's footstool, where plenty might be enjoyed, and the sorrows of the desert forgotten. It was midnight before we could get them all satisfied with their knowledge of our experience. . . .

Just as we were ready to leave . . . we took off our hats, and then overlooking the scene of so much trial, suffering and death spoke the thought uppermost saying:—"*Good bye Death Valley!*" then faced away and made our steps toward camp. Ever after this in speaking of this long and narrow valley over which we had crossed into its nearly central part, and on the edge of which the lone camp was made, for so many days, it was called Death Valley.

217

Many accounts have been given to the world as to the origin of the name and by whom it was thus designated but ours were the first visible footsteps, and we the party which named it the saddest and most dreadful name that came to us first from its memories.

William Lewis Manly, *Death Valley in '49*
(San Jose, 1894), 196-203, 215-217.

San Francisco Vignettes

BY VICENTE PEREZ ROSALES

Vicente Pérez Rosales eventually found his career as promoter of the colonization of southern Chile. In the forties he was more restlessly seeking an outlet for his talents that would yield him a modest fortune. He joined the rush of his countrymen to California not profitably, except that out of the experience came the brightest chapters in his much esteemed reminiscences, Recuerdos del pasado.

The things I saw and heard at that time in California were so unusual, so beyond the natural order of human events, so extraordinary in the speed with which they followed one another, that only by having noted them down as they occurred and seeing them in my own hand later can I believe that all I am stating is not a dream.

We leaped resolutely to dry land—or rather mud, for the outgoing tide had left nothing between the point at which our ship became grounded in the slime and the base of the slope of solid earth on which the town began. To the right of our landing place stood a kind of plank fence enclosing some beeves. Perched on the boards sat a row of crows croaking their appreciation of the odor of blood.

Some of our friends had stressed the necessity for leaving the ship armed, and always in the company of at least one other person. This is in fact how we went, and how most of the tradesmen of

218

the town also went, displaying not only their merchandise but a dagger at the waist or else a revolver, a weapon that was then becoming common. In order to hit upon Price's house we were obliged to cover the greater part of this most extravagant and singular town. The streets were wide arcs each of whose ends came down to the beach, arcs broken by other streets at right angles that came down to the water, in each case to piers that hindered rather than facilitated the unloading of vessels. Some of the buildings arrayed in lines at either side of the streets of this maze must have been worth $100,000. But there was no uniformity among them. By the side of a costly though rough and simple structure stood rows of tents covered with wretched awnings, board shacks and cabins, some already set up, others in the very active process of construction. The Parker House Hotel was leased for $175,000 a year. There were no sidewalks in the streets, nor anything resembling them, and the center was a slough of trampled mud whose solidest parts were formed by the thousands of broken bottles thrown from the buildings as emptied. The inhabitants, of heterogeneous nationality, numbering about fifteen hundred permanent residents and as many transients, might have been thought to be celebrating a vast and noisy masquerade ball, such were their exotic costumes, their language, and the very nature of their occupations. Even the women we thought must be dressed as men, for seek as one might through that Babylon, one found never a skirt recognizable as such. The furs of the Oregonion with his hectoring look, the Maule cap, the parasol-like headgear of the Chinese, the enormous boots of the Russian that appeared to swallow up their wearer, the Frenchman, the Englishman, the Italian in sailor attire, the rustic whose coat was about to take its last farewell, the gentleman with no coat at all; everything, in short, that might have been found in some gigantic carnival was here to be found gathered together and whirling in movement. At every step we were compelled to get out of the way, plunging our legs into the mire to give passage to some former dandy now arrayed in woolen shirt and rolled up pants and sweating under the weight of some load he was carrying from the beach to the dwellings at four dollars a burden. Or perhaps we had to avoid being picked up by a more fortunate porter who, the proud owner of a wheelbarrow, strode stiffly ahead with perfect un-concern exciting the envy of those who lacked a comparable tool. Quiet and ease were words without meaning in San Francisco. In the midst of the tremendous din of hammering that went on all about, some men were setting up tents, others were sawing boards; one man rolled a barrel, another struggled with a post or pounded loudly to fix it in the ground. A tent was scarccly erected when business was in full swing, the goods displayed in the open: boots and flimsy clothing, Chanco cheeses, bundles of jerked beef, piles of dried pears, shovels, picks, powder and liquors, objects which, like toasted and untoasted flour, brought their weight in gold. Chilean brandy sold for seventy dollars a four-gallon jug, and the sweetened soda water that they called champagne for eight to twelve dollars a bottle. These prices were due not so much to the small supplies of commodities, as to the necessity for economy of time, which no one wasted in haggling, even though things might be cheaper a bit farther on. Gold dust was the commonest currency, and the best evidence of its abundance lay in the manner in which it was handled in making a payment, little care being taken to return to the leather bag the excess that fell into the scale. . . .

How different was the San Francisco of my second visit! The city of canvas and a few more or less pretentious structures had disappeared. Tents and shelters had been metamorphosed into buildings in regular rows, though of hurried and rough construc-tion. Foundations had been laid for splendid hotels; and the streets, formerly cut off by mire at the high water level, had been extended out over the water by means of piers resting on redwood logs driven into the bottom. Lots that had diligently been given away were now measured by feet, and their value was more than sky high.

The progress of this town, especially surprising to men like our-selves accustomed only to the tortoise pace of the Chilean villages, convinced me of our mistake in having refused the property offered us on condition we put up on it our fine tents. Could I do otherwise than regret underestimating what was to be worth so much in so short a period? It may be said here, with no intention of injuring feelings, that in California the only men to heap up fortunes were those who had not the daring to go out and seek them in the face of hunger, exertion and danger. Instead, some accepted free lots, others bought up property for next to nothing, and some simply stood in ambush behind goods that chance rather than design had led them to bring; and it was these men who found themselves over night the possessors of positive riches.

The bay was crowded with ships, all of them deserted. Passengers and crews were raising the unstable population to over 30,000. And so intense was the activity of transient and permanent residents alike, that the city was growing and being transformed as if by magic. Long wharves had already been built out over huge redwood piles, but were being lengthened; and others, only half finished as yet, ran out from every street that came down to the water's edge, disputing with the mud of low tide room for thoroughfare and new buildings. Owing to the shortage of other material right at hand for pier construction, boxes and sacks of earth were heaped up at the muddy waterline in one place, while in another spot piers, warehouses and streets were improvised by grounding a row of ships in a line from the ends of the city streets. Shops were then built over beams and boards resting upon the ships.

One of the inventors of this method of changing ships into land dwellings was the young Chilean Wenceslao Urbistondo. He made use of a full moon to prolong with his deserted and useless ship the street situated at the base of a hill that forms the lefthand boundary of the port, and created a bridge with his masts in order to cross the mud lying between his stern and the street. Since there were no cheaper or quicker sidewalks to be had, footpaths were made in the streets even with bundles of jerked beef, sunk into the clay along the houses to provide passage without the necessity for plunging up to the knees in mud. . . .

The hordes of men, always men, for women had as yet not come into fashion, had made it necessary to establish at least a pretense of civil government in this Tower of Babel. Indeed, an approach was created in the office of alcalde, an officer whose duties were exactly those of our old sheriffs. All that distinguished the former from the latter was the fact that the latter's orders and decrees, just or unjust, were carried out, whereas only convenience gave any weight to those of the Californian or San Franciscan alcalde.

Brought to the scene once by the bustle, shouting and swearing of a crowd of people, I saw that they were pushing one of their number into the presence of the Alcalde. Casually joining them, I went with the rest into the courtroom, a large, bare hall with a door at one end and a low window at the other, where the judge sat. The latter, after a brief exchange of words with plaintiffs and defendant, considered himself informed—again *time was money*—and standing up, loudly said, "Hear, hear! I condemn the culprit to fifty lashes, to be administered at once!"

At the mention of fifty lashes, another voice, alcoholic and broken by hiccoughs, also pronounced a "Hear, hear!" All of us turned to the direction from which the bellow had issued, and saw with amazement that it came from an Oregonian who, precariously poised on a speaker's platform made by the shoulders of three heavy-faced companions, after another command of "Hear, hear!" cried out: "Citizens! Inasmuch as the Alcalde is in favor of the immediate application of fifty strokes to this citizen of the United States, I propose that ten of us escort the Alcalde for a distance of one mile with kicks in the —!"

"Hurray!" exclaimed all present with one voice. The culprit himself and all the rest rushed toward the Alcalde, who, swifter than a hare, leaped out the window and evaporated among the adjoining alleys. With such judges and such litigants, it was not surprising that suits of the first and second instance were adjusted with pistols and knives.

Vicente Pérez Rosales, *Recuerdos del pasado* (Santiago, 1890);
translated by Edwin S. Morby and Arturo Torres-Rioseco as *California Adventure* (San Francisco, Book Club of California, 1947), 19-21, 63-67.

The Mining Life

BY LOUISE AMELIA KNAPP SMITH CLAPPE

For a picture of life in the mines the most favored reference is the Shirley Letters. Written in 1851 and 1852 from Rich Bar and Indian Bar on the North Fork of the Feather, they were serialized three years later in The Pioneer *and subsequently have been collected in book form. Louise Amelia Knapp Smith Clappe, or Dame Shirley, as she signed herself, never washed a pan of "dirt" and lived somewhat apart from the general run of the miners, but she was most observant and she wrote with grace and feeling.*

From our Log Cabin, Indian Bar, July 5, 1852

Dear M:—Our Fourth of July celebration, which came off at Rich Bar, was quite a respectable affair. I had the honor of making a flag for the occasion. The stripes were formed of cotton cloth and red calico, of which last gorgeous material, no possible place in California is ever destitute. A piece of drilling, taken from the roof of the Humboldt, which the rain and the sun had faded from its original, somber hue, to just that particular shade of blue, which you and I admire so much—served for a Union. A large star in the center, covered with gold leaf, represented California. Humble as were the materials of which it was composed, this banner made quite a gay appearance, floating from the top of a lofty pine, in front of the Empire, to which it was suspended.

I went over to Rich Bar at six in the morning, not wishing to take so fatiguing a walk in the heat of the day. After breakfast, I assisted Mrs. B. and one of the gentlemen, in decorating the dining-room; the walls of which, we completely covered with grape-vines, relieved here and there, with bunches of elder-blow. We made several handsome bouquets, and arranged one of syringas, white lilies and the feathery green of the cedar, to be presented, in the name of the ladies, to the Orator of the Day. You can imagine my disgust, when the ceremony was performed, to observe that some officious Goth, had marred the perfect keeping of the gift, by thrusting into the vase, several ugly, purple blossoms.

The exercises were appointed to commence at ten o'clock, but they were deferred for half an hour, in expectation of the arrival of two ladies, who had taken up their abode in the place within the last six weeks, and were living on Indian Bar Hill. As they did not come, however, it was thought necessary to proceed without them; so Mrs. B. and myself, were obliged to sit upon the piazza of the Empire, comprising in our two persons, the entire female audience.

The scene was indeed striking. The green, garlanded hills girdling Rich Bar, looked wonderfully beautiful, rising with their grand, abrupt outlines into the radiant summer sky. A platform reared in front of the Empire, beneath the banner-tasseled pine, and arched with fragrant fir-boughs, made the prettiest possible rustic rostrum. The audience, grouped beneath the awnings of the different shops, dressed in their colored shirts,—though here and there, one might observe a dandy miner, who had relieved the usual vestment, by placing beneath it one of calico or white muslin—added much to the picturesqueness of the scene. Unfortunately, the Committee of Arrangements had not been able to procure a copy of the Declaration of Independence. Its place was supplied by an apologetic speech from a Mr. J., who will, without doubt, be the Democratic candidate for State Representative at the coming election. This gentleman finished his performance, by introducing Mr. B., the Orator of the Day, who is the Whig nominee for the abovementioned office. . . .

Mr. B. prounounced beautifully a very splendid Oration. Unlike such efforts in general, it was exceedingly fresh and new; so that instead of its being that infliction that Fourth of July Orations commonly are, it was a high pleasure to listen to him. Perhaps, where Nature herself is so original, it is impossible for even thought to be hackneyed. . . .

About half an hour after the close of the Oration, the ladies from the hill arrived. They made a pretty picture descending the steep, the one with her wealth of floating curls turbaned in a showy nubie, and her white dress set off by a crimson scarf; the other, with a little Pamella hat, placed coquettishly upon her brown, braided tresses, and a magnificent Chinese shawl enveloping her slender figure. So lately arrived from the States, with everything fresh and new, they quite extinguished poor Mrs. B. and myself, trying our best to look fashionable in our antique mode of four years ago.

The dinner was excellent. We had a real, live Captain, a very gentlemanly person, who had actually been in action during the Mexican War, for president. Many of the toasts were quite spicy and original; one of the new ladies sang three or four beautiful songs, and everything passed off at Rich Bar quite respectably. To be sure, there was a small fight in the bar-room—which is situated just below the dining-room—during which much speech and a little blood were spouted; whether the latter catastrophe was caused by a blow received, or the large talking of the victim, is not known. Two peacefully inclined citizens who, at the first battle-shout, had rushed manfully to the rescue, returned at the sub-siding of hostilities with blood-bespatered shirt-bosoms; at which fearful sight, the pretty wearer of the Pamella hat—one of the delinquents being her husband—chose to go faint, and would not finish her dinner, which, as we saw that her distress was real, somewhat marred our enjoyment. . . .

August 4, 1852

The Committee tried five or six Spaniards, who were proven to have been the ringleaders in the Sabbath-day riot. Two of them were sentenced to be whipped, the remainder to leave the Bar that evening; the property of all to be confiscated to the use of the wounded persons. Oh Mary! imagine my anguish when I heard the first blow fall upon those wretched men. I had never thought that I should be compelled to hear such fearful sounds, and, al-though I immediately buried my head in a shawl, nothing can efface from memory the disgust and horror of that moment. I had heard of such things, but heretofore had not realized, that in the nineteenth century, men could be beaten like dogs, much less that other men, not only could sentence such barbarism, but could actually stand by and see their own manhood degraded in such disgraceful manner. One of these unhappy persons was a very gentlemanly young Spaniard, who implored for death in the most moving terms. He appealed to his judges in the most eloquent manner—as gentlemen, as men of honor; representing to them that to be deprived of life, was nothing in comparison with the never-to-be-effaced stain of the vilest convict's punishment—to which they had sentenced him. Finding all his entreaties dis-regarded, he swore a most solemn oath, that he would murder every American that he should chance to meet alone, and as he is a man of the most dauntless courage, and rendered desperate by a burning sense of disgrace, which will cease only with his life, he will doubtless keep his word. . . .

September 4, 1852

There is nothing which impresses me more strangely than the fluming operations. The idea of a mighty river being taken up in a wooden trough, turned from the old channel, along which it has foamed for centuries, perhaps, its bed excavated many feet in depth, and itself restored to its old home in the fall, these things strike me as almost a blasphemy against Nature. And then the idea of men succeeding in such a work, here in the mountains, with machinery and tools of the poorest description, to say nothing of the unskillful workmen, doctors, lawyers, ministers, scholars, gentlemen, farmers, etc. . . .

When we arrived at—what may be called in reference to the Bar—the country seat of Don Juan, we were ushered into the parlor, two sides of which opened upon the garden, and the grand old mountains which rise behind it, while the other two sides and the roof were woven with fresh willow boughs, crisply green, and looking as if the dew had scarcely yet dried from the polished leaves.

After opening some cans of peaches, and cutting up some watermelons gathered from the garden, our friends went into, or rather *out* to the kitchen fire (two or three stones is generally the extent of this useful apartment in the mines), to assist in preparing the breakfast—and *such* a breakfast! If "Tadger could do it when it chose," so can we miners. We had—but what did we *not* have? There were oysters, which, I am sure, could not have been nicer had they just slid from their shells on the shore at Amboy; salmon, in color like the "red, red gold"; venison, with a fragrant, spicy gusto, as if it had been fed on cedar buds; beef cooked in the Spanish fashion—that is, strung on to a skewer, and roasted on the coals—than which, I never tasted better; preserved chicken, and almost every possible vegetable bringing up the rear. Then, for drinkables, we had tea, coffee and chocolate, champagne, claret and porter, with stronger spirits for the stronger spirits. . . . Our mountain pic-nic, with its attendant dandies, in their blue and red flannel shirts, was the most charming affair of the kind that I ever attended.

226

On our return, we called to see "Yank's" cub, which is fast rising into young grizzly-bear-hood. It is about the size of a calf, very good-natured, and quite tame. Its acquirements, as yet, are few, being limited to climbing a pole. Its education has not been conducted with that care and attention which so intelligent a beast merits, but it is soon, I hear, to be removed to the valley, and placed under teachers capable of developing its wonderful talents to the utmost. . . .

Last night, one of our neighbors had a dinner party. He came in to borrow a teaspoon. "Had you not better take them all?" I said. "Oh, no," was the answer, "that would be too much luxury. My guests are not used to it, and they would think that I am getting aristocratic, and putting on airs. One is enough; they can pass it round from one to the other."

Louise Amelia Knapp Smith Clappe,
"The Shirley Letters," The Pioneer (1854-1855).

In the Diggings

BY FRANK MARRYAT

Fresh from writing a travel book on Borneo, perhaps in emulation of his more famous father, Frank Marryat came to California intent on doing another such book. In the fashion of travel writers, he was at times more attentive to personal experiences than to the larger things that were going on, but his descriptions are lively.

A turn of the road presented a scene of mining life, as perfect in its details as it was novel in its features. Immediately beneath us the swift river glided tranquilly, though foaming still from the great battle which, a few yards higher up, it had fought with a mass of black obstructing rocks. On the banks was a village of canvas that the winter rains had bleached to perfection, and round it the miners were at work at every point. Many were waist-deep in the water, toiling in bands to construct a race and dam to turn the river's course; others were intrenched in holes, like grave-

DEVIL'S WASHBOWL, KINGS RIVER *by Stagner*

diggers, working down to the "bed rock." Some were on the brink of the stream washing out "prospects" from tin pans or wooden "batteas," and others worked in company with the long-tom, by means of water-sluices artfully conveyed from the river. Many were coyote-ing in subterranean holes, from which from time to time their heads popped out, like those of squirrels, to take a look at the world, and a few with drills, dissatisfied with nature's work, were preparing to remove large rocks with gunpowder. All was life, merriment, vigor, and determination, as this part of the earth was being turned inside out to see what it was made of.

Small patches of garden surrounded the village, which bore so palpably the stamp of cheerfulness and happy industry, that I was disappointed on learning that its name was "Murderer's Bar."

One would ask how it is that Murderer's Bar, despite its name, is a peaceable village, where each man's wealth, in the shape of ten feet square of soil, is virtuously respected by his neighbor; it is not because there is enough for all, for every paying claim has long ago been appropriated, and the next comer must go further on. There is a justice of the peace (up to his arms in the river just at present), and there is a constable (who has been "prospecting" a bag of earth from the hill, and been rewarded with a gold flake of the value of three cents); these two, one would suppose, could scarcely control two or three hundred men, with rude passions and quick tempers, each of whom, as you observe, carries his revolver even while at work. But these armed, rough-looking fellows themselves elected their judge and constable, and stand, ever ready, as "specials," to support them.

If a man wanted a pickax or a shovel, and thought to help himself to one of those that lie about at all times at Murderer's Bar, he would find it inconvenient if discovered; for, as there is no extenuating clause of hunger or misery in the diggings, theft is held to be a great crime; in all probability the offender would be whipped at the tree; and this brings us again to the perplexing subject of Lynch law as relating to the miners.

I venture to say that it will puzzle the theorist to determine how far the roving population of the mining regions in California have been justified in taking measures to eject the bad and worthless from among them; for all rules and precedents fall before the strong argument of self-preservation. When Christian and his shipmates landed at Pitcairn's Island and made laws for the regulation of their small colony (happily little needed), they acted as much upon the principle of Lynch law as did the miners; for these latter were equally without the reach of the laws under which they had been born. Where, after all, was the great difference in the first trial by jury and the Lynch execution among a colony of men living far from civilization? Was the peace of a community of honest men to be disturbed by crime and bloodshed, unpunished, when, from circumstances, the law of their country was unable to protect them? These and similar questions would form the basis of the argument in defense of Lynch law in the mountains.

On the other hand, the opponent would point to the fearful instances on record of men being hurried to eternity without preparation—victims to the over-wrought feelings of an excited mob. The defense of self-constituted law is untenable, yet there are instances in which small communities have seemed to me justified in enforcing, by the only means at their command, the order so necessary in such a state of society as that of the mountain gorges of California.

But when we see this law "subverting law" in a city like San Francisco, then we are forced sweepingly to condemn, once and for all, all that bears the name of Lynch, and we feel loth to admit that in any case the end can ever justify the means. Still it is a question, taken from first to last, that one may split straws on, when we see how peacefully Murderer's Bar progresses, not under the *execution*, but under the *fear* of Lynch law. In most mining villages public indignation has been confined to ordering men to "leave the camp" in twenty-four hours, or otherwise to take the consequences; and after being thus warned, the nefarious digger invariably "slopes."

The mining population have been allowed to constitute their own laws relative to the appointment of "claims," and it is astonishing how well this system works. Had the Legislature, in ignorance of the miner's wants, interfered and decided that a man should have so much, and no more, of the soil to work on, all would have been anarchy and confusion.

In the Diggings

I have had my claim in the digging more than once, of ten feet square; if a man "jumped" it, and encroached on my boundaries, and I didn't knock him on the head with a pickax, being a Christian, I appealed to the "crowd," and my claim being carefully measured from my stake, and found to be correct, the "jumper" would be ordered to confine himself to his own territory, which of course he would do with many oaths.

Frank Marryat, *Mountains and Molehills, or*
Recollections of a Burnt Journal (New York, 1855), 213-217.

Take Your Bible in One Hand

BY GEORGE R. STEWART

George R. Stewart is best known as a novelist with titles such as Storm; Fire; *and* Man. *He also is the historian of the Donner tragedy and of Highway 40 and the biographer of Francis Bret Harte, George F. (John Squibob) Derby, and, more lightly, of William Henry Thomes. The subject matter here treated is the spirit of New England and its export to California.*

One afternoon in November, 1848, a group of a dozen young men, of whom [William Henry] Thomes seems to have been one, met in a room on Exchange Street [in Boston] for discussion of plans. They came to what certainly seemed the reasonable conclusion "that gold-digging could be made a matter of science by the aid of wisdom and well-directed endeavors, and that a strong force could keep the wealth which would be unearthed better than a small one." This was the beginning of the *Boston and California Joint Stock Mining and Trading Company*. The plan was to enlist one hundred fifty members, who would make the voyage and work the mines in common. Each was to contribute $300. Thomes implies that he himself had difficulty in raising this stake. But he raised it, and so did plenty of others. The company, in fact, was soon filled to the limit, and recruits were turned away. Captain Henry Smith was chosen president. For $15,000 and a mortgage of equal amount the "good noble ship, *Edward Everett*," was purchased, and the $30,000 remaining in the treasury was sufficient to purchase equipment and food, everything, in fact, which might conceivably be needed by the company for a two-year period. The voyagers also purchased outfits on their own account, and generally succeeded in arming themselves to the teeth with revolvers, shotguns, and rifles.

Nor was good advice lacking. As Thomes wrote in a passage not unworthy of Mark Twain, they were looked upon as pioneers of civilization:

"Reverend Mr. Kirk of the Asburton-Place Orthodox Church, one Sunday evening delivered a special discourse before the company or such as chose to attend. He said we were going to a far-off country, where all were in ignorance and sin, and that we should take our Bibles in one hand, and our great New England civilization in the other and conquer all the wickedness that stood in our path or obstructed our course. We promised to follow his advice.

"Dr. Abbe . . . whose two sons were members of the company, gave to each of us a Bible. He told us when the good books were presented, that we were going to a strange wild and immoral country, and that we must take our Bibles in one hand, and our New England civilization in the other and implant our principles upon the soil. Honorable Edward Everett, then President of Harvard College, made us a present of one hundred volumes, and, in his letter conveying the gift, said:

" 'You are going to a strange country. Take the Bible in one hand and your New England civilization in the other, and make your mark upon the people and the country.'

"The United States Secretary of State . . . sent us charts and reports of the gold discoveries and told us that we must take our Bibles, guns, and our great New England civilization with us, and act as pioneers of Christianity. They sent for us at the State House and the Secretary of State solemnly gave us State passports (didn't charge anything for them, for a wonder) and said to each of us:

" 'You are going to a strange country, and will meet many desperate people. You must overcome them. Take your Bibles in one hand, and your great New England civilization in the other and always remember that you are Christians, and carry light into darkness.' "

Thus admonished, they went aboard on a January day, carrying their shotguns in one hand and their hopes of growing wealthy in the other. . . .

They reached the mines, and immediately found that gold-digging was the hardest work imaginable. You stood with your feet in ice-water while the blazing sun beat on your head. Many reported themselves sick, too sick to work. Some undoubtedly were. But how many were "soldiering"? The strong and conscientious found themselves burdened by the task of working for the support and profit of all who could not or would not work. Accordingly (after about two days of actual digging!) a meeting was called, and the company by formal vote disbanded.

Thomes remained at Benicia while the company's affairs were being settled. Ship and cargo were sold at a great loss. The little steamer, however, brought a good profit, being sold for $6000 at Sacramento, only to be snagged and sunk a short time later on the upper river. The company finally paid a dividend of $175, so that Thomes found no reason to regret his association with it; transportation to California had cost him only $125. He prepared to go to the mines. One day before leaving Benicia he went into a saloon, and saw lying on the bar a considerable number of volumes which the keeper of the grog-shop said he had taken in exchange for drinks at twenty-five or fifty cents apiece. Thomes did not need to look inside them; he knew them too well. They were the Bibles which the "civilizers" had been so often bidden to take in one hand.

George R. Stewart, *Take Your Bible in One Hand:*
The Life of William Henry Thomes
(San Francisco, The Colt Press, 1939), 30-32, 40-41.

The Scotch Bar Case

BY CHARLES HOWARD SHINN

Charles Howard Shinn's Mining Camps *originated as a thesis for the bachelor's degree at Johns Hopkins University. It was grounded on years of reporting and free lance writing in California, where Shinn, as a roving reporter for the San Francisco* Bulletin,

had opportunity to chat with veterans of the placer mining. This
is the source he indicates for the anecdote that follows.

Scotch Bar is rather indefinitely located by my informant as "in
the Siskiyou-Klamath region." It was a highly prosperous camp,
"booming" as the miners said; and the fame of its rich placers had
already extended to Trinity, Shasta, and Butte, attracting traders,
prospectors, and parasites of the camp. Exactly what local laws
and local officers the camp had, we do not know; but probably
much the same that were known to districts in the central part of
the State. It is likely that they had elected a justice of the peace,
allowing him to settle their disputes over boundaries and to keep
a record of their claims. At least, so it appears; the camp had been
peaceable, law-abiding, and contented; the miners had dwelt together in concord, much in the spirit of the Arcadian days of '48;
and it was "a royally good camp to live in."

Some time early in 1851, a discovery of some very "rich gravel,"
or mining ground, was made, and made in such a way, also, that
two equally strong parties of prospectors laid claim to it at the
same time. There were about a dozen men in each party, and both
groups were entirely honest in their belief of the justice of their
respective claims. Each clan at once began to increase its fighting
numbers by enlistments from the rest of the camp, till twenty or
thirty men were sworn to each hostile assembly. The ground in
dispute was so situated that it was best worked in partnership,
and thirty claims of the ordinary size allowed in the district would
occupy all the desirable territory of the new find. So there were
two rival companies ready to begin work, and no law whatever
to prevent a pitched battle.

It began to look more and more like fighting. Men were asked
to join, and bring their bowies, revolvers, and shotguns. Men were
even forced to refuse the honor, against their wills, because, for-
sooth, there were no more weapons left in camp. The two opposing
parties took up their stations on the banks of the gulch; there was
further and excited talk; at last there were eight or ten shots inter-
changed, fortunately injuring no one. But by this time the blood
of the combatants was fairly roused; the interests at stake were
very large; neither side proposed to yield: and the next minute

there probably would have been a hand-to-hand conflict, except for an unlooked-for interference.

The camp, the commonwealth, the community at large, had taken the field the very moment the first shot was fired. Dozens and hundreds of men, five minutes before mere spectators of the difficulty, at once compelled a parley, negotiated a truce, and urged a resort to legal methods. The moment this compromise was suggested, the combatants laid aside their weapons. They knew there was no legal authority within twenty miles, and not even in the camp itself any force able to keep them from fighting; for persuasion was the only argument used, and it is not supposable that the rest of the miners would have actually fought to prevent fighting. It was a victory of common sense, a triumph of the moral principles learned in boyhood in New England villages and on Western prairies. "Men more thoroughly fearless never faced opposing weapons"; but the demand for a fair and full trial in open court found an answer-chord in every bosom. Both parties willingly agreed to submit to arbitration; but not to the ordinary arbitration of the "miners' court," or of the "miners' committee," or of the "miner's alcalde," all of which we have heretofore described. They thought out a better plan, and adopted it after a few moments' discussion.

The rude and often biassed jury of the camp was repudiated by both contestants alike. None of the ordinary forms of tribunal known to the mining region seemed to them entirely adequate to this momentous occasion. They chose a committee, and sent it to San Francisco. There they had three or four of the best lawyers to be found, engaged for each party; and they also engaged a judge of much experience in mining cases. It was a great day at Scotch Bar when all this legal talent arrived to decide the ownership of the most valuable group of claims on the river—claims that had been lying absolutely idle, untouched by any one, guarded by camp opinion and by the sacred pledges of honor, ever since the day of the compact between the rival companies.

Well, the case was tried with all possible formality, and as legally as if it had occurred within the civil jurisdiction of a district court. It is not reported in any of the California law-books; but no mining case ever commanded better talent or elicited more exhaustive and brilliant arguments. The lawyers and judge were there to settle the case; the entire camp wanted it settled; both parties to the dispute were anxious to find out who the real owners were. In order to show the childlike sense of fairness the miners had, we should mention that before the trial began it was arranged by mutual consent that the winners should pay costs. To the losers, it was sufficient to have failed to prove title to such rich claims: they must not be made still poorer.

Now, in ordinary cases of camp rule there is often too much compromise: one claimant gets less than he deserves, while the other gets more. But in this justly famous Scotch Bar case there was in the end a verdict squarely for one side and squarely against the other. The defeated party took it placidly, without a murmur; nor then, nor at any other time, were they ever heard to complain. The cheerfulness of their acceptance of the verdict was not the least gratifying episode of the famous trial.

"Ah! it was a great case," writes our informant, after an interview with Mr. Roman. "The whole camp was excited over it for days and weeks. At last, when the case was decided, the claim was opened by the successful party; and when they reached bed-rock, and were ready to 'clean up,' we all knocked off work, and came down and stood on the banks, till the ravine on both sides was lined with men. And I saw them take out gold with iron spoons, and fill pans with solid gold, thousands upon thousands of dollars. Ah! it was a famous claim, worth hundreds of thousands of dollars."

On the bank, along with these hundreds of spectators, stood the defeated contestants, cheerful and even smiling: it was not their gold, any more than if it had been in Africa. And the successful miners brought their gold out on the bank, divided it up among themselves—so many pounds apiece—and each went to his tent to thrust the treasure under his blankets till a good opportunity arrived for sending it to San Francisco.

The community capable of that Scotch Bar case was a community which could be trusted to the uttermost. Put it down on a desert island, and it would organize a government, pick out its best men, punish its criminals, protect its higher interests, develop local institutions; and soon, unless its natural surroundings forbade, there would be a healthy, compact, energetic state, with capital city, seaports, commerce, navy, and army. Put it down on a new continent, and it would eventually possess, control, and develop all its resources and energies; doing the work that Rome did for Italy, that the Puritans did for New England, and through New England for the United States. And if the evidence of travellers, of the pioneers themselves, and of the institutions they organized can be trusted, there were many such camps in California. The Siskiyou region did not monopolize that habit of self-control, of acceptance of the situation, of submitting questions to the best obtainable courts, and of abiding by their decisions. From Klamath to Colusa, from Siskiyou to Fresno, from Lake Bowman to Trinity Peak, manhood and honesty ruled the camps of the miners. Some were ruled better than others, but all were ruled well.

Charles Howard Shinn, *Mining Camps: A Study in American Frontier Government* (New York, 1885), 219-224.

The Lucky Louse, or, Blood Will Tell

BY G. EZRA DANE

G. Ezra Dane was a leading spirit in the reorganization of the ancient and honorable order of E Clampus Vitus. In the same spirit he assembled an anthology of folktales of the mines, some of them based on authenticated episodes, but all appropriated to one camp, Columbia.

It was one day in the rainy winter of '54 and '55, and too wet to work in the mines, so the boys begun to wander in early down at the Long Tom. By noon all the tables was full and the gambling got more exciting as the day wore on. Some of the boys set right there at the tables from morning through all the day and on into the evening, without stopping except to take on a drink or to make room for more.

If you once get the gambling fever, you know, in a place like that, the longer you keep at it, the higher the fever gets. That fever's catching and it'll spread through a crowd like any other fever. So monte, faro, seven-up, and the different brands of poker got too slow for some, and they begun laying bets on any chance that offered. At some of the tables they was betting on the turn of a card, and they was one crowd having a spitting tournament at the stove. Then they was some fellows betting which of two flies on the wall would move first, and others at the door laying bets whether or not the next man to come in would be Irish. But the greatest bet in betting history was laid that night by young Ad Pence. An inspiration it was, no less.

"Boys," says Ad, pounding on the bar to get the attention of the crowd, "Boys," says he, "luck's been agin me so far, but I've got five hundred here that says I've a louse that can beat, in a fair race, any louse that ever cut his teeth on any miner's hide."

He'd caught a good lively one and held him up for all the boys to see.

"I say this louse is the champeen," says Ad, "for I've been chasing him around my carcass for a week and I've only just caught up with him. Five hundred backs him against all comers."

Well, at that all the games stopped short, and everybody crowded up to the bar where Ad was showing off this champeen louse. But none of the boys would admit that he kept this kind of stock and it begun to look as though nobody was going to take the bet. Then a stranger, a big Irishman with a red beard, come elbowing his way through the crowd and up to the bar where Ad was standing.

"Will ye let me have a look at that louse?" he says.

So Ad held it out and the stranger squinted at it from one side and then from the other. "A dainty crayther indade he is," says he, "but I think he's no racer. His belly's too low and his legs are too short by a long ways. Now wait just a bit and I'll have something to show ye."

So the stranger put his hand inside his shirt, and scrabbled around in there for a minute, and when he pulled it out again, between his thumb and finger he held a struggling louse.

"Me boy," he says, "your five hundred is as good as gone. But before I take it from ye, I want to have a good look at *this* louse. Ye'll never see the likes of him again. Ye say yours is the champeen, but ye've only had him a wake, and he has not so much as a name. I say he's but a mongrel. Now *this* one is the greatest racing louse

238

in all the world, and he has the most distinguished pedigray that ever a louse did boast. And I don't want to be taking your money under any false pretenses, so I'm going to tell ye his history, and when ye've heard it, if ye want to withdraw, I'll freely let ye do so.

"Just before me old grandfather died, back in Ireland, he called me to his bedside and he said to me: 'Grandson', says he, 'I'm a pore man. I've no money to lave ye, nor any property. But there's wan threasure I have, Grandson', says the old man, 'Katie, the finest little seam squirrel in all of Ireland, and a direct discindent of one that fed on Saint Patrick.

" 'Take her, Grandson', says he, 'kape good care of her and fade her well, and she'll surely bring ye luck'.

"Now, me boy, this louse ye see here is Larry, Katie's great-great-great-grandson, and the blood of Saint Patrick himself runs in his veins, so he's bound to bring me luck. And to show the faith I have in him and in Holy Saint Patrick, bejayziz, I'll lay a thousand to that five hundred ye bet on yer mongrel louse! Now, do ye still want to make the bet?"

"I do", says Ad. "Your louse may be good, but I know what mine can do from long chasing of him, and my bet on him still stands."

So Ad and the stranger placed their stakes with Doc Johns, and side betting begun in the crowd.

"There can be no race without a racetrack", says the stranger, and he calls to the bar-tender. "Bring us a plate", he says. "Now, boys, the middle's the start, the edge is the goal, and the first little pants rabbit over the rim is the winner."

So the bar-tender brought the plate, and the stranger felt of it. "No louse", says he, "would ever set a good pace on this cold plate. Let's hate it up a bit, and then you'll see them kick up their heels and run."

So they heated the plate piping hot over the stove and set it on a table where all could see. And when Doc Johns counted off: "One, two, three, go!" each man dropped his louse in the middle of the plate and they were off, a-scrambling and a-jumping because it was so hot, you know. The boys was cheering and yelling and standing on chairs to see, and laying bets right and left.

Well, neck and neck it was at the start acrost the bottom of the plate, but Ad's louse pulled ahead a bit and he was the first to reach the rise of the rim. Then come the last hard pull for the edge. He started up the rise, but when he got about half-way up he lost his footing on the slippery rim and slid down again. So he backed up and he took another run for it, and got up a little further, but again he slid back. He was a game one, that louse was. He tried it again and again, but he couldn't quite make it. No sir, it was on that last hard pull up the rim of the plate that the blood of Saint Patrick begun to tell, for Larry, the stranger's lucky louse, he started up slow and careful, and he kept on a-pulling and a-scrambling and up and up he went and *over* the edge to victory and into his master's hand. A hero he was, for sure!

The fellows jumped down from the tables then and Jack White, he says: "Three cheers for Larry and the blood of Saint Patrick!" So the boys roared out the three cheers. And they *was* cheers too, for them young fellows didn't have no colds, nor consumption neither.

Well, then Doc Johns paid over the fifteen hundred dollars to the stranger, and Ad went up to shake his hand. "Stranger," he says, "it was a fair race, and the best louse won. The money's yours and I don't begrudge it to you. But I've one request to make of you, stranger, and if you'll grant it, I'll be forever grateful."

"And what may that be?" says the stranger.

"Just let me borrow Larry till tomorrow," says Ad.

"But what for?" says the stranger. "Why might ye be wanting to borry me pet?"

"Why man!" says Ad, "I want to improve my breed!"

G. Ezra Dane, *Ghost Town* (New York, Alfred A. Knopf, 1941), 13-18.

The Mines in Retrospect

BY RODMAN W. PAUL

Rodman W. Paul's California Gold *is a well documented balance sheet on the economics of gold mining from 1848 to 1873.*

When the second number of the *Overland Monthly* appeared on the San Francisco newsstands in August, 1868, it included among its offerings a story entitled "The Luck of Roaring Camp," by "F. B. Harte." Within the space of a half dozen double columned pages this little sketch told a sentimental yet vivid tale of the birth, brief life, and tragic death of a baby whose mother was a prostitute.

So frank a reference to a forbidden topic might perhaps have earned for the romance a momentry burst of attention in that era of literary circumlocutions, but it could hardly have given the story the nation-wide popularity that it so quickly won. What distinguished "The Luck of Roaring Camp" from other fictional writings of its time was the setting in which it was laid. The scene was a raw California mining camp of 1850. The actors were rough, bearded miners. The dialogue was picturesquely indecorous.

This was not Bret Harte's first venture into what critics now call "local color." As far back as 1860 he had tried his hand at tales that had a California mining camp for their setting. Not satisfied with the results, he abandoned the field for eight years.

His literary colleague in San Francisco, Mark Twain, followed much the same course. In 1865 Twain published a humorous anecdote called "The Notorious Jumping Frog of Calaveras County," based upon an incident supposed to have taken place at a camp in the Southern Mines of California. Despite the applause with which this was greeted, Twain did not for the moment attempt any further exploitation of this promising vein.

It was not until the close of the sixties and the opening of the seventies that Harte, Mark Twain, the poet Joaquin Miller, and several lesser writers awoke to a recognition of the literary treasure that lay at their feet. Harte's "The Luck of Roaring Camp" was the first indication that there was a new western awareness of the possibilities of the western mining scene. "The Luck of Roaring Camp" was soon followed by a succession of similar mining-camp tales and poems by Harte, by Mark Twain's *Roughing It*, an amusing description of life on the Comstock Lode and in California, and by *Songs of the Sierras*, a slim volume in which Miller sang of

> The valor of these men of old—
> The mighty men of 'Forty-nine.

The use of the colorful aspects of mining life for the purposes of fiction and poetry was thus postponed until after the mineral regions themselves had passed out of their period of picturesque boisterousness and into the later, more mature era when comparatively peaceful conditions prevailed. Apparently it was only after the flush days in the gold camps had changed from reality into folk history that they could take on the rosy glow of sheer romance. Apparently it was only when one could look back from a safe distance that the hardships and disappointments of life in the mines could be forgotten, that the all-important struggle to improve the techniques of the industry could be thrust aside in favor of the purely dramatic. Only then could one find readers for tales of miners who lived an attractively bizarre existence, and who drank, gambled, swore, and joked a great deal, but rarely mined.

It is not hard to understand why a writer, whose purpose is to entertain, sometimes selects and exaggerates in so unbalanced a fashion, but neither is it difficult to perceive that the narratives which result from such treatment are far from giving an accurate representation of the life they claim to portray. In so far as the changing fortunes of the miner are concerned, one could come nearer the truth by reading quite a different literary effort of the period, Henry George's *Progress and Poverty*, a book which has the somber theme of increasing want amidst increasing wealth. Or, for a picture of a special type of miner, one could read Prentice Mulford's reminiscent sketches, which tell much about the stubborn individualists who sought to continue their independent existence in the Southern Mines long after that way of life had ceased to be economically justifiable. Books such as these contrast sharply with the fictional and near-fictional accounts, especially those by Bret Harte's imitators, but because the former are few, while the writings that stress "color" are many, a thick haze of romantic legend and mythology has settled over the California mining scene. This must be cleared away if one is to understand the significance of the quarter-century that began in 1848.

Within that span of twenty-five years, California mining passed successively through a short period of flush times, during which the rudiments of the trade were learned, then through a longer interval of transition, while the adjustment was being made to better methods of exploitation, and, finally, after the discovery of the Comstock Lode, through an era which was simultaneously a time of colonization beyond California's borders and of mature progress within the state itself.

By 1873 the trends that characterized this last epoch had been carried to a point of full development, and conditions had appeared which were in the sharpest contrast to those that had obtained in 1848, 1849, and 1850. In place of the pan, rocker, pick, and shovel, the miner now had sluices a thousand feet long, dynamite, the diamond drill, and a hydraulic instrument so powerful that no one knew its limits. The miner could now destroy mountains, where once he had struggled to dig away hillocks.

In place of the crude wooden stamp mill and the slow, mule-powered arrastre, he had now the efficient "California stamp mill" and its auxiliary, the steam-driven arrastre. Instead of wasting the greater part of his quartz-gold, the miner now used the chlorination process and the several mechanical devices that increased the proportion of gold saved. If he needed expert guidance for his operations, the miner of the later day could turn to the new state university, where the business of extracting minerals from the earth had been officially recognized as a science.

Where once the system of law and property ownership had been dependent solely upon the coöperation of one's neighbors, now it was founded upon the statutes of the United States and was enforceable in the courts of the state and federal governments. In the camps where Sunday had been a saturnalia and ladies as few as ministers, the miner could now find a reasonable degree of peacefulness and a goodly number of families, churches, and other evidences of normal life. If he were oppressed by his employers, the miner could, in the quartz industry at least, have some hope of the organized support of his fellow workers.

To be sure, there had been much loss along with the gains. Towns and districts had boomed noisily into prominence and then had disappeared as completely as dew before the morning sun. Whole counties had fallen into decline and were not likely to recover. And yet, if much of the mineral region was destined for oblivion, nevertheless its hectic life had not been useless. Vast states and territories in the West beyond the Great Plains had been pioneered by men who had learned their lessons in the old California camps, while within California itself the demands of the mining population had built up one of the nation's great cities —San Francisco—and had encouraged the development of an agriculture that by 1873 was making its influence felt in the wheat and wool markets of both Old World and New. Further still, the rise of population centers in California and the other mining commonwealths had been one of the several factors that inspired the railroad boom which in 1869 joined the Atlantic to the Pacific, and which soon afterwards opened the way to the full exploitation of the West by all forms of American enterprise.

Both in its direct and indirect results, then, the evolution of California mining was a phenomenon that had both intrinsic importance and significance in the broader field of American development. But when assigning to it a place of consequence in the nation's past, it is well to remember that this was an experience in which the whole world shared. The Gold Rush which inaugurated the mining era was in every sense an international movement that brought to California the ideas, methods, and men without which the gold deposits of the Sierras would have long remained little more than a local curiosity.

Nor did the contributions from outside the United States cease with the ending of the great migration. Cornishmen, Austrians, Italians, and Irish came in increasing numbers to work in the quartz mines, the Chinese labored wherever the lords of the land would permit, and in the quicksilver mines and the Southern Mines the Latin Americans were for many years an important element. Similarly, just as the stamp mill and arrastre of the early period were copied from Europe and Latin America, partly through the agency of the Georgia and Carolina gold regions, so in the later day the diamond drill was borrowed from France and the formula for dynamite from Sweden.

If, therefore, modern California and much of the West beyond the Great Plains owe their foundations to the mining boom which began in 1848, then they are decisively the product of the joint efforts of men from many lands. Thereby they become not less

"American" but more so, for throughout her history the United States has been a country in which the course of development has not been confined to a narrow path cut by the descendants of a single racial stock, but rather has been routed over a broad thoroughfare dug by the hands of men and women of diverse origins. In California at least a dozen nationalities and half that number of racial strains made major contributions to the progress of mining, and the great state which flourishes today upon America's western border stands as a lasting monument to the effectiveness of their joint labors.

Rodman W. Paul, *California Gold*
(Cambridge, Harvard University Press, 1947), 334-341.

6

THE YOUNG STATE

ONE OF THE passing consequences of the gold rush was that the prospectors took over a large area that up to that time had been in undisturbed Indian possession. The Indians sometimes resisted; casual violence resulted and at times expanded into campaigns by posse or volunteer troops. L. H. Bunnell of the Mariposa Battalion tells of the military aspects of one such campaign, mentions the treaty-reservation system that was in the background, and has much to say about the Indians and the interior discovered by these explorers.

The era produced other culture conflicts. In Los Angeles society, as Horace Bell reports, the friction was between the oldtimers (American and Spanish) and the uncouth newcomers. Often the conflict was racist, with the Spanish Americans as the particular target. That is said to be what drove Joaquin Murieta to outlawry. Significantly he found his chief literary champion in a Cherokee American, John R. Ridge, otherwise known as Yellow Bird.

The contributions by Lt. George Derby and editor Ferdinand C. Ewer depict the state of journalism, politics, and civic pride in the early fifties. Men were conscious that California for all its wealth had the rawness of a frontier and they looked particularly to transportation improvements to advance it to a more civilized status. Waterman L. Ormsby, the one through passenger on the first running of the Butterfield Overland Mail, writes of one much acclaimed improvement. Mark Twain's tribute is to another that was more spectacular but more evanescent. Richard Henry Dana's "Twenty-four Years After" has a double purpose here. It deals with maritime transportation, coastal and intercoastal, and for

246

JEFFREY PINE, SENTINEL DOME *by Nancy May*

the first American decades that of course was nine tenths of the story. Against the yardstick of the old days of the hide trade Dana also measures the vast change that had occurred in San Francisco and the smaller but noteworthy changes down the coast.

For the southern part of the state one of the more striking descriptions is to be found in the journal of William H. Brewer of the Geological Survey. He comments on the climate, scenery, economy, and general lawlessness. He combined picnicking, botanizing, touring the mission remains at Santa Barbara, and practicing with his revolvers the better to survive the venture into this sparsely settled land where a murder a week was the boasted average.

Prentice Mulford and Francis Bret Harte are illustrative that the literary mode of this epoch permitted a good deal of license. At a point not always precisely defined this lapsed over into the tall tale, a vogue that persisted sturdily, as witness the Freeman-Barker-Bynum colloquy.

Historical research as applied to this epoch pretty well corroborates the informal and off-the-cuff descriptions by travelers and literary people. William B. Rice's paragraphs on crime and punishment are out of a study of the beginnings of journalism in southern California and the way in which the Los Angeles *Star* mirrored the scene. Raymond A. Rydell writes of what was, at least architecturally, the noblest chapter in American maritime history. Jerry MacMullen's interest runs to the navigation of the inland waterways, but he manages to work in choice data on the foibles of the people of that day, just a short time removed from California pastoral.

Discovery of the Yosemite

BY L. H. BUNNELL

Although Yosemite was first sighted by Joseph Reddeford Walker and his men in 1833, effective discovery had to wait until 1851. In that year the Mariposa Battalion stumbled on the valley while seeking to capture Chief Tenieya and several hundred Yosemites and Chowchillas. Fortunately the battalion included L. H. Bunnell, a New Yorker by birth who started to write a short article on his Yosemite adventures. The article grew into a book, which won an immediate audience and did much to popularize the natural beauties of the area.

During the winter of '49-50 while ascending the old Bear Valley trail from Ridley's Ferry on the Merced River, my attention was attracted to the stupendous rocky peaks of the Sierra Nevadas. In the distance an immense cliff loomed, apparently to the summit of the mountains. Although familiar with nature in her wildest moods, I looked upon this awe-inspiring column with wonder and admiration, and turned from it with reluctance to resume the search for gold; yet the impressions of that scene were indelibly fixed in my memory. On a second visit to Ridley's, not long after, the towering mountain was invisible, an intervening haze obscuring the scenery of that locality, but few of the miners had noticed any of its special peculiarities. A year or more passed before the mysteries of the land were satisfactorily solved.

During 1850 the Indians in the Mariposa district became very troublesome to the miners and settlers. Their depredations and numerous assaults were continued until the arrival of the U.S. Indian Commissioners, in 1851, when the general government assumed control over them. Through the agency of the commissioners treaties were made and many of the Indians were transferred to locations reserved for their special occupancy.

It was in the early days of the operations of this commission that the Yosemite Valley was first entered by a command employed to perform the special police duty of capturing and bringing the Indians before the representatives of the Government so that treaties might be made with them. These wards of the Government were then provided with supplies at the expense of the public treasury provided they confined themselves to the reservations. . . .

After supper, guards stationed, and the camp fires plentifully provided for, we gathered around the burning logs of oak and pine. The hearty supper and cheerful blaze created a general good feeling. After the jollity of the camp had somewhat subsided the valley became the topic of conversation around the camp fire.

None of us at that time surmised the vastness of those cliffs, although before dark we had seen El Capitan looking down upon our camp, and spray from the Bridal Veil was being wafted about us in the breeze.

I suggested that the valley should have an appropriate name. Different names were proposed but none were satisfactory to a majority about the circle. Some romantic and foreign names were offered and a large number canonical and scriptural, from which I inferred that I was not the only one in whom religious emotions or thoughts had been aroused by the mysterious power of the surrounding scenery.

I did not like any of the names proposed and suggested that it would be better to give the valley an Indian name than to import a strange and inexpressive one; and that the name of the tribe who had occupied it would be more appropriate than any which I had heard suggested. I then proposed that we give the valley the name of Yosemite, that by so doing the name of the tribe of Indians which we met leaving their homes in the valley, perhaps never to return, would be perpetuated.

I was interrupted by Mr. Tunnehill with: "Devil take the Indians and their names! Why should we honor these vagabond murderers by perpetuating their name?"

"Damn the Indians and their names," said another. "Let's call this Paradise Valley."

Before an opportunity was given for any others to object to the name, John O'Neil, a rollicking Texan, vociferously announced: "Hear ye! Hear ye! A vote will now be taken to decide what name shall be given to this valley." A *viva voce* vote was taken and the name of Yosemite was almost unanimously adopted. The name that was there and thus adopted by us, while seated around our camp fire, on the first visit of a white man to this remarkable locality, is the name by which it is now known to the world. At the time its signification—grizzly bear—was not generally known to our battalion. Neither was it pronounced with uniformity. Savage, who could speak the dialects of most of the mountain tribes in this part of California, told us that the correct pronunciation was Yo-sem-i-ty and that it signified a full grown grizzly; and that the name was given to old Tenieya's band because of their lawless and predatory character.

The date of our discovery and entrance into the Yosemite Valley was about the 21st of March, 1851. We were afterwards assured by Tenieya and others of his band that this was the first visit ever made to this valley by white men. Tenieya said that a small party of white men once crossed the mountains on the north side, but were so guided as not to see it. . . .

After an early breakfast on the morning following our entrance into the Yosemite we equipped ourselves for duty, and as the word was passed to "fall in," we mounted and filed down the trail to the lower ford, ready to commence our explorations. The water in the Merced had fallen somewhat during the night but the stream was still in appearance a raging torrent. The ford was found to be rocky but we passed over it without difficulty although several repeated their morning ablutions while stumbling over the boulders.

Soon after crossing the ford smoke was seen to be rising from a cluster of manzanita shrubs, commanding a view of the trail. The smoking brands indicated that it had been a picket fire and we now felt assured that our presence was known and our movements watched by the vigilant Indians we were hoping to find. Moving rapidly we discovered near the base of El Capitan a large collection of Indian huts and from the condition of things it was evident that the occupants had but recently left and that some of the wigwams had been occupied during the night. Not far from the camp upon posts, rocks and in trees was a large "cache" of acorns and other provisions.

As we moved on smoke was again seen in the distance. The trail brought us again to the ford and crossing and recrossing we pursued our course. The river had again become swollen from melting snow but by this time our horses and ourselves had become used to the icy waters, and when at times our animals lost their footing at the fords they were not at all alarmed but vigorously swam to shore.

Abundant evidence was again found that the huts had been but just deserted. A rigid search was made but no Indians were found.

Scouting parties were sent out and beneath a huge rock near the base of the North Dome I was for a moment startled by the movement of a living object. Involuntarily my rifle was brought to bear upon it when I discovered it to be a female, an extremely old squaw with a countenance that could only be likened to a vivified Egyptian mummy. She was huddled over a nearly exhausted fire, which I replenished for her but she neither spoke nor exhibited any curiosity as to my presence. Savage soon came up but he could elicit nothing from her. Subsequently when Tenieya was interrogated as to her age he replied: "No one knows her age. When I was a boy, it was a favorite tradition of the old members of the tribe that when she was a child the peaks of the Sierras were little hills."

We left her and passed on. Scouting parties reported a small *rancheria* above Cathedral Rocks, its huts unoccupied, and other detachments found huts in groups but no Indians. At all these localities the stores of wood were abundant. . . .

An expedition was now urged by Savage against the Chowchillas which succeeded in bringing most of the Indians along the San Joaquin headwaters, but Tenieya and his tribe still remained under cover. Our preparations made, under Capt. Boling, we started for the Merced in search of the Yosemites. It was our design to surprise the Indians, if possible, and if not, to cut off the escape of their women and children, the capture of whom would soon bring the warriors to terms. With this plan in view we made a rapid march direct for their valley, now crossing the streams without much difficulty and without accident.

The advance detachment quietly entered the valley but no Indians were seen. A few wigwams had been built on the south side near the lower ford. Without halting for more than a glance at these vacant huts the detachment rode rapidly on following a trail up the south side. On seeing the deserted wigwams, I reached the conclusion that our approach had been heralded. As we rode on up the valley I became more observant of the scenery than watchful for signs when suddenly my attention was attracted by shadowy objects flitting past rocks and trees on the north side, some distance above El Capitan. Halting, I caught a glimpse of Indians as they passed an open space opposite us. Seeing that they

were discovered they made no further efforts to hide their movements but came out into open view, at long rifle range. There were
five of them. They saluted us with taunting gestures and fearlessly
kept pace with us as we resumed our march. The river was here
a roaring impassable torrent and the warriors looked with great indifference on our repeated efforts to find a fording place.

As we approached a stretch of comparatively quiet water I announced my intention of swimming the stream to capture the
Indians. With Firebaugh, Stone and four others, I started for a
sloping bank where our animals would least unwillingly enter
the stream; but Stone spurred past me and, when Firebaugh's
mustang refused the water and all the mules refused to leave the
horse, Stone backed his mule over the bank and we swam our
mules after the boy leader across the Merced. Alarmed, the Indians sped up the valley at the top of their speed and we followed
at our best gait until we found the trail obstructed. Without hesitation we abandoned our mules and continued the pursuit on
foot up to the rocky spur known as the Three Brothers, where they
disappeared. Find them we could not, and with utmost reluctance
we reentered the cold water and swam our mules back to the south
side. Luckily, Firebaugh, having failed to get his mustang to follow us, had run up on the south side and had seen where the Indians had hidden behind a ledge of rocks. Our Indian scouts were
now sent across to hunt out the hidden Indians, and by means of
fair promises, if they would come down voluntarily, the five Indians were brought in. Three of them were known to us, being
sons of Tenieya. From the strange coincidence of the three brothers
being taken captive near the rocky peaks, we designated the peaks
"The Three Brothers."

Tenieya's sons said that the old sachem would come in and have
a talk with the white chief when he knew that they had been
captured, and were most anxious to be permitted to go after him.
The captain at length decided to send one of Tenieya's sons and
another of the captives along with me, to find Tenieya, holding the
other three as hostages. Arming myself, I started alone with the
two prisoners, keeping them ahead of me on the trail as I always
did when traveling with any of that race. We passed along the
westerly base of the North Dome at a rapid pace when suddenly

the Indians sprang back in great fright and jumped behind me. I stepped forward to see what so alarmed them and looked into the leveled rifle of one of our men. Behind him was Sergeant Cameron with an injured man on his shoulders. With extreme difficulty I succeeded in preventing our scouts from shooting the Indians while I examined the injured man. The party, it appeared, had run into an ambush and narrowly escaped being killed by rocks hurled down upon them by Indians hiding above. Although no bones were broken, Spencer was cruelly bruised and prostrated by the shock induced by his injuries.

Our camp was undisturbed that night, although doubtless we were watched from the adjacent cliffs. The prisoners silently occupied places by the camp fire, probably expecting their lives might be forfeit, for they could see little sympathy in the countenances about them. The energetic remarks of the men caused the captain to have a special guard detailed from those who were not supposed to be prejudiced against the Indians, as it was deemed all-important to the success of the campaign that Tenieya should be conciliated or captured; therefore, the detail was as much for the protection of the hostages as to prevent their escape.

In the morning our Indian guide brought word from Tenieya that the old chief refused to consider any plan which would involve leaving the valley, and our scouts were sent out with instructions to bring him in, alive if possible. Knowing where Tenieya had talked with the messenger, scouting parties started out and cutting off his retreat on all sides, brought him in, unharmed. The first sight which greeted him as he entered the camp was the dead body of his favorite son, shot while attempting to escape. At the sight he halted without visible emotion, except a slight quivering of the lips. As he raised his head, his feelings were exhibited in the glaring expression of deadly hatred with which he gazed at Capt. Boling and cast his eyes over the camp as though in search of his other sons. Boling expressed his regret and had the circumstances explained to him, but not a word did Tenieya utter. Passively he accompanied us to our camp on the south side of the valley. The boy's body was left where he had fallen, and permission was given for the Indians to take it away for burial; and during the following night, unobserved by us, the body disappeared.

For days Tenieya rebuffed all attempts to talk to him. Finding that nothing could be accomplished through the old chief, the captain gave orders to recommence our search for his people. Scouts were sent out who explored all the ravines of the valley but without finding any trace of the Yosemites, so Capt. Boling sent back for a pack train with supplies and we started over the high Sierras, Tenieya firmly tied with a rope whose other end I held. Over trails, seemingly impossible for a man to follow, from which some of our party turned back, we climbed out of the valley to the north. Savage had despatched a new Indian guide to us, Cowchitty, a traditional enemy of the Yosemites; and partly by following his counsel and partly by doing the opposite of what Tenieya wished at critical moments, we at length wound around a mountain spur and saw opposite a dim circle of blue smoke. Old Tenieya was standing in front of me, but he exhibited no interest in the discovery.

Resting in fancied security, upon the border of a most beautiful little lake, to which I later gave the name of Tenieya, the village was seemingly not more than half a mile away. As the captain was studying the location and planning how to capture the village, our scouts were discovered in full chase of an Indian picket who was running toward the village as though his life depended upon his efforts. In the excitement of the moment Capt. Boling ordered us to double quick and charge, thinking that the huts were not more than half a mile away. Such a mistake could originate only in the transparent air of the mountains. The village was fully two miles or more away; we did, however, double quick, and I kept a gait that soon carried Tenieya and myself ahead of our scattered column. Finding the rope with which I held Tenieya an encumbrance in our rapid march, I wound it around his shoulder and kept him in front of me. While passing a steep slope of overlapping granite rock, the old chief made a sudden spring to the right and attempted to escape down the ragged precipice. His age was against him for I caught him just as he was about to let himself drop from the projecting ledge to the ground below; angered at the trick of the old fellow in attempting to relieve himself of my custody, I resumed our advance at a gait that hurried the old sachem forward less carefully than comported with his years and dignity.

The Yosemites discovered our approach too late for either concerted resistance or successful escape, for Lieutenant Crawford at the head of a portion of the command, dashed at once into the center of the encampment and the terror-stricken Indians threw up their bare hands in token of submission and piteously cried out "Peace! Peace!" No show of resistance was offered us, neither did any escape. After he had counted the prisoners and corralled them with a guard, Capt. Boling told me to send Tenieya over among the women who were grouped a little aside, as he was now about as harmless. I acted upon the suggestion and upon being told that he had the liberty of the camp provided he made no further attempts to escape, the old fellow stepped off briskly to meet his four squaws who seemed as pleased as himself at the reunion.

Finding themselves completely surprised, notwithstanding their extreme vigilance, and comparing the well-kept appearance of their old chief with their own worn out dilapidated condition, the Indians expressed a willingness to live in the future at peace with the Americans. All hopes of avoiding a treaty or of preventing their transfer to the reservation appeared to be at once abandoned. "Where can we now go that the Americans will not follow us?" asked the young chief in charge of that particular band. "Where can we make our homes that you will not find us?"

Before dawn, unable to sleep because of the penetrating cold, Boling aroused the camp and began preparations for the start to the valley. After a hasty breakfast the word was passed to assemble, when all at once there was turmoil and strife in the camp and what sounded to me very much like a Chinese concert. Boling had ordered the Indians to carry the packs—burdens they had imposed upon the squaws—and the order brought down upon him the vituperations of the squaws and sullen murmurs of the noble red men. The real object was to facilitate our return to the valley by making it easy for the squaws and children to accompany us without delays. One interesting feature in the arrangement was that long after the braves had been silenced their squaws continued to murmur at the indignity practised on their disgraced lords.

As we climbed the mountains I looked back on the lovely little lake from which we were leading the last remnant of the once dreaded Yosemites to a territory from which it was designed they should never return as a people. I waited for Tenieya to come up and told him that we had given his name to the lake and the river. At first he seemed unable to comprehend our purpose, repeating: "It already has a name." Upon telling him that we had named it Tenieya because it was upon the shores of the lake that we had found his people, who would never return to it to live, his countenance fell, and he at once left us and rejoined his own family circle. His expression as he left us indicated that he thought the naming of the lake no equivalent for the loss of the territory.

L. H. Bunnell, *The Discovery of the Yosemite*
and the Indian War of 1851
(Chicago, 1880) 272-273, 283-286, 291-296.

The Washington Birthday Ball

BY HORACE BELL

Horace Bell's Reminiscences of a Ranger, *the first hard-cover history published in Los Angeles, initiated the trend of tongue-in-cheek writing about the City of the Angels. Arriving on the scene in 1852, Bell had abundant opportunity to observe. As a journalist, editor of the* Porcupine, *he also had experience in the gentle art of hyperbole. Most of his anecdotes had some basis in fact—perhaps every one of them did—but he let them grow in the telling.*

Soon after my arrival in Los Angeles it was my good fortune to attend a first-class ball at the house of Don José Antonio Carrillo, a first-class citizen, who had been honored with a seat in the Sovereign Congress of Mexico. He had also been the military head of the country, and was at the head of native California *ton*.

The ball was the first of the season, and was attended by the *elite* of the country from San Diego to Monterey. The dancing hall was large, with a floor as polished as a bowling saloon. The music was excellent—one splendid performer on an immense harp.

The assembled company was not only elegant—it was surpassingly brilliant. The dresses of both ladies and gentlemen could not be surpassed in expensive elegance. The fashions of the *gringo* world had made little innovation on the gorgeous and expensive attire of the country as to the gentlemen, while the ladies were resplendent in all the expense of fashion that could be supplied by unlimited resources. The writer had read Major Emery's book on California, in which, after lauding the California horsemen above the Comanche Indian and the Bedouin Arab, he went on to say that "the ladies excelled in dancing more than did the men in horsemanship."

Being thus prepared, the writer expected to witness reasonably elegant Terpsichorean performances, but the dancing on that occasion was something more than elegant, it was wonderful, while the most dignified and staid decorum was observed to the end of the festivities, which broke up about two o'clock in the morning. It was at this ball that I first met my old Ranger comrade, Captain J. Q. A. Stanley. Among other distinguished characters at the ball were the celebrated Juan Bandini, a learned man of the country, Doctor Don Ricardo Den of generous and chivalrous memory, who being a subject of Great Britain during the war with Mexico, gave his services gratuitously to both sides in the war, and deservedly won the love and gratitude of all, and Don Tomas Sanchez, a true son of chivalry, who had wielded a good lance at San Pasqual.

Some two and a half months thereafter we had one of those very elegant and exclusive affairs that ended in blood, its very exclusiveness being the cause of its very sanguinary termination. The ball was given at the house of Don Abel Stearns, a very wealthy American, on Washington's birthday, February 22, 1853, and was a grand and patriotic affair, but very exclusive. Somehow or other two or three gamblers were invited guests at the ball, which gave grave offense to the fraternity in general, among whom were many first class Americans, good and patriotic fellows, who loved their country and venerated the name of the immortal hero in honor of whose memory the grand affair was gotten up. These gentlemen maintained that on national occasions one American was as good as another, and that the whole community were on an equal footing, and that to attempt an exclusive national celebration was tomfoolery of the first order. So about two hundred of them assembled to *bust up* and disperse the exclusive humbug. The first move was to get the old canon, which had grown rusty for lack of revolutions, and place it in position directly in front of the house and bearing on one of the doors. They then procured a large beam, to be used as a battering ram when the time arrived for the general assault—all of which was done with the utmost silence.

At about midnight, when the patriotic dancing was at fever heat, and everything was hilarious within, the old gun was let off, and the battering-ram was driven with terrific force against the other door. Fortunately the cannon was badly trained, and the charge missed the door. The battering-ram, however, did its work well, and the door burst in with a tremendous crash. It fortunately happened that one game little fellow, who was one of the exclusives, was dancing directly in front of the burst-in door, and had a battery of Colts buckled to him, either of which was nearly as large as himself.

This patriotic exclusive stepped directly to the door and plugged the first gentleman who attempted to enter. Then another, and another, and by this time the affair had assumed all the beautiful proportions of a first-class revolution, and the firing became general. Of the assailants several were shot down, and the assault effectually repulsed; while of the exclusives but one man was wounded, and he the gay and festive Myron Norton, the chivalric vanquisher of the great Largo in that memorable game of billiards heretofore referred to. The brilliant Norton received a gentle perforation, that placed him *hors du combat* for some time thereafter.

For the next few days the angels were on a war footing; the community was divided; the defeated gamblers swore vengeance; the well-heeled exclusives were on the alert, determined not to be taken unawares; a general conflict seemed imminent; on retiring at night doors were barricaded and arms carefully examined; a silent, moody gloom prevailed; the gamblers would meet in groups and menacingly discuss the situation; the business part of the community was greatly alarmed. Confidence was only re-stored when Don Andres Pico came out and gave the gamblers to emphatically understand that, on the first hostile demonstration, he would raise the native Californians *en masse* against them, and that he would not be responsible for the consequences. It never-theless took months to cool off the bad blood engendered by that affair of the 22nd of February, 1853, and for some time individual collisions were of frequent occurence.

Horace Bell, *Reminiscences of a Ranger*
(Los Angeles, 1881), 79-82.

Return of the Editor

BY GEORGE H. DERBY

In the fifties Lieutenant George H. Derby, John Phoenix, né John Squibob, was acclaimed as the wittiest man in California. Wit was then measured by its breadth, and Derby, besides being addicted to puns, was an inveterate practical joker. In the passage quoted, he was indulging in understatement. Left in charge of the San Diego Herald *for six weeks at election time, he reversed its politics, espousing Waldo and Democracy whereas the absent owner was staunch for Bigler and the Whigs. The whole state thought this capital fun—the whole state, that is, with the excep-tion of Judge Ames.*

"*Te Deum Laudamus*."—Judge Ames has returned! With the com-pletion of this article my labors are ended; and wiping my pen on my coat-tail, and placing it behind my sinister ear, with a grace-ful bow and bland smile for my honored admirers, and a wink of intense meaning for my enemies, I shall abdicate, with dignity, the "Arm-Chair," in favor of its legitimate proprietor.

By the way, this "Arm-Chair" is but a pleasant fiction of "the Judge's,"—the only seat in the Herald Office being the empty nail keg, which I have occupied while writing my leaders upon the inverted sugar box, that answers the purpose of a table. But such is life. Divested of its poetry and romance, the objects of our highest admiration become mere common-places, like the Herald's chair and table. Many ideas which we have learned to love and reverence, from the poetry of imagination, as tables, become old sugar boxes on close inspection, and more intimate acquaintance. "Sic—but I forbear that sickening and hackneyed quotation.

During the period in which I have had control over the Herald, I have endeavored to the best of my ability to amuse and interest its readers, and I cannot but hope that my good humored efforts have proved successful. If I have given offence to any by the tone of my remarks, I assure them that it has been quite unintentional, and to prove that I bear no malice, I hereby accept their apologies. Certainly no one can complain of a lack of versatility in the last six numbers. Commencing as an Independent Journal, I have gradually passed through all the stages of incipient Whiggery, decided Conservatism, dignified Recantation, budding Democracy and rampant Radicalism, and I now close the series with an entirely literary number, in which, I have carefully abstained from the mention of Baldo and Wigler, I mean, Wagler and Bildo, no— never mind—as Toodles says, I haven't mentioned *any of 'em*, but been careful to preserve a perfect armed neutrality.

The paper this week will be found particularly stupid. This is the result of deep design on my part; had I attempted any thing remarkably brilliant, you would all have detected it, and said, probably with truth;—Ah, this is Phoenix's last appearance, he has tried to be very funny, and has made a miserable failure of it. Hee! hee! hee! Oh! no, my Public, an ancient weasel may not be detected in the act of slumber, in that manner. I was well aware of all this, and have been as dull and prosy as possible to avoid it. Very little news will be found in the Herald this week: the fact is, there never is much news in it, and it is very well that it is so; the climate here is so delightful, that residents, in the enjoyment of their *dolce far niente*, care very little about what is going on elsewhere, and residents in other places, care very little about what is going on in San Diego, so all parties are likely to be gratified with the little paper, "and long may it wave."

In conclusion, I am gratified to be able to state that Johnny's office (the fighting department), for the last six weeks, has been a sinecure, and with the exception of the atrocious conduct of one miscreant, who was detected very early one morning, in the act of chalking A S S on our office door, and who was dismissed with a harmless kick, and a gentle admonition that he should not write his name on other persons' property, our course has been peaceful, and undisturbed by any expression of an unpleasant nature.

So, farewell Public, I hope you will do well; I do, upon my soul. This leader is ended, and if there be any man among you who thinks he could write a better one, let him try it, and if he succeeds, I shall merely remark, that I could have done it myself if I had tried. Adios!

Respectably Yours.
San Diego *Herald*, October 1, 1853,
reprinted in the *Pioneer* and in *Phoenixiana*
(New York, 1855) 110-112.

An Anti-Chinese Decision

In this opinion written in 1854 by Hugh C. Murray, Chief Justice, the California Supreme Court held that Chinese were constructively barred from testifying against whites, a ruling which consigned them to far less than equal protection of the laws.

The appellant, a free white citizen of this State, was convicted of murder upon the testimony of Chinese witnesses.

The point involved in this case, is the admissibility of such evidence.

The 394th section of the Act Concerning Civil Cases, provides that no Indian or Negro shall be allowed to testify as a witness in any action or proceeding in which a White person is a party.

The 14th section of the Act of April 16th, 1850, regulating Criminal Proceedings, provides that "No Black, or Mulatto person, or Indian, shall be allowed to give evidence in favor of, or against a white man."

The true point at which we are anxious to arrive, is the legal signification of the words, "Black, Mulatto, Indian and White person," and whether the Legislature adopted them as generic terms, or intended to limit their application to specific types of the human species.

Before considering this question, it is proper to remark the difference between the two sections of our Statute, already quoted, the latter being more broad and comprehensive in its exclusion, by use of the word "Black," instead of Negro.

Conceding, however, for the present, that the word "Black," as used in the 14th section, and "Negro," in 394th, are convertible terms, and that the former was intended to include the latter, let us proceed to inquire who are excluded from testifying as witnesses under the term "Indian."

When Columbus first landed upon the shores of this continent, in his attempt to discover a western passage to the Indies, he imagined that he had accomplished the object of his expedition, and that the Island of San Salvador was one of those Islands of the Chinese sea, lying near the extremity of India, which had been described by navigators.

Acting upon this hypothesis, and also perhaps from the similarity of features and physical conformation, he gave to the Islanders the name of Indians, which appellation was universally adopted, and extended to the aboriginals of the New World, as well as of Asia.

From that time, down to a very recent period, the American Indians, and the Mongolian, or Asiatic, were regarded as the same type of the human species....

That this was the common opinion in the early history of American legislation, cannot be disputed, and, therefore, all legislation upon the subject must have borne relation to that opinion....

In using the words, "No Black, or Mulatto person, or Indian shall be allowed to give evidence for or against a White person," the Legislature, if any intention can be ascribed to it, adopted the most comprehensive terms to embrace every known class or shade of color, as the apparent design was to protect the White person from the influence of all testimony other than that of persons of the same caste. The use of these terms must, by every sound rule of construction, exclude every one who is not of white blood....

We have carefully considered all the consequences resulting from a different rule of construction, and are satisfied that even in a doubtful case we would be impelled to this decision on grounds of public policy.

The same rule which would admit them to testify, would admit them to all the equal rights of citizenship, and we might soon see them at the polls, in the jury box, upon the bench, and in our legislative halls.

This is not a speculation which exists in the excited and over-heated imagination of the patriot and statesman, but it is an actual and present danger.

The anomalous spectacle of a distinct people, living in our community, recognizing no laws of this State except through necessity, bringing with them their prejudices and national feuds, in which they indulge in open violation of law; whose mendacity is proverbial; a race of people whom nature has marked as inferior, and who are incapable of progress or intellectual development beyond a certain point, as their history has shown; differing in language, opinions, color, and physical conformation; between whom and ourselves nature has placed an impassable difference, is now presented, and for them is claimed, not only the right to swear away the life of a citizen, but the further privilege of participating with us in administering the affairs of our Government. . . .

For these reasons, we are of opinion that the testimony was inadmissible.

People v. *Hall*, 4 Cal. 399 (1854).

Riding with the Overland Mail

BY WATERMAN L. ORMSBY

As reporter for the New York Herald, *Waterman L. Ormsby drew the rough assignment of riding on the first running of the Butterfield Overland Mail. No employee of the line and no other passenger had the fortitude to attempt the twenty-five-day ride. The*

*parts of his report excerpted find the stage at Pacheco Pass and,
the next morning, entering San Francisco.*

FAST DRIVING

Most drivers would have been content to drive slowly over this
spot—a distance of twelve miles and every foot of it requiring the
most skillful management of the team to prevent the certain destruction of all in the coach. But our Jehu was in a hurry with the
"first States' mail" and he was bound to put us through in good
time. I suggested to him that a bad man riding on this road was
on the very brink of the bad place and likely to depart thence at almost any moment if anything should break. He said, "Yes, but
they didn't expect anything to break," and whipped up his horses
just as we started down a steep hill. I expected to see him put down
the brakes with all his might but he merely rested his foot on them,
saying, "It's best to keep the wheels rolling, or they'll slide"; so
he did keep the wheels rolling, and the whole coach slid down the
steepest hills at the rate of fifteen—yes, twenty—miles an hour,
now turning an abrupt curve with a whip and crack and "round
the corner, Sally," scattering the loose stones, just grazing the
rocks, sending its rattling echoes far away among the hills and
ravines, frightening the slow teamsters on the road and making
them haul off out of the way, and nearly taking away the breath
of all.

The driver seemed to enjoy the fun, and invited me up to ride
with him on the box. I got up, taking off my hat and throwing a
blanket over my head; I held on tight as we dashed along—up and
down, around the curves, and in straight lines, all at the same railroad speed. The loosening of a nut, the breaking of a strap, the
shying of one of the four spirited horses, might—indeed would—
have sent us all to "kingdom come," without a chance for saying
prayers. But just as I made such a reflection, crack went the whip
and away we flew, at a rate which I know would have made old
John Butterfield, the president of the mail company, and a very
experienced stage man, wish himself safely at home. For my part,
I held on to the seat and held my breath, hoping we might get
through safe. If I thought I was destined to be killed in a stage-
coach I most certainly should have considered my time come.

We ran the twelve miles in an hour and five minutes, and, con-
. sidering the ups and downs, I thought it pretty good travelling.
The mountain is covered with stunted oak trees, making it much
resemble an orchard. On the east side I noticed very few rocks, and
none large. On the west this was made up by huge rusty looking
crags, towering high in air, or with heavy boulders on their sides
or at their feet, as if just fallen. The road over the mountains is
excellent for the place and is much improved by Mr. Firebaugh,
who appears to be the enterprising man of the region. He has a
toll gate at the base of the mountain, charging two dollars for the
passage of a single four horse team, which is cheerfully paid in
consideration of what he does to the road.

How the Californians Received the Mail

The next twenty miles, to Gilroy, we travelled in two hours, and
took supper. The scene here was much like that at the other stop-
ing places of any note along the route since we left Franklin. The
villagers gathered around, asking all sorts of questions: "Have you
got the States mail?" "What's the news from the States?" "Is the
cable working yet?" "Have you got any through passengers?"
"Only the correspondent of the *Herald*." "Why, then, we shall
hear all about it." "How did you like your trip, sir?" "Very well."
"How did you manage to sleep?" "What, slept in the wagons?"
"Did you ride day and night?" "Well, I declare, I should think
you would be tired." "Have plenty to eat?" "What, beans and
jerked beef?" "Glad to hear you say they'd have better soon."
"Meet any Injuns?" "None at all, eh?" "Well, that's some com-
fort." "How long have you been?" "Left St. Louis on the 16th of
September." "Well, that beats all stage ridin'." "Going to come
through twice a week, eh?" "Well, that is good, now, ain't it?"
"How's the line on the other end?" "Slow, eh?" "Of course, all the
States people are slow." "Let em come out here and see a little life."
"Here we do live—live fast, too. . . ."

It was just after sunrise that the city of San Francisco hove in
sight over the hills, and never did the night traveller approach a
distant light, or the lonely mariner descry a sail, with more joy
than did I the city of San Francisco on the morning of Sunday,
October 10. As we neared the city we met milkmen and pleasure

seekers taking their morning rides, looking on with wonderment as we rattled along at a tearing pace.

IN SAN FRANCISCO—DELIVERING THE MAILS

Soon we struck the pavements, and, with a whip, crack, and bound, shot through the streets to our destination, to the great consternation of everything in the way and the no little surprise of everybody. Swiftly we whirled up one street and down another, and round the corners, until finally we drew up at the stage office in front of the Plaza, our driver giving a shrill blast of his horn and a flourish of triumph for the arrival of the first overland mail in San Francisco from St. Louis. But our work was not yet done. The mails must be delivered, and in a jiffy we were at the post office door, blowing the horn, howling and shouting for somebody to come and take the overland mail.

I thought nobody was ever going to come—the minutes seemed days—but the delay made it even time, and as the man took the mail bags from the coach, at half-past seven A.M. on Sunday, October 10, it was just twenty-three days, twenty-three hours and a half from the time that John Butterfield, the president of the company, took the bags as the cars moved from St. Louis at 8 A.M. on Thursday, 16th of September, 1858. And I had the satisfaction of knowing that the correspondent of the New York *Herald* had kept his promise and gone through with the first mail—the sole passenger and the only one who had ever made the trip across the plains in less than fifty days.

Waterman L. Ormsby, dispatch of October 13, 1858 to the
New York *Herald*, reproduced in Lyle L. Wright and Josephine M. Bynum, eds.,
The Butterfield Overland Mail (San Marino, 1942), 124-126, 129-130.

The Pony Express

BY SAMUEL CLEMENS

Samuel Clemens, better known as Mark Twain, opens Roughing It *with a lament on staging. What he and his fellow travelers had endured put them in frame of mind to idealize the pony rider putting the mail through in about a third of the time required by stage.*

We had had a consuming desire, from the beginning, to see a pony-rider, but somehow or other all that passed us and all that met us managed to streak by in the night, and so we heard only a whiz and a hail, and the swift phantom of the desert was gone before we could get our heads out of the windows. But now we were expecting one along every moment, and would see him in broad daylight. Presently the driver exclaims:

"HERE HE COMES!"

Every neck is stretched further, and every eye strained wider. Away across the endless dead level of the prairie a black speck appears against the sky, and it is plain that it moves. Well, I should think so! In a second or two it becomes a horse and rider, rising and falling, rising and falling—sweeping toward us nearer and nearer—growing more and more distinct, more and more sharply defined—nearer and still nearer, and the flutter of the hoofs comes faintly to the ear—another instant a whoop and a hurrah from our upper deck, a wave of the rider's hand, but no reply, and man and horse burst past our excited faces, and go winging away like a belated fragment of a storm!

So sudden is it all, and so like a flash of unreal fancy, that but for the flake of white foam left quivering and perishing on a mail-sack after the vision had flashed by and disappeared, we might have doubted whether we had seen any actual horse and man at all, maybe.

Samuel Clemens, *Roughing It*
(Hartford, 1871), I, 71-72.

Twenty-four Years After

BY RICHARD HENRY DANA

In 1859 Richard Henry Dana dropped in on the scene he had known so well during the hide trade. It surprised and gratified him, at forty-one, to be lionized as a real old-timer who had known the San Francisco waterfront so long ago. He also marveled at the changes that had come about.

On the evening of Saturday, the 13th of August, 1859, the superb steamship *Golden Gate*, gay with crowds of passengers, and lighting the sea for miles around with the glare of her signal lights of red, green, and white, and brilliant with lighted saloons and state-rooms, bound up from the Isthmus of Panama, neared the entrance to San Francisco, the great centre of a world-wide commerce. Miles out at sea, on the desolate rocks of the Farallones, gleamed the powerful rays of one of the most costly and effective light-houses in the world. As we drew in through the Golden Gate, another light-house met our eyes, and in the clear moonlight of the unbroken Californian summer we saw, on the right, a large fortification protecting the narrow entrance, and just before us the little island of Alcatraz confronted us,—one entire fortress. We bore round the point towards the old anchoring-ground of the hide ships, and there, covering the sand-hills and the valleys, stretching from the water's edge to the base of the great hills, and from the old Presidio to the Mission, flickering all over with the lamps of its streets and houses, lay a city of one hundred thousand inhabitants. Clocks tolled the hour of midnight from its steeples, but the city was alive from the salute of our guns, spreading the news that the fortnightly steamer had come, bringing mails and passengers from the Atlantic world. Clipper ships of the largest size lay at anchor in the stream, or were girt to the wharves; and capacious high-pressure steamers, as large and showy as those of the Hudson or Mississippi, bodies of dazzling light, awaited the delivery of our mails, to take their courses up the Bay, stopping at Benicia and the United States Naval Station, and then up the great tributaries—the Sacramento, San Joaquin, and Feather Rivers—to the far inland cities of Sacramento, Stockton, and Marysville.

The dock into which we drew, and the streets about it, were densely crowded with express wagons and hand-carts to take luggage, coaches and cabs for passengers, and with men,—some looking out for friends among our hundreds of passengers,—agents of the press, and a greater multitude eager for newspapers and verbal intelligence from the great Atlantic and European world.

Through this crowd I made my way, along the well-built and well-lighted streets, as alive as by day, where boys in high-keyed voices were already crying the latest New York papers; and between one and two o'clock in the morning found myself comfortably abed in a commodious room, in the Oriental Hotel, which stood, as well as I could learn, on the filled up cove, and not far from the spot where we used to beach our boats from the *Alert*. . . .

August 17th. The customs of California are free; and any person who knows about my book speaks to me. The newspapers have announced the arrival of the veteran pioneer of all. I hardly walk out without meeting or making acquaintances. I have already been invited to deliver the anniversary oration before the Pioneer Society, to celebrate the settlement of San Francisco. Any man is qualified for election into this society who came to California before 1853. What moderns they are! I tell them of the time when Richardson's shanty of 1835—not his adobe house of 1836—was the only human habitation between the Mission and the Presidio, and when the vast bay, with all its tributaries and recesses, was a solitude—and yet I am but little past forty years of age. They point out the place where Richardson's adobe house stood, and tell me that the first court and first town council were convened in it, the first Protestant worship performed in it, and in it the first capital trial by the Vigilance Committee held. I am taken down to the wharves, by antiquaries of a ten or twelve years' range, to identify the two points, now known as Clark's and Rincon, which formed the little cove of Yerba Buena, where we used to beach our boats,—and now filled up and built upon. The island we called "Wood Island," where we spent the cold days and nights of December, in our launch, in getting wood for our year's supply, is clean shorn of trees; and the bare rocks of Alcatraz Island, an entire fortress. I have looked at the city from the water, and at the water and island from the city, but I can see nothing that recalls the times gone by, except the venerable Mission, the ruinous Presidio, the high hills in the rear of the town, and the great stretches of the bay in all directions.

Today I took a Californian horse of the old style,—the run, the loping gait,—and visited the Presidio. The walls stand as they did, with some changes made to accommodate a small garrison of

United States troops. It has a noble situation, and I saw from it a clipper ship of the very largest class coming through the Gate, under her fore-and-aft sails. Thence I rode to the Fort, now nearly finished, on the southern shore of the Gate, and made an inspection of it. It is very expensive and of the latest style. One of the engineers here is Custis Lee, who had just left West Point at the head of his class,—a son of Colonel Robert E. Lee, who distinguished himself in the Mexican War. . . .

In one of my walks about the wharves, I found a pile of dry hides lying by the side of a vessel. Here was something to feelingly persuade me what I had been, to recall a past scarce credible to myself. I stood lost in reflection. What were these hides—what were they not?—to us, to me, a boy, twenty-four years ago? These were our constant labour, our chief object, our almost habitual thought. They brought us out here, they kept us out here, and it was only by getting them that we could escape from the coast and return to home and civilized life. If it had not been that I might be seen, I should have seized one, slung it over my head, walked off with it, and thrown it by the old toss—I do not believe yet a lost art—to the ground. How they called up to my mind the months of curing at San Diego, the year and more of beach and surf work, and the steeving of the ship for home? I was in a dream of San Diego, San Pedro,—with its hills so steep for taking up goods, and its stones so hard to our bare feet,—and the cliffs of San Juan! All this, too, is no more! The entire hide-business is of the past, and to the present inhabitants of California a dim tradition. The gold discoveries drew off all men from the gathering or cure of hides, the inflowing population made an end of the great droves of cattle; and now not a vessel pursues the—I was about to say dear—the dreary, once hated business of gathering hides upon the coast, and the beach of San Diego is abandoned, and its hide-houses have disappeared. Meeting a respectable-looking citizen on the wharf, I inquired of him how the hide trade was carried on, "Oh," said he, "there is very little of it, and that is all here. The few that are brought in are placed under sheds in winter, or left out on the wharf in summer, and are loaded from the wharves into the vessels alongside. They form parts of cargoes of other materials." I really felt too much, at the instant, to express to him the cause of

271

my interest in the subject, and only added, "Then the old business of trading up and down the coast and curing hides for cargoes
is all over?" "Oh, yes, sir," said he, "those old times of the *Pilgrim*
and *Alert* and *California*, that we read about, are gone by."

Saturday, August 20th. The steamer *Senator* makes regular
trips up and down the coast, between San Francisco and San Diego,
calling at intermediate ports. This is my opportunity to revisit the
old scenes. She sails to-day, and I am off, steaming among the
great clippers anchored in the harbor, and gliding rapidly round
the point, past Alcatraz Island, the light-house, and through the
fortified Golden Gate, and bending to the southward,—all done
in two or three hours, which, in the *Alert*, under canvas, with
head tides, variable winds, and sweeping currents to deal with,
took us full two days. . . .

The points in the country, too, we noticed, as we passed them—
Santa Cruz, San Luis Obispo, Point Año Nuevo, the opening to
Monterey, which to my disappointment we did not visit. No;
Monterey, the prettiest town on the coast, and its capital and seat
of customs, had got no advantage from the great changes, was out
of the way of commerce and of the travel to the mines and great
rivers, and was not worth stopping at. Point Conception we passed
in the night, a cheery light gleaming over the waters from its tall
lighthouse standing on its outermost peak. Point Conception! That
word was enough to recall all our experiences and dreads of gales,
swept decks, topmast carried away, and the hardships of a coast
service in the winter. But Captain Wilson tells me that the climate
has altered; that the south easters are no longer the bane of the
coast they once were, and that vessels now anchor inside the kelp
at Santa Barbara and San Pedro all the year round. I should have
thought this owing to spending his winters on a rancho instead of
the deck of the *Ayacucho*, had not the same thing been told me
by others. . . .

There is the old white mission [of Santa Barbara] with its bel-
fries, and there the town, with its one-story adobe houses, with
here and there a two-story wooden house of later build; yet little
is it altered—the same repose in the golden sunlight and glorious
climate, sheltered by its hills; and then, more remindful than anything else, there roars and tumbles upon the beach the same grand

surf of the great Pacific as on the beautiful day when the *Pilgrim*, after her five months' voyage, dropped her weary anchors here; the same bright blue ocean, and the surf making just the same monotonous, melancholy roar, and the same dreamy town, and gleaming white Mission, as when we beached our boats for the first time, riding over the breakers with shouting Kanakas, the three small hide-traders lying at anchor in the offing. But now we are the only vessel, and that an unromantic, sail-less, spar-less, engine-driven hulk!

I landed in the surf, in the old style, but it was not high enough to excite us, the only change being that I was somehow unaccountably a passenger, and did not have to jump overboard and steady the boat, and run her up by the gunwales. . . .

The breeze freshened as we stood out to sea, and the wild waves rolled over the red sun, on the broad horizon of the Pacific; but it is summer, and in summer there can be no bad weather in California. Every day is pleasant. Nature forbids a drop of rain to fall by day or night, or a wind to excite itself beyond a fresh summer breeze.

The next morning we found ourselves at anchor in the Bay of San Pedro. Here was this hated, this thoroughly detested spot. Although we lay near, I could scarce recognise the hill up which we rolled and dragged and pushed and carried our heavy loads, and down which we pitched the hides to carry them barefooted over the rocks to the floating long-boat. It was no longer the landing-place. One had been made at the head of the creek, and boats discharged and took off cargoes from a mole or wharf, in a quiet place, safe from south easters. A tug ran to take off passengers from the steamer to the wharf,—for the trade of Los Angeles is sufficient to support such a vessel. . . . A stage-coach, I found, went daily between this place and the Pueblo. I got a seat on the top of the coach, to which were tackled six little less than wild Californian horses. Each horse had a man at his head, and when the driver had got his reins in hand he gave the word, all the horses were let go at once, and away they went on a spring, tearing over the ground, the driver only keeping them from going the wrong way, for they had a wide level pampa to run over the whole thirty miles to the Pueblo. This plain is almost treeless, with no grass, at least none now in the drought of midsummer, and is filled with squirrel-holes, and alive with squirrels. As we changed horses twice, we did not slacken our speed until we turned into the streets of the Pueblo.

The Pueblo de los Angeles I found a large and flourishing town of about twenty thousand inhabitants, with brick sidewalks, and blocks of stone or brick houses. The three principal traders when we were here for hides in the Pilgrim and Alert are still among the chief traders of the place,—Stearns, Temple, and Warner, the two former being reputed very rich. I dined with Mr. Stearns, now a very old man, and met there Don Juan Bandini, to whom I had given a good deal of notice in my book. From him, as indeed from every one in this town, I met with the kindest attentions. The wife of Don Juan, who was a beautiful young girl when we were on the coast, Doña Refugio, daughter of Don Santiago Argüello, the commandant of San Diego, was with him, and still handsome. This is one of several instances I have noticed of the preserving quality of the Californian climate.

Richard Henry Dana, Two Years before the Mast
(second edition, Boston, 1869), 433-434, 435-444, 446-448.

Los Angeles and Santa Barbara in 1860-61

BY WILLIAM H. BREWER

William H. Brewer was a member of the team sent in 1860 by Yale University to make a geological survey of California. Its work stressed the Sierra Nevada, but parties were deployed in other parts of the state. Brewer's book-length journal, more broadly descriptive, was an extra dividend from the survey.

In Camp at Los Angeles.
December 7.

Well, we are in camp. It is a cold rainy night, but I can hardly realize the fact that you at home are blowing your fingers in the cold, and possibly sleighing, while I am sitting here in a tent, without fire, and sleeping on the ground in blankets, in this month. We are camped on a hill near the town, perhaps a mile distant, a pretty place.

Los Angeles is a city of some 3,500 or 4,000 inhabitants, nearly a century old, a regular old Spanish-Mexican town, built by the old *padres*, Catholic Spanish missionaries, before the American independence. The houses are but one story, mostly built of *adobe* or sun-burnt brick, with very thick walls and flat roofs. They are so low because of earthquakes, and the style is Mexican. The inhabitants are a mixture of old Spanish, Indian, American, and German Jews; the last two have come in lately. The language of the natives is Spanish, and I have commenced learning it. The only thing they appear to excel in is riding, and certainly I have never seen such riders.

Here is a great plain, or rather a gentle slope, from the Pacific to the mountains. We are on this plain about twenty miles from the sea and fifteen from the mountains, a most lovely locality; all that is wanted naturally to make it a paradise is *water*, more *water*. Apples, pears, plums, figs, olives, lemons, oranges, and "the finest grapes in the world," so the books say, pears of two and a half pounds each, and such things in proportion. The weather is soft and balmy—no winter, but a perpetual spring and summer. Such is Los Angeles, a place where "every prospect pleases and only man is vile."

As we stand on a hill over the town, which lies at our feet, one of the loveliest views I ever saw is spread out. Over the level plain to the southwest lies the Pacific, blue in the distance; to the north are the mountains of the Sierra Santa Monica; to the south beneath us, lies the picturesque town with its flat roofs, the fertile plain and vineyards stretching away to a great distance; to the east, in the distance, are some mountains without name, their sides abrupt and broken, while still above them stand the snow covered peaks of San Bernardino. The effect of the pepper, fig, olive, and palm trees in the foreground, with the snow in the distance, is very unusual.

This is a most peculiar climate, a mingling of the temperate with the tropical. The date palm and another palm grow here, but do not fruit, while the olive, fig, orange, and lemon flourish well.

The grapes are famous, and the wine of Los Angeles begins to be known even in Europe.

We got in camp on Tuesday, December 4. We had been invited to a ranch and vineyard about nine miles east, and went with a friend on Tuesday evening. It lies near San Gabriel Mission, on a most beautiful spot, I think even finer than this. Mr. [Benjamin D.] Wilson, our host, uneducated, but a man of great force of character, is now worth a hundred or more thousand dollars and lives like a prince, only with less luxury. His wife is finely educated and refined, and his home to the visitor a little paradise. We were received with the greatest cordiality and were entertained with the greatest hospitality. A touch of the country and times were indicated by our rig—I was dressed in colored woolen shirt, with heavy navy revolver (loaded) and huge eight-inch bowie knife at my belt; my friend the same; and the clergyman who took us out in his carriage carried along his rifle, he said for game, yet owned that it was "best to have arms after dark."

Here let me digress. This southern California is still unsettled. We all continually wear arms—each wears both bowie knife and pistol (navy revolver), while we have always for game or otherwise, a Sharp's rifle, Sharp's carbine, and two double-barrel shotguns. Fifty to sixty murders per year have been common here in Los Angeles, and some think it odd that there has been no violent death during the two weeks that we have been here. Yet with our care there is no considerable danger, for as I write this there are at least six heavy loaded revolvers in the tent, besides bowie knives and other arms, so we anticipate no danger. I have been practicing with my revolver and am becoming expert.

Well, to return to my story, and to Mr. Wilson's. We found a fine family, with two lovely young ladies. The next day, Wednesday, December 5, we went up into the mountain, followed up a canyon (gorges are called *cañons* or canyons), and then separated. I climbed a hill 2,500 or more feet, very steep and rocky, gathered some plants, and had one of the most magnificant views of my life—the plain, and the ocean beyond. The girls went with us into the canyon, but did not climb higher. After our climb and a lunch, a ride of eight miles over the fields (for no fences obstruct the land) brought us back; then dinner and return here. We had a delightful time—I ought to say "we" were the field assistant Mr. Ashburner and I. We will try to visit them again when Professor Whitney comes.

It is cold, wet, and cheerless, so good night! Rain patters on the tent and dribbles within. . . .

In Camp at Santa Barbara.
Sunday, March 10, 1861.

We came here on Thursday, March 7, arriving in the afternoon. The steamer was to leave that night for San Francisco, the only public communication with the outer world. I tried to make a raise and get some money from express agents, merchants, etc.— no go—so wrote on to Professor Whitney that we would wait here until either funds or he arrived. Friday we visited the Mission, examined the foothills, etc. More of the Mission anon.

Saturday, with Averill, I visited a hot spring about five miles from here. First a good road, past some pretty ranches, then up a wild ravine by such a path as you would all put down as entirely impassable to horses, but it was mere fun for our mules.

Santa Barbara lies on the seashore, and until lately it was isolated from the rest of the world by high mountains. No wagon road or stage route ran into it from without, only mere trails or paths for horses over the mountains. For a few years they had had a mail once in two weeks by steamer from San Francisco—two mails per month was the only news of the world outside. But the Overland has been working the road—or the county has—and will run this way after the first of April. Here is a village of about 1,200 inhabitants. A wealthy Mission formerly existed here, but like all the rest, is now poor after the robbery by the Mexican Government. I have not seen before in America, except at Panama, such extensive ruins.

The Mission was founded about the time of the American Revolution—the locality was beautiful, water good and abundant. A fine church and ecclesiastical buildings were built and a town sprang up around. The slope beneath was all irrigated and under high cultivation—vineyards, gardens, fields, fountains, once embellished that lovely slope. Now all is changed. The church is in good preservation, with the monastery alongside—all else is ruined.

It was with a feeling of much sadness that I rode through the old town. Here were whole streets of buildings, built of *adobes*, their roofs gone, their walls tumbling, squirrels burrowing in them—all now desolate, ruined, deserted. Grass grows in the old streets and cattle feed in the gardens. Extensive yards *(corrals)* built with stone walls, high and solid, stand without cattle. The old threshing floor is ruined, the weeds growing over its old pavement. The palm trees are dead, and the olive and fig trees are dilapidated and broken.

We went into the church—a fine old building, about 150 feet long (inside), 30 wide, and 40 high, with two towers, and a monastery, sacristy, etc., 250 feet long at one side, with long corridors and stone pillars and small windows and tile roofs. The interior of the church was striking and picturesque. Its walls were painted by the Indians who built it. The cornice and ornaments on the ceiling were picturesque indeed—the colors bright and the designs a sort of cross between arabesques, Greek cornice, and Indian designs, yet the effect was pretty. The light streamed in through the small windows in the thick walls, lighting up the room. The floor was of cement. The sides and ceiling were plastered with the usual accompaniment of old pictures, shrines, images, altar, etc.

Up the canyon two or three miles a strong cement dam had been built, whence the water was brought down to the Mission in an aqueduct made of stone and cement, still in good repair. Near the Mission it flows into two large tanks or cisterns, reservoirs I ought to call them, built of masonry and cement, substantial and fine. These fed a mill where grain was ground, and ran in pipes to supply the fountains in front of the church and in the gardens, and thence to irrigate the cultivated slope beneath. But all now is in ruin—the fountains dry, the pipes broken, weeds growing in the cisterns and basins. The bears, from whose mouths the water flowed, are broken, and weeds and squirrels are again striving to obtain mastery as in years long before.

I find it hard to realize that I am in America—in the *United States*, the young and vigorous republic as we call her—when I see these ruins. They carry me back again to the Old World with its decline and decay, with its histories of war and blood and strife and desolation, with its conflict of religions and races.

William H. Brewer, Journal, in Francis P. Farquar, ed.,
Up and Down California in 1860-1864
(New Haven, Yale University Press, 1930), 12-15, 55-58.

My California School

BY PRENTICE MULFORD

Prentice Mulford became a writer by accident. One morning, after the whole population of one of the mining camps had gone on a binge, he treated his hangover by putting on paper a graphic description. The camp clamored for more and Mulford embarked on this new career. An essay on California cooking is his most famous contribution. "My California School" is in the same spirit.

I was not confident of my ability to teach even a "common school" when the situation was offered me in a little Tuolumne County mining camp. I said so to my old friend, Pete H., who had secured me the position. "Well," said he, after a reflective pause, "do you retain a clear recollection of the twenty-six letters of the alphabet? For, if you do, you are the equal to any educational demand this camp will make on you."

It was a reckless "camp." No phase of life was viewed or treated seriously. They did walk their horses to the grave slowly at a funeral, but how they did race back!

It was legally necessary, however, that I should be examined as to my ability by the school trustees. These were Dr. D., Bill K., a saloonkeeper, and Tom J., a miner. I met them in the Justice's office. The doctor was an important appearing man, rotund, pompous, well-dressed, and spectacled. He glared at me with an expression betwixt sadness and severity. I saw he was to be the chief inquisitor. I expected from him a searching examination, and trembled. It was years since I had seen a school-book. I knew that in geography I was rusty and in mathematics musty.

Before the doctor lay one thin book. It turned out to be a spelling book. The doctor opened it, glared on me leisurely, and finally said: "Spell cat." I did so. "Spell hat." I spelled. "Rat," said the doctor, with a look of explosive fierceness and in a tone an octave higher. I spelled, and then remarked: "But, doctor, you surely must know that I can spell words of one syllable?" "I don't," he shouted, and propounded "mat" for me to spell, with an increase of energy in his voice, and so went on until I had so spelled long enough to amuse him and the other two trustee triflers. Then he shut the book, saying: "Young man, you'll do for our camp. I wouldn't teach that school for $5,000 a year; and there are two boys you'll have for scholars that I advise you to kill, if possible, the first week. Let's all go over and take a drink."

Prentice Mulford, Prentice Mulford's Story
(New York, 1889), 145-146.

The Expansive Power of Beans

BY JOHN BARKER

Among the Californians the tall tale is a hardy perennial. The one that follows was composed or more probably collected by John Barker, pioneer miner, rancher, irrigator, editor, and occasional contributor to the Bakersfield Californian.

"Why," [said General Freeman], "you do not know the first principles of the expansive power of beans.

"When I was mining up on Greenhorn, at my mill, I had for partners in the mine Sam May, Long Moore, Leon Mathews—four including myself. We always laid off and took a holiday on Sunday. We went on Saturday evening to Whiskey Flat, now known as Kernville, and did not return until Sunday night or Monday morning. Of course we were at church all this time.

"One Saturday evening when it was my turn to cook, I told the boys not to wait for me; that I had some chores to attend to, and that I would be at the prayer meeting almost as soon as they would. We had a large open fire place that occupied very nearly the whole width of the cabin on the hearth, and we could roll an oak log in that would answer as a back log for several days. We also had a large copper kettle that would hold about forty gallons. I concluded that as the weather was cool, I would cook enough beans to last a week and not be troubled cooking them every day. So I filled the kettle nearly full of water and took the sack of beans. After I had hung the kettle on the hook that hung in the chimney, and started to empty the beans into the kettle, I slipped forward as I was in the act, and emptied the whole sack into the kettle. I thought I would let it go anyway, and finished up my work and started for the church at Whiskey Flat.

"We had a protracted meeting then and we did not return home until after dark on Sunday evening.

"Our cabin was a substantial one built of pine logs, and the doors all opened toward the inside. One of us attempted to open the door. It would not budge. I tried it, and I said, 'I think some one is inside and has fastened the door.' We tried a rear door with the same results. One of us then climbed up with the intention of crawling down the chimney, but the chimney seemed choked by something. I then climbed up myself, got into the chimney, reached down to feel what I stood on, when behold, it was beans! I then remembered what I had done, and I said, 'Boys, get an ax and split that door to pieces. The devil has been here while we were worshipping at Whiskey Flat.'

"No sooner said than done. The door was split out, and out rolled the beans. We got shovels and shoveled them out and then shoveled them into a pile away from the cabin. We found it full to the roof, and everything steaming like a Turkish bath. We had to send away for the whole tribe of Indians on the South Fork to help us get away with those beans before they got sour and created an epidemic. After that I knew enough not to try any experiments with beans. . . ."

[Lindley Bynum tells a story that links this episode with what follows. Another parcel of hardrock miners working in this same vicinity struck some extra hard going. Hammering away at their drills they were able to gain only a few inches a day. When Saturday night came, and their drill holes were only about six inches deep, they were glad to knock off, as General Freeman and his partners did, and go in to Whiskey Flat for Sunday. "But that rock was so hard," so the informant states, "that when we came back to the hills on Monday morning, those holes stuck out a good two inches."]

"But to return to our beans. A short time after . . . , we ran out of blasting powder at the mine. In those days we knew nothing of the high and powerful explosives used in the mines of today, and as there was no powder to be got before the arrival of the next train of ox teams from Stockton, it set us to thinking of the highly expansive power of beans. I called the attention of my partners to the fact, historically established, that Pizarro, when he invaded the domain of the Incas of Peru, found great works that had been constructed by this remarkable and wonderful people, in the construction of canals for the purpose of irrigation, which exist to this day, in which their courses had been excavated for long distances by way of open work as well as tunnels through the hardest kind of rock formation and this without the aid of steel or the agency of explosives. I argued that as they had nothing but the simplest tools at their command that they must have used some of the forces provided by nature for the purpose of disintegrating the rock. Ergo, what would have suggested itself more naturally to them than the expansive power of one of the staple articles of their food, viz., beans?

"I suggested that we go to work and try an experiment by drilling four holes into the face of the drift in our mine, one at the top, one at the bottom and one on each side about half way up. We did so accordingly, and then filled the holes about two-thirds full of dry beans, rammed them in tight and forced warm water in—sufficient to saturate them well. We then tamped them hard and tight in the usual way of tamping a blast with sand. When we had that all done we leisurely sat down and awaited developments. In about a half hour we began to hear an occasional snap or crack, and soon we began to see the rock in the face of the drift begin to bulge out. Then gradually the whole face of the drift began to disintegrate and to bulge more and more, until with a crash such as would be made by a mass of falling mortar, the vein matter that formed the face of the drift fell out all broken up to the full depth of the holes we had drilled, which was about two feet.

"We were of course delighted. We had wrested the secret of the Incas from the oblivion in which it had been shrouded, and demonstrated the power of one of the hidden forces of nature, simplified the art of mining and provided a cheap and effectual means of unlocking the great treasure house of the Sierra Nevada. No longer were men to be killed and maimed by premature explosions of dangerous compounds; and we, the discoverers of this simple, safe and powerful agent, would go down to posterity as amongst the foremost of the great army of discoverers like Fulton, Columbus, Sir Isaac Newton and a host of others.

"After that we never used anything except beans as an explosive as long as we worked the mine, after which we went our various ways and our great discovery remains non-patented to this day. And if any of you enterprising young men want to make a fortune the way is open for you."

> John Barker, Bakersfield *Daily Californian*, June 28, 1904;
> reprinted in William Harland Boyd and Glendon J. Rodgers, eds.,
> *San Joaquin Vignettes* (Bakersfield, 1955), 87-90.

Crime and Punishment in Los Angeles

BY WILLIAM B. RICE

William B. Rice, a historian of great promise, lost his life in 1942 just after earning his Ph.D. He had published on Salt Lake to Los Angeles freighting, Olive Oatman after her ransom from Indian captivity, Clarence King and the Atlantic, *and Muir and his reviewers. He wrote a small book on William Money, a Los Angeles eccentric. The selection that follows is from his principal book, a study of the life and times of southern California's earliest newspaper.*

A local subject particularly in need of editorial attention was that of crime and disorder, for Los Angeles in the early 'fifties was a spa for the state's criminally inclined. The *Star* promptly took a stand that would brook no compromise with criminality. In its third issue, that of May 31, 1851, it announced that of the advantages with which cities were blest, only one—law and order—was lacking in Los Angeles. "Is it not a fact," it asked, "that at this moment the laws have lost their force among us?" It called for the aid of public opinion in the fight against crime, "a bold, unflinching voice to speak in thunder tones against the abuses and daring outrages. . . ." In August it warned all rogues to search elsewhere for a skulking-place, or they would get a warm reception.

The continued lawlessness of the city began to force upon the *Star* a realization that strong measures were necessary. Once it proposed that peaceable citizens abandon the town to the criminals. "If anarchy is to rule," it stated, "if assassinations are to be matters of nightly occurrence, then the sooner good men betake themselves to more congenial climes, the better, for the ruffians can then war only upon one another, and the hope will exist that in time their extermination may be accomplished." It maintained, however, its faith in established legal procedure. "The people of this city, it is believed, are in favor of punishing offenses by due process of law. A few, indeed, have hinted at a Vigilance committee, not because the laws of the land are insufficient to protect us, but that they are not rigidly administered. Let is not be said of Los Angeles that her citizens were obliged to resort to this measure."

In spite of this view, events occurred to force the *Star* into a more favorable outlook toward vigilantism. One of these was the achievement of the San Francisco Vigilance Committee of 1851. In commenting on the organization's proposed disbandment, the paper praised it for the immense amount of good it had accomplished, saying that the people of San Francisco had the committee to thank for their present tranquility. The *Star* also complimented the members "for their readiness to disband when a reason for their existence was no longer manifest."

Occurrences which brought about organized vigilantism in Los Angeles were the murders of two American travelers in July, 1852, and the assassination of General Joshua H. Bean, the Indian fighter, in November of the same year at San Gabriel. The first incident resulted in the formation of a citizens' court and the hanging of two culprits; the second was more notorious, since it involved the death of a prominent soldier and local politician. After the murder of Bean, a public meeting was held at the courthouse, with W. H. Rand and M. C. Rojo of the *Star* delegated to act as secretaries. Six suspects had been apprehended and were to be tried by a self-constituted court. "There can certainly be no objection to this mode of procedure," remarked the paper, "when we hear that our very court officers acknowledge that the law is utterly incapable of bringing them to justice." "It is to be hoped, however," it added, "that passion will not get the better of justice and judgment, but let everything be conducted in a manner worthy of an American community.

On February 26, 1853, the *Star* continued to fight against crime and disturbance with an editorial which recommended that in the people's court such example be made of violators as would demonstrate "that there shall be no discrimination in men—only in crime." It went on to hope that all citizens would support the campaign for law and order, so that "our social relations shall resemble the natural conformations that surround us, and which are so pleasant to look upon."

Soon after the foregoing remark, the editors noticed an uptrend in local conditions, citing the fact that fewer drunken Indians had encumbered the streets the previous Sunday. Consequently the day had passed without its usual noise and brawling. Credit for this the journal bestowed on the newly elected city marshal. That official did not, however, repose for long in the good graces of the *Star*. Two weeks later some twenty prisoners emerged stealthily from the jail and escaped. The paper severely censured the marshal, attributing the whole affair to his carelessness and inexperience.

Worse than this was to come. On July 16, 1853, the *Star* printed an editorial which showed the alarm with which it looked upon the renewed activity of the criminal element:

"This county is in a state of insurrection, and clearly and plainly so. A large gang of outlaws . . . are in open rebellion against the laws, and are daily committing the most daring murders and robberies. Good citizens should devise plans to defend themselves. One of two things must result: the orderly industrious inhabitants must drive out this worthless scum of humanity, or they must give way before the pirates and be driven out themselves. In the times of Micheltoreno [sic] when the country was infested by a horde of Cholos, thieves and murderers, the citizens mustered and drove the scamps to the seaboard, and then shipped them off to Mexico, where they belonged. This was called a revolution; and just such another revolution is needed now. It is needed for self-protection, but will be too late when the assassin's knife has deprived the county of half of her best citizens. Let good citizens combine and drive the rascals headlong into the sea."

William B. Rice, *The Los Angeles Star, 1851-1864: The Beginning of Journalism in Southern California* (Berkeley, University of California Press, 1947), 44-46.

The California Clipper

BY RAYMOND A. RYDELL

Raymond A. Rydell, one-time sailor and importer as well as historian, is vice-chancellor of the State Colleges of California. His Cape Horn volume recounts the rise and decline of this ocean highway.

The boom years of the clipper era were 1850-1853. Then freight rates were the highest, profits the heaviest, and most of the record passages took place. The older China clippers *Architect* and *Memnon*—first of their type to pass through the Golden Gate after the discovery of gold—were soon followed by the larger California clippers, ships of more than twice their tonnage, built during 1849 expressly for the trade with San Francisco. These sleek and powerful vessels embodied in their design and construction all the lessons American shipbuilders had learned since the Declaration of Independence. Their concave lines forward and their fine lines aft were meant to slip them through the water with minimum resistance, to help them clip through the waves rather than crash into them—hence the popular name. They were, in fact, streamlined.

Their hulls were designed to permit the maximum amount of canvas aloft, and, most significantly, their rugged construction was predicated upon their being driven to the limit under the most formidable weather conditions. These material factors, added to

286

the efficiency of Yankee captains, most of whom had learned their profession in the transatlantic packets or the China trade, and the availability of Maury's *Sailing Directions* and *Wind and Current Charts*, go far toward explaining the remarkable performances of American merchant vessels in the 'fifties.

Of all the passages made in 1851, none is as celebrated as the maiden voyage of McKay's *Flying Cloud*. Built specifically for the California trade for the account of Enoch Train, and commanded by Josiah P. Cressy, she was the last word in sail that season. On her maiden voyage she cleared New York at 2:00 P.M., June 2, carrying a full cargo of general merchandise for San Francisco. Five hours later she dropped the pilot off Sandy Hook and pointed southeast in fine weather. Three days later she carried away her main and mizzen topgallant masts and main topsail yard off Cape Hatteras. But Cressy sent up new spars during the next two days and kept driving, passing other ships which were laboring under reefed topsails only, while he was carrying full sail. She crossed the equator on June 26 and began to round Cape St. Roque the same day. July 10 found her off the Plata. The next day she ran into a violent pampero; Cressy wrote in the log:

"Heavy Gales, Close Reefed Topsails split fore Staysail & Main Topmast Staysail at 1 P.M. Discovered Main Masthead Sprung (same time Brig in Company to leeward lost fore & Main topmast) sent down Royal & Topmast Yards & Booms off Lower & Topsail Yard to releave the mast, very turbulent sea Running Ship Laboring hard & shipping large quantities of Water over lee Rail. Middle & latter parts hard Gales & Harder squalls. No observations."

July 26 found the vessel five miles off Cape Horn; the next day Cressy pointed North. On July 31, off Valparaiso, the log shows that the ship, for a time, was going through the water at better than eighteen knots and that the official distance run that day was 374 nautical miles, a mark that steamships would not surpass for a generation. The weather continued favorable for the remainder of the passage, and on August 31, at 7:00 A.M., the *Flying Cloud* took on a pilot near the Farallones. She let go her anchor at 11:30 A.M., off North Beach, San Francisco, eighty-nine days, twenty-one hours from New York. This record stood until 1854, when she bettered it by thirteen hours, the permanent record from anchor to anchor.

On her 1851 voyage, the *Sea Serpent*, Captain William Howland, carried a freight manifest ten feet long. All her bills of lading show the same rate: $1 per cubic foot with 5 per cent added for primage. On 1,304 tons of freight (the approximate tonnage of the vessel), total charges were $54,528.36 to the shippers; the ship herself had cost considerably less to construct. Reading straight down her freight list from item number one, one finds:

30 grt. casks Brandy	4 Packages Hatchets
30 ⅛ " "	1 Cask & Box Hardware
2 cases Mdze.	1 Box Axe Handles
28 " "	5 bales Blankets & box Samples
24 dozin Shovels	15 Bbls Alcohol
10 Pkg Axes	13 Box Mdze
2 Boxes Axes	200 Coils Rope
4 Broad Axes	15 Kegs Shot

Hardware, liquor, and food made up most of her cargo.

In all, forty-eight clippers arrived in San Francisco in 1851, each realizing enough, or nearly enough, to pay for itself in one voyage. Some came back over the same route to New York; more pushed on to China and England before crossing the North Atlantic to home ports. . . .

The greatest year of the clippers was 1853. More passages were made, their average elapsed time shorter, and their cargoes heavier than in any other. Virtually every "shipbuilder in the United States launched his clipper *beau ideal*." Never before or after was there such an abundance of glamor in the United States merchant marine. On several occasions, three clippers stood in through the Golden Gate within twenty-four hours, and on two others, five arrived within forty-eight hours. Notwithstanding unusually heavy weather in the Cape Horn region, a number of new records were set. Less than a month after McKay's great voyage home, the *Northern Light*, driven all the way by her master, Freeman Hatch, completed the passage from San Francisco to New York in seventy-six days. Hatch was so impressed with the accomplishment that he asked that it be recorded on his tombstone with no other data except his name. And it was . . . .

The passing of the towering clippers from public attention in the late 'fifties foreshadowed the passing of the United States as a leading commercial and maritime nation of the nineteenth century. The blazing records of the *Flying Cloud, Great Republic,* and others were in part the result of unusual economic conditions; when the situation reverted to normal, the interests of the American people were drawn to other matters far removed from maritime enterprise: the Civil War, Reconstruction, the exploitation of the West, the industrialization of the nation. These responsibilities and opportunities left little room in the national house for ocean commerce.

Yet the clippers had had a fair share in facilitating the westward expansion of the United States, and, for a moment, they had made the American merchant marine the greatest in the world. No nobler nor more ephemeral ships would ever pass Cape Horn.

Raymond A. Rydell, *Cape Horn to the Pacific*
(Berkeley, University of California Press, 1952), 133-136, 138, 142-143.

The Slim Princess

BY JERRY MACMULLEN

In Paddle-wheel Days *and* Ships of the Redwood Coast *Jerry Mac-Mullen may be thought of as the rediscoverer of the role of shipping in California's intrastate traffic, a role that was paramount in the fifties and sixties and highly significant to the turn of the century. Journalism is MacMullen's profession, history his avocation.*

When you think of the California clippers, the name which first flashes across your mind is *Flying Cloud*; speak of the British tea and wool ships, and it is *Cutty Sark*. And just as each of these symbolized the finest of its class, so did slim, dainty *Chrysopolis* catch the fancy of the rivermen that even today she is remembered with affection. Chrysopolis—The Golden City. . . .

John North designed and built her, for the California Steam Navigation Company, and both he and Captain James Whitney saw to it that nothing which went into her construction was anything but the best. Each stick of wood which formed the slender hull was the pick of the forests—and each piece was painted before it was carefully spiked into place. They intended that *Chryssie* should last a long time, which indeed she did. Her hull was 245 feet long, with a beam of 40 and a depth of 10 feet; she drew 4½ feet of water, and her tonnage was 1,050.

Below decks—or more correctly, through all of them—she carried a single-cylindered, vertical-beam engine with a bore of 5 feet and a stroke of 11, which rated 1,357 horsepower. There were two boilers, located on the guards, weighing 32 tons each, and their working pressure was 55 pounds. (There was a popular tradition that, if the boilers were on the guards instead of inside the hull, the vessel might "blow up and be damned, sir," without causing the slightest inconvenience to the passengers. It was a pretty theory.) Her paddle wheels were 36 feet in diameter, with 8-foot buckets, and even turning over at well under twenty revolutions a minute they gave her a speed which enabled her, on December 31, 1861, to come down from Sacramento to San Francisco in five hours and nineteen minutes—a record which still stands. Her cabins were the picture of Victorian elegance—elaborately turned moldings, plate-glass mirrors, marble-topped tables, red plush upholstery, and glistening brass lamps. She could carry a thousand passengers and 700 tons of cargo, and her fuel capacity was 25 tons. Leading artists of the time were engaged to set off her interior with murals of California scenes—and all this for $200,-000. . . .

Others could go in for racing if they wished, but not the *Chrysopolis*. If she wanted to, she could show up the whole lot of them, so why strain herself in trying? She was content to dwell in the esteem and respect of her friends without getting her name into the papers in an unpleasant way, and her life passed in complete innocence of explosions.

And yet there was one explosion, but it wasn't her fault. . . . After the Mexican War and in Civil War days, the state erupted with a veritable rash of more or less official militia companies, many of which persisted for years as marching and elbow-bending societies. There were the Sutter Rifles and the Coloma Grays, and there were the Knight's Ferry Dragoons. A large element of the California population being, even as now, of Hibernian stock, it is not surprising that there also were the McMahon Guards and the Emmett Guards, which boasted two companies—one in Sacramento, the other in San Francisco. They held clambakes and free-for-alls and encampments, the latter always attended by some local Pooh-Bah, preferably with a military background. Before he marched away to the Civil War, to achieve fame as Fightin' Joe, General Joe Hooker of Sonoma County was much in demand as "Inspector" at the encampments of the more socially prominent companies. The Blue Book rating of these swashbuckling militia outfits was in many cases determined by the social standing of the volunteer fire company of which they often were an adjunct.

The Emmett Guards of Sacramento decided that St. Patrick's Day of 1869 would be an appropriate time to engage in a bit of serious wassailing and marching with their comrades-in-arms, the Emmett Guards of San Francisco. It was the misfortune of the *Chrysopolis* to be the down boat that night. During the day, two worthies attached to the outfit asked their company commander if it would be all right if they brought a small cannon with them. He stated flatly that it would not, and the master of the steamer backed him up. However, they were down nearly to Steamboat Slough before it was discovered that the pair had, in some manner, smuggled not only the cannon but also a keg of powder aboard. There was no more peace that night. The next morning when the *Chrysopolis* was approaching the wharf in San Francisco the two mountebanks loaded up for what they planned as a grand finale. It was. When the smoke cleared away—the keg as well as the cannon having gone off—a lot of planking was loosened, several of the nice red plush seats were on fire, and sixteen of the Emmett Guards were injured. Unfortunately the two who were responsible were not killed. That was her only explosion. The rest of her life on the river was one of gracious service, of comfortable speed, of meals which will go down in history.

Jerry MacMullen, *Paddle-Wheel Days in California*
(Stanford, Stanford University Press, 1944), 34-37.

7

THE PASSING OF THE
FRONTIER

PARTLY BECAUSE the forty-niners were youthful and partly because their activities were so flamboyant, the gold rush era gave
way only grudgingly. Yet rapid build-up of poulation, wealth,
and substance hastened the passing of the frontier. In time the
Argonauts aged and calmed down, and the sons of the pioneers
took over, drafting a new constitution, gearing their life to the
railroad, wheat, and the orange, and accommodating themselves
to the tourist, the health seeker, and the real estate promoter. And
since Californians acclimate readily, many of these were tourists,
health seekers, or in real estate.

In history as it was studied and in literature as it was written
the people of this latter day showed more sophistication than their
predecessors. With Hubert Howe Bancroft, Josiah Royce, and
Theodore H. Hittell as the representatives, for the first time on the
local scene history as a reflective study was being pursued. Bancroft the businessman, Royce the philosopher, and Hittell the lawyer had their differences, but they emphatically agreed that the
climax of the state's history was in the span between 1846 and
1865. Bancroft, for instance, gave ten times as much space to that
period as to the longer stretch from 1865 to 1890. Their biblio-
graphical place is elsewhere, but as members of this generation
they are of significance.

Sophistication is not the characteristic of Ina Coolbrith's lyrics
nor of the selection here presented from Charles Nordhoff's promotional handbook or Mark Twain's jest about Catgut Cañon.
But much late century writing had the strength of expert scientific

JOHN MUIR

informedness. Ambrose Bierce at times had the impulse merely to be caustic, but when he appraised the veterans of '49 or the aberrations of California speech and letters he got beyond epigram and cleverness. In his treatment of land monopolization Henry George was intent on analyzing consequences. Clarence King's tribute to the sequoias and their neighbors has emotional appeal, but its strength comes from his scientific awareness of the qualities of these trees and their relationship to the environment. What Robert Louis Stevenson was able to see and therefore to describe may be mostly a tribute to his sensitive spirit. Yet here too the impact of his writing is enhanced by the technical accuracy of his description of the processes of nature that were involved. With John Muir it is apparent that as a nature writer he gained immeasurably because of his knowledge of geology and botany. It was because he could read the geological record of a former glacier that he made the discovery of one still alive.

In the sixties, Bret Harte lost out on an appointment in the University of California—or, more accurately, it was the university that lost out—because he had written jocosely about an earthquake. In 1890 T. S. Van Dyke could mercilessly lampoon the boom and bust of the eighties; the business interest apparently was not altogether sacred. Yet Californians of this era had quite a capacity for sentimentality. Charles F. Lummis' eulogy of the California lion is suffused with it, and the urban counterpart can be seen in Gelett Burgess' tribute to the cable car.

Alongside this that may be called escapist, writers of the literary persuasion were more attentive to the major problems of the day than were the state's historians. That of course was Henry George's preoccupation, and Muir entered vigorously into the conservation fight. The Chinese exclusion question inspired diatribe rather than literary masterpieces, and Los Angeles' fight for a free harbor was waged at the lower political level. But the uphill struggle to break the political and economic stranglehold of the Southern Pacific enlisted Josiah Royce in his role as novelist (*The Feud of Oakfield Creek*) and provided the theme for Frank Norris' crusading novel *The Octopus*. There the reader's sympathy is invited for the embattled farmers caught in the toils of the great corporation.

Life went on, some of it in quite direct carryover from earlier days as is suggested in Arnold R. Rojas' cowboy anecdote. In many fields there was noteworthy material improvement—in railroading with the oil-burning locomotive and the refrigerator car, in citrus raising with the Washington navel, and with other technological gains such as the Stockton gang plow for which Wallace Smith gives the specifications. Technology of another sort, the style current in medical prescription, was basic to the great health rush. Life went on, but, as Franklin Walker's roll call tells, the generation that witnessed the passing of the frontier made its own exit from the scene.

The California Poppy

BY INA COOLBRITH

Conscious that they had acted out a momentous drama, veterans of the gold rush called for a poet to do justice to this epic theme. None responded, but poetry was a much exercised form. There was a long epidemic of anecdotal poems, introspective verse, rhymed declamations for public occasions, and comic and tragicomic parodies. Perhaps least emphasized was serious verse, western in theme. Among the host of versifiers Ina Coolbrith stands out with a long career of competent production. She was, in addition, the rallying point for California's literary frontiersmen. They enthusiastically applauded her selection as poet laureate.

Thy satin vesture richer is than looms
Of Orient weave for raiment of her kings.
Not dyes of old Tyre, not precious things
Regathered from the long forgotten tombs
Of buried empires, not the iris plumes
That wave upon the tropic's myriad wings,
Not all proud Sheba's queenly offerings,
Could match the golden marvel of thy blooms.

For thou art nurtured from the treasure veins
Of this fair land; thy golden rootlets sup
Her sands of gold—of gold thy petals spun.
Her golden glory, thou! on hills and plains
Lifting, exultant, every kingly cup,
Brimmed with the golden vintage of the sun.

Ina Coolbrith, *Songs from the Golden Gate*
(Boston, 1895), 152.

Snatches from the Town Crier

BY AMBROSE BIERCE

Grim, sardonic, bitter, Ambrose Bierce was ruthless in criticizing inferior writing and meticulous in sharpening his own shafts. His Civil War stories are held up as the best of his writing. To California readers he poured forth forty years of columns, not every one inspired, but what prudent reader would have dared to skip one! Here, from assorted outlets, are samples:

It is with grim satisfaction that we record the destruction by fire of Bierstadt's celebrated picture of Yosemite Valley. The painting has been a prolific parent of ten thousand abominations. We have had Yosemite in oils, in water colors, in crayon, in chalk and charcoal until in our very dreams we imagine ourselves falling from the summit of El Capitan or descending in spray from the Bridal Veil cataract. Besides, that picture has incited more unpleasant people to visit California than all our conspiring hotel-keepers could compel to return. . . . We are glad a blow has finally been struck at the root of immigration. If we can now corral Hill's painting and send East all the rest we may hope for peace. If not, we trust some daring spirit will be found to blow up the infernal valley with Giant powder or glycerine soap.

—San Francisco *News-Letter*, September 4, 1869.

Twenty pioneers, who have not seen "God's Country" since '49, have arranged to go east in June. We warn that tributary section that a treat is in store for it. The gentlemen in question are a rarity —each is six feet four in his moccasins, and with a beard as long as your arm. Each carries three Colt revolvers and a bowie-knife, and usually an exaggerated rifle. They all pack about them habitually their picks and rockers, and one adobe house to four men. They are addicted to profanity, tobacco, hanging, chivalry, and weeping at the sight of babies. Every man of them carries about fifteen pounds of gold dust in his belt, and is accustomed to bestow it upon whomever will accept. We must not omit, among other qualities, to notice their slouch hats, red shirts, and top-boots. Such, dear eastern friends, are these '49ers, as you yourselves have created them—such the homely virtues, for which they are indebted to your own lively fancy. If you find them a bevy of asthmatic old gentlemen in stove-pipe hats and clean shirts, mild-mannered to the point of inanity, and somewhat given to lying, you may justly decline to receive them; they are imposters, and you may keep the dinner warm until the genuine heroes shall appear. Meantime, hold your breath till you see them.

—News-Letter, May 5, 1870.

A writer in a Nevada journal thinks I am not as nobly merciful as I could afford to be to the local poets, and comes near losing his head in restless speculation as to the origin of my animosity. I really do not clearly apprehend the matter myself—am unable to determine the cause of my resentment, trace its progress, or assign a date to its perfection. The knowledge of their existence and the revelation of my contempt for them came to me so nearly together than I don't know if I read them before despising, or despised them before reading. If it is pretty much the same thing to them it certainly is to me, and they may profitably turn to the mending of their verses, and I to the manner of their mending.

Argonaut, April 6, 1878.

Messrs. Perrine and Moleter having been perpetually enjoined from making artificial stone pavement, perhaps they might profitably undertake the making of handy little pocket bowlders to fling at Chinamen. One can hardly ever get his hands on a rock of just the right size and weight until his opportunity has passed into an adjacent wash-house.

—*Wasp*, May 21, 1881.

We do not know how to make a harrow, and if we did we should not tell you. It is the policy of this paper to discourage agriculture, which seems to us a very useless industry.

—*News-Letter*, August 27, 1870.

California is a word that does not lend itself very readily to the schemes of the philologer. It makes an excellent noun and adjective, but the latter is having a mighty hard struggle to get into use. We call ourselves "Californians" readily enough, but it requires a good deal of coaxing to say "Californian" climate, or "Californian" anything. Heaven has somehow put it into our hearts that that is a tenderfooted way of speaking, and we won't have it—just as we will have "sheep-herder" for "shepherd," and be consciously and delightedly guilty of a multitude of other verbal absurdities. The Sierras are not rugged enough; we must have a philological and grammatical frontier.

—San Francisco *Examiner*, February 12, 1888.

I found a young man, the youngest young man, it seemed to me, that I had ever confronted. His appearance, his attitude, his manner, his entire personality suggested extreme diffidence. I did not ask him in, instate him in my better chair (I had two) and inquire how we could serve each other. If my memory is not at fault I merely said: "Well," and awaited the result.

"I am from the San Francisco *Examiner*," he explained in a voice like the fragrance of violets made audible, and backed a little away.

"O," I said, "you come from Mr. Hearst."

Then that unearthly child lifted its blue eyes and cooed: "I am Mr. Hearst."

—"A Thumb-Nail Sketch," *Works*, XII, 305.

The Effect of Land Monopolization

BY HENRY GEORGE

Struck by the juxtaposition of wealth and poverty in California, Henry George, without benefit of formal tutelage in economics, adumbrated his theory that land speculation and greed for the unearned increment were at the bottom of all economic ills. He carried this theme to the world with Progress and Poverty *(1880) and his gospel of the single tax is still accepted by many.* Our Land and Land Policy *in 1871 was a preliminary exercise toward this larger work.*

It is not we, of this generation, but our children of the next, who will fully realize the evils of the land monopolization which we have permitted and encouraged; for those evils do not begin to fully show themselves until population becomes dense.

But already, while our great State, with an area larger than that of France or Spain or Turkey—with an area equal to that of all of Great Britain, Holland, Belgium, Denmark and Greece, combined—does not contain the population of a third class modern city; already, ere we have commenced to manure our lands or to more than prospect the treasures of our hills, the evils of land monopolization are showing themselves in such unmistakable signs that he who runs may read. This is the blight that has fallen upon California, stunting her growth and mocking her golden promise, offsetting to the immigrant the richness of her soil and the beneficence of her climate.

It has already impressed its mark upon the character of our agriculture—more shiftless, perhaps, than that of any State in the Union where slavery has not reigned. For California is not a country of farms, but a country of plantations and estates. Agriculture is a speculation. The farm houses, as a class, are unpainted frame shanties, without a garden or flower or tree. The farmer raises wheat; he buys his meat, his flour, his butter, his vegetables and frequently, even his eggs. He has too much land to spare time for such little things, or for beautifying his home, or he is merely a renter, or an occupant of land menaced by some adverse title, and his interest is but to get for this season the greatest crop that can be made to grow with the least labor. He hires labor for his planting and his reaping, and his hands shift for themselves at other seasons of the year. His plow he leaves standing in the furrow, when the year's plowing is done; his mustangs he turns upon the hills, to be lassooed when again needed. He buys on credit at the nearest store, and when his crop is gathered must sell it to the Grain King's agent, at the Grain King's prices.

And there is another type of California farmer. He boards at the San Francisco hotels, and drives a spanking team over the Cliff House road; or, perhaps, he spends his time in the gayer capitals of the East or Europe. His land is rented for one-third or one-fourth of the crop, or is covered by scraggy cattle, which need to look after them only a few half-civilized vaqueros; or his great wheat fields, of from ten to twenty thousand acres, are plowed and sown and reaped by contract. And over our ill-kept, shadeless, dusty roads, where a house is an unwonted land-mark, and which run frequently for miles through the same man's land, plod the tramps, with blankets on back—the laborers of the California farmer—looking for work, in its seasons, or toiling back to the city when the plowing is ended or the wheat crop is gathered. I do not say that this picture is a universal one, but it is a characteristic one.

It is not only in agriculture, but in all other avocations, and in all the manifestations of social life, that the effect of land monopoly may be seen—in the knotting up of business into the control of little rings, in the concentration of capital into a few hands, in the reduction of wages in the mechanical trades, in the gradual decadence of that independent personal habit both of thought and action which gave to California life its greatest charm, in the palpable differentiation of our people into the classes of rich and poor. Of the "general stagnation" of which we of California have been so long complaining, this is the most efficient cause. Had the unused land of California been free, at Government terms, to those who would cultivate it, instead of this "general stagnation" of the past two years, we should have seen a growth unexampled in the history of even the American States. For with all our hyperbole, it is almost impossible to overestimate the advantages with which nature has so lavishly endowed this Empire State of ours. "God's

Country," the returning prospectors used to call it, and the strong expression loses half of its irreverence as, coming over sage brush plains, from the still frost-bound East, the traveler winds, in the early Spring, down the slope of the Sierra, through interminable ranks of evergreen giants, past laughing rills and banks of wild flowers, and sees under their cloudless sky the vast fertile valleys stretching out to the dark blue Coast Range in the distance. But while nature has done her best to invite new comers, our land policy has done its best to repel them. We have said to the immigrant: "It is a fair country which God has made between the Sierra and the sea, but before you settle in it and begin to reap His bounty, you must pay a forestaller roundly for *his* permission." And the immigrant having far to come and but scanty capital, has as a general thing stayed away.

Henry George, *Our Land and Land Policy,*
National and State (San Francisco, 1871), 24-25.

The Sequoias

BY CLARENCE KING

Many of his friends thought Clarence King the greatest of all conversationists. He had other charms and other talents. As geologist he supervised the survey along the 40th parallel. As engineer he advised many mining companies. Combining these talents he exploded the great diamond hoax of 1872. Aside from a few scattered articles Mountaineering in the Sierra Nevada *is his one contribution to humane letters.*

The mill-people and Indians told us of a wonderful group of big trees *(Sequoia gigantea)*, and about one particular tree of unequalled size. We found them easily, after a ride of a few miles in a northerly direction from our camp, upon a wide, flat-topped spur, where they grew, as is their habit elsewhere, in company with several other coniferous species, all grouped socially together, heightening each other's beauty by contrasts of form and color.

301

In a rather open glade, where the ground was for the most part green with herbage, and conspicuously starred with upland flowers, stood the largest shaft we observed. A fire had formerly burned off a small segment of its base, not enough, however, to injure the symmetrical appearance. It was a slowly tapering, regularly round column of about forty feet in diameter at the base, and rising two hundred and seventy-four feet, adorned with a few huge branches, which start horizontally from the trunk, but quickly turn down and spray out. The bark, thick but not rough, is scored up and down at considerable intervals with deep, smooth grooves, and is of brightest cinnamon color mottled in purple and yellow.

That which impresses one most after its vast bulk and grand, pillar-like stateliness, is the thin and inconspicuous foliage, which feathers out delicately on the boughs like a mere mist of pale apple-green. It would seem nothing when compared with the immense volume of tree for which it must do the ordinary respirative duty; but doubtless the bark performs a large share of this, its papery lamination and porous structure fitting it eminently for that purpose.

Near this "King of the Mountains" grew three other trees; one a sugar-pine *(Pinus Lambertiana)* of about eight feet in diameter, and hardly less than three hundred feet high (although we did not measure it, estimating simply by comparison of its rise above the *Sequoia*, whose height was quite accurately determined). For a hundred and fifty feet the pine was branchless, and as round as if turned, delicate bluish-purple in hue, and marked with a network of scorings. The branches, in nearly level poise, grew long and slenderly out from the shaft, well covered with dark yellow-green needles. The two remaining trees were firs *(Picea grandis)*, which sprung from a common root, dividing slightly, as they rose, a mass of feathery branches, whose load of polished blue-green foliage, for the most part, hid the dark wood-brown trunk. Grace, exquisite spire-like taper boughs, whose plumes of green float lightly upon the air, elasticity, and symmetry, are its characteristics.

In all directions this family continue grouping themselves always with attractive originality. There is something memorable

302

in the harmonious yet positive colors of this sort of forest. First, the foliage and trunk of each separate tree contrasts finely,—cinnamon and golden apple-green in the *Sequoia*, dark purple and yellowish-green for the pine, deep wood-color and bluish-green of fir.

The sky, which at this elevation of six thousand feet is deep pure blue and often cloudless, is seen through the tracery of boughs and tree-tops, which cast downward fine and filmy shadows across the glowing trunks. Altogether, it is a wonderful setting for the *Sequoia*. The two firs, judging by many of equal size whose age I have studied, were about three hundred years old; the pine, still hale and vigorous, not less than five hundred; and for the "King of the Mountains" we cannot assign a probable age of less than two thousand years.

A mountain, a fossil from deepest geological horizon, a ruin of human art, carry us back into the perspective of centuries with a force that has become, perhaps, a little conventional. No imperishableness of mountain-peak or of fragment of human work, broken pillar or sand-worn image half lifted over pathetic desert, —none of these link the past and to-day with anything like the power of these monuments of living antiquity, trees that began to grow before the Christian era, and, full of hale vitality and green old age, still bid fair to grow broad and high for centuries to come. Who shall predict the limits of this unexampled life? There is nothing which indicates suffering or degeneracy in the *Sequoia* as a species. I find pathological hints that several other far younger species in the same forest are gradually giving up their struggle for existence. That singular species *Pinus Sabiniana* appears to me to suffer death-pains from foot-hill extremes of temperature and dryness, and notably from ravenous parasites of the mistletoe type. At the other extreme the *Pinus flexilis* has about half given up the fight against cold and storms. Its young are dwarfed or huddled in thickets, with such mode of growth that they may never make trees of full stature; while higher up, standing among bare rocks and fields of ice, far above all living trees, are the stark white skeletons of noble dead specimens, their blanched forms rigid and defiant, preserved from decay by a marvellous hardness of fibre, and only wasted by the cutting of storm-driven crystals of snow. Still the *Sequoia* maintains perfect health.

It is, then, the vast respiring power, the atmosphere, the bland, regular climate, which give such long life, and not any richness or abundance of food received from the soil.

Clarence King, *Mountaineering in the Sierra Nevada* (Boston, 1871), 40-43.

Haven for Invalids

BY CHARLES NORDHOFF

A man of broad experience and wide interests, Charles Nordhoff wrote on such subjects as life at sea, slavery, the Civil War, communistic societies, and the reasons for coming to California. Claims such as his about the healing power of the California climate played no small role in generating the health rush of the eighteen-seventies, eighties, and nineties, a phenomenon best described in John E. Baur's Health Seekers of Southern California.

A friend and neighbor of my own, consumptive for some years, and struggling for his life in a winter residence for two years at Nice and Mentone, and during a third at Aiken, in South Carolina, came last October to Southern California.

He had been "losing ground," as he said, and as his appearance showed, for two years, and last summer suffered so severely from night sweats, sleeplessness, continual coughing, and lack of appetite, that it was doubtful whether he would live through the winter anywhere; and it was rather in desperation than with much hope of a prolonged or comfortable life that he made ready for the journey across the continent with his family.

In January I was one day standing in the door-way of a hotel at Los Angeles, when I saw a wagon drive up; the driver jumped out, held out his hand to me, and sung out in a hearty voice, "How do you do?" It was my consumptive friend, but a changed man.

He had just driven sixty miles in two days, over a rough road, from San Bernardino; he walked with me several miles on the evening we met; he ate heartily and slept well, enjoyed his life, and coughed hardly at all. It was an amazing change to come about in three months, and in a man so ill as he had been.

"I shall never be a sound man, of course," he said to me when I spent some days with him, later, at San Bernardino; "but this climate has added ten years to my life; it has given me ease and comfort; and neither Nice, nor Mentone, nor Aiken are, in my opinion, to be compared with some parts of Southern California in point of climate for consumptives."

In Santa Barbara, San Diego, and San Bernardino, one may find abundant evidence corroborative of my friend's assertion. In each of these places I have met men and women who have been restored to health and strength by residence there; and though no one whom I met had had the wide experience of my friend in other winter resorts, I found not a few people of intelligence and means who bore the strongest testimony to the kindly and healing influences of the climate of Southern California.

I think I shall be doing a service, therefore, to many invalids if I give here some details concerning the places I have named, and some others, but little known as yet in the East, which are now accessible, and whose beneficial influences upon diseases of the throat and lungs are undoubtedly remarkable.

The whole of Southern California has a very mild and equable winter climate. Stockton, for instance, which lies at the head of the San Joaquin Valley, has a temperature all the year singularly like that of Naples, as is shown by observations kept for some years by one of the most eminent and careful physicians of the place. But local peculiarities cause in some places daily extremes which are not, I think, favorable for invalids; and in other points the winds are too severe for weakly persons. At Los Angeles, for instance, the days in January are warm and genial, but as soon as the sun sets the air becomes chilly, and quickly affects tender throats. San Diego, Santa Barbara, San Bernardino, with Stockton and Visalia, are the points most favorable for consumptives and persons subject to throat difficulties.

Of these, the friend of whom I spoke above found San Bernardino the most beneficial; and a physician, who had removed from an Eastern city to the new Riverside Colony near San Bernardino, told me that he lived nowhere so comfortably as there. He could not live in New York at all, being prostrated with severe throat disease; and he enjoyed, he told me, perfect health at Riverside. . . .

San Diego seems to me to possess the mildest and sunniest winter climate on the coast. It has the advantage of a large and excellent hotel, and very good shops, and the disadvantage of an almost entire absence of shade and trees. It has pleasant society, and within thirty miles very fine and varied scenery. If I were spending a winter in California for my health, I think I should go first to San Diego, and stay there the months of December and January. It is the most southern town in the State, and presumably warmer than either Santa Barbara or San Bernardino, though the difference is but slight. It affords some simple amusements, in fishing, shell-hunting, and boat-sailing; and here, as all over Southern California, horses are cheap; and to those who are fond of driving or riding, very fair roads are open. There is less rain here than in any other part of the State; and as the so-called winter in the State is a rainy season, San Diego has the advantage over other places of less mud in December and January. In fact, I doubt if it is ever muddy there.

Santa Barbara is on many accounts the pleasantest of all the places I have named; and it has an advantage in this, that one may there choose his climate within a distance of three or four miles of the town. It has a very peculiar situation. If you will examine a map of California, you will see that, while the general "trend" of the coast-line is from north-north-west to south-south-east, at Point Conception it makes a sharp and sudden turn, and runs to Rincon Point, below Santa Barbara, nearly due east and west. Thus Santa Barbara faces directly south. . . .

Wherever you go, you need to take with you a cheerful and also an inquiring spirit. The whole of Southern California is full of novelties and wonders to an intelligent person; but oftenest he must discover them for himself. You will not find highly cultivated and ornamented gardens; but from January onward to June, you will, if you have eyes for them, discover in your rambles a succession of beautiful, and to you new wild flowers. Theatres and other places of amusement you will not find in the towns I have mentioned; but for all healthful open-air enjoyments you will have extraordinary facilities, because the life is free and untrammeled. You are expected to do what you please; horses are cheap; roads are almost invariably excellent; every place has a good livery-stable; you can get competent guides; and you carry with you, wherever you go, fine mountain scenery, bright sunshine—so constant that, when I remarked to a citizen of San Diego that it was a fine day, he looked at me in amazement, and said, after a pause, "Of course it is a fine day; why not? Every day is fine here." Moreover, at all these places you will meet pleasant, intelligent, and hospitable people, who will add somewhat to your enjoyment. Santa Barbara has even a circulating library. There are good schools for children, if you have such with you; and with a little enterprise to plan excursions, your time will not hang heavily on your hands.

Charles Nordhoff, *California for Health, Pleasure, and Residence*
(New York, 1872), 109-112, 116.

Mining Methods in Catgut Cañon

BY SAMUEL CLEMENS

A good dozen years after he left California, Clemens put his western experience through the pan once more and came up with this bit of color. It was packaged as a letter to the editors of the New York Evening Post, *September 17, 1880.*

I have just seen your despatch from San Francisco, in Saturday's *Evening Post*, about "Gold in Solution" in the Calistoga Springs, and about the proprietor's having "extracted $1,060 in gold of the utmost fineness from ten barrels of water" during the past fortnight, by a process known only to himself. This will surprise many of your readers, but it does not surprise me, for I once owned those springs myself. What does surprise me, however, is the falling off in the richness of the water. In my time the yield was a dollar a dipperful. I am not saying this to injure the property, in case a sale is contemplated. I am only saying it in the interest of history. It may be that this hotel proprietor's process is an inferior one— yes, that may be the fault. Mine was to take my uncle—I had an extra uncle at that time, on account of his parents dying and leaving him on my hands—and fill him up, and let him stand fifteen minutes to give the water a chance to settle well, then insert him in an exhausted receiver, which had the effect of sucking the gold out through his pores. I have taken more than eleven thousand dollars out of that old man in a day and a half. I should have held on to those springs but for the badness of the roads and the difficulty of getting the gold to market.

I consider that gold-yielding water in many respects remarkable; and yet not more remarkable than the gold bearing air of Catgut Cañon, up there toward the head of the auriferous range. This air—or this wind—for it is a kind of a trade wind which blows steadily down through six hundred miles of rich quartz croppings during an hour and a quarter every day except Sundays, is heavily charged with exquisitely fine and impalpable gold. Nothing precipitates and solidifies this gold so readily as contact with human flesh heated by passion. The time that William Abrahams was disappointed in love, he used to stop out doors when that wind was blowing, and come in again and begin to sigh, and his brother Andover J. would extract over a dollar and a half out of every sigh he sighed, right along. And the time that John Harbison and Aleck Norton quarrelled about Harbison's dog, they stood there swearing at each other all they knew how—and what they didn't know about swearing they couldn't learn from you and me, not by a good deal—and at the end of every three or four minutes they had to stop and make a dividend—if they didn't their jaws would clog up so that they couldn't get the big nine syllabled ones out at all—and when the wind was done blowing they cleaned up just a little over sixteen hundred dollars apiece. I know these facts to be absolutely true, because I got them from a man whose mother I knew personally. I do not suppose a person could buy a water privilege at Calistoga now at any price; but several good locations along the course of the Catgut Cañon Gold-Bearing Trade-Wind are for sale. They are going to be stocked for the New York market. They will sell, too; the people will swarm for them as thick as Hancock veterans—in the South.

Reproduced by Edwin H. Carpenter, Jr.,
Pacific Historical Review, XVIII (1949), 109-111.

The Sea Fogs

BY ROBERT LOUIS STEVENSON

*Although Robert Louis Stevenson was in California less than a
year, that was long enough for an identification with Monterey,
San Francisco, and Mount St. Helena. The California experience
shows in* Treasure Island; The Wrecker; The Great North Road;
and particularly in The Silverado Squatters, *the strangest narrative of a honeymoon ever written.*

A change in the colour of the light usually called me in the morning. By a certain hour, the long, vertical chinks in our western
gable, where the boards had shrunk and separated, flashed suddenly into my eyes as stripes of dazzling blue, at once so dark and
splendid that I used to marvel how the qualities could be combined. At an earlier hour, the heavens in that quarter were still
quietly coloured, but the shoulder of the mountain which shuts
in the canyon already glowed with sunlight in a wonderful compound of gold and rose and green; and this too would kindle, although more mildly and with rainbow tints, the fissures of our
crazy gable. If I were sleeping heavily, it was the bold blue that
struck me awake; if more lightly, then I would come to myself in
that earlier and fairer light.

One Sunday morning, about five, the first brightness called me.
I rose and turned to the east, not for my devotions, but for air.
The night had been very still. The little private gale that blew
every evening in our canyon, for ten minutes or perhaps a quarter of an hour, had swiftly blown itself out; in the hours that followed not a sigh of wind had shaken the treetops; and our barrack,
for all its breaches, was less fresh that morning than of wont. But
I had no sooner reached the window than I forgot all else in the
sight that met my eyes, and I made but two bounds into my clothes,
and down the crazy plank to the platform.

The sun was still concealed below the opposite hilltops, though
it was shining already, not twenty feet above my head, on our
mountain slope. But the scene, beyond a few near features, was
entirely changed. Napa valley was gone; gone were all the lower

slopes and woody foothills of the range; and in their place, not a thousand feet below me, rolled a great level ocean. It was as though I had gone to bed the night before, safe in a nook of in-land mountains, and had awakened in a bay upon the coast. I had seen these inundations from below; at Calistoga I had risen and gone abroad in the early morning, coughing and sneezing, under fathoms on fathoms of gray sea vapour, like a cloudy sky—a dull sight for the artist, and a painful experience for the invalid. But to sit aloft one's self in the pure air and under the unclouded dome of heaven, and thus look down on the submergence of the valley, was strangely different and even delightful to the eyes. Far away were hilltops like little islands. Nearer, a smoky surf beat about the foot of precipices and poured into all the coves of these rough mountains. The colour of that fog ocean was a thing never to be forgotten. For an instant, among the Hebrides and just about sun-down, I have seen something like it on the sea itself. But the white was not so opaline; nor was there, what surprisingly increased the effect, that breathless, crystal stillness over all. Even in its gentle-est moods the salt sea travails, moaning among the weeds or lisp-ing on the sand; but that vast fog ocean lay in a trance of silence, nor did the sweet air of the morning tremble with a sound.

As I continued to sit upon the dump, I began to observe that this sea was not so level as at first sight it appeared to be. Away in the extreme south, a little hill of fog arose against the sky above the general surface, and as it had already caught the sun, it shone on the horizon like the topsails of some giant ship. There were huge waves, stationary, as it seemed, like waves in a frozen sea; and yet, as I looked again, I was not sure but they were moving after all, with a slow and august advance. And while I was yet doubting, a promontory of the hills some four or five miles away, conspicuous by a bouquet of tall pines, was in a single instant over-taken and swallowed up. It reappeared in a little, with its pines, but this time as an islet, and only to be swallowed up once more and then for good. This set me looking nearer, and I saw that in every cove along the line of mountains the fog was being piled in higher and higher, as though by some wind that was inaudible to me. I could trace its progress, one pine tree first growing hazy and then disappearing after another; although sometimes there was none of this forerunning haze, but the whole opaque white ocean gave a start and swallowed a piece of mountain at a gulp. It was to flee these poisonous fogs that I had left the seaboard, and climbed so high among the mountains. And now, behold, here came the fog to besiege me in my chosen altitudes, and yet came so beautifully that my first thought was of welcome.

The sun had now gotten much higher, and through all the gaps of the hills it cast long bars of gold across that white ocean. An eagle, or some other very great bird of the mountain, came wheeling over the nearer pine-tops, and hung, poised and something sideways, as if to look abroad on that unwonted desolation, spying, perhaps with terror, for the eyries of her comrades. Then, with a long cry, she disappeared again towards Lake County and the clearer air. At length it seemed to me as if the flood were beginning to subside. The old landmarks, by whose disappearance I had measured its advance, here a crag, there a brave pine tree, now began, in the inverse order, to make their reappearance into daylight. I judged all danger of the fog was over. This was not Noah's flood; it was but a morning spring, and would now drift out seaward whence it came. So, mightily relieved, and a good deal exhilarated by the sight, I went into the house to light the fire.

I suppose it was nearly seven when I once more mounted the platform to look abroad. The fog ocean had swelled up enormously since last I saw it; and a few hundred feet below me, in the deep gap where the Toll House stands and the road runs through into Lake County, it had already topped the slope, and was pouring over and down the other side like driving smoke. The wind had climbed along with it; and though I was still in calm air, I could see the trees tossing below me, and their long, strident sighing mounted to me where I stood.

Half an hour later, the fog surmounted all the ridge on the opposite side of the gap, though a shoulder of the mountain still warded it out of our canyon. Napa valley and its bounding hills were now utterly blotted out. The fog, sunny white in the sunshine, was pouring over into Lake County in a huge, ragged cataract, tossing treetops appearing and disappearing in the spray. The air struck with a little chill, and set me coughing. It smelt strong of the fog, like the smell of a washing-house, but with a shrewd tang of the sea salt.

Had it not been for two things—the sheltering spur which answered as a dyke, and the great valley on the other side which rapidly engulfed whatever mounted—our own little platform in the canyon must have been already buried a hundred feet in salt and poisonous air. As it was, the interest of the scene entirely occupied our minds. We were set just out of the wind, and but just above the fog; we could listen to the voice of the one as to music on the stage; we could plunge our eyes down into the other, as into some flowing stream from over the parapet of a bridge; thus we looked on upon a strange, impetuous, silent, shifting exhibition of the powers of nature, and saw the familiar landscape changing from moment to moment like figures in a dream.

The imagination loves to trifle with what is not. Had this been indeed the deluge, I should have felt more strongly, but the emotion would have been similar in kind. I played with the idea, as the child flees in delighted terror from the creations of his fancy. The look of the thing helped me. And when at last I began to flee up the mountain, it was indeed partly to escape from the raw air that kept me coughing, but it was also part in play.

As I ascended the mountain-side, I came once more to overlook the upper surface of the fog; but it wore a different appearance from what I had beheld at daybreak. For, first, the sun now fell on it from high overhead, and its surface shone and undulated like a great nor'land moor country, sheeted with untrodden morning snow. And next the new level must have been a thousand or fifteen hundred feet higher than the old, so that only five or six points of all the broken country below me still stood out. Napa valley was now one with Sonoma on the west. On the hither side, only a thin scattered fringe of bluffs was unsubmerged; and through all the gaps the fog was pouring over, like an ocean, into the blue clear sunny country on the east. There it was soon lost; for it fell instantly into the bottom of the valleys, following the water-shed; and the hilltops in that quarter were still clear cut upon the eastern sky.

Through the Toll House gap and over the near ridges on the other side, the deluge was immense. A spray of thin vapour was thrown high above it, rising and falling, and blown into fantastic shapes. The speed of its course was like a mountain torrent. Here and there a few treetops were discovered and then whelmed again; and for one second, the bough of a dead pine beckoned out of the spray like the arm of a drowning man. But still the imagination was dissatisfied, still the ear waited for something more. Had this indeed been water (as it seemed so, to the eye), with what a plunge of reverberating thunder would it have rolled upon its course, dis-embowelling mountains and deracinating pines! And yet water it was, and seawater at that—true Pacific billows, only somewhat rarefied, rolling in mid-air among the hilltops.

I climbed still higher, among the red rattling gravel and dwarf underwood of Mount Saint Helena, until I could look right down upon Silverado, and admire the favoured nook in which it lay. The sunny plain of fog was several hundred feet higher; behind the protecting spur a gigantic accumulation of cottony vapour threatened with every second, to blow over and submerge our homestead; but the vortex setting past the Toll House was too strong; and there lay our little platform, in the arms of the deluge, but still enjoying its unbroken sunshine. About eleven, however, thin spray came flying over the friendly buttress and I began to think the fog had hunted out its Jonah after all. But it was the last effort. The wind veered while we were at dinner, and began to blow squally from the mountain summit; and by half-past one, all that world of sea fogs was utterly routed and flying here and there into the south in little rags of cloud. And instead of a lone sea-beach, we found ourselves once more inhabiting a high moun-tain-side with the clear green country far below us, and the light smoke of Calistoga blowing in the air.

This was the great Russian campaign for that season. Now and then, in the early morning, a little white lakelet of fog would be seen far down in Napa valley; but the heights were not again as-sailed, nor was the surrounding world again shut off from Sil-verado.

Robert Louis Stevenson, *The Silverado Squatters* (London, 1883), 155-169.

FAWN   *by Cedric Wright*

Discovering the Sierra Glaciers

BY JOHN MUIR

Naturalist extraordinary, lone wanderer in the wilds, founder of the Sierra Club, and staunchest exponent of the preservation of the wilderness, John Muir was one of California's most effective citizens. That as a writer he could evoke the beauty of Nature was one of his strengths. He was a good scientist too, as he proved by the correctness of his theory that the polished rock canyons such as Yosemite were products of glaciation.

Prior to the autumn of 1871 the glaciers of the Sierra were unknown. In October of that year I discovered the Black Mountain Glacier in a shadowy amphitheater between Black and Red Mountains, two of the peaks of the Merced group. This group is the highest portion of a spur that straggles out from the main axis of the range in the direction of Yosemite Valley. At the time of this interesting discovery I was exploring the *névé* amphitheaters of this group, and tracing the courses of the ancient glaciers that once poured from its ample fountains through the Illilouette Basin and the Yosemite Valley, not expecting to find any active glaciers so far south in the land of sunshine.

Beginning on the northwestern extremity of the group, I explored the chief tributary basins in succession, their moraines, roches moutonnées, and splendid glacier pavements, taking them in regular succession without any reference to the time consumed in their study. The monuments of the tributary that poured its ice from between Red and Black Mountains I found to be the most interesting of them all; and when I saw its magnificent moraines extending in majestic curves from the spacious amphitheater between the mountains, I was exhilarated with the work that lay before me. It was one of the golden days of the Sierra Indian summer, when the rich sunshine glorifies every landscape however rocky and cold, and suggests anything rather than glaciers. The path of the vanished glacier was warm now, and shone in many places as if washed with silver. The tall pines growing on the moraines stood transfigured in the glowing light, the poplar groves on the levels of the basin were masses of orange-yellow, and the late-blooming goldenrods added gold to gold. Pushing on over my rosy glacial highway, I passed lake after lake set in solid basins of granite, and many a thicket and meadow watered by a stream that issues from the amphitheater and links the lakes together; now wading through plushy bogs knee-deep in yellow and purple sphagnum; now passing over bare rock. The main lateral moraines that bounded the view on either hand are from 100 to nearly 200 feet high, and about as regular as artificial enbankments, and covered with a superb growth of Silver Fir and Pine. But this garden and forest luxuriance was speedily left behind. The trees were dwarfed as I ascended; patches of the alpine bryanthus and cassiope began to appear, and arctic willows pressed into flat carpets by the winter snow. The lakelets, which a few miles down the valley were so richly embroidered with flowery meadows, had here, at an elevation of 10,000 feet, only small brown mats of carex, leaving bare rocks around more than half their shores. Yet amid this alpine suppression the Mountain Pine bravely tossed his storm-beaten branches on the ledges and buttresses of Red Mountain, some specimens being over 100 feet high, and 24 feet in circumference, seemingly as fresh and vigorous as the giants of the lower zones.

Evening came on just as I got fairly within the portal of the main amphitheater. It is about a mile wide, and a little less than two miles long. The crumbling spurs and battlements of Red Mountain bound it on the north, the somber, rudely sculptured precipices of Black Mountain on the south, and a hacked, splintery *col*, curving around from mountain to mountain, shuts it in on the east.

I chose a camping-ground on the brink of one of the lakes where a thicket of Hemlock Spruce sheltered me from the night wind. Then, after making a tin-cupful of tea, I sat by my camp-fire reflecting on the grandeur and significance of the glacial records I had seen. As the night advanced the mighty rock walls of my mountain mansion seemed to come nearer, while the starry sky in glorious brightness stretched across like a ceiling from wall to wall, and fitted closely down into all the spiky irregularities of the summits. Then, after a long fireside rest and a glance at my note-

316

book, I cut a few leafy branches for a bed, and fell into the clear, death-like sleep of the tired mountaineer.

Early next morning I set out to trace the grand old glacier that had done so much for the beauty of the Yosemite region back to its farthest fountains, enjoying the charm that every explorer feels in Nature's untrodden wildernesses. The voices of the mountains were still asleep. The wind scarce stirred the pine-needles. The sun was up, but it was yet too cold for the birds and the few burrowing animals that dwell here. Only the stream, cascading from pool to pool, seemed to be wholly awake. Yet the spirit of the opening day called to action. The sunbeams came streaming gloriously through the jagged openings of the *col*, glancing on the burnished pavements and lighting the silvery lakes, while every sun-touched rock burned white on its edges like melting iron in a furnace. Passing round the north shore of my camp lake I followed the central stream past many cascades from lakelet to lakelet. The scenery became more rigidly arctic, the Dwarf Pines and Hemlocks disappeared, and the stream was bordered with icicles. As the sun rose higher rocks were loosened on shattered portions of the cliffs, and came down in rattling avalanches, echoing wildly from crag to crag.

The main lateral moraines that extend from the jaws of the amphitheater into the Illilouette Basin are continued in straggling masses along the walls of the amphitheater, while separate boulders, hundreds of tons in weight, are left stranded here and there out in the middle of the channel. Here, also, I observed a series of small terminal moraines ranged along the south wall of the amphitheater, corresponding in size and form with the shadows cast by the highest portions. The meaning of this correspondence between moraines and shadows was afterward made plain. Tracing the stream back to the last of its chain of lakelets, I noticed a deposit of fine gray mud on the bottom except where the force of the entering current had prevented its settling. It looked like the mud worn from a grindstone, and I at once suspected its glacial origin, for the stream that was carrying it came gurgling out of the base of a raw moraine that seemed in process of formation. Not a plant or weather-stain was visible on its rough, unsettled surface. It is from 60 to over 100 feet high, and plunges forward at an angle of 38°. Cautiously picking my way, I gained the top of the moraine and was delighted to see a small but well-characterized glacier swooping down from the gloomy precipices of Black Mountain in a finely graduated curve to the moraine on which I stood. The compact ice appeared on all the lower portions of the glacier, though gray with dirt and stones embedded in it. Farther up the ice disappeared beneath coarse granulated snow. The surface of the glacier was further characterized by dirt-bands and the outcropping edges of the blue veins, showing the laminated structure of the ice. The uppermost crevasse, or "bergschrund," where the *névé* was attached to the mountain, was from 12 to 14 feet wide, and was bridged in a few places by the remains of snow avalanches. Creeping along the edge of the schrund, holding on with benumbed fingers, I discovered clear sections where the bedded structure was beautifully revealed. The surface-snow, though sprinkled with stones shot down from the cliffs, was in some places almost pure, gradually becoming crystalline and changing to whitish porous ice of different shades of color, and this again changing at a depth of 20 or 30 feet to blue ice, some of the ribbon-like bands of which were nearly pure, and blended with the paler bands in the most gradual and delicate manner imaginable. A series of rugged zigzags enabled me to make my way down into the weird under-world of the crevasse. Its chambered hollows were hung with a multitude of clustered icicles, amid which pale, subdued light pulsed and shimmered with indescribable loveliness. Water dripped and tinkled overhead, and from far below came strange, solemn murmurings from currents that were feeling their way through veins and fissures in the dark. The chambers of a glacier are perfectly enchanting, notwithstanding one feels out of place in their frosty beauty. I was soon cold in my shirt-sleeves, and the leaning wall threatened to engulf me; yet it was hard to leave the delicious music of the water and the lovely light. Coming again to the surface, I noticed boulders of every size on their journeys to the terminal moraine—journeys of more than a hundred years, without a single stop, night or day, winter or summer.

The sun gave birth to a network of sweet-voiced rills that ran gracefully down the glacier, curling and swirling in their shining channels, and cutting clear sections through the porous surface-ice into the solid blue, where the structure of the glacier was beautifully illustrated.

The series of small terminal moraines which I had observed in the morning, along the south wall of the amphitheater, correspond in every way with the moraine of this glacier, and their distribution with reference to shadows was now understood. When the climatic changes came on that caused the melting and retreat of the main glacier that filled the amphitheater, a series of residual glaciers were left in the cliff shadows, under the protection of which they lingered, until they formed the moraines we are studying. Then, as the snow became still less abundant, all of them vanished in succession, except the one just described; and the cause of its longer life is sufficiently apparent in the greater area of snow-basin it drains, and its more perfect protection from wasting sunshine. How much longer this little glacier will last depends, of course, on the amount of snow it receives from year to year, as compared with melting waste.

After this discovery, I made excursions over all the High Sierra, pushing my explorations summer after summer, and discovered that what at first sight in the distance looked like extensive snow-fields, were in great part glaciers, busily at work completing the sculpture of the summit-peaks so grandly blocked out by their giant predecessors.

John Muir, *The Mountains of California*
(New York, 1894), 28-34.

The Great Southern California Boom

BY T. S. VAN DYKE

T. S. Van Dyke came to California as a health seeker and found relief in the warmth and dryness of San Diego and its back country. Assigned an outdoor life, he began to write about it in pieces purely descriptive and in others addressed to hunters and fishermen, vacationers and irrigators. The most enduring of his books is the one here quoted on the boom of the eighties. It strikes what seems

*a happy medium between Glenn S. Dumke's carefully measured
history and Stewart Edward White's more roseate fiction.*

"I wouldn't have missed it for all I have lost. It was worth living
a lifetime to see."

So said to the author last year one of the ex-millionaires. And
in truth he was not far from right. One who has not, as an actor,
been through a first-class "boom" has missed one of the most interesting points of view of human nature.

Now that we have had plenty of time to look back upon the
great boom that raged so long in the six southern counties of
Southern California and gauge its immensity, we can see that it
had never its like on earth. There have indeed been times of wilder
excitement, when property has changed hands oftener in twenty-
four hours and brought perhaps higher prices, but they were limited to a single point or to a brief period, and nearly always to
both. But this boom (for convenience we will drop the quotation-
marks hereafter) lasted nearly two years, embraced a vast area of
both town and country, and involved an amount of money and
players almost incredible to even those who were in it.

There was nothing in this analogous to any South Sea Bubble,
or oil or mining stock swindle, or any other of the great humbugs
of the past. The actors in this great game were not ignorant or
poor people, and from end to end there was scarcely anything in
it that could fairly be called a swindle. What few misrepresenta-
tions there were, were mere matters of opinion such as no one of
sense ever relies on, any more than he does on the assurance that
he will double his money within so many days. With a very few
exceptions the principal victims were men of means. Most of
them, and certainly the most reckless of them, were men who in
some branch of business had been successful. Very many of them
were "self-made men" who had built up fortunes by their own
exertions, and were supposed to know right well the value of a
dollar, and to have some idea of the value of property. All had the
amplest time to revise their judgments and investigate the conditions of the game. The country all lay open, was easily and quickly traversed, and the advantages or disadvantages of any point
could be readily seen. Over and over again the shrewdest of them

did revise their judgments, debated with themselves the question whether they were fools or not, and the more they debated the more they were convinced that they were underestimating instead of overestimating the situation. And some of the silliest of the lot were men who, during the first three fourths of the excitement, kept carefully out of it, and did nothing but sneer at the folly of those who were in it.

The history of such a craze seems worth writing. Much has, of course, been told about it; but no one, unless he had a hand in it and could see its inside working, can tell of it in its most important phases, and nothing would be history that did not follow the results of the folly to their end.

To the people of the older States much of this will seem mere burlesque, and they will toss it aside as unworthy of belief. But the Californian will say that instead of being an exaggeration many interesting facts have been suppressed, probably because the writer dare not tell them. But enough has been told to interest all who were in it, thought it will awaken many a painful recollection, and enough to warn any one who will study it from ever gambling on a margin on any prospects, no matter how good a judge he may think himself of booms and conditions of growth. Of course no warning will have any effect upon the great majority; but one thing is certain—the Californians want no more booms. A steady and substantial growth they do want, are having now, and will continue to have if Eastern boomers do not again set them crazy. They want nothing that will again check true development as the great boom did, and will advise all who think of coming to California to read this brief sketch of the greatest piece of folly that any country has even seen.

T. S. Van Dyke, *Millionaires of a Day*
(New York, 1890), 1-4.

The California Lion

BY CHARLES F. LUMMIS

Charles F. Lummis hiked out to California to become city editor of the Los Angeles Times, *city librarian, founder of the Southwest Museum, the Landmarks Club, and the Sequoyah Club, and editor of a promotional and cultural magazine,* The Land of Sunshine. The Bear Flaggers, *the designer of the state seal, and Bret Harte on the cover of the* Overland, *all honored the bear. On his magazine Lummis, a man of enthusiasms, honored* felis concolor paseandose *and called his editorial column The Lion's Den.*

Of all animate creation, science recognizes the cat family as the most perfect workmanship. No other animal—not even Man—is so unimprovably adjusted to its environments, so absolutely fitted for the life it has to lead. Even evolution, the supreme, slow Afterthought, has found nothing to better in the *felidae*. . . .

No other animal remained so unchanged through the geologic aeons; no other is so unchangeable now. Domesticated for as many millenniums as the dog—and therefore far longer than any other quadruped—he stands in look, in motion, in dignity and independence unchanged from the beginning of the world. He is today the most archaic of all living types; and to the scientist that means that the type was practically perfect. If there had been any room for improvement, Nature would have found it out.   few million

The American lion is *felis concolor*—the puma, cougar, mountain-lion or California lion. His build is essentially leonine, not tigerish; and so are his color and his character. He is most supple of all the great cats. The lither body and lack of mane make him a very different presence from his old-world namesake; but he is very much like the African lioness. . . .

The California lion is not a coward and not a fool. He has learned what civilized man is; he *sabes* "gun." The reflections upon his honor because he has learned this lesson are not creditable to the intelligence of his critics. All the higher animals have learned it, and have become prudent within half a century; only the bull and the average man continue to charge upon the red rag and cold steel of Fate.

322

I know the puma not only in the cage but in his habitat; and every student with that acquaintance respects not only his armature but his character. Barring the jaguar (which does not range north of Mexico) he is the most beautiful creature in the New World; the most graceful, the most dignified, the most superbly competent. He is the highest type of sinewy strength, of agility, of dexterity, of balanced power. Stalking his prey, he is more graceful than a perfect woman, and inevitable as the End. In repose, he is the last word of contained force. Noblest of all is he when he promenades—"walking with himself," as my *paisano* friends have it; *paseandose*, not for prey, but just for joy of his legs. I have studied all the large animals of the New World in their native haunts; and there is none other so lordly.

Charles F. Lummis, *Land of Sunshine*, II
(1895), 80-81.

The Watch

BY ARNOLD R. ROJAS

Although the California cowboy was throwing a longer rope and flourishing before the Texas cowboy began his spread over the Great Plains, comparatively little has been written about him. Jo Mora provides analytical descriptions illustrated most appropriately with his own sketches. For anecdotal detail, one of the best informants is an old-time San Joaquin Valley vaquero, Arnold R. Rojas.

Nacho, one of the vaqueros, always wore a vest in the pockets of which he carried pencils and a notebook like a regular bossman. As though this were not enough useless weight to carry, on a trip to Buttonwillow he bought a "dollar watch" to add to his impedimenta. On his return to the wagon Lupe Valenzuela, the cook, gave him a piece of buckskin to use in lieu of a watch chain. He tied one end of the thong to the watch and the other to a buttonhole of the vest and put the watch in one of the pockets. Buckskin is the strongest of leathers so the watch was secure.

A day or two later he was riding a cold-backed gray. The other men, watching the horse travel with a hump in its back, looked at each other and grinned expectantly. The crew rode on and in a short time came to a narrow gully and jumped their horses over it. The gray jumped over too, but when he landed on the other side he kept right on jumping. At the first jump the watch dropped out of the vest pocket and swung in an arc and hit the buckeroo on the nose. The next jump, the watch gave him a black eye and as long as the horse bucked the watch swung. As we have said, buckskin is the strongest of leathers so if the horse had not quit bucking the watch "would have beat me to death" as the vaquero afterward said. He untied the buckskin thong, took the pencils out of the pockets (he had lost the notebook) and with what was left of the watch threw them as far away as he could.

Arnold R. Rojas, *Lore of the California Vaquero*
(Fresno, Academy Library Guild, 1958), 95-96.

The Railroad and the Ranchers

BY FRANK NORRIS

Force and violence are common themes in the novels of Frank Norris, a San Francisco disciple of Emile Zola's naturalism. McTeague *is favored by the connoisseurs, but it was outstripped in popularity by* The Octopus. *Based on the Mussel Slough incident, it narrates the clash between the Central Valley wheat growers and the railroad, an industrial octopus with tentacles of steel.*

The morning was fine; there was no cloud in the sky, but as Harran's buggy drew away from the grove of trees about the ranch house, emerging into the open country on either side of the Lower Road, he caught himself looking sharply at the sky and the faint line of hills beyond the Quien Sabe ranch. There was a certain indefinite cast to the landscape that to Harran's eye was not to be mistaken. Rain, the first of the season, was not far off.

"That's good," he muttered, touching the bays with the whip, "we can't get our ploughs to hand any too soon."

324

These ploughs Magnus Derrick had ordered from an Eastern manufacturer some months before, since he was dissatisfied with the results obtained from the ones he had used hitherto, which were of local make. However, there had been exasperating and unexpected delays in their shipment. Magnus and Harran both had counted upon having the ploughs in their implement barns that very week, but a tracer sent after them had only resulted in locating them, still *en route*, somewhere between The Needles and Bakersfield. Now there was likelihood of rain within the week. Ploughing could be undertaken immediately afterward, so soon as the ground was softened, but there was a fair chance that the ranch would lie idle for want of proper machinery. . . .

Magnus climbed into the buggy, helping himself with Harran's outstretched hand which he still held. The two were immensely fond of each other, proud of each other. They were constantly together and Magnus kept no secrets from his favorite son.

"Well, boy."

"Well, Governor."

"I am very pleased you came yourself, Harran. I feared that you might be too busy and send Phelps. It was thoughtful."

Harran was about to reply, but at that moment Magnus caught sight of the three flat cars loaded with bright-painted farming machines which still remained on the siding above the station. He laid his hands on the reins and Harran checked the team.

"Harran," observed Magnus, fixing the machinery with a judicial frown, "Harran, those look singularly like our ploughs. Drive over, boy." . . .

"Ah, I was right," said the Governor. " 'Magnus Derrick, Los Muertos, Bonneville, from Ditson & Co., Rochester.' These are ours, boy."

Harran breathed a sight of relief. . . .

"It means money to us, Governor," remarked Harran.

But as he turned the horses to allow his father to get into the buggy again, the two were surprised to hear a thick, throaty voice wishing them good-morning, and turning about were aware of S. Behrman, who had come up while they were examining the ploughs. Harran's eyes flashed on the instant and through his nostrils he drew a sharp, quick breath, while a certain rigour of carriage stiffened the set of Magnus Derrick's shoulders and back. Magnus had not yet got into the buggy, but stood with the team between him and S. Behrman, eyeing him calmly across the horses' backs. S. Behrman came around to the other side of the buggy and faced Magnus. . . .

S. Behrman was the banker of Bonneville. But besides this he was many other things. He was a real-estate agent. He bought grain; he dealt in mortgages. He was one of the local political bosses, but more important than all this, he was the representative of the Pacific and Southwestern Railroad in that section of Tulare County. The railroad did little business in that part of the country that S. Behrman did not supervise, from the consignment of a shipment of wheat to the management of a damage suit, or even to the repair and maintenance of the right of way. . . . The position he occupied on the salary list of the Pacific and Southwestern could not readily be defined, for he was neither freight agent, passenger agent, attorney, real-estate broker, nor political servant, though his influence in all these offices was undoubted and enormous. . . . S. Behrman was the railroad.

"Mr. Derrick, good-morning," he cried as he came up. "Good-morning, Harran. Glad to see you back, Mr. Derrick." He held out a thick hand. . . .

"Well, Mr. Derrick," continued S. Behrman, wiping the back of his neck with his handkerchief, "I saw in the city papers yesterday that our case had gone against you."

"I guess it wasn't any great news to *you*," commented Harran, his face scarlet. "I guess you knew which way Ulsteen was going to jump after your very first interview with him. You don't like to be surprised in this sort of thing, S. Behrman."

"Now, you know better than that, Harran," remonstrated S. Behrman blandly. "I know what you mean to imply, but ain't going to let it make me get mad. I wanted to say to you governor —I wanted to say to you, Mr. Derrick—as one man to another— letting alone for the minute that we were on opposite sides of the case—that I'm sorry you didn't win. Your side made a good fight, but it was in a mistaken cause. That's the whole trouble. Why, you could have figured out before you ever went into the case that such rates are confiscation of property. You must allow us—must allow

326

the railroad—a fair interest on the investment. You don't want us to go into the receiver's hands, do you now, Mr. Derrick?"

"The Board of Railroad Commissioners was bought," remarked Magnus sharply, a keen, brisk flash glinting in his eye.

"It was part of the game," put in Harran, "for the Railroad Commission to cut rates to a ridiculous figure, far below a *reasonable* figure, just so that it *would* be confiscation. Whether Ulsteen is a tool of yours or not, he had to put the rates back to what they were originally."

"If you enforced those rates, Mr. Harran," returned S. Behrman calmly, "we wouldn't be able to earn sufficient money to meet operating expenses or fixed charges, to say nothing of a surplus left over to pay dividends - - - - -"

"Tell me when the P. and S.W. ever paid dividends."

"The lowest rates," continued S. Behrman, "that the legislature can establish must be such as will secure us a fair interest on our investment."

"Well, what's your standard? Come, let's hear it. Who is to say what's a fair rate? The railroad has its own notions of fairness sometimes."

"The laws of the State," returned S. Behrman, "fix the rate of interest at seven per cent. That's a good enough standard for us. There is no reason, Mr. Harran, why a dollar invested in a railroad should not earn as much as a dollar represented by a promissory note—seven per cent. By applying your schedule of rates we would not earn a cent; we would be bankrupt."

"Interest on your investment!" cried Harran, furiously. "It's fine to talk about fair interest. I know and *you* know that the total earnings of the P. and S.W.—their main, branch, and leased lines for last year—was between nineteen and twenty millions of dollars. Do you mean to say that twenty million dollars is seven per cent of the original cost of the road?"

S. Behrman spread out his hands, smiling.

"That was the gross, not the net figure—and how can you tell what was the original cost of the road?"

"Ah, that's just it," shouted Harran, emphasizing each word with a blow of his fist upon his knee, his eyes sparkling, "you take cursed good care that we don't know anything about the original cost of the road. But we know you are bonded for treble your value; and we know this: that the road *could* have been built for fifty-four thousand dollars per mile and that you *say* it cost you eighty-seven thousand. It makes a difference, S. Behrman, on which of these two figures you are basing your seven per cent."

"That all may show obstinacy, Harran," observed S. Behrman vaguely, "but it don't show common sense."

"We are threshing out old straw, I believe, gentlemen," remarked Magnus. "The question was thoroughly sifted in the courts."

"Quite right," assented S. Behrman. "The best way is that the railroad and the farmer understand each other and get along peaceably. We are both dependent on each other. Your ploughs, I believe, Mr. Derrick." S. Behrman nodded toward the flat cars.

"They are consigned to me," admitted Magnus.

"It looks a trifle like rain," observed Behrman, easing his neck and jowl in his limp collar. "I suppose you will want to begin plowing next week."

"Possibly," said Magnus.

"I'll see that your ploughs are hurried through for you then, Mr. Derrick. We will route them by fast freight for you and it won't cost you anything extra."

"What do you mean?" demanded Harran. "The ploughs are here. We have nothing more to do with the railroad. I am going to have my wagons down here this afternoon."

"I am sorry," answered S. Behrman, "but the cars are going north, not, as you thought, coming *from* the north. They have not been to San Francisco yet."

Magnus made a slight movement of the head as one who remembers a fact hitherto forgotten. But Harran was as yet unenlightened.

"To San Francisco!" he answered, "we want them here—what are you talking about?"

"Well, you know, of course, the regulations," answered S. Behrman. "Freight of this kind coming from the Eastern points into the State must go first to one of our common points and be reshipped from there."

Harran did remember now, but never before had the matter so

struck home. He leaned back in his seat in dumb amazement for the instant. Even Magnus had turned a little pale. Then, abruptly, Harran broke out violent and raging.

"What next? My God, why don't you break into our houses at night? Why don't you steal the watch out of my pocket, steal the horses out of the harness, hold us up with a shotgun; yes, 'stand and deliver; your money or your life.' Here we bring our ploughs from the East over your lines, but you're not content with your long-haul rate between Eastern points and Bonneville. You want to get us under your ruinous short-haul rate between Bonneville and San Francisco, *and return.* Think of it! Here's a load of stuff for Bonneville that can't stop at Bonneville, where it is consigned, but has got to go up to San Francisco first *by way* of Bonneville, at forty cents per ton and then be reshipped from San Francisco back to Bonneville again at *fifty-one* cents per ton, the short-haul rate. And we have to pay it all or go without. Here are the ploughs right here, in sight of the land they have got to be used on, the season just ready for them, and we can't touch them. Oh," he exclaimed in deep disgust, "isn't it a pretty mess! Isn't it a farce! the whole dirty business!"

S. Behrman listened to him unmoved, his little eyes blinking under his fat forehead, the gold chain of hollow links clicking against the pearl buttons of his waistcoat as he breathed.

"It don't do any good to let loose like that, Harran," he said at length. "I am willing to do what I can for you. I'll hurry the ploughs through, but I can't change the freight regulations of the road."

"What's your blackmail for this?" vociferated Harran. "How much do you want to let us go? How much have we got to pay you to be *allowed* to use our own ploughs—what's your figure? Come, spit it out."

"I see you are trying to make me angry, Harran," returned S. Behrman, "but you won't succeed. Better give up trying, my boy. As I said, the best way is to have the railroad and the farmer get along amicably. It is the only way we can do business."

Frank Norris, *The Octopus* (New York, 1901),
58-59, 61-68.

The Ballad of the Hyde Street Grip

BY GELETT BURGESS

Author, editor, and teacher, Gelett Burgess (1866-1951) won a considerable reputation as an American humorist. After teaching briefly at the University of California he launched a short-lived journal which had the dubious distinction of being printed on wallpaper. (There was a different pattern for each issue.) Making good use of another talent, he illustrated many of his own stories. Some of his better known books are The Purple Cow; Goops and How To Be Them; Are You a Bromide; *and* Burgess Unabridged.

Oh, the rain is slanting sharply, and the Norther's blowing cold,
When the cable strands are loosened, she is nasty hard to hold;
There's little time for sitting down and little chance for gab,
For the bumper guards the crossing, and you'd best be keeping tab!
Two-and-twenty "let-go's" every double trip—
It takes a bit of doing, on the Hyde Street Grip!

Throw her off at Powell Street, let her go at Post,
Watch her well at Geary and at Sutter, when you coast,
Easy at the Power House, have a care at Clay,
Sacramento, Washington, Jackson, all the way!
Drop your rope at Union, never make a slip—
The lever keeps you busy, on the Hyde Street Grip!

Foot-brake, wheel-brake, slot-brake and gong,
You've got to keep 'em working, or you'll soon be going wrong!
Rush her on the crossing, catch her on the rise,
Easy round the corners, when the dust is in your eyes!
And the bell will always stop you, if you hit her up a clip;
You are apt to earn your wages, on the Hyde Street Grip!

North Beach to Tenderloin, over Russian Hill,
The grades are something giddy, and the curves are fit to kill!
All the way to Market Street, climbing up the slope,
Down upon the other side, hanging to the rope;
But the view of San Francisco, as you take the lurching dip,
There is plenty of excitement on the Hyde Street Grip! ...

330

Oh, the lights are in the Mission, and the ships are in the Bay,
And Tamalpais is looming from the Gate, across the way;
The Presidio trees are waving, and the hills are growing brown,
And the driving fog is harried from the Ocean to the town!
How the pulleys slap and rattle! How the cables hum and whip!
Oh, they sing a gallant chorus, on the Hyde Street Grip!

When the Orpheum is closing, and the crowds are on the way,
The conductor's punch is ringing, and the dummy's light and
    gay;
But the wait upon the table by the beach is dark and still—
Just the swashing of the surges on the shore below the mill;
And the flash from Angel Island breaks across the channel rip
As the hush of midnight falls upon the Hyde Street Grip!

Gelett Burgess, *A Gage of Youth*
(Boston, 1901), 48-49.

The Utopia of Madame Modjeska

BY ROBERT V. HINE

The utopian urge which produced Brook Farm, Oneida, and dozens of other experiments in communitarian life in the eastern states also had generous play in California. There were enough such ventures to form the basis for a book on the subject, California's Utopian Colonies, *by Robert V. Hine of the University of California, Riverside. In such adventures in nonconformity no one is average. The Modjeska fling embraced more notables and was more short-lived than most.*

In Cracow, Poland, Count Charles Bozenta Chlapowski and his actress-wife, Helena Modjeska, were frequently entertaining a circle of intellectual radicals bitter over Russian domination of their homeland. From this coterie one winter evening in 1875, after a period of excessively oppressive censorship and a siege of ill health for Madame Modjeska, a scheme of emigrating to America was hatched, and in the elated conversations that followed, the plan narrowed to the establishment in California of a utopian colony on the model of the earlier Brook Farm in Massachusetts. Serious meetings through the winter carried the enterprise nearer maturity. The members drafted statutes, vowed to obey their own laws, and pooled financial resources. Madame Modjeska reflected the group's enthusiasm when she described her dreams of California:

"Oh, but to cook under the sapphire-blue sky in the land of freedom! What Joy!" I thought. "To bleach linen at the brook like maidens of Homer's 'Iliad'! After the day of toil, to play the guitar and sing by moonlight, to recite poems, or to listen to the mockingbird! And listening to our songs would be charming Indian maidens, our neighbors, making wreaths of luxuriant wild flowers for us! And in exchange we should give them trinkets for their handsome brown necks and wrists! And oh, we should be so far away from everyday gossip and malice, nearer to God, and better."

The group which eventually left Poland for California consisted of Count Chlapowski, Madame Modjeska, and Rudolphe (later Ralph) Modjeska, son of her first marriage; Henryk Sienkiewicz, whose fame as an author rests on his later work, *Quo Vadis?*; Julian Sypniewski, his wife and two children; Paprocki, a painter; and Anusia, a flighty girl of sixteen who had been hired to care for the children. In the early spring of 1876 the group sent two of its members, Sienkiewicz and Sypniewski, to explore the land of southern California. After investigation, the committee chose the area of Anaheim because many citizens of that town spoke German, a familiar language for the Poles. Sypniewski returned to Poland with glowing accounts; Sienkiewicz waited in California at Anaheim Landing writing letters which were no less enticing. In July, 1876, the little band sailed aboard the *Donau* from Bremen. They landed in New York, stopping long enough for an excursion to Washington where they eagerly received boxes of pamphlets on farming from the Department of Agriculture; proceeded to the Isthmus on a steamer which suffered an explosion from a bursting boiler; journeyed from Panama to San Francisco on an antique side-wheeler; and finally entrained for Los Angeles. Reuniting with Sienkiewicz, they made the last lap of their journey in wagons to the ranch near Anaheim.

After the long trek and the glowing prospects, the immigrants arrived at their utopia to find a wooden house of two bedrooms, a dining room, and a parlor with an upright piano and a sofa. To Modjeska "the commonplaceness of it all was painfully discouraging." Sypniewski and his family took the large bedroom; Chlapowski and his wife, the small one; Ralph slept on the parlor sofa; Anusia, in a nook of the kitchen; and Sienkiewicz and Paprocki made shift in the barn.

Utopia suffered problems from the very first morning. Madame Modjeska, who in the assignment of tasks had drawn the kitchen, soon learned that even breakfast for a group of intellectual Poles was no simple affair. Each one wanted something different. Tea, coffee, milk, chocolate, and wine-soup had to be served every morning, to mention the drink alone.

The first day's work in the fields was glorious—Nature's sons and daughters returning to her bosom. But on the following morning lame backs and sore arms kept Nature's children abed. In the weeks that followed, when muscles reacted better but the spirit lagged from toil and homesickness, the whole colony often took to its buggies for a picnic or a drive to Anaheim Landing. It required the combined efforts of three men to kill a turkey on the occasion of a festive dinner. Even Sypniewski, the sole possessor of agricultural experience, had gained his knowledge in a fundamentally different soil and climate.

Trouble came and agricultural reverses, but the colony never lost its high spirits. A visitor reported that he found the men practicing Wagner while a mule and a cow died from improper food. Another neighbor, Lyman Busby, once said, "You ought to have seen how jolly they used to be when everything on the farm was drying up in the sun and the animals were all sick and dying." Sienkiewicz came gradually to divorce himself from the agricultural labor, setting up a table under the trees in a far corner of the ranch where he read, smoked, and wrote most of the day.

After six months on the new Brook Farm, the colony counted $15,000 spent and almost nothing returned. "We all came to the conclusion," wrote Modjeska, "that our farming was not a success.

"We had several cows, but there was no one to milk them, and we had to buy milk, butter, and cream from the neighbors. We had chickens, but our fine dogs made regular meals of the eggs. We had a vineyard, which yielded beautiful muscat grapes, but there was nobody to buy them, and often people would come and fill their wagons with them without more ado; they said that such was the custom of the country. . . . Our winter crop of barley was fast disappearing in the mouths of the neighboring cattle, although I tried myself to shoot at the latter with my revolver."

In the spring of 1877 the actress laid down her gun and her skillet, perfected her English, and returned to the stage, paving the way for those triumphs with Edwin Booth and Otis Skinner which placed her so prominently in the history of the American theater. Money from the sale of the farm provided return passage for the other homesick colonists. Madame Modjeska and her family, however, remained in America, building a summer house surrounded by her Forest of Arden in Santiago Canyon, only a few miles from the site where the rudeness of agricultural reality had disrupted a captivating utopian dream.

Robert V. Hine, *California's Utopian Colonies*
(San Marino, Huntington Library, 1953), 137-140.

The Stockton Gang Plow

BY WALLACE SMITH

In addition to this book on the San Joaquin Valley, Wallace Smith, professor of history at Fresno State College, has written on the Sierra crossings and on the train robberies by Evans and Sontag.

Independently of these commercial plows, the wheat growers of the San Joaquin busied themselves with the invention of a plow which was to became famous throughout the world wherever wheat was grown. In 1860 Westley Underwood, a wheat grower near the present Manteca, secured two plows from his neighbors and bolted them to his own. Each plow had a ten-inch share. In his experimentation Underwood was aided by his wife's brother, Henry Mills. This three-bottom plow was used for the first time in the fall of 1861. The next year John A. Perry, a New England

334

Yankee and the grandson of a Revolutionary soldier, came to California in search of health. Although he arrived late in the season he decided to plant some wheat. In order to make haste he bought Underwood's three-bottom plow. He employed three yokes of oxen to pull it and finished on scheduled time. The plow did excellent work but was hard to handle on the turns. The three heavy timbers bolted diagonally across the beams of the three plows made it cumbersome and at that stage of its development it had no wheels. One of the phenomena of the San Joaquin which impressed Perry was the absence of stones. In his native New Hampshire he maintained that each hundred square feet of field contained more than a thousand large stones. The unobstructed soil of the San Joaquin Valley was a marvel to eastern men, and was to project itself through them into a series of mechanical inventions pertaining to agriculture.

A wheat grower on the west side of the valley, Lowell Alexander Richards, improved the Underwood plow, which had been used in 1861 and 1862, by placing the standards of the three plows on a single beam. The patent rights to this plow were then sold by these men to H. C. Shaw of Stockton, who operated a foundry, and Matteson & Williamson, implement dealers of the same city. Additional improvements were then made by adding wheels, reversible shares, levelers to adjust the depth of plowing, and a gauge to adjust the width. Thereafter no improvements were necessary; it was complete. It was manufactured and shipped to all parts of the world under the name of the Stockton Gang Plow and brought the first fame of this type to the Delta City. Much of a similar nature was to follow. . . .

The invention of the Stockton Gang Plow resulted in a new and unique manner of handling the several spans of horses required to pull it. An improvisation of the vocal method of driving oxen together with the system of checks and lines then in vogue among freighters was combined to develop the first jerk-line team in the world. The first method could not be adopted entirely since horses are not as amenable to control as oxen; the second was too cumbersome and costly. The farmer who walked all day beside his plow did not want to carry the many reins necessary to handle his teams.

In 1868 Stephen V. Porter, Henry W. Lander, and Ransome McCapes, all natives of Wisconsin, rented land near the present site of Manteca. Irwin S. Wright, employed by Lander as a teamster, went to the Coast Range and procured four wild mules which he broke to the plow. Lander owned a strawberry roan broncho mare named Hannah. She and her team mate were placed at the head of these four mules. A long baling rope was attached to the left ring of Hannah's bit. This line was then inserted through the rings in the hames of the near pointer and wheeler and fastened to the lever of the plow where Wright could reach it easily. A steady pull on the rope naturally turned Hannah to the left. The other members of the team, each fastened by a head-strap to the single-tree of the preceding animal, followed the leaders. In order to turn the team to the right, a strap was fastened between the right ring in Hannah's bit and the ring in her hame. This was barely long enough for her to walk comfortably. A quick jerk would cause her to throw up her head and the short strap then pulled her to the right. A sharp command "Gee!" at the same time finally taught her to turn right without any undue pressure or pain. She was then "broken to the word." Her team mate was forced to turn at the same moment by a short jockey stick extending from Hannah's hame to the right ring of the off leader's bit. In order to enable the near leader to take precedence on the turns, the off leader was held back by a check strap extending from his bridle to the near leader's single-tree.

The off-wheeler, unlike the other horses, was usually not fastened to the animal in front of him. This enabled him, when the plow showed a tendency to crawl out into the unplowed ground, to swing out and pull it back into place. Sometimes this wheeler swung out too far and failed to get back into the furrow. Then he was either crippled or killed by the heavy plow. This caused a strap to be snapped into the single tree of the off pointer which permitted only a forty-five degree turn. Since the rancher or teamster always walked in the hard, unplowed ground, it became customary to designate the horses to the left as the near horses; those to the right then became the off horses. This jerk-line form of driving a long string of work stock won favor immediately and was adopted, not only by other wheat growers, but replaced the old form of hitch on the big freight wagons throughout the nation.

The first quadrupeds hitched to the Stockton Gang Plow were inferior as draft stock. Usually they were bronchos, or mules out of broncho mares. They were as hard to handle as dynamite. Young men who crave excitement in modern times are too prone to jeopardize the lives of pedestrians by the reckless manner in which they manipulate the long, low cars which come so high. In those days they found ample vent for surplus vitality by taming these vicious brutes who, besides leaving their footprints in the sands of time on the Stockton plains also left their marks on the broken bodies of the men whom they maimed or killed.

In time native California horseflesh was supplemented by the excessively tall Cleveland Bay mares, originally imported from England as carriage horses for wealthy urban residents, which found their way into the San Joaquin and, together with Percheron mares, produced mules which weighed from 1400 to 1600 pounds, and stood six feet or more at the withers. They walked twenty-five miles a day with the Stockton Gang Plow and had enough energy left at nightfall to run away if opportunity offered. These great animals were matched by the rangy young men employed as teamsters. The latter often walked to the nearest town of an evening to get tired enough to sleep. So they said. There may have been other attractions. A few old-time freighters, who became gang plow teamsters, followed their old custom of riding the near wheeler. Occasionally a rude seat was improvised on the plow. However, as a general rule, the teamsters walked beside their plow.

Wallace Smith, *Garden of the Sun: A History of the San Joaquin Valley, 1772-1939* (Los Angeles, Lymanhouse, 1939), 222-226.

The Passing of a Literary Frontier

BY FRANKLIN WALKER

In San Francisco's Literary Frontier *and* Literary History of Southern California *Franklin Walker interprets two epochs in California writing reaching forward to the First World War. His more specialized interests are Frank Norris and Jack London.*

337

Already beginning to talk of the period when Bret Harte and Mark Twain walked down Montgomery Street as "those good old days," a group of journalists and artists founded the Bohemian Club in 1872, unmindful of the fact that the desire to organize appears only after true Bohemianism has died. The club was hard pressed to find illustrious names for its roster, for surprisingly few of the writers of the golden fifties and silver sixties were left in the city. Some of them, like Avery and Swift and Daggett, had gone to the Orient as United States ministers, while others, like Webb and Harte and Mark Twain, had moved to the East to further their careers. Among the European pilgrims only Bierce had returned, and he had come back reluctantly. As he looked around a city nearly empty of talent, he announced: "It is my intention to purify journalism in this town by instructing such writers as it is worth while to instruct, and assassinating those that it is not."

Death had not been waiting for Bierce's pen, however, to reap its toll. The old-timers among California journalists were fast disappearing. In 1867 Yellow Bird had died of softening of the brain; his friend Old Block followed him to the Grass Valley cemetery in 1874. In the following year J. Ross Browne's funeral cortege set out from Pagoda Hill, in the next, Caxton ceased combining law and poetry, and in another three years John C. Cremony had told his last tall tale and succumbed to eating toadstools. . . .

There was a moment during the days of the exodus that Ina Coolbrith hoped she might go with the others to Europe. A book of her poems was in the offing, and there would be no great difficulty in arranging to publish her travel letters. But still another disappointment was awaiting the poetess who had had a martyr for a father and a scoundrel for a husband. Her widowed sister, falling ill, needed a home for herself and her two small children. Six months after she arrived from Los Angeles, she died, and Ina found herself with two orphans to rear. How could she leave now, particularly as her mother, who was also dependent on her, was rapidly failing in health? To add to her problems, Joaquin Miller has deposited his Indian daughter, Cali-Shasta, on her doorstep before returning to London, and, as there was no one else to take care of the girl, Ina had assumed the task. It was ridiculous for her to think any more of going to Europe. Instead she went to work behind the desk in the Oakland Public Library, kept herself and her family of four alive and cheerful on her salary of eighty dollars a month augmented by any odd sums that Miller might send her, and still managed to write poetry. Her friends did not forget her; at one time the artists of the Bohemian Club auctioned some of their paintings at a benefit and turned a thousand dollars over to her to help pay the landlord and the grocer.

For thirty years Ina served as a librarian, first for the Oakland Library and later for the Bohemian Club. She brought up her nephew and niece; she cared for Cali-Shasta until the latter was married; and she interested herself in many of the children who came to the library, including a ragged urchin named Jack London. She even saw a volume of her poems issue from the press. But she did not go to Europe. As the years passed by in San Francisco, she heard of the triumphs and failures of her friends, her companions in the halcyon days of the *Californian* and the *Overland Monthly*. Sometimes they wrote to her; sometimes they came to see her. One by one, as the turn of the century approached, they dropped their parts in the drama.

The first to go was dear old Prentice Mulford. Word came in 1891 that he was found one bright May morning lying in a small boat on Sheepshead Bay, Long Island, wrapped in his blankets, his banjo by his side. No one knew how he had died, for it was several days since he had set out with provisions and spirit lamp on his voyage from New York City to Sag Harbor. His followers made a mystery of his death, just as they did of the strange jumble of words found on his writing-pad, which they maintained had been dictated from the spirit world. His unusual death was no more extraordinary than the career he had led since returning from England. First he and Josie had separated. It was rumored that the issue which disrupted their union was his refusal to let his pretty wife continue posing in the nude for commercial artists, a practice which he discovered when he received a picture of her naked figure in a package of cheap cigarettes.

Then he had become a hermit in a New Jersey swamp, where he had emulated Thoreau in both economy and reflection. He had emerged from his retreat with the conviction that he had thought out a philosophy that would make people healthy, happy, and efficient. With his few remaining dollars he had begun to publish the five-cent tracts of the White Cross Library, in which he set forth in a disarmingly serious manner his doctrine containing approximately equal amounts of spiritualism, mental healing, and common sense. Interrupting the didactic stream just once, he had included in the White Cross series his vivid and amusing account of frontier experiences entitled *Prentice Mulford's Story*. His little pamphlets had made their way so well that by the time of his death many considered him an important leader in the occult sciences. Ina felt that after all his failures Prentice Mulford had found his niche in life, albeit a strange one.

Six years later Ina knew with all of the rest of the nation that Henry George was dead. After the success of *Progress and Poverty*, he had become a front-page newspaper figure, a social reformer whose spectacular career was followed in every town in America. Forcefully and continuously he had preached his single-tax doctrine from the Pacific to the Atlantic and had even carried his gospel to Ireland. On a reform ticket he had nearly beaten Theodore Roosevelt in a campaign for the mayorship of New York City. In 1897 the prophet of San Francisco had been persuaded, against the advice of his physician, to champion his theories at the New York polls a second time. In the midst of the heated contest he died. The newspapers said that his funeral was the most impressive tribute the people had paid to a leader since the passing of Lincoln.

In 1902 word sped across the Atlantic from London that Bret Harte had succumbed to cancer of the throat. After his ordeal of the seventies, those last twenty years in England had treated him kindly. Though he had shown something of his former magic touch in a half-dozen stories, he had for the most part resigned himself to being an efficient and regular hack writer; "I grind out the old tunes on the old organ and gather up the coppers," he wrote to his wife and children, who had remained in America and were receiving a large share of the coppers. He continued to set most of his stories in a California society that had long since disappeared, and, as his memory began to play him tricks, he put woods beside the Carquinez Straits and spoke of crimson poppies growing near the Golden Gate. But while the slim, dapper, white-haired gentleman was listening to his cronies of the Royal Yacht Club, a new generation of Californians was growing up, a generation that looked upon Bret Harte as the most romantic figure in a romantic era. Already the Bret Harte country had become one of the showplaces of the state.

Ina suffered her hardest blow when she heard in 1909 that Charlie Stoddard had died in Monterey. She had seen him frequently since his return to the coast a few years before, fat and bald, but still personally charming. As of old, he had been full of enthusiasms, but just as restless as ever—only he had learned to take his idiosyncrasies more as a matter of course. How characteristic was a comment in his diary: "How awfully glad I shall be to get out of this and to long for it with tears, afterwards!" Equally self-revealing was the fact that, because he could not make up his mind, his autobiographical novel, *For the Pleasure of His Company*, appeared with two conflicting endings, published unabashedly in the same book. . . .

When Mark Twain died in 1910, the world paid him such a tribute that it seemed to Ina hardly possible she had once known him as the rough young journalist who had pretended to be a rival with Harte for her hand. Of all her friends, he had gone the furthest; people no longer referred to him as an amusing frontier humorist, but as one of the great American authors. His books had been many, but as she looked back it seemed as if the early ones like *The Innocents Abroad, Roughing It, Tom Sawyer, and Huckleberry Finn*, books that dealt with his boyhood in Missouri and his life on the frontier, were the best. They were written before he had lost a fortune, a wife, and two daughters; now men said that he played billiards late into the night because he could not sleep and that he had more than once declared he hated " the damned human race," himself most of all. Perhaps she wondered why the restless author had crossed the Atlantic at least twenty times but had never come back to San Francisco. It was surely not because he had forgotten the West, for not long ago, he had written a friend in Nevada: "Those were the old days! those old ones! They will come no more. Youth will come no more. They were so full to the brim with the wine of life; there have been no others like them. Would you like to have me come out there and cry?" And now she knew that he would never come back.

Joaquin Miller had played his part up to his last breath, drawn one February morning in 1913. When Europe had tired of him he had returned to America and for a while had posed as a wild Western poet in a log cabin situated in a park in Washington, D.C. When the real-estate boom of the late eighties brought new life to the West, he came back to California and bought one hundred acres on the hills above Oakland, where he planted thousands of trees, built three small houses, and erected monuments to Frémont, Moses, and Browning, as well as a funeral pyre for himself. His assumption that the Californians one generation removed from the frontier days would cherish a poet who had worked in the diggings and fought the Indians proved to be thoroughly justified.

On "The Hights" he continued to produce abundantly, turning out novels, poems, plays, and even a history; he rewrote his autobiography in several versions; and he discarded the role of a frontier Byron for that of a Pacific Coast Moses, beginning his poems with such lines as "I cry aloud from my mountain top, as a seer." Joaquin invited other poets to come and stay with him as long as they pleased; he showed curious visitors how to throw the tomahawk; and he entertained clubwomen by producing rain from a cloudless sky, relying on a mixture of nonsense and profanity, which he called an Indian chant, to confound his audience, and on a sprinkler, which he had installed on the roof of his cabin, to create the shower. Ina had never greatly minded his spoofing, knowing how much he enjoyed it, and she was glad to hear that he had kept his jug of corn whisky handy under his bed to the very last.

That same year Ambrose Bierce made the most dramatic exit achieved by any member of the group. A long life of journalism in San Francisco and Washington had not broken his spirit nor exhausted the gall from his pen. Though he had wasted much of his strength on unimportant issues, he had exerted a much-needed influence in his crusade for high standards in literature and he had written some excellent short stories. In private life he had

342

suffered more than his share of disappointments and tragedies. He had separated from his beautiful wife, he had lost his two sons by tragic deaths, and he had broken with his favorite pupils, George Sterling and Jack London, when they had taken up socialism. But at seventy his body was straight, his silver-white head was high, and his blue eyes were clear. Once more he visited the Civil War battlefields, the scenes of his fighting and the settings for many of his stories, and then he walked across the Mexican border at Laredo, Texas, never to return. The manner of his death, if ever fully ascertained, will add little to the record; the fact remains that by disappearing into Chihuahua he realized most literally the ambition of every frontiersman, to die with his boots on.

By the beginning of the World War they were all gone except Ina. As the last of the giants—and, from 1915 until her death in 1928, as the recognized poet laureate of the State of California—she took her place as the matriarch of a group of local enthusiasts called the California Literary Society, which met with due seriousness and earnestness of purpose every third Sunday in her flat. That purpose was frequently enunciated at the meetings by Ella Sterling Cummins Mighels, the perpetual secretary of the organization: "Why do we have this society? We have it, my good friends, so we can pass on to the next generation the memory of our writers. We have it so that the old traditions and customs of California may not die out and be forgotten. We must not forget the *pioneers*." Then, as though she were repeating the litany, she would add: "What can we do for California authors?" And the answer came in unison: "We can buy their books."

Franklin Walker, *San Francisco's Literary Frontier*
(New York, Alfred A. Knopf, 1939), 352-360.

8

INTO THE TWENTIETH CENTURY

EARLY IN THE twentieth century the study of California history for the first time came to be university-centered. The initial impulse was the purchase of the Bancroft Library by the University of California. Then in 1911 Herbert E. Bolton was brought to the staff and a beehive of historical studies soon sprang up. Over the next three decades Berkeley became the foremost training ground on the history of the American West and the history of Latin America. Many of the studies bore at least tangentially on California. The Americanists of this group showed a strong preference for the eighteen-forties and fifties, the epoch that had held such fascination for the earlier free-enterprise historians. The Latin Americanists stressed the Spanish frontier advance into the northern borderlands of which California was one. The vigor of this California school of historical scholarship was noteworthy, its contributions major, most of them concerning a rather distant past.

The literary figures of this generation were at least as brilliant, probably more so. Jack London was a more adept story teller than the state had enjoyed. Mary Austin is one of the few repeaters in this anthology, her forte the description of the Land of Little Rain and its people. Will Irwin, primarily a newspaperman, is best known for his moving tribute to San Francisco written in a burst of emotion on hearing of its disaster in 1906. The sensitive verse of George Sterling is especially associated with that city.

For all the march of civilization it had witnessed, California in

ORCHARD NEAR SOLANO   *by Edward Weston*

the first decades of the new century still had its wilds. The average traveler seldom saw more than was reached by rail. It was possible, thus, for a visitor such as J. Smeaton Chase who was willing to leave the beaten path to report on features relatively unfamiliar. Chase has three volumes of such descriptions, one on Yosemite, one on a horseback ride through the coastal belt from Mexico to Oregon, and the third on the desert. More integral to the society was another recent arrival, Sister Aimee Semple McPherson. Her narrative here quoted is important for its central theme and not merely for the surrounding detail about the Tournament of Roses, the local construction industry, and so on.

James Rorty's "Dissonance" is primarily a social document called forth by the real estate boom of the twenties, less famous than the one of the eighties, though by every measure except ratio to base it was times over larger. The record does not show how many court jesters of old actually registered solid criticism under the cover of their buffoonery. For Americans, and sometimes for Californians in particular, Will Rogers showed how it could be done, as these almost random selections indicate.

Not all the writers of this period insisted on burning issues or on a moral or a call to action. Edwin Corle's "The Ghost of Billy the Kid" stands first of all as a character sketch. Idwal Jones' "China Boy" may have the ring of antiquarian discourse; perhaps it is not to be taken literally, yet it could have happened. This sort of sympathetic writing about a Chinese, however, would have been less to be expected a generation earlier. It belongs at this later time when the attitude toward the Chinese had mellowed.

Entering the twentieth century, Californians were more alarmed over a new influx from the Orient, the Japanese, and vented their feelings in the San Francisco segregated school incident and by passing a law forbidding land ownership by any alien ineligible for citizenship. In the fullness of time, forty years later, the state supreme court discovered this law to be unconstitutional. Meanwhile, it was enforced.

With even more vigor, leading citizens turned to reform drives aimed at cleaning up city government in San Francisco, Sacramento, Los Angeles, and elsewhere, and to free the state government from domination by the one great corporation doing business in the state. With Hiram Johnson as standard bearer the men of the Lincoln-Roosevelt League succeeded brilliantly.

Another quite contrary force was rising, the Industrial Workers of the World, with its bizarre effort to organize the low-skilled laborers of the farms, forests, and waterfront. Almost to a man, the people who were dedicated to striking off the fetters imposed by the Southern Pacific machine were as firmly opposed to the emancipation of labor that the I.W.W. advocated. By direct action and by criminal syndicalism prosecutions the Wobblies were ruthlessly combated.

Viewed retrospectively, some of these phenomena take on a different coloration. Candidate Johnson is revealed by George E. Mowry as not altogether certain about the meaning of reform, but a dynamic leader nonetheless. The anti-Wobblies are taken to task by Wallace Stegner in a way that would have been sensational in the twenties. And practicing historians, through Oscar Lewis' composite recreation, have their foibles pricked out.

The first United States mariners who visited California were on their way to the far side of the Pacific. The first American to arrive by an overland route was in search of an outlet to the Pacific. The region beyond continued to beckon and when a transcontinental railroad was built the word "Pacific" was prominent in its name and trans-Pacific traffic was one of its main objectives. When the Panama Canal was completed, California celebrated with a Panama Pacific Exposition. But in point of fact, Californians most of the time and in heavy majority have lived and live with their backs to the Pacific and their attention (political, economic, and intellectual) riveted eastward. Perhaps it will not always be so. The idea that the future lies with the Pacific is a hardy perennial. Historian John Carl Parish did not invent it in 1932; indeed, his theme is the more modest proposition that the people of the west coast will do well to take better note of this larger environment of theirs, the Pacific area.

The Abalone Song

Although sometimes attributed to George Sterling, this ballad benefitted, as ballads should, from many collaborators in the convivial artists colony at Carmel.

Oh! some folks boast of quail on toast,
Because they think it's tony;
But I'm content to owe my rent,
And live on abalone.

We sit around and gaily pound,
And hold no acrimony,
Because our object is a gob
Of toothsome abalone.

He hides in caves beneath the waves—
His ancient patrimony,
And so, 'tis shown that faith alone
Reveals the abalone.

The more we take, the more they make
In deep-sea matrimony;
Race-suicide cannot betide
The fertile abalone.

Printed by Albert M. Bender for the friends of
George Sterling (San Francisco, 1937).

The Little Town of the Grape Vines

BY MARY AUSTIN

Mary Austin is perhaps best known for her nature writing, particularly on what she called The Land of Little Rain and for The Flock (1906), in which she dealt intimately with the California sheep herders. The vignette that follows describes the carry-over of Mexican ways.

There are still some places in the west where the quails cry "*cuidado*"; where all the speech is soft, all the manners gentle; where

348

all the dishes have *chile* in them, and they make more of the Sixteenth of September than they do of the Fourth of July. I mean
in particular El Pueblo de Las Uvas. Where it lies, how to come at
it, you will not get from me; rather would I show you the heron's
nest in the tulares. It has a peak behind it, glinting above the tam-
arack pines, above a breaker of ruddy hills that have a long slope
valley-wards and the shoreward steep of waves toward the Sierras.

Below the Town of the Grape Vines, which shortens to Las Uvas
for common use, the land dips away to the river pastures and the
tulares. It shrouds under a twilight thicket of vines, under a dome
of cottonwood-trees, drowsy and murmurous as a hive. Hereabouts
are some strips of tillage and the headgates that dam up the creek
for the village weirs; upstream you catch the growl of the arrastra.
Wild vines that begin among the willows lap over to the orchard
rows, take the trellis and roof-tree.

There is another town above Las Uvas that merits some attention, a town of arches and airy crofts, full of linnets, blackbirds,
fruit birds, small sharp hawks, and mockingbirds that sing by
night. They pour our piercing, unendurably sweet cavatinas
above the fragrance of bloom and musky smell of fruit. Singing is
in fact the business of the night at Las Uvas as sleeping is for mid-
day. When the moon comes over the mountain wall new-washed
from the sea, and the shadows lie like lace on the stamped floors
of the patios, from recess to recess of the vine tangle runs the thrum
of guitars and the voice of singing.

At Las Uvas they keep up all the good customs brought out of
Old Mexico or bred in a lotus-eating land; drink, and are merry
and look out for something to eat afterward; have children, nine
or ten to a family, have cock-fights, keep the siesta, smoke cigarettes and wait for the sun to go down. And always they dance;
at dusk on the smooth adobe floors, afternoons under the trellises
where the earth is damp and has a fruity smell. A betrothal, a
wedding, or a christening, or the mere proximity of a guitar is sufficient occasion; and if the occasion lacks, send for the guitar and
dance anyway.

All this requires explanation. Antonio Sevadra, drifting this
way from Old Mexico with the flood that poured into the Tappan
district after the first notable strike, discovered La Golondrina. It

was a generous lode and Tony a good fellow; to work it he brought in all the Sevadras, even to the twice-removed; all the Castros who were his wife's family, all the Saises, Romeros, and Eschobars,— the relations of his relations-in-law. There you have the beginning of a pretty considerable town. To these accrued much of the Spanish California float swept out of the southwest by eastern enterprise. They slacked away again when the price of silver went down, and the ore dwindled in La Golondrina. All the hot eddy of mining life swept away from that corner of the hills, but there were always those too idle, too poor to move, or too easily content with El Pueblo de Las Uvas.

Nobody comes nowadays to the town of the grape vines except, as we say, "with the breath of crying," but of these enough. All the low sills run over with small heads. Ah, ah! There is a kind of pride in that if you did but know it, to have your baby every year or so as the time sets, and keep a full breast. So great a blessing as marriage is easily come by. It is told of Ruy Garcia that when he went for his marriage license he lacked a dollar of the clerk's fee, but borrowed it of the sheriff, who expected reëlection and exhibited thereby a commendable thrift.

Of what account is it to lack meal or meat when you may have it of any neighbor? Besides, there is sometimes a point of honor in these things. Jesús Romero, father of ten, had a job sacking ore in the Marionette which he gave up of his own accord. "Eh, why?" said Jesús, "for my fam'ly."

"It is so, señora," he said solemnly, "I go to the Marionette, I work, I eat meat—pie—frijoles—good, ver' good. I come home sad'day nigh' I see my fam'ly. I play lil' game poker with the boys, have lil' drink wine, my money all gone. My family have no money, nothing eat. All time I work at mine I eat, good, ver' good grub. I think sorry for my fam'ly. No, no, señora, I no work no more that Marionette, I stay with my fam'ly." The wonder of it is, I think, that the family had the same point of view.

Every house in the town of the vines has its garden plot, corn, and brown beans and a row of peppers reddening in the sun; and in damp borders of the irrigating ditches clumps of *yerba santa*, horehound, catnip, and spikenard, wholesome herbs and curative, but if no peppers then nothing at all. You will have for a holiday

350

dinner, in Las Uvas, soup with meat balls and chile in it, chicken with chile, rice with chile, fried beans with more chile, enchilada, which is corn cake with a sauce of chile and tomatoes, onion, grated cheese, and olives, and for a relish chile tepines passed about in a dish, all of which is comfortable and corrective to the stomach. You will have wine which every man makes for himself, of good body and inimitable bouquet, and sweets that are not nearly so nice as they look.

There are two occasions when you may count on that kind of a meal; always on the Sixteenth of September, and on the two-yearly visits of Father Shannon. It is absurd, of course, that El Pueblo de Las Uvas should have an Irish priest, but Black Rock, Minton, Jimville, and all that country round do not find it so. Father Shannon visits them all, waits by the Red Butte to confess the shepherds who go through with their flocks, carries blessings to small and isolated mines, and so in the course of a year or so works around to Las Uvas to bury and marry and christen. Then all the little graves in the *Campo Santo* are brave with tapers, the brown pine headboards blossom like Aaron's rod with paper roses and bright cheap prints of Our Lady of Sorrows. Then the Señora Sevadra, who thinks herself elect of heaven for that office, gathers up the original sinners, the little Elijias, Lolas, Manuelitas, Josés, and Felipes, by dint of adjurations and sweets smuggled into small perspiring palms, to fit them for the Sacrament.

I used to peek in at them, never so softly, in Doña Ina's living-room; Raphael-eyed little imps, going sidewise on their knees to rest them from the bare floor, candles lit on the mantel to give a religious air, and a great sheaf of wild bloom before the Holy Family. Come Sunday they set out the altar in the schoolhouse, with the fine-drawn altar cloths, the beaten silver candlesticks, and the wax images, chief glory of Las Uvas, brought up mule-back from Old Mexico forty years ago. All in white the communicants go up two and two in a hushed, sweet awe to take the body of their Lord, and Tomás, who is priest's boy, tries not to look unduly puffed up by his office. After that you have dinner and a bottle of wine that ripened on the sunny slope of Escondito. All the week Father Shannon has shriven his people, who bring clean conscience to the betterment of appetite, and the Father sets them an example. Father Shannon is rather big about the middle to accommodate the large laugh that lives in him, but a most shrewd searcher of hearts. It is reported that one derives comfort from his confessional, and I for my part believe it.

The celebration of the Sixteenth, though it comes every year, takes as long to prepare for as Holy Communion. The señoritas have each a new dress apiece, the señoras a new *rebosa*. The young gentlemen have new silver trimmings to their sombreros, unspeakable ties, silk handkerchiefs, and new leathers to their spurs. At this time when the peppers glow in the gardens and the young quail cry *"cuidado,"* "have a care!" you can hear the *plump, plump* of the metate from the alcoves of the vines where comfortable old dames, whose experiences gives them the touch of art, are pounding out corn for tamales.

School-teachers from abroad have tried before now at Las Uvas to have school begin on the first of September, but got nothing else to stir in the heads of the little Castros, Garcias, and Romeros but feasts and cock-fights until after the Sixteenth. Perhaps you need to be told that this is the anniversary of the Republic, when liberty awoke and cried in the provinces of Old Mexico. You are aroused at midnight to hear them shouting in the streets, *"Viva la Libertad!"* answered from the houses and the recesses of the vines, *"Viva la Mexico!"* At sunrise shots are fired commemorating the tragedy of unhappy Maximilian, and then music, the noblest of national hymns, as the great flag of Old Mexico floats up the flagpole in the bare little plaza of shabby Las Uvas. The sun over Pine Mountain greets the eagle of Montezuma before it touches the vineyards and the town, and the day begins with a great shout. By and by there will be a reading of the Declaration of Independence and an address punctured by *vivas*; all the town in its best dress, and some exhibits of horsemanship that make lathered bits and bloody spurs; also a cock-fight.

By night there will be dancing, and such music! Old Santos to play the flute, a little lean man with a saintly countenance, young Garcia whose guitar has a soul, and Carrasco with the violin. They sit on a high platform above the dancers in the candle flare, backed by the red, white, and green of Old Mexico, and play fervently such music as you will not hear otherwhere.

352

At midnight the flag comes down. Count yourself at a loss if you are not moved by that performance. Pine Mountain watches whitely overhead, shepherd fires glow strongly on the glooming hills. The plaza, the bare glistening pole, the dark folk, the bright dresses, are lit ruddily by a bonfire. It leaps up to the eagle flag, dies down, the music begins softly and aside. They play airs of old longing and exile; slowly out of the dark the flag drops down, bellying and falling with the midnight draught. Sometimes a hymn is sung, always there are tears. The flag is down; Tony Sevadra has received it in his arms. The music strikes a barbaric swelling tune, another flag begins a slow ascent,—it takes a breath or two to realize that they are both, flag and tune, the Star Spangled Banner,—a volley is fired, we are back, if you please, in California of America. Every youth who has the blood of patriots in him lays ahold on Tony Sevadra's flag, happiest if he can get a corner of it. The music goes before, the folk fall in two and two, singing. They sing everything, America, the Marseillaise, for the sake of the French shepherds hereabout, the hymn of Cuba, and the Chilian national air to comfort two families of that land. The flag goes to Doña Ina's, with the candlesticks and the altar cloths, then Las Uvas eats tamales and dances the sun up the slope of Pine Mountain.

You are not to suppose that they do not keep the Fourth, Washington's Birthday, and Thanksgiving at the town of the grape vines. These make excellent occasions for quitting work and dancing, but the Sixteenth is the holiday of the heart. On Memorial Day the graves have garlands and new pictures of the saints tacked to the headboards. There is great virtue in an *Ave* said in the Camp of the Saints. I like that name which the Spanish speaking people give to the garden of the dead, *Campo Santo*, as if it might be some bed of healing from which blind souls and sinners rise up whole and praising God. Sometimes the speech of simple folk hints at truth the understanding does not reach. I am persuaded only a complex soul can get any good of a plain religion. Your earthborn is a poet and a symbolist. We breed in an environment of asphalt pavements a body of people whose creeds are chiefly restrictions against other people's way of life, and have kitchens and latrines under the same roof that houses their God. Such as these go to church to be edified, but at Las Uvas they go for pure worship and to entreat their God. The logical conclusion of the faith that every good gift cometh from God is the open hand and the finer courtesy. The meal done without buys a candle for the neighbor's dead child. You do foolishly to suppose that the candle does no good.

At Las Uvas every house is a piece of earth—thick walled, whitewashed adobe that keeps the even temperature of a cave; every man is an accomplished horseman and consequently bow-legged; every family keeps dogs, flea-bitten mongrels that loll on the earthen floors. They speak a purer Castillian than obtains in like villages of Mexico, and the way they count relationship everybody is more or less akin. There is not much villainy among them. What incentive to thieving or killing can there be when there is little wealth and that to be had for the borrowing! If they love too hotly, as we say "take their meat before grace," so do their betters. Eh, what! shall a man be a saint before he is dead? And besides, Holy Church takes it out of you one way or another before all is done. Come away, you who are obsessed with your own importance in the scheme of things, and have got nothing you did not sweat for, come away by the brown valleys and full-bosomed hills to the even-breathing days, to the kindliness, earthiness, ease of El Pueblo de Las Uvas.

Mary Austin, *The Land of Little Rain*
(Boston 1903), 263-281.

Demetrios Contos

BY JACK LONDON

Jack London of the Oakland water front, the oyster flats, and the sea, came up the hard way. He was at his best in narratives in which he had or might well have played a part. No one can read much of his writing without a feeling of knowing him intimately.

It must not be thought, from what I have told of the Greek fishermen, that they were altogether bad. Far from it. But they were rough men, gathered together in isolated communities and fighting with the elements for a livelihood. They lived far away from the law and its workings, did not understand it, and thought it tyranny. Especially did the fish laws seem tyrannical. And because of this, they looked upon the men of the fish patrol as their natural enemies.

We menaced their lives, or their living, which is the same thing, in many ways. We confiscated illegal traps and nets, the materials of which had cost them considerable sums and the making of which required weeks of labor. We prevented them from catching fish at many times and seasons, which was equivalent to preventing them from making as good a living as they might have made had we not been in existence. And when we captured them, they were brought into the courts of law, where heavy cash fines were collected from them. As a result, they hated us vindictively. As the dog is the natural enemy of the cat, the snake of man, so were we of the fish patrol the natural enemies of the fishermen.

But it is to show that they could act generously as well as hate bitterly that this story of Demetrios Contos is told. Demetrios Contos lived in Vallejo. Next to Big Alec, he was the largest, bravest, and most influential man among the Greeks. He had given us no trouble, and I doubt if he would ever have clashed with us had he not invested in a new salmon boat. This boat was the cause of all the trouble. He had had it built upon his own model, in which the lines of the general salmon boat were somewhat modified.

To his high elation he found his new boat very fast—in fact, faster than any other boat on the bay or rivers. Forthwith he grew proud and boastful: and, our raid with the *Mary Rebecca* on the Sunday salmon fishers having wrought fear in their hearts, he sent a challenge up to Benicia. One of the local fishermen conveyed it to us: it was to the effect that Demetrios Contos would sail up from Vallejos on the following Sunday, and in the plain sight of Benicia set his net and catch salmon, and that Charley LeGrant, patrolman, might come and get him if he could. Of course Charley and I had heard nothing of the new boat. Our own boat was pretty fast, and we were not afraid to have a brush with any other that happened along.

Sunday came. The challenge had been bruited abroad, and the fishermen and seafaring folk of Benicia turned out to a man, crowding Steamboat Wharf till it looked like the grand stand at a football match. Charley and I had been skeptical, but the fact of the crowd convinced us that there was something in Demetrios Contos's dare.

In the afternoon, when the sea-breeze had picked up in strength, his sail hove into view as he bowled along before the wind. He tacked a score of feet from the wharf, waved his hand theatrically, like a knight about to enter the lists, received a hearty cheer in return, and stood away into the Straits for a couple of hundred yards. Then he lowered sail, and, drifting the boat sideways by means of the wind, proceeded to set his net. He did not set much of it, possibly fifty feet; yet Charley and I were thunderstruck at the man's effrontery. We did not know at the time, but we learned afterward, that the net he used was old and worthless. It *could* catch fish, true; but a catch of any size would have torn it to pieces.

Charley shook his head and said:

"I confess, it puzzles me. What if he has out only fifty feet? He could never get it in if we once started for him. And why does he come here anyway, flaunting his lawbreaking in our faces? Right in our home town, too."

Charley's voice took on an aggrieved tone, and he continued for some minutes to inveigh against the brazenness of Demetrios Contos.

In the meantime, the man in question was lolling in the stern of his boat and watching the net floats. When a large fish is meshed in a gillnet, the floats by their agitation advertise the fact. And they evidently advertised it to Demetrios, for he pulled in about a dozen feet of net, and held aloft for a moment, before he flung it into the bottom of the boat, a big, glistening salmon. It was greeted by the audience on the wharf with round after round of cheers. This was more than Charley could stand.

"Come on, lad," he called to me; and we lost no time jumping into our salmon boat and getting up sail.

The crowd shouted warning to Demetrios, and as we darted out from the wharf we saw him slash his worthless net clear with a long knife. His sail was all ready to go up, and a moment later it fluttered in the sunshine. He ran aft, drew in the sheet, and filled on the long tack toward the Contra Costa Hills.

356

By this time we were not more than thirty feet astern. Charley was jubilant. He knew our boat was fast, and he knew, further, that in fine sailing few men were his equals. He was confident that we should surely catch Demetrios, and I shared his confidence. But somehow we did not seem to gain.

It was a pretty sailing breeze. We were gliding sleekly through the water, but Demetrios was slowly sliding away from us. And not only was he going faster, but he was eating into the wind a fraction of a point closer than we. This was sharply impressed upon us when he went about under the Contra Costa Hills and passed us on the other tack fully one hundred feet dead to windward.

"Whew!" Charley exclaimed. "Either that boat is a daisy, or we've got a five-gallon coal-oil can fast to our keel!"

It certainly looked it one way or the other. And by the time Demetrios made the Sonoma Hills, on the other side of the Straits, we were so hopelessly outdistanced that Charley told me to slack off the sheet, and we squared away for Benecia. The fishermen on Steamboat Wharf showered us with ridicule when we returned and tied up. Charley and I got out and walked away, feeling rather sheepish, for it is a sore stroke to one's pride when he thinks he has a good boat and knows how to sail it, and another man comes along and beats him.

Charley mooned over it for a couple of days; then word was brought to us, as before, that on the next Sunday Demetrios Contos would repeat his performance. Charley roused himself. He had our boat out of the water, cleaned and repainted its bottom, made a trifling alteration about the centre-board, overhauled the running gear, and sat up nearly all of Saturday night sewing on a new and much larger sail. So large did he make it, in fact, that additional ballast was imperative, and we stowed away nearly five hundred extra pounds of old railroad iron in the bottom of the boat.

Sunday came, and with it came Demetrios Contos, to break the law defiantly in open day. Again we had the afternoon sea-breeze, and again Demetrios cut loose some forty or more feet of his rotten net, and got up sail and under way under our very noses. But he had anticipated Charley's move, and his own sail peaked higher than ever, while a whole extra cloth had been added to the after leech.

It was nip and tuck across to the Contra Costa Hills, neither of us seeming to gain or to lose. But by the time we had made the return tack to the Sonoma Hills, we could see that, while we footed it at about equal speed, Demetrios had eaten into the wind the least bit more than we. Yet Charley was sailing our boat as finely and delicately as it was possible to sail it, and getting more out of it than he ever had before.

Of course, he could have drawn his revolver and fired at De- metrios; but we had long since found it contrary to our natures to shoot at a fleeing man guilty of only a petty offence. Also a sort of tacit agreement seemed to have been reached between the pa- trolmen and the fishermen. If we did not shoot while they ran away, they, in turn, did not fight if we once laid hands on them. Thus Demetrios Contos ran away from us, and we did no more than try our best to overtake him; and, in turn, if our boat proved faster than his, or was sailed better, he would, we knew, make no resistance when we caught up with him.

With our large sails and the healthy breeze romping up the Carquinez Straits, we found that our sailing was what is called "ticklish." We had to be constantly on the alert to avoid a capsize, and while Charley steered I held the main-sheet in my hand with but a single turn round a pin, ready to let go at any moment. De- metrios, we could see, sailing his boat alone, had his hands full.

But it was a vain undertaking for us to attempt to catch him. Out of his inner consciousness he had evolved a boat that was better than ours. And though Charley sailed fully as well, if not the least bit better, the boat he sailed was not so good as the Greek's.

"Slack away the sheet," Charley commanded; and as our boat fell off before the wind, Demetrios's mocking laugh floated down to us.

Charley shook his head, saying, "It's no use. Demetrios has the better boat. If he tries his performance again, we must meet it with some new scheme."

This time it was my imagination that came to the rescue.

"What's the matter," I suggested, on the Wednesday following,

358

"with my chasing Demetrios in the boat next Sunday, while you wait for him on the wharf at Vallejo when he arrives?"

Charley considered it a moment and slapped his knee.

"A good idea! You're beginning to use that head of yours. A credit to your teacher, I must say."

"But you mustn't chase him too far," he went on, the next moment, "or he'll head out into San Pablo Bay instead of running home to Vallejo, and there I'll be, standing lonely on the wharf and waiting in vain for him to arrive."

On Thursday Charley registered an objection to my plan.

"Everybody'll know I've gone to Vallejo, and you can depend upon it that Demetrios will know, too. I'm afraid we'll have to give up the idea."

This objection was only too valid, and for the rest of the day I struggled under my disappointment. But that night a new way seemed to open to me, and in my eagerness I awoke Charley from a sound sleep.

"Well," he grunted, "what's the matter? House afire?"

"No," I replied, "but my head is. Listen to this. On Sunday you and I will be around Benicia up to the very moment Demetrios's sail heaves into sight. This will lull everybody's suspicions. Then, when Demetrios's sail does heave in sight, do you stroll leisurely away and up-town. All the fishermen will think you're beaten and that you know you're beaten."

"So far, so good," Charley commented, while I paused to catch breath.

"And very good indeed," I continued proudly. "You stroll carelessly up-town, but when you're once out of sight you leg it for all you're worth for Dan Maloney's. Take the little mare of his, and strike out on the county road for Vallejo. The road's in fine condition, and you can make it in quicker time than Demetrios can beat all the way down against the wind."

"And I'll arrange right away for the mare, first thing in the morning," Charley said, accepting the modified plan without hesitation.

"But, I say," he said, a little later, this time waking *me* out of a sound sleep.

I could hear him chuckling in the dark.

"I say, lad, isn't it rather a novelty for the fish patrol to be taking to horseback?"

"Imagination," I answered. "It's what you're always preaching —'keep thinking one thought ahead of the other fellow, and you're bound to win out.' "

"He! he!" he chuckled. "And if one thought ahead, including a mare, doesn't take the other fellow's breath away this time, I'm not your humble servant, Charley LeGrant."

"But can you manage the boat alone?" he asked, on Friday. "Remember, we've a ripping big sail on her."

I argued my proficiency so well that he did not refer to the matter again till Saturday, when he suggested removing one whole cloth from the after leech. I guess it was the disappointment written on my face that made him desist; for I, also, had a pride in my boat-sailing abilities, and I was almost wild to get out alone with the big sail and go tearing down the Carquinez Straits in the wake of the flying Greek.

As usual, Sunday and Demetrios Contos arrived together. It had become the regular thing for the fishermen to assemble on Steamboat Wharf to greet his arrival and to laugh at our discomfiture. He lowered sail a couple of hundred yards out and set his customary fifty feet of rotten net.

"I suppose this nonsense will keep up as long as his old net holds out," Charley grumbled, with intention, in the hearing of several of the Greeks.

"Den I give-a heem my old-a net-a," one of them spoke up, promptly and maliciously.

"I don't care," Charley answered. "I've got some old net myself he can have—if he'll come around and ask for it."

They all laughed at this, for they could afford to be sweet-tempered with a man so badly outwitted as Charley was.

"Well, so long, lad," Charley called to me a moment later. "I think I'll go up-town to Maloney's."

"Let me take the boat out?" I asked.

"If you want to," was his answer, as he turned on his heel and walked slowly away.

Demetrios pulled two large salmon out of his net, and I jumped into the boat. The fishermen crowded around in a spirit of fun, and when I started to get up sail overwhelmed me with all sorts of jocular advice. They even offered extravagant bets to one another that I would surely catch Demetrios, and two of them, styling themselves the committee of judges, gravely asked permission to come along with me to see how I did it.

But I was in no hurry. I waited to give Charley all the time I could, and I pretended dissatisfaction with the stretch of the sail and slightly shifted the small tackle by which the huge sprit forces up the peak. It was not until I was sure that Charley had reached Dan Maloney's and was on the little mare's back, that I cast off from the wharf and gave the big sail to the wind. A stout puff filled it and suddenly pressed the lee gunwale down till a couple of buckets of water came inboard. A little thing like this will happen to the best small-boat sailors, and yet, though I instantly let go the sheet and righted, I was cheered sarcastically, as though I had been guilty of a very awkward blunder.

When Demetrios saw only one person in the fish patrol boat, and that one a boy, he proceeded to play with me. Making a short tack out, with me not thirty feet behind, he returned, with his sheet a little free, to Steamboat Wharf. And there he made short tacks, and turned and twisted and ducked around, to the great delight of his sympathetic audience. I was right behind him all the time, and I dared to do whatever he did, even when he squared away before the wind and jibed his big sail over—a most dangerous trick with such a sail in such a wind.

He depended upon the brisk sea breeze and the strong ebb tide, which together kicked up a nasty sea, to bring me to grief. But I was on my mettle, and never in all my life did I sail a boat better than on that day. I was keyed up to concert pitch, my brain was working smoothly and quickly, my hands never fumbled once, and it seemed that I almost divined the thousand little things which a small-boat sailor must be taking into consideration every second.

It was Demetrios who came to grief instead. Something went wrong with his centre-board, so that it jammed in the case and would not go all the way down. In a moment's breathing space, which he had gained from me by a clever trick, I saw him working impatiently with the centre-board, trying to force it down. I gave him little time, and he was compelled quickly to return to the tiller and sheet.

The centre-board made him anxious. He gave over playing with me, and started on the long beat to Vallejo. To my joy, on the first long tack across, I found that I could eat into the wind just a little bit closer than he. Here was where another man in the boat would have been of value to him; for, with me but a few feet astern, he did not dare let go the tiller and run amidships to try to force down the centre-board.

Unable to hang on as close in the eye of the wind as formerly, he proceeded to slack his sheet a trifle and to ease off a bit, in order to outfoot me. This I permitted him to do till I had worked to windward, when I bore down upon him. As I drew close, he feinted at coming about. This led me to shoot into the wind to forestall him. But it was only a feint, cleverly executed, and he held back to his course while I hurried to make up lost ground.

He was undeniably smarter than I when it came to manoeuvring. Time after time I all but had him, and each time he tricked me and escaped. Besides, the wind was freshening constantly, and each of us had his hands full to avoid capsizing. As for my boat, it could not have been kept afloat but for the extra ballast. I sat cocked over the weather gunwale, tiller in one hand and sheet in the other; and the sheet, with a single turn around a pin, I was very often forced to let go in the severer puffs. This allowed the sail to spill the wind, which was equivalent to taking off so much driving power, and of course I lost ground. My consolation was that Demetrios was as often compelled to do the same thing.

The strong ebb-tide, racing down the Straits in the teeth of the wind, caused an unusually heavy and spiteful sea, which dashed aboard continually. I was dripping wet, and even the sail was wet half-way up the after leech. Once I did succeed in outmanoeuvring Demetrios, so that my bow bumped into him amidships. Here was where I should have had another man. Before I could run forward and leap aboard, he shoved the boats apart with an oar, laughing mockingly in my face as he did so.

We were now at the mouth of the Straits, in a bad stretch of water. Here the Vallejo Straits and the Carquinez Straits rushed directly at each other. Through the first flowed all the water of

Napa River and the great tide-lands; through the second flowed all the water of Suisun Bay and the Sacramento and San Joaquin rivers. And where such immense bodies of water, flowing swiftly, clashed together, a terrible tide-rip was produced. To make it worse, the wind howled up San Pablo Bay for fifteen miles and drove in a tremendous sea upon the tide-rip.

Conflicting currents tore about in all directions, colliding, forming whirlpools, sucks, and boils, and shooting up spitefully into hollow waves which fell aboard as often from leeward as from windward. And through it all, confused, driven into a madness of motion, thundered the great smoking seas from San Pablo Bay.

I was as wildly excited as the water. The boat was behaving splendidly, leaping and lurching through the welter like a race-horse. I could hardly contain myself with the joy of it. The huge sail, the howling wind, the driving seas, the plunging boat—I, a pygmy, a mere speck in the midst of it, was mastering the elemental strife, flying through it and over it, triumphant and victorious.

And just then, as I roared along like a conquering hero, the boat received a frightful smash and came instantly to a dead stop. I was flung forward and into the bottom. As I sprang up I caught a fleeting glimpse of a greenish, barnacle-covered object, and knew it at once for what it was, that terror of navigation, a sunken pile. No man may guard against such a thing. Water-logged and floating just beneath the surface, it was impossible to sight it in the troubled water in time to escape.

The whole bow of the boat must have been crushed in, for in a few seconds the boat was half full. Then a couple of seas filled it, and it sank straight down, dragged to bottom by the heavy ballast. So quickly did it all happen that I was entangled in the sail and drawn under. When I fought my way to the surface, suffocating, my lungs almost bursting, I could see nothing of the oars. They must have been swept away by the chaotic currents. I saw Demetrios Contos looking back from his boat, and heard the vindictive and mocking tones of his voice as he shouted exultantly. He held steadily on his course, leaving me to perish.

There was nothing to do but to swim for it, which, in that wild confusion, was at the best a matter of but a few moments. Holding my breath and working with my hands, I managed to get off my heavy sea-boots and my jacket. Yet there was very little breath I could catch to hold, and I swiftly discovered that it was not so much a matter of swimming as of breathing.

I was beaten and buffeted, smashed under by the great San Pablo whitecaps, and strangled by the hollow tide-rip waves which flung themselves into my eyes, nose, and mouth. Then the strange sucks would grip my legs and drag me under, to spout me up in some fierce boiling, where, even as I tried to catch my breath, a great whitecap would crash down upon my head.

It was impossible to survive any length of time. I was breathing more water than air, and drowning all the time. My senses began to leave me, my head to whirl around. I struggled on, spasmodically, instinctively, and was barely half conscious when I felt myself caught by the shoulders and hauled over the gunwale of a boat.

For some time I lay across a seat where I had been flung, face downward, and with the water running out of my mouth. After a while, still weak and faint, I turned around to see who was my rescuer. And there, in the stern, sheet in one hand and tiller in the other, grinning and nodding good-naturedly, sat Demetrios Contos. He had intended to leave me to drown,—he said so afterward,—but his better self had fought the battle, conquered, and sent him back to me.

"You all-a right?" he asked.

I managed to shape a "yes" on my lips, though I could not yet speak.

"You sail-a de boat verr-a good-a," he said. "So good-a as a man."

A compliment from Demetrios Contos was a compliment indeed, and I keenly appreciated it, though I could only nod my head in acknowledgment.

We held no more conversation, for I was busy recovering and he was busy with the boat. He ran in to the wharf at Vallejo, made the boat fast, and helped me out. Then it was, as we both stood on the wharf, that Charley stepped out from behind a net-rack and put his hand on Demetrios Contos's arm.

"He saved my life, Charley," I protested; "and I don't think he ought to be arrested."

A puzzled expression came into Charley's face, which cleared immediately after, in a way it had when he made up his mind.

"I can't help it, lad," he said kindly. "I can't go back on my duty, and it's plain duty to arrest him. To-day is Sunday; there are two salmon in his boat which he caught to-day. What else can I do?"

"But he saved my life," I persisted, unable to make any other argument.

Demetrios Contos's face went black with rage when he learned Charley's judgment. He had a sense of being unfairly treated. The better part of his nature had triumphed, he had performed a generous act and saved a helpless enemy, and in return the enemy was taking him to jail.

Charley and I were out of sorts with each other when we went back to Benicia. I stood for the spirit of the law and not the letter; but by the letter Charley made his stand. As far as he could see, there was nothing else for him to do. The law said distinctly that no salmon should be caught on Sunday. He was a patrolman, and it was his duty to enforce that law. That was all there was to it. He had done his duty, and his conscience was clear. Nevertheless, the whole thing seemed unjust to me, and I felt very sorry for Demetrios Contos.

Two days later we went down to Vallejo to the trial. I had to go along as a witness, and it was the most hateful task that I ever performed in my life when I testified on the witness stand to seeing Demetrios catch the two salmon Charley had captured him with.

Demetrios had engaged a lawyer, but his case was hopeless. The jury was out only fifteen minutes, and returned a verdict of guilty. The judge sentenced Demetrios to pay a fine of one hundred dollars or go to jail for fifty days.

Charley stepped up to the clerk of the court.

"I want to pay that fine," he said, at the same time placing five twenty-dollar gold pieces on the desk. "It—it was the only way out of it, lad," he stammered, turning to me.

The moisture rushed into my eyes as I seized his hand. "I want to pay—" I began.

"To pay your half?" he interrupted. "I certainly shall expect you to pay it."

In the meantime Demetrios had been informed by his lawyer that his fee likewise had been paid by Charley.

Demetrios came over to shake Charley's hand, and all his warm Southern blood flamed in his face. Then, not to be outdone in generosity, he insisted on paying his fine and lawyer's fee himself, and flew half-way into a passion because Charley refused to let him.

More than anything else we ever did, I think, this action of Charley's impressed upon the fishermen the deeper significance of the law. Also Charley was raised high in their esteem, while I came in for a little share of praise as a boy who knew how to sail a boat. Demetrios Contos not only never broke the law again, but he became a very good friend of ours, and on more than one occasion he ran up to Benicia to have a gossip with us.

Jack London, *Tales of the Fish Patrol*
(New York, 1905), 177-207.

The City That Was

BY WILL IRWIN

Will Irwin, San Francisco-trained journalist, was in New York when word came of the 1906 earthquake and fire. Sensing that things would never be exactly the same again, he immediately composed a tribute to the city he had known and loved so well.

The old San Francisco is dead. The gayest, lightest hearted, most pleasure loving city of the western continent, and in many ways the most interesting and romantic, is a horde of refugees living among ruins. It may rebuild; it probably will; but those who have known that peculiar city by the Golden Gate, have caught its flavor of the Arabian Nights, feel that it can never be the same. It is as though a pretty, frivolous woman had passed through a great tragedy. She survives, but she is sobered and different. . . .

One usually entered San Francisco by way of the Bay. Across its yellow flood, covered with the fleets from the strange seas of the Pacific, San Francisco presented itself in a hill panorama. Probably no other city of the world, excepting perhaps Naples, could

366

SAN ANDREAS FAULT, CARRIZO PLAIN   *by William Garnett*
Displacement of stream beds can be seen.

be so viewed at first sight. It rose above the passenger, as he reached dockage, in a succession of hill terraces. At one side was Telegraph Hill, the end of the peninsula, a height so abrupt that it had a one hundred and fifty foot sheer cliff on its seaward frontage. Further along lay Nob Hill, crowned with the Mark Hopkins mansion, which had the effect of a citadel, and in later years, by the great, white Fairmount. Further along was Russian Hill, the highest point. Below was the business district, whose low site caused all the trouble.

Except for the modern buildings, the fruit of the last ten years, the town presented at first sight a disreputable appearance. Most of the buildings were low and of wood. In the middle period of the '70's, when a great part of San Francisco was building, the newly-rich perpetrated some atrocious architecture. In that time, too every one put bow windows on his house to catch all of the morning sunlight that was coming through the fog; and those little houses, with bow windows and fancy work all down their fronts, were characteristic of the middle class residence districts....

The Californian is the second generation of a picked and mixed ancestry. The merry, the adventurous, often the desperate, always the brave, deserted the South and New England in 1849 to rush around the Horn or to try the perils of the plains. They found there a land already grown old in the hands of the Spaniards—younger sons of hildalgos and many of them of the best blood of Spain. To a great extent the pioneers intermarried with Spanish women; in fact, except for a proud little colony here and there, the old, aristocratic Spanish blood is sunk in that of the conquering race. Then there was an influx of intellectual French people, largely overlooked in the histories of the early days; and this Latin leaven has had its influence.

Brought up in a bountiful country, where no one really has to work very hard to live, nurtured on adventure, scion of a free and merry stock, the real, native Californian is a distinctive type, as far from the Easterner in psychology as the extreme Southerner is from the Yankee. He is easy going, witty, hospitable, lovable, inclined to be unmoral rather than immoral in his personal habits, and easy to meet and to know.

Above all there is an art sense all through the populace which

368

sets it off from any other population of the country. This sense is almost Latin in its strength, and the Californian owes it to the leaven of Latin blood. The true Californian lingers in the north; for southern California has been built up by "lungers" from the East and middle West and is Eastern in character and feeling. . . .

The eating was usually better than the surroundings. Meals that were marvels were served in tumbledown little hotels. . . .

Listen! O ye starved amidst plenty, to the tale of the Hotel de France. This restaurant stood on California street, just east of Old St. Mary's Church. One could throw a biscuit from its back windows into Chinatown. It occupied a big ramshackle house, which had been a mansion of the gold days. Louis, the proprietor, was a Frenchman of the Bas Pyrenees; and his accent was as thick as his peasant soups. The patrons were Frenchmen of the poorer class, or young and poor clerks and journalists who had discovered the delights of his hostelry. The place exhuded a genial gaiety, of which Louis, throwing out familiar jokes to right and left as he mixed salads and carried dishes, was the head and front.

First on the bill of fare was the soup mentioned before—thick and clean and good. Next, one of Louis' three cherubic little sons brought on a course of fish—sole, rock cod, flounders or smelt— with a good French sauce. The third course was meat. This came on en bloc; the waiter dropped in the centre of each table a big roast or boiled joint together with a mustard pot and two big dishes of vegetables. Each guest manned the carving knife in turn and helped himself to his satisfaction. After that, Louis, with an air of ceremony, brought on a big bowl of excellent salad which he had mixed himself. For beverage, there stood by each plate a perfectly cylindrical pint glass filled with new, watered claret. The meal closed with "fruit in season"—all that the guest cared to eat. I have saved a startling fact to close the paragraph—the price was fifteen cents!

If one wanted black coffee he paid five cents extra, and Louis brought on a beer glass full of it. Why he threw in wine and charged extra for after-dinner coffee was one of Louis' professional secrets.

Will Irwin, *The City That Was: A Requiem of Old San Francisco* (New York, B. W. Huebsch, 1906), 7, 14-16, 25-27, 32, 34-36.

The Color of the Desert

BY J. SMEATON CHASE

*Born and educated in England, J. Smeaton Chase (1864-1923)
came to California in 1890 and immediately fell in love with the
state's natural beauty. He spent many hours on horseback following little known trails along the coast and in the mountains and
deserts. His writings reflect his love of the outdoors and are noted
for their vivid and accurate descriptions. His books include:* Yosemite Trails, California Coast Trails, California Desert Trails,
and Our Araby.

One feature of loveliness the desert has, however, that is essential:
in one field of beauty it is supreme. That is the field of color. . . .
The marvellous air, wholly free from the vapors and impurities
of coast and valley places, while it sharpens detail and reduces
difference of plane, at the same time throws over every object in
far or middle distance a veil of lilac atmosphere wonderfully thin
and transparent. Owing, perhaps, to the high power of these color-
waves, the eye is hardly interfered with in penetrating shadows.
As a result, one receives the full effect of every tone of color,
whether in light or shade: while all come to the eye softened but
enriched, and with that indefinable opaline quality that gives
magic and fascination to the most poetic of gems.

The geological simplicity of sand and rock does not result, as
might be expected, in poverty of color. Sand, particularly, might
seem to be capable of little change of hue. But, on the contrary, its
reflecting power gives it special value as a color agent, a means
of taking on varying effects from the ever-changing sky. In the
northwestern arm of the Colorado Desert are two great masses of
sand. Flattened domes in shape, the higher one rises, I would
guess, to five hundred feet above the surrounding levels. The sand
probably overlies a rocky abutment of the adjacent foothills, and
has been heaped there by that scarifying wind, the terror of railway employés whose lines are cast in the division which includes
the San Gorgonio Pass. For months these sand-hills were in my
daily view, and to describe the shades of color I have noted on
them would make tedious paragraphs. From almost snow-white

they have taken often in rapid turn, all the hues of gray, of blue, of rose, of chrome, of brown, and purple, reaching even, under gloom of storm, an approach to absolute black. Sand is actually as responsive as a chameleon, and I could never tire of the vagaries of those dunes.

But most they charmed me at sunset—that hour when the soul itself is suffused with changing hues, and comes to its best perception. Then none but warm and gentle shades are seen, and the mind, like a tranquil lake, receives them and renders them into something clearer and deeper than thought. . . .

Rock, contrary to sand, gives back its own color; but here it is pure and vivid color, untinged with overlying hues of vegetation that elsewhere come in to perplex the eye. The prevailing surface hue of desert rock is a dark rust-red. I should name it Egyptian red, for in my mental picturings of the land of the Nile this same dull but powerful note rules like absolute Pharaoh. The color, however, is not inherent in the stone, which is mainly granite of the common gray. But in course of ages this material, lying usually in huge slabs, has taken on a surface sheen and coloring due to weathering and baking by the sun. It is spoken of as "desert glaze," and is really something like the artificial glaze of pottery. Even when the rocks take boulder form they are generally great, house-like cubes or rhomboids, offering flat surfaces which sun and weather have painted in the same broad, strong hue. Only where cañons choked with more freshly shattered rock score the mountain walls does one catch the native tint of the granite, making a startling contrast. From these cañon mouths wide, fan-like sheets of similar débris sweep down to the level. Up these the eye ranges, higher and higher, into gloomy galleries and chasms until the thread is lost in a maze of braided folds of mountain, these overlooked often by some far, high crest, in winter white with snow, in summer gray with iron crag and precipice of granite, but always softly clouded with humanizing pines. . . .

The great stretches of level desert also show some diversity of color, arising partly from absence or presence (and kind) of vegetation, and partly from difference of surface material. But it is only when seen in great extent, from a good elevation, that atmosphere and grouping of shades lend enchantment. In near view, seen from slightly above the level, a vast drab tinged usually with olive, is the general hue. The olive comes from an infinite stipple of low shrubs, so uniform in spacing—for each plant jealously guards its little territory—as to show no cloudings of heavier and sparser growth. The effect is about as lively and original as fifty square miles of tweed in "pepper-and-salt mixture." But though not themselves in the least degree stimulating to fancy, these dull plains have value as foil and foreground to the color display of ever-present hills and mountains. And when, as often may be the case, the close foreground is laid in blocks of that deep, powerful red, the landscape, though bare of any recognized elements of beauty, yet is perfect, in its way incomparable.

In places the drab gives way to other tones. There are large extents of unmixed sand, boulders, gravel, or of pavement-like rock-mosaic in yellow, red, lava-black. On these the vegetation is so sparse as to yield no element of color. This is the desert entire and austere, the realm of geology alone among the sciences. Here Time and all things of Time seem to have ended or not to have begun. The sun rises, flames through the sky, and sets; the moon and stars look coldly down; the traveller seems to himself the last life on the planet. Awe that is close on terror grasps him: he feels himself alone in the universe—he, and God. His footsteps cease: why should he go on? and whither? for there is no whither. Nothing moves, nor can move, but the elemental wind, vacantly roaming the empty earth (and those great airs, what a sense they bring of age, of eternal solitude, of cold, sidereal space!) . . .

Of all those thin, spiritual hues that make the color-charm of the desert and that painters find so baffling, lilac is the prevailing note. It is the most ethereal of tints, hardly to be termed color, and seemingly more of the mind than of the eye. Yet, once realized, one finds it universal. Between you and the gray boulder three feet away you half see, half feel a veil of lilac light, and the distance is suffused with it in varying degrees. Overlying the reds and browns of the mountain walls it makes its delicate presence felt, and covers the crudest facts of geology with a film of fancy, a touch almost of faëry.

Desert shadows fall into the same high tone. There is nothing of darkness in them, no weight, no sense of dimness, but always

that aerial tint of lilac infinitely thin and refined. Over wastes of
sand aching and throbbing with light one catches the same faint
hue, lilac, always lilac.

J. Smeaton Chase, California Desert Trails
(Boston, Houghton Mifflin and Company, 1919), 4-7, 9-10, 106.

Dedication of the Temple

BY AIMEE SEMPLE MC PHERSON

*To many a Californian in the twenties and thirties the cultural
note of most significance was that sounded at Angelus Temple by
Sister Aimee. In so far as mere words can convey, the selection that
follows suggests the extraordinary combination of showmanship
and sincerity.*

Slowly, majestically the old year faded and the new year dawned
over the green fragrance and beauty of Echo Park in Los Angeles,
California. The booming of the midnight bell had found hundreds
of saints with bowed heads wrapped in earnest prayer. . . . Many
had crossed the continent or come from abroad for the opening of
Angelus Temple, Church of the Four-Square Gospel. . . .

The darkness faded. Night gathered the purple fringed folds of
her garments together and lifted them clear of the mountains that
surround Los Angeles. . . . Hurry, sun, hurry! Lift your shining
golden face above eastern hills, and kiss the fields, the flowers, the
trees, the shining lake, the park, the streets to wakefulness, peep
through drawn shades, bid every sleeper wake—this is the day of
days. . . .

Hold your breath, watchers in the streets below. . . , the sun has
kissed the first point of the dome! It is creeping down the rounded
sides. See it flash and twinkle, scintillate and glow as though en-
crusted in gems. Dew, you ask? No, crushed abalone shells from
the sea shore have been powdered and sprinkled through the concrete of the dome and now catch the sun and flash, making the
beauty which newspaper writers call "the jewelled dome". . . .

The footsteps on the pavement increase in numbers. Other automobiles are drawing up from every side. Happy voices, singing

voices, drift up to our windows. The streets are filling with people who are determined to gain admittance when the doors of the Temple swing open. . . . They are assured . . . that the building does not open till 2:30 in the afternoon. They reply that they are fully aware of that fact. . . .

We realize that we who wait also are trembling with excitement and the greatness of the day almost frightens us. We turn away and bathe our faces and fully dressed, run to the Temple doors to assure ourselves that all will be in readiness. Yes, there are the workers who have toiled within its gates, armies of them since midnight putting on the finishing touches required for opening. Brooms are sweeping, carpet is being laid, the piano is being brought in, and the golden harp of Miss Carter of Australia is lifted to the platform; Dickey, the little canary bird given to the House that God Built . . . is being carried in and hung by the piano. . . . Yonder ushers are drilling and planning as to how they shall handle the crowds. . . .

The crowds are growing. . . . It is a wonderful sight, specially wonderful on this New Year's day when hundreds of thousands are in Pasadena to witness the Tournament of Roses, wherein, in a most beautiful and impressive way, California displays to the onlooking world the flowers that God has given her while the rest of the country is buried in ice and snow. But those in Pasadena must know the Temple, too! The whole world, we feel, must know! So while at Echo Park, assembled thousands gaze up at the real Temple, in Pasadena other thousands gaze upon the Temple in miniature (yet large enough to cover entirely the largest truck in Los Angeles), made entirely of roses and fragrant dew-kissed flowers. We have a float in the parade advertising the Temple and its opening as the Church of the Four-Square Gospel. And this float being a replica of the real Temple with its choir girls singing like angels to the strains of the organ within, is awarded a prize and bears it home to Angelus Temple triumphantly. . . .

As we mount the steps we hear the doors of the Temple flung wide. We hear a murmur of voices like the billows of the sea. And then the crowd surging over the steps and up the aisles, filling the main auditorium, filling the balcony, climbing the balcony, packing each available inch of space. . . .

And now with a coterie of ministers on either side and Mr. Brook Hawkins, Temple builder, taking our arm, we are on our way....

"Don't tremble like that, Sister; keep steady, you mustn't be nervous...."

"Oh, it isn't nervousness, brother, but with joy," we answer. "This, this is the greatest day of our lives...." Hallelujah! You wonder I am trembling, but now with this Temple as a mighty monument to God's power and the crowning blessing of fifteen years of humble but adoring ministry, could I but see it endowed ... I think I could say: "Now, Lord, let thy servant depart in peace, for mine eyes have beheld Thy glory."

The meeting is on. How the volume of their singing fills the Temple. We lift our eyes to the great concrete dome, the largest unsupported concrete dome in America, if not in the world, we are told. We lift our eyes to the azure blue of heaven flecked with bright clouds as of blessing, and again our eyes are suffused with tears....

We are on our feet reading from the Book of Ezra the story of a rejoicant people when the foundation of the house of the Lord was laid. How among their number on that far-distant day some shouted with a great voice, some wept aloud for joy till they made such a noise that the prophet declared he could not tell the noise of them that wept from the voice of them that shouted. And their jubilance was only over the foundation being laid, and we had the walls up and the roof on. Glory to Jesus!

Then we are talking out of the fulness of our bursting hearts about the worship of the Lord. Telling how though God is so great the heavens can not contain him and the earth but a stool for His blessed feet. It has been the custom and longing of believing hearts to assemble themselves together to call upon His Name. Starting with the first recorded altar—that of Abel, then the altar of Noah, of Abraham, Isaac and Jacob; on to the days of Moses in the wilderness and on to the magnificent Temple which Solomon did build; the altar fires, whereunto Samuel didst minister; then to the days of the Son of Man when he gathered His little flock about Him; the Lord's sermons in the Temples and Synagogues and from house to house was rapidly sketched.... Then likewise rapidly we sketch the story of our own life. The calling of Jesus to our own

375

soul from that Canadian farm to preach the Gospel of the crucified, resurrected Savior. The years of toiling, battling wind and rain and weather in tents and open fields; the blessing of the ever-present Lord, the call to build unto Him a house in the city of Los Angeles for the cause of Evangelism and the training of workers.

All over the building people are weeping and praising the Lord. How good He has been! And now we are giving the first altar call in the new Temple. Even though it is the first and the dedication service we feel we must not let the opportunity slip past unheeded. And now they are coming, down the aisle, swarming up yonder passage way; they are coming from the balconies, trooping down the ramparts, coming from the gallery and from every direction. The communion rail is filled, again and again. They are crowding the orchestra with their instruments from before the platform and filling the space reserved for them and yet they come. Thank You, O thank You, dear Jesus, for this token at the first service. We are unworthy, but Thou, Thou art worthy; let them come unto Thee and be saved.

Aimee Semple McPherson, *This Is That:
Personal Experiences, Sermons and Writings*
(Los Angeles, Echo Park Evangelistic Association, [1923]), 518-526.

California Dissonance

BY JAMES RORTY

Poet and essayist, James Rorty has contributed frequently to several leading magazines, including Harper's *and* Collier's.

> There is a pewee bird that cries
> "La, sol, me,
> "La, sol, me."
> He is the only thing that sighs
> Beside the western sea.
>
> The blue jays chatter "Tcha! Tcha! Tcha!"
> And cheer for California.
> The real estate men chortle "Whee!"
> And toot the loud calliope.

The sky is blue, the land is glad—
The pewee bird alone is sad
And sings in minor key
"La, sol, me,
"La, sol, me."
He is the only thing that sighs
Beside the western sea.

It was a shock, I own, to see
Sedition sitting in a tree,
Remarking plainly, "La, sol, me,
"La, sol, me."

George Sterling, Genevieve Taggard,
and James Rorty, *Continent's End*
(San Francisco, Book Club of California, 1925), 37-38.

The People's Jester

BY WILL ROGERS

In his day Will Rogers was as well known and as much admired as any Californian has ever been. He belonged, of course, not just to California, but to the world.

Bishop, August 30, 1932:

California always did have one custom that they took serious, but it amused the rest of the United States. That was in calling everything a "ranch." Everything big enough to spread a double mattress on is called a "ranch." Well, up here is these mountains where there is lots of fishing, why every house you pass they sell fishing worms, and it's called a "worm ranch." Well, I always did want to own a "ranch," so I am in the market for a good worm ranch. I never was so hot as a cowboy, but I believe I would make a good "worm herder." If I can land our Presidents as clients, I could make it sound like England when they sell to the king, "Rogers worm ranch, purveyor to His Excellency, the President."

Beverly Hills, September 6:

Don't miss seeing the building of Boulder Dam. It's the biggest thing that's ever been done with water since Noah made the flood look foolish. You know how big the Grand Canyon is. Well, they just stop up one end of it, and make the water come out through a drinking fountain.

They have only been bothered with two things: one is silt and the other is Senatorial investigations. They both clog everything up. It's called "Hoover Dam" now, subject to election returns of November 8.

The dam is entirely between Nevada and Arizona. All California gets out of it is the water.

Beverly Hills, September 9:

Eighty-two years ago today California entered the Union, on a bet. The bet was that the country would eventually be called California and not America.

We took it away from Mexico the next year after we found it had gold. When the gold was all gone we tried to give it back, but Mexico was too foxy for us. In '49 the wayward sons out of 10,000 families crossed the country, and the roads was so rough they couldn't get back.

From Will Rogers' syndicated column,
August and September, 1932.

The Mooney Case in the Context of Enlightened Criminal Justice

BY RICHARD H. FROST

Mooney had no Zola, but to the great advantage of history, his trial and the subsequent machinations have been meticulously researched and effectively exposed in Richard H. Frost's The Mooney Case.

The Mooney case festered unresolved for more than twenty years, its causes widespread, its consequences pernicious. The trials and imprisonment of Mooney and Billings revealed dramatically

378

the intolerance and injustice accorded radical dissenters before, during, and long after the First World War. The case, developing out of class social tensions and public anxieties accompanying the Preparedness Day crime, was forged through the repeated abuse of fair procedures by local law enforcement officials. It came ultimately to involve the inadequacies of the law itself (including the state constitution), the bias of the State Supreme Court, and the timidity of California's governors. The attitudes of Governor Olson's predecessors reflected public indifference and hostility to the defendants rather than the merits of the case. By and large, the public—particularly in California—preferred not to consider legal abuses and the law's inadequacies, but insisted that respect for law and order took precedence over the fate of two radicals.

A generation and more has passed since the freeing of Mooney and Billings. The law has changed since their days in court. In recent years the United States Supreme Court, preceptor to a reluctant nation, has handed down constitutional interpretations designed to compel scrupulously fair procedures in the prosecution of state criminal cases. Although these decisions have provoked widespread resentment ("There is no substitute for law and order," writes former Congressman Hamilton Fish, calling to mind the San Francisco *Examiner* of 1916), the Supreme Court has significantly advanced the centuries-old libertarian aim of English and American constitutional law—to protect the individual from zealous and unscrupulous exercise of authority. Under the leadership of Earl Warren, California's once intractable Attorney General who succeeded Olson as Governor before being appointed Chief Justice, the Supreme Court has made binding on state courts the provisions of the Bill of Rights essential to a fair trial. The Warren Court has required the prompt arraignment of criminal suspects; it has condemned incommunicado interrogation, and upheld the right of a suspect to counsel during police questioning; it has ruled that evidence illegally gathered in unreasonable searches and seizures is inadmissible in state criminal courts as in federal courts; and it has found that "massive, pervasive, and prejudicial publicity" attending a state trial may constitute a violation of due process. In all these

379

respects, Mooney and Billings had been denied fair proceedings; and it is not too much to infer that had the United States Supreme Court established these same safeguards half a century ago, there would have been no Mooney case. Certainly there would have been no Mooney case after the appellate courts had finished with it.

Moreover, if the California Supreme Court had subscribed to the principles of criminal procedure that it has recently upheld, there would have been no need to seek redress in the federal courts; for the California Supreme Court is one of the most libertarian state supreme courts in the nation, and in some respects has anticipated the Warren Court. For instance, it anteceded the Warren Court by several years in barring state use of evidence secured through illegal search and seizure. Since 1956 it has progressively established the principle of "criminal discovery"— the sharing of information by both sides before the trial—in order to minimize the sporting element in criminal trials and increase the likelihood that cases will proceed on their merits. A defendant in California now generally has the right to know in advance the names and addresses of prosecution witnesses, and to examine documents that may be used against him. Had such rules existed in 1916, they would have enabled Mooney's attorneys to obtain the Eilers Building photographs before Billings's trial, and to make a careful advance check on Frank Oxman's assorted surprises.

For many years Mooney lacked access to the United States Supreme Court—access that has been available since the 1930's to many petitioners seeking protection of their rights in state criminal cases. The Mooney case itself contributed to the protection of these rights, by providing the occasion for expanding the writ of habeas corpus. Over the years since Chief Justice Hughes announced the Court's opinion, the Supreme Court has made *Mooney* v. *Holohan* bedrock constitutional law. The Court has cited the decision in more than fifty cases since 1935. In 1967, explaining a unanimous reversal of an Illinois rape-murder conviction (and death sentence), Associate Justice Potter Stewart said bluntly: "More than 30 years ago this Court held that the Fourteenth Amendment cannot tolerate a state criminal convic-

tion obtained by the knowing use of false evidence. There has
been no deviation from that established principle. There can
be no retreat from that principle here." That principle, guaran-
teeing the constitutional rights of the accused, is a living monument to Tom Mooney and Warren Billings, and to those who
defended them.

Richard H. Frost, *The Mooney Case*
(Stanford, Stanford University Press, 1968), 489-491.

The Ghost of Billy the Kid

BY EDWIN CORLE

*Edwin Corle sometimes wrote nonfiction as in his books on the
Grand Canyon, the southwestern deserts, and Highway 101, but
his more natural vein was the short story as sampled here.*

The Ghost of Billy the Kid haunts the Panamint country north of
the Slate Range. Of course it is all nonsense because nobody believes in ghosts and Billy the Kid was never in California. But the
rumor started and it continues to persist as rumors will.

Billy the Kid, since his death at the age of twenty-one, and his
record of chivalry and deadliness (twenty-one men sent to eternity
by this youth not counting Mexicans and Indians) has become
the Robin Hood of New Mexico. The boy must have had charm
and generosity and loyalty, for he has become something of a folk-
hero in the half century since his death at the hand of Sherriff Pat
Garrett in the Maxwell House at Old Fort Sumner in the early
eighteen-eighties. But he also had a cold eye and a lightning trig-
ger finger that allowed him to empty with accuracy a six-shooter a
split second sooner than any other man in the southwest. . . .

After the Kid's death there were several absurd rumors to the
effect that he had escaped to Mexico, that he was living in disguise
in the Pecos Valley, and that he had fled to Arizona. All of these
were absolutely groundless and it is an established fact that Billy

the Kid is buried at the abandoned military burying ground at old Fort Sumner. The old military post was trail's end for Billy, and any further account of his life is sheer fiction and the embroidery of imaginative minds. What, then, of this ghost of Billy the Kid who lives in the Panamint Valley? Is it all a wild yarn with no truth to back it up? Yes, it's a wild yarn, but yet . . . ?

In one of the half deserted mining towns lives an old man whose only name seems to be "The Kid," but whose initials are W. B. And as every one knows who has been interested in the real Billy, his legitimate name was William Bonney.

This old man is close to eighty and his mind is not as coherent as it might be. His speech rambles. He has a white beard and blue eyes. He is only about five feet eight inches tall and he has very small hands. Those hands are no longer steady, but in spite of that fact he can whip out a six-shooter and put six bullets in a target with astounding speed and accuracy. He won't tell any one his name, but insists that he has been "The Kid" for eighty years, and "The Kid" he intends to remain. He never mentions Billy the Kid, and never plays upon the idea that he was ever William Bonney. When asked if he has ever visited New Mexico, he says yes, but as it was almost sixty years ago, it seems like another life to him.

When asked what he did in New Mexico, The Kid replies that he roamed around, and punched cattle, and worked for some of the big cattle men of the time. And he always adds, "And I learned how to handle a gun." But at the mention of the Lincoln County War, and Murphy and McSween and Governor Lew Wallace, he says nothing.

It is possible, however, to get this old man to admit that he has been outside the law several times in his life. But he will never be specific about it, and the most he ever says about New Mexico is that "life was pretty fast there in the old days."

Only a few people have associated this Panamint Valley Kid with Billy the Kid, and one of the more curious deliberately mentioned the name of Bob Ollinger to him. Now Bob Ollinger was a bad man of the eighteen-eighties and he wanted everybody to know it. He wasn't in trouble with the law, but he went around with the proverbial chip way out on the edge of his shoulder. He liked to be considered dangerous. Of course such a man was naive and even childish. Billy the Kid had none of the theatrical desperado about him. He had nothing but scorn for Ollinger. And it so happened that when Billy the Kid was in jail in Lincoln under sentence to be hung, Ollinger, and a man named Bell, were his guards. Bell was a decent sort, but Ollinger, who hated The Kid because he was jealous of his reputation, loved to irritate him and to talk about the approaching hanging. Ollinger must have had a sadistic streak, for he kept rubbing it into The Kid about his imminent death on the gallows, and how few days of life were remaining to him, and how he would dance in the air, and how the rope would choke the rotten life out of him, and how his body would stiffen, and how he himself would put a load of buckshot into the remains of The Kid if he had half a chance.

All that sort of thing must have made Billy writhe, but he said little or nothing in reply. But if he said nothing, he did plenty. A few days before the date of the hanging Ollinger was eating his dinner across the street from the jail in Lincoln. That left The Kid with the remaining guard, Bell. There has been much speculation as to how it was done, and some authorities romantically visualize it as over a card game, but by whatever means possible, Billy managed to get Bell's revolver. That was a costly mistake for Bell, and not being shrewd enough to placate The Kid, who bore him no particular malice, he tried to dash out of the room. The Kid, naturally enough, shot him through the heart.

Ollinger, finishing his meal across the street, gulped the remains of a cup of coffee, and went running back to the jail. The room in which The Kid had been confined was the second story of the old court house. And as Ollinger came lumbering across the street, a quiet, "Hello, Bob," stopped him in his tracks. He looked up at the second story window and saw The Kid smiling down at him with a smile that had little good humor in it. And that's the last thing he ever saw.

Every one in Lincoln knew the desperado was loose, and no one dared do anything about it. Billy the Kid took the county clerk's horse and rode out of town never to return. The entire episode was perhaps the most sensational jail break in the history of New Mexico, and certainly a high spot in the vivid escapades of The Kid.

Now if this old man living alone in the Panamint country were the real Billy, the entire Ollinger episode must have remained forever in his memory. So, of course, must his experiences with Sheriff Pat Garrett. But whenever Garrett's name is mentioned the old man fails to express any kind of an emotion or even recognition of the name. It is a discouraging test for any one who romantically hopes that he has stumbled upon the ghost of a bad man, or who wants to believe that this old man may have been Billy the Kid. And that is just as it should be. For he cannot be the real Billy if the real Billy died over fifty years ago at old Fort Sumner.

But to return to the incident of Bob Ollinger. Apparently, only one· man ever mentioned Ollinger to this Panamint Valley Kid, and he got a reaction. The old man was sitting in the shade of his little shack which was on a slight rise of ground overlooking a dry wash. He and the stranger were making small talk of sidewinders and gila monsters. Leading the conversation to reptiles in general, the stranger casually said:

"I knew a rattlesnake once whose name was Bob Ollinger. Ever hear of him?"

The old man stared at the distant mountains, and very slowly began to smile. It was a cool and deliberate and extremely satisfied smile. He picked up a revolver that he had been toying with in his lap.

"Now he comes out of the hotel onto the porch," he remarked. "He's lookin' around to see where that first shot came from. He's wipin' the coffee off his mouth with one hand, and he trots across the street toward the jail. Now he's half way. Now he's right there where that tin can is settin'."

The stranger didn't say a word. He held his breath while the old man leveled the revolver at a tin can twenty feet away. The old man's hand was steady and his face had a cold, mirthless smile.

"Hello, Bob," he said softly with a slight drawl.

Then he fired and the tin gave six spasmodic jumps along the ground as six bullets went through it.

"And take that to hell with you," he said, and he put the revolver down beside him.

Then both men were quiet, and the stranger didn't know what to say. But presently the old man scratched the back of his neck.

"Ollinger, did you say?" He was looking blank and the smile was gone. "Ollinger, eh? Nope. Don't recollect that I ever heard of him."

Edwin Corle, *Mojave* (New York, Liveright Publishing Company, 1934), 163-169.

China Boy

BY IDWAL JONES

Idwal Jones contributes frequently to regional and national magazines. His specialty is the free rendition of a historic anecdote or one preserved in folklore, though Ark of Empire *is a whole book on San Francisco's Montgomery Building, and* The Vineyard *and* Vermilion *are novels tied to two historic elements in the California economy. Throughout there is a dwelling on the details that establish the local color.*

I first beheld Pon Look twelve years ago, and even then he was the oldest human creature in Fiddle Creek township. It was on top of Confidence Hill one August day, when the pines were withering in the terrific heat and the road was a foot deep in white dust. Pon Look came over the brow of the hill, from below.

He waddled like a crab, leaning on a staff, and extreme age had bent his body at a right angle to his stunted legs. His physiognomy was fearsome, like a Chinese actor's in a print. His head was sunk forward, so that his ears were in line with his shoulders, and the protuberant chin was adorned with sparse, silvery hairs. For all he had the aspect of a crippled galley-slave, he progressed smartly, slewing that head continually from side to side with a strange grace. He seemed to be propelling himself through the heat waves with that sculling movement. He had something alive, which he held in check with a rope. It was a large, feline animal, with a bobbed tail and a funny wicker hat fitting over its head, like a muzzle. At intervals this beast leaped into the air, and, uttering frantic cries, tore furiously at the muzzle with its forefeet. It had eyes as glittering as topazes. It was a superb catamount. Pon Look no more minded its antics than if they were the antics of a mosquito.

I offered Pon Look a cigar. His face wreathed instantly with smiles, and he took it shyly. Laughter wrinkles creased his smooth high forehead.

"You are taking your pet out for a breath of air?"

"Pet?" he queried. Meanwhile the catamount was whirring insanely in the dust, at taut rope, with the velocity of a squirrel in a cage. "Pet?—oh, no—I jus' catch heem now in the canyon."

"What are you going to do with him?"

Pon Look gave a fierce yank at the rope. "Oh—I tame him first. Then in two weeks, if not fliendly, I kill him." . . .

Across from the Flat was a narrow pass in a long mountain of black, igneous rock. The mountain was in a semi-circle, and encompassed many square miles of the only green land in the countryside. It was moist from hidden springs, and the virgin soil, overlaid with a humus of centuries, was phenomenal in its richness. Old Man Summerfield owned it. He was a hard-scrabble Vermont farmer who lived in a good house with his haggard wife. He waylaid cattle from the ox-trains, and decoyed them into the enclosure. They bred calves, and he grew passably rich. He dwelt in antipathy with his neighbors, who at night frequently took potshots at him. It was on the domains of this ogre that Pon Look trespassed. The owner came riding out with a rifle.

"What do you want here, you yellow limb? Get off my place!"

"A job," responded Pon Look.

After some reflection, the farmer manoeuvred Pon Look, as if he were a stray ox, and drove him to the cow-house.

"Live there," he snarled. "You'll find some sacks to sleep on."

Pon Look entered upon his duties, and became known as Summerfield's China Boy. There were twenty-five head of cattle, and it was his function to ride about on horseback and keep a wary eye on them, and if they showed symptoms of bursting, to dismount and stab them in the belly with a trochar. Because of the succulence of the grass they would overeat and suffer from bloat.

He acquired a sympathy with these animals, and in his solicitude would keep them moving incessantly, and try to retain them where the grass was somewhat less luxuriant. One night a handsome black bull escaped through the pass and vanished. Probably it got carved into steaks by unscrupulous neighbors. Old Man Summerfield frothed through his beard. He raged at Pon Look.

"What am I paying you board for, hey? To lose cattle for me? If that happens again—you get kicked out!"

The boy was aghast. There was every likelihood that it would happen again. It was then that he conceived the idea of building a wall around the ranch. It was a felicitous idea. Along one side of the low cliff was a talus of lava boulders; material right to hand. The stuff was in every size, from pebbles to bigness of a fist to rocks the size of a huge hog, and all rounded by aeons of time. The most of them resembled footballs, and were known locally as niggerheads.

He built a stone-boat, trained a cadgy old ox to haul it, and began to close the pass. He built a wall six feet high, and three and a half wide, with a wooden gate in the middle. The quarry was a quarter mile distant, and his tools were a crowbar and an end of plank. The job was finished after a year of back-breaking toil and the cost of Pon Look's right toe. Old Man Summerfield was so proud of this entrance that he spent hours sitting on the gate so people could see him as they drove by.

It was a notably fine gate, portentous and eye-taking. It was a gate that connoted landed respectability, and its psychological effect was curious. Old Man Summerfield swelled with self-esteem. He loafed at the saloons in the camp, and leading talk to the job, arrogated to himself all the credit for its design and building.

"It's all in handling the ma-terial," he would say. "You got to know how to lay them boulders and lock 'em so they won't roll off like balloons. They's nothing like a good gate to keep the cattle in."

"A better gate 'ud be one that kept other folks' cattle out," some neighbor would remark, after Old Man Summerfield had left.

The China Boy's task was only just started. He now began to haul boulders to close in the southern and open arc of the circle. He lived on a diet of boiled beef and rice, which he cooked at his end of the cowhouse, where he also slept. He arose before dawn, ate breakfast, then hitched the ox and boated a load of nigger-heads to the scene of operations. These he laid down before he returned to do the chores and attend to the milch cows. Not even after the rainy season was past was danger to the cattle over, and he had to be vigilant against the bloat. His masonry plan was to lay down the bottom tier, for the space of four miles, large boulders that required a trip apiece; then to superimpose smaller boulders, then loads upon loads of nigger-heads, until the wall was complete.

Progress was slow. The stone-boat ox would cough, then die very soon, and Pon Look had to train another one; or the vehicle would wear out, and he had to build another. Old Man Summerfield's wife, who had kept within the house and was wont to shout loud at night, gave up the ghost, so the master went to San Francisco to do some wooing, and being, as he said, "a particular man to please," it was three months before he returned with her successor. The boy did the work of two men in the meanwhile, but had to suspend work on the wall.

The new mistress was a fat shrew of a body, with a clacking tongue, and much displeased Pon Look by her interference. She made him beat carpets, trudge about the country to buy laying hens, and dig a garden. He submitted to it all, and arose an hour earlier, making a return trip with the stone-boat before sun-up. On one occasion, as he was passing by the house, she called to him to come in and wash the dishes. He said no. Whereupon she rushed at him with a broom and smote him violently as he stood in the yard. Pon Look took the blows without a murmur, and remained like a statue, with hands folded, while his mistress, still plying the broom, waxed hysterical.

There was no budging Pon Look. She spun round to beat at his face. It was serene, but pallid. The lips bespoke an obstinate resolve, but the eyes gleamed mistly at her with pity and forgiveness. Mrs. Summerfield's arms dropped, then she clutched at her throat, and staring at him walked backward into the house.

When Pon Look returned to the cow-house that night, he found on his table a hot raisin pie. On the window-sill the next morning, Mrs. Summerfield found the pie plate, scrubbed with the sand so bright that it reflected the sun like a mirror, and upon it a handful of the white daisies that grew nowhere except near the bog a mile distant. Pon Look had dined that night, as usual, on rice and beef.

388

The mystified hens, before going to roost, had filled their craws with pastry and raisins.

Thenceforward, Mrs. Summerfield treated Pon Look with a respect that was a compound of both affection and fear. On no pretext could he be induced to enter her house. She did not know what to make of him, so she left him alone. She ran the domestic establishment, but Pon Look, since the old man spent all day and half the night in the camp saloon, saw to the running of the ranch, the sale of the cattle, and of course, the construction of the wall.

"You don't have ter build that wall entire of rocks, China Boy," she said one evening, when the indomitable mason, scrubbed, and in his fresh alpaca coat, stood surveying in the dusk the lengthening boundary of the ranch. "Wire's just as good, and fence-stakes is cheaper than they was."

Pon Look gave a smile so expansive that his eyes disappeared in the creases. "Make 'um all stone, Mis' Sommyfeel'—begin 'um stone, and finish 'um stone, allee same niggy haid."

She plucked timorously at her alpaca apron. "Oh, well, it's you're doing it, not us."

Yet she took a pride in the fabulous immensity of the task. The editor of the county-town paper drove over one day and watched China Boy wrestling with the boulders. The next week he published a page story on the Summerfields' stone wall. It was a monument to Mr. Summerfield's enterprise and vision, he said; a testimony to the will, the perseverance and crag-like virtues that made New England great, etc. He dragged in quotations from the Latin poets. This story attracted a surprising lot of attention. Old Man Summerfield bought several copies, and wore them to rags in making a boozy tour of all the saloons in the county. People came to see, and amongst them were women who owned family coaches. Mrs. Summerfield made social contacts in this way, and finally joined the Ladies' Aid Society, and bought a bombazine dress and a landaulette so she could ride over to the meetings. Her period of ostracism was over.

The year 1879 was memorable in the annals of the family. Pon Look had completed the southern wall after the unremitting labors of twenty-seven years. Death enfolded Mrs. Summerfield that Autumn, while she was pruning a rose-bush in her garden. Pon

Look worked by lantern-light in the barn and built an enormous hexagonal coffin to house her frail body. It was so heavy that eight men buckled under the weight as they carried it to the hearse. Old Man Summerfield bought a new silk hat for the occasion, and was very proud of it. The minister held a service in the parlor, with no less than six families in attendance; and all throughout the widower nursed the hat on his knees, in full view of the admiring assemblage. Pon Look participated by looking in through the open window. He did not attend the funeral at the Odd Fellows' Cemetery, for there was much to do.

He trudged all over the ground with a tape-measure, and made mental calculations. He returned very late, and sat on the veranda to smoke a pipe in the moonlight. The old lady had latterly been quiet, and his thoughts were tinged with regret that she had gone. He was gratified that the master had taken things sensibly. A wind arose, and because it was cool, and he was afraid of the moon shining on his temples and making him mad, he got up to retire to the cow-shed. Between the lower bars of the gate something white caught his eye. He thought it one of the fluffy pom-poms that had been blown thither from the garden where the old lady had planted a clump of Holy Thistles. He drew nearer, picked up wonderingly a new silk hat, and found that the object was Old Man Summerfield's snowy head. Whiskey and grief had done for him.

There was some wearisome business with the coroner. Pon Look wanted to attend the funeral, but could not, for some excitable men detained him for a week in a stone room with bars at the window. He was released with palliative back-slappings and a handful of cigars after the inquest. He had been put to a great inconvenience, for the rains were now on, coming down like firm and slanting spears without let-up for days and days. He had to slosh around in the bog to lay a timber road across which to sled his rock. The Summerfield heir, an elderly nephew, took over the place a month afterwards. He was a city man, with a waxed moustache and a square-cut derby. He drank somewhat, and was inclined to be companionable. China Boy avoided him, looking rigidly ahead every time they passed.

"How much longer that job, John?" he asked one day.

"No can say."

"Well, then, how long did it take to build all that wall?"

"Oh—thirty—thirty-five year."

"Good God!" murmured the heir.

He sat under the trees dismally, like a strange bird. Then he panned for gold in various corners of the ranch, and did other foolish things. He would sit hunched on the sacred gate, mope about whistling with a dirge-like note, or keep to the house and drink. He was a lonely and wistful interloper. All his actions lowered himself in China Boy's esteem, and he knew it. China Boy strutted about with aloof and cold arrogance, and the heir's morale ebbed. Finally he accosted the mason and came to an understanding. China Boy was to keep an eye on the place, market the stock and keep a percentage for himself. Then he packed up his things in a wicker suit-case, and went away forever.

The Chinaman had the place to himself now, and sold off most of the heifers so they wouldn't breed and rob him of time he could apply to building. The wall progressed handsomely. He had stretched barbed wire across the northerly side of the farm until the work should be finished. When that was done the place would be a paradise for cattle. They could cram themselves with lush grass in one part of the ranch, then chew the cud in the cropped field adjoining. That would be the end of bloat. China Boy worked incessantly, visited by no one except the banker who came along every quarter to represent the routed heir. In time the wall got itself done. It undulated for miles over uneven ground, but plumb. as straight as a furrow, without a single bend. The job had taken China Boy forty years to complete. By this time he was doubled with age, his pigtail white, and his hands rock-hard and stumpy.

It was in August, when China Boy went up to ring the nose of the little black bull, that he saw the ground was parched. Down he went on his knees in the middle of the field and pulled up a handful of soil. It was as dry as ashes. The cattle came around with their tongues, leathery and swollen, hanging out. Palsied with terror, China Boy arose, and shading his myopic eyes, turned around and round like a weather cock, and stared for a glimpse of green. The entire ranch was as brown as a brick. Drouth had laid waste the ground as if with torches.

He saddled a pony and galloped, pigtail a-flying, to the bank.

The banker, when he heard the plaint, grumbled:

"I knew there was a hoodoo on the damned place. It's cooking hot, but I'll come down and see."

Together they rode back. The banker drew up in the buggy before a new mine in the field adjoining the Summerfield ranch. Here were a tall gallows-hoist, with sheaves whirring, a mill from which poundings emanated, and an engine house with a high stick. The ditch alongside the road was filled with a roaring flood of water.

"Ye-ah," he grunted, pointing at the ditch with his whip. "That's what I expected. The shaft has tapped the springs underlying the Summerfield flat. Might as well sell off the cattle, the place will be as dry as a volcano from now on." Then he scratched his head. "I'll have to send down some goats, Angora goats. Mebbe they'll pay off the taxes. Guess we can cut down some timber, too. I'll have a look at it."

China Boy got out and walked in a daze to the grove. The banker followed afoot, then paused when his guide appeared at the door of his cabin with a musket in his hands.

"Cattle can go," China Boy informed him, "but these trees they stay up, I watch 'um."

And up they stayed. The story got about, for the banker, who had been taken by the handsomeness of the grove, told it on himself. "An arbor-maniac, that's what he is. He made that wall business a life-long job, so he could live right there among those trees. Poor old chap, I'll have him pensioned off."

The banker kept his word, but China Boy drove a hard bargain. His terms for being superannuated were the weekly dole of five pounds of corn flour, a piece of bacon, six cartridges and a quart of whiskey, all to be delivered at the cabin.

Thereafter China Boy lived in the grove. Two hundred trees! Lordly sugar-pines, gold traced with black, like Porto-Venere marble. Five sequoias, so colossal that only after staring at them for twenty minutes did their size dawn upon you, and then with a finality that took you in the pit of the stomach like a blow. Winestemmed manzanitas, gnarled chaparral. The rest were all redwoods, with high fluted columns; and through their branches interlaced overhead the sunlight streamed in lines and cast disks

392

of silver upon the dark trunks and the ochre ground twinkling with ants. It was something like the inside of a church.

There was a wood for you! Visitors came rarely. Bearded blanket-stiffs, homeless men, tarried for a night on their way to the Middle Fork of the Stanislaus. An occasional prospector, reverent among trees, stayed sometimes two days. China Boy was their invisible host. He peered at them through the foliage, as if he were a bird, but never spoke to them, unless he perceived their shoes needed cobbling and he felt sure they could pay for the job, nothing less than a dollar, for even a philosopher must live. Aloof, and wrapped in an old army overcoat, he sometimes watched them all night, being afraid they would be careless with their pipes or forget to stamp out the embers of their camp fires.

His house, hidden away in the trees, was rather a nice one, of a single large room, very high, and built of brick. Decades before, he had come across an abandoned express office, and had carried it thither, piecemeal, a bushel of brick at a time, and set it up exactly as it was before, even to the legend board above the doorway: "Wells-Fargo Express."

It was a forest lover's house, with blackberry bushes climbing into the window, hedgehogs and gray squirrels sunning themselves on the step, and pine cones dropping like cannon-balls on the roof. It held a cot, a stove, a shoe-last, and a library that consisted in a wisdom-banner that hung on the wall. If he found you, after years of acquaintance, worthy enough, he would translate the wiggly ideographs thus:

"It is shame to be ignorant at sixty, for time flies like a mountain stream."

Here in this tree sanctuary that was of hoary age long before the Sung dynasty had started, China Boy had gone to school. He listened to the wind wrestling with the tree tops, to the language of the birds, the 'cries of the coyotes and owls, and other sounds that made the air articulate and vibrant. He loved to sit in the middle of his grove at night, still and pensive amid the falling leaves, like a rheumy-eyed hamadryad.

At intervals he straggled afoot to Sonora, with shirt-tail out and the sun warded off by an umbrella: quite the gentleman of leisure. But these excursions bored him finally, and he desisted, except when he had to call at the bank to complain about the quality of the whiskey. It was surprising what an educated palate he had. He wouldn't let the grocer's boy depart until he had first sampled the liquor ration.

Two years ago he trapped a pair of fine wildcats, and carted them off to town, and tarried overlong. Some campers came to the grove and were careless with their fire. China Boy's woods made a gorgeous blaze, singing and burning for ten hours, with the gray squirrels plumping down roasted, and the philosopher's house turning to a black lump like fused glass.

The story made five lines in the county paper. The forest ranger said afterwards that he had seen the Old-Man-Mad-About-Trees pull up to the ruins in his buckboard, look on a few minutes, then drive away.

The banker was dubious. "Must have checked out through old age in the city," he said, "else he would have come up to the bank. He drove an awful hard bargain over that whiskey. He had me paying eleven dollars a bottle for the stuff I used to get for him at two before Prohibition. If anybody's ahead of the game, it's me."

Idwal Jones, <i>China Boy</i>
(Los Angeles, Primavera Press, 1936), 9-10, 18-32.

Reform Governor

BY GEORGE E. MOWRY

George E. Mowry is a specialist on Theodore Roosevelt and the Progressives. The paragraphs that follow are drawn from his book on the California variant, the reformers banded together as the Lincoln-Roosevelt League.

During most of the campaign of 1910 Hiram Johnson was reasonably sure that he would be defeated. But one day, shortly before the election, he remarked to his traveling companion, Edward A. Dickson, that for the first time he felt he was going to win. Apparently, that was a sobering thought. For a long time he sat silent and looked at the road ahead. Then, obviously agitated, he turned to his companion again and asked, "What in the world are we going to do after we do get in?" His friend replied that they could institute a system of direct legislation, for one thing, so that when they were defeated at some inevitable date in the future, the old machine could never again have the power over the people of California it once enjoyed. Johnson was silent again for a period, and then, confessing that he did not know what direct legislation was, he asked Dickson to explain how the initiative, referendum, and recall worked. As Chester Rowell remarked afterward, the governor never seemed to realize throughout most of the campaign that if he were elected, he would actually have to outline and defend a long list of reform measures.

Once sure of office, Johnson tried to make up for his previous lack of reform knowledge. He spent over a month in the East, where he talked to Theodore Roosevelt, Robert LaFollette, and Lincoln Steffens about the things that could be done in the state. With the benefit of these talks and a number of books recommended by Roosevelt, the new governor felt that he had a much better grasp of the meaning of the progressive movement. But his colleagues at home were still not confident of his abilities to devise a sound reform program. Rowell, Lissner, Dickson, and Stimson were agreed that if a comprehensive reform program were planned, it would have to be conceived and worked out by the governor's friends and advisors. So sure of this was Meyer Lissner, the new chairman of the Republican State Central Committee, that without consulting the governor-elect, he appointed a series of committees to investigate all proposed reform measures. The committees were to report to a meeting of the progressive legislators at San Francisco a week before the legislature opened. There Lissner hoped that a comprehensive program of legislation would be agreed to, and made binding on the legislative members of the League. When Johnson returned and heard of the committees and the proposed "legislative conference," he was angry. In apology for his precipitate action, Lissner wrote that he thought he had spoken to the governor about the plan. But Johnson would not be mollified. At the conference he made an obvious point of refusing to sit beside Lissner, and for a long time thereafter he referred to the meeting with heavy irony as, "your famous San Francisco conference."

After that, Lissner and his colleagues were more careful of the governor's *amour propre*. Nevertheless, the San Francisco conference, attended by practically all the progressive members of the legislature, served an extremely useful purpose. During its sessions every pledge in the platform was thoroughly discussed, and on the basis of the committee reports, measures were drafted which subsequently were presented as bills to the legislature. Without the committee work and the conference, the story of the famous reform legislature of 1911 might have been materially different.

If Johnson depended upon his advisors for a constructive legislative program, they were even more dependent upon him in a political sense. . . .

The Johnson administration was then and has since been criticized for building up as tight a political organization as ever existed in California, and rather invidious comparisons have been made between it and the "creaking" Southern Pacific organization that preceded it. As far as such comparisons go, they are usually correct. The Johnson organization was extensive, devoted to its own purposes, and sometimes ruthless with opponents. To a degree, its methods were the methods of any exceptionally efficient political organization. The three qualifying words are important. There was no discernible corruption in the Johnson administration, and certainly no bribery in the ordinary sense. As much cannot be said for most other political organizations in the history of the state to that time. And the comparison falls down entirely when one looks at the goals of the reformers. The Johnson group sought to serve what they called the people of the state. Perhaps their definition of the people was sometimes a little narrow, as most such definitions are. But by any measure, the group the progressives sought to serve was so much broader than the group served in the past that to press the point further is to belabor the obvious. If a few of these reformers were extremely ambitious and used their positions for their own success, they were acting in an ancient and recognizable human pattern. But granted that one assumes a faith in democracy and in Christian ethics, a serious resemblance of the Johnson machine to the Southern Pacific political organization, either in their ends or means, becomes slightly fantastic.

"A successful and permanent government," Hiram Johnson observed in his first inaugural address, "must rest primarily upon the recognition of the rights of men and the absolute sovereignty of the people." The special interests of big business and the machine politician had prevented that in the past. Between "the political thug of the waterfront" and "the smugly respectable individual in broadcloth" who employed the processes of the state for his own private gain, he considered the latter much more dangerous to the common welfare. The governor proposed to wipe out vested privilege by making the people and their agents supreme. For that purpose, he recommended passage of the long list of reforms which the leaders of the Lincoln-Roosevelt League had written into the Republican platform. These included a railroad act empowering a commission to fix absolute rates on the basis of physical evaluation, the initiative, referendum, and recall (the last to include even judicial officers), an uncomplicated and direct primary, a short ballot, home rule for political subdivisions, and an employers' liability law. It was a good forthright reform speech; for the first time the governor talked about specific issues.

George E. Mowry, *The California Progressives*
(Berkeley, University of California Press, 1951), 135-139.

The Bindle Stiff

BY WALLACE STEGNER

At Stanford University Wallace Stegner teaches and practices creative writing. This selection is from his evocation of the surge and suppression of the Wobblies.

He traveled fast and light, with only a little bread and a couple of cans of beans in his balloon. Three days after he hooked a manifest out of Seattle he was soaking up steam in an Oakland Turkish bath. That night a strike of trainmen on the Southern Pacific stalled him in San Jose, but by the next evening, after talking with pickets and learning that the engineers and firemen had not yet voted to come out, he hung around the yards. There were so many railroad dicks around that there was no show to get aboard anything; he would have to snag one on the fly. Just at dark he started down the tracks out of town, through straggling shacks and Mexican *barrios*, until he was at the fringe of town, past where he estimated the yard dicks would have to drop off as the train gathered speed. Then he sat down by the trackside and waited, drowsing over his knees until a locomotive's light poked down the laddered track and roused him.

All the next morning he sat alone in a boxcar and dangled his heels out the open door, watching the picture-postcard ocean between San Luis Obispo and Santa Barbara twinkle and flow inward to the white beaches and break in big surf on the points. Outside of Santa Barbara he ditched the freight, walked clear through town, and picked it up again on the other side, clear out by Montecito, rising from his covert at a place where bums had jungled at the very edge of a big estate.

In Ventura a pair of shacks, going in pairs like nuns for protection, looked in one side of the car just as Joe went out the other. The train was still moving slowly. Before they could come through after him he had ducked through a ruck of rabbit hutches and chicken pens and littered backyards and out onto a dustry street. Again he walked through the town. This time he found a little jungle camp under some pepper trees, where about a dozen hoboes were lying around waiting for a stew. He chipped in a can of beans and ate with them, and after he had eaten he lay down with his hat over his face and slept. After dark he awoke, ate a tincup full of mulligan, washed the cup with sand and seawater down at the shore. There was a game of cooncan going on on a blanket by the fire; he sat off to one side, watching it.

After almost an hour word came down that a freight was coming. Joe stood up, and a man next to him said, "I'll be glad when their dam strike is over and the shacks are takin' bo money again. You really got to earn your ride, this way."

The bos were scattering along the grade. The headlight reached over them, the locomotive shook the ground as it passed in a moment of glare and steam and power. Back up the tracks Joe saw the lanterns of the yard dicks drop off, two of them, and bob and plunge and come to a stop. Figures were running desperately along the grade, but the chances were not good. The train was already rolling as fast as a man could run. The dark cars drew past him as he sprinted on the uneven footing, trying to keep his feet in the dark and still spot an open door. The man ahead of him swerved and gave it up, and in desperation Joe shifted his bindle over his back on the dead run and hooked a ladder with his right hand, jumping to get his feet clear as the train yanked him into the air. Panting, he clung to the throbbing rods, and then climbed carefully, his breath coming hard and his heart pounding, and made his way along the roof in the wind and the rain of cinders until he found the propped hatch of an empty reefer. His cautious call got no answer, but when he let himself down he found two other bos already there. They shifted over for him without a word.

At daylight the three of them ditched the freight together as it began to jerk and crawl into the Los Angeles yards. By nine o'clock Joe was riding the PE car down the Shoestring toward San Pedro. . . .

The self-regulating life of the mission went on, ignoring Joe Hillstrom where he sat. Two men drifted outside. Two others came to Lund for paper and pencil and sat down to write letters. A checker game, interrupted by the services, started up again. The dead afternoon slid toward evening. Finally Joe stood up, wandered over to the piano, put out a finger and touched a key. The single pure note hung in the air, and he felt that everything in the room momentarily stopped. He half wished he had played the piano for Lund. What difference would it have made?

But he felt sullen and irritable now, and he did not turn toward Lund. For a little while there had been here the welcome he had hungered for—which was a sour thought when you pondered it, that you had no place to go except a mission or a YMCA. But he didn't belong here, really, he didn't want a lot of greasy preaching thrown at his head, he didn't want his soul saved. Lund was not his kind. The room was full of his kind, sailors and working men on the drift, but when he looked at them from the platform he saw no face that he knew and no one to whom he had anything

399

to say. If he had been a user of tobacco he might have borrowed a match or a pinch of *snus*. If he had been a drinking man he might have said to one of them, "Let's go get a can of beer someplace." Out of the casual opiates of his kind he might have manufactured some bond, at least a temporary one, between himself and these others. But he didn't even have beer and tobacco in common with them.

He laid his hand again on the piano, tried a whole handful of keys, a jangling discord. Then he hooked the stool with his toe and pulled it over and sat down, swinging on the rotating seat until he faced the keyboard.

For a while he fooled around, building up chords and listening to the way they mounted. There was a pleasure in the sounds like the pleasure of being clean and in good clothes. He limbered his stiff fingers on scales, and from scales he wandered off into little hesitating tunes, feeling out the combinations with hands and ears. Across the piano's corner he could see Lund's big solid back, and he let his fingers work out on the keys the orderly pattern of Lund's beliefs. Live a Christian life and work hard and develop your talents and stay away from bad companions and turn the other cheek and organize in some good sound AFL union and make well-bred demands and thank the bosses when they raise your wages ten cents a day, or forgive them when they lay you off or cut your pay envelope. Above all, take your licking philosophically when they break your strikes with Pinkertons and gunmen. Be polite and the plutocrats might toss you a bone. Maybe there'll be a job scabbing on someone less polite. You might get to be Casey Jones the Union Scab, and blow a whistle on the S.P. line.

The tune came to his fingers and he played it through. Casey Jones the Union Scab. All the engineers and firemen who wouldn't come out in support of the trainmen. All the boomers who jumped up to form scab crews and beat the trainmen before their strike got a start. All the scissorbills who were good and faithful to the bosses, and got their reward in heaven, or in the neck. He could prophesy the course of this strike from the earful he had got from pickets in the San Jose yards.

His fingers were still working over the tune of "Casey Jones." Words began to fit themselves to it, an ironic parody that made

400

him go without a word to Lund's desk and grab up a piece of paper. He wrote the song almost as if from dictation, with very little crossing out and thinking, and when he stopped to read them over cold he had two verses and two choruses.

The Workers on the S.P. line to strike sent out a call;
But Casey Jones, the engineer, he wouldn't strike at all;
His boiler it was leaking, and its drivers on the bum,
And his engine and its bearings, they were all out of plumb.

Casey Jones kept his junkpile running;
Casey Jones was working double time; . . .
Casey Jones got a wooden medal,
For being good and faithful on the S.P. line.

The Workers said to Casey: "Won't you help us win this strike?"
But Casey said: "Let me alone, you'd better take a hike."
Then someone put a bunch of railroad ties across the track,
And Casey hit the river with an awful crack.

Casey Jones hit the river bottom;
Casey Jones broke his blooming spine;
Casey Jones was an Angeleno,
He took a trip to heaven on the S.P. line.

A line at a time he coaxed it along, juggling St. Peter, the Pearly Gates, harps, wings, angels, until they fell into place, erasing and changing until he had another verse:

When Casey got to heaven to the Pearly Gate,
He said: "I'm Casey Jones, the guy that pulled the S.P. freight."
"You're just the man," said Peter: "our musicians went on strike;
You can get a job a-scabbing any time you like."

Now Lund was looking over his shoulder. "Inspiration?"

Rotating on the stool, Joe passed him the sheet. "Communication to the Brotherhood of Railway Engineers." He swung gently, indifferently, but he kept Lund's face in the periphery of his vision, and the way Lund's smile widened as he read was a thing of importance. He waited for the laugh, and it came.

"Wonderful!" Lund said. "You've really got it coming. But why make poor St. Peter into the image of Collis P. Huntington?"

"Not Huntington," Joe said. "St. Pete isn't that big a bug. He's just a labor shark in heaven. He runs the hiring hall."

Still laughing, Lund beckoned to a man reading at one of the tables. The man came over, a short wiry man with an enormous Adam's apple. "This is something you'd like, Mac," the missionary said. "Sing it for him, Joe. This is Frank McGibbeney, he's a train-man himself."

McGibbeney shook hands, impassive, and listened with an expressionless face as Joe played and sang the first verse and chorus half under his breath. But by the fourth line he was grinning. At the end of the chorus his face was reddening and his eyes were half closed with a suspended guffaw and his mouth was hanging as he listened. When Joe finished the railroader was almost hopping up and down.

"Say!" he said. "Say, that's a daisy, Jack. That's really a peacherino."

Lund had put on his bartender scowl. "Are you going to leave that scab in heaven? Isn't there any solidarity among the angels?"

"All right," Joe said. "Let's get him out of there." Their eyes were on him as he leaned on his elbows and thought. His mind worked like a watch, little wheels turning, gears meshing, a controlled and triumphant mechanism. After no more than two or three minutes he spread the paper against the music rack and wrote:

> The angels got together and they said it wasn't fair
> For Casey Jones to go around a-scabbing everywhere
> The Angels' Union No. 23 they sure were there,
> And they promptly fired Casey down the Golden Stair.

The abrupt laughter at his back inspired him, and he tossed off another chorus as fast as he could write.

> Casey Jones went to Hell a-flying.
> "Casey Jones," the Devil said, "Oh fine;
> Casey Jones, get busy shoveling sulphur;
> That's what you get for scabbing on the S.P. line."

McGibbeney was almost lyrical with admiration. "Oh, that's a pip," he kept saying. "Boy, that's really first class." For a marveling second he looked at Joe, but he spoke to Lund, as if one didn't quite talk to a man who could write such songs. "The boys over at the hall would like to hear that, they sure would."

"Take it along," Joe said, and thrust the paper at him.

> Wallace Stegner, *The Preacher and the Slave*
> (Boston, Houghton Mifflin Company, 1950), 13-15, 24-27.

The Way of a Historian

BY OSCAR LEWIS

Oscar Lewis is one of the more prolific writers on California. His works include The Big Four; Sea Routes to the Gold Fields; Silver Kings; *and* San Simeon. *The traits of the historian limned in* I Remember Christine *seem to be borrowed from real life and the temptation has been strong to try to identify. The truth, we think, is that the Casebolt of the novel is really a composite with something borrowed from historian A, something else from historian B, historian C, and so on down the line.*

Casebolt has been writing so voluminously on California history, and so successfully, and over a period of so many years, that he has come to feel a sort of proprietory interest in the whole subject. It is perhaps an exaggeration to say that he regards the publication of a book on California by someone other than himself as a personal affront, but one often gets that impression. Because of his standing in academic circles and his wide popular following, his services as a reviewer are in demand both by the scholarly journals and the literary weeklies. Casebolt has reviewed almost every California book of importance, except his own, that has appeared during the past twenty years. His reviews are always models of impartiality. He goes into the subject in detail and with authority. He weighs the book's good and bad qualities, points out errors of fact and interpretation, and tells what field the author has attempted to cover and why he has failed. After reading one of these comprehensive analyses no one ever feels any desire to look into the book itself. Moreover, although Casebolt invariably finds that the volume under discussion is worthless, his reasons for reaching that conclusion are stated so fairly and with so engaging an air of detachment that no one (except, perhaps, the wretched author) ever thinks of accusing him of bias.

The fact that writers of books on California fail to gain Casebolt's approval is very largely their own fault. He has ideas on the subject and he has never hesitated to express them. I suppose he has delivered "The Winning of the Golden Empire"—the most popular of his lectures—at least five hundred times during the past twenty years. If there is a Chamber of Commerce, or a Rotary or Lions or Kiwanis club from Redding to El Centro that has not heard that spirited talk, it can only be because their managers lacked the enterprise to invite him. I once heard Casebolt lament the fact that his services as a lecturer were so much in demand, and I don't doubt that his constant traveling up and down the state is a drain on even his abundant energy. But when I asked him why, if lecturing was burdensome, he continued to do it, Casebolt confessed that he enjoyed it.

"I've never been an armchair historian," he added, "and I guess I'm too old to begin now. It's not that I don't envy you fellows who can retire to your studies and come out in a few weeks with a new book under your arm. It's just that I can't work that way—I often wish I could. I can't let myself get detached from my subject. I've got to get out where I can see it and touch it, where I can grapple with it at close quarters. You know what I mean, Walter?"

"No," I said.

"I suppose it is different with you fiction-writers," he acknowledged. "You don't have to worry about names or dates or the reliability of sources or the hundred other things that give us historians gray hairs. You invent your tales as you go along, and stir in a bit of love interest and a complication or two, and presto! you've got another novel. Another 'gripping romance of Old California'!"

I was well aware of the source of Casebolt's grievance against us fiction-writers who sometimes use California as the locale of our tales. The fact that every now and then one of these novels has a mild popularity and outsells his own solid historical works doesn't alter his conviction that all such books are trash. His chief complaint is that their authors haven't a proper knowledge of the periods of which they presume to write. If, in a review of one of these innocuous romances, he finds a historical error (he usually finds more than one), he drags it out and corrects it, citing chapter and verse to prove his point. But his attitude is more often one of sorrow than of anger; no fair-minded reader ever believes there is any rancor behind his judgments. He leaves one with the feeling that he would gladly have said something nice about the book if only its author had done one thing right and so have given him an opportunity to be generous.

Anyone who has listened to Casebolt's "Golden Empire" lecture—and who has not?—will recall that telling phrase of his: "When it comes to history, ladies and gentlemen, I'll take mine straight." That is a good example of his informal platform manner. He is not afraid to say that something he likes is "swell" (twenty-five years ago he would have said "bully") or that something he doesn't like is "lousy." That puts his audiences at their ease and, as he says, takes the curse off his academic connection. Than Casebolt there is not in all California a more striking exemplification of the fact that a college professor can be, in another of his phrases, a good egg.

Of course, Casebolt's prestige here on the Coast is not based solely on such grounds. He has been writing industriously for a third of a century and he has produced more than a score of books. Besides that he has held a series of progressively more important jobs at his university, ending with a full professorship and the chairmanship of his department. There are those who think he is in line for even higher honors when old President Van Amberg retires, as he inevitably will soon. Casebolt has been a leading spirit in the Historical Association from its founding, and a director since 1926 of the First National Bank of his home town. And of course everyone recalls his venture into politics a few years ago, when he ran far ahead of his ticket and missed becoming lieutenant governor only because of the Democratic land-slide that year.

But Casebolt's reputation is primarily based on his historical writings. Although I feel that his books make heavy going, I must add that this is a personal reaction and that many think otherwise. Besides, my belief that he is a bad writer does not prevent my recognizing that he is an influential one. It is well known that an inability to express oneself lucidly has never prevented a scholar from receiving the homage to which his other talents entitle him. At worst this is looked on as a minor blemish that throws one's other qualities into relief, like a well-placed mole on the cheek of a beauty.

Casebolt's theories are not in the least complicated. I am not over-simplifying when I state that his entire professional career has been devoted to furthering the belief that from the early nineteenth century until about the year 1865 every man who entered California from the east coast underwent a remarkable transformation at the moment he set foot on our soil, and that everyone who came from any other place whatsoever suffered changes equally drastic, but for the worse. The convenience of such a belief is evident. Once Casebolt had established that point in mind he was relieved from the necessity of ever giving it another thought. In his subsequent writings his heroes and villains fell automatically into their proper categories and thereafter they gave him no further trouble. It is a great boon to a member of any of the learned professions to be able to do all one's thinking at the outset of one's career.

It has done a lot for Casebolt. While he was still at college he decided what was to be his life's work. He would teach California history and he would write about California history, and his field should be that period from the coming of the first Yankee until the close of the Civil War. Both his theory and his method are well exemplified in the work that first established his reputation, his two volume *Conquest of California*, published in 1916. Many thousands of sets have been sold; one sees the stout red volumes on the shelves of every California library that amounts to anything, and I don't doubt that most of their owners have made conscientious attempts to read them. That the *Conquest* is not easy

406

going Casebolt himself candidly admits. "You won't find the nuggets lying on the surface," he tells his students in History B-1, the most popular of his lecture courses. "You've got to dig for them." Six generations of college students have heard that warning—Casebolt never hesitates to make his own books required reading in his courses—and it must be admitted that those who dig industriously enough often feel that they are rewarded.

Those who believe that California was conquered and annexed and settled by a race of idealists who acted on all occasions out of motives of pure benevolence will find in Casebolt's books much to admire. On the other hand, anyone who suspects that the rough shirts of the Yankee trappers and traders and miners did not invariably conceal hearts of pure gold are likely to regard much of Casebolt's writings as pernicious nonsense.

I felt no pressing urge to read his life of Jim Horton.

Oscar Lewis, *I Remember Christine*
(New York, Alfred A. Knopf, 1942), 4-9.

Perspective on the Pacific

BY JOHN CARL PARISH

John Carl Parish was a historian of the American move west, in which he had participated from Iowa to California. The following editorial which he composed for the first issue of the Pacific Historical Review *states the proposition that the American West faces the Pacific and prophesies that in time to come the Pacific area will be worthy of increased attention.*

The Pacific Coast through many generations was the far edge of the world for a people moving west. Balboa climbed over the mountains and found it. Magellan discovered a passage by which ships could reach it. Thereafter by land and sea men visited the western shore of the continent. Conquistador and priest, trader and pirate, rancher and miner and town-builder fashioned the rim of land into a place of legend and a lure for the adventurous.

407

Ships that beat their way around the Horn, pack-trains that toiled across the southern mountains, wagons whose creaking wheels rolled over interminable miles of dust, converted into a part of America this farthest margin of expansion.

But its dwellers looked across the mountains to the lands from which they had come. Their backs were to the sea. The ocean behind them seemed at best but an avenue by which ships could bring them news and supplies from the East. The sea was an empty room in the dwelling place of mankind—a vacant space setting them apart from an ancient and disregarded world. For the most part the inhabitants of the Pacific Coast forgot that the ocean itself was the scene and center of a great history. They ceased to remember that Magellan, having found the water route to the Pacific, was killed in battle in the Philippine Islands; that Captain Cook, after visiting the Northwest coast was killed in the Hawaiian Islands; that Chinese had probably crossed the ocean to California long before the Europeans arrived; that Spanish galleons had plied back and forth from Manila to the California and Mexican coasts before Jamestown was founded; that Kendrick and Robert Gray and other skippers carried Northwestern furs to China and there bought oriental goods for New England consumption; that Oregon learned of gold in California by way of Hawaii and that Peruvians and Australians beat the overland 49ers into the gold fields.

The Pacific Coast frontiersmen were engrossed with their own task—the conquest and development of their continent. But the time came when the struggle for the possession of the West was finished. Railways supplanted the ox-cart and the pack-train. The movement was still westward but it became less of a push and more of a drift. The spirit was gone from it. They were a numerous people now. Material comforts had followed them. Culture was finding its home among them. Less often did they look back toward the East. They glanced over their shoulders and saw Hawaii. They turned about and there was an awakened Japan, a China with its eternal problems, a Russia on the sea at the end of a transcontinental march like their own. The Pacific was no longer an empty room, a vacant space setting them apart from the Old East. It introduced them to a strange world. They had

408

settled and tamed a land. Now they found themselves in the open doorway of a new life.

As America had been coming into equality with Europe, so was the Pacific coming into an equality with the Atlantic. The Atlantic brought an old world in touch with a new. The Pacific brought a new world in touch with an old. California and China, Oregon and Hawaii, Mexico and the Philippines, Peru and Australia made each other's acquaintance. They came to see that instead of a dividing factor, a river or an ocean is bound to become a unifying force. The Basin of the Pacific was an entity. Its history was a unity. A community of interest and experience bound together the peoples that looked out upon the great ocean.

Pacific Historical Review I (1932), 135-136.

9

FROM DEPRESSION
TO AFFLUENCE

FROM THE HEADY EXPLOITS of the effervescent twenties. Californians plunged into the abyss of the Great Depression, a rough decade with business failures, plants shut down, cascading real estate prices, widespread unemployment, and hunger. But because these were the lot of the nation and the world and because relief and recovery were left mostly to the federal government and the New Deal, the tendency is to regard this subject matter as American rather than Californian.

On the local scene two topics are stressed—the wracking experiences of the Oakies and Arkies and the visionary and radical proposals advanced, particularly Upton Sinclair's plan to end poverty and Dr. Francis Townsend's formula for old age pensions. A generation later, with Social Security taken for granted and President Nixon as advocate of a federally guaranteed minimum income, Sinclair and Townsend seem merely to have been ahead of their time. From a literary standpoint Sinclair's I, *Governor and How I Ended Poverty* is greatly overshadowed by the epic treatment of the agony of the migratory farm workers in Dorothea Lange's pictorial *American Exodus*, John Steinbeck's *Grapes of Wrath*, and Carey McWilliams' *Factories in the Field*.

How the Second World War rescued the economy and ushered in a long-lasting era of affluence is also very much in the stream of the nation's history and related to the Cold War and the Nuclear Age. Eventually there should be monographs on California's war industries, on individual companies, the flood of new residents, and the prodigies in construction, as there have been

SAN FRANCISCO FROM TWIN PEAKS   *by Ansel Adams*

in the twentieth century on the gold rush, the building of the Pacific railroad, the health rush, and the boom of the eighties. To date, aside from the textbooks, written history stresses some of the grievous problems of the thirties, forties, and fifties.

In the ancient tradition of their craft, creative writers Steinbeck, Saroyan, Stegner, and company have approached this period similarly. They have dwelt but slightly on the captains of industry and the holders of power. As subjects they have preferred characters more ordinary, not to say underprivileged. More than with the building of things and the making of money they have been concerned with human beings as such and with problems of human welfare.

Some of this writing is descriptive with no apparent intention to summon to action. This is how most of Saroyan reads, His people are down but not quite out, and he is most vivid on what the Depression felt like and what in more prosperous times it meant to belong to the depressed quarter or tenth of the population. Social criticism is sometimes implied, as in the essay on Fresno, but it is not made an indictment.

On minute scale Sally Carrigher's *One Day on Beetle Rock* carries on the tradition of calm contemplative nature writing. François E. Matthes' *The Incomparable Valley* is similar in spirit though on the grandest of scales. Other examples occur in such books as *The Coast Ranges* and *The Sierra Nevada*, edited by Roderick Peattie, and in the pocket-size paperbacks on the natural history of the San Francisco Bay region, issued by the University of California Press. On occasion too, so social-minded a writer as Carey McWilliams embarks upon pure description as in the introductory pages of his *Southern California Country*. Writers such as these are worthy successors to King, Muir, and Austin.

Other writings, almost certainly to be accounted more noteworthy address crucial problems of the time. Steinbeck set the pace. His *Long Valley* and *Tortilla Flat* are compassionate descriptions. *In Dubious Battle* takes sides in a labor dispute, and *The Grapes of Wrath* outdoes such crusading novels as *Ramona* and *The Octopus*.

On other sectors criticism has been robust. Budd Schulberg's

412

What Makes Sammy Run? chooses Hollywood as appropriate setting for examining the drive for power, or what Americans will do for success. A more refined treatment of the same theme in the same setting is Libbie Block's *The Hills of Beverly*. F. Scott Fitzgerald's unfinished *The Last Tycoon* gives straighter reporting on the movie-makers. Just one suburb away are Aldous Huxley's *After Many a Summer* and Evelyn Waugh's *The Loved One*, excoriations of the necromantics but also a gloss on other facets of southern California life. In *The Preacher and the Slave*, quoted above, Wallace Stegner illuminates a recurrent theme, popular repression of a hated minority. Cynthia Lindsay's *The Natives Are Restless*, and Lawrence Lipton's *The Holy Barbarians* are acidulous comments.

A corpus of studies centers on the darkest blot of our war record, the mass removal of the Japanese Americans, aliens and citizens alike. With no pretense of individual evaluation they were conscripted into imprisonment. In a powerful novel, less adroit than Steinbeck or Huxley could have written, James Edmiston's *Home Again* follows the Mio family to Tanforan, Heart Mountain, and back to Synnyvale. Morton Grodzin's *Americans Betrayed*, and Allan R. Bosworth, *America's Concentration Camps* assess the forces that brought about the evacuation, and tenBroek, Barnhart, and Matson in *Prejudice* find the popular rationalization altogether inadequate. In *American Racism*, Roger Daniels and Harry H. L. Kitano analyze California indulgences in race prejudice from statehood to the present.

The machinations of the Cold War security program offers an equally poignant theme. In his opinion in *Pockman* v. *Leonard* Justice Jesse W. Carter analyzes and excoriates this folly. Several creative writers have examined its consequences: Martha Dodd in *The Searching Light*, camouflaged with a Pennsylvania setting; Abraham Polonsky in *A Season of Fear*; John Beecher in *Land of the Free*; and Seymour Kern in *The Golden Scalpel*. "A Battlefield Revisited" deals with another facet of this hypertension.

On what must be counted the over-riding issue of this epoch—atomic fission, what to do with it, and how to co-exist with it—California through its scientists had a leading role in giving dimension to the problem. That is true, not merely as to the researches that gave it rise, but in analyzing the consequent problems. Linus Pauling and Harrison Brown on the one side and Edward Teller and Willard F. Libby on the other represent a substantial part of the nationwide debate. On this grave issue the state's historians would express themselves later. Soon after Hiroshima, Robinson Jeffers dealt with it devastatingly in "The Inquisitors."

Fresno

BY WILLIAM SAROYAN

Born in 1908 in the Armenian section of Fresno, William Saroyan has acquired fame as a novelist, playwright, and short story writer. Stylistically, he is an impressionist and his writings are marked with a sense of the basic goodness of all men. His well-known works include The Daring Young Man on the Flying Trapeze, Inhale and Exhale, *and* The Time of Your Life.

A man could walk four or five miles in any direction from the heart of our city and see our streets dwindle to land and weeds. In many places the land would be vineyard and orchard land, but in most places it would be desert land the weeds would be the strong dry weeds of desert. In this land there would be the living things that had had their being in the quietness of deserts for centuries. There would be snakes and horned-toads, prairie-dogs and jack-rabbits. In the sky over this land would be buzzards and hawks, and the hot sun. And everywhere in the desert would be the marks of wagons that had made lonely roads.

Two miles from the heart of our city a man could come to the desert and feel the loneliness of a desolate area, a place lost in the earth, far from the solace of human thought. Standing at the edge of our city, a man could feel that we had made this place of streets and dwellings in the stillness and loneliness of the desert, and that we had done a brave thing. We had come to this dry area that was

414

without history, and we had paused in it and built our houses and we were slowly creating the legend of our life. We were digging for water and we were leading streams through the dry land. We were planting and ploughing and standing in the midst of the garden we were making.

Our trees were not yet tall enough to make much shade, and we had planted a number of kinds of trees we ought not to have planted because they were of weak stuff and would never live a century, but we had made a pretty good beginning. Our cemeteries were few and the graves in them were few. We had buried no great men because we hadn't had time to produce any great men. We had been too busy trying to get water into the desert. The shadow of no great mind was over our city. But we had a playground called Cosmos Playground. We had public schools named after Emerson and Hawthorne and Lowell and Longfellow. Two great railways had their lines running through our city and trains were always coming to us from the great cities of America and somehow we could not feel that we were wholly lost. We had two newspapers and a Civic Auditorium and a public library one-third full of books. We had the Parlor Lecture Club. We had every sort of church except a Christian Science church. Every house in our city had a Bible in it, and a lot of houses had as many as four Bibles in them. A man could feel our city was beautiful.

Or a man could feel that our city was fake, that our lives were empty, and that we were the contemporaries of jack-rabbits. Or a man could have one viewpoint in the morning and another in the evening. The dome of our court-house was high, but it was ridiculous and had nothing to do with what we were trying to do in the desert. It was an imitation of something out of Rome. We had a mayor but he wasn't a great man and he didn't look like a mayor. He looked like a farmer. He *was* a farmer, but he was elected mayor. We had no great men, but the whole bunch of us put together amounted to something that was very nearly great. Our mayor was not above carrying on a conversation with an Armenian farmer from Fowler who could speak very little English. Our mayor was not a proud man and he sometimes got drunk with his friends. He liked to tell folks how to dig for water or how to prune muscat vines in order to get a good crop, and on the

415

whole he was an admirable man. And of course we had to have a mayor, and of course *somebody* had to be mayor.

Our enterprise wasn't on a vast scale. It wasn't even on a medium-sized scale. There was nothing slick about anything we were doing. Our enterprise was neither scientific nor inhuman, as the enterprise of a growing city ought to be. Nobody knew the meaning of the word efficiency, and the most frightening word ever used by our mayor in public orations was *progress*, but by *progress* he meant, and our people understood him to mean, the paving of the walk in front of the City Hall, and the purchase by our city of a Ford automobile for the mayor. Our biggest merchant was a small man named Kimball, who liked to loaf around in his immense department store with a sharpened pencil on his right ear. He liked to wait on his customers personally, even though he had over two dozen alert clerks working for him. They were alert during the winter, at any rate, and if they sometimes dozed during the long summer afternoons, it was because our whole city slept during those afternoons. There was nothing else to do. This sort of thing gave our city an amateur appearance, as if we were only experimenting and weren't quite sure if we had more right to be in the desert than the jack-rabbits and the horned-toads, as if we didn't believe we had started something that was going to be very big, something that would eventually make a tremendous change in the history of the world.

But in time a genius appeared among us and he said that we would change the history of the world. He said that we would do it with raisins.

He said that we would change the eating habits of man.

Nobody thought he was crazy because he wore spectacles and looked important. He appeared to be what our people liked to call *an educated man*, and any man who had had an education, any man who had gone through a university and read books, must be an important man. He had statistics and the statistical method of proving a point. He proved mathematically that he would be able to do everything he said he was going to do. What our valley needed, he said, was a system whereby the raisin would be established as a necessary part of the national diet, and he said that he had evolved this system and that it was available for our valley.

416

He made eloquent speeches in our Civic Auditorium and in the public halls of the small towns around our city. He said after we got America accustomed to eating raisins, we would begin to teach Europe and Asia and maybe Australia to eat raisins, our valley would become the richest valley in the whole world. China! he said. He shouted the exact number of Chinese in China. It was a stupendous figure, and the farmers in the Civic Auditorium didn't know whether to applaud or protest. He said that if he could get every living Chinaman to place one raisin, only *one* mind you, in every pot of rice he cooked, why, then, we could dispose of all our raisins at a good price and everybody in our valley would have money in the bank, and would be able to purchase all the indispensable conveniences of modern life, bath-tubs, carpet-sweepers, house electricity, and automobiles.

Rice, he said. That's all they eat. But we can teach them to drop one raisin in every pot of rice they cook.

Raisins had a good taste, he said. People liked to eat raisins. People were so fond of eating raisins that they would be glad to pay money for them. The trouble was that people had gotten out of the habit of eating raisins. It was because grocers all over the country hadn't been carrying raisins for years, or if they had been carrying them, the raisins hadn't been packed in attractive packages.

All we needed, he said, was a raisin association with an executive department and a central packing and distributing plant. He would do the rest. He would have an attractive package designed, and he would create a patented trade-name for our raisins. He would place full-page advertisements in *The Saturday Evening Post* and other national periodicals. He would organize a great sales force. He would do everything. If our farmers would join this raisin association of his, he would do everything, and our city would grow to be one of the liveliest cities in California. Our valley would grow to be one of the richest agricultural centers of the world. He used big words like *co-operation, mass production, modern efficiency, modern psychology, modern advertising*, and *modern distribution*, and the farmers who couldn't understand what he was talking about felt that he was very wise and that they must join the raisin association and help make raisins famous.

He was an orator. He was a statistician. He was a genius. I forget his name. Our whole valley has forgotten his name, but in his day he made something of a stir.

The editor of the *Morning Republican* studied this man's proposal and found it sound, and the editor of the *Evening Herald* said that it was a good thing, and our mayor was in favor of it, and there was excitement all over our valley. Farmers from all over our valley came to town in surreys and buggies. They gathered in small and large groups in front of our public buildings, and they talked about this idea of making the raisins famous.

It *sounded* all right.

The basic purpose of the raisin association was to gather together all the raisins of our valley, and after creating a demand for them through national advertising, to offer them for sale at a price that would pay for all the operating expenses of the association and leave a small margin for the farmers themselves. Well, the association was established and it was called the Sun-Maid Raisin Association. A six-story Sun-Maid Raisin Building was erected, and an enormous packing and distributing plant was erected. It contained the finest of modern machinery. These machines cleaned the raisins and took the stems from them. The whole plant was a picture of order and efficiency.

Every Thursday in those days I went down to Knapp's on Broadway and got a dozen copies of *The Saturday Evening Post*. The magazine was very thick and heavy. I used to carry a dozen of them in a sack slung over my shoulder. By the time I had walked a block my shoulder would be sore. I do not know why I ever wanted to bother about selling *The Saturday Evening Post*, but I suppose it was partly because I knew Benjamin Franklin had founded it, and partly because I liked to take a copy of the magazine home and look at the advertisements. For a while I even got in the habit of reading the stories of George Agnew Chamberlain. One Thursday evening I had a copy of *The Saturday Evening Post* spread before me on our living-room table. I was turning the pages and looking at the things that were being advertised. On one page I read the words, *Have you had your iron today?* It was a full-page advertisement of our Raisin Association. The advertisement explained in impeccable English that raisins contained iron and that wise people were eating a five-cent package of raisins every afternoon. Raisins banished fatigue, the advertisement said. At the bottom of the page was the name of our Association, its street address, and the name of our city. We were no longer lost in the wilderness, because the name of our city was printed in *The Saturday Evening Post*.

These advertisements began to appear regularly in *The Saturday Evening Post*. It was marvelous. People were hearing about us. It was very expensive to have a full-page advertisement in the *Post*, but people were being taught to eat raisins, and that was the important thing.

For a while people actually *did* eat raisins. Instead of spending a nickel for a bottle of Coca-Cola or for a bar of candy, people were buying small packages of raisins. The price of raisins began to move upward, and after several years, when all of America was enjoying prosperity, the price of raisins became so high that a man with ten acres of vineyard was considered a man of considerable means, and as a matter of fact he was. Some farmers who had only ten acres were buying brand-new automobiles and driving them around.

Everybody in our city was proud of the Raisin Association. Everything looked fine, values were up, and a man had to pay a lot of money for a little bit of desert.

Then something happened.

It wasn't the fault of our Raisin Association. It just happened, People stopped eating raisins. Maybe it was because there was no longer as much prosperity as there had been, or maybe it was because people had simply become tired of eating raisins. There are other things people can buy for a nickel and eat. At any rate, people stopped eating raisins. Our advertisements kept appearing in *The Saturday Evening Post* and we kept asking the people of America if they had had their iron, but it wasn't doing any good. We had more raisins in our Sun-Maid warehouse than we could ever sell, even to the Chinese, even if they were to drop *three* raisins in every pot of rice they cooked. The price of raisins began to drop. The great executives of the Association began to worry. They began to think up new ways to use raisins. They hired chemists who invented a raisin syrup. It was supposed to be at least as

419

good as maple syrup, but it wasn't. Not by a long shot. It didn't taste like syrup at all. It simply had a syrupy texture. That's all. But the executives of our Association were desperate and they wanted to dispose of our surplus raisins. They were ready to fool themselves, if necessary, into believing that our valley would grow prosperous through the manufacture and distribution of raisin syrup, and for a while they believed this. But people who were buying the syrup didn't believe it. The price of raisins kept on going down. It got so low it looked as if we had made a mistake by pausing in the desert and building our city in the first place.

Then we found out that it was the same all over the country. Prices were low everywhere. No matter how efficient we were, or how cleverly we wrote our advertisements, or how attractive we made our packages of raisins, we couldn't hope for anything higher than the price we were getting. The six-story building looked sad, the excitement died away, and the packing house became a useless ornament in the landscape. Its machinery became junk, and we knew a great American idea had failed. We hadn't changed the taste of man. Bread was still preferable to raisins. We hadn't taught the Chinese to drop a raisin in their pots of cooking rice. They were satisfied to have the rice without the raisins.

And so we began to eat the raisins ourselves. It was amazing how we learned to eat raisins. We had talked so much about them we had forgotten that they were good to eat. We learned to cook raisins. They were good stewed, they had a fine taste with bread. All over the valley people were eating raisins. People couldn't buy raisins because they were a luxury, and so we had to eat them ourselves although they were no luxury to us.

William Saroyan, *The Saroyan Special*,
(New York, 1934), 58-62.

And It Came to Pass, in the
Fields of California

BY JOHN STEINBECK

John Steinbeck seems most at ease in his stories about the paisanos of Monterey. He has ranged much farther afield, to the fisheries of Baja California, to Scandinavia, to New England. In Dubious Battle *(1936) concerned the plight and aspirations of farm labor, and to that theme Steinbeck returned in the most significant of his novels,* The Grapes of Wrath.

Once California belonged to Mexico and its land to Mexicans; and a horde of tattered feverish Americans poured in. And such was their hunger for land that they took the land—stole Sutter's land, Guerrero's land, took the grants and broke them up and growled and quarreled over them, those frantic hungry men; and they guarded with guns the land they had stolen. They put up houses and barns, they turned the earth and planted crops. And these things were possession, and possession was ownership.

The Mexicans were weak and fed. They could not resist, because they wanted nothing in the world as frantically as the Americans wanted land.

Then, with time, the squatters were no longer squatters, but owners; and their children grew up and had children on the land. And the hunger was gone from them, the feral hunger, the gnawing, tearing hunger for land, for water and earth and the good sky over it, for the green thrusting grass, for the swelling roots. They had these things so completely that they did not know about them any more. They had no more the stomach-tearing lust for a rich acre and a shining blade to plow it, for seed and a windmill beating its wings in the air. They arose in the dark no more to hear the sleepy birds' first chittering, and the morning wind around the house while they waited for the first light to go out to the dear acres. These things were lost, and crops were reckoned in dollars, and land was valued by principal plus interest, and crops were bought and sold before they were planted. Then crop failure, drought, and flood were no longer little deaths within life, but simple losses of money. And all their love was thinned with money, and all their fierceness dribbled away in interest until they were no longer farmers at all, but little shopkeepers of crops, little manufacturers who must sell before they can make. Then those farmers who were not good shopkeepers lost their land to good shopkeepers. No matter how clever, how loving a man might be with earth and growing things, he could not survive if he were not also a good shopkeeper. And as time went on, the business men had the farms, and the farms grew larger, but there were fewer of them.

Now farming became industry, and the owners followed Rome, although they did not know it. They imported slaves, although they did not call them slaves: Chinese, Japanese, Mexicans, Filipinos. They live on rice and beans, the business men said. They don't need much. They wouldn't know what to do with good wages. Why, look how they live. Why, look what they eat. And if they get funny—deport them.

And all the time the farms grew larger and the owners fewer. And there were pitifully few farmers on the land any more. And the imported serfs were beaten and frightened and starved until some went home again, and some grew fierce and were killed or driven from the country. And the farms grew larger and the owners fewer.

And the crops changed. Fruit trees took the place of grain fields, and vegetables to feed the world spread out on the bottoms: lettuce, cauliflower, artichokes, potatoes—stoop crops. A man may stand to use a scythe, a plow, a pitchfork; but he must crawl like a bug between the rows of lettuce, he must bend his back and pull his long bag between the cotton rows, he must go on his knees like a penitent across a cauliflower patch.

And it came about that owners no longer worked on their farms. They farmed on paper; and they forgot the land, the smell, the feel of it, and remembered only that they owned it, remembered only what they gained and lost by it. And some of the farms grew so large that one man could not even conceive of them any more, so large that it took batteries of bookkeepers to keep track of interest and gain and loss; chemists to test the soil, to replenish; straw bosses to see that the stooping men were moving along the rows as swiftly as the material of their bodies could stand. Then such a farmer really became a storekeeper, and kept a store. He paid the men, and sold them food, and took the money back. And after a while he did not pay the men at all, and saved bookkeeping. These farms gave food on credit. A man might work and feed himself; and when the work was done, he might find that he owed money to the company. And the owners not only did not work the farms any more, many of them had never seen the farms they owned.

And then the dispossessed were drawn west—from Kansas, Oklahoma, Texas, New Mexico; from Nevada and Arkansas families, tribes, dusted out, tractored out. Carloads, caravans, homeless and hungry; twenty thousand and fifty thousand and a hundred thousand and two hundred thousand. They streamed over the mountains, hungry and restless—restless as ants, scurrying to find work to do—to lift, to push, to pull, to pick, to cut—anything, any burden to bear, for food. The kids are hungry. We got no place to live. Like ants scurrying for work, for food, and most of all for land.

We ain't foreign. Seven generations back Americans, and beyond that Irish, Scotch, English, German. One of our folks in the Revolution, an' they was lots of our folks in the Civil War—both sides. Americans.

They were hungry, and they were fierce. And they had hoped to find a home, and they found only hatred. Okies—the owners hated them because the owners knew they were soft and the Okies strong, that they were fed and the Okies hungry; and perhaps the owners had heard from their grandfathers how easy it is to steal land from a soft man if you are fierce and hungry and armed. The owners hated them. And in the towns, the storekeepers hated them because they had no money to spend. There is no shorter path to a storekeeper's contempt, and all his admirations are exactly opposite. The town men, little bankers, hated Oakies because there was nothing to gain from them. They had nothing. And the laboring people hated Oakies because a hungry man must work, and if he must work, if he has to work, the wage payer automatically gives him less for his work; and then no one can get more.

And the dispossessed, the migrants, flowed into California, two hundred and fifty thousand, and three hundred thousand. Behind them new tractors were going on the land and the tenants were being forced off. And new waves were on the way, new waves of the dispossessed and the homeless, hardened, intent, and dangerous.

And while the Californians wanted many things, accumulation, social success, amusement, luxury, and a curious banking security, the new barbarians wanted only two things—land and food; and to them the two were one. And whereas the wants of the Californians were nebulous and undefined, the wants of the Oakies were beside the roads, lying there to be seen and coveted: the good fields with water to be dug for, the good green fields, earth to crumble experimentally in the hand, grass to smell, oaten stalks to chew until the sharp sweetness was in the throat. A man might look at a fallow field and know, and see in his mind that his own bending back and his own straining arms would bring the cabbages into the light, and the golden eating corn, the turnips and carrots.

And a homeless hungry man, driving the roads with his wife beside him and his thin children in the back seat, could look at the fallow fields which might produce food but not profit, and that man could know how a fallow field is a sin and the unused land a crime against the thin children. And such a man drove along the roads and knew temptation at every field, and knew the lust to take these fields and make them grow strength for his children and a little comfort for his wife. The temptation was before him always. The fields goaded him, and the company ditches with good water flowing were a goad to him.

And in the south he saw the golden oranges hanging on the trees, the little golden oranges on the dark green trees; and guards with shotguns patrolling the lines so a man might not pick an orange for a thin child, oranges to be dumped if the price was low.

He drove his old car into a town. He scoured the farms for work. Where can we sleep the night?

Well, there's Hooverville on the edge of the river. There's a whole raft of Oakies there.

He drove his old car to Hooverville. He never asked again, for there was a Hooverville on the edge of every town.

The rag town lay close to water; and the houses were tents, and

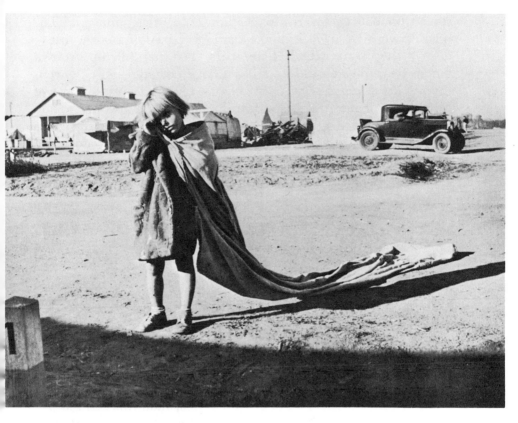

CHILD WITH COTTON SACK *by Dorothea Lange*
An early morning picture in Kern County;
time for this girl to go into the field with her parents.

weed-thatched enclosures, paper houses, a great junk pile. The man drove his family in and became a citizen of Hooverville— always they were called Hooverville. The man put up his own tent as near to water as he could get; or if he had no tent, he went to the city dump and brought back cartons and built a house of corrugated paper. And when the rains came the house melted and washed away. He settled in Hooverville and he scoured the countryside for work, and the little money he had went for gasoline to look for work. In the evening the men gathered and talked together. Squatting on their hams they talked of the land they had seen.

There's thirty thousan' acres, out west of here. Layin' there. Jesus, what I could do with that, with five acres of that! Why, hell, I'd have ever'thing to eat.

Notice one thing? They ain't no vegetables nor chickens nor pigs at the farms. They raise one thing—cotton, say, or peaches, or lettuce? 'Nother place'll be all chickens. They buy the stuff they could raise in the dooryard.

Jesus, what I could do with a couple pigs!

Well, it ain't yourn, and it ain't gonna be yourn.

What we gonna do? The kids can't grow up this way.

In the camps the word would come whispering, There's work at Shafter. And the cars would be loaded in the night, the highways crowded—a gold rush for work. At Shafter the people would pile up, five times too many to do the work. A gold rush for work. They stole away in the night, frantic for work. And along the roads lay the temptations, the fields that could bear food.

That's owned. That ain't our'n.

Well, maybe we could get a little piece of her. Maybe—a little piece. Right down there—a patch. Jimson weed now. Christ, I could git enough potatoes off'n that little patch to feed my whole family!

It ain't our'n. It got to have Jimson weeds.

Now and then a man tried; crept on the land and cleared a piece, trying like a thief to steal a little richness from the earth. Secret gardens hidden in the weeds. A package of carrot seeds and a few turnips. Planted potato skins, crept out in the evening secretly to hoe in the stolen earth.

426

Leave the weeds around the edge—then nobody can see what we're a-doin'. Leave some weeds, big tall ones, in the middle.

Secret gardening in the evenings, and water carried in a rusty can.

And then one day a deputy sheriff: Well, what you think you're doin'?

I ain't doin' no harm.

I had my eye on you. This ain't your land. You're trespassing.

The land ain't plowed, an' I ain't hurtin' it none.

You goddamned squatters. Pretty soon you'd think you owned it. You'd be sore as hell. Think you owned it. Get off now.

And the little green carrot tops were kicked off and the turnip greens trampled. And then the Jimson weed moved back in. But the cop was right. A crop raised—why, that makes ownership. Land hoed and the carrots eaten—a man might fight for land he's taken food from. Get him off quick! He'll think he owns it. He might even die fighting for the little plot among the Jimson weeds. . . .

The men squatted on their hams, sharp-faced men, lean from hunger and hard from resisting it, sullen eyes and hard jaws. And the rich land was around them.

D'ja hear about the kid in that fourth tent down?

No, I jus' come in.

Well, that kid's been a-cryin' in his sleep an' a-rollin' in his sleep. Them folks thought he got worms. So they give him a blaster, an' he died. It was what they call black-tongue the kid had. Comes from not gettin' good things to eat.

Poor little fella.

Yeah, but them folks can't bury him. Got to go to the county stone orchard.

Well, hell.

And hands went into pockets and little coins came out. In front of the tent a little heap of silver grew. And the family found it there.

Our people are good people; our people are kind people. Pray God some day kind people won't all be poor. Pray God some day a kid can eat.

427

And the associations of owners knew that some day the praying would stop.

And there's the end.

John Steinbeck, *The Grapes of Wrath*
(New York, The Viking Press, 1939), 315-326.

On Beetle Rock

BY SALLY CARRIGHAR

One Day on Beetle Rock is a one-act, one-scene drama, recited from the perspective of one after another of the inhabitants of this famous feature of Sequoia National Park. Sally Carrighar is well steeped in the scientific lore necessary for this kind of nature writing and she had schooled herself also by writing for radio and the press.

The Buck . . . finally stood on the inner edge of the Rock. Before him lay the two acres of granite field, almost square, divided like a beetle's back. The forest rose behind the north and east sides. The other sides ended in a sharp rim out over the canyon.

Most of the Rock's terraces were smooth, but some were broken up into domes, knobs, and angular boulders. A few pine and cedar trees had found rootholds in the crevices. Their shade lay cool on the gray and ivory-white stone. Brush was growing from soil blown into the cracks; rock flowers and grasses leaned from smaller pockets; back under the ledges were cliff-brake and moss. On the May morning when the Buck came to the Rock, a green fuzz was showing in some of the shallow depressions. A month later golden-throated gilia and baby's-breath would be blooming there.

Energetically the birds were singing their claims to their particular trees and bushes, and small furred creatures were chasing each other, settling the boundary lines between their private areas of the Rock. Before the Buck had gone many steps he came to a bluffing contest. The Lizard and a neighbor who coveted his gully were pumping up and down on their forelegs, trying to intimidate each other by displaying their bulging blue throat-spots.

The Buck moved from one terrace to another, browsing on the Manzanita bushes, straying towards the north side of the Rock. The deer did not often go to the south side, for there they found a disturbing bear scent. It rose from a small meadow below, and from a wooded shelf on the face of the cliff where several bears stayed in the daytime. This morning the Buck caught none of their odor. The air was lightly pungent with the fragrance of new needles on the trees and new leaves on the brush. And everywhere was the sound, which never ceased here, of the canyon wind flowing among the crevices, turning between the boulders, blowing upon thin edges of stone, the wind that had given sound to the mountain before any leaves grew there to rustle, the wind that the Buck would not hear forever.

But now he has leapt to a higher ledge, is ready to bound away from the Rock, and into the forest. For a turn past a chinquapin has disclosed the Coyote, stalking granite-hoppers in a space hidden by brush. The Coyote sensed that the Buck could escape, and gave no sign that he heard the scattering gravel and the hoofs' landing upon the ledge. The Buck looked down from above. The Coyote was new here; for three years no coyotes had lived in the deer's immediate range.

This summer, then, the herd leader would need even more than his usual caution. Wariness was his skill, his most significant quality. In the Buck was the best example, among all the Beetle Rock animals, of the willing tension that keeps a wilderness society stable. His was the finest alertness, but every creature had much of it. Since long before he was born the community here had been holding together, because each of its members was ready to leap, to chase, to freeze, to threaten, to love, or to step aside—in an instant.

Sally Carrighar, *One Day on Beetle Rock*, (New York, Alfred A. Knopf, 1944), 8-10.

South of Tehachapi

BY CAREY MCWILLIAMS

In the early 1950's Carey McWilliams became editor of the Nation *and perforce a New Yorker. Prior to that he was one of the most active writers on California with such important titles as* Factories in the Field; Ill Fares the Land; Brothers under the Skin; Prejudice; *and* California, the Great Exception.

From San Francisco south, the coast-line extends in a north-south direction until Point Conception is reached at latitude 34.30 degrees; then the line swerves abruptly east and the shoreline begins to face almost due south. Once Point Conception has been rounded in an ocean liner, once the Tehachapi range has been crossed by train or car, even the most obtuse observer, the rankest neophyte, can feel that he has entered a new and distinct province of the state. If Southern California is entered from the east, through El Cajon Pass or San Gorgonio Pass, the impression is even more vividly sensed. On the Pacific side, the coast range turns east. The mountains no longer shut off the interior from the sea. The air is softer, the ocean is bluer, and the skies have a lazy and radiant warmth. South of Point Conception, a new Pacific Ocean emerges: an ocean in which you can actually bathe and swim, an ocean that sparkles with sunlight, an ocean of many and brilliant colors. Here is California del Sur, the Cow Counties, subtropical California, the land South of Tehachapi.

Physically the region is as distinct, as unlike any other part of the state, as though it were another country. But this separateness is not accurately reflected in county boundaries. Southern California, properly speaking, is one of the smallest geographic regions in America. It includes part of Santa Barbara County (the portion south of Tehachapi), all of Ventura, Los Angeles, and Orange Counties, and those portions of San Bernardino, Riverside, and San Diego Counties "west of the mountains." It does *not* include Imperial County, for Imperial Valley belongs, geographically and otherwise, to the Colorado River basin. Southern California is a coastal stip of land—"the fortunate coast" as Hamlin Garland once called it—275 miles in length and with a depth that ranges from a few miles to nearly a hundred miles "from the mountains to the sea." The land area itself embraces approximately 11,729 square miles.

As a region, Southern California is rescued from the desert by the San Bernardino and San Jacinto Mountains on the east and is walled off from the great Central Valley by the transverse Tehachapi range which, running in an east-west direction, unites the Sierra Nevada and the coast ranges. Not only do these towering mountain ranges serve to keep out the heat and dust of the desert, but they are high enough to snatch moisture from the ocean winds and to form clouds. The land itself faces west, toward the Pacific, from which the winds blow with great regularity. It is this combination of mountain ranges, ocean breezes, and semi-desert terrain that makes the "climate," and the climate in turn makes the land.

Offshore are the Channel Islands, definitely a part of the region although traditionally detached from its social life. At one time several of the islands were thickly populated with Indians, but the Spaniards removed the Indians to the mainland, leaving the islands as deserted as they are today (with the exception of resort-ridden Santa Catalina). To the north, near Point Conception, are the islands of the Santa Barbara group: perennially fog-bound San Miguel, the Anacapas, Santa Rosa, Santa Cruz, and San Nicholas well offshore. About a hundred miles south of Santa Barbara are the Catalina Islands: Santa Catalina and San Clemente; while still further south, near San Diego, are the islands of the Los Coronados group.

In all of Southern California, there are no fully mature soils. Stretching from "the Sierras to the Sea," the lowlands are covered with huge coalescing alluvial fans formed of materials washed down from the mountains. The coastal plains are broken, here and there, by branches of the Sierra Madre range and by three of the driest rivers in America: the Los Angeles, the San Gabriel, and the Santa Ana. It was surely of these rivers that Mark Twain spoke when he said that he had fallen into a California river and "come out all dusty." Today the three rivers carry only a limited amount of surface and drainage waters, although each has an excellent underground flow. Here, in Southern California, as J.

431

Russell Smith has observed, "rain makes possible the homes of man where otherwise there would be only jack rabbits, pastures, a little extensive farming, and a few small irrigated oases."

Basically the region is a paradox: a desert that faces an ocean. Since it is desert or semi-desert country, maximum sunshine prevails most of the year. The sunshine makes up for what the soils lack—a discovery that both Anglo and Hispano settlers were slow to make. Before man completely changed the ecology of the region, the natural landscape was not particularly prepossessing. The native vegetation consisted of chaparral on the moist mountain slopes and bunch grass on the lowlands. The real richness of the land is not to be found in the soils but in the combination of sky and air and ocean breezes. The wisecrack that Los Angeles is half wind and half water describes a real condition. As a region, Southern California lacks nearly everything: good soils; natural harbors (San Diego has the one natural harbor); forest and mineral resources; rivers, streams, and lakes; adaptable flora and fauna; and a sustaining hinterland. Yet the region has progressed amazingly by a succession of swift, revolutionary changes, from one level of development to another, offsetting natural limitations with an inventive technology. Its one great natural asset, in fact, is its climate.

The climate of Southern California is palpable: a commodity that can be labeled, priced, and marketed. It is not something that you talk about, complain about, or guess about. On the contrary, it is the most consistent, the least paradoxical factor in the environment. Unlike climates the world over, it is predictable to the point of monotony. In its air-conditioned equability, it might well be called "artificial." The climate is the region. It has attracted unlimited resources of manpower and wealth, made possible intensive agricultural development, and located specialized industries, such as motion pictures. It has given the region its rare beauty. For the charm of Southern California is largely to be found in the air and the light. Light and air are really one element: indivisible, mutually interacting, thoroughly interpenetrated. Without the ocean breezes, the sunlight would be intolerable; without the sunlight and imported water, virtually nothing would grow in the region.

432

When the sunlight is not screened and filtered by the moisture-laden air, the land is revealed in all its semi-arid poverty. The bald, sculptured mountains stand forth in a harsh and glaring light. But let the light turn soft with ocean mist, and miraculous changes occur. The bare mountain ranges, appallingly harsh in contour, suddenly became wrapped in an entrancing ever-changing loveliness of light and shadow; the most commonplace objects assume a matchless perfection of form; and the land itself becomes a thing of beauty. The color of the land is in the light and the light is somehow artificial and controlled. Things are not killed by the sunlight, as in a desert; they merely dry up. A desert light brings out the sharpness of points, angles, and forms. But this it not a desert light nor is it tropical for it has neutral tones. It is Southern California light and it has no counterpart in the world.

The geographers say that the quality of Southern California's climate is pure Mediterranean—the only specimen of Mediterranean climate in the United States. But such words as "Mediterranean" and "subtropical" are most misleading when applied to Southern California. Unlike the Mediterranean coast, Southern California has no sultry summer air, no mosquito-ridden malarial marshes, no mistral winds. A freak of nature—a cool and semi-moist desert—Southern California is climatically insulated, shut off from the rest of the continent. As Helen Hunt Jackson once said, and it is the best description of the region yet coined, "It is a sort of island on the land." Is is an island, however, of sharp contrasts. To William Rose Benét, the land suggests, "a flowing life circle cut into contrasting angles . . . hills change over a week from garish green to golden brown; days are hot in the sun and cool in the shade; dense fog and spotless sky; giant trees or bare slopes; burnt sand or riotous flowers."

Traveling west from Chicago, the transition from one landscape to another although often abrupt is altogether logical. The rich, black Mississippi bottom lands shade off imperceptibly into the Kansas wheat lands; the Kansas plains lead naturally up to the foothills of the Rocky Mountains; once over the mountains, stretches of desert alternate with high piñon-covered plateaus; and, across the Colorado River, the desert climbs slowly to the last mountain range. Up to this point, the contrasting landscapes have seemed pleasing and appropriate; the eye has not been offended nor the emotions shocked. But, once the final descent has been made from the desert, through Cajon Pass, to the floor of the coastal plain at San Bernardino, one has entered a new world, an island tenuously attached to the rest of the continent. "My first impression," wrote L. P. Jacks, "was such as one might receive on arriving in a City of Refuge, or alternatively on entering the atmosphere of a religious retreat. Here, it seems, is the place where harassed Americans come to recover the joy and serenity which their manner of life denies them elsewhere, the place, in short, to study America in flight from herself." Logically Southern California should be several miles offshore, so that one might be prepared for the transition from the desert and the intermountain West. But, if the long train trip is thought of, as it should be, as an ocean crossing, then the island-like character of the region is properly revealed.

Southern California is the land of the "sun-down sea," where the sun suddenly plummets into the ocean, disappearing "like a lost and bloody cause." It is a land where "the Sun's rim dips—at one stride comes the Dark." Of landward rolling mists, but not of clouds; of luminous nights, but not of stars; of evanescent light, but not of sunsets; of rounded rolling hills and mountains without trees. Here the sun glares out of a high blue sky—a sun that can beat all sense from your brains, that can be "destructive of all you have known and believed": a relentless, pounding, merciless sun. But when the mists roll in at evening, the skies brighten with "blue daylight" and the air is like "a damp cloth on the forehead of the hills." Cool and fragrant and alive, the nights engulf the glaring pavements, the white stucco homes, the red-tiled roofs, the harsh and barren hills. From Mt. Wilson, late at night, one can look down on a vast pulsating blaze of lights, quivering like diamonds in the dark. Here, as Frank Fenton notes, the land does not hug the sky; it is the sky that is solid and real and the land that seems to float. At times you feel as though you were far away "on the underside of the earth."

Carey McWilliams, *Southern California Country*
(New York, Duell, Sloan and Pearce, 1946), 4-8.

Whispering Glades

BY EVELYN WAUGH

A Londoner and an Oxford man and intermittently a Californian, Evelyn Waugh has written several biographies, travel books, and war novels but is best known for his biting satire, The Loved One, *a fugue on the funerary mores of southern California.*

Dennis was a young man of sensibility rather than of sentiment. He had lived his twenty-eight years at arm's length from violence, but he came of a generation which enjoys a vicarious intimacy with death. Never, it so happened, had he seen a human corpse until that morning when, returning tired from night duty, he found his host strung to the rafters. The spectacle had been rude and momentarily unnerving; perhaps it had left a scar somewhere out of sight in his subconscious mind. But his reason accepted the event as part of the established order. Others in gentler ages had had their lives changed by such a revelation; to Dennis it was the kind of thing to be expected in the world he knew and, as he drove to Whispering Glades, his conscious mind was pleasantly exhilarated and full of curiosity.

Times without number since he first came to Hollywood he had heard the name of that great necropolis on the lips of others; he had read it in the local news-sheets when some more than usually illustrious body was given more than usually splendid honours or some new acquisition was made to its collected masterpieces of contemporary art. Of recent weeks his interest had been livelier and more technical for it was in humble emulation of its great neighbour that the Happier Hunting Ground was planned. The language he daily spoke in his new trade was a *patois* derived from that high pure source. More than once Mr. Schultz had exultantly exclaimed after one of his performances: "It was worthy of Whispering Glades." As a missionary priest making his first pilgrimage to the Vatican, as a paramount chief of equatorial Africa mounting the Eiffel Tower, Dennis Barlow, poet and pets' mortician, drove through the Golden Gates.

They were vast, the largest in the world, and freshly regilt. A notice proclaimed the inferior dimensions of their Old World rivals. Beyond them lay a semi-circle of golden yew, a wide gravel roadway and an island of mown turf on which stood a singular and massive wall of marble sculptured in the form of an open book. Here, in letters a foot high, was incised:

THE DREAM

BEHOLD I DREAMED A DREAM AND I SAW A NEW EARTH SACRED TO HAPPINESS. THERE AMID ALL THAT NATURE AND ART COULD OFFER TO ELEVATE THE SOUL OF MAN I SAW THE HAPPY RESTING PLACE OF COUNTLESS LOVED ONES. AND I SAW THE WAITING ONES WHO STILL STOOD AT THE BRINK OF THAT NARROW STREAM THAT NOW SEPARATED THEM FROM THOSE WHO HAD GONE BEFORE. YOUNG AND OLD, THEY WERE HAPPY TOO. HAPPY IN BEAUTY, HAPPY IN THE CERTAIN KNOWLEDGE THAT THEIR LOVED ONES WERE VERY NEAR, IN BEAUTY AND HAPPINESS SUCH AS THE EARTH CANNOT GIVE.

I HEARD A VOICE SAY: "DO THIS."

AND BEHOLD I AWOKE AND IN THE LIGHT AND PROMISE OF MY DREAM I MADE WHISPERING GLADES.

ENTER STRANGER AND BE HAPPY.

And below, in vast cursive facsimile, the signature:

WILBUR KENWORTHY, THE DREAMER.

A modest wooden signboard beside it read: Prices on enquiry at Administrative Building. Drive straight on.

Dennis drove on through green parkland and presently came in sight of what in England he would have taken for the country seat of an Edwardian financier. It was black and white, timbered and gabled, with twisting brick chimneys and wrought iron wind-vanes. He left his car among a dozen others and proceeded on foot through a box walk, past a sunken herb garden, a sun-dial, a bird-bath and fountain, a rustic seat and a pigeon-cote. Music rose softly all round him, the subdued notes of the "Hindu Love-song" relayed from an organ through countless amplifiers concealed about the garden.

When as a newcomer to the Megalopolitan Studios he first toured the lots, it had taxed his imagination to realize that those solid-seeming streets and squares of every period and climate were

436

in fact plaster facades whose backs revealed the structure of bill-boardings. Here the illusion was quite otherwise. Only with an effort could Dennis believe that the building before him was three-dimensional and permanent; but here, as everywhere in Whispering Glades, failing credulity was fortified by the painted word.

This perfect replica of an Old English Manor, a notice said, *like all the buildings of Whispering Glades, is constructed throughout of Grade A steel and concrete with foundations extending into solid rock. It is certified proof against fire, earthquake and* ⸻ *. Their name liveth for evermore who record it in Whispering Glades.*

At the blank patch a signwriter was even then at work and Dennis, pausing to study it, discerned the ghost of the words "high explosive" freshly obliterated and the outlines of "nuclear fission" about to be filled in as substitute.

Followed by music he stepped as it were from garden to garden for the approach to the offices lay through a florist's shop. Here one young lady was spraying scent over a stall of lilac while a second was talking on the telephone: ". . . Oh, Mrs. Bogolov, I'm really sorry but it's just one of the things that Whispering Glades does not do. The Dreamer does not approve of wreaths or crosses. We just arrange the flowers in their own natural beauty. It's one of the Dreamer's own ideas. I'm sure Mr. Bogolov would prefer it himself. Won't you just leave it to us, Mrs. Bogolov? You tell us what you want to spend and we will do the rest. I'm sure you will be more than satisfied. Thank you, Mrs. Bogolov, it's a pleasure. . . ."

Dennis passed through and opening the door marked *Enquiries* found himself in a raftered banqueting hall. The "Hindu Love-song" was here also, gently discoursed from the dark oak panel-ling. A young lady rose from a group of her fellows to welcome him, one of that new race of exquisite, amiable, efficient young ladies whom he had met everywhere in the United States. She wore a white smock and over her sharply supported left breast was embroidered the words, *Mortuary Hostess.*

"Can I help you in any way?"

"I came to arrange about a funeral."

437

"Is it for yourself?"

"Certainly not. Do I look so moribund?"

"Pardon me?"

"Do I look as if I were about to die?"

"Why, no. Only many of our friends like to make Before Need Arrangements. Will you come this way?"

She led him from the hall into a soft passage. The decor here was Georgian. The "Hindu Love-song" came to its end and was succeeded by the voice of a nightingale. In a little chintzy parlour he and his hostess sat down to make their arrangements.

"I must first record the Essential Data."

He told her his name and Sir Francis's.

"Now, Mr. Barlow, what had you in mind? Embalmment of course, and after that incineration or not, according to taste. Our crematory is on scientific principles, the heat is so intense that all inessentials are volatilized. Some people did not like the thought that ashes of the casket and clothing were mixed with the Loved One's. Normal disposal is by inhumement, entombment, inurnment, or immurement, but many people just lately prefer insarcophagusment. That is *very* individual. The casket is placed inside a sealed sarcophagus, marble or bronze, and rests permanently above ground in a niche in the mausoleum, with or without a personal stained-glass window above. That, of course, is for those with whom price is not a primary consideration."

"We want my friend buried."

"This is not your first visit to Whispering Glades?"

"Yes."

"Then let me explain the Dream. The Park is zoned. Each zone has its own name and appropriate Work of Art. Zones of course vary in price and within the zones the prices vary according to their proximity to the Work of Art. We have single sites as low as fifty dollars. That is in Pilgrims' Rest, a zone we are just developing behind the Crematory fuel dump. The most costly are those on Lake Isle. They range about a thousand dollars. Then there is Lovers' Nest, zoned about a very, very beautiful marble replica of Rodin's famous statue, the Kiss. We have double plots there at seven hundred and fifty dollars the pair. Was your Loved One married?"

438

"No."

"What was his business?"

"He was a writer."

"Ah, then Poets' Corner would be the place for him. We have many of our foremost literary names there, either in person or as Before Need reservations. You are no doubt acquainted with the works of Amelia Bergson?"

"I know of them."

"We sold Miss Bergson a Before Need reservation only yesterday, under the statue of the prominent Greek poet Homer. I could put your friend right next to her. But perhaps you would like to see the zone before deciding?"

"I want to see everything."

"There certainly is plenty to see. I'll have one of our guides take you round just as soon as we have all the Essential Data, Mr. Barlow. Was your Loved One of any special religion?"

"An Agnostic."

"We have two non-sectarian churches in the Park and a number of non-sectarian pastors. Jews and Catholics seem to prefer to make their own arrangements."

"I believe Sir Ambrose Abercrombie is planning a special service."

"Oh, was your Loved One in films, Mr. Barlow? In that case he ought to be in Shadowland."

"I think he would prefer to be with Homer and Miss Bergson."

"Then the University Church would be most convenient. We like to save the Waiting Ones a long procession. I presume the Loved One was Caucasian?"

"No, why did you think that? He was purely English."

"English are purely Caucasian, Mr. Barlow. This is a restricted park. The Dreamer has made that rule for the sake of the Waiting Ones. In their time of trial they prefer to be with their own people."

"I think I understand. Well, let me assure you Sir Francis was quite white."

Evelyn Waugh, *The Loved One*
(Boston, Little, Brown and Company, 1948), 37-45.

439

The Clampers

BY CARL I. WHEAT

In the interstices of his law practice Carl I. Wheat has found time to contribute extensively on such topics as the maps of Jedediah Smith, the maps of the Gold Rush, the Death Valley forty-niners, Theodore Judah and the Pacific railway, and monumentally on the maps of the Trans-Mississippi West. Here he discusses an institution in which his interest is strong and proprietary.

It was early in the 'fifties that "The Ancient and Honorable Order of E Clampus Vitus" first appeared on the California scene. The time was one of vast upheaval, human as well as physical. And after a hard day in the dirt and muck of some Sierra diggin's, where else but in the Clampers' "Hall of Comparative Ovations" could a man rediscover those values that seemed otherwise so lacking in the hard life of the California canyons?

E Clampus Vitus spread like wildfire through the mountains. Few, indeed, were the camps where the order's great horn—the "Hewgag"—did not on occasion hoarsely bray. Surely, the succint Constitution of the Order displayed its roisterous spirit as could nothing else.

"Article One," read that unorthodox document: "All members are Officers."

"Article Two," it eloquently continued: "All Officers are of equal indignity."

That was all. But it was enough. When the Hewgag blew, the brethren gathered from far and near. It was a signal that a sucker had appeared in camp—some "Poor Blind Candidate" ripe for a new experience. For the only ritual of this significant organization of gold rush days was that of initiation, and the only stated meeting was before or after the full moon when such a one should come upon the scene ready for immolation on the altar of merriment.

On those gala occasions when—in the vociferous spirit of the mid-nineteenth-century Yankee—a parade was to be staged along the camp's lone street, it was usually the Clampers who stole the show, marching behind a stalwart soul carrying a pole that bore a hoop skirt with the strange device, "This Is the Banner We Fight Under." Nor was it only in connection with such celebrations that the Clampers shone, for were they not brethren ready at the merest hint of their mysterious Sign of Distress to come to one another's assistance, and did not their well-known sign of recognition—the Sign of the Well Jackass—betoken a vitality that even the drab life of the diggin's could not destroy?

"All for one and one for all" could, indeed, have been the motto of this lusty Order. As a matter of fact, however, the Order's hortatory watchword was: "For the benefit of widows and orphans—but more especially of widows!" And when a brother, worn by toil and broken in the search for gold, could no longer carry on, the brethren, one and all, would come to his assistance. It is said that fifteen dollars a month from the Clampers would keep a miner in bacon and flour, beans, and saleratus, and that in those better days E Clampus Vitus had but two rules to guide its members in their eleemosynary roles:

(1) A man shall come in person to the Hall of Comparative Ovations for this helpful dole; and

(2) Payments shall commence two years after death.

When, in the late 'twenties of this softer century, a band of latter-day enthusiasts sought once more to capture the spirit of the Order's elder days, it was found that little in the way of written data could be found to describe and explain those small and intimate details of the past that at such times bear so great significance. It was the late lamented Ezra Dane who suggested the answer. "During those early days," said he, "no Clamper in attendance at a stated meeting was ever in any condition to take minutes of the ceremonies." And, he would add, "After the meeting had concluded no one could be found who could remember what had happened."

The Grand Lodge of the Order convened at Mokelumne Hill, but from the far north of Downieville and Sierra City to the southernmost diggin's, even beyond Mariposa, chapters of E Clampus Vitus flourished. Let no benighted individual place a period after that fateful "E" (as was done—ignominiously—in a recently celebrated catalogue of Californiana), and let no person

441

of whatever race, color or previous condition succumb to the heretical placing of an "s" after the "p" of Clampus.

The actual revival of the Order began at Yerba Buena early in the 'thirties, and by a happy circumstance there came to the group a voice from the past in the person of Adam Lee Moore, last Noble Grand Humbug of the Order in that earlier Dispensation. Before he passed from the scene a few years ago at the ripe age of ninety and nine, he—the *Clampatriarch* of the revival—brought to these younger and later Clampers not only a Charter of Apostolic Succession but a youthful spirit that pervaded many a Pilgrimage to the Diggin's with mirth and lusty human wisdom. Soon another chapter was erected in the Queen of the Cow Counties, far to the south, and others later were convened at Camptonville, Nevada City, Auburn, Hangtown, Columbia, Murphy's Camp, Skunks Misery, and other memorable spots. The New Dispensation carries on, often incredulous of the tales it hears of the Clampers of old.

In *The Enigmatical Book of Vitus* the story of the resuscitation of the Order has been told, and the spirit of *Credo quia absurdum* has been outlined in *The Curious Book of Clampus*. Later, *The Esoteric Book of E* and *Ye Preposterous Booke of Brasse* carried the tale farther. The literature of the revival grows apace.

Once each year the brethren gather at Yerba Buena on a night nigh unto the twenty-fourth of January, when their lamented one-time Clampatriarch, James W. Marshall turns over in his grave three times in their favor. Once, also, in each year, "before or after the Full Moon," they devote themselves to a pilgrimage to some spot hallowed by the picks and pans of forty-niner days, there to imbibe by some obscure but revivifying osmosis the spirit of the elder days.

E Clampus Vitus was a force of no little significance in those earlier decades. It represented release from toil—respite from sweat—a chance to laugh with and at one's fellows. And so, when the sonorous echoes of the Hewgag resounded through the Sierra silences, few there were who did not drop their picks and haste them to the Great Hall, where amid Comparative Ovations and mighty mirth "Poor Blind Candidates" were brought out and instructed in the mysteries of the Order. To the query "What say

442

the Brethren?" the assembled Clampers would shout "Satisfactory!" and the Grand Noble Recorder would reply, with august
dignity, "And so recorded."

What is the significance of the mystic words which designate
the Order? What can "E" or "Clampus," or even "Vitus," mean in
this connection? That is a secret the answer to which reposes only
in the astral memories of Clampers long since gone to their reward. It is, in fact, the only true secret still recorded and remembered by the Order, for no member now in good standing knows
the answer. An odd situation? Yes, but wholly in keeping with
those other factors which render this agreeable fraternity of the
gold days memorable and worthy of perpetuation.

Pacific Historical Review, XVIII (1949), 67-69.

A Dissent

BY JESSE W. CARTER

*Jesse W. Carter was a justice of the California Supreme Court from
1939 to 1959, a period when the nation, on edge about subversion,
indulged in many invasions of the rights and immunities of individuals. Notwithstanding the set of public opinion, Carter stood
firm on the constitutional guaranties, unfazed that this often put
him in dissent. On the Levering Oath case not one of his colleagues sided with him, though his marshalling of state and national history, precedent, and logic seems incontrovertible.*

The only word of commendation which I can speak for the opinions of the court in these cases is that they bring into sharp focus
the loyalty oath hysteria which has pervaded this country and
particularly this state during the past five or six years. The concept that a person exposed to subversive activity may be immunized
against such exposure by the taking of a so-called loyalty oath
opens the door for vast exploration in the field of metaphysical
research. While this process is taking place the loyalty of every
public employee is impugned even though he has taken the oath
prescribed by the Constitution many times and has obeyed it re-
ligiously. It must be conceded, however, that those who have been
loyal may become disloyal and that "eternal vigilance is the price

443

of liberty," but it should not follow that vigilance against disloy-
alty of public employees requires that they take an oath proscribed
by the Constitution. The holding of the majority in these cases
requires the taking of such an oath.

From the records before us in the various cases decided by the
opinions this day filed, it would appear that many days, weeks and
possibly months were consumed by the state Legislature, the
Board of Regents of the University of California and the various
boards of supervisors and city councils of the counties and cities
of California in the preparation, discussion and adoption of various loyalty oath proposals. In addition to the time consumed in
the legislative field, these cases have been before the various courts
of this state during the past two or three years where thousands of
pages of transcripts and briefs have been prepared and filed and
the time and effort of numerous judges and lawyers has been consumed in their disposition. In my opinion all of this time and
effort, as well as the money necessarily expended in connection
with the legislation and judicial proceedings, which must have
amounted to thousands, if not millions of dollars, was, and is entirely wasted, and has been and will be of no benefit whatsoever
either to the general public or the individuals affected thereby.
There can be no escape from this conclusion when we consider
that the Constitution of this state expressly and specifically declares the form of oath required of all persons holding any public
position under the law of this state, and expressly provides that:
"No other oath, declaration or test shall be required as a qualification for any office or public trust." (Cal. Const., Art. XX, § 3.) The
oath prescribed by the Constitution is a simple, concise declaration, solemnly made by the person taking it, that he will support
the Constitution of the United States and the Constitution of the
State of California and faithfully discharge the duties of the office
or employment which he is undertaking to the best of his ability.
The constitutional provision, by implication at least confers upon
the Legislature the power to require that this oath be taken by all
who occupy any office or public trust under the law of this state
and the Legislature saw fit to require that all state employees take
such oath. (See Gov. Code, § 18150 et seq.) It is a conceded fact in
each of these cases that every employee of the state here involved

444

took the constitutional oath long before the enactment of the acts which constitute the basis of this litigation. Notwithsanding this undisputed fact, the majority of this court holds in each of these cases that these petitioners are required to take another oath prescribed by the so-called Levering Act (Stats., 1951 [3d ex. sess. 1950, ch. 7, p. 15]) which, it is said, is no different than the oath prescribed by the Constitution. The majority nevertheless holds that because each of the petitioners has failed to take the oath prescribed by the Levering Act, they have forfeited their position with the state in accordance with the provisions of that act. This is indeed strange and paradoxical reasoning. In effect the majority says: No employee of the state is required to take any other oath than that prescribed by the Constitution, but even though all employees of the state have taken the constitutional oath, they must also take the Levering Act oath which is the same as that prescribed by the Constitution, and if they do not take the Levering Act oath, they are ineligible for employment by the state. If there is any logic or common sense in such reasoning, it is not apparent to me and I have grave doubt that it will appeal to any thinking person. . . .

We are therefore met at the outset of this discussion with the problem of what was intended by the framers of the Constitution when they wrote into article XX, section 3, the words: "And no other oath, declaration, or test shall be required as a qualification for any office or public trust. . . ."

If anything can be gleaned from this legislative history, it is that the delegates of 1878 determined to leave the provision as it had always been—in simple language meaning what it said. That only *one* oath could be required for those in the public employ and *one* only. The abhorrence for test oaths for the servants of the public which prevailed in Monterey in 1849 and in Philadelphia in 1787 prevailed in Sacramento in 1878. It would prevail today were it not for the hysteria and name calling which has tended to obscure the traditional concept of the framers of both Constitutions.

It should be noted that the Levering Act oath is strikingly similar in its language and tone to the third and fourth amendments suggested at the Constitutional Convention in 1878. Indeed the

445

first paragraph of the Levering Act is almost identical, word for word, with the first paragraph of the defeated 1878 amendments. And the second paragraph resounds as though in echo to the sentiments which moved the gentlemen in 1878 to propose an oath that one had not employed Asiatics.

But historical coincidence aside, the Levering Act oath and the constitutional oath are as different as day from night both in content and intent. In the first place, the constitutional oath is not a perjury oath. It relates to a state of mind, a promise in good faith to perform one's duties to the best of one's abilities. That an oath of office as relates to the future performance of duties does not relate to perjury was recognized by the Legislature even before the 1879 Constitution was enacted. (See Pen. Code, § 120.) Furthermore, it is clear that the constitutional oath is a promissory declaration intended to solemnize an occasion and to impress upon the mind of the employee the trust upon which he is about to enter. It is not intended to inhibit one's thinking nor one's associations.

The majority holds that "We are satisfied that there is nothing in the Levering oath which goes beyond the object or meaning of section 3 of Article XX and that it is not the type of 'other oath, declaration or test' which was intended to be prohibited by that section." With this statement, I most emphatically disagree. The constitutional oath relates to the future: "I do solemnly swear (or affirm, as the case may be) that I *will* support the Constitution of the United States and the Constitution of the State of California, and that I *will* faithfully discharge the duties of . . . ." There can be no other meaning that *that from the time of taking employment and the oath the affiant will support the constitutions*. The Levering oath, on the other hand, calls for an oath regarding past activities: "that within the five years immediately preceding the taking of this oath (or affirmation) I have not been a member of any party or organization, political or otherwise, that advocated . . . ." So far as the balance of the Levering Act is concerned, it might possibly be inferred from the constitutional oath that in swearing to support the two constitutions, the affiant impliedly swears to defend them "against all enemies, foreign and domestic" and that he would not become a member of any organization advocating the overthrow of the two governments by force and violence since

446

the two matters just set forth would be, in reality, one and the same thing. But the fact remains that the words so stating are *not* in the constitutional oath except by implication. No such implication may be read into the constitutional oath with respect to that portion of the Levering Act relating to *past* affiliations. The above quoted statement from the majority opinion is deceptive in its simplicity in that it seeks to uphold the Levering Act, since that is the popular thing to do, but must in some manner avoid the clear, positive and unequivocal mandate of the Constitution that "no other oath, declaration or test shall be required as a qualification for any office or public trust." The only way to avoid that provision is to say that there is no substantial difference between the two oaths. And to say that there is no substantial difference between the two is the height of absurdity. . . ."

If, as stated by the majority, there is no substantial difference between the two oaths, it would appear that the Levering Act adds nothing to the constitutional oath and is, therefore, a nullity. All these petitioners have taken the constitutional oath and, if the two are the same, there appears to be no sound reason why they should lose their positions and means of earning a livelihood because they have refused to do a useless act. The law does not require useless acts (or so we have always been told), but if we follow the reasoning of the majority to its illogical conclusion, the law does require, on pain of dismissal from employment, the doing of such an act. . . .

The principle here involved is of tremendous importance to those who believe in preserving the constitutional guarantees of fundamental civil liberties. These constitutional guarantees were written in the light of bitter experiences arising out of the exercise of arbitrary power or usurpation of power by the legislative or executive branch of the government. Constitutions were written to protect the individual against the exercise of such arbitrary power. The lessons of history reveal that at various times under the stress of inflamed public opinion both the Legislature and the Executive have attempted to circumvent constitutional restrictions by adopting measures which seemed expedient in view of the exigencies of the situation at hand. In my opinion the Levering Act is such a measure. I think it is apparent from the language of the act that its proponents believed that the Legislature had the power to prescribe a different oath for all employees of the state except the constitutional officers, and that it was under this mistaken belief that the act was adopted. Now that this court has held that the constitutional prohibition against any other oath, declaration or test applies to every state and local officer and employee, the Levering Act which was designed to apply to all employees of the state except constitutional officers, should fall.

To my mind it is too plain to permit of argument that it was the intention of the framers of the Constitution that "no other oath, declaration or test" should ever be required of any public officer or employee of the state or any of its political subdivisions than that specifically provided for in article XX, section 3 of the Constitution. The action taken at the constitutional conventions clearly demonstrates the correctness of this position. The defeat of proposed amendments which sought to enlarge the scope of the oath, the failure to confer upon the Legislature power to do anything other than *exempt* such inferior officers as it saw fit from taking the prescribed oath and the specific prohibition against requiring any "other oath, declaration or test . . . as a qualification for any office or public trust," makes it crystal clear that the framers of the Constitution intended to prevent just what the Levering Act is designed to accomplish. . . .

But the majority of this court by its decisions in these cases is forsaking its sworn duty to support the Constitution of the State of California, and has abdicated its power, for the sake of expediency, to uphold an act which invades the constitutional guarantees of civil liberties of those affected by its mandates.

There is no question of loyalty involved in any of these cases. So far as appears from the records before us every employee here involved was fully investigated and there is no suggestion of any conduct even bordering on subversive activity on the part of any of them. They have merely sought to stand on their constitutional right to take the one and only oath which the Constitution prescribed. On this stand I unqualifiedly join them.

I would, therefore, grant the writ prayed for and restore petitioner to his position.

Jesse W. Carter, *Pockman* v. *Leonard*,
39 A.C. 25 at pp. 705-714.

Hyperion to a Satyr

BY ALDOUS HUXLEY

*As a transplanted Californian, Aldous Huxley was intrigued by
the scene in which he found himself and by bits and pieces of
its history.* After Many a Summer *is his principal California
title, but his "Ozymandias" is an essay on the attempted Utopia
at Llano del Rio in Antelope Valley, and essays such as the one
here excerpted have California setting.*

A few months before the outbreak of the Second World War I
took a walk with Thomas Mann on a beach some fifteen or twenty
miles southwest of Los Angeles. Between the breakers and the
highway stretched a broad belt of sand, smooth, gently sloping
and (blissful surprise!) void of all life but that of pelicans and
godwits. Gone was the congestion of Santa Monica and Venice.
Hardly a house was to be seen; there were no children, no prom-
enading loincloths and brassieres, not a single sun-bather was
practicing his strange and obsessive cult. Miraculously, we were
alone. Talking of Shakespeare and the musical glasses, the great
man and I strolled ahead. The ladies followed. It was they, more
observant than their all too literary spouses, who first remarked
the truly astounding phenomenon. "Wait," they called, "wait!"
And when they had come up with us, they silently pointed. At
our feet, and as far as the eye could reach in all directions, the
sand was covered with small whitish objects, like dead caterpillars. Recognition dawned. The dead caterpillars were made
of rubber and had once been contraceptives of the kind so eloquently characterized by Mantegazza as *"una tela di ragno
contro l'infezione, una corazza contro il piacere."*

> Continuous as the stars that shine
> And twinkle in the milky way,
> They stretched in never-ending line
> Along the margin of a bay:
> Ten thousand saw I at a glance . . .

Ten thousand? But we were in California, not the Lake District.
The scale was American, the figures astronomical. Ten million

saw I at a glance. Ten million emblems and mementoes of Modern Love.

> O bitter barren woman! what's the name,
> The name, the name, the new name thou hast won?

And the old name, the name of the bitter fertile woman—what was that? These are questions that can only be asked and talked about, never answered in any but the most broadly misleading way. Generalizing about Woman is like indicting a Nation—an amusing pastime, but very unlikely to be productive either of truth or utility.

Meanwhile, there was another, a simpler and more concrete question: How on earth had these objects got here, and why in such orgiastic profusion? Still speculating, we resumed our walk. A moment later our noses gave us the unpleasant answer. Offshore from this noble beach was the outfall through which Los Angeles discharged, raw and untreated, the contents of its sewers. The emblems of modern love and the other things had come in with the spring tide. Hence that miraculous solitude. We turned and made all speed towards the parked car.

Since that memorable walk was taken, fifteen years have passed. Inland from the beach, three or four large cities have leapt into existence. The bean fields and Japanese truck gardens of those ancient days are now covered with houses, drugstores, supermarkets, drive-in theaters, junior colleges, jet-plane factories, laundromats, six-lane highways. But instead of being, as one would expect, even more thickly constellated with Malthusian flotsam and unspeakable jetsam, the sands are now clean, the quarantine has been lifted. Children dig, well-basted sunbathers slowly brown, there is splashing and shouting in the surf. A happy consummation—but one has seen this sort of thing before. The novelty lies, not in the pleasantly commonplace end—people enjoying themselves—but in the fantastically ingenious means whereby that end has been brought about.

Forty feet above the beach, in a seventy-five-acre oasis scooped out of the sand dunes, stands one of the marvels of modern technology, the Hyperion Activated Sludge Plant. . . .

An underground river rushes into Hyperion. Its purity of 99.7 per cent exceeds that of Ivory Soap. But two hundred million gallons are a lot of water; and the three thousandth part of that daily quota represents a formidable quantity of muck. But happily the ratio between muck and muckrakers remains constant. As the faecal tonnage rises, so does the population of aerobic and anaerobic bacteria. Busier than bees and infinitely more numerous, they work unceasingly on our behalf. First to attack the problem are the aerobes. The chemical revolution begins in a series of huge shallow pools, whose surface is perpetually foamy with the suds of Surf, Tide, Dreft and all the other monosyllables that have come to take the place of soap. For the sanitary engineers, these new detergents are a major problem. Soap turns very easily into something else; but the monosyllables remain intractably themselves, frothing so violently that it has become necessary to spray the surface of the aerobes' pools with overhead sprinklers. Only in this way can the suds be prevented from rising like the foam on a mug of beer and being blown about the countryside. And this is not the only price that must be paid for easier dishwashing. The detergents are greedy for oxygen. Mechanically and chemically, they prevent the aerobes from getting all the air they require. Enormous compressors must be kept working night and day to supply the needs of the suffocating bacteria. A cubic foot of compressed air to every cubic foot of sludgy liquid. What will happen when Zoom, Bang and Whiz come to replace the relatively mild monosyllables of today, nobody, in the sanitation business, cares to speculate.

When, with the assistance of the compressors, the aerobes have done all they are capable of doing, the sludge, now thickly concentrated, is pumped into the Digestion System. To the superficial glance, the Digestion System looks remarkably like eighteen very large Etruscan mausoleums. In fact it consists of a battery of cylindrical tanks, each more than a hundred feet in diameter and sunk fifty feet into the ground. Within these huge cylinders steam pipes maintain a cherishing heat of ninety-five degrees—the temperature at which the anaerobes are able to do their work with maximum efficiency. From something hideous and pestilential the sludge is gradually transformed by these

451

most faithful of allies into sweetness and light—light in the form of methane, which fuels nine supercharged Diesel engines, each of seventeen hundred horsepower, and sweetness in the form of an odorless solid which, when dried, pelleted and sacked, sells to farmers at ten dollars a ton. The exhaust of the Diesels raises the steam which heats the Digestion System, and their power is geared either to electric generators or centrifugal blowers. The electricity works the pumps and the machinery of the fertilizer plant, the blowers supply the aerobes with oxygen. Nothing is wasted. Even the emblems of modern love contribute their quota of hydrocarbons to the finished products, gaseous and solid. And meanwhile another torrent, this time about 99.95 per cent pure, rushes down through the submarine outfall and mingles, a mile offshore, with the Pacific. The problem of keeping a great city clean without polluting a river or fouling the beaches, and without robbing the soil of its fertility, has been triumphantly solved.

Aldous Huxley, *Tomorrow and Tomorrow and Tomorrow and Other Essays*
(New York, Harper & Brothers, 1956), 149-151. 163-165.

They Were Putting Up the Statue

BY LAWRENCE FERLINGHETTI

An outsider might hesitate to make light of the Beniamino Bufano statue or of the gentle Saint Francis who used to preach to the birds, but Lawrence Ferlinghetti is a San Franciscan and proprietor of its City Lights Bookshop.

They were putting up the statue
        of Saint Francis
    in front of the church
        of Saint Francis
            in the city of San Francisco
in a little side street
            just off the Avenue
                        where no birds sang
and the sun was coming up on time
                        in its usual fashion
        and just beginning to shine

452

They Were Putting Up the Statue

on the statue of Saint Francis
where no birds sang

And a lot of old Italians
were standing all around
in the little side street
just off the Avenue
watching the wily workers
who were hoisting up the statue
with a chain and a crane
and other implements
And a lot of young reporters
in button-down clothes
were taking down the words
· of one young priest
who was propping up the statue
with all his arguments
And all the while
while no birds sang
any Saint Francis Passion
and while the lookers kept looking
up at Saint Francis
with his arms outstretched
to the birds which weren't there
a very tall and very purely naked
young virgin
with very long and very straight
straw hair ·
and wearing only a very small
bird's nest
in a very existential place
kept passing thru the crowd
all the while
and up and down the steps
in front of Saint Francis
her eyes downcast all the while
and singing to herself

Lawrence Ferlinghetti, *A Coney Island of the Mind*
(New York, New Directions, 1955), 17.

A Supermarket in California

BY ALLEN GINSBERG

Poet Allen Ginsberg, an émigré from metropolitan New York, is a leading light in San Francisco's coterie of creative writers.

What thoughts I have of you tonight, Walt Whitman, for I walked down the sidestreets under the trees with a headache self-conscious looking at the full moon.

In my hungry fatigue, and shopping for images, I went into the neon fruit supermarket, dreaming of your enumerations!

What peaches and what penumbras! Whole families shopping at night! Aisles full of husbands! Wives in the avocados, babies in the tomatoes!—and you, Garcia Lorca, what were you doing down by the watermelons?

I saw you, Walt Whitman, childless, lonely old grubber, poking among the meats in the refrigerator and eyeing the grocery boys.

I heard you asking questions of each: Who killed the pork chops? What price bananas? Are you my Angel?

I wandered in and out of the brilliant stacks of cans following you, and followed in my imagination by the store detective.

We strode down the open corridors together in our solitary fancy tasting artichokes, possessing every frozen delicacy, and never passing the cashier.

Where are we going, Walt Whitman? The doors close in an hour. Which way does your beard point tonight?

(I touch your book and dream of our odyssey in the supermarket and feel absurd.)

Will we walk all night through solitary streets? The trees add shade to shade, lights out in the houses, we'll both be lonely.

Will we stroll dreaming of the lost America of love past blue automobiles in driveways, home to our silent cottage?

Ah, dear father, graybeard, lonely old courage-teacher, what America did you have when Charon quit poling his ferry and you got out on a smoking bank and stood watching the boat disappear on the black waters of Lethe?

Allen Ginsberg, *Howl and Other Poems*
(San Francisco, City Lights Books, 1956), 23-24.

454

The Sign-Up

BY ABRAHAM POLONSKY

Abraham Polonsky had a distinguished career writing for radio and as writer and director in Hollywood. After a sojourn in Europe he returned to New York where he wrote The World Above *and this, his second novel.*

All day long the light had become hotter and more crystalline and now from the Water and Power building where the men had been sitting for hours the city moved into absolute focus under the blazing sun. Each thing stood in its own unique and marvelous dimension. It was a delight just to look, to have human eyes and see.

For these water engineers the world was divided in two: above, an oasis lavish with green, and below, the eternal desert in which hollow pipes endlessly branching formed two great veins, one going to the high Sierra snows and the other to a hot and muddy river. Sorenson, the chief engineer and general manager of the water department, had planned and built the great system and Charles Hare had driven the last two-hundred-and-thirty-mile aqueduct to the Colorado River. It was their system, it was their work, and more profoundly their idea. They knew it all from the first drip of melting ice to the mapped millions of flowering arterial capillaries that lay in the waste beneath the city.

As usual when he was irritated, Sorenson fanned himself. He never felt the heat any more, being so old, he said, and dried up, his eyes perpetually crinkled against the memory of the inland suns. He fanned himself with his yellow envelope. On Hare's desk there was another which glowed in the sunlight glancing off the pigeon guano on the concrete cornices of the building.

"Well, Charles," Sorenson asked, "what do you think?" His voice was dry and monotonous, strongly accented like the ordinary talk of the plains.

"I don't know, Chief. On hot days like this I don't think. It's every man for himself."

The chief engineer put the yellow envelope to his lips and whistled. "Anyhow," and he seemed to be saying goodby to the city, to be putting it away in memory now that it would never be actual again, "anyhow, it's a good view."

"You know what my friend Pickett says?"

"What does he say?"

"He says if only the Spaniards had won, we would have a civilization here in California instead of a real estate development."

Sorenson wrinkled his nose with distaste. "I know the type." He seemed to smell a leaking drain. "Antiques, a shelf full of odd herbs, dirt, and diarrhea." Sorenson got up and moved restlessly about the room. "I don't get it," he said. "I just don't get it. I mean I'm a Protestant. My mind belongs to God and me and no one, theological, political, economical, has the right to ask me what's in it. I have a basic and fundamental morality. You have. We could never violate it."

Charley grinned uncomfortable within this intimacy. He joked about it. "Well, Chief, the truth is I never had to. I never had to cheat at school. I knew the answers. I liked my work. I fell in love and married young and did my job and voted. You know how it is. I did what I had to do and no one ever asked me to do anything I would really consider wrong. That's life for most people."

"What about the time you were offered a bribe to put the pipe through ten miles on the other side of Great Flats?"

Charley laughed. "All they offered was money."

Sorenson's face crinkled with a fond smile. "How naïve we both are!"

"Naïve?"

"Innocent. We think morality is a question of majority vote."

"Well," Charley said slowly, estimating it, "morality is something that people have together, isn't it?"

"Yes," Sorenson replied, "that's when it's comfortable and right. But just you wait until it's right and uncomfortable."

The door swung open with a rush and Commissioner O'Brien's soft wet laugh came in like a dog's tongue. "Up, men," he called. "To the gas chamber!" He reversed in his track, yellow envelope in hand, and each man took his yellow envelope and followed.

In the calm, cold corridor faced with marble and as wide as a city street they joined the division heads, each of whom was tailed by his assistants, technicians, clerical staff, until a long lumpy line like an intestine wound through the corridor past the banked elevators to a small office near the fire stairs. Here behind a temporary desk sat a notary public. She was a middle-aged woman from the mayor's office and wore heavy glasses on her amiable face. As she took each signature she checked the names against the civil service registry and counterchecked it from a secret list compiled by the attorney general's office.

Counting faces, Commissioner O'Brien looked down the great line which hummed with conversation and the break in routine. "Well," he said to Sorenson, "it looks like we're all here and accounted for, patriots all."

Hare looked vaguely over their heads to the familiar, famous view. Above the flat gridiron of boulevards and streets, above the mountains, above the far yellow hills pinned to earth with oil derricks, a cloud slightly flattened at the bottom floated immense and motionless in the bright sky. There was no smoke and there was no wind. A ledge from the story above cut the direct sun from his eyes and he seemed to float out into a fine and constant light which had no source but glowed, so it appeared, from an infinite number of grains of air delicately tinted in pink and dazzling blue.

Hare slouched on the line, his eyes half closed against the window, hearing the separate conversations behind him as separate waves make surf. He was a big, easy muscled man who liked lots of room, a house and yard with size, collars not too tight, a big roomy car, a roomy life. He was uncomfortable now and disliked standing on line. He never did when he could help it. He wouldn't shop in stores where you had to take tickets and wait your turn. When he saw a queue before a movie house he didn't try to go in. He sent away for his license plates by mail. For him there was something peculiar about a line and being on it. A line violated his adulthood, his independence. It changed a man from an American and the abundant life to a European and the parsimonious one where there never was enough of anything and all existence was a waiting. Although like many Americans he had been ticketed and fingerprinted and listed during the various wars and government jobs, he deliberately carried in his wallet only the essential driving license and never less than one hundred dollars in cash.

O'Brien said, "Charley, do you have a brother?"

"No." Curiously Hare observed the innocent fatness of the Commissioner's head that was really shrewd and nimble in the brain. "Why?"

"Well, there was a man in here a few weeks ago, from one of the state security boards, I'll be damned if I know which, I get so many, and he was asking about a brother of yours."

"I have no brother."

"It must be some other Hare, then."

"What did he want to know?"

"We never got around to it."

Sorenson said, "They're around all the time now. It's a way to live."

O'Brien laughed again in his fat wet way. He always laughed his way in and out of conversations, meetings, crises, and small talk, and no one could tell which was which in his mind. "All right, all right. We're in the water business. The hell with it."

Down the corridor the general hum gave way to a single voice raised in suppressed anger. "Well, do something, then. Do something. Everybody says we *ought*, but no one *does*."

Hare turned as did everyone else and there in the center of the line a knot of arguing men had suddenly bulged out, a sudden swell of figures, a spasm, undigested and indigestible.

There was the heavy silence of all the others now listening and the little group as quickly straightened out and lost themselves in the line again, and yet there was an unusual movement there, an obstacle. Everyone felt it even though there was no more talk, and the marble corridor magnified the wait and the quiet.

A thin little man with a shock of golden hair above a pointed face stepped from the line. He looked more like a bright child than a man, and he wore a blue shirt with rolled up sleeves and an open collar. The yellow envelope was in his hand. He stood away from the line, outside all the others, and the line felt it as he did. Automatically the line drew closer together, protecting itself with anonymity while this little man waited outside of it. Someone

458

reached a hand out to pull the little man back and a voice said, Come back. We were only kidding." The man in the blue shirt continued to hesitate. The yellow envelope was bright against the dark blue and then it disappeared as the man turned and began to move away. He went rapidly, almost trotting. He hurried down the length of the line and never stopped until he disappeared into one of the many rooms.

Like pale sequins the faces were all turned the same way and all caught the light the same way.

"Who's that?" Commissioner O'Brien asked sharply.

The chief and his assistant exchanged embarrassed looks but they didn't answer. From the anonymous line the reply came, "Al Hamner."

The faces all waited for the Commissioner to say something else but all he did was turn away, and in a rush the voices began, humming and buzzing. Without even intending to, the people on the line straightened out the kinks and bends and slowly the line became more unified, the shortest distance between the door to the notary and the very last man. He stood as close to the man in front of him as he could so no one would think he was not part of the line.

The line began to move.

Charles Hare signed that he was loyal, that he was not now nor had he ever been a Communist, that he did not belong to any organization which had as its aim the overthrow of the government by force and violence or the teaching or advocacy of the same.

His one idea as he smiled and exchanged a little joke with the notary was to get away from the line. He hurried back to his office and busied himself for a half hour with some work. He tried to put all of it from his mind, the line, little Al Hamner walking off, the questions about a nonexistent brother, yet nevertheless he felt oppressed with something alien, as if among the thousands of kisses which are love, one was different, the beginning of the end, suspicions, agonies, betrayal.

Abraham Polonsky, *A Season of Fear*
(New York, Cameron Associates, 1956), 9-14.

Jeeney Ray

BY IRIS DORNFELD

Iris Dornfeld has taught school, acted, and worked at such jobs as modeling, teaching music, and canning peaches. Jeeney Ray, *her first novel, is a touching characterization and story of a baffled human being.*

The summer is a bird summer and there is no trouble in it; the eggs overflow in paper boxes, and taking some to a banty hen she broods them warm till she got two pheasant and a quail, and Zeke said they'd be good eating some day and scared me to move them way out past the Chinaman's grave to the old outhouse that no one uses any more. There is no stink left to it; sunshine and old vines cram through the roof cracks, and a few spiders hang around. It is a good hiding place. Here is where I start care of birds; I watch life come naked and weak and grow wings for flying and let it go; I am a feeding mother till summer passes too dry and old for hatching, and silence of the young is everywhere, and the pause begins. All is dry ground and dry grass and a white sun baking day by day, and fruit rot coming in the dampness of night, saying summer is almost dead. . . .

In the passing of these things and times it comes easy to stay in the woods more than not and grow in the way that was set for me by early teaching that [old Grandma] give me—into the old way of learning, stretching back to summers with the word song of her Book and the birds come and go, and the secret strange of all living. I wander far and deep to new meadows laying quiet and forgot, and climb new hills and lay to sleep in new places. I look down on the shape of earth and up to the shape of sky, and there is sad happiness and wild happiness and imagining. I go to myself and live inside.

Standing alone is one day.

I come upon a lone cabin; it is high up the ditch water walk. I stand off its yard and shape it for remembering. It is little and bare at the windows, and a dog lives there, from the look of a water pan; a horse is someplace, from the look of the back shed and droppings round about. I listen. It is in the middle of singing; old gray pines skirt a circle up above, and the air brushes their needles in sound. There is a well with a bucket hanging from a rope and a tin cup hanging from a nail.

I walk around to the front and see it has a car; and right off I hear it coming, grinding up the steep curves from Rattlesnake Bridge, where only one can go at a time. I hear the blat of cattle guards covering the ditch, and then see dust spreading. I kneel back to cover myself and watch it drive in; a dog bounds over and away to the back yard before it can stop.

I lean closer. A man gets out from the other side and stands up; he is pale; and the cool looned air of calm is written over him; he speaks when the horse whinnies up from the shed; he takes a box from the car and goes in his cabin.

It is the ditchwalker.

Tears sting my eyes without want, and there is the terrible lone-liness for a person of my own; he will be the person of my own, my hidden person, with his cabin and dog and horse and his car. I look it all over careful once more and take myself away.

The ditchwalker begins to take my mind till he is there all the time. I range high up off the P. G. and E. ditch and see him walking the paths, guarding water and snapping his stick to kill a rat-tler; I see him write in his book and frown; I see his boots are high and shining bright as new; I see his gun hitched close. He is my first friend; he that took me home; he that is calm.

I study him well and receive the kindred of one to another.

It is a long heat when water at the crick runs low that I take to the P. G. and E. ditch. I put my eggs in spider silk to lay safe at the bridge, then go down under, slipping mud along my hind end to get in and sit cool. The water sweeps and hums on and on through pine shade and sun and white sky. I sit and rub toes on the orange water dogs; freckled sun falls down the cattle guard and squints between the cracks like a ladder.

A quick rustle starts the grass above, and a lizard must be moving from fear; he splits off to a whisper, and coming steady and soft above I hear feet along the ditch path. I skim under the cattle guard and hide for them to pass. The steps stop and a long shadow falls across the water.

"Come out from under there!" he says, and it is his voice.

I am still.

His boots send dirt through the cattle guard.

"You got no right to be swimming in the ditch, Jeeney Ray."

His shadow sits down.

"If you don't come out from there I'll take your eggs."

I scrounge up the bank and see him squatting with them in his hands already, but I know from his way that he won't take them.

"Don't you know it's dangerous to swim in the ditch?" His hand moves the eggs while he talks; he looks down and lays his head sideways, and there are mean marks between his eyes, but they don't cover him from me. He is not mean. And he is not pale like I thought; he is tan as old gunny sacks and wrinkled heavy; his hair is winter straw and that is his paleness. He is long-fingered and long-footed and long-faced.

"Don't you?" He looks square at me, and I look square at him but don't answer, and he don't push me to it.

He holds an egg out to me, way out over the water to me, and turns it in his fingers.

"You know what bird lays this egg?"

I know what bird it is; I know as well as it was myself.

"What bird?" He holds it higher with a question all over him. I like the way he does and lift up inside and out, and laugh.

"What bird?" He lays his head sideways again; and the little egg is pink and funny to me like the bird herself, and I am her and sprinkle out her cry and song, and watching him listen I know the kindred of us is true; when I finish he is concerning with surprise.

He is concerning; he don't smile; a question look comes between his eyes.

"This is a wren egg. Can you say wren, Jeeney Ray?" His voice is pushing me now.

"Say *wren!*"

There is all the sunlight baking the water and throwing up mirrors in his face and pointing his eyes close. He is real hard now; but it is not wrong and it is not against. It is for talking, and it raises hope for talking that went dead under failure of school.

I do not falter. My lips go out strong to take the very shape of his and plead for sound to follow, and it does, and the word is made, but not good as his.

462

"Lopsided for a wren," he says and cracks his eyes to make me laugh; then he laughs too and when it is over he puts me to practicing. He is strict with showing the way to talking that I heard from old Grandma and the Book. I do every last word he tells me, and care for every one in a new listening way.

"Jeeney Ray, you practice those words like you do the bird songs, you hear me?" He has a steady frown in his long face.

"And keep out of the ditch water. It runs swift through here and you might drown." He picks up his stick and whales the air for a bit and then goes with the curve of the path to guard the P. G. and E. water, that is his job for a living; and leaves me the need and the want and the how of talking and a wilder heart to do it.

I yip and plunge down the cool of the ditch and swim full length to the curve, and see him grow small in the slope of meadow. I laugh; my swimming is good as a water dog and come long ago in the crick when walking failed.

From now on I have a person of my own. At first I call him "Mister," the way Zelda did, but before long he says a friend should call a friend by name and that his name is Jim.

Jim is strong kindness that I never knew was in a person till now. He brings me a spyglass to see the birds better and shows me the use and care of it. It is a gift of greatness; it is the eye to secret life and brings me closer than touching.

I use it to see the world from Rocky Ridge; down through the low hills are some farmhouses, and farther down is the town of Rose with trains worming in and out, and stretching way to nothing are more and more towns and roads streaming up and down with cars. Up through the back hills I find snow on the great mountains and the sky small above. I range the glass round and round and come upon a gold dome blazing against the sun; it is strange glory in the green hills, and wondrous.

I ask Jim what it is.

"That's the county seat in Ophir where gold was discovered in 'forty-nine. Mother Ophir was the richest gold mine in the world, with veins stretching all through this country. They took millions out of her and named the county after her, and then they forgot her." He grins.

I tell him to go on about the gold dome.

"It's the law for Ophir County now; it's a big firetrap with a gold dome, and inside there is the law. It's a hundred years old, same as Mother Ophir, and dead, but don't know it!"

Jim has got to understand me same as Zelda, and he talks of bigger things more and more. He knows the hills and mountains like the back of his hand, being born and grown up in Ophir, and tells of every ghost town left from 'forty-nine and every gold mine that petered out; and how chinks and ragheads shipped over to work; and about hangings and beatings and killings come every day from nothing better to do. And how everyone left when Mother Ophir was old with her veins give out. It was long ago, and how he knows it is from his wooden-legged Grandpa, who hunted gold all his life and died without a pot to piss in, and from his pa, who was poisoned with the same poison and lives in Ophir off the old-age pension that come to be law just in time for him.

Every day I wait for Jim at the cattle guard, and we talk back and forth, making words better and stronger with him guiding; with him telling of his own, showing the greatness of his own, till I cram to tell of old Grandma and the back summers, same as he done; showing the root of my own.

And I do.

I start slow and tangle her and the Book till pages and hands fall a picture of sound with birds and green sunlight in gabbling slop and babble talk and no sense in it from excitement of doing— till Jim says, "First one and then the other. Take old Grandma first."

He is helping me to go back for her, but there is no doing her without the Book.

"They are together," I cry.

He waits.

The ease comes; the yard trees and summer and her old hand and walking and teeth; then the words stream into brightness and hold themselves proud like she showed them to be and leave the seed of their keeping and break out sound.

. . . Save me, O God; for the waters are come in unto my soul. . . .

I sink in deep mire, where there is no standing: I am come into deep waters, where the floods overflow me. I am weary of my crying: my throat is dried: mine eyes fail while I wait for my God. . . .

They that hate me without cause are more than the hairs of mine head: they that would destroy me, being mine enemies wrongfully, are mighty: then I restored that which I took not away. . . .

Words fall down through the dead and walk out; they cry the song of my half-wit self and I am in pain of snot and tears and shamed in weakness.

Jim moves up close to me.

"Stop bawling, Jeeney Ray!" He shakes me hard.

"You got no cause to bawl. You got cause to be proud. There's no one but a preacher I ever heard could do that—no one! That's the Bible you been reciting!" Jim is wide-open astonishment. "Learned by heart!"

He takes his hand away; I reach as far into his eyes as I can to understand the fullness of what he says and the way he looks me over; puzzled back in thinking is how he is, and grinning and frowning, then going way down to pierce darkness; down like Zeke, but not like Zeke. It is when thinking is coming from the other person into yourself and touching the same thinking as the other person; it is quiet then, and words come from their hiding heart.

I ask: "Am I a half-wit and a idiot?"

"No." He frowns.

"What am I then, having the ways I do, that holds me from others, that scrabbles legs and arms in their crazy way and put a key on my mouth to lock up talking. What am I?"

Jim don't answer. After a long time I see him get ready; he fills with air and decides.

"One thing is sure"—he thumps his brain—"you're smart up here." He grins.

"You're better with birds than any game warden I know, and I bet your egg collection is the best in Ophir County. You're a whiz at bird songs and Bible reciting—and you're a good friend for an old ditchwalker." He is looking at me with his sideways look and grinning the saddest way I can remember.

He is finished; but that is not my truth. If I am not the truth of half-wit and idiot, what is my truth? my own truth? the truth of myself? It seems like Jim could tell me; he is old enough and strong enough and if he tried hard it seems to me he could tell me.

I touch arms and legs and feet and face and head and belly; my complete self; I stand up for him to see clear; I hold my arms out with asking.

He shakes his head.

"I don't know," Jim says.

Iris Dornfeld, Jeeney Ray (New York,
The Viking Press, 1962), 24-25, 43-51.

Expulsion of the Japanese

BY JACOBUS TENBROEK, EDWARD N. BARNHART, AND FLOYD W. MATSON

As part of a University of California study project on the wartime evacuation of the Japanese Americans, Professors tenBroek, Barnhart, and Matson probe the animation of the decision to remove this whole racial group, place responsibility for the action, and analyze the judicial ruling that equal protection of the laws had not been abridged. Their conclusions, here summarized, differ somewhat from those of the other principal book on the subject, Morton Grodzins' Americans Betrayed.

Viewed in the perspective of a decade, with all the advantages of hindsight and subsequent disclosure, the Japanese American episode of World War II looms as a great and evil blotch upon our national history. The whole vast, harsh, and discriminatory program of uprooting and imprisonment—initiated by the generals, advised, ordered, and supervised by the civilian heads of the War Department, authorized by the President, implemented by Congress, approved by the Supreme Court, and supported by the people—is without parallel in our past and full of ominous forebodings for our future.

The entire Japanese American program violated and degraded the basic individualism which sustains a democracy. It impaired the trial tradition of the common law. It disparaged the principle

466

that guilt is individual. It sapped the vitality of the precept of equality. It made racism a constitutional principle. It tolerated preventive incarceration for assumed disloyal beliefs and attitudes —unaccompanied by acts—attributing them without proof, probable cause, or reasonable suspicion to an entire group on a basis of race. Recklessly and unnecessarily, it loosened judicial control of the military and produced dangerous imbalance in our government.

The episode embodied one of the most "sweeping and complete deprivations of constitutional rights in the history of this nation." It destroyed basic and precious rights of personal security: the right—without arbitrary or constitutionally irrelevant interference—to move about freely, to live and work where one chooses, to establish and maintain a home; the right not to be deprived of constitutional safeguards except upon an individual basis and after charges, notice, hearing, fair trial, and all of the procedural requirements of due process. It destroyed, as well, basic and precious rights of democratic participation; the right of peaceable assembly to discuss the general welfare and problems of government; the rights of free speech and a free press; the right freely to hear, read, and learn; the rights of petition and remonstrance; the rights of franchise and election, of seeking and holding office; and, not least of all, the right and responsibility to defend one's native land, if need be, with one's life.

The Japanese American episode culminated in a constitutional sanctification of these deprivations by the highest court in the land —a court dedicated to justice, defense of the Constitution, determination of the powers and limitations of government, and protection of the rights of men.

In the historical view, the wisdom of a decision is treated principally by subsequent events. Contemporary plausibility is only a minor criterion. Judged by the historical test, military necessity arising out of the war emergency does not provide justification of the program of removal and imprisonment. It is true that Japanese armies, in the winter of 1941-42, advanced rapidly in southeast Asia and the southwest Pacific. Damaging blows were dealt the American navy. A foothold was gained on Attu and Kiska in the Aleutians, Dutch Harbor in Alaska was bombed. But it is also

467

true that Japanese strength had been fully committed in the far Pacific. The mainland Pacific coastline of the United States was adequately protected even before December was out. The Battle of Midway on June 6, 1942, brought Japanese naval expansion in the Pacific to an end. Thereafter, the enemy forces on Attu and Kiska withered from lack of support.

There was no invasion of the coastal mainland. There were not even commando raids or air strikes upon it. One submarine lobbed a few shells harmlessly near an oil installation not far from Santa Barbara (February 23, 1942). Another sent a midget airplane with an incendiary bomb over an Oregon forest (September 9, 1942); the bomb ignited nothing. A third submarine fired on coast defences at Astoria, Oregon (June 21, 1942). In December, 1941, there were only three successful enemy submarine attacks on ships leaving West Coast ports. In January, 1942, there were none; in February none; in March none; in April none; in May none. No Japanese surface ship ever operated in the eastern part of the Pacific between Hawaii and the mainland.

Thus, in the calm retrospect of history, it is evident that military necessity warranting the program simply did not exist. After Midway, there was no justification at all for either mass detention or mass exclusion. Even before Midway, there was no justification for mass detention or for the mass exclusion of American citizens of Japanese ancestry. There was no justification at any time for treating Japanese aliens differently from other enemy aliens.

The absence of any acts of espionage and sabotage by Japanese Americans between Pearl Harbor and evacuation—while numerous persons of other extractions were being convicted of such acts —sufficiently testifies (1) to the active or passive loyalty of the major part of the Japanese American population, and (2) to the adequacy of existing methods of control and prevention. Even were this not so, alternative methods of control were available, less drastic than evacuation and detention combined or than either of them separately, more consonant with the Constitution and wholly adequate to meet the actual danger.

All this can now be seen clearly. But even if we abandon the vantage point of history and judge the military only by what they then knew, the same conclusion must be reached. For the fact is that much of what was learned by the public only years later was, at the time, known to our military leaders. It was their judgment then that Japanese strength had been fully committed elsewhere; that, after December, the Pacific Coast was adequately protected. They knew the Japanese strength on land, sea, and in the air. They knew where it was deployed and what its capabilities were. The Navy especially believed that invasion was virtually out of the question by the spring of 1942. The significance of Midway was correctly appraised at the time. Yet it was after that battle that the inland Japanese Americans were evacuated and all Japanese Americans removed from assembly centers to relocation centers.

The weakness of the case for military necessity was spotlighted rather than concealed by General DeWitt's *Final Report*, which is a flimsy tissue of misstatements, preposterous absurdities, patently fallacious reasoning, unacknowledged quotations, and uses facts and arguments developed after the event in an obvious attempt to show that, at the time the decision for evacuation was made, it was based on facts and sound reasoning. Most remarkable of all are these two assertions, contained in a single paragraph: "The very fact that no sabotage has taken place to date is a disturbing and confirming indication that such action will be taken"; and "The Japanese race is an enemy race and while many second and third generation Japanese born on United States soil, possessed of United States citizenship, have become 'Americanized', the racial strains are undiluted".....

The primary responsibility of the people for the action taken against the Japanese Americans cannot be shifted to the shoulders of pressure groups and politicians. The activity of such organizations and individuals before the basic decision of mid-February, 1942, (and indeed after) has been greatly exaggerated both as to extent and influence. . . .

Responsibility for the episode rests, secondarily, with the military, particularly with General DeWitt and the Western Defense Command. . . .

Even greater responsibility rests upon President Franklin D. Roosevelt and his civilian aids in the War Department, Secretary Henry L. Stimson and Assistant Secretary John J. McCloy, and upon the Congress of the United States. . . .

Responsibility rests, finally, with the courts, and especially with the Supreme Court of the United States. In many ways the failure of the Supreme Court was the greatest failure of all. . . .

If the court had struck down the program, the Japanese American episode would have lived in history as nothing worse than a military blunder. But the court approved the program as constitutional, a step with implications and consequences accurately described by Justice Jackson in his dissenting opinion on the *Korematsu* case:

"Once a judicial opinion rationalizes such an order to show that it conforms to the Constitution, or rather rationalizes the Constitution to show that the Constitution sanctions such an order, the Court for all time has validated the principle of racial discrimination in criminal procedure and of transplanting American citizens. The principle then lies about like a loaded weapon ready for the hand of any authority that can bring forward a plausible claim of an urgent need."

Jacobus tenBroek, Edward N. Barnhart, and Floyd W. Matson,
Prejudice, War and the Constitution
(Berkeley, University of California Press, 1954), 325-332.

A Battlefield Revisited

BY JOHN CAUGHEY

Eighteen years have gone by since the University of California suffered its ordeal of the oath. For a participant to go back to that travail is an act of masochism—not that I as one of the nonsigners have not reviewed the unhappy experience many a time. Comes now from the University of California Press David P. Gardner's *The California Oath Controversy*, a guided tour of the battlefield; in fact, almost an official guided tour.

No university official was so crass as to commission an authorized history. On the contrary, Gardner's study came of the purest of motives, the preparation of a dissertation to meet one of the requirements for a doctorate. He gained full access to the official records—the executive as well as open-session minutes of the regents, various committee files, the minutes of the two divisions of the Academic Senate, and President Robert Gordon Sproul's files. Interviews with Sproul and other administrative officers and with several of the regents yielded additional information. Perhaps most determinative, Regent John Francis Neylan's widow and her attorney granted access to the Neylan papers.

On the other side of the aisle, Gardner consulted a substantial number of the changing guard of faculty leaders and the files of several of the committees that functioned at different stages in the controversy. Except in the papers of the Group for Academic Freedom, active mainly in the period of litigation, he elicited less from nonsigners. The latter are less available and in all likelihood proved less communicative.

The imbalance in the records that he scanned confirmed an inclination toward the perspective of the administration. Gardner is frank that his affection for the university is great, and by that he means the institution as such. He most admires those who tempered principle with pragmatism and stayed in the university. And among all the participants, he finds none to compare with Regent Neylan.

The oath controversy was extremely complex. It began with an unpublicized action by the regents in March, 1949, voting an addition to the affirmative oath of allegiance already filed by each member of the faculty. Only at the close of the school year did the faculty learn of this action and that the addition was a required denial of membership in the Communist party. At Berkeley the northern division of the Senate protested this requirement, asked its repeal, and instructed a standing committee to advise the president. This committee soon found itself in an unprecedented consultation with a committee of the regents. A revision of the wording of the oath resulted, but there was no serious consideration of withdrawing the requirement.

Over the summer the faculty felt pressures to sign the oath, among others that contracts for the fiscal year beginning July 1 were issued only after an executed oath had been sent in. When full-scale operations resumed in the fall, both divisions of the Senate made more vigorous objections to the oath of denial and to the pressures exerted for signatures. In October the regents were persuaded to release the rest of the contracts.

Regent Neylan, who had been out of the state when the oath was first voted and had spoken out sharply against it in discussions with the regents and president, took umbrage over what he charged was bad faith in the faculty representations. He became the champion of the oath and, at the same time, brought into the open that it was the president who had introduced the oath and asked that it be required.

President Sproul, by this time, had second thought on the advisability of the oath requirement. Had he acted earlier he might have been able to persuade the regents to withdraw it. Now it appeared to most of the regents that revocation would have the appearance of being soft on Communism and of abdicating a power that belonged to the regents. Negotiations through the president availed nothing. A new committee sent to confer with a regents' committee failed as miserably.

On the floor of the Senate at Berkeley a resolution was put together attempting to make clear that objection to requiring every professor to swear that he was not a Communist did not mean that the faculty demanded that the regents repeal their order forbidding employment of a Communist. There is a significant difference; most of the regents could not or would not see it. Nor does Gardner.

With Governor Earl Warren and a couple of new regents attending, a faction more favorable to the faculty arose but could not prevent passage of a "sign-or-be-fired" ultimatum in February, 1950. The anti-oath regents encouraged an alumni effort to work out a compromise which was voted in April. On its face it seemed to set up an alternative of retaining membership on the faculty by submitting oneself and record to examination by the faculty committee on privilege and tenure. That committee's normal function had always been to handle the last appeal of a professor facing demotion or dismissal. That it should be a loyalty appeals board was a quite different assignment.

At the opening of the school year there had been well over a thousand nonsigners. By May there were only about seventy who asked hearings by the committee on privilege and tenure. There were others who chose to leave the university rather than submit to such a check-up on their patriotism. There also were teaching assistants, secretaries, librarians, custodians, and others for whom no tenure was established and no standing committee to which they could appeal. For them the alternative of appeal looked much more hazardous.

In the summer of 1950 the pressures for signatures were compounded by the outbreak of war in Korea. In time of war a loyalty hearing was a more forbidding prospect. By July there were only forty-five of the committee-examined professors to be reported to the regents. On five the committee gave a Scotch verdict in reverse; it was "not favorably reported," which was intended as far less opprobrious than "reported unfavorably." Without hesitation the regents fired these five. After long debate on the other forty, a plurality voted to issue notices of reappointment. Regent Neylan thereupon changed his vote to aye and moved reconsideration, postponing decision for a month.

By August further attrition reduced the number to thirty-one. Challenging Governor Warren's declaration that the Neylan motion was out of order, the Board over-ruled the chair, 12 to 10. By the same vote it dismissed the thirty-one remaining nonsigners. Later it developed that five were on the list by inadvertence; they were out of the country or out of touch and later were permitted to sign in. The vote was prefaced by disavowal of any accusation of communism; the dismissals were for disobedience.

In his chronicle of events through these first seventeen months of the oath, Gardner offers the most detailed narrative thus far available. On the next developments he is more cursory. He mentions the Senate resolutions of protest, the fund raising for relief of the jobless, appeal to the American Association of University Professors, and the litigation begun by the Berkeley nonsigners.

He reports the legislature's quick enactment of the Levering oath, which required every state employee to swear to nonmembership in any organization committed to the violent overthrow of the government. He describes regent discussions on whether this oath should be allowed to apply in the university. He is carelessly speculative on Warren's role in the enactment of the state test oath.

He briefly summarizes the District Court decision that the university oath was violative of the state constitution. He does not dwell on the opinion written by Justice Peek eloquently supporting the contention of the nonsigners that intellectual freedom was at stake.

Although only a minority of the regents wanted it done, their counsel filed an appeal. The State Supreme Court took the case under review along with other oath cases. Moving from the constitutional grounds that would have made *Tolman* v. *Underhill* a landmark case, the court found a much narrower basis. It held that, many years earlier, the legislature had occupied the field of oath legislation. Therefore the regents' oath was an unlawful trespass. Gardner mistakenly assumes that it was through the Levering oath that the legislature had pre-empted the field.

In accompanying decisions, to which Justice Carter filed a classic dissent, the court validated the Levering oath and held it to be a condition of employment in the university. There was no sentiment and presumably no basis for appealing the decision on the regents' oath.

Gardner sees the oath controversy ending thus in futility. It was not the glorious victory that would have been gained had the District Court's ruling been upheld. But the regents' oath was struck down. And the Levering oath, rather than being worse as Gardner rates it, was in three respects less obnoxious. It was part of the law of the state rather than by order of the regents; it proceeded by language which defined rather than by naming the Communist party; and it was general in application rather than required only of university personnel.

For the next several years Gardner has only a few pages. A handful of the nonsigners returned to the classrooms. Discovering shortly that they were classified as new appointees having to start over to qualify for tenure, sabbaticals, and the like, sixteen of them lodged a new suit against the regents. Another five nonsigners, who had resigned in 1950 on promise of a year's severance pay, had been denied that payment. They sued. In 1954 the regents settled with these resigners for what was due, with interest at 7 per cent. The other suit dragged on until 1956 when, by

474

coincidence, the AAUP had under consideration a motion to censure the University of California administration. Then finally the regents settled out of court without interest but to the satisfaction of the claims entered. This settlement mended tenure and certain rights of nontenured professors broken by the firings in 1950.

This University of California Press publication gives useful detail on the steps from the unfolding of the university's special test oath to its outlawing three and a half years later. Much less can be said for the validity of the interpretations offered and the judgments expressed.

Gardner is wrong in insisting that the controversy which began over the oath shifted to the regents' ban on employment of Communists and shifted again to tenure as the issue. Seemingly he fails to realize that from the outset a major objection to the oath was that it negated tenure. He fails to recognize that the Senate resolution on banning Communists was no more than a partial diversion from the abiding issue of the demanded personal denials. He forgets that the breaches of tenure rose from the oath and its substitutes and that the litigation covered the rights of nontenured as well as tenured professors.

Gardner is strangely insensitive to the mismatch in a conflict between regents and faculty. No regent had his career or livelihood at stake. The regents had a corporate unity, staff, and all expenses paid. The professors had given personal hostages to fortune. They were scattered on eight campuses, outfitted with a two-division Senate designed for deliberations rather than action, shut off by precedent from direct dealings with the regents, and committed to a scholarly, reasoned approach rather than to adversary proceedings. In the end the only resistance the regents could not put down was represented by the few who would not sign and would not concede the regents' right to fire them.

Gardner writes of the controversy almost as though following the moves in a game of chess. He does not convey a feeling of the agony that beset many of the participants on both sides and many students, alumni, and citizens only less directly involved. The professors mentioned come over as two-dimensional figures. Even John Francis Neylan, Gardner's hero, is presented as insistent but cold and colorless. The facts come out that he relentlessly outmaneuvered the faculty negotiators, planted editorials, directed his cohorts in the faculty, and took principled stands on such matters as offering ten days to the fired nonsigners who might prefer to resign and arguing against admitting the Levering oath in the university. Gardner does not begin to give Neylan due credit as an advocate, haranguing the president, the regents, or a committee of the faculty. In this genre the Neylan tirades were masterpieces.

Gardner's studied opinion of the oath controversy has many expressions. As he sees the nonsigners, their prime attribute was intransigence. They were unrealistic in not taking into account the damage to the university that their stand would cause. They were not of sufficient renown to make the regents hesitate about firing them. Gardner writes off the whole resistance as "a futile struggle," an exercise in "personal hostility, stubbornness, pride of opinion, ill manners and bad faith," and a "self-imposed conflict." It ended, he says, in "a hollow victory," greater suspicion of free inquiry, and "no victory for intellectual and academic freedom."

It is on record that the regents were much relieved that none of their Nobel laureates was a nonsigner. The case history seems to demonstrate that firings are more likely if only a token number of protestants is involved. Calculated tactics, however, did not determine the number of nonsigners; ultimately each person made his own decision whether to risk being fired.

The ridding of the university of its oath requirement was not so hollow a victory as Gardner makes out. Many scholars in other institutions have asserted that this California example was a deterrent preventing imposition of comparable oaths. The AAUP, having censured on the basis of the 1949-1956 record of the University of California, went on to become a much more robust defender of academic freedom nationally.

Within the university the oath controversy certainly left resentments and scars. It may be questioned whether faculty voice in crucial determinations is as effective as it was from 1925 to 1949. The larger imponderable is what would have resulted from complete and quiet submission to the oath requirement.

Law in Transition, IV (1967), 172-178.

The Sierra Nevada

BY FRANÇOIS MATTHES, WITH EDITING
BY FRITIOF FRYXELL

*Upon his retirement from the Geological Survey, François Mat-
thes moved to California intent on writing a nontechnical book on
the geological history of Yosemite. Major scientific reports of his on
this incomparable valley were already in print. Death interrupted
the task before it was well begun, but by using notes, drafts, and
earlier writings Fritiof Fryxell was able to fashion a manuscript
to serve the purpose Matthes had had in mind.*

Were we to start from San Francisco in an airplane and fly due
east, we would pass first over the wooded crests of the Coast
Ranges; next over the broad, level expanse of the Great Valley of
California, checkered with irrigated fields, vineyards, and orchards; and then, after a flight of about a hundred miles, we would
come to a huge mountain barrier, stretching north and south at
right angles to our course and rising in a long, gradual slope to a
resplendent row of snow-flecked peaks. This is the Sierra Nevada,
the longest, the highest, and the grandest single mountain range
in the United States.

The Sierra Nevada may be likened to a gigantic ocean wave
rolling landward from the west. Rising in a grand sweep from the
trough of the Great Valley, this giant wave culminates in a somewhat sinuous snowy top, as in a foam crest, and with its precipi-
tous front threatens the low-lying deserts to the east. At its northern end the wave splits into three lesser crests, the altitudes there
ranging between 7,000 and 9,000 feet; but throughout the greater
part of its length it has a single clean-cut crest line, rising southward by degrees to 13,000 feet, opposite Mono Lake, and reaching a climax in the 14,000-foot peaks about Mount Whitney. Still
farther south the range declines to 6,000 feet and curving toward
the west, merges with the Coast Ranges near Tehachapi Pass. So
strongly asymmetric is the Sierra Nevada that its crest line is for
the most part within a few miles of its eastern base but thirty to
seventy miles from its western base.

Share with me, in imagination, the thrilling experience of an
ascent of the range, from its parched western foothills, where the

477

scanty grass assumes the lush green of springtime for only a few weeks, and wears the golden tint of autumn for the rest of the year; up through the less desolate chaparral belt, where the slopes are densely clad with small-leaved, impenetrable bushes; up into the majestic forests of the middle slope, where, favored by summer warmth and prodigious winter snows, pine and fir and cedar lift their tops 200 to 250 feet above the ground; to the zone of superlative tree growth, where the columnar sugar pine with its twenty-inch cones, vies in height with the thousand-year-old sequoia; still farther up, into the lodgepole belt, where the snows linger until midsummer, and where tree stature dwindles; into the timber-line zone, with its recumbent dwarf trees, its emerald short-grass meadows, and its rock-bound sapphire lakelets; and finally up the stark summit peaks, in whose deeply sculptured recesses snow fields and tiny glaciers blaze under a sky of immaculate blue. Thence one may look northward and southward over an array of boldly carved, snow-flecked peaks and eastward over the empty vastness of the "land of little rain. . . ."

The Sierra Nevada, geologists are agreed, consists essentially of a single, huge, massive block of the earth's crust lying in a tilted position, with its eastern edge raised to great height and its broad surface slanting westward to the Great Valley of California. The eastern side of the block, exposed as the result of a tremendous dislocation of the crust, rises like an imposing façade thousands of feet above the Owens Valley and the other lowlands farther to the north. The Sierra does not owe its great elevation to a wrinkling of the crust, as do many other ranges. In the eastern half of California, apparently, the crust was too rigid and brittle to yield by bending and folding to the push and heave of disturbances within the earth, but cracked into angular blocks and slabs, like a badly laid cement sidewalk. . . .

The colossal proportions of the Sierra Nevada are best appreciated if comparisons are made with other well-known western mountain ranges. The Rocky Mountains are popularly regarded as the great mountain bulwark of the Far West; but the Rockies in reality comprise a vast system of ranges and groups of mountains, somewhat loosely woven together and interspersed with valleys and gaps. The largest mountain units in that system are less than

478

two hundred miles long—less than half as long as the Sierra Nevada. And the 14,000-foot peaks of the Rocky Mountains rise only about 7,000 feet above the Great Plains, which attain elevations of from 5,000 to 7,000 feet at the foothills; but the highest peaks of the Sierra Nevada tower 10,000 and even close to 11,000 feet above the Great Valley of California. . . .

The manner in which the originally flat Sierra block became tilted has long puzzled geologists. The Sierra Nevada is so large that no geologist can become familiar with all its features. Its outlines, inner structure, and surface sculpture vary from place to place, so that several equally competent geologists, examining different sections of the range, may arrive at somewhat different conclusions about certain aspects of its evolution.

On one point all geologists are agreed—that the dislocation of the earth's crust that caused the Sierra Nevada to stand so high and with so steep a front overlooking the country to the east was produced by slipping, or faulting, movements on a line of fractures reaching deep into the earth and extending for hundreds of miles along the eastern base of the range and around its curving southern portion, as far as the vicinity of Tehachapi Pass. The Sierra block and the contiguous valley block are conceived to have sheared past each other, the one upward, the other downward, relative to each other.

The great eastern front of the Sierra Nevada is unquestionably a "fault escarpment," one of the grandest features of its kind in the world. The actual declivity of the escarpment at no point exceeds 25°; though this is a moderate angle, the effect upon a beholder stationed in the lowland to the east of the range is that of a formidable, well-nigh unscalable mountain wall. It is not merely the height of the escarpment that produces this effect, but the combination of great height and abrupt rise, without intermediate foothills or sprawling spurs, from the level plain at the base. Supremely impressive is the long, straight wall, facing the Owens Valley, that averages two miles in height. It is said that Albrecht Penck, the dean of European geomorphologists, upon viewing this stupendous mountain front, was visibly affected by its grandeur and begged his guide to leave him for several hours that he might contemplate and study it in solitude.

The scientists who have come here, even from distant lands, have viewed the Sierra fault escarpment with awe, and have usually departed without offering more than a tentative explanation. The precise manner of the escarpment's origin is not patent at a glance. There are, indeed, several ways in which the dislocation could have taken place: (1) The Sierra block may have been thrust up by itself, leaving the country to the east lying low. (2) Both blocks may have risen, the Sierra block faster and to greater height than the valley block. (The lowest part of the Owens Valley has an elevation of 3,700 feet, and Mono Lake lies at an altitude of about 6,400 feet.) (3) The Sierra block and the valley block may first have risen together in one piece, as parts of a great bulge in the earth's crust that extended far to the east; then, when the bulge collapsed, the Owens Valley and the other valley lands may have sunk to their present levels, leaving the Sierra block standing high. (4) The Sierra block may have been thrust eastward and up onto the valley block, pushing the latter down. . . .

Much of the uncertainty in regard to the nature of the faulting movements that have taken place at the eastern base of the Sierra Nevada is due to the fact that most of the fractures are concealed from view. So much time has elapsed since the last major faulting movements that the sheer cliffs produced by them have long since crumbled back to slopes, and the mountain front throughout its length has become gashed by canyons. The fractures at the base of the range are buried under accumulations of rock debris, under masses of gravel swept out of the canyons by torrential floods, and under lava, cinders, and pumice ejected by volcanoes that spouted through the cracks.

Fortunately, however, renewed faulting on a small scale has occurred in fairly recent times, so recently that the resulting little "scarps" are still fresh and easily recognized. Most of them are only 10 or 20 feet high, but some measure 40 to 100 feet, and have the aspect of smooth, sheer cliffs at the immediate base of the range, or of steep bluffs where they cut across masses of loose rock debris or gravel. Some of the lava flows in the Owen Valley are broken by parallel faults, and "step down" 10 or 15 feet at each fracture. One small volcanic cone, seven miles to the south of Big

Pine, is neatly cut in two by one of these recent faults.

Perhaps the reader would prefer not to have his attention drawn to these fresh breaks in the earth's crust, while he is pleasantly touring up the Owens Valley and northward to Mono Lake, feeling reasonably secure in the thought that the solid-looking mountains have been standing for ages and are not likely to heave, or fall, just when one is passing. For it is disquieting to reflect that even these little scarps, that seem insignificant in a landscape framed by mile-high peaks, were produced instantaneously by a sudden snapping of the earth's crust accompanied by an earthquake. Many minor faulting movements have taken place in recent geologic time and right up to the present—evidence that the stresses within the earth which have built the Sierra Nevada have by no means spent themselves. . . .

North of Mono Lake the Sierra front is extremely irregular; long spur ranges branch from it, mostly in northerly directions, while the main mountain mass trends northwestward. All those spur ranges, which are not unlike huge splinters torn from the side of the Sierra block, are bounded by faults, and small fresh scarps occur here and there along their bases. Lake Tahoe occupies a basin between the Sierra block and one of these great splinters—the Carson Range. Its great depth, 1,685 feet, cannot be accounted for either by stream cutting or glacial erosion, but must have been produced by the subsidence of an earth block. The dislocations occurred long ago, and the fault scarps have lost their characteristic forms, but at the eastern base of the Carson Range, near Genoa, Nevada, are fresh cliffs 40 to 50 feet high that still retain the vertical grooves and the polish (slickensides) produced by recent slipping movements under great pressure. . . .

As we have seen, the recent small dislocations along and near the eastern base of the Sierra Nevada were produced not by a rise of the mountain block but by subsidence of the valley blocks. There remains the question: How was the imposing front of the range produced—the great Sierra escarpment, which varies in height from 2,000 feet at the north to 7,000 feet at Owens Lake? Was it by uplift of the Sierra block, the Owens Valley remaining at its present low level; or was it by the sinking of the valley block, the Sierra remaining standing with its previously attained height;

or was it a combination of both kinds of movements?

The answer is found in the positions of the deposits of ice-borne debris (moraines) built by the glaciers which occupied the canyons in the escarpment during the Ice Age. The moraines indicate not only the character of the faulting movements but the approximate time of the movements.

The moraines are ridges composed of rock debris that accumulated along the flanks of the glaciers as it was released by the melting ice. They are typically sharp-crested and extend unbroken for miles, almost as regular in form as railroad embankments. The so-called Ice Age consists really of four successive glaciations, or glacial stages, separated by long intervals of approximately normal climate. As a consequence, there are four sets of moraines differing greatly in antiquity and degree of preservation. The moraines of the latest glaciation have remarkably perfect forms, but the moraines of the preceding glaciations, which are hundreds of thousands of years old, are poorly preserved and relatively obscure, the more so the older they are. The oldest are in large part destroyed but they are still recognizable in spots.

From the mouths of many canyons the sharp-crested moraines of the latest glaciation extend into the lowland to the east of the range.They show by their positions that when the last glaciers advanced the canyons had already attained their present depth. Some of these moraines "step down" abruptly 50 feet or more where they cross the fault line at the foot of the range. In those places only one small dislocation has occurred within, perhaps, the last 25,000 years. Few of the older moraines extend into the lowland. Most of them are cut off at the fault line, in some instances at heights of 1,000 to 1,500 feet. Thus we know that faulting movements of that order of magnitude must have taken place since those moraines were deposited—that is, during the last 500,000 years.

The oldest moraines, which may be from 750,000 to 1,000,000 years old, lie not in the canyons or at their mouths but high on their shoulders, thousands of feet above the lowland. The finest example is the partially disintegrated moraine lying on the mountains west of McGee Canyon. It terminates at the brink of the escarpment, 3,000 feet above Long Valley. To judge from its gentle slope, moreover, this ancient moraine was built by a glacier that lazily wended its way through a rather flat, shallow valley high on the Sierra block. McGee Canyon evidently had not yet been cut. But this implies that there was as yet no escarpment. It is, then, an inescapable conclusion that the major faulting movements did not begin until after the first glaciation—that is, roughly, less than 750,000 years ago. The great Sierra escarpment, accordingly, appears to be only about 750,000 years old.

But how was it formed? Did the Sierra rise 3,000 feet, or did Long Valley drop 3,000 feet? The ancient McGee Moraine is of about the same dimensions as the moraines of the later glaciations, and that fact, together with similar evidence from other parts of the range, warrants the inference that during the first glaciation the Sierra Nevada was about as extensively mantled with glaciers as during the later glaciations. That, however, could not have been true unless at that time the range was already as high as it was during the later glaciations. It might have been somewhat lower, but it could not have been 3,000 feet lower, for then its summit would have lain below the level of the snow line and would have borne no glaciers. The three main peaks at the head of McGee Canyon—Red and White Mountain (12,840 feet), Mount Crocker (12,448 feet), and Mount Stanford (12,826 feet) —would have stood only 9,000 to 10,000 feet high, yet from detailed glaciologic studies it is evident that in this part of the Sierra Nevada the snow line during glacial times never lay much below 11,000 feet.

It follows from this, inevitably, that the Sierra Nevada could not have risen 3,000 feet since the first glaciation. The 3,000-foot escarpment below the ancient McGee Moraine could not have been produced by uplift of the Sierra block; it must have been produced by subsidence of the adjoining valley block. It is, of course, probable that the successive downward movements of the lowlands were accompanied by upward jerks of the mountain mass, but, if so, the jerks were relatively small and did not materially increase the height of the range.

François E. Matthes, *The Incomparable Valley:*
A Geologic Interpretation of the Yosemite
(Berkeley, 1950), 33-48.

The Inquisitors

BY ROBINSON JEFFERS

Coming around a corner of the dark trail . . .
    what was wrong with the valley?
Azevedo checked his horse and sat staring: it was all
    changed. It was occupied. There were three hills
Where none had been: and firelight flickered red on their
    knees between them: if they were hills:
They were more like Red Indians around a camp-fire,
    grave and dark, mountain-high, hams on heels
Squatting around a little fire of hundred-foot logs. Aze-
    vedo remembers he felt an ice-brook
Glide on his spine; he slipped down from the saddle and
    hid
In the brush by the trail, above the black redwood forest.
    This was the Little Sur South Fork,
Its forest valley; the man had come in at nightfall over
    Bowcher's Gap, and a high moon hunted
Through running clouds. He heard the rumble of a voice,
    heavy not loud, saying, "I gathered some,
You can inspect them." One of the hills moved a huge
    hand.
And poured its contents on a table-topped rock that stood
    in the firelight; men and women fell out;
Some crawled and some lay quiet; the hills leaned to eye
    them. One said: "It seems hardly possible
Such fragile creatures could be so noxious." Another
    answered,
"True, but we've seen. But it is only recently they have
    the power." The third answered, "That bomb?"
"Oh," he said, "—and the rest." He reached across and
    picked up one of the mites from the rock, and held it
Close to his eyes, and very carefully with finger and
    thumbnail peeled it: by chance a young female
With long black hair: it was too helpless even to scream.
    He held it by one white leg and stared at it:

484

The Inquisitors

"I can see nothing strange: only so fragile." The third
    hill answered, "We suppose it is something
Inside the head." Then the other split the skull with his
    thumbnail, squinting his eyes and peering, and said,
"A drop of marrow. How could that spoil the earth?"
    "Nevertheless," he answered,
"They have that bomb. The blasts and the fires are
    nothing: freckles on the earth: the emanations
Might set the whole planet into a tricky fever
And destroy much." "Themselves," he answered. "Let
    them. Why not?" "No," he answered, "life."
                                  Azevedo
Still watched in horror, and all three of the hills
Picked little animals from the rock, peeled them and
    cracked them, or toasted them
On the red coals, or split their bodies from the crotch
    upward
To stare inside. They said, "It remains a mystery. How-
    ever," they said,
"It is not likely they can destroy all life: the planet is
    capacious. Life would surely grow up again
From grubs in the soil, or the newt and toad level, and be
    beautiful again. And again perhaps break its legs
On its own cleverness: who can forecast the future?" The
    speaker yawned, and with his flat hand
Brushed the rock clean; the three slowly stood up,
Taller than Pico Blanco into the sky, their Indian-beaked
    heads in the moon-cloud,
And trampled their watchfire out and went away south-
    ward, stepping across the Ventana mountains.

Robinson Jeffers, *The Double Axe and Other Poems*
(New York, 1948), 147-149.

10

A TIME OF RECKONING

The fabulous prosperity of the postwar years stretched through the forties and fifties and kept on going. The longer it lasted the more unbelievable it became but, at the same time, the more taken for granted. Before long, no one under thirty could remember the Great Depression, perhaps the best key to the generation gap. California rode the crest of the wave. Throughout the sixties its population kept on zooming, carrying the state ahead of New York and past the 20 million mark. Through the Brown-Reagan years the economy flourished to the point that the Gross State Product of goods and services reached $100 billion, a figure which only five nations exceeded.

The explanation was multiple. Scenery and climate, though somewhat depreciated, continued to attract. Farmers and businessmen, industry and construction made new applications of science and technology. As the War in Vietnam added heat to the arms race, California firms claimed the largest share of contracts. The race to the moon was another sweepstakes in which California scored another first, though pressed by Houston and Cape Kennedy. And as in the past the price of land and improvements kept on rising. Californians could use a system of accounting in which there was no depreciation—except for tax purposes. Taxes they did have; that was one of the ties with reality.

In these continuing years of the Great Boom, Californians made many adjustments geared to the immediate needs and opportunities. That is what Remi Nadeau describes in "The Spiralling Growth of Los Angeles" and is the footing for Richard

486

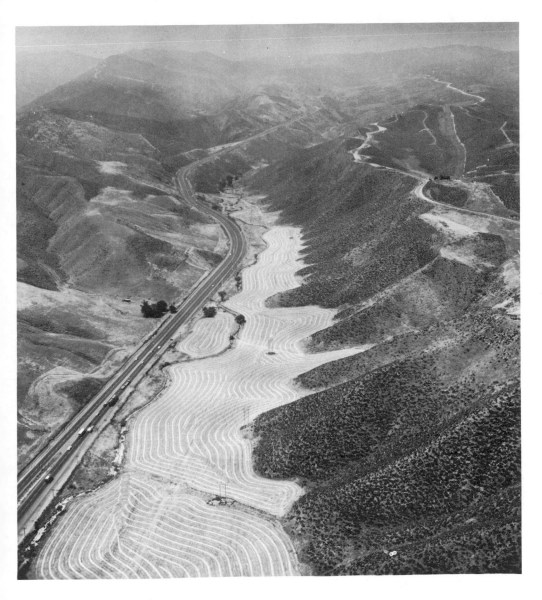

THE OLD RIDGE ROUTE AND THE NEW,
NORTH OF CASTAIC
Note the magnitude of the protective terracing.

G. Lillard's essay, "The Soil Beneath the Blacktop." Gavin Lambert's "The Slide Area" and Jim Murray's "H₂O'Malley" are commentaries on the growth ethic that prevailed. The growth pattern did prompt some planning ahead, by business concerns and by government agencies. Governor Brown's California Water Project is a $12 billion instance, and the Master Plan for Higher Education, also accepting bold projections for continuing expansion, had as its essence to make the higher-education dollar go farther. The fact of adjustment to the new California is communicated in Neil Morgan's embellishment on William Bronson's fable, "Home Is a Freeway." Rapid population increase is the clue to the baffling behavior of the California voter and in particular those who really count, the swingers, or as Gladwin Hill calls them, "The Capricious Million."

Early in the sixties California minorities began to be more insistent on equal rights and fair treatment. Concessions were very slow in coming, and in 1964 the state by a million-vote majority adopted the patently racist Proposition 14, the Anti-Fair Housing Amendment. Counterpoint to it was the riot in Los Angeles' Negro ghetto, an example soon followed across the country. The Berkeley students with their Free Speech Movement also set in motion a nationwide trend. Before long other minorities were demanding compsatorily equal rights, fair treatment, and power. Out-of-state influences from such varied sources as Martin Luther King, Malcolm X, the John Birch Society, the Minute Men, and the Weathermen came to bear, to some extent melding the youth movement, the drives for race and student power, and the peace movement. Conciliation gave way to confrontations which skidded into violence and counterviolence.

Superintendent Max Rafferty, Governor Reagan, Huey Newton of the Black Panthers, Eldredge Cleaver, and many others have fulminated about this grating underside of California's age of affluence, but it still awaits its Thucydides and its Steinbeck. With pomp and ceremony the McCone Commission viewed the battle scene in Watts. Jack Jones' "Watts Was Called Mudtown" opened a newspaper serial report that was much more illuminating. Ed Cray, "The Curious Incident of the Raided Mosque," describes an episode preceding the withdrawal of the troops.

LaRee Caughey's "A Graduation That Troubles the Conscience" protests the holding of the line against school integration; a few school districts have distinguished themselves by integrating. César Chávez' "The Organizer's Tale" describes the impetus for a most remarkable program that led to effective collective bargaining for California's migratory farm labor. Banker Louis B. Lundborg re-assesses the burning of the Isla Vista branch of his bank and the larger issues between the youthful protestants and the establishment.

These crises in human relations, as grave as ever faced, have recently been matched by a crisis in man's relation to the environment. Ecologists claim priority on the score that solutions of the problems in human relations would be worth nothing if the state or the nation or the world ceased to be inhabitable. Committes and societies for the care and preservation of the ecology abound in this the age of the ecology. The task of saving from ruination one small but beautiful part of California, the Big Sur coast, is told by a participant in Margaret Wentworth Owings' "Winning a Reprieve." The broader problem of averting the destruction of California is sketched in John Caughey's "Our Way of Life May Be the Death of Us," together with an explanation why past generations, much less burdensome to the land, had far less occasion for this worry.

The Soil Beneath the Blacktop

BY RICHARD G. LILLARD

Richard G. Lillard, a professor at San Fernando Valley State College, is the author of Desert Challenge: An Interpretation of Nevada *(1942),* Great Forest *(1947), and* Eden in Jeopardy *(1966).*

Ever since that fateful publicity event, the Gold Rush, California ranching and agriculture have been special marvels. Whether expanding to grandiose proportions or contracting because of unusual disasters, they have been a conditioning part of the exceptional, imagination-catching role of California. The good earth of the spacious Golden State, graced by the only areas of Mediterranean climate in the United States, has enabled California to be the leader of innovations in crops and marketing, in labor relations, and in automation. The state is also a leader in obliterating the best soils and in devising projects to rescue them and keep them in production.

Commercial growing in California has been tied to the unparalleled variety of local climates and soils in the plains and valleys and mountains, from the fog-cooled coasts to the hot, wind-swept interior deserts. It is related to the limited and irregular natural water supply and the long, dry summers, which have led men to carry out extraordinary water works, pumping dry the earth's crust and creating the longest rivers in the known geological history of the state.

A century ago the problem for California agriculture was the distance between its orchards and fields and the consuming population back east. The solution was transcontinental railroads and, later, trucks and airplanes. Now the problem is that too many millions of Californians spill from the cities onto good farming land. The solution, up to now, has been to bulldoze the farm and import food from distant states to the east.

Though the population burgeons its millions more per decade and becomes increasingly a market for the state's produce, fewer and fewer citizens are willing to pick crops under traditional California conditions. As a result, California farm workers now lead America in trying to upgrade their lives, and farm owners lead America in trying to replace workers with machinery.

Nowhere have nonsouthern farmers more abused workers or resisted attempts to improve working conditions; yet nowhere else have farmers been quicker to run to federal and state agricultural agencies, especially the state university, to get socialized help in solving every sort of problem except the "labor problem."

In its way, California agriculture has made radical breaks with the past. Though farmers have been Republicans, and ever ready to rally to the cause of free enterprise, they have since the 1890s set precedents in forming co-operative water and irrigation systems and weather-predicting agencies. They have created scores of large and efficient co-operative marketing associations, dominated by the big growers and backed by state and federal laws on controlled marketing. Walnut growers made the trademark "Diamond" famous. Raisin growers established their "Sun Maid," and avocado raisers gave "Calavo" to the retail world. Prune and apricot people likewise pooled their efforts, as did almond growers, cattlemen, and others. The lemon and orange growers' exchanges merged into California Fruit Growers Exchange and later Sunkist Growers, Inc.; now the Sunkist teletype systems span the United States and Canada and link the principal markets of the globe.

During the first century of statehood California's agriculture was a biological triumph. Early explorers of the coasts and river valleys—Portolá, Anza, Vancouver—saw much sand and rock, much seared grass and dry plain. But after heavy-eating gold seekers created a local consumers' market and the long railroads opened up the continent, Californians turned square miles of nondescript bottom and foothill land into cattle or sheep ranches, grain and vegetable fields, and vineyards and orchards. Scattered over a distance of 900 miles, favored spots became oases of almonds, figs, apricots, cherries, prunes, peaches, hops, oranges, lemons, English walnuts, celery, lettuce, wheat, barley, alfalfa, wine grapes. Individuals and government agents experimented endlessly with imported livestock, including camels and ostriches, and with plants from all the green continents.

There have been notable successes in adapting plants and their environments to each other, as, for example, dates, grapefruit and winter vegetables near Palm Springs; alfalfa, cantaloupe, and cattle feeding in the Imperial Valley; apple orchards along the coast near Monterey, Easter lilies along the extreme northwest coast, or rice on the hot plains alongside the Sacramento River. California developed the world capitals for lima beans, asparagus, figs and raisins, avocados. Portions of four Southern California counties became the Orange Empire. Coastal valleys produced more than half of the world's flower seeds.

The gigantic task in landscape architecture took place largely between 1870 and 1940. It turned entire flatland vistas, the flanks of long ranges, and vast blanched desert slopes into carefully

491

tended open space. It was beautiful and enchanting; in the blossom seasons it was as fragrant as later it was profitable. Far from destroying natural beauty, most farmers had improved upon the original brush, flood plains and willow bottoms.

California, a leading commercial and industrial state, has balanced its economy by also being the leading agricultural state in value and variety of production. It grows commercially more than 200 crops, and ranks first in forty-three of them. The Experiment Station Extension Service calmly claims that California "productivity and variety [have] never been matched anywhere in the world's history"....

In pilot social reform as in sheer gigantism of production, California agriculture is also showing the way. Growers now confront an economic revolution that they have long tried to prevent or delay. There is an unprecedented push to unionize hands in field and orchard and in packing sheds. After a century, farmers can foresee an end to their variation on the hacienda system of old Mexico....

Related to the development of farm workers' unions—making them possible and also perhaps making both unions and workers largely obsolete—is the new drive to mechanize agriculture. The machines invented to replace workers are designed at several branches of the University of California and in the shops of private engineers like those employed by Sunkist....

The present technical development goes far beyond the earlier eastern inventions for harvesting grains and the early California concern with machines to level and work farm soils and to cut drainage or irrigation systems. The California challenge to engineers has not been hay or barley or cotton but specialties like carrots, melons, dates, lemons, celery, bell peppers, and oranges that take relatively huge amounts of hand labor. As this labor has become scarce or expensive or firmly self-respecting, the interlocking United States Department of Agriculture, California State Department of Agriculture and the university have set to work redesigning crops and inventing machinery to harvest them.

Men are at work breeding asparagus, grapes, melons, even sesame seed that can be machine harvested. Tomato plants, the result of computer-controlled genetic breeding, have fruits of the same size, conveniently shaped, mostly ripening at the same time, and allegedly tasting like tomatoes; they can be picked all at once by a machine that pulls up the plant.

Citrus fruits, first and most famous of the California orchard bonanzas, have undergone the longest studies. These began in the 1890s with mechanical sorting, and have since included fruit washers, bulk handling in the orchard, natural coloring of fruits by use of ethylene, trade-marking directly on each fruit, orchard heating on frosty nights, and systems planning of everything from placement of trees to layout in packing houses and warehouses. Instead of climbing a ladder, the picker rides in a cockpit on the end of a boom. He uses a push button to position himself. He picks an orange and deposits it in a tube that gently drops it to a box at the bottom of the machine. Studies are under way to devise machines for shaking citrus fruit off trees into canvas catchers, or for harvesting by means of an oscillating air blast.

More serious than the weather, the insects, the labor organizers, and the difficulties of mechanizing the harvest is the ominous urban growth. The very population that hungers for fresh produce threatens to crowd agriculture out of the state. . . . In the old and famous parts of California, agriculture is being steadily paved or roofed over. The change in the areas surrounding Ventura and Los Angeles, San Jose and Santa Clara, Sacramento and San Diego is as visible and as significant as that from one geological epoch to another. Though minor California officials—experts —mutter now and then, there is no wide public concern over the destruction of the fertile oases of prime, unparalleled, irreplaceable land. The masses are too preoccupied with bowling alleys, race tracks, and drive-in theaters to care about the soil beneath the blacktop.

After World War II, Southern California began the ever more rapid alteration of its landscape. Olives, muscat grapes, bee culture, and turkey raising were already centered in Northern California; now from the broad sweep of established agriculture south of the Tehachapi Mountains, Southern California specialties began to depart for the eastern deserts or for the northern valleys, where walnuts, head lettuce, olives, celery, artichokes, and dairying developed new production enclaves.

During and after World War II, as millions arrived to make ships and planes or to ride them off to the wars, the trend to put homes and factories on farmland took over in Northern California as well. This time there were fewer opportunities for agriculture to move. Though government at all levels began to tinker with zoning and planning, it made no plans for agriculture. For the building and loan companies, the mortgage companies, the big real estate operators (often Easterners), the contractors with their fleets of bulldozers and other earth-moving apparatus, the state highway engineers (who hate trees, dislike curves, and shudder at the word *beauty*), and allied county supervisors and state legislators—for all those who profited from "Progress," the rancher and farmer were like the Indian of yore. They were wasters of open space. Sound investment, the needs of a forward-looking population, GNP, and other mystical phrases called for action; they turned orchards and fields, flower-seed farms, feed lots and dairy barns, range land, and forests of second-growth timber into housing tracts, new towns, freeways, airfields, reservoirs, drive-in churches, department stores, amusement parks, factories, warehouses, junk yards, military camps, missile bases, golf links (themselves vulnerable to apartment house builders), and parking lots for square miles of motionless motor vehicles.

The new space users, said to be good economics, were created at a heavy cost in scenery and environment, regional flavor, and local identity. The new users threatened the balance of the state's economy, for a state without agriculture is badly off. Prices of fruits, vegetables and milk went up. . . . In the late 1950s, men began to foresee the end of agriculture in the most productive parts of California. . . .

Grave concern over the loss of farm land to subdivisions and industrial and military uses has stimulated radical proposals for salvation—California pioneers in cures as in catastrophes. One device used by farmers to save their occupations from city people has been to incorporate their lands to form "cities"— Dairy Valley, to save milk farms, or Fremont, to save orchards. But a basic problem has been a constitutional provision that

494

county assessors must value all land for tax purposes on the basis of "the highest and best use"—a rule that dooms a cauliflower field if a "de luxe" housing tract goes up next to it. Thanks to leapfrog and "scatteration" developments, many farmers have their taxes suddenly spurt up above their income from the land. One Sacramento almond grower had a 2,446 per cent tax increase in one year.

In 1966, the voters passed an amendment that bases assessments and taxes for open space on actual use, not on development potential. . . . The 1966 Amendment, if properly implemented by legislative action, will greatly help Californians to retain the nonurban landscape that still remains. The legislature will bear close watching, and this will be done by enlightened farming interests, including some big old ranches, and by new nonprofit organizations, bright, alert, properly aggressive, such as California Tomorrow, with its quarterly *Cry California*, and the Planning and Conservation League for Legislative Action, which keeps a full-time lobbyist in Sacramento.

The one over-all cure for the loss of agricultural domain is statewide planning, administered by a state commission as removed from monetary pressures and politics as is the state supreme court. Such a body could apply suggestions such as those in . . . the State Development Plan, years in preparation, which considers agricultural and other open space, as well as cities, fish and game, and varied amenities. The plan, pushed by the forward-looking Edmund Brown administration, has dropped out of sight under Brown's successor, Ronald Reagan, well publicized as a private land speculator and an "economy-minded" governor. . . .

Anyone who views the present chaotic surface of the state may find it hard to believe that California will—soon enough—create an all-powerful state planning commission. But then it is also hard to believe that Californians will let their agriculture, like their scenery, like their clean sea water and clear atmosphere, pass into oblivion. Unless the state has changed utterly from what it was in the past, answers will come out of California as the pinch, already felt, becomes an ultimatum. The state that has led the way in crop production, co-operative selling, unionization of grape pickers, mechanization of orchards, and calculated destruction of agricultural marvels can also lead the way in planning.

California can do whatever it wants. It can use its mountains to fill in San Francisco Bay and the ocean above the continental shelf and there build more suburbs and parking lots. It can exterminate any and all species of birds, mammals, and plants. Or it can restrict or ban the car, the bulldozer, the subdivider, and the speculator. It can save or reconstitute much of its agriculture, as it can much of its shore line and mountain back country. Salvation is as possible as destruction.

Carey McWilliams, editor,
The California Revolution (New York, Grossman Publishers, 1968), 147-158.

The Spiralling Growth of Los Angeles

BY REMI NADEAU

Remi Nadeau, scion of an early Los Angeles family, is the author of two important works on southern California history: City-Makers *(1948), a study of the men who presided over the boom of 1868-1876, and* The Water Seekers *(1950), a chronicle of the region's search for its prime necessity. A more recent work of his offers an excellent insight into the startling postwar growth.*

Young couples stood in line at tract offices to buy homes before the foundations were laid.

Biggest operator by far was Louis H. Boyar, who had started as a developer in 1939 with $700 in borrowed capital. Through FHA guarantees he secured huge loans covering most of the development costs, and then built enormous tracts with comparatively little personal investment. His greatest promotion was Lakewood Park, which he launched by purchasing 3,375 acres of farm land for $8.8 million in 1950. Here, with the help of professional city planners, he laid out a community of 17,000 homes for a population of 70,000—the biggest single-ownership development in the nation and twice as big as the famed Levittown of Long Island, New York.

While the farmers were harvesting the last crop from the land Boyar's construction crews were starting to lay 133 miles of paved streets. Small teams of specialists moved down one side of each street with fantastic new machinery. Great power diggers gouged out a foundation trench for a house in fifteen minutes. Lumber arrived pre-cut for each home. Conveyor belts carried shingles to the roofs. Carpenters used automatic nailing machines and powered door-hanging machines. Expediters with radio cars moved from one home to another looking for bottlenecks. On some days as many as 100 new homes were started; 10,000 were finished in the first two years. Mass construction was matched by mass sales; by late 1950 the volume reached 107 sales in a single hour.

Lakewood was only the most spectacular project in a real estate boom that burst over the entire Los Angeles area. Neighboring Orange County, which had been largely an agricultural region before the war, suddenly became the fastest growing county in the nation. Since the war the population has quadrupled to 710,000 people—the vast rows of orange trees giving way to rows of tract homes. Along the Sierra Madre foothills more communities blossomed; the homes replaced the orange groves so swiftly that for the first time in decades Los Angeles lost its place as the number one agricultural county in the nation, and relinquished to Florida the leadership in the citrus industry.

While this was a blow to Angeleno boosters, the fact was that Los Angeles had outgrown its pastoral age at last. With the pressure of population still rising, the land was too valuable for farming. Los Angeles was no longer a garden city, but an urban city in the traditional eastern sense—with all the problems of urban congestion. . . . In all, the tract boom was a conspicuous tribute to the explosive vitality of Los Angeles business. It provided comfortable homes by the tens of thousands at reasonable prices and low terms. It solved a desperate housing shortage. It gave employment to thousands at a time when Los Angeles heavy industry had retrenched. . . .

Nowhere was southern California's growth more spectacular than in San Fernando Valley, which was chiefly responsible for the growth of the city of Los Angeles from 1.5 million just before the war to 2.5 million by [1960]. As late as 1944, when about

497

170,000 valley people lived in an area the size of Chicago, grass was growing in the streets and there was an annual appropriation from the gas tax fund to remove it. The area was chiefly agricultural, with a few scattered towns serving as market centers for the farmers.

As the war ended in 1945 valley land prices began to rise. By 1946 the tract home craze was fairly launched. In the longest uninterrupted real estate boom in the city's history San Fernando Valley's population multiplied five times, to 850,000, [by 1960].

Such an overwhelming inpouring of people was bound to create shortages. The telephone company found itself more than a year behind in filling orders for new subscribers. The valley's sewer lines were so overloaded that many developers in the west end were forced to use cesspools; for a time, in one section where the earth was unsuited for cesspools, the effluent ran down the streets. By 1953 some 38,000 city school children were on half-day sessions due to the classroom shortage—most of them in San Fernando Valley. Evidence of overcrowding was everywhere. Ex-GI's who had vowed never to stand in line again found themselves queuing up for everything from the grocery counter to the parking lot. During one holiday rush a valley supermarket became so crowded that an employee was stationed at the door to bar customers—admitting one person at a time for every one leaving.

The valley's growth might have been less painful had the Los Angeles authorities been alert to their responsibilities. Though valleyites made themselves a nuisance at city hall demanding the simple necessities, the city refused to accept the valley as anything but a rural community. Most of the other sections of Los Angeles had long since had their curbings, storm drains, sewers, and sidewalks; but the City Council continued to allocate public works money so that each councilman could go back to his district with a piece of the pie. When the issue of giving a baseball stadium site to the Dodgers came before the voters, most of the opposition came from the valley; its people were not so much opposed to the idea of the gift as to the expenditure of several million dollars in county funds for access streets and allied improvements which were more desperately needed in the valley. On a rainy day in 1958 so many children could not reach school because of flooded streets that two thirds of the valley's public schools

498

(sixty-four) were closed; no public schools were closed in the rest of the city.

The valley's worst single difficulty is its inadequate street system; except for the widening of a few arteries, it is substantially the same as it was before the war. In essence, a community the size of San Francisco is trying to make out with country roads. Equally difficult is the problem of commuters in getting out of the valley in the rush hour. Only two arteries lead out of this vast area to the industrial centers of Los Angeles and these are jammed bumper to bumper. Public transportation is wholly inadequate; in the early fifties the last Pacific Electric rail lines were abandoned and their place was taken by buses, which added to the street congestion. It requires twice as long to commute from the valley to downtown Los Angeles by bus as by auto. Reaching many other areas of the city by bus is a practical impossibility. . . .

Los Angeles is the car-craziest town in the country, and getting worse. It has more autos, more miles of streets, and more intersections than any other city in the United States. Unlike other communities, Los Angeles County has a car for every two persons, which means that practically every family has a car, and many have two. Numbering more than 2.8 million, the autos in the metropolitan area are increasing, due to the influx of population, by approximately 120,000 per year.

Serious traffic congestion first appeared in downtown Los Angeles during the boom of the twenties and has grown ever since. The police have adopted one expedient after another—"no left turn" signs, one-way streets, parking restrictions, lane switching for peak hours, special left-turn lanes—in an attempt to make the rickety street system carry the load.

As early as 1938 a special traffic study led to a state law for the creation of nonstop parkways, since known as freeways. A magnificent freeway complex was planned for Los Angeles and the first link was completed from the downtown district to Pasadena just before wartime building restrictions interrupted its progress. In 1947 the opening of a short freeway across Cahuenga Pass from Hollywood to San Fernando Valley launched an intensive new building program that has not yet stopped. Through the most populous sections of Los Angeles marched the right-of-way agents with their condemnation notices. Outward from downtown Los

Angeles the six-lane concrete ribbons stretched toward Hollywood, Pomona, Santa Ana, and Long Beach.

As each new link was opened, the eager motorists thundered into it from the jammed side streets, only to find another jam wherever the concrete stopped. It was even difficult to get onto a freeway in the rush hours; before the Ventura Freeway was extended through San Fernando Valley, morning traffic was often backed up nine miles on Ventura Boulevard. Sometimes the new stretches of freeway were, and still are, as crowded as the side streets. Over Cahuenga Pass on a hot summer evening, idling cars compound the trouble by developing vapor lock and boiling radiators. On such a day the entire pass presents a spectacle of tortured humanity. The side strips are lined with parked cars, their hoods raised and their drivers sitting in silent desperation. Policemen make their way through the jam with buckets of water to help those with dead engines. Tow trucks, hitchhikers with red gasoline cans, and other signs of misfortune complete the picture. At police headquarters the switchboards are continually lighted with calls from frantic wives who wonder what has happened to their husbands.

"The freeways are wonderful," wrote newspaper columnist Paul Coates. "They take all the little traffic jams and combine them into one big traffic jam."

Today, because some of the links have been joined up to make a continuous flow of traffic, freeway driving is often quite bearable. Sometimes, say in the middle of the night, it is a pleasure. While the freeway network is still only partly built, it is now possible to drive from the coast to the desert for more than 170 miles without a stop—that is, a signal stop. At nearly any time of day a car traversing this route will be halted by a traffic bottleneck through the main interchange in downtown Los Angeles.

Colloquially known as the mixmaster, the interchange exhibits five levels of converging and diverging traffic. Although it is considered among experts to be an engineering triumph, the average motorist has some strong opinions about some of its bottlenecks. Actually the mixmaster is doing its best considering the fact that as soon as it was opened it began carrying more traffic than it was designed for. . . .

The basic difficulty with the freeway system is not engineering, which is generally superb, but overcrowding. Nowhere has the relentless growth of Los Angeles been more apparent than in the clogging of the freeways. A 1949 prediction of freeway usage for the year 1970 had been exceeded by 1954. Every new link has been burdened beyond its planned capacity as soon as it was opened.

Remi Nadeau, *Los Angeles from Mission to Modern City*
(New York, Longmans, Green, and Company, 1961), 275-281.

The Slide Area

BY GAVIN LAMBERT

Well-known in movie and television circles, Gavin Lambert is a script writer, film critic, and editorial advisor for the Film Quarterly, *as well as being a novelist of note.*

I find myself remembering how the summer began. The cliffs weakened under heavy spring rains, rocks and stones rolled away, then whole sections crumbled and fell. Houses skidded down with them. There were some deaths. For several miles the coast highway was closed. The newspapers rumoured that a long geological survey would be undertaken. Had the highway been cut too deep into the cliffs? Would the land go on falling? Perhaps the area would have to be abandoned and a causeway built out over the ocean. Meanwhile, the ruins were shovelled away, FOR RENT signs went up on beach houses, a few bars and restaurants closed. After three months, the highway was opened again without explanation. Driving along, you saw jagged hollows and craters scarring the cliffs. They looked almost volcanic. WATCH FOR ROCKS. The sun grew stronger. Cars massed along the highway, the long pale stretch of pleasure beaches became filled with people. And the slides were forgotten, nobody talked about them any more.

"Well, there's no point in scaring people. Remember those old ladies who went over the edge? I told them then it wouldn't be the end of it, but I told them not to scare anybody." The engineer who said this was stocky and unruffled. He had thickly-rimmed spectacles and a briar pipe. The city authorities had consulted him after the houses fell down. "We'll handle the whole thing quietly, in our own way. That's what I told them."

501

"Then how serious are the slides?" I asked.

"I guess you could call the last one a little serious." He puffed at his pipe. "Quite a bit of land fell away that time. Took quite a few houses with it."

"People, too?"

"Sure. People, too."

"Shouldn't something be done?"

"We need more information." The engineer's pipe was drawing badly. He lit another match. "We want to see what happens after the rains next year."

"You mean, wait for the same thing to happen again?"

"So what else can you do?" The engineer shrugged. "Make a big project out of it and spend a lot of money? Scare a lot of people and take their business away? It's not worth it. Time's on our side." He gave a reassuring nod. "Maybe the foundations *are* shaky, maybe we'll have another slide after the rains next year, but it's a slow, easy process. It'll take years and years before you notice a real difference."

"A few houses more or less don't really matter," I said.

"Well, that's not exactly the way I'd put it." he shrugged again. "You know what I think? People should be a little careful and not live too near the edge, that's all."

Gavin Lambert, *The Slide Area*
(New York, The Viking Press, 1959), 222-223.

H₂O 'Malley, or, Let 'em Drink Beer

BY JIM MURRAY

Jim Murray, formerly a writer for Sports Illustrated, *is featured columnist in the sports section of the Los Angeles* Times.

I first heard about the great Chavez Ravine water shortage from my secretary, Vi Stevens. Vi was helpless with laughter. "You've got lots of mail," she said. "From people who say they can't get a drink of water in Dodger Stadium." She added laughing, "There's not a drinking fountain in the place! Did you ever hear of such a boo-boo in your life?!"

I waited till the peals of laughter subsided. "Vi," I told her, "there are lots of boo-boos in O'Malley Stadium, but lack of drinking fountains ain't one of them. It's the oldest carnie trick in the game."

I lit a cigarette. "You see, Vi," I went on, like the Ancient Mariner, "years ago a movie exhibitor found a long line at his drinking fountain in the lobby. He asked one the customers why. 'It's the popcorn', the fellow told him. 'Popcorn! What popcorn?' the exhibitor shouted. 'The popcorn we got in the Greek Candy Kitchen next door', the fellow shrugged. 'Makes you thirsty.'

"Well, you know what happened. The exhibitor thereupon put in his own popcorn. Then he shut off the water fountain to a trickle you'd be lucky to brush your teeth with. It's known in the trade as putting in 'Coca-Cola plumbing.'

"The Greek Candy Kitchen went out of business, but the Greeks got even by building candy kitchens with theaters attached. The next thing they did was make lousier movies because it is well established that the lousier movies are, the hungrier customers get. They improved the strain of popcorn, the better theater chains bought their own hybrid cornfields, but they didn't give a hoot what kind of schlock they put on the screen.

"Now, O'Malley has the same kind of 'out.' If the team gets lousier, the crowds will get smaller. But they'll eat and drink more. The day the Giants beat them, 19-8, in Chavez will be the day all records will fall. They'll need a stomach pump for every second person. In the meantime, he can't guarantee they'll be hungry, but he can be damn sure they're thirsty. Either that, or they'll start seeing mirages—like the Angels winning the pennant.

"O'Malley has pointed out repeatedly that concession revenues are frequently the difference between a profit and loss season. Many an All-Star shortstop has been paid for on a million bags of popcorn. And I shudder to think how many cans of beer it took to get Frank Howard.

"For some reason, people eat their fool heads off when they go to ball games, sad movies, or funerals, or anything else they enjoy—like a guy getting stuck in a cave. The psychologists can explain it. O'Malley is just channeling this wholesome morbidity into money. It's just good old American know-how, after all. I mean, supplying water fountains is just an extension of the damn welfare state, isn't it?"

Vi was impressed. So was I, to tell the truth. I mean, I didn't think I had it in me.

I even got a kick out of the Dodgers' explanation which was also in the finest American tradition. Why, there were a couple hundred water faucets in the powder rooms, they said defensively. Of course, not everybody likes hot water. And those paper towels leak. You can, to be sure, drink direct from the tap. All you have to do is hang by your heels from the water pipes like a sloth. This way, you get more exercise than the left-fielder.

The Dodgers might also have pointed out there is plenty of water under the ground, too, if the patrons would only take the trouble to drill for it.

The biggest danger, as I see it, is that O'Malley may have unwittingly furnished Arizona with a powerful argument in its water fight with California. If it can be shown that over 2½ million Californians subsisted without water during the 1962 pennant chase, it can be argued they don't need the Colorado River as much as they need a pipeline from Anheuser-Busch.

"Let 'em drink beer" may some day rival "54-40 or Fight" as a slogan for a cold war over boundary rights.

The City Council is loudly threatening to get into the act. I don't know what they can do except send a mercy fleet of Sparkletts trucks into the Ravine with Red Cross flags on them so O'Malley won't shoot them down—or charge them for parking.

But they like to point out that the Coliseum had 150 drinking fountains. On the other hand, you have to remember the Coliseum didn't have anything stronger than water. At least, not legally, it didn't. The Ravine has everything but the chaser. But then, O'Malley is Irish—or half so—and you all know the old story about the Irishman who went in and ordered a double whiskey and when asked if he wanted water on the side, roared, "When I want to take a bath, I'll let you know." When someone asked O'Malley if he was going to put water in Chavez, he probably thought they meant showers.

Clearly, he never reckoned on the Lace Curtain Set. Next thing you know they'll be wanting tea.

Los Angeles Times, April 19, 1962.

The Organizer's Tale

BY CESAR CHAVEZ

Early in this century the IWW made a futile drive to organize California farm labor. In the 1930's, stimulated by the New Deal, unionism scored gains in Los Angeles which had been a citadel for the open shop. The growers joined hands as the Associated Farmers, but there was no comparable organizing of farm labor until César Chávez came along in the 1960's to draw together the predominantly Mexican casual laborers, strike the table-grape growers, draw astonishing support for a boycott of the grape, and in 1970 win a settlement which established union recognition and collective bargaining with good chance of spreading to all such labor in the state.

It really started for me 16 years ago in San Jose, California, when I was working on an apricot farm. We figured he was just another social worker doing a study of farm conditions, and I kept refusing to meet with him. But he was persistent. Finally, I got together some of the rough element in San Jose. We were going to have a little reception for him to teach the *gringo* a little bit of how we felt. There were about 30 of us in the house, young guys mostly. I was supposed to give them a signal—change my cigarette from my right hand to my left, and then we were going to give him a lot of hell. But he started talking and the more he talked, the more wide-eyed I became and the less inclined I was to give the signal. A couple of guys who were pretty drunk at the time still wanted to give the *gringo* the business, but we got rid of them. This fellow was making a lot of sense, and I wanted to hear what he had to say.

His name was Fred Ross, and he was an organizer for the Community Service Organization (CSO) which was working with Mexican-Americans in the cities. I became immediately really involved. Before long I was heading a voter registration drive. All the time I was observing the things Fred did, secretly, because I wanted to learn how to organize, to see how it was done. I was impressed with his patience and understanding of people. I thought this was a tool, one of the greatest things he had.

It was pretty rough for me at first. I was changing and had to

505

take a lot of ridicule from the kids my age, the rough characters I worked with in the fields. They would say, "Hey, big shot. Now that you're a *politico*, why are you working here for 65 cents an hour?" I might add that our neighborhood had the highest percentage of San Quentin graduates. It was a game among the *pachucos* in the sense that we defended ourselves from outsiders, although inside the neighborhood there was not a lot of fighting.

After six months of working every night in San Jose, Fred assigned me to take over the CSO chapter in Decoto. It was a tough spot to fill. I would suggest something, and people would say, "No, let's wait till Fred gets back," or "Fred wouldn't do it that way." This is pretty much a pattern with people, I discovered, whether I was put in Fred's position, or later, when someone else was put in my position. After the Decoto assignment I was sent to start a new chapter in Oakland. Before I left, Fred came to a place in San Jose called the Hole-in-the-Wall and we talked for half an hour over coffee. He was in a rush to leave, but I wanted to keep him talking; I was that scared of my assignment.

There were hard times in Oakland. First of all, it was a big city and I'd get lost every time I went anywhere. Then I arranged a series of house meetings. I would get to the meeting early and drive back and forth past the house, too nervous to go in and face the people. Finally I would force myself to go inside and sit in a corner. I was quite thin then, and young, and most of the people were middle-aged. Someone would say, "Where's the organizer?" And I would pipe up, "Here I am." Then they would say in Spanish—these were very poor people and we hardly spoke anything but Spanish—"Ha! This *kid?*" Most of them said they were interested, but the hardest part was to get them to start pushing themselves, on their own initiative.

The idea was to set up a meeting and then get each attending person to call his own house meeting, inviting new people—a sort of chain letter effect. After a house meeting I would lie awake going over the whole thing, playing the tape back, trying to see why people laughed at one point, or why they were for one thing and against another. I was also learning to read and write, those late evenings. I had left school in the 7th grade after attending 67 different schools, and my reading wasn't the best.

506

At our first organizing meeting we had 368 people: I'll never forget it because it was very important to me. You eat your heart out; the meeting is called for 7 o'clock and you start to worry about 4. You wait. Will they show up? Then the first one arrives. By 7 there are only 20 people, you have everything in order, you have to look calm. But little by little they filter in and at a certain point you know it will be a success.

After four months in Oakland, I was transferred. The chapter was beginning to move on its own, so Fred assigned me to organize the San Joaquin Valley. Over the months I developed what I used to call schemes or tricks—now I call them techniques—of making initial contacts. The main thing in convincing someone is to spend time with him. It doesn't matter if he can read, write or even speak well. What is important is that he is a man and second, that he has shown some initial interest. One good way to develop leadership is to take a man with you in your car. And it works a lot better if you're doing the driving; that way you are in charge. You drive, he sits there, and you talk. These little things were very important to me; I was caught in a big game by then, figuring out what makes people work. I found that if you work hard enough you can usually shake people into working too, those who are concerned. You work harder and they work harder still, up to a point and then they pass you. Then, of course, they're on their own.

I also learned to keep away from the established groups and so-called leaders, and to guard against philosophizing. Working with low-income people is very different from working with the professionals, who like to sit around talking about how to play politics. When you're trying to recruit a farmworker, you have to paint a little picture, and then you have to color the picture in. We found out that the harder a guy is to convince, the better leader or member he becomes. When you exert yourself to convince him, you have his confidence and he has good motivation. A lot of people who say OK right away wind up hanging around the office, taking up the workers' time.

During the McCarthy era in one Valley town, I was subjected to a lot of redbaiting. We had been recruiting people for citizenship classes at the high school when we got into a quarrel with the naturalization examiner. He was rejecting people on the grounds that they were just parroting what they learned in citizenship class. One day we had a meeting about it in Fresno, and I took along some of the leaders of our local chapter. Some redbaiting official gave us a hard time, and the people got scared and took his side. They did it because it seemed easy at the moment, even though they knew that sticking with me was the right thing to do. It was disgusting. When we left the building they walked by themselves ahead of me as if I had some kind of communicable disease. I had been working with these people for three months and I was very sad to see that. It taught me a great lesson.

That night I learned that the chapter officers were holding a meeting to review my letters and printed materials to see if I really was a Communist. So I drove out there and walked right in on their meeting. I said, "I hear you've been discussing me, and I thought it would be nice if I was here to defend myself. Not that it matters that much to you or even to me, because as far as I'm concerned you are a bunch of cowards." At that they began to apologize. "Let's forget it," they said. "You're a nice guy." But I didn't want apologies. I wanted a full discussion. I told them I didn't give a damn, but that they had to learn to distinguish fact from what appeared to be a fact because of fear. I kept them there till two in the morning. Some of the women cried. I don't know if they investigated me any further, but I stayed on another few months and things worked out.

This was not an isolated case. Often when we'd leave people to themselves they would get frightened and draw back into their shells where they had been all the years. And I learned quickly that there is no real appreciation. Whatever you do, and no matter what reasons you may give to others, you do it because you want to see it done, or maybe because you want power. And there shouldn't be any appreciation, understandably. I know good organizers who were destroyed, washed out, because they expected people to appreciate what they'd done. Anyone who comes in with the idea that farmworkers are free of sin and that the growers are all bastards, either has never dealt with the situation or is an idealist of the first order. Things don't work that way.

For more than 10 years I worked for the CSO. As the organization grew, we found ourselves meeting in fancier and fancier motels and holding expensive conventions. Doctors, lawyers and politicians began joining. They would get elected to some office in the organization and then, for all practical purposes, leave. Intent on using the CSO for their own prestige purposes, these "leaders," many of them, lacked the urgency we had to have. When I became general director I began to press for a program to organize farmworkers into a union, an idea most of the leadership opposed. So I started a revolt within the CSO. I refused to sit at the head table at meetings, refused to wear a suit and tie, and finally I even refused to shave and cut my hair. It used to embarrass some of the professionals. At every meeting I got up and gave my standard speech: we shouldn't meet in fancy motels, we were getting away from the people, farmworkers had to be organized. But nothing happened. In March of '62 I resigned and came to Delano to begin organizing the Valley on my own.

By hand I drew a map of all the towns between Arvin and Stockton—86 of them, including farming camps—and decided to hit them all to get a small nucleus of people working in each. For six months I traveled around, planting an idea. We had a simple questionnaire, a little card with space for name, address and how much the worker thought he ought to be paid. My wife, Helen, mimeographed them, and we took our kids for two or three day jaunts to these towns, distributing the cards door-to-door and to camps and groceries.

Some 80,000 cards were sent back from eight Valley counties. I got a lot of contacts that way, but I was shocked at the wages the people were asking. The growers were paying $1 and $1.15, and maybe 95 per cent of the people thought they should be getting only $1.25. Sometimes people scribbled messages on the cards: "I hope to God we win" or "Do you think we can win?" or "I'd like to know more." So I separated the cards with the pencilled notes, got in my car and went to those people.

We didn't have any money at all in those days, none for gas and hardly any for food. So I went to people and started asking for food. It turned out to be about the best thing I could have done, although at first it's hard on your pride. Some of our best members came in that way. If people give you their food, they'll give you their hearts. Several months and many meetings later we had a working organization, and this time the leaders were the people.

None of the farmworkers had collective bargaining contracts, and I thought it would take ten years before we got that first contract. I wanted desperately to get some color into the movement, to give people something they could identify with, like a flag. I was reading some books about how various leaders discovered what colors contrasted and stood out the best. The Egyptians had found that a red field with a white circle and a black emblem in the center crashed into your eyes like nothing else. I wanted to use the Aztec eagle in the center, as on the Mexican flag. So I told my cousin Manuel, "Draw an Aztec eagle." Manuel had a little trouble with it, so we modified the eagle to make it easier for people to draw.

The first big meeting of what we decided to call the National Farm Workers Association was held in September 1962, at Fresno, with 287 people. We had our huge red flag on the wall, with paper tacked over it. When the time came, Manuel pulled a cord ripping the paper off the flag and all of a sudden it hit the people. Some of them wondered if it was a Communist flag, and I said it probably looked more like a neo-Nazi emblem than anything else. But they wanted an explanation, so Manuel got up and said, "When that damn eagle flies—that's when the farmworkers' problems are going to be solved."

One of the first things I decided was that outside money wasn't going to organize people, at least not in the beginning. I even turned down a grant from a private group—$50,000 to go directly to organize farmworkers—for just this reason. Even when there are no strings attached, you are still compromised because you feel you have to produce immediate results. This is bad, because it takes a long time to build a movement, and your organization suffers if you get too far ahead of the people it belongs to. We set the dues at $42 a year per family, really a meaningful dues, but of the 212 we got to pay, only 12 remained by June of '63. We were discouraged at that, but not enough to make us quit.

Money was always a problem. Once we were facing a $180

gas bill on a credit card I'd got a long time ago and was about to lose. And we *had* to keep that credit card. One day my wife and I were picking cotton, pulling bolls, to make a little money to live on. Helen said to me, "Do you put all this in the bag, or just the cotton?" I thought she was kidding and told her to throw the whole boll in so that she had nothing but a sack of bolls at the weighing. The man said, "Whose sack is this?" I said, well, my wife's, and he told us we were fired. "Look at all that crap you brought in," he said. Helen and I started laughing. We were going anyway. We took the $4 we had earned and spent it at a grocery store where they were giving away a $100 prize. Each time you shopped they'd give you one of the letters of M-O-N-E-Y or a flag: you had to have M-O-N-E-Y plus the flag to win. Helen had already collected the letters and just needed the flag. Anyway, they gave her the ticket. She screamed, "A flag? I don't believe it," ran in and got the $100. She said, "Now we're going to eat steak." But I said no, we're going to pay the gas bill. I don't know if she cried, but I think she did.

It was rough in those early years. Helen was having babies and I was not there when she was at the hospital. But if you haven't got your wife behind you, you can't do many things. There's got to be peace at home. So I did, I think, a fairly good job of organizing her. When we were kids, she lived in Delano and I came to town as a migrant. Once on a date we had a bad experience about segregation at a movie theater, and I put up a fight. We were together then, and still are. I think I'm more of a pacifist than she is. Her father, Fabela, was a colonel with Pancho Villa in the Mexican Revolution. Sometimes she gets angry and tells me, "These scabs—you should deal with them sternly," and I kid her, "It must be too much of that Fabela blood in you."

The movement really caught on in '64. By August we had a thousand members. We'd had a beautiful 90-day drive in Corcoran, where they had the Battle of the Corcoran Farm Camp 30 years ago, and by November we had assets of $25,000 in our credit union, which helped to stabilize the membership. I had gone without pay the whole of 1963. The next year the members voted me a $40 a week salary, after Helen had to quit working in the fields to manage the credit union.

Our first strike was in May of '65, a small one but it prepared us for the big one. A farmworker from McFarland named Epifanio Camacho came to see me. He said he was sick and tired of how people working the roses were being treated, and he was willing to "go the limit." I assigned Manuel and Gilbert Padilla to hold meetings at Camacho's house. The people wanted union recognition, but the real issue, as in most cases when you begin, was wages. They were promised $9 a thousand, but they were actually getting $6.50 and $7 for grafting roses. Most of them signed cards giving us the right to bargain for them. We chose the biggest company, with about 85 employees, not counting the irrigators and supervisors, and we held a series of meetings to prepare the strike and call the vote. There would be no picket line; everyone pledged on their honor not to break the strike.

Early on the first morning of the strike, we sent out 10 cars to check the people's homes. We found lights in five or six homes and knocked on the doors. The men were getting up and we'd say, "Where are you going?" They would dodge, "Oh, uh . . . I was just getting up, you know." We'd say, "Well, you're not going to work, are you?" And they'd say no. Dolores Huerta, who was driving the green panel truck, saw a light in one house where four rose-workers lived. They told her they were going to work, even after she reminded them of their pledge. So she moved the truck so it blocked their driveway, turned off the key, put it in her purse and sat there alone.

That morning the company foreman was madder than hell and refused to talk to us. None of the grafters had shown up for work. At 10:30 we started to go to the company office, but it occurred to us that maybe a woman would have a better chance. So Dolores knocked on the office door, saying, "I'm Dolores Huerta from the National Farm Workers Association." "Get out!" the man said, "you Communist. Get out!" I guess they were expecting us, because as Dolores stood arguing with him the cops came and told her to leave. She left.

For two days the fields were idle. On Wednesday they recruited a group of Filipinos from out of town who knew nothing of the

512

strike, maybe 35 of them. They drove through escorted by three sheriff's patrol cars, one in front, one in the middle and one at the rear with a dog. We didn't have a picket line, but we parked across the street and just watched them go through, not saying a word. All but seven stopped working after half an hour, and the rest had quit by mid-afternoon.

The company made an offer the evening of the fourth day, a package deal that amounted to a 120 per cent wage increase, but no contract. We wanted to hold out for a contract and more benefits, but a majority of the rose-workers wanted to accept the offer and go back. We are a democratic union so we had to support what they wanted to do. They had a meeting and voted to settle. Then we had a problem with a few militants who wanted to hold out. We had to convince them to go back to work, as a united front, because otherwise they would be canned. So we worked—Tony Orendain and I, Dolores and Gilbert, Jim Drake and all the organizers—knocking on doors till two in the morning, telling people. "You have to go back or you'll lose your job." And they did. They worked.

Our second strike, and our last before the big one at Delano, was in the grapes at Martin's Ranch last summer. The people were getting a raw deal there, being pushed around pretty badly. Gilbert went out to the field, climbed on top of a car and took a strike vote. They voted unanimously to go out. Right away they started bringing in strikebreakers, so we launched a tough attack on the labor contractors, distributed leaflets portraying them as really low characters. We attacked one—Luis Campos—so badly that he just gave up the job, and he took 27 of his men out with him. All he asked was that we distribute another leaflet reinstating him in the community. And we did. What was unusual was that the grower would talk to us. The grower kept saying, "I can't pay. I just haven't got the money." I guess he must have found the money somewhere, because we were asking $1.40 and we got it.

We had just finished the Martin strike when the Agricultural Workers Organizing Committee (AFL-CIO) started a strike against the grape growers, DiGiorgio, Schenley liquors and small growers asking $1.40 an hour and 25 cents a box. There was a lot of pressure from our members for us to join the strike, but we had some misgivings. We didn't feel ready for a big strike like this one, one that was sure to last a long time. Having no money—just $87 in the strike fund—meant we'd have to depend on God knows who.

Eight days after the strike started—it takes time to get 1,200 people together from all over the Valley—we held a meeting in Delano and voted to go out. I asked the membership to release us from the pledge not to accept outside money, because we'd need it now, a lot of it. The help came. It started because of the close, and I would say even beautiful relationship that we've had with the Migrant Ministry for some years. They were the first to come to our rescue, financially and in every other way, and they spread the word to other benefactors.

We had planned, before, to start a labor school in November. It never happened, but we have the best labor school we could ever have, in the strike. The strike is only a temporary condition, however. We have over 3,000 members spread out over a wide area, and we have to service them when they have problems. We get letters from New Mexico, Colorado, Texas, California, from farmworkers saying, "We're getting together and we need an organizer." It kills you when you haven't got the personnel and resources. You feel badly about not sending an organizer because you look back and remember all the difficulty you had in getting two or three people together, and here *they're* together. Of course, we're training organizers, many of them younger than I was when I started in CSO. They can work 20 hours a day, sleep four and be ready to hit it again; when you get to be 39 it's a different story.

The people who took part in the strike and the march have something more than their material interest going for them. If it were only material, they wouldn't have stayed on the strike long enough to win. It is difficult to explain. But it flows out in the ordinary things they say. For instance, some of the younger guys are saying, "Where do you think's going to be the next strike?" I say, "Well, we have to win in Delano." They say, "We'll win, but where do we go next?" I say, "Maybe most of us will be working in the fields." They say, "No, I don't want to go and work in the fields. I want to organize. There are a lot of people that need our help." So I say, "You're going to be pretty poor then, because when you strike you don't have much money." They say they don't care about that.

And others are saying, "I have friends who are working in Texas. If we could only help them." It is bigger, certainly, than just a strike. And if this spirit grows within the farm labor movement, one day we can use the force that we have to help correct a lot of things that are wrong in this society. But that is for the future. Before you can run, you have to learn to walk.

There are vivid memories from my childhood—what we had to go through because of low wages and the conditions, basically because there was no union. I suppose if I wanted to be fair I could say that I'm trying to settle a personal score. I could dramatize it by saying that I want to bring social justice to farmworkers. But the truth is that I went through a lot of hell, and a lot of people did. If we can even the score a little for the workers then we are doing something. Besides, I don't know any other work I like to do better than this. I really don't, you know.

Ramparts, July, 1966, pp. 43 50.

Home Is a Freeway

BY NEIL MORGAN

William Bronson, editor of Cry California *and polemicist against pollution and all profaning of the California environment, is here reported and extrapolated by Neil Morgan, prolific commentator on the western scene, best known for* Westward Tilt *(1963) and* The California Syndrome *(1969).*

During the year 1966, in the pithy but unsensational little journal called *Cry California*, there was a picture story that appeared to document a novel case: a family who lived on the freeways of Los Angeles in their motor home, one of those outsized vehicles with sleeping area, kitchenette and bathroom. When their first baby had come, the story related, Marilee Farrier had given up her job. Installment payments and bills had mounted, and her husband had taken a second, nighttime job. Still they were in trouble. Rather than sell their motor home, which they enjoyed for weekend holidays, the Farriers had sold their tract home and their car.

A night photograph in the magazine showed their motor home parked in a public lot not far from the Los Angeles Music Center. At 7:00 each morning, Marilee Farrier was quoted as saying, she got up, changed the baby, plugged in the coffee, and began driving out the Hollywood Freeway. Mike Farrier noted proudly that his wife didn't wake him until they passed the Cahuenga off-ramp. They parked for a light breakfast outside the Burbank factory where he worked. Then she drove back over the Golden State and San Bernardino freeways to her mother's home, where she left the baby and went to a half-day job. Later she reversed the route to pick up her child and her husband. He drove back to downtown Los Angeles as she prepared dinner. More photographs showed the Farrier family making a deposit at a drive-in teller's window at their bank, attending a drive-in movie, and pulling into a drive-in restaurant for a dinner out.

With the story, the editor of *Cry California* produced a map of metropolitan Los Angeles freeways, tracing the Farrier family's daily route. It was a jumble of circuitous dots and arrows indicating runs totaling 128 miles. Farrier was quoted:

"One day is about the same as another: about ten gallons of gas a day. We've begun to feel that the freeways, particularly the Hollywood Freeway, belong to us. It's not the same feeling you get about a house on a lot, but it's definitely a sense of ownership. We don't have any neighbors, of course, but actually we had a few neighbors before that we were happy to leave behind."

When the story appeared, I was one of several newsmen who went to the magazine's editor, William Bronson, in an attempt to locate the Farriers. Bronson told us the story was a hoax, and that he had used friends and borrowed a motor home for the photographs. He has insisted doggedly ever since that it seemed to him to be so patent a farce that he did not think it necessary to label it. But in California the Farriers did not seem outrageous enough to lead readers to doubt them. I still do not entirely accept Bronson's disclaimer. I suspect people like the Farriers are driving about Los Angeles today.

In California the automobile assumes tribal significance. Limitless ingenuity is displayed in adapting it to man's desire. Freeway commuters grow so blasé that a Los Angeles mortuary has directed its radio and roadside advertising toward those who daydream or read, shave, study or neck while they drive along at sixty or seventy miles an hour. When traffic slows toward the stop-and-go commuter rush hours, the student can be seen grasping his slide rule or turning to an anatomy chart. Businessmen are dictating into tape recorders. Others are plugged into tutor tapes, learning languages. Women are applying lipstick, brushing their hair, hooking their dresses. The automobile serves as office, bedroom and signboard. In San Francisco, a neighborhood divorcée became the talk of the service stations by gluing her phone number in plastic tape to her car's oil stick. At Laguna Beach, a blonde's Volkswagen bore the legend "Have Pills—Will Go." When freeways and beaches grow too crowded, young people can be found embracing in their cars on the top floors of public garages. Teenagers prize ancient hearses as personal vehicles; they can be equipped to carry surfboards and sleep two. The automobile is even used as a mobile listening post to maintain the sanctity of the home. In San Diego, a photographer answered a newspaper advertisement offering a camera for sale, and discovered that he had telephoned a pay booth outside a drive-in restaurant. "That's right," a voice answered, "you wanted the guy with the camera. He drove up here this morning with a book to read, parked outside the phone booth and answered the phone for about half an hour until he'd made his deal. I asked him if he didn't have a phone at home. "Sure," he said, 'but this way I can sell the camera and not have to sit around listening to the damn phone ring all day and night.' "

Since there is now relatively little rapid mass transit in California cities, every man's car is his mobile castle. The number of motor vehicles in the metropolitan Los Angeles area alone is approaching five million; only the states of New York, Pennsylvania and Texas have more cars than Los Angeles. In Southern California there is a car for about every two people; in New York

City, there is one for every six. Close to eight million gallons of gasoline are burned each day in the Los Angeles Basin. Throughout California one finds the greatest concentration of motor vehicles in the world, and it shows no sign of diminishing. In 1968 the California Department of Motor Vehicles was seeking a new method of license plate numbering. Under its system using three letters and three digits on each plate, there were only about sixteen million possible combinations, and they were being exhausted. Officials were predicting that twenty-two million cars would be registered in California by 1980. San Francisco is choking with cars, the highest density of automobiles of any city: 7000 per square mile. The San Francisco freeways, blocked from completion because outraged citizens regarded them as eyesores on the lovely San Francisco skyline, now dump their daily burden of cars at the edges of downtown. The city awaits completion of the Bay Area Rapid Transit District, an interurban rail commuter system which has been mired in debt and debacle during its construction. Meanwhile, from off the Bayshore Freeway, the Golden Gate and the Oakland Bay Bridges, motor vehicles are funneled into the city until it seems sure to burst in an exploding aneurysm of steel, rubber and fume.

In Los Angeles, which has desperately accepted all proffered freeways—sightly or not—almost half a million cars roll each day through the central interchange known as The Slot. Only for about four hours each day, at peak commuter rushes, does the intricate freeway system overload enough to bring automobile speeds down below maximum. By the early 1980's the three Southern California counties of Los Angeles, Orange and Ventura alone will be slashed by a network of 1535 miles of freeway costing more than five billion dollars; close to one-half of it is already in existence. It is possible to drive on freeways from San Diego almost five hundred miles northward through Los Angeles and through the Great Central Valley without encountering any traffic signal, stop sign or toll station; for cars with sufficient fuel capacity and drivers of adequate durability, there is no compulsion to pause. It is not a sightseers' route.

Neil Morgan, The California Syndrome
(Englewood Cliffs, Prentice-Hall, 1969), 38-41.

The Capricious Million

BY GLADWIN HILL

For many years Gladwin Hill commanded the far western news gathering outpost for the New York Times. *His expert knowledge on California politics is distilled into* Dancing Bear *(1968), an analytical exposition of political science as malpracticed in California.*

Ronald Reagan's election could be attributed to Democrats rather than Republicans. It had been expected that he would get the Republican vote. But if little more than half the Democrats who voted for him had voted for Brown, Brown would have won the election.

The results were all that was needed to complete the documentation of the most important immediate fact of California politics:

The Democrats' nominal advantage of more than a million in registrations over the Republicans is illusory.

Approximately a million Democrats are Democrats-in-name-only. They will vote Democratic sometimes. But they are just as likely to vote Republican—in the same election. They are the ticket-splitters. And, composing about 16 per cent of actual election-day turnouts, they hold in their unpredictable hands far more than the margin of votes by which candidates generally win and lose elections.

Whether the Capricious Million are a fairly fixed group of individuals or a revolving portion of the electorate of particular mental bent remains to be determined. But they have been mathematically evident in every election since at least 1958.

In 1958, the Capricious Million swung Democratic. Brown got all of the Democratic turnout and beat Knowland by more than 1 million votes. Moving down the ticket, the Capricious Million strayed more and more, until, in the vote for secretary of state, a majority had swung to the Republican side: the Democratic candidate, Henry Lopez, in losing to Frank M. Jordan, ran some 600,000 *under* the Democratic turnout.

It was the Capricious Million that crossed up Richard Nixon

in 1962. Most of them voted for Senator Thomas Kuchel, giving him about 750,000 votes over the Republican turnout. But in the gubernatorial race they split between Brown and Nixon; and, considering the smaller Republican registration, half a loaf for Nixon was not enough.

In 1964, the same bloc swung against Pierre Salinger and gave George Murphy the senatorship. Salinger's deficiency in Democratic votes corresponded closely to Murphy's excess over the Republican vote.

In 1966, to zero in on the phenomenon precisely, the Republican turnout on Election Day was about 2,808,000. This can be measured from the party's total registration, minus the non-voters, who under California law are stricken from the rolls after every state election. The Democratic turnout was 3,629,000— some 800,000 more than the Republican.

Thus for this election the Democrats' registration advantage of 1,370,000 was reduced by 500,000 non-voters. Reagan ran 934,000 over the Republican turnout. Brown ran 880,000 under the Democratic turnout. (For simplicity, the votes of the 187,000 unaffiliated voters are consolidated here with the major-party vote.)

Robert Finch, in the lieutenant governor contest, polled 1,026,-000 more votes than the Republican turnout; Lieutenant Governor Glenn Anderson, the weakest Democratic candidate, ran 1,051,000 under the Democratic turnout. Moving down the roster of candidates, the Capricious Million shifted slowly back to a Democratic vote, until, in the attorney general contest, the Democratic incumbent, Thomas Lynch, corralled about 250,000 of his party's ambivalent mavericks and beat the Republican entry, Spencer Williams, by nearly 500,000.

(The aggregate votes in the different contests do not match because of a progressive drop-off in voting; some 234,000 persons who voted for governor did not vote for secretary of state.)

Overall, the election results indicated that, as of 1966, from a practical standpoint the Republicans were the majority party. The only measure of hard-core Democratic strength was the minimal vote of 2,578,000 for Lieutenant Governor Anderson. Since no Republican candidate polled less than the party turnout, the Republican hard-core can only be gauged from the party turnout, which was 2,808,000.

The Capricious Million undoubtedly include some habitual ticket-splitters who are registered Republicans, as well as the 250,000 perennial registrees outside the major parties. But the pattern of voting figures from election to election indicates that the Million are mostly nominal Democrats.

The principal reason for their concentration under the Democratic label is believed to be that much of the heavier migration to California in recent years has been "one-party" states where people habitually registered Democratic even if they were conservative, and a Republican vote meant a lost vote. California gave these people their first chance to really vote Republican.

But an equally important factor probably is the looseness of party ties that applies to all California voters—the tendency to vote "the man, not the party."

In any case, the import of the Capricious Million is that it is fallacious to extrapolate from national-election behavior and try to classify California in state affairs as either a Republican or a Democratic state.

California can only be classified as bipartisan. It belongs to whoever, regardless of party, can convince the Capricious Million.

Gladwin Hill, *Dancing Bear: An Inside Look at California Politics* (Cleveland, World Publishing Company, 1968), 219-221.

Watts Was Called "Mudtown"

BY JACK JONES

On October 10-17, 1965, two months after the riot, the Los Angeles Times *published a series of reports by Jack Jones under the general heading,* The View from Watts. *In the studied judgment of the California Advisory Committee to the United States Commission on Civil Rights, this series provided "a far better and more well-informed picture" of the realities than did the cele-*

brated report of the blue-ribbon McCone Commission. The following section set the background for this series.

Watts, according to a UCLA Institute of Industrial Relations report on poverty in Los Angeles, was once known as "Mudtown." Just when it lost that undignified appellation is unclear, but residents of the area say it has been Watts as long as they can recall.

A pre-World War I novel described it:

"The streets of Mudtown were three or four dusty wagon paths. In the moist grass along the edges cows were staked. Ducks were sleeping in the weeds, and there was in the air a suggestion of pigs and slime holes.

"Tiny hoot owls were sitting bravely on fence posts while bats wavered overhead like shadows. Mudtown was like a tiny section of the deep South literally transplanted."

Watts, says an early history of Los Angeles, drew its name from C. H. Watts, a Pasadena real estate and insurance man of the late 1800s who also operated a livery business in Los Angeles. When he retired, he devoted himself to managing his 125-acre ranch in what is now the Watts area. As Watts, it was annexed to Los Angeles in 1926.

Now, observes the UCLA report, "the rustic setting has disappeared completely."

"Several large public housing projects occupy much of the land. It remains a Negro ghetto . . . with a steady immigration from the Deep South, populated by people who are seeking escape from a system which denies them and their children even the barest of opportunity . . . people who are often unfamiliar with the complexities of living in a large and impersonal metropolitan area."

The report traced Negro migration here back to post-Civil War days when railroad workers began to settle along Central Avenue and Jefferson Boulevard, when one of the shrewdest and wealthiest property developers in central Los Angeles was Mrs. Biddy Mason, a former slave.

Concentrated at the end of World War II along Central and Avalon Boulevard, Los Angeles' black belt has spread out, Jefferson and Adams Boulevards to Crenshaw Boulevard and beyond, bringing sprinkles of Negro residents to the Baldwin Hills.

Restricted for years by real estate covenants (ruled unenforceable in 1949) and other devices to "designated areas," the county's Negro population has increased by 600% since 1940, that is, in twenty-five years, to an estimated 560,000. Negroes have been arriving at the rate of 2,000 a month. There are about 420,000 in the City of Los Angeles—most of them trapped for one reason or another inside the rising walls of the expanding poor Negro area.

The Negro who has fled the oppression of Dixie for what he hoped was a better life may not get over the wall—but he is close enough to see what the system won't let him have.

He has reached the banks of the Jordan—in this case the Harbor Freeway—and can look across it to where the middle-class Negro lives comfortably in View Park, so close and still so distant.

Los Angeles Times, October 10, 1965.

The Curious Incident of the Raided Mosque

BY ED CRAY

This vignette of a repercussion of the Watts riot is reported by Ed Cray, editor of Open Forum *and author of* The Big Blue Line *(1967), an exposé of police practices that overstep rights of individuals.*

Los Angeles' riot had settled into a state of fatigued collapse by the early morning hours of August 18 when squad car after squad car of Los Angeles police officers rolled up in front of the Black Muslims' mosque in the heart of the Negro ghetto. The officers jumped into the street with guns blazing.

Ostensibly, the squad cars came to the rescue of two officers who said they were fired on by a shotgun-wielding sniper from the roof or second story of the temple. The two policemen were, they said, investigating a report that firearms were being unloaded from a truck and cached in the mosque. Considering the tense truce over the riot-torn ghetto, the police naturally would wish to check such an ominous story, for if it were true, here surely appeared to be the headquarters for a new outbreak.

Within minutes, the front of the mosque was pockmarked with bullet holes, every window had been shot out, and a platoon of policemen had stormed the beleaguered building.

Inside, police found nineteen members of the sect, four of them badly cut by flying glass, but not a single weapon. Rushing through the building, the officers fired wildly into empty rooms, shooting into the floor and furniture—even at the risk of hitting one of their own men—and ransacked the group's files.

No arms cache was found. No sniper was found. No weapon was found. Police were certain that armed men had slipped out the back door. No, the back of the building was covered. They must have used a secret passageway.

Police hurried back into the street where waiting national guardsmen obliged by dropping tear gas grenades through manholes into the city's sewage system. That would flush out suspected fugitives. While troops and police hovered around manholes with weapons ready, the tear gas mingled with the sewage, but no Muslims were discovered.

Meanwhile, forty members of the sect walked into the battle area and promptly were arrested and charged with conspiring to obstruct justice. According to a police officer, the new arrivals said they "had been called to protect the temple." These defenders came unarmed. Could they have expected to be supplied from the vanishing arms cache?

The nineteen found lying on the floor of the second story were booked on charges of assault with intent to commit murder and, curiously enough, arson. Two small fires, the sort which can be ignited by bullets hitting inflammable materials, were burning.

But the morning's shoot-up hadn't ended. An hour after the temple had been secured, two police officers started shooting into the United Veterans' Club three-tenths of a mile south of the mosque. At first they said they had come under sniper fire, then the police changed their account to explain that they had been charged by two Muslims who tried to shoot it out with officers in front of the club building and adjoining barbershop.

In a brisk, if one-sided action, the police poured more than 500 rounds into the front of the club building and barbershop, thirty shots into a sign twenty-five feet above the sidewalk on the roof of the club and another thirty into an inside wall between the barbershop and the club office. Police shot off the locks and assaulted the empty building, sprayed another twenty bullets into the interior walls of the club, peppered adjoining apartment houses with no fewer than 100 shots, and riddled a parked car in front of the barbershop. Despite the fusilade, the sniper or escaping Muslims or whoever had vanished. Just why it was necessary to enter the locked club and barbershop and shoot up the interior, the police didn't say. What happened to the $400 reportedly stolen from a locked cabinet during the melee? Neither the club owner nor the police said they knew. According to the president of the members-only club, it was there when he locked up, and not there after the police left. Police did not explain why it was necessary to fire into the parked car, which was owned by the club's president, a man known to resent what he terms police harassment.

More than a thousand rounds had been fired in the two engagements. Total casualties: eight Muslims cut by flying glass. The District Attorney refused to issue felony indictments against the forty Muslims arrested outside the temple, but police went to the City Attorney who drew up misdemeanor charges against them. Nineteen Muslims were jailed and the mosque's membership records were neatly placed in police department files.

Assault charges against the nineteen were later dismissed for lack of evidence, but the forty other men arrested still face misdemeanor complaints.

Supposedly, police are still looking for that secret passageway. And the guns. And the sniper. And the escaped Muslims.

Frontier, October, 1965, p. 16.

A Graduation That Troubles the Conscience

BY LAREE CAUGHEY

A memorial to the Los Angeles City Board of Education, June, 1967.

This year's graduating class has a distinction that should trouble the conscience of Los Angeles. The boys and girls of this class entered kindergarten thirteen years ago in the auspicious year of the Supreme Court's school desegregation decision, yet almost half of those who are Mexican Americans and more than four-fifths of those who are Negroes have come all the way up to graduation in schools predominantly Mexican-American or Negro. According to the official 1966-67 *Racial and Ethnic Survey* for Los Angeles that is the present concentration in segregated schools—and this in a community which gives no endorsement to Jim Crow.

Beginning five years ago, and we deeply regret that it was not thirteen, the American Civil Liberties Union began calling this Board's attention to the plight of the growing number of young people trapped in the ghetto schools of Los Angeles. We pointed to methods of desegregating applied in other school districts. We urged formulation of a district-wide, long-range program, and we urged immediate steps.

Our unsuccessful efforts at persuasion are summed up in *School Segregation on Our Doorstep: The Los Angeles Story*. A further report, *Segregation Blights Our Schools*, utilizing the racial census and the 1967 report of the United States Civil Rights Commission, appeared on May 17. Copies of these booklets were sent immediately on publication to the Superintendent and members of this Board.

Although the 1954 ruling by the Supreme Court had certain limitations, particularly in the phrase "with all deliberate speed," the findings on which this great decision rested were broadly stated. "In the field of public education," the Court said, "the doctrine of 'separate but equal' has no place. Separate educational

526

facilities are inherently unequal." In the sentence that set the rationale for the decision, the Court said "opportunity [for an education], where the state has undertaken to provide it, is a right which must be made available to all on equal terms."

A child in Watts was and is justified in feeling that in these findings the Supreme Court was speaking for him as well as for Linda Brown and her fellow litigants.

The scholarly-based 1967 study of the United States Civil Rights Commission corroborates the findings of the Court. "Negro children," the Commission says, "suffer serious harm when their education takes place in public schools which are racially segregated, *whatever the source of such segregation may be.*" [emphasis added.] The Commission goes on to report that in most cases in which children from the ghetto have been brought to a preponderantly white school "the results have been of benefit to all children, white and Negro alike."

The Commission finds that "Negro children attending desegregated schools that do not have compensatory education programs perform better than Negro children in racially isolated schools with such programs." It finds that "compensatory education programs on the present scale are unlikely to improve significantly the achievement of Negro students isolated by race and social class." Noting that the gains made through remedial programs wear off quickly if the pupil is thrust back into a segregated school, the Commission points to integration as the greatest benefit that can be conferred on minority pupils.

The Commission warns that there is "a growing deficit for Negroes who remain in racially isolated schools." "The time has come," the Commission concludes, "to put less emphasis on 'deliberate' and more on 'speed.' "

Last month the Supreme Court confirmed that discriminations such as were imposed by California's Proposition 14 are unconstitutional. At about the same time the House of Representatives amended the education bill to specify that federal school desegregation guidelines shall apply with the same force in the North and West as in the South. These are added signs that this nation cannot long endure an educational Mason and Dixon line with integrated schools required in the South and segregated schools tolerated elsewhere.

We in the ACLU are saddened that in the era enlightened by the landmark school desegregation decision so many Negro and Mexican-American boys and girls of the class of 1967 have been kept in segregated schools. What is most disheartening is that this Board and Superintendent, so far as we can see, have no plan or program for ultimate elimination of segregated schools or for immediate reduction of the number of pupils under this handicap.

Pandora's Box

BY LOUIS B. LUNDBORG

The burning of the Isla Vista branch of the Bank of America was an episode in a prolonged altercation between the police and a sizeable fraction of the residents of this bedroom suburb of the University of California, Santa Barbara. In these excerpts from his speech to the Rotary Club of Seattle on June 18, 1970, the chairman of the board of Bank of America discusses the much larger issues that were at stake.

While the actual burning of our Isla Vista branch may have been perpetrated by a violent few, there is no question that there was widespread agreement among the students on the Santa Barbara campus that the causes leading to the protest were both serious and legitimate. Apparently a substantial majority of the campus community deplored the use of violent action. But an almost equally substantial majority sympathized with and shared in the frustrations leading to that violence. . . .

It is clear to me that it was our involvement in Vietnam that opened Pandora's Box and that each passing year and each additional degree of entanglement have increased the bitterness and intensity of the feeling. Having once been aroused by the war, having felt trapped into it by their elders, and impotent and frustrated in all their attempts to make themselves heard, these young people have begun to question everything their elders were doing, and to question everything about the society their elders have created. . . .

There is a new value system emerging in this country. For generations we have been mouthing the cliché, "You can't stand in the way of progress." Now there is a new generation that is saying, "The hell you can't." That generation—and an increasing number of its elders—are saying, "Prove to us that it really is progress." In a sense, that is the essence of everything that is stirring and boiling and seething. Thoughtful people in increasing numbers are asking about one thing after another, "Is it really progress—progress for the human condition?"

What they say they want doesn't sound so different, you know, from what our founding fathers said they wanted. They said they wanted the freedom to be their own men, the freedom for self-realization. We have lost sight of that a bit in this century, but the young people are prodding us and saying, "Look, Dad— this is what it's all about." . . .

Let me leave no doubt about it—there are some real, hardcore radicals bent on the destruction of what they call "the system." I know, because I have talked to a few of them. At the other end of this spectrum there is another group—and I have no way of knowing how many there are in either group—that is as committed to the system as anyone in this audience. But in between is the great, great majority of students and other young people, troubled, disturbed, questioning, but uncommitted.

We have two choices as to which way we can go. We can divide into camps and shoot it out, or we can try to find common grounds so that we can grow together again. One course is easy but is blind; the other course is hard and slow, but is the path of wisdom. One course leaves all the thinking to someone else; the other requires deep, painful thought in a never-ending search for answers. One course will bring bloodshed, destruction, and ultimate crushing of the human spirit; the other course can bring peace and with it a hope for the rekindling of the American Dream.

Winning a Reprieve

BY MARGARET WENTWORTH OWINGS

The people of Monterey, Carmel, and the rugged Big Sur Coast are legendary for standing up successfully against the entrenched bureaucracy bankrolled by the gas tax and obsessively determined to thrust freeways into every underdeveloped part of the state. Margaret Wentworth Owings, famous also as protector of the sea otter, gives a low-key description of the juggernaut that the Big Sur town meeting undertook to roadblock. She communicates the spirit that gave force to the "scenic highway" concept and achieved the setting of a precedent.

The regret we feel for fallen leaves is seasonal, for we know about the imminent renewal of springtime. The regret stirred by the death of a landscape, however, is long lasting and singularly probes our thinking; we may well wonder whether we have taken the immobility of stone too much for granted.

We have taken for granted for more than a century the rocky coastlands of the Santa Lucias down the Big Sur Coast. We assumed that Rancho San José y Sur Chiquito would always stretch south from Point Lobos as a permanent pasture, edged with some twenty-five miles of shoreline, radiant green in spring, often veiled in fog, parched to gold in summer. There was an inviolable quality to the shore which suggested a birthright for all the people.

Farther south was a grant received from the Spanish Throne in the 1830's by a whaling captain, John Bautiste Roger Cooper. This holding penetrated the deep forks of the Little Sur River, embraced the fields that rose above the mouth of the Big Sur River, and ran back into the secluded Sur Valley, where the redwood groves, the sycamore, and the clumps of wind-carved laurel grew. . . .

South of Big Sur there were only the sea and rugged trails. The Upper Coast Trail laboriously climbed some 3,000 feet to where black oaks, Coulter pines, and madrone topped the ridge and stood dark against the sky. Robinson Jeffers describes what happens here:

I, gazing at the boundaries of granite and spray, the
Established sea-marks, felt behind me
Mountain and plain, the immense breadth of the continent
Before me, the mass and doubled stretch of water.

The Lower Coast Trail threaded its way into redwood canyons, where deer browsed the deep walls of the running streams. It climbed the steep slopes of chaparral out onto the "lion-colored hills" spotted with yucca. The Castros, the Grimes, and the Torres built their homes along this trail and lived a life that accepts wilderness as a neighbor.

There was a rendezvous here, where seventy-two miles of wild coast country lay dazzling in the sun. Rachel Carson called such meeting "a place of compromise, conflict and eternal change." Here sea and land consorted, the seeping moisture in each fold of the mountain range emerged and slipped musically into the shifting continents of kelp. The conflict and change was a natural interplay in the balance of life. Then came the road.

The new road intruded upon a dynamic ecological balance, divided what had been the indivisibility of the living whole. The old coach road from Monterey to Big Sur, carved out by settlers in 1886, accepted the terrain, explored each canyon and scouted each ridge. By 1932 road engineers set about to stabilize, widen and shorten—and to span the deep canyon at Bixby Landing with a boldly fashioned concrete arch. South of Big Sur Valley, the road cut hard into "the hundred-fold ridges." Blocks of landscape were spilled into the redwood canyons or tumbled into the sea seven hundred feet below. Man's intrusion left erosive scars that would not heal in his time. The earth, jarred by dynamite, still seeks the balance that was, and each winter loosens the rocks that block the natural channels on the cliffs, letting a rain of slides thunder over the narrow road. Perhaps the gray fox is agile enough still to climb and descend through the new chaos; few other living things could count on a foothold—not even the chaparral.

The new road brought new settlers, writers, artists, retired or active, industrialists and soldiers who, pricking with the needle of civilization, sought here a partial exile. In their new solitude, all these people had one element in common—the background of the superb landscape.

Twenty-five years after the improved coast road was cut through, the pressures to modernize it began—to realign its curves, to build straight slices for speed that could serve a fast-traveling public—mass-recreation seekers, and the projected real-estate developers. State engineers proposed to put this road into the freeway system. To demand a straight broad freeway along these unstable cliffs was to ask for disaster—a laying waste of environment, of integrity, of natural balance, of the very quality man was willing to travel far to experience. Real-estate developments, out of harmony with the land, threatened to spread unguided down the coast from the north and up from the south, to deface the scenery with roadside buildings, with shelves bulldozed in the mountains for house sites, girdling the smooth hills with roads. They planned a phalanx of houses between the road and the sea. Some developers advocated "a reasonable space between houses along the shore," others advised "clear the land of its natural growth to prevent fires." But where, in all this, would the brodeia hills of childhood be? Where in the years to come would we find the slopes covered by blooms reflecting the sky in their petals? Where the Jeffers' fields, "veiled in a late rain, wreathed with wet poppies," awaiting spring?

It was in 1960 that a group of Big Sur citizens called a meeting at the Grange Hall. Recent residents joined with some of the early settlers in sensing that the mountain shoreline could remain the same only if wisdom and foresight prevented its misuse. Together they began to view their environment with a new perspective, appreciating that future plans thrust upon their country, plans that would be considered normal developments in other portions of the state, could here destroy those things they most valued. They set about to defend them.

Out of the movement grew a master plan, encompassing the full length of the south coast. Its formulators listened hard for the words of the earth. Their goal was to preserve the coast without imposing unjustifiable restrictions on landowners. It was necessary to secure a consensus in the effort to solve a dilemma—

the kind of dilemma the American of the future will be facing more and more. The master plan called for clustering, for open space, for controls for future commercial developments that would be economically sound and resourceful.

As a key step, the Legislature was persuaded to remove Highway 1 from the State Freeway system. It would be instead, the "scenic highway" prototype for a concept adopted throughout California. Since the road would be inadequate if, in addition to summer tourist travel, large developments fed into it, the master plan proponents set about to control densities and draw up plans for scenic corridors. After two years of controversy, the plan was passed. Its proponents had reached high and had not achieved their highest aims but the final compromise was well worth the long struggle. In the course of the struggle we learned to face and accept new responsibilities in dealing with the land itself, to respect its fragile character, to perceive the meaning of the road.

Those of us privileged to live on this coast, in the immensity of its scope and in its great proportion, enjoy a strong sense of belonging. Perched on the buttresses of the range, we might with Sigurd Olson call them "the final bastions of the spirit of man." In our lifetime, may we thus hold them in our hearts—for the unknown date and hour of our return.

David Brower, ed., *Not Man Apart*
(San Francisco, Sierra Club, 1965), 28-29.

Our Way of Life May Be
the Death of Us

BY JOHN CAUGHEY

Robinson Jeffers, California's greatest poet and compassionately concerned for mankind's plight, made himself unpopular by his strictures on our impact on the planet and by his conclusion that man did not deserve to survive and would not survive. He wrote:

Mourning the broken balance, the hopeless prostration of
    the earth   .
Under men's hands and their minds,
The beautiful places killed like rabbits to make a city,
The spreading fungus, the slime-threads
And spores; my own coast's obscene future: I remember
    the farther
Future, and the last man dying
Without succession under the confident eyes of the stars.

Portions of that message have not yet been translated to the Californians, but the warning on the ecology began to come through, mainly in the late sixties. Simply stated, it was that current practices were creating an intolerable strain on the ecological round and were pointing toward its complete breakdown.

At the same time cosmic scientists delivered a more strident alarm. They denounced modern man, of whom the Californians are the shining example, for applying the fearsome skills of science and technology, the weight of rapidly expanding numbers, and an extravagance of consumption and pollution that could destroy the life-supporting functioning of the biosphere. These scientists subscribe to a domino or chain reaction theory. They see the tipping point already passed, the breaking point in the very near future, and Doomsday just around the corner.

The scientific basis for this gloom, along with the damage to the ecology, includes such elements as an overheating of the atmosphere, the build-up of an upper level float of pollution in the stratosphere, and accumulation of toxic wastes and by-products of nuclear fission and fusion, matters difficult for non-scientists to comprehend. Perhaps it was to be expected that Californians would not immediately or unanimously accept the scientists' forecast and timetable on the cataclysmic wiping out of all life on this planet.

As to the gasping and faltering of the California ecology, much more tangible evidence has been pressing on our senses. Smog, which in the early forties was a Los Angeles monopoly, has worsened and spread to San Fernando and Pomona valleys,

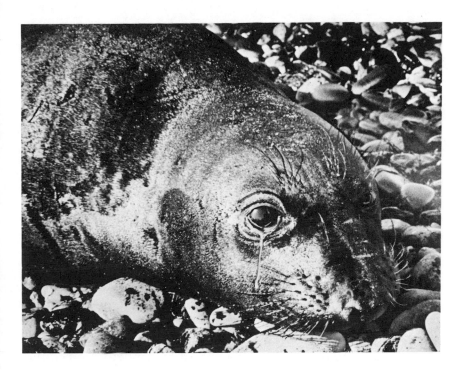

A VICTIM OF THE SANTA BARBARA OIL SPILL

Orange County, San Diego, and even San Francisco. The blight it has put on close-in agriculture is notorious. The Santa Barbara oil spill is but one of many incidents of industrial pollution. Waste and garbage threaten to engulf us. Los Angeles plies the not altogether safe or satisfactory technique of cut and fill at convenient canyons in its surrounding mountains. San Francisco has been considering a contract with Western Pacific to run a daily garbage train to interested and willing Lassen County. Residential, industrial, shopping-center, airport, and educational sprawl, blacktop parking-lot sprawl, and freeway swath have denatured millions of acres of the best farmland. The cumulative effect is damaging to the beauty of the state and clearly a violence to the ecology. And the horsemen of this apocalypse are the ones the scientists identify—the explosions in population, science, technology, and pollution-producing consumption.

California history as written and accepted has taken a much more comfortable view of the uses made of this remarkable part of the globe from earliest times almost up to the present. It dwells on the taming of the frontier, the struggles against a land often refractory, the gradual then rapid maximizing of population, and the build-up of a sophisticated, cultured urban life.

In the process the land was drawn on, some of its stockpiled resources were used up, and the flora and fauna were altered. In fact, part of the heroic work that Californians did was to re-engineer the land to what appeared to be better advantage, as in redistributing water, and to enter the ecology as ringmaster putting the subhuman participants through their paces and substituting at will. Here too. improvements on Nature were credited. California history could be optimistic. The material indexes mounted gratifyingly and, as to the environment, it had been tested by many successive sets of occupants and had shown itself rich, varied, and resilient.

The antiquity of man in California is on the order of 20,000 years, give or take a few millenia. Through the first 99 per cent of that span the Indians monopolized the region. Along with hunting and fishing, they harvested acorns, pine nuts, grass seeds, and much else that was edible. Because they put little emphasis on war, government, or agriculture, Spanish and

American pioneers and some historians thought them very backward. Anthropologists see them in much better light because of their acorn process, basketry, oral literature, and philosophy, and because they were numerous. In the continental area north of Mexico they constituted approximately one-seventh of the total. These Indians left few marks on the land—shellmounds, mortars where the acorn grinding took place, and cave paintings. To their everlasting credit they lived in harmony with the environment, did not exterminate a single species, and passed the land on to their successors unsullied and undamaged.

In 1769 Spain sent soldiers and missionaries to establish an outpost of empire. After six lean years, the Anza reinforcement of slightly over 200 persons doubled the population. Another six years later 44 men, women, and children were sent to found the pueblo of Los Angeles. The Spaniards introduced wheat, maize, beans, fruit trees, the vine, horses, and cattle. They began to till and to irrigate. Eventually the colony had 20 missions, 4 presidios, and 2 civilian pueblos strung out from San Diego to San Rafael. After fifty years Spain's representatives, the so-called *gente de razón*, had passed 2,000 in number and the mission Indian work force was another 20,000.

Twenty-five years later, at the close of the Mexican pastoral period, the *gente de razón* were perhaps three times as numerous, but the Indian work force, to everyone's regret, was much reduced. An inheritance appraiser in 1848, checking the estate left by the late Hispanic ownership, would have listed improvements in houses and corrals, dams and zanjas, orchards and vineyards, fields made tillable, oxen broken to the yoke, horses gentled and thousands of head of cattle and horses on the open range. As to the bionomics, two species had been virtually eliminated, the sea otter killed off by American and Russian poachers and the beaver by American trappers entering without consent. The ecology as a whole was approximately as sound as it had been when the first Indian arrived on the scene.

The next twenty years belonged to the gold seekers. By accident and on purpose these newcomers liquidated at least three-fourths of the Indians of the interior while running their own number up to half a million. They gave California a new face, making San Francisco an instant city and touching off a boom in agriculture, lumbering, and transportation as well as in mining.

Except as stages and wagon freighters stirred up dust, the transportation was easy on the land. The dashing stages, paddle-wheel river boats, and majestic clippers were objects of interest and beauty. Lumbermen cut ruthlessly into every convenient stand of timber, demolishing oak groves and sawing up thousand-year-old redwoods. The placer miners, swarming over the Mother lode, made relatively small disturbance of the terrain as they skimmed off the alluvial gold. The gold dredgers and the hydraulic miners, though few in number, set in motion a flow of debris that fouled the Mother Lode streams, ended the salmon runs, buried good farmland, and multiplied flood damage all the way to the mouth of the Sacramento. A 1970 footnote is that the dosage of quicksilver applied in the gold washings lingers on to produce mercury poisoning. These forty-niners were rambunctious, they committed localized atrocities, but the tools available for altering the land were modest, and most of the ecological damage Nature could repair.

Then followed a fifty-year railroad age. Population mounted; urban residence came to predominate. There was diversified industrial and business activity along with expansion of agriculture, lumbering, and mining, and a health rush, hyperactive real estate promotion, and tourists in large numbers.

Smelters, tanneries, sawmills, and oil fields and refineries were blemishes on the land. Lumbering was more aggressive and, when it appeared that loggers would destroy the whole stands of giant sequoias and coast redwoods, conservationists were alerted—John Muir and the Sierra Club in the 1890's and the Save-the-Redwoods League, organized in 1918.

Especially after conversion to oil burning, the railroad was not offensive to the environment. In many a scene the passing train was a pleasing accent, its whistle a welcome sound, and its pulsating machinery a delight. Its steel rails lay innocently on the roadbed, and native vegetation persisted along the right of way when virtually eliminated elsewhere. Transportation by rail also had the virtue of channeling travelers across the deserts and through the Sierra without giving them much chance to harm these delicate balances of land and biota. The bulk of California residents and visitors kept to coastal and valley lowlands.

The agricultural expansion of this period graced the landscape. Vineyards, orange groves, orchards of apricots, peaches, and pears, and fields of alfalfa were esthetically pleasing. Reclamation projects such as Chaffey's at Ontario and Imperial Valley made parts of California greener. Making the desert bloom and produce seemed an altogether desirable alternative to allowing Colorado River water to waste into the Gulf of California. Leaving aside issues of municipal morality and private profit grabbing, Owens Valley water yielded more when allotted to agriculture in San Fernando Valley. In a much less visible project in the lower Sacramento Valley, federal aid, engineering, and management combined with private-enterprise farming exorcised the worst flood hazards and multiplied agricultural output and profits through what was also an ecological improvement.

With the 1920's and 30's the pace quickened. New oil strikes made California the number one producer. The state was first in movie making, first in automobiles, high in installment buying and in tourists attracted, and first in population growth. The oil strikes resulted in ungainly growths of derricks at Signal Hill, Kettlemen Hills, and elsewhere, but to the ecology it mattered little whether the petroleum was extracted or left dormant below the surface and the amount burned in California was not critical. The morals of the movie industry were questioned, but it and most other industries flourishing did not mar the physical environment.

The great construction projects of these decades also had respectability. Boulder Dam ended flood hazard for Imperial Valley, produced hydroelectric power which no one criticized, and made water available to Los Angeles and environs. Although Coloradans and others upstream groused that it was their water the Angelenos were syphoning off, the national economy would be enhanced and at no discernible cost to the continental or global ecology. The Central Valley project raised acrimonious debate on the 160-acre limitation, but its reduction of flood hazard for the Sacramento Valley and restoration of the water table in the San Joaquin Valley seemed the sort of readjustment "that God would have made had He known the facts in the case." San Francisco's bridge builders retired one sentimental favorite, the ferries, but substituted a thing of beauty in the Golden Gate span.

Adding 3.5 million to the population appeared a more dubious benefit. Subdividers hacked into orange groves to make room for bungalows and moved well ahead of the builders with the result that much productive land became nothing better than vacant lots. Stray individuals deplored the population growth, a premonition of Lee A. DuBridge's plug for Zero Population Growth and Art Seidenbaum's more subversive campaign for Lesser Los Angeles. A few Californians such as Lindley Bynum lamented not having lived a hundred years earlier in the good old days of the pastoral period, but the Chambers of Commerce, the All-Year Club, and every right-thinking Californian saw a direct correlation between population increase, prosperity, and progress, a conviction which the Great Depression only accentuated.

The automobile, suddenly dominant, can be blamed for littering at every roadside and road's end, for billboards, and for discarded tires and cars distressingly slow in disintegrating once taken out of service. The motorists of the twenties put the choke on streetcars and electric interurbans, though these systems limped along for another few years. Motorists set an immediate strain on Yosemite and other preservations of wilderness. Undoubtedly they also contributed to pollution of the air and overtaxed the natural agents in photosynthesis, though neither the scientists nor Calvin Coolidge told us about it at the time. The major concern then was about the prodigal burning of the world's limited supply of petroleum, a concern easy to put out of mind in the delicious new experience of being able to drive almost anywhere anytime. To the ecology there were plusses as well as minusses in the twenties and thirties. In sum the adverse pressures came less from the mechanical innovations than from the greatly increased population.

In the course of the onrushing forties, fifties, and sixties 7 million prideful Californians became 20 million; the state pushed farther in front as the agricultural leader; the Gross State Product in goods and services climbed to $100 billion; the state budget under Governor Edmund G. Brown reached $4 billion and under Ronald Reagan went on to a recommended $6.35 billion; the state led in space and defense industries and in contracts from the Pentagon and NASA. Gas tax money had built the finest set of freeways in the world, and California was investing more in higher education than any other state except New York.

The bright side of the picture showed challenging work available in research and development in the universities and in industry, particularly the air, space, and electronics complex. California had a full roster of professional sports and Disneyland to boot. On paper it had two new national parks, one at the Point Reyes seashore and the other in the redwoods. A third was proposed on the Santa Barbara Channel Islands. There were cultural showplaces such as San Francisco's Opera House and the Los Angeles Music Center. Statistics indicated that life was better in California than ever before; indeed, an Ivy League inventor of a yardstick for measuring the quality of living reported that California scored highest. Science, technology, and managerial skill applied to the California environment had produced this remarkable construct, the new Terrestrial Paradise.

There was, however, the smogged side of the picture that impelled some persons to announce that they could not abide California any longer. One reason assigned was simply too many people, too much competition on the freeways, at the shopping centers, and at the resorts. Another was deterioration of the environment. The sardines disappeared, whole fields of kelp ceased to exist, and the brown pelicans lost capacity to lay hatchable eggs. Waste and sewage and other solid fill reduced San Francisco Bay to a fraction of its original dimensions, a desecration which, if not stayed, would turn it into an open sewer. By installing concrete sides and bottom, the Army Engineers made the Los Angeles River look like an open sewer. What saved it, along with other California rivers, was that it runs only when it rains. Campgrounds throughout the state had turnaway crowds and reservation lists as much as a year in advance. Yosemite Valley became a traffic jam and a slum, and the Park Service found it necessary to airlift two government-gray outhouses to the summit of Mt.

Whitney. Public beach frontage, meanwhile, shrank to one quarter inch per Californian.

In book titles, cries of dismay and anger came from Raymond Dasmann in *The Destruction of California*, Richard Lillard in *Eden in Jeopardy*, and William Bronson in *How To Kill a Golden State*, while Samuel E. Wood said *California, Going, Going*, and left the reader waiting in ellipsis for the word *Gone*.

A revulsion against pollution set in, stimulated by descriptions of the filth in the Danube, the Seine, the Thames, and the Hudson. California's Sierra Club was already so vigorous a spokesman for conservation of wilderness that it had lost its tax exemption. Its much more militant spin-off, Friends of the Earth or FOE, declared war on desecrations everywhere on the planet. Antipollution and pro-ecology organizations such as the San Francisco Bay Conservation and Development Commission, Get Oil Out [of Santa Barbara Channel], and Save Elysian Park proliferated to such an extent that California could be called the ecological capital of the world.

Yet for all this fanfare Californians hardly budged. Their track record—that is to say their history—contains little to suggest that they will voluntarily surrender present enjoyments for future benefits somewhat conjectural. The natural setting has accommodated such a procession of life styles from the Indian to the mid-twentieth century that it would seem ungrateful now to sell it short. Confidence runs higher that science and technology, which have conferred better living in the past, will do it again.

The fabulous growth history of the state also prompts optimism. Of course a great many Californians are of such recency that this history is not really theirs, and many others know it only in broadest outline. But if they were to study it, they would see the fantastic bulging of the cornucopia with each coil monstrously larger than the one before, and they would discern a formula. As soon as one pattern of production was exploited to capacity, ingenuity or circumstance provided another base on which to build larger. If the cornucopia from 1848 to 1970 can be believed, why not count on one more gigantic swirl?

As of this writing it may be that the breakthrough for this

next round of better living has appeared: inventor Bill Lear has confided to the press that, with a magic fluid "Learium" and a $7 million rotary motor that can be reproduced for $30, steam-clean cars can blow away the smog. With that leverage perhaps we could placate the ecology and roll on for a time with our historic value system intact in which progress is measured by the tangible increases in population and production.

A more accurate reading of California history would indicate that this fragile environment cannot sustain continuation of the dizzy growth rate. Evidence such as historians are accustomed to handling confirms that the present course is toward disaster and that the horsemen of this apocalypse are precisely the ones that the scientists identify. To save ourselves we must roll back population and consumption, restrain the machines, and house-break science.

We have entered the age of the ecological imperative. Instead of behaving like malignant parasites we must become, as the biologists would say, symbionts, that is, organisms living in an association that is advantageous rather than harmful to Nature. Our motto must be Peace with the Environment.

Other Books to Read

GENERAL

Hubert Howe Bancroft. *History of California.* 7 vols. San Francisco, 1884-90.
Walton Bean. *California, an Interpretive History.* New York, 1968.
John W. Caughey. *California: A Remarkable State's Life History.* Englewood Cliffs, N. J., 1970.
Charles E. Chapman. *History of California: The Spanish Period.* New York, 1921.
Robert G. Cleland. *From Wilderness to Empire.* New York, 1944.
———. *California in Our Time.* New York, 1947.
Aubrey Drury. *California, an Intimate Guide.* New York, 1935.
Zoeth S. Eldredge. *History of California.* 5 vols. New York, 1915.
Theodore H. Hittell. *History of California.* 4 vols. San Francisco, 1885-97.
Joseph Henry Jackson. *The Western Gate.* New York, 1952.
Carey McWilliams. *California the Great Exception.* New York, 1949.
Robert Pearsall and Ursula Spier Erickson. *The Californians.* 2 vols. San Francisco, 1961.
Andrew F. Rolle. *California, a History.* New York, 1963.
Jeanne Van Nostrand and Edith M. Coulter. *California Pictorial.* Berkeley, 1948.
Edward Weston. *California and the West.* New York, 1940.
Writers' Project. *California: A Guide to the Golden State.* New York, 1939.

THE INDIANS

David P. Barrows. *The Ethno-Botany of the Coahuilla Indians.* Chicago, 1900.
C. Gregory Crampton, ed. *The Mariposa Indian War.* Salt Lake City, 1957.
Edward E. Dale. *The Indians of the Southwest.* Norman, 1949.
Jaime De Angulo. *Indian Tales.* New York, 1953.
R. F. Heizer and J. E. Mills. *The Four Ages of Tsurai.* Berkeley, 1952.
R. F. Heizer and M. A. Whipple. *The California Indians, A Source Book.* Berkeley, 1951.
George Wharton James. *Indian Basketry.* New York, 1904.
Theodora Kroeber. *Almost Ancestors.* San Francisco, 1968.
———. *Ishi in Two Worlds.* Berkeley, 1961.
———. *Ishi, Last of His Tribe.* Berkeley, 1964.
Annie B. Mitchell. *Jim Savage and the Tulareño Indians.* Los Angeles, 1957.
Keith A. Murray. *The Modocs and Their War.* Norman, 1959.

THE COMING OF THE SPANIARDS

John A. Berger. *The Franciscan Missions of California.* New York, 1948.
Herbert E. Bolton. *The Padre on Horseback.* San Francisco, 1932.
———. *Rim of Christendom* [a life of Kino]. New York, 1936.
Charles E. Chapman. *The Founding of Spanish California.* New York, 1916.

Donald C. Cutter. *Malaspina in California*. San Francisco, 1960.
Peter M. Dunne. *Black Robes in Lower California*. Berkeley, 1952.
Zephyrin Engelhardt. *The Missions and Missionaries of California*. 4 vols. San Francisco, 1908-15.
California Historical Society. *Drake's Plate of Brass*. San Francisco, 1937.
George Wharton James. *In and Out of the Old Missions*. Boston, 1916.
Peveril Meigs, 3d. *The Dominican Mission Frontier of Lower California*. Berkeley, 1935.
Francisco Palou. *Junípero Serra*. Mexico, 1787; translated by C. S. Williams, Pasadena, 1913, and by Maynard J. Geiger, Washington, 1955.
Richard F. Pourade. *The Explorers*. San Diego, 1960.
———. *Time of the Bells*. San Diego, 1961.
Herbert I. Priestley. *A Historical, Political, and Natural Description of California by Pedro Fages*. Berkeley, 1937.
———. *José de Gálvez, Visitador-General of New Spain*. Berkeley, 1916.
Irving B. Richman. *California under Spain and Mexico*. Boston, 1911.
William L. Schurz. *The Manila Galleon*. New York, 1939.
Lesley B. Simpson, ed. *California in 1792: The Expedition of José Longinos Martínez*. San Marino, 1938.
Sigismundo Taraval. *The Indian Uprising of Lower California*. Translated by Marguerite Eyer Wilbur. Los Angeles, 1931.
Theodore E. Treutlein. *San Francisco Bay: Discovery and Colonization*. San Francisco, 1968.
Miguel Venegas. *Juan María Salvatierra*. Translated by Marguerite Eyer Wilbur. Cleveland, 1929.
Henry Raup Wagner. *Juan Rodríguez Cabrillo, Discoverer of the Coast of California*. San Francisco, 1941.
———. *Sir Francis Drake's Voyage around the World*. San Francisco, 1926.
R. K. Wyllys. *Pioneer Padre* [a life of Kino]. Dallas, 1935.

PASTORAL

Hubert Howe Bancroft. *California Pastoral*. San Francisco, 1888.
Hector Chevigny. *Lost Empire: The Life and Adventures of Nikolai Petrovich Rezanov*. New York, 1937.
Robert G. Cleland. *This Reckless Breed of Men*. New York, 1950.
Owen C. Coy. *The Great Trek*. Los Angeles, 1931.
Susanna B. Dakin. *The Lives of William Hartnell*. Stanford, 1949.
———. *Scotch Paisano: Hugo Reid's Life in California*. Berkeley, 1939.
William Heath Davis. *Seventy-Five Years in California*. San Francisco, 1929.
William H. Ellison, ed. *The Life and Adventures of George Nidever*. Berkeley, 1937.
Alexander Forbes. *California: A History of Upper and Lower California*. London, 1839.
George L. Harding. *Don Agustin V. Zamorano*. Los Angeles, 1934.
J. J. Hill. *History of Warner's Ranch and Its Environs*. Los Angeles, 1927.
Rockwell D. Hunt. *John Bidwell, Prince of Pioneers*. Caldwell, 1942.
C. Allan Hutchinson. *Frontier Settlement in Mexican California*. New Haven, 1969.

Zenas Leonard. *Narrative of Adventures.* Clearfield, Pa., 1839.
George D. Lyman. *John Marsh, Pioneer.* Chautauqua, 1930.
Charles McGlashan. *History of the Donner Party.* Truckee, 1879.
Dale L. Morgan. *Jedediah Smith and the Opening of the West.* Indianapolis, 1953.
Samuel E. Morison. *The Maritime History of Massachusetts.* Boston, 1921.
Adele Ogden. *The California Sea Otter Trade.* Berkeley, 1941.
Paden, Irene D. *The Wake of the Prairie Schooner.* New York, 1943.
James Ohio Pattie. *Personal Narrative.* Cincinnati, 1831.
W. D. Phelps. *Fore and Aft.* Boston, 1871.
Alfred Robinson. *Life in California.* New York, 1846.
W. W. Robinson. *Land in California.* Berkeley, 1948.
Andrew F. Rolle. *An American in California: The Biography of William Heath Davis.* Berkeley, 1956.
Nellie V. Sánchez. *Spanish Arcadia.* Los Angeles, 1929.
George R. Stewart. *Ordeal by Hunger.* New York, 1936.
Tracy I. Storer and Lloyd P. Tevis, Jr. *California Grizzly.* Berkeley, 1955.
M. S. Sullivan, ed. *The Travels of Jedediah Smith.* Santa Ana, 1934.
Stanley Vestal. *Kit Carson.* Boston, 1928.
James P. Zollinger. *Sutter: The Man and His Empire.* New York, 1939.

THE CONQUEST

J. Ross Browne. *Report of Debates in the Convention of California.* Washington, 1850.
Charles H. Carey, ed. *The Journals of Theodore Talbert.* Portland, 1931.
S. N. Carvalho. *Incidents of Travel and Adventure.* New York, 1857.
Bernard De Voto. *The Year of Decision, 1846.* Boston, 1941.
William H. Ellison. *A Self-Governing Dominion.* Berkeley, 1950.
John C. Frémont. *Memories of My Life.* New York, 1887.
Cardinal L. Goodwin. *Establishment of State Government in California.* New York, 1914.
———. *John Charles Frémont: An Explanation of His Career.* Stanford, 1930.
Howard Lamar, ed. *The Cruise of the Portsmouth.* New Haven, 1958.
Werner Marti. *Messenger of Destiny: Archibald H. Gillespie.* San Francisco, 1960.
Allan Nevins. *Frémont, Pathmarker of the West.* New York, 1939.
Catherine C. Phillips. *Jessie Benton Frémont.* San Francisco, 1935.
Fred D. Rogers. *Bear Flag Lieutenant: The Life Story of Henry L. Ford.* San Francisco, 1951.
———. *Filings from an Old Saw.* San Francisco, 1956.
———. *A Navy Surgeon in California.* San Francisco, 1957.
———. *Montgomery and the Portsmouth.* San Francisco, 1958.
James A. B. Scherer. *Thirty-First Star.* Indianapolis, 1942.
Irving Stone. *Immortal Wife.* New York, 1944.
Reuben L. Underhill. *From Cowhides to Golden Fleece.* Stanford, 1939.
Arthur Woodward. *Lances at San Pascual.* San Francisco, 1948.

GLINTS OF GOLD

Hubert Howe Bancroft. *California Inter Pocula.* San Francisco, 1888.

Ralph P. Bieber. *Southern Trails to California in 1849.* Glendale, 1937.
Franklin A. Buck. *A Yankee Trader in the Gold Rush.* Boston, 1930.
California Historical Society. *California Gold Discovery.* San Francisco, 1947.
Chauncey L. Canfield. *Diary of a Forty-Niner.* New York, 1906.
John W. Caughey. *Gold Is the Cornerstone.* Berkeley, 1948.
———. *Rushing for Gold.* Berkeley, 1949.
W. A. Chalfant. *Gold, Guns, and Ghost Towns.* Stanford, 1947.
W. A. Chalfant. *Tales of the Pioneers.* Stanford, 1942.
Enos Christman. *One Man's Gold.* New York, 1930.
Owen C. Coy. *Gold Days.* Los Angeles, 1929.
John G. Ellenbecker. *The Jayhawkers of Death Valley.* Marysville, Kansas, 1938.
Grant Foreman. *Marcy and the Gold Seekers.* Norman, 1939.
Friederich Gerstäcker. *Narrative of a Journey around the World.* New York, 1853.
Octavius T. Howe. *Argonauts of '49.* Cambridge, 1931.
A. B. Hulbert. *Forty-Niners.* Boston, 1931.
Joseph Henry Jackson. *Anybody's Gold.* New York, 1941.
———. *Gold Rush Album.* New York, 1949.
Olaf P. Jenkins. *Geologic Guidebook along Highway 49.* San Francisco, 1948.
William McCollum. *California as I Saw It.* Los Gatos, 1960.
Charles Pancoast, *A Quaker Forty-Niner.* Philadelphia, 1930.
Rodman W. Paul. *The California Gold Discovery.* Georgetown, Calif., 1966.
David M. Potter, ed. *Trail to California.* New Haven, 1945.
Sarah Royce. *A Frontier Lady.* New Haven, 1932.
William R. Ryan. *Personal Adventures.* 2 vols. London, 1851.
Howard L. Scamehorn. *The Buckeye Rovers in the Gold Rush.* Athens, Ohio, 1965.
John Steele. *In Camp and Cabin.* Lodi, Wisc., 1901.
Joseph E. Ware. *The Emigrants' Guide to California.* St. Louis, 1849; edited by John W. Caughey, Princeton, 1932.
Walker D. Wyman, ed. *California Emigrant Letters.* New York, 1952.

THE YOUNG STATE

Hubert Howe Bancroft. *Popular Tribunals.* 2 vols. San Francisco, 1887.
William Banning and George Hugh Banning. *Six Horses.* New York, 1930.
George W. and Helen P. Beattie. *Heritage of the Valley* (San Bernardino). Pasadena, 1939.
Horace Bell. *On the Old West Coast.* New York, 1930.
A. Russell Buchanan. *David S. Terry of California, Dueling Judge.* San Marino, 1956.
Vincent P. Carosso. *The California Wine Industry.* Berkeley, 1951.
Stanton A. Coblentz. *Villains and Vigilantes.* New York, 1936.
Owen C. Coy. *The Humboldt Bay Region.* Los Angeles, 1929.
Henry George. *Progress and Poverty.* New York, 1880.
Benjamin S. Harrison. *Fortune Favors the Brave.* Los Angeles, 1953.
Francis Bret Harte. *Outcroppings.* San Francisco, 1866.

Other Books to Read

W. Turrentine Jackson. *Wagon Roads West*. Berkeley, 1952.
Pauline Jacobsen. *City of the Golden Fifties*. Berkeley, 1941.
John H. Kemble. *The Panama Route to California*. Berkeley, 1943.
Lewis B. Lesley. *Uncle Sam's Camels*. Cambridge, 1929.
Harris Newmark. *Sixty Years in Southern California*. New York, 1916.
W. W. Robinson. *Ranchos Become Cities*. Pasadena, 1939.
Constance Rourke. *Troupers of the Gold Coast*. New York, 1928.
James A. B. Scherer. *The Lion of the Vigilantes*. Indianapolis, 1939.
May Wentworth. *Poets of the Pacific*. San Francisco, 1865.
R. K. Wyllys. *The French in Sonora*. Berkeley, 1932.

THE PASSING OF THE FRONTIER

J. A. Alexander. *The Life of George Chaffey*. Melbourne, 1928.
Charles A. Barker. *Henry George*. New York, 1955.
John E. Baur. *The Health Seekers of Southern California*. San Marino, 1959.
Edwin R. Bingham. *Charles F. Lummis*. Berkeley, 1955.
John W. Caughey. *Hubert Howe Bancroft, Historian of the West*. Berkeley, 1946.
Charles C. Dobie. *San Francisco's Chinatown*. New York, 1936.
Glenn S. Dumke. *The Boom of the Eighties*. San Marino, 1944.
Henry George. *Progress and Poverty*. New York, 1880.
Anne Roller Issler. *Stevenson at Silverado*. Caldwell, 1939.
Helen Hunt Jackson. *Ramona*. Boston, 1884.
Holway R. Jones. *John Muir and the Sierra Club*. San Francisco, 1965.
Idwal Jones. *Vermilion*. New York, 1947.
———. *The Vineyard*. New York, 1942.
Oscar Lewis. *The Big Four*. New York, 1938.
Oscar Lewis and Carroll D. Hall. *Bonanza Inn*. New York, 1939.
Joaquin Miller. *Memorie and Rime*. New York, 1884.
Remi A. Nadeau. *City-Makers*. New York, 1948.
Amelia R. Neville. *Fantastic City*. Boston, 1932.
Earl R. Pomeroy. *In Search of the Golden West*. New York, 1957.
Stephen Powers. *Afoot and Alone*. Hartford, 1872.
Glenn C. Quiett. *They Built the West*. New York, 1934.
Josiah Royce. *The Feud of Oakfield Creek*. Boston, 1887.
Sarah Bixby Smith. *Adobe Days*. Los Angeles, 1925.
John R. Spears. *Illustrated Sketches of Death Valley*. Chicago, 1892.
Robert Louis Stevenson. *Across the Plains*. London, 1892.
Charles W. Stoddard. *In the Footprints of the Padres*. San Francisco, 1901.
Benjamin F. Taylor. *Beyond the Gates*. Chicago, 1878.
Franklin Walker. *A Literary History of Southern California*. Berkeley, 1950.
Evelyn Wells. *Champagne Days in San Francisco*. New York, 1939.
Thurman Wilkins. *Clarence King*. New York, 1958.

INTO THE TWENTIETH CENTURY

Mary Austin. *Earth Horizons*. New York, 1932.
———. *The Flock*. New York, 1906.

549

Mary Austin. *The Flood*. New York, 1917.

Walton E. Bean. *Boss Ruef's San Francisco*. Berkeley, 1952.

William Bronson. *The Earth Shook, the Sky Burned*. New York, 1959.

W. A. Chalfant. *The Story of Inyo*. Chicago, 1922.

Roger Daniels. *The Politics of Prejudice*. Berkeley, 1962.

Eldredge F. Dowell. *A History of Criminal Syndicalism Legislation in the United States*. Baltimore, 1939.

R. L. Duffus. *The Innocents at Cedro*. New York, 1944.

Emmett A. Greenwalt. *The Point Loma Colony*. Berkeley, 1955.

Joseph Henry Jackson. *Continent's End*. New York, 1944.

George Wharton James. *The Wonders of the Colorado Desert*. 2 vols. Boston, 1906.

Edwin Markham. *Songs and Stories*. Los Angeles, 1931.

Alice Barr Mavity. *Sister Aimee*. New York, 1931.

Morrow Mayo. *Los Angeles*. New York, 1933.

Remi A. Nadeau. *The Water Seekers*. New York, 1950.

Fremont Older. *My Story*. San Francisco, 1919.

Spencer C. Olin, Jr., *California's Prodigal Sons*. Berkeley, 1968.

Robert W. de Roos. *The Thirsty Land: The Story of the Central Valley Project*. Stanford, 1948.

Charles Francis Saunders. *Under the Sky in California*. New York, 1913.

J. Lincoln Steffens. *Autobiography*. 2 vols. New York, 1931.

George Sterling and James Rorty. *Continent's End*. San Francisco, 1925.

W. A. Swanberg. *Citizen Hearst*. New York, 1961.

John Tebbel. *The Life and Good Times of William Randolph Hearst*. New York, 1952.

Lately Thomas. *The Vanishing Evangelist*. New York, 1959.

Hyman Weintraub. *Andrew Furuseth*. Berkeley, 1959.

Charles D. Willard. *The Free Harbor Contest at Los Angeles*. Los Angeles, 1899.

FROM DEPRESSION TO AFFLUENCE

Edward L. Barrett. *The Tenney Committee*. Ithaca, 1951.

Libbie Block. *The Hills of Beverly*. New York, 1957.

Leonard Bloom and Ruth Riemer. *Removal and Return*. Boston, 1949.

Allan R. Bosworth, *America's Concentration Camps*. New York, 1967.

Myron Brinig. *The Flutter of an Eyelid*. New York, 1933.

Eugene Burdick. *The Ninth Wave*. Boston, 1956.

Robert E. Burke. *Olson's New Deal for California*. Berkeley, 1952.

James M. Cain. *Mildred Pierce*. New York, 1941.

Edwin Corle. *Desert Country*. New York, 1941.

George Edmiston. *Home Again*. New York, 1953.

Frank Fenton. *A Place in the Sun*. New York, 1942.

F. Scott Fitzgerald. *The Last Tycoon*. New York, 1941.

Morton Grodzins. *Americans Betrayed*. Chicago, 1949.

Aldous Huxley. *After Many A Summer*. New York, 1939.

Robinson Jeffers. *Selected Poems*. New York, 1938.

Seymour Kern. *The Golden Scalpel*. New York, 1960.

Dorothea Lange and Paul S. Taylor. *An American Exodus*. New York, 1939; New Haven, 1969.
Carey McWilliams. *Factories in the Field*. Boston, 1939.
Arthur Mizener. *The Far Side of Paradise*. Boston, 1951.
Miné Okubo. *Citizen 13660*. New York, 1936.
Roderick Peattie. *The Pacific Coast Ranges*. New York, 1946.
———. *The Sierra Nevada*. New York, 1947.
J. B. Priestley. *Midnight on the Desert*. New York, 1937.
Budd Schulberg. *What Makes Sammy Run?* New York, 1941.
Upton Sinclair. *I, Governor and How I Ended Poverty in California*. Los Angeles, 1934.
Hans Otto Storm. *Count Ten*. New York, 1940.
Dorothy S. Thomas. *The Spoilage*. Berkeley, 1946.
Dorothy S. Thomas. *The Salvage*. Berkeley, 1952.
Judy Van der Veer. *Brown Hills*. New York, 1938.
———. *The Quiet Pasture*. New York, 1936.
Nathanael West. *The Day of the Locust*. New York, 1939.

A TIME OF RECKONING

Edmund G. Brown and others. *California the Dynamic State*. Santa Barbara, 1966.
John and LaRee Caughey. *School Segregation on Our Doorstep: The Los Angeles Story*. Los Angeles, 1966.
Roger Daniels and Harry H. L. Kitano. *American Racism*. Englewood Cliffs. N. J., 1970.
Raymond F. Dasmann. *The Destruction of California*. New York, 1965.
Royce D. Delmatier, Clarence F. McIntosh, and Earl G. Waters. *The Rumble of California Politics*. New York, 1970.
R. L. Duffus. *Queen Calafia's Island*. New York, 1965.
John Gregory Dunne. *Delano, The Anatomy of the Great California Grapeworkers' Strike*. New York, 1967.
Ernesto Galarza. *Merchants of Labor: The Mexican Bracero Story*. Santa Barbara, 1964.
Irving G. Hendrick. *The Development of a School Integration Plan in Riverside*. Riverside, 1968.
Theodora Kroeber. *Alfred Kroeber, A Personal Configuration*. Berkeley, 1970.
Richard G. Lillard. *Eden in Jeopardy*. New York, 1966.
Seymour Lipset and Sheldon S. Wolin. *The Berkeley Student Revolt*. New York, 1965.
Helen Manfull. *Additional Dialogue: Letters of Dalton Trumbo*. New York, 1970.
Remi A. Nadeau. *California, the New Society*. New York, 1963.
Art Seidenbaum. *Confrontation on Campus*. Los Angeles, 1969.
Neil V. Sullivan and Evelyn S. Stewart. *Now Is the Time: Integration in the Berkeley Schools*. Bloomington, Ind., 1969.

Index of Authors

Index of Authors